Instructor's Annotated Edition

PRIMERA PARTE

Invitaciones

An Interactive Worktext for Beginning Spanish

Deana Alonso-Lyrintzis
Southwestern College

Esther Alonso
Southwestern College

Brandon Zaslow
Occidental College

❖

Lab Activities

Beverly Burdette
Pellissippi State Community College

VISTA
HIGHER LEARNING

Boston, Massachusetts

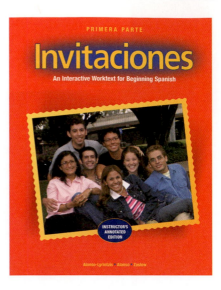

Publisher: José A. Blanco

President: Stephen Pekich

Editorial Director: Denise St. Jean

Director of Production: Nancy Jones

Art Director: Linda Jurras

Senior Designer: Polo Barrera

Design Team: Linde Gee

Staff Editors: Sarah Kenney, Alicia Spinner

Contributing Writers and Editors: Francisco de la Rosa, Gabriela Ferland, Claudi Mimó, Lourdes Murray

Production Team: María Eugenia Castaño, Oscar Díez, Mauricio Henao, Charles Leo, Ray Levesque, Kristin Mehring

Student Text ISBN 1-59334-219-5

Instructor's Annotated Edition ISBN 1-59334-220-9

Library of Congress Card Number: 2003108948

1 2 3 4 5 6 7 8 9 VH 08 07 06 05 04 03

Table of Contents

Getting to Know INVITACIONES

INVITACIONES was conceived with the methodological needs of the instructors, the pedagogical needs of the students, and the time constraints of both in mind. You will find that teaching with **INVITACIONES** is easy because it provides you, the instructor, with all of the materials and activities needed to deliver a communicative language program successfully. The focus of **INVITACIONES** is to develop learners' ability to carry out language tasks by providing the knowledge, vocabulary, and linguistic structures necessary for students to use Spanish immediately for communication. Aligned with professional moves towards proficiency-oriented programs, **INVITACIONES** provides students with adequate time to assimilate vocabulary and forms, as well as ample opportunities to use Spanish in meaningful communication by means of a realistic realignment of the grammatical syllabus.

The authors of **INVITACIONES** believe the best way to meet students' pedagogical needs and to engage them in language learning is through a story. **INVITACIONES** tells a story through the episodes of the **INVITACIONES** video and throughout the lessons of the worktext. Every phase of each lesson presents, deepens, discusses, and elaborates on the lives of six Spanish-speaking college students as they confront the challenges and experience the joys of daily life. Their stories invite students to share their own lives. Students identify with the characters because the story reflects their own experiences as students.

With its unique story-driven, student-centered, task-oriented, interactive worktext, **INVITACIONES** delivers a comprehensive, all-inclusive set of materials that will enable students to interact in informal, transactional, and interpersonal situations with native speakers of Spanish.

To get the most out of pages IAE-5–IAE-16 of your **Instructor's Annotated Edition**, you should familiarize yourself with the front matter to the **INVITACIONES** student worktext, especially the Introduction (page v), the **INVITACIONES-at-a-glance** (pages xiv–xxv), **Video program** (pages xxvi–xxvii), and **Ancillaries** (pages xxviii–xxix).

Getting to Know Your Instructor's Annotated Edition

The **Instructor's Annotated Edition (IAE)** of **INVITACIONES** contains a wealth of instructional resources. For your convenience, answers to all activities have been overprinted on the pages of the student worktext. In addition, to save you time in class preparation and course management, marginal annotations complement and support varied teaching styles and extend the rich content of the student worktext. Here are some of the principle types of annotations you will find in the **INVITACIONES IAE:**

• **Instructor's Resources** A correlation to all instructor supplements available to reinforce each lesson (**episodio**) section or subsection

> **Instructor's Resources**
> • Overheads
> • VHS Video
> • Worktext CD
> • **IRM:** Videoscript, Tapescript, Comprehensible input
> • Testing Program
> • Website

• **Video Synopsis** A brief synopsis of each **INVITACIONES** video episode on the first page of each lesson

• **Additional Activity** Supplemental activities, including games, that provide even more practice of the language of the corresponding section of the lesson

• **Script** Transcripts of the recordings for the listening activities in the four-color worktext pages, or references on where to locate the scripts, in the event that they are too long to fit in the margins of the **IAE**

• **Suggestions** Ideas and techniques for presenting, expanding, or varying individual instructional elements

---

Please check our website, *www.vistahigherlearning.com,* periodically for program updates and additional teaching support.

INVITACIONES, the *ACTFL Proficiency Guidelines*, and the *Standards for Foreign Language Learning*

INVITACIONES uses the *ACTFL Proficiency Guidelines* to create instructional objectives that meet the specific needs of first-year Spanish language learners. Students are provided language-use activities that enable them to:

- function in informal, transactional, and interpersonal situations (contexts)

- understand the overall meaning, key ideas, and some supporting details of simple narration, description, and explanation (the receptive functions of listening and reading)

- ask and answer questions; produce simple narration, description, and explanation (the productive functions of speaking and writing)

- deal with topics related to self and the immediate environment (content)

- understand and produce sentences and simple paragraphs (text types)

- comprehend and be understood by sympathetic language users (accuracy).

INVITACIONES uses *the Standards for Foreign Language Learning in the 21st Century* to create activities that develop competence in each of the areas captured in the 5C's. Students are provided opportunities to:

- participate in interpersonal, interpretive, and presentational communication

- experience cultural products and practices and reflect on the perspectives that underlie them

- acquire knowledge and new perspectives from Spanish language sources

- learn about the nature of language and culture and how each manifests itself in human communication

- take language beyond the classroom and into real-world interactions with Spanish speakers.

Orienting Students to the Worktext

The first day of class, take some time to orient your students to their worktext. Point out the different sections, features, and icons. Refer students to the **Español al instante** section on the inside back cover of their books, so they are aware of this handy reference to words and expressions to use in classroom interactions. Explain to them that their books have been designed for them to write in directly, so as to personalize their learning experience.

Point out that icons provide on-the-spot visual cues for the kinds of activities they will encounter: video-based activities, listening activities, pair work, group work, reading activities, and writing activities. Make sure they understand that they can do the video-based activities outside of class using the Video CD-ROM, provided with their worktext, and the listening activities using the Worktext & Lab MP3 Files Audio CD-ROM, also provided with their worktext.

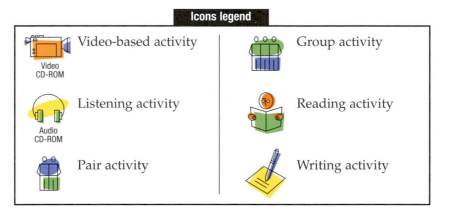

Show them a **Práctica adicional** reference and tell them that these boxed features indicate precisely when they should make use of their print and technology ancillaries. Point out that the abbreviations **WB** and **LM** list the page numbers and the exact activities in the **Cuaderno de tareas** workbook and lab manual sections they should complete for each section; **Pron.** refers to the **Pronunciación** section in the lab manual. Reinforce this information by having students turn to the **Cuaderno de tareas** pages referenced in the **Práctica adicional** box so that they realize those black and white pages appear at the end of each lesson.

Inform students that all words and expressions appearing in the charts, lists, and illustrations of the **Gramática** and **Vocabulario** sections of **Para comunicarnos mejor** in the four-color pages of their worktext are considered active vocabulary. Additionally, point out that, at the end of each lesson, **Vocabulario del episodio** provides a convenient summary of the active vocabulary, as well as a section they can fill in with vocabulary important to their own lives and experiences. Finally, tell students that they are responsible for knowing the words and expressions in **Vocabulario del episodio**, and that they will appear on quizzes and exams.

Suggestions for Using Escenas de la vida

These opening pages of each lesson serve as advanced organizers that will help you set the stage and preview the story presented in the **INVITACIONES** video. By previewing vocabulary and structures in the context of the story, you will prepare students to understand and derive meaning from the video episode.

- **Objetivos comunicativos** This feature provides students with a list of tasks they will be able to carry out after completing the lesson's activities. Always go over the objectives with students so they have a real-life framework for their work in and outside of class.

- The tasks contained in **Escenas de la vida** are designed to spark students' interest in the content of the lesson, to tap into their knowledge of the topic presented in the video episode, and to familiarize them with the language necessary to comprehend and produce messages. Overhead transparencies provide the visual support you need to make the content of the story comprehensible.

- The illustrations and transparencies provide the tools you need for presenting grammar and vocabulary in real-life contexts. Use comprehensible input and involve students in your presentation. Share your personal experiences, and encourage students to share their stories as you help them to relate to the content and the characters in the video episode. Teach for meaning, but also focus your students' attention on form by writing key words on the board or on an overhead transparency. Check students' comprehension by means of questions that require **sí/no** or short answers. Since this phase of the lesson provides students with the knowledge, vocabulary, and structures of the episode, it is one of the most important parts of the communicative lesson. It may take between 20 and 40 minutes. See the **Instructor's Resource Manual (IRM)** for already-scripted sample comprehensible input that you can use with the **Escenas de la vida** section of each lesson.

- **Cultura a lo vivo** Everyday culture is an integral part of the **INVITACIONES** video episodes, which provide a window on the many manifestations of Hispanic culture and through which vocabulary and grammar are highlighted. **Cultura a lo vivo** appears in every **Escenas de la vida** section to deepen students' understanding of culture. Assign **Cultura a lo vivo** for in-class reading and discussion or as homework. Also, encourage students to learn more about the famous places, authors, music, and history mentioned in these boxes through research at the library, or on the **INVITACIONES** text-specific website that can be accessed through *www.vistahigherlearning.com*.

- **Learning Strategy** These sections present general processes that students use to maximize opportunities for learning. When available, discuss these strategies in class, model using them with the students, and provide practice in order to ensure student success.

Suggestions for Using the INVITACIONES Video

INVITACIONES is a video-driven program. Photos from the video, events from the storyline, and characters from the episodes are systematically integrated into virtually every section of each lesson, including the workbook and lab activities. It is important that you make students accountable for the content of the video, since it provides models for carrying out communicative tasks and establishes a common base of knowledge for meaningful discussions in class.

For each lesson, it is critical that students watch the video episode after you have previewed its contents by presenting the **Escenas de la vida** visual cues in tandem with comprehensible input as described on the previous page. Even with this initiation to the vocabulary, grammar, and language functions of the video episode, students may not be able to understand everything they hear, but they will be successful because they will have been prepared for the core content and will be able to respond to the prompts in the **Escenas de la vida** activities in the worktext.

It is strongly recommended that you show the video in class at least once, especially when students first see each episode. Ideally, students should view the video episode at least three times for each lesson: once for overall comprehension (no tasks involved), an additional viewing in order to complete the tasks in the **Escenas de la vida** activities, and a final viewing to summarize the content in their own words by doing the **¡A ver de nuevo!** activity in the **La correspondencia** section of each lesson in their worktext.

You may also choose to assign the **¡A ver de nuevo!** activity for homework and have students complete the third viewing outside of class—in the language lab, at home, in their dormitories—by using the Video CD-ROM that comes with their worktext or by listening to the audio track of the video episode on the Worktext & Lab MP3 Files Audio CD-ROM that also accompanies their worktext. Alternatively, if you do not have access to a VCR and monitor in your classroom, you can have students watch the video outside of class, and you can play the audiotrack of the video episode in class, using the Worktext Audio CD.

The first section in the workbook activities in **Cuaderno de tareas** for each lesson consists of video-based activities. You can have students watch the video and do these activities in class or you can assign them for homework, and students can watch the video or listen to the audiotrack of the video episode outside of class.

You might also want to use the **INVITACIONES** video in class when working with the **Para comunicarnos mejor** sections in the worktext. You could play the parts of the video episode that exemplify the vocabulary topics or grammar points being presented and ask students to identify them. You might try this technique as you progress through the section, or as a review of the entire section after you have completed it.

Suggestions for Using Para comunicarnos mejor

Para comunicarnos mejor highlights the grammar in **Gramática** or vocabulary in **Vocabulario** necessary to carry out the functions of the episode.

- **Analizar y descubrir** Lead students through these activities to help them discover the rules governing structures they will need for communication.

- **Model sentences and charts** Give students time to read the examples, so they understand what they will be repeating. Model the pronunciation of the words and phrases and have students repeat after you. Whenever possible, ask personalized questions using the vocabulary and grammar being taught.

- **Práctica** Activities provide highly contextualized guided practice. They generally begin by requiring only comprehension and move to those in which students manipulate form in meaningful and personalized ways. Students develop listening, reading, speaking, and writing skills through guided, yet meaningful exercises that increase their confidence and accuracy. The activities may be done orally as a class, in pairs or in small groups. They may also be assigned as homework. Remind students to refer to **Español al instante**, on the inside back cover of their worktext, in order to better understand activity direction lines in Spanish. The vocabulary and linguistic markers that characterize different varieties of Spanish as represented by the characters in the video have been used in the exercises and activities throughout the worktext as much as possible and within the acceptability of "standard" Spanish.

- **También se dice....** This features provides an avenue for different varieties of Spanish to be validated and discussed, if you so desire. Every effort has been made to include as many varieties as feasible to present a truly diverse look at the linguistic richness of the Spanish-speaking world.

Suggestions for Using Actividades comunicativas

The **Actividades comunicativas** section of each lesson provides highly motivating, interactive activities through which students receive the support they need to internalize vocabulary and grammar of the episode in a non-threatening environment. The activities promote cooperative learning and help develop a sense of community as students work together to accomplish learning goals. They include information gap, class surveys, and role-plays and may be completed in pairs, in groups, or in whole-class formats.

- Explain to students the importance of this section for developing oral proficiency in Spanish. Remind students to refer to the **Español al instante** section on the inside back cover of their worktexts in order to be able to interact with their classmates exclusively in Spanish.

- These activities should take from eight to ten minutes each. Monitor students' work by circulating around the class as they do the activites. Review answers with the entire class after the activities are completed. When applicable, have students report and summarize the information gathered from their classmates.

Suggestions for Using La correspondencia

With its three subsections, **La correspondencia** integrates language, culture, and real-world tasks. **El correo** contains a variety of informal texts such as e-mails and letters, many of which are written or received by the characters. Lively and relevant, they serve as models for students' written communication. Questions guide students in focusing on the main ideas and important details necessary to understand the text. Although students will not understand every word, they should be considered successful if they are able to accomplish the tasks. **Reading** and **Writing Strategies** guide students through more difficult texts and aid them in the reading and writing processes. **En papel** is a writing task in which students are invited to write their own materials in direct reaction to the **El correo** selection. **¡A ver de nuevo!** provides closure to the episode; students watch the video a final time and summarize its content, thereby realizing how much more of the **Escenas de la vida** story they understand, and how much language they have learned overall.

- **El correo** This activity may be assigned as homework. When available, review the **Reading Strategy** with students. If done in class, have students read the questions, ask for volunteers to read several sentences from the text, and have students finish reading the selection silently. Then, you may want to have students answer the questions as a class.

- **En papel** This activity may be assigned for homework. When available, review the **Writing strategy** with students, modeling the strategy and having students apply it. Give students the opportunity to engage in peer editing by editing a classmate's writing before assignments are turned in for a grade. Assign a grade based on task completion, focusing on the vocabulary and structures of the episode at hand, as well as the use of connectors and transition words. You are encouraged to display students' work, so that other students can learn from their classmates. Oral presentations based on an individual student's or a classmate's written work can be wonderful follow-up activities to the **En papel** assignments.

- **¡A ver de nuevo!** For the first few lessons, you may want to demonstrate the process of writing a summary, using a blank transparency on the overhead projector as you play the video segment. Ask students to tell you what happened in the **Escenas de la vida** episode, reminding them to paraphrase using the language they have learned and stressing the use of transition words. Once students have learned the process, you can assign the activity as homework, telling students to watch the video episode on the Video CD-ROM that comes with their worktext, or have students create their summaries in class in pairs.

- **Invitación a...**   This section is written exclusively in Spanish, with English glosses where necessary. Read the captions with students in class. Encourage them to visit the **INVITACIONES** website in order to learn more about each country.

Suggestions for Using Vocabulario del episodio

Each episode concludes with a summary of the vocabulary and the structures practiced. The **Vocabulario personal** sections encourage students to personalize their learning so they are better able to talk about themselves and the world around them.

- As homework, the day before you start a new episode, ask students to look over the episode in order to get an idea of what they will be learning. Have them create flash cards with the new vocabulary. This task will build schema that will prepare them to better understand the episode's content.

- **Objetivos comunicativos** Remind students to review the communicative objectives in order to determine if they have attained all of the competencies taught in the episode.

- **Vocabulario personal** Have students write down all of the words they need to talk about the episode's theme with respect to themselves. You may wish to ask different students to share their personal vocabulary with the class. It will vary from student to student. For communication to be meaningful, it is important that students develop the ability to talk about themselves and gain a sense of "ownership" of words that are important to them.

Suggestions for Using Cuaderno de tareas

The **Cuaderno de tareas** is divided into two parts: **¡A escribir!** (workbook activities) and **¡A escuchar!** (lab activities). The activities on these black and white pages of the worktext are designed to provide students with out-of-class support and practice with the materials they are learning. **Práctica adicional** boxes in the color pages correlate each activity to the lessons.

- **¡A escribir!** Point out to students that the practice activities occur within the context of the story and the culture it reflects. The exercises are varied and include: discrete, form-and-meaning focused practice, open-ended questions, and reading and writing activities. Vocabulary, grammar, and language functions from the corresponding and previous lessons are consistently recycled throughout the materials. You may assign and collect these pages regularly to assess the progress of your students as you work through each lesson.

- **¡A escuchar!** The characters and storyline of the video are frequently integrated into these listening comprehension activities and pronunciation practice. The exercises are varied and include real-world listening, speaking, and writing activities. You may want to assign and collect these activities at the end of each lesson as you are working with the **La correspondencia** section. Students may complete the activities in the language lab or they may listen to them wherever they prefer, using the Worktext & Lab MP3 Files Audio CD-ROM that comes with their worktext.

Course and Lesson Planning

Overall Course Planning

INVITACIONES consists of two volumes, **Primera parte** and **Segunda parte. Primera parte** contains **Episodios 1–15** and **Segunda parte** contains **Episodios 16–30.** Each episode is designed to be completed in four to five contact hours. Students learn, practice, process, and acquire manageable quantities of language weekly. A modular instructional program, **INVITACIONES** can be used effectively in a variety of settings and may be divided as follows:

Option A (2 semesters, 5 contact hours per week)

Semester 1:   **Semester 2:**
Episodes 1–15   Episodes 16–30

With 4 contact hours per week, instructors may assign the **La Correspondencia** module as homework.

Option B (3 quarters, 5 contact hours per week or 3 semesters, 3 contact hours per week)

Quarter/semester 1:	Quarter/semester 2:	Quarter/semester 3:
Episodes 1–10	Episodes 11–20	Episodes 21–30

Lesson Planning

Here is a sample lesson for **Episodio 4: ¡Qué internacionales!**

Day 1

1. Read the **Objetivos comunicativos** on p. 81 so that students will know what they will be able to do at the end of the episode. (2 minutes)

2. Before playing the video, use comprehensible input to preview the content of **Escenas de la vida** by talking about the tasks and describing the pictures on p. 81. Complete sample comprehensible input is available in the **IRM**; an abbreviated version is provided below. Be sure to preview **ser de** + [*country*], family terms (**papá, mamá, hermanos, hijos**), and **tener... años** in the context of the story.

Sample comprehensible input: **Vamos a ver este mapa. ¿Qué país es éste?... Sí, es México. ¿Quién es de México? ¿Adriana o Sofía?... Bien, Sofía es de México. Los padres de Sofía también son de México. ¿De dónde es Adriana?... Adriana es de Puerto Rico. No sabemos de dónde es Manolo. Vamos a escuchar la conversación para indicar de dónde es Manolo. Aquí tenemos a los padres de Manolo. La mamá y el papá. Mi mamá se llama... y es de... Y tu mamá, ¿cómo se llama?... ¿De dónde es?** (Ask several students.) **Yo soy de... ¿Y tú? ¿Eres de aquí? ¿De dónde eres?** (Do not expect students to produce complete answers.) **Después de escuchar vamos a indicar de dónde son los padres de Ramón,** etc.

Ahora miren esta foto. Es la familia de Ramón. ¿Es una familia grande o pequeña? Sí, es grande, ¿verdad? Son seis. Mi familia es... somos... Y tu familia, ¿es grande o pequeña? (Ask several students.) **Vamos a ver: éste es el papá de Ramón; ¿cuántos años tiene el papá de Ramón? Humm, 48 ó 50, ¿qué creen? ¿Y la mamá? Mi mamá tiene... años. ¿Cuántos años tiene tu mamá?** (Ask several students.) **¿Y tú papá?** (Ask several students.) **Bueno ellos tienen cuatro hijos, ¿no? Ramón, Ana Mari y otros dos.** Question several students until you feel satisfied that they understand **soy de, es de, tengo hijos, tienes hermanos,** etc. (20–25 minutes)

3. Ask students to close their books and watch the **Escenas de la vida** video segment. Play the video. (3 minutes)

4. Have students open their books and complete the task in activity **A. ¡Mira cuánto puedes entender!** on p. 81. Read activities **B** and **C** on p. 82 with students. Play the video again in order for students to respond to the prompts. Go over the answers. (10 minutes)

5. Go over the **Learning Strategy** on p. 82 with students. Ask them to make up some associations for the vocabulary on p. 83 so they may share them the next day with the class. (3 minutes)

6. Model the pronunciation of **La familia, los familiares y más** on p. 83 and have students repeat after you. (3 minutes)

7. Briefly present the key points in *Expressing possession* on pp. 83–84, **Gramática 1** on pp. 86–87, and **Gramática 2** on p. 89 that you previewed through comprehensible input. (4 minutes)

8. For homework, have students study pp. 82–84 and do **Práctica** activities **A, B,** and **C** on pp. 84–86 and the **Escenas de la vida** workbook activities in **Cuaderno de tareas** on pp. 101–102. (1 minute)

Day 2

1. Begin class by reviewing the material from Day 1 and by collecting the **Escenas de la vida** workbook activities that were assigned as homework. Have students tell you what they remember about the characters. Use the family tree on p. 85 to review all of the relationships. Tell them about your family and ask students personalized questions about their own families. (10 minutes)

2. Have students work with a partner to check each other's answers to **Práctica** activities **A, B,** and **C** that were assigned as homework. (5 minutes)

3. Have students change partners and complete **Práctica D. ¿Y tus parientes?** on p. 86. (5 minutes)

4. Review *Expressing age* and model the pronunciation of **tener,** using the examples on p. 86. Ask students questions. Highlight the use of **tener** for expressing age. (4 minutes)

5. Complete **Práctica E. ¿Cierto o falso?** on p. 87 in a whole–class format. Ask volunteers to read each question. (4 minutes)

6. Model the pronunciation of a few numbers on p. 87, then write other numbers on the board and have students tell you what they are. (3–4 minutes)

7. Have students complete **Práctica F. El inventario** on p. 87 and **Práctica G. ¿Cuántos años tiene...?** on p. 88 in pairs. Students take turns playing each role. (6 minutes)

8. Have students complete **Práctica H. ¿Cuál es tu teléfono?** on p. 88 in groups of four. (5–7 minutes)

9. Refer students back to p. 81, asking them questions about where the characters' families are from. Emphasize the use of the preposition **de** to indicate origin. You may also want to do a quick review of the conjugation of **ser** (students already learned the verb in **Episodio 3**). (5 minutes)

10. Assign **Práctica** activities **I, J,** and **K** on pp. 88–89 for homework. (1 minute)

Day 3

1. Begin class by reviewing the material from Day 2. Ask students to share something about their families and ask personalized questions as well as questions about the characters, for example: **¿De dónde es Adriana? ¿Cuántos hijos tiene? ¿De dónde es Ramón? ¿De dónde es Manolo?** (4–6 minutes)

2. Have students interview a partner based on the questions from **Práctica** activity **I** that was assigned for homework. (5 minutes)

3. Go over the answers to **Práctica** activities **J** and **K** that were assigned for homework. Ask for volunteers. (5 minutes)

4. In groups of three, have students complete **Práctica L. ¿De dónde es tu familia?** on p. 90. Invite students to share their findings. (6–8 minutes)

5. Play the Worktext Audio CD or read the tapescript for **Práctica M. Una familia internacional** on p. 90 and have students complete the chart. Play or read it a second time so students can verify their answers. Have students share their responses. (5 minutes)

6. Have students complete the activities in **Actividades comunicativas** on pp. 91–96 with a partner. Remind students of the importance of accomplishing the tasks without looking at their partner's page. Circulate around the classroom, making note of students' mistakes for later review. If a pair of students finishes early, have them switch roles and complete the activity again. (15–20 minutes)

7. Assign the *Identifying family members and friends, Expressing age,* and *Telling where someone is from* workbook activities in **Cuaderno de tareas** on pp. 102–106. (1 minute)

Day 4

1. Begin class by reviewing the material from Day 3 and by collecting the **Cuaderno de tareas** workbook activities that were assigned as homework. Have students share their experiences with the communicative activities. (5 minutes)

2. Complete **El correo: Sofía te escribe** on p. 97. Focus students' attention on the information they need to understand when reading Sofía's letter by reviewing the questions before students begin to read. Provide students with sufficient time to read the letter either by themselves or with a partner. Have students respond to the questions, asking volunteers to share their answers. Discuss the content of the reading. (10 minutes)

3. In a whole-class format, guide students in using Sofía's letter as a model for **En papel: Una carta para Sofía** on p. 97. Have students write their first draft. (8–10 minutes)

4. Give students time to work with a partner to read each other's work and give feedback to their partner. Have them focus on the content first and on form second. (10–15 minutes)

5. For homework, have students type a final draft of their letter to Sofía and attach a picture of their family, for posting in class the next day. The first time that you ask students to bring something that will be displayed, be sure to prepare a model. In this case, you might paste a paragraph on cardstock and attach a picture, so students can see a sample of what they are expected to do. (5 minutes)

6. Review the objectives of the episode and announce and outline the content of the quiz to be given during the next class. Assign the lab activities in **Cuaderno de tareas** on pp. 107–108 as homework. (5 minutes)

Day 5

1. Collect the typed **En papel** assignments and the **Cuaderno de tareas** lab activities that were assigned for homework. Post students' writing and allow time for them to read three or four samples of their classmates' work. Talk about their families and ask them personal questions. Ask students to share what they have learned about their classmates' families. (20 minutes)

2. Play the video episode again and have students complete **¡A ver de nuevo!** on p. 98. (3–5 minutes)

3. Go over students' answers to **¡A ver de nuevo!** and have them summarize the content of the video episode. (8–10 minutes)

4. Administer the **Episodio 4 prueba**. (15 minutes)

5. Ask students to glance at the next episode to familiarize themselves with its content, and ask them to prepare flash cards with the new vocabulary for homework. (2 minutes)

Invitaciones

An Interactive Worktext for Beginning Spanish

Deana Alonso-Lyrintzis
Southwestern College

Esther Alonso
Southwestern College

Brandon Zaslow
Occidental College

❖

Lab Activities

Beverly Burdette
Pellissippi State Community College

VISTA
HIGHER LEARNING

Boston, Massachusetts

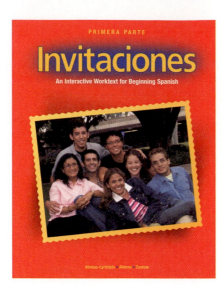

Publisher: José A. Blanco

President: Stephen Pekich

Editorial Director: Denise St. Jean

Director of Production: Nancy Jones

Art Director: Linda Jurras

Senior Designer: Polo Barrera

Design Team: Linde Gee

Staff Editors: Sarah Kenney, Alicia Spinner

Contributing Writers and Editors: Francisco de la Rosa, Gabriela Ferland, Claudi Mimó, Lourdes Murray

Production Team: María Eugenia Castaño, Oscar Díez, Mauricio Henao, Charles Leo, Ray Levesque, Kristin Mehring

Student Text ISBN 1-59334-219-5

Library of Congress Card Number: 2003108875

1 2 3 4 5 6 7 8 9 VH 08 07 06 05 04 03

Dedication

At the time of his tragic death on August 15, 1996, my husband, **Costas Lyrintzis,** was a professor of Aerospace Engineering at San Diego State University. He was loved and respected by his students and colleagues because of his friendliness, his intelligence and his ability to smile and make others feel better, even in the worst of times.

Even though his death made the process of writing this book so much more difficult, he has been with us all along the way. His memory gave us strength, his faith in us and our ability to contribute to the teaching of Spanish kept us going at times when we wanted to quit. Our desire to write a book worthy of him and his memory raised our spirits.

We all love you, Costas. Our lives will never be the same without you.

Deana Alonso-Lyrintzis

Introduction

Bienvenido a INVITACIONES, your invitation to the rich language and the diverse cultures of the Spanish-speaking world! This program takes a communicative approach to developing your ability to use and understand Spanish in practical, everyday contexts. It also aims at building your cultural knowledge and competency.

▶ Unique interactive worktexts

A brand new program, **INVITACIONES** consists of two volumes, **Primera parte** and **Segunda parte**. Both are interactive worktexts, the first of their kind published for introductory college Spanish. Because you write in and otherwise "interact" with the lessons, the worktexts are spiral-bound, with paperback covers and perforated pages for easy removal.

▶ Five resources in one package

Each **INVITACIONES** worktext contains fifteen lessons, called *episodes*, and each episode is organized in exactly the same way: full-color lesson pages, immediately followed by black-and-white pages with workbook and lab activities. As a result, the worktext offers you three printed learning tools you need for learning Spanish in one self-contained volume. In addition, each new worktext comes packaged with the **INVITACIONES** Video CD-ROM and the Worktext & Lab MP3 Files Audio CD-ROM, ensuring that you have one convenient package with the multimedia ancillaries you need for success in your introductory Spanish course.

▶ Video-driven program

Specially shot for **INVITACIONES**, the video revolves around the everyday lives and relationships of a group of Spanish-speaking friends from various countries as they attend college in the United States. Photos from the video, events from the storyline, and characters from the episodes are systematically integrated into virtually every section of each lesson, including the workbook and lab activities.

▶ Personalized learning experience

Throughout the full-color pages of its lessons, **INVITACIONES** invites you to interact with the worktext by filling in information that interests you, prompting personalized reactions, and by providing ideas for use with a partner, small groups, or the entire class. As you work through each lesson, you will find that the worktext consistently gives you the support you need to carry out real-life tasks in Spanish.

To familiarize yourself with the worktext's organization and features, turn to page xiv and take the **INVITACIONES: Primera parte**-at-a-glance tour. For more information on **INVITACIONES: Segunda parte**, see page xxx.

¡Bienvenidos al mundo hispano!

Escenas de la vida	Para comunicarnos mejor

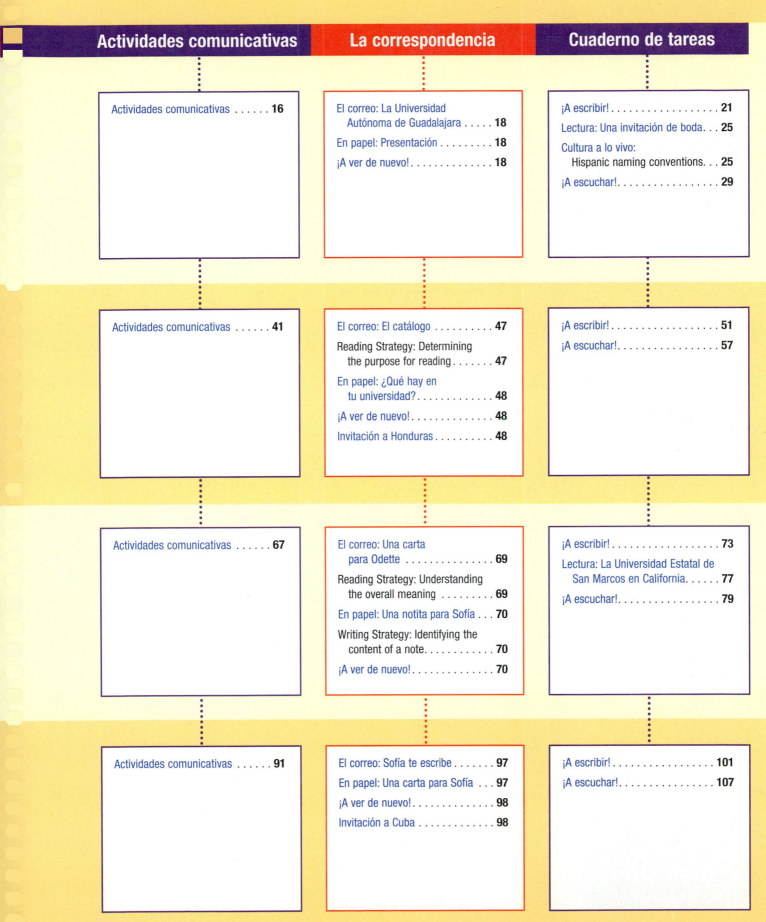

	Escenas de la vida	Para comunicarnos mejor

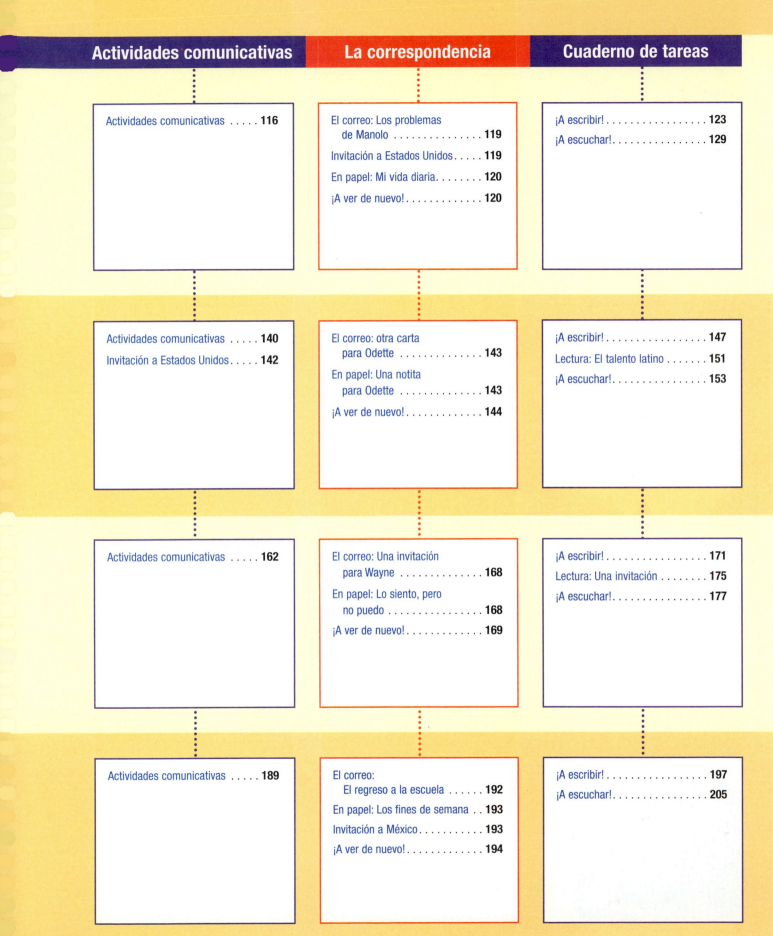

	Escenas de la vida	Para comunicarnos mejor

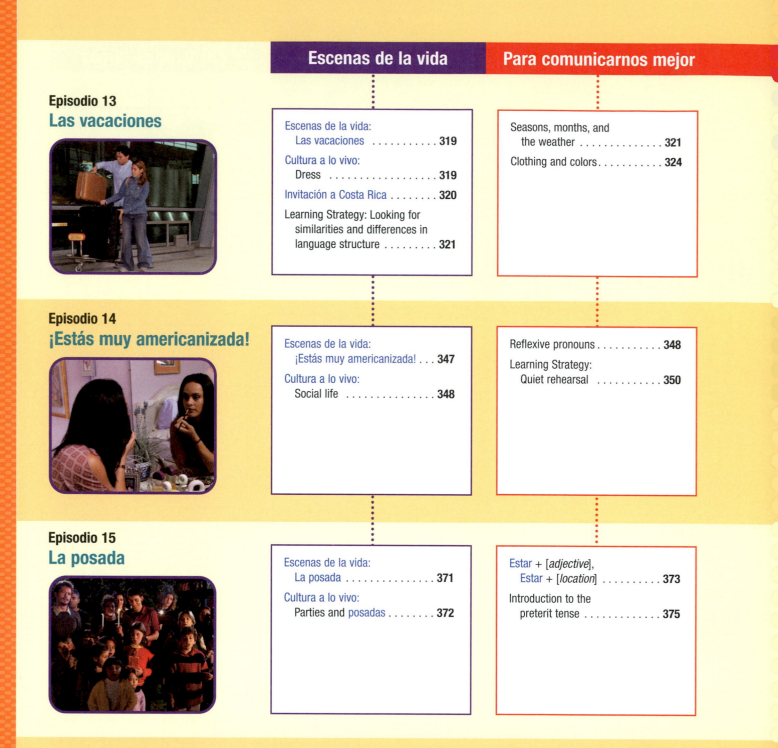

	Escenas de la vida	**Para comunicarnos mejor**

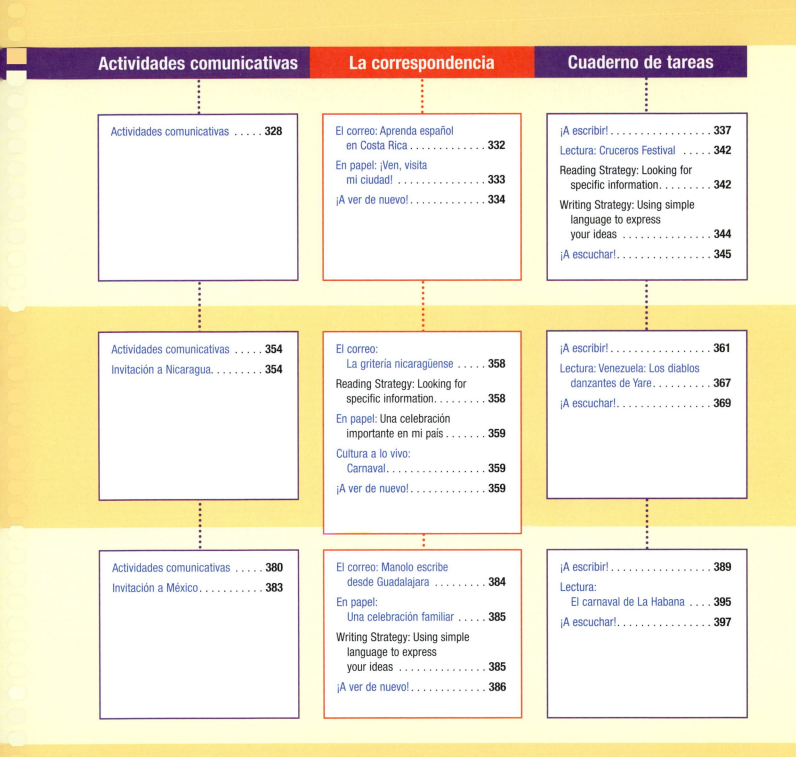

Escenas de la vida

opens every lesson with an input-driven *and* video-based introduction to the lesson's theme, vocabulary, and grammar.

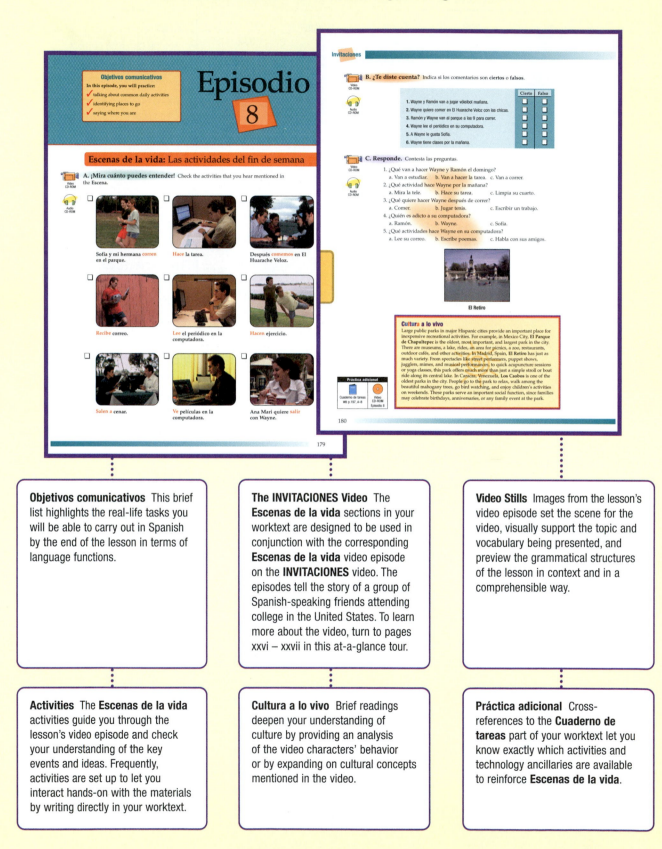

Objetivos comunicativos This brief list highlights the real-life tasks you will be able to carry out in Spanish by the end of the lesson in terms of language functions.

The INVITACIONES Video The **Escenas de la vida** sections in your worktext are designed to be used in conjunction with the corresponding **Escenas de la vida** video episode on the **INVITACIONES** video. The episodes tell the story of a group of Spanish-speaking friends attending college in the United States. To learn more about the video, turn to pages xxvi – xxvii in this at-a-glance tour.

Video Stills Images from the lesson's video episode set the scene for the video, visually support the topic and vocabulary being presented, and preview the grammatical structures of the lesson in context and in a comprehensible way.

Activities The **Escenas de la vida** activities guide you through the lesson's video episode and check your understanding of the key events and ideas. Frequently, activities are set up to let you interact hands-on with the materials by writing directly in your worktext.

Cultura a lo vivo Brief readings deepen your understanding of culture by providing an analysis of the video characters' behavior or by expanding on cultural concepts mentioned in the video.

Práctica adicional Cross-references to the **Cuaderno de tareas** part of your worktext let you know exactly which activities and technology ancillaries are available to reinforce **Escenas de la vida**.

Para comunicarnos mejor

presents the grammatical structures necessary to carry out the real-life tasks of the lesson.

D. Emparejar. Empareja las personas con las frases.

Video CD-ROM

Audio CD-ROM

____ 1. Santiaguito   a. tiene un hermano.
____ 2. Carlos   b. es el mayor.
____ 3. Manolo   c. tiene quince años.
____ 4. Sofía   d. tiene una hermana.

Práctica adicional

Cuaderno de tareas Wb pp.147–148, A–C

Video CD-ROM Episodio 6

Cultura a lo vivo
When Spanish speakers are successful in the United States, they are viewed as examples of how dreams can come true by both those who have remained in the home country, as well as by those who have immigrated to the United States. A notable example is Chicago Cubs home-run hitter Sammy Sosa, hailed as a national hero in his native Dominican Republic, for his success on the playing field.

Para comunicarnos mejor

Gramática 1

Describing people and things
- Descriptive adjectives
- Placement of adjectives

Analizar y descubrir
In the conversation, you heard the following statements.

¡Qué **guapos** son sus hijos! — Your children are so good-looking!
Tú eres **alto** y muy **guapo**. — You're tall and very handsome.
Tu hermana es **alta** y **rubia**. — Your sister is tall and blonde.

1. Notice that the adjectives **guapo** and **alto** have more than one form. Study the previous statements and answer these questions:
   a. Which word was used to describe Adriana's children? _____
   b. Which words were used to describe Manolo? _____ and _____
   c. Which words were used to describe Manolo's sister ? _____ and _____

   Circle the correct answer in items d-f, and answer g.
   d. **Guapos** is used in (a) because it matches **hijas / hijos.**
   e. **Alto** and **guapo** are used in (b) because they match **Manolo / Sofía.**
   f. **Alta** and **rubia** are used in (c) because they match **él / ella.**
   g. Which form of **guapo** would be used to describe Sofía and Viviana? _____

2. Unlike English, Spanish adjectives change their form to match the gender (masculine or feminine) and number (singular or plural) of the nouns they describe.

   La clase es **divertida.** — The class is fun.
   Manolo es alto; **él y Carlos** son morenos. — Manolo is tall; he and Carlos are dark-haired.
   Las amigas de Sofía son graciosas. — Sofía's friends are funny.

3. Some adjectives (ending in -e or in some consonants) do not change form to indicate gender. All, however, change form to indicate number.

   La casa es **grande**; el estadio es **grande.** — The house is big; the stadium is big.
   Los salones no son **grandes.** — The classrooms are not big.

132

Here are some adjectives used to describe physical appearance.

Adjetivos descriptivos: La apariencia física

guapo/a	handsome, good-looking	joven	young
bonito/a	good-looking, pretty	viejo/a*	old
feo/a	ugly, plain	grande	large, big
alto/a	tall	pequeño/a	small
bajo/a	short (height)	rubio/a	blond(e)
gordo/a	fat	moreno/a	dark (haired)
delgado/a	thin		

*In some Spanish-speaking countries, it is impolite to describe an older person as **viejo** or **vieja.** It is better to say **Es una persona mayor.**

Below are some adjectives used to describe character and personality.

También se dice...
delgado → flaco
perezoso → flojo
gracioso → chistoso
rubio → güero

Adjetivos descriptivos: El carácter y la personalidad

agradable	pleasant, nice	grosero/a	rude
antipático/a	unpleasant, nasty	amable	kind, friendly
bueno/a	good, nice	cariñoso/a	affectionate
malo/a	bad	reservado/a	reserved
gracioso/a	funny	listo/a	smart
serio/a	serious	tonto/a	dumb, silly
trabajador(a)	hard-working	perezoso/a	lazy

Learning Strategy: Focus on word clusters and word families.
You will understand more if you are able to relate words with similar roots: for example, persona, personal, and personalidad or arte, artista, and artístico. Use the words you know to figure out what other words mean: knowing perezoso, what could perza mean? It means laziness. Try to guess the meaning of groseria, amabilidad, aburrimiento, and cariño.

Here are some words and expressions used to describe people and things.

Descripciones: Las personas y las cosas

nuevo/a	new	fácil	easy	mayor	older
viejo/a	old	difícil	hard, difficult	menor	younger
aburrido/a	boring	rico/a	rich, tasty	hijo/a único/a	only child
divertido/a	fun	pobre	poor	soltero/a	single
diferente	different	casado/a	married	similar	similar

133

Gramática Grammatical concepts previewed in **Escenas de la vida** activities and featured in the corresponding **Escenas de la vida** video episode are presented in the grammar section of your worktext.

Analizar y descubrir This section appears, when appropriate, to guide you in analyzing and discovering grammatical structures and patterns featured in **Escenas de la vida**, before you use them in upcoming practice activities.

Examples Examples, frequently taken from the lesson's video episode, highlight the language and structures you are studying and put them in real-life contexts.

Charts Colorful, easy-to-use charts call out key grammatical structures and forms, as well as vocabulary fundamental to communicating with the structures at hand.

Learning Strategy Learning strategy boxes, related to specific language-learning tasks, present general techniques you can use to maximize your learning opportunities.

Para comunicarnos mejor
also focuses on the vocabulary necessary to carry out
the real-life tasks of the lesson.

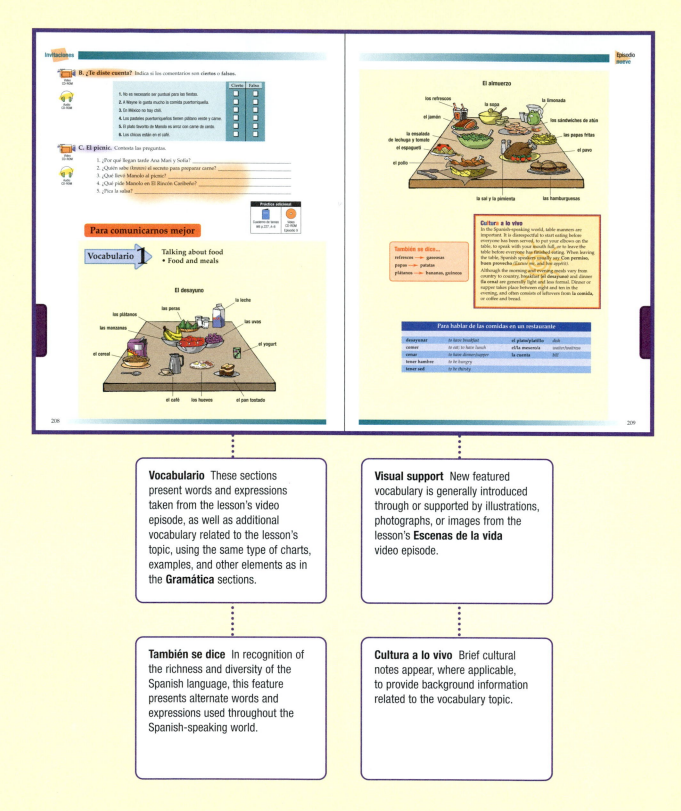

Vocabulario These sections present words and expressions taken from the lesson's video episode, as well as additional vocabulary related to the lesson's topic, using the same type of charts, examples, and other elements as in the **Gramática** sections.

Visual support New featured vocabulary is generally introduced through or supported by illustrations, photographs, or images from the lesson's **Escenas de la vida** video episode.

También se dice In recognition of the richness and diversity of the Spanish language, this feature presents alternate words and expressions used throughout the Spanish-speaking world.

Cultura a lo vivo Brief cultural notes appear, where applicable, to provide background information related to the vocabulary topic.

Para comunicarnos mejor
provides varied types of guided, yet meaningful practice.

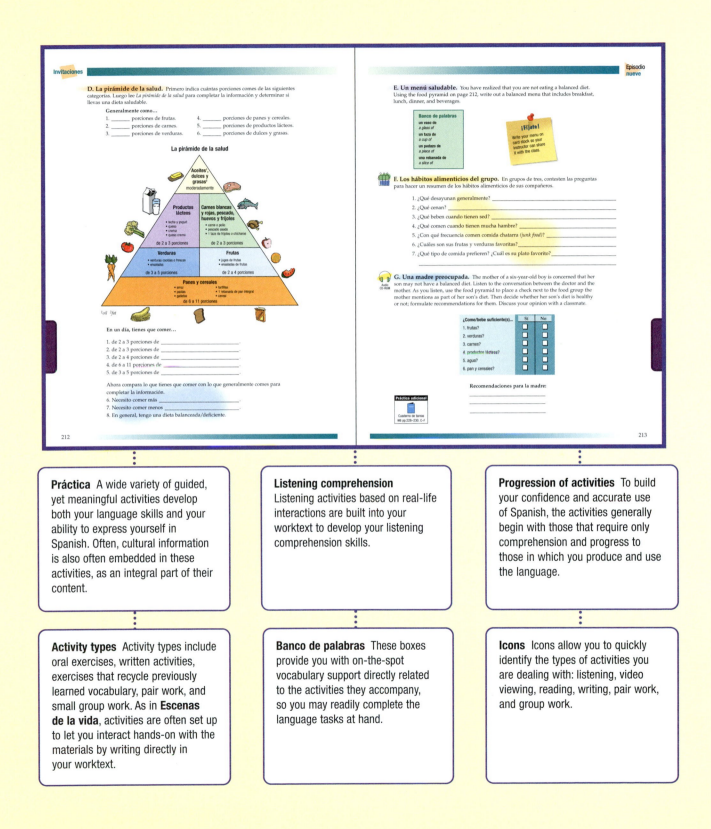

Práctica A wide variety of guided, yet meaningful activities develop both your language skills and your ability to express yourself in Spanish. Often, cultural information is also often embedded in these activities, as an integral part of their content.

Listening comprehension Listening activities based on real-life interactions are built into your worktext to develop your listening comprehension skills.

Progression of activities To build your confidence and accurate use of Spanish, the activities generally begin with those that require only comprehension and progress to those in which you produce and use the language.

Activity types Activity types include oral exercises, written activities, exercises that recycle previously learned vocabulary, pair work, and small group work. As in **Escenas de la vida**, activities are often set up to let you interact hands-on with the materials by writing directly in your worktext.

Banco de palabras These boxes provide you with on-the-spot vocabulary support directly related to the activities they accompany, so you may readily complete the language tasks at hand.

Icons Icons allow you to quickly identify the types of activities you are dealing with: listening, video viewing, reading, writing, pair work, and group work.

Para comunicarnos mejor
also features personalized and video-related activities.

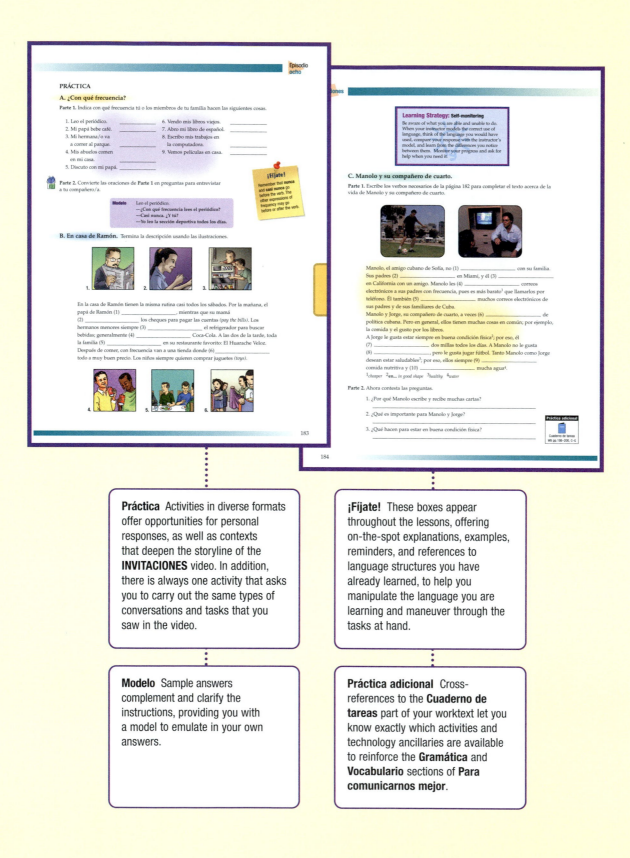

Práctica Activities in diverse formats offer opportunities for personal responses, as well as contexts that deepen the storyline of the **INVITACIONES** video. In addition, there is always one activity that asks you to carry out the same types of conversations and tasks that you saw in the video.

¡Fíjate! These boxes appear throughout the lessons, offering on-the-spot explanations, examples, reminders, and references to language structures you have already learned, to help you manipulate the language you are learning and maneuver through the tasks at hand.

Modelo Sample answers complement and clarify the instructions, providing you with a model to emulate in your own answers.

Práctica adicional Cross-references to the **Cuaderno de tareas** part of your worktext let you know exactly which activities and technology ancillaries are available to reinforce the **Gramática** and **Vocabulario** sections of **Para comunicarnos mejor**.

Actividades comunicativas

uses information gap activities to strengthen your communication skills.

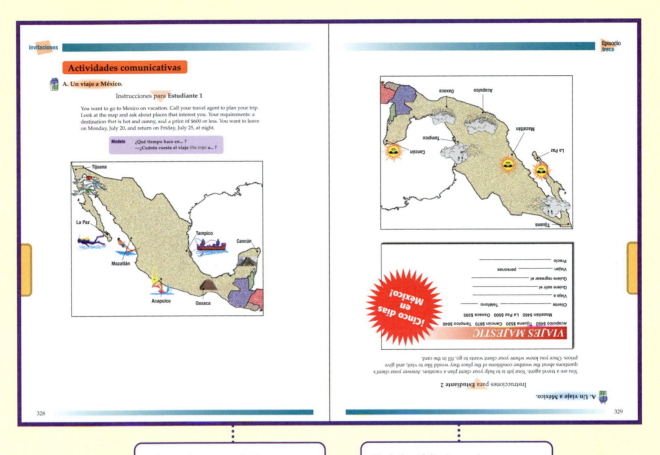

Information gap activities
Information gap activities support you as you practice the vocabulary and grammar of the lesson in problem-solving or other situations. These activities are frequently culturally-oriented. You and a partner each have only half of the information you need, so you must work together to accomplish the task at hand.

Varied activity types In **Crucigrama**, you and a partner give each other hints in order to complete a crossword puzzle, while in **En imágenes**, you work together to interpret a series of pictures. **Sopa de palabras** is based on scrambled sentences, and **Diferencias** deals with different versions of an illustration. Other information gap activities involve completing stories and enacting role-plays.

Actividades comunicativas

includes other creative and interactive activities that build your communication skills.

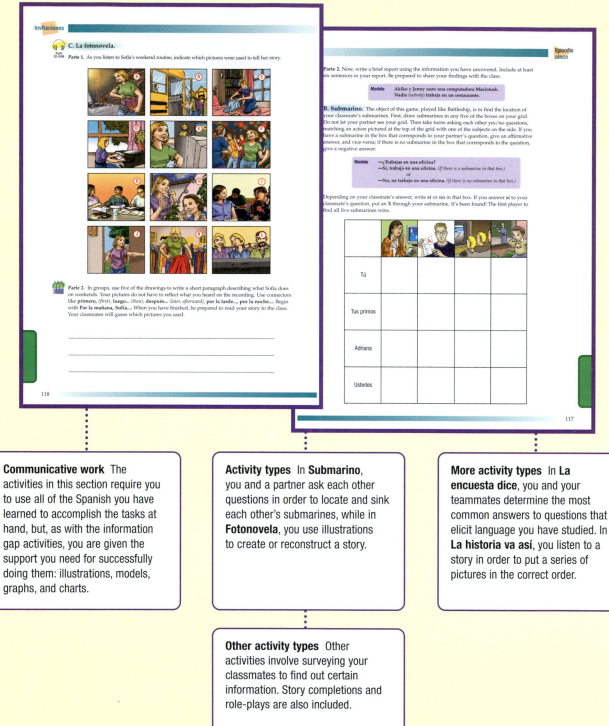

Communicative work The activities in this section require you to use all of the Spanish you have learned to accomplish the tasks at hand, but, as with the information gap activities, you are given the support you need for successfully doing them: illustrations, models, graphs, and charts.

Activity types In **Submarino**, you and a partner ask each other questions in order to locate and sink each other's submarines, while in **Fotonovela**, you use illustrations to create or reconstruct a story.

More activity types In **La encuesta dice**, you and your teammates determine the most common answers to questions that elicit language you have studied. In **La historia va así**, you listen to a story in order to put a series of pictures in the correct order.

Other activity types Other activities involve surveying your classmates to find out certain information. Story completions and role-plays are also included.

La correspondencia

develops your reading and writing skills in the context of the lesson theme.

Types of readings Among the kinds of readings you will encounter are e-mails, letters, newspaper and magazine articles, and brochures. Questions guide you in focusing on main ideas and overall comprehension.

El correo A variety of realia and other texts, many of which are written or received by the characters in the **INVITACIONES** video, develop your reading skills and cultural knowledge.

Reading Strategy Reading strategies help you focus your reading, navigate more difficult texts, and respond to questions about the readings.

En papel In this writing activity, spun off from the topic of **El correo**, you use the grammar and vocabulary of the lesson to write about your personal experiences, using the **El correo** reading as a model.

Writing Strategy Writing strategies guide you through the process of creating different kinds of texts in Spanish and help you to maximize the accuracy of your work.

La correspondencia
also synthesizes the language of the lesson and spotlights culture.

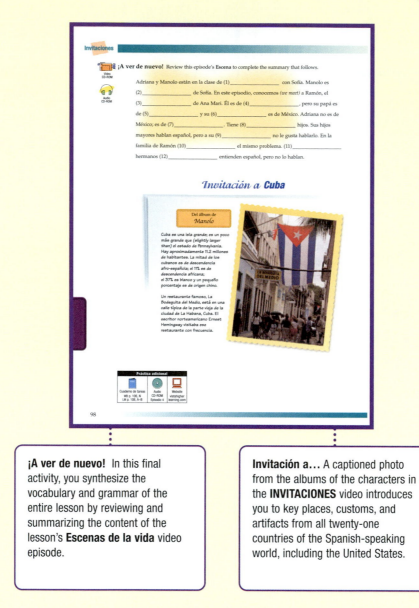

¡A ver de nuevo! In this final activity, you synthesize the vocabulary and grammar of the entire lesson by reviewing and summarizing the content of the lesson's **Escenas de la vida** video episode.

Invitación a... A captioned photo from the albums of the characters in the **INVITACIONES** video introduces you to key places, customs, and artifacts from all twenty-one countries of the Spanish-speaking world, including the United States.

Vocabulario and Español al instante
serve as important vocabulary references.

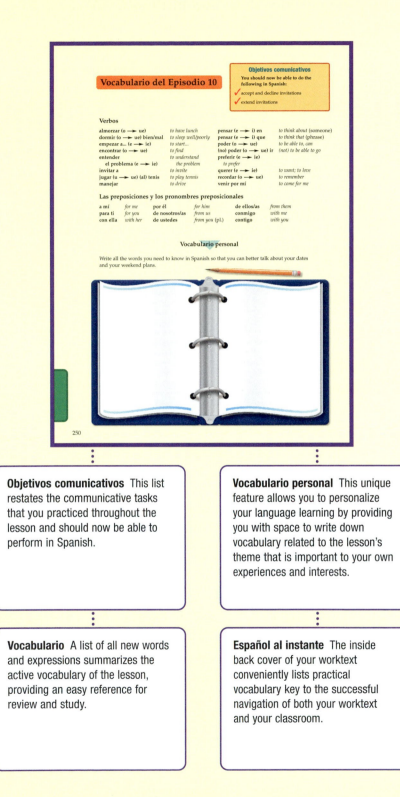

Objetivos comunicativos This list restates the communicative tasks that you practiced throughout the lesson and should now be able to perform in Spanish.

Vocabulario personal This unique feature allows you to personalize your language learning by providing you with space to write down vocabulary related to the lesson's theme that is important to your own experiences and interests.

Vocabulario A list of all new words and expressions summarizes the active vocabulary of the lesson, providing an easy reference for review and study.

Español al instante The inside back cover of your worktext conveniently lists practical vocabulary key to the successful navigation of both your worktext and your classroom.

Cuaderno de tareas: ¡A escribir!
provides workbook activities that reinforce and expand
on the materials in the lesson.

Cuaderno de tareas

Nombre _____ Fecha _____

Quinta etapa: *El compromiso*

Esta etapa debe considerarse el período de entrenamiento[1] antes del matrimonio. Una vez que hemos encontrado a la persona ideal para nosotros, es el momento de comprometerse. Este período es ideal para crear memorias duraderas del amor especial que sienten y comparten. Las parejas que tienen de cinco a ocho meses de compromiso están mejor preparados para la prueba del matrimonio. Es el momento de prepararse para los rigores del matrimonio, de formar una familia, de vivir juntos, de compartir una vida.

Según Grey, los marcianos deben recordar que en Venus, pedir la mano es la segunda cosa más importante (la primera es la boda) en los recuerdos personales de las venusianas. Es esencial que planeen el día o el momento cuidadosamente.

En la quinta etapa, la pareja debe practicar una de las cualidades más importantes en un matrimonio entre marcianos y venusianas: el arte de pedir perdón y el arte de perdonar.

"Cuando un hombre no reconoce sus errores, la mujer se los recordará hasta que lo haga". (pág. 114) El doctor añade que no es suficiente pedir perdón, sino saber hacerlo: no es suficiente explicar por qué llegó tarde, aunque tenga una excelente razón, sino que debe entender y validar los sentimientos de enojo de la mujer. Por otro lado, la mujer debe perdonar al hombre de manera que quede claro que lo acepta y lo quiere de todas maneras. Decir simplemente, "Te perdono", no es suficiente. Es necesario añadir algo como "Está bien, pero la próxima vez llámame, estaba preocupada por ti".

[1]*training*

Quinta etapa: El compromiso

17. ¿Para qué sirve la última etapa?
_____

18. ¿Qué puede hacer el hombre para que la mujer tenga recuerdos inolvidables del compromiso?
_____

19. ¿En qué consiste el arte de pedir perdón y saber perdonar?
_____

20. ¿Te gustó la reseña? ¿Por qué?
_____
_____

395

Cuaderno de tareas

Nombre _____ Fecha _____

G. ¡Tú eres el experto! A friend of yours has had a history of unsuccessful dates. After reading the book review **Marte y Venus en una cita**, give them six or seven suggestions and recommendations to improve their dating techniques. Use the following pairs of expressions.

es importante que…	para que/hasta que	dudo que… cuando…
(no) te aconsejo que…	a menos que…	es necesario que… antes de que…
(no) te recomiendo que…	hasta que…	es bueno que… para que…

Primera etapa: la atracción

> **Modelo** Es importante que sientas genuino interés en la persona para que compartan la conversación.

_____
_____
_____

Segunda etapa: la duda
_____
_____
_____

Tercera etapa: la exclusividad
_____
_____
_____
_____

Cuarta etapa: la intimidad
_____
_____
_____

Quinta etapa: el compromiso
_____
_____
_____

396

Workbook activities A series of workbook activities directly follow the color pages of each lesson in your worktext. You will know precisely when to complete these activities because they are referenced in the **Práctica adicional** boxes throughout the preceding pages of the lesson.

Lesson reinforcement A wide range of exercise types, often placed in the context of the **INVITACIONES** video and/or featuring the video characters, gives you ample written practice of the vocabulary and structures in the **Escenas de la vida**, **Gramática**, and **Vocabulario** sections of each lesson.

Cultural focus and language use The **Para terminar** section contains open-ended activities that synthesize the vocabulary and grammar of the lesson and recycle language from previous lessons. Cultural readings—realia, letters, and other formats—followed by comprehension and personal reaction questions are frequently included.

Cuaderno de tareas: ¡A escuchar!
develops listening comprehension skills while reinforcing the lesson's theme, vocabulary, and grammar.

Page 1 (left)

Nombre _____ Fecha _____

¡A escuchar!

Episodio 1

Comprensión

A. Las clases.

Parte 1. You are going to listen to Ana Mari and some of her classmates say which classes they are taking this semester. First, listen to the list of classes and repeat each one after the speaker.

economía	inglés	filosofía	matemáticas
astronomía	química	tenis	historia

Now, listen to Ana Mari and her friends and check off the classes each person is taking.

	Ana Mari	Raúl	Cristina	Carmen
astronomía	☐	☐	☐	☐
economía	☐	☐	☐	☐
filosofía	☐	☐	☐	☐
historia	☐	☐	☐	☐
inglés	☐	☐	☐	☐
matemáticas	☐	☐	☐	☐
química	☐	☐	☐	☐
tenis	☐	☐	☐	☐

Parte 2. You will now hear four questions. Look at the list of classes in **Parte 1** and answer the questions that you hear. Then repeat the correct answer after the speaker.

Modelo	You hear:	¿Cuántos estudiantes toman tenis?
	You say:	Tres estudiantes: Ana Mari, Raúl y Cristina toman tenis.

B. ¿Cuántos? How many are there of the following items? Listen and write the numerals for the numbers that you hear.

1. _____ sillas
2. _____ banderas
3. _____ lápices
4. _____ plumas
5. _____ diccionarios
6. _____ escritorios
7. _____ cuadernos
8. _____ libros
9. _____ profesores
10. _____ mapas

Page 2 (right)

Nombre _____ Fecha _____

Pronunciación

Las vocales. The vowels in Spanish, **a**, **e**, **i**, **o**, and **u**, are important sounds to master. Unlike English, each vowel in Spanish has only one pronunciation. In addition, the vowel sounds are shorter and crisper than the vowel sounds in English. Repeat these letters, words, and sentences after the speaker.

a

Ana	lápiz	habilidad	Ana camina a la casa.
Adán	papa	América	Adán habla con las amigas de Ana.

e

Pepe	me	septiembre	Pelé bebe leche.
te	le	televisión	Héctor lee lentamente.

i

Ignacio	igual	importante	Allí está mi diccionario de inglés.
Víctor	química	librería	Perdí el lápiz de Lilí.

o

Octavio	kiosko	oportunidad	Manolo dejó las fotocopias.
poco	hombre	fotocopias	El pobre hombre come poco.

u

Humberto	número	universidad	Lupe usa la computadora.
Lupe	mujer	unidad	La mujer usa su pluma.

Más escenas de la vida

A. ¿Quién lo dijo? Wayne is calling Ramón, and Ramón's mother answers. Listen to their conversation, and indicate who said each statement: Wayne **(W)** or Ramón **(R)**. You will hear the conversation twice.

1. Buenos días, señora.
2. Bien gracias, ¿y usted?
3. Hola Wayne, ¿cómo estás?
4. Más o menos. Estoy un poco enfermo.
5. Hasta luego.
6. Gracias. Hasta mañana.

B. ¿Cierto o falso? Sofía and Ana Mari run into Adriana at school. Indicate whether the following statements are **cierto** or **falso**, according to their conversation. You will hear the conversation twice.

	Cierto	Falso
1. Adriana runs into Ana Mari and Sofía in the afternoon.	☐	☐
2. Adriana has met Ana Mari before.	☐	☐
3. Sofía wishes Adriana a good day.	☐	☐
4. Ana Mari and Sofía are going to work.	☐	☐
5. Adriana will see Sofía again tomorrow.	☐	☐

Lab activities Two pages of lab activities appear right after the workbook activities for each lesson. As with the workbook activities, **Práctica adicional** boxes throughout the lesson let you know exactly when to complete these activities.

Pronunciación A pronunciation section explains and practices the sounds and pronunciation of Spanish and discusses topics like accent marks that are related to spelling.

Comprensión These activities, which are frequently placed in the context of the **INVITACIONES** video, build your listening comprehension skills as they practice the grammar and vocabulary of the lesson.

Más escenas de la vida A new, additional conversation between the video characters deepens the storyline of the lesson's **Escenas de la vida** video episode, while once again reinforcing the lesson's target structures and vocabulary.

Video Program

Fully integrated with your worktext, the **INVITACIONES: Primera parte** video contains fifteen episodes, one for each lesson in your worktext. The episodes follow a group of Spanish-speaking students attending college in the United States as they confront the challenges and experience the joys of daily life. Several of the friends hold down part-time jobs. One is an American man who speaks good Spanish, while yet another is a Puerto Rican housewife who is returning to school and the workforce. The video, shot in southern California, follows the characters through an academic year and focuses on the Latino experience and influence in the United States.

Before you see each video episode, your instructor will use the **Escenas de la vida** section to preview the vocabulary and grammatical structures the characters will use and that you will study in the corresponding lesson. As the video progresses, the video conversations carefully combine new vocabulary and grammar with language taught in earlier lessons in your worktext. In this way, the video provides comprehensible input as it puts the language you are learning in action in real-life contexts.

The Cast

Here are the main characters you will meet when you watch the **INVITACIONES: Primera parte** video:

From Mexico,
Sofía Blasio Salas

From Cuba,
Manolo Báez Rodríguez

From the United States, of Mexican and Honduran heritage,
Ana Mari Robledo Suárez

From Puerto Rico,
Adriana Ferreira de Barrón

Ana Mari's brother,
Ramón Robledo Suárez

From the United States,
Wayne Reilly

A powerful and important learning tool, the video is integrated into every section of all the lessons in your worktext. The opening section each lesson, **Escenas de la vida**, prepares you for the video episode and checks your comprehension. Vocabulary and grammar used by the video characters appear throughout the **Para comunicarnos mejor** explanations and activities. The **Actividades comunicativas** and **La correspondencia** sections of each lesson reference the events and characters of the corresponding video episode, and both the workbook and lab activities in each lesson's **Cuaderno de tareas** pages are often set in the context of the video episode.

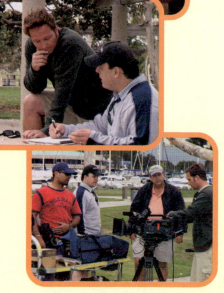

Student Ancillaries

Video CD-ROM

Free-of-charge with each new copy of **INVITACIONES: Primera parte**, this easy-to-navigate CD-ROM contains the complete **INVITACIONES** video with videoscript.

Worktext & Lab MP3 Files Audio CD-ROM

Free-of-charge with each new copy of **INVITACIONES: Primera parte**, the MP3 Files Audio CD-ROM contains all of the recordings you need to complete the listening activities in both the color pages of your worktext and the lab activities in the **Cuaderno de tareas: ¡A escuchar!**

Companion Website (accessed through *www.vistahigherlearning.com*)

The **INVITACIONES** website offers Internet activities and a wide range of on-line resources for you and your instructor that directly correlate to your worktext and go beyond it.

Instructor Ancillaries

Instructor's Annotated Edition (IAE)

The **Instructor's Annotated Edition** provides a wealth of information designed to support classroom teaching and management. The same size as the student worktext, the **IAE** provides answers overprinted on the student pages, as well as resources and suggestions for implementing and extending the worktext activities.

Instructor's Resource Manual (IRM)

The **Instructor's Resource Manual** offers materials that reinforce and expand upon the lessons in the student worktext. The **Comprehensible Input** section provides guidance on what language to pre-teach before showing the video for the **Escenas de la vida** section. The **Additional Activities** section offers suggestions and materials for additional activities to accompany the worktext episodes. The **Videoscript** and **Tapescript** sections provide transcriptions of all of the conversations from the **Escenas de la vida** video and the recorded activities, respectively.

VHS Video

This VHS version of the **INVITACIONES** video is ideal for showing the episodes in class.

Worktext CD

This audio CD contains the audio tracks of the **Escenas de la vida** video episodes on the **INVITACIONES** video and the recordings for all of the listening activities on the color pages of the lessons in the worktext. The printed scripts are available in the **IRM.**

Lab Audio CDs

These audio CDs contain the recordings that are used in conjunction with the lab activities in the **Cuaderno de tareas: ¡A escuchar!** section of each worktext lesson.

Cuaderno de tareas Answer Key

The **Answer Key** provides answers to the workbook and lab activities in the **Cuaderno de tareas** section of the worktext, should instructors wish to distribute them to students for self-correction.

Overhead Transparencies

This set of overhead transparencies contains maps of the Spanish-speaking world, as well as selected images from the student worktexts, for use in presenting and reinforcing the language introduced throughout the lessons.

Testing Program

The **Testing Program** contains a quiz for every lesson in **INVITACIONES**, as well as midterm and final exams.

Test Files CD-ROM for Windows® and Macintosh®

This CD-ROM contains the complete, printed **Testing Program** as Microsoft Word® files, so instructors can readily customize the tests and exams for their courses.

INVITACIONES: Segunda parte

This companion volume completes the course, continuing the video storyline and building on the grammatical structures and vocabulary presented in **INVITACIONES: Primera parte.**

SEGUNDA PARTE

Invitaciones

An Interactive Worktext for Beginning Spanish

Alonso-Lyrintzis • Alonso • Zaslow

INVITACIONES: Segunda parte offers the same features, input-driven instructional approach, and ancillary package as **Primera parte**, as it both reviews the first volume and rounds out the entire **INVITACIONES** program with **Episodios 16–30**.

Reviewers

The authors and the publishing professionals at Vista Higher Learning express their sincere appreciation to the college instructors nationwide who reviewed portions of the **INVITACIONES** program. Their comments and suggestions were invaluable to the final product.

Beatrice L. Bongiorno
Bellevue Community College, WA

Jose A. Carmona
Daytona Beach Community College, FL

Sharon Cherry
University of South Carolina Spartanburg, SC

Maritza Chinea-Thornberry
University of South Florida, FL

Conxita Domenech
Front Range Community College, CO

Marcella Fierro
Mesa Community College, AZ

Jennifer Garson
Pasadena City College, CA

Judy Getty
California State University, Sacramento, CA

Pamela A. Gill
Gaston College, NC

Andrew S. Gordon
Mesa State College, CO

Irene B. Hodgson
Xavier College, OH

Patricia Houston
Pima Community College, East Campus, AZ

Teresa Dee Kennedy
Lenoir Community College, NC

Marta F. Loyola
Trinity College, DC

Matthew Luke
Lane Community College, OR

John Markovich
Messiah College, PA

Kathryn McConnell
Point Loma Nazarene University, CA

Lori L. McGee
Kent State University, Stark Campus, OH

Susan McMillen Villar
University of Minnesota, Twin cities, MN

Silvina Montrul
University of Illinois at Urbana Champaign, IL

Eduardo Pacheco
Judson College, AL

Mercedes Palomino
Florida Atlantic University, FL

Marcela Ruiz-Funes
East Carolina University, NC

Loreto Sánchez
Johns Hopkins University, MD

Phillip Santiago
Buffalo State College, NY

Jennifer Schaber
St. Louis Community College, MO

Nidia A. Schuhmacher
Brandeis University, MA

Theresa Ann Sears
University of North Carolina at Greensboro, NC

Wendy Woodrich
Lewis and Clark College, OR

Susan Yoder-Kreger
University of Missouri-St. Louis, MO

Student Reactions

The authors would like to thank the students at California State University San Marcos, where the program was class tested in the summer of 1999, and at Southwestern College, where the **INVITACIONES** program was class-tested from the fall of 1999 until the time of publication. Their patience and candid remarks about the activities, the characters, and the philosophy of the text were invigorating and truly useful to the completion of the project. Below are some of their reactions.

"What I liked the most is that it was not a bunch of conjugating. It actually teaches you useful conversations."

"It is a brilliant idea to have everything in one book; I feel I am getting my money's worth."

"All the side notes helped me learn things!"

"I really liked the layout of the book. The activities help to break down your inhibitions about using the language."

"I loved having the vocabulary at the end of every episode."

"I enjoy learning about the characters and their lives; it helps to personalize the material for me."

"I enjoyed being able to write all my notes directly on the book. I know that in the future, I can look back and review my Spanish."

"Everything in the episodes was relevant and related to what we were learning!"

"This book made it fun to learn, and the language is sticking to me."

"I really appreciate not carrying three books around!"

Acknowledgments

The long process of writing this textbook was challenging and full of unexpected changes. It took a lot of tenacity, endurance, and our unappeasable dream that many more students would be successful in learning Spanish, if only the materials they used were more inviting, realistic, interactive, and fun.

Our most heartfelt gratitude goes to José Blanco and Denise St. Jean, who share our dream and were willing to take the inherent risk of bringing to the market a new, "out of the box" set of books. We are delighted to have been given the opportunity to work with them and their outstanding team of professionals, who made this program a reality.

We are grateful to Beverly Burdette, of Pellissippi State Community College, for creating lab activities to accompany our text; her conscientious contributions have always been in keeping with our own intentions, and round-out our Spanish program.

We would like to thank our editors, Sarah Kenney and Gabriela Ferland, for their astute observations, unfaltering hard work and dedication, and, most of all, for their patience and cheery responses to our inquiries.

We are also indebted to our colleagues and friends, whose advice and contributions during the different stages of the manuscript helped us shape the book: Dinorah Guadiana-Costa and Concetta Calandra, of Southwestern College, for their support, constructive suggestions and enthusiasm while using our materials in their classes; Cuban poet Pedro Báez, Ana Hami, of Chapman University, and Francisco Zabaleta, of San Diego State University, for helping us create culturally and linguistically authentic Cuban, Puerto Rican, and Spanish characters, respectively; Diana Rossner and Nancy Barley, of Lake Tahoe Community College, for always offering sincere and encouraging remarks; Gary Anderson for sharing his ideas unselfishly; Virginia Young, of Grossmont College, for adding activities to our Instructor's Resource Manual; Hal Wingard, the Executive Director of the California Language Teachers Association, for embracing our materials and speaking on our behalf at the Foreign Language Conference of the California Community Colleges. We also give a special thanks to our colleagues and friends at the different institutions in San Diego, who have openly and warmly supported us, both personally and professionally.

A project of this magnitude could not be undertaken without the support of our families and close friends, who have unselfishly shared a piece of their lives by taking care of our children and pets, allowing us to use their pictures, their names, and their stories. Thank you for enduring the joys and sorrows of the past few years with us.

We would also like to thank Southwestern College, for not only class testing our program, but also for being so cooperative and accommodating when we shot our video on the campus. Last but not least, we offer our sincere thanks to our wonderful team of adjunct instructors, who have served as anonymous reviewers.

Deana Alonso-Lyrintzis, Esther Alonso, and Brandon Zaslow

¡Bienvenidos al mundo hispano!

A. How much do you know about the Spanish language? Indicate whether you believe the following statements are true or false.

Instructor's Resources
• Overheads
• Website

	Cierto	Falso
1. After English, Spanish is the most frequently spoken language in the United States.	✓	☐
2. One out of every ten United States residents speaks Spanish.	✓	☐
3. The United States has the fifth largest population of Spanish speakers in the world.	✓	☐
4. The first Europeans to settle in the modern-day United States were Spanish speakers.	✓	☐
5. Spanish is spoken in twenty-one countries.	✓	☐
6. More than 350 million people speak Spanish.	✓	☐
7. Spanish is a modern derivative of Latin.	✓	☐

A. Allow students to respond to prompts and highlight the importance of the Spanish language throughout the world.

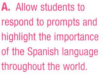

B. Let's meet each other! Listen to your instructor as they model the pronunciation of the following exchange. Then practice the conversation with three or four classmates. Answers will vary.

Estudiante 1:	¡Hola! ¿Cómo estás?
Estudiante 2:	Bien, ¿y tú?
Estudiante 1:	Bien, gracias.
Estudiante 2:	Me llamo _____ (*your name*). Y tú, ¿cómo te llamas?
Estudiante 1:	_____ ¡Mucho gusto!
Estudiante 2:	Igualmente.

B. Greet several students modeling the dialogue, and invite them to respond to you. You may do choral repetition as well. Give them time to practice with three or four classmates.

C. The Spanish-speaking world. Spanish speakers are a diverse group of ethnicities, religions, and cultures. Learn about exciting places and facts, using your knowledge of English and of the world, as you read the captions under the following photographs.

Learning Strategy: Using cognates

A cognate is a word that is similar in two or more languages because of a common origin. The English word *publication* and the Spanish word **publicación** are cognates. Cognates in Spanish and English are always pronounced differently, are often spelled differently, and sometimes differ in meaning. Most of the time, however, you can guess what a Spanish cognate means by associating it with an English word you know. Can you guess the meaning of these cognates?

colonial	**falsos**	**indicar**	**contraste**	**fotografía**	**millones**
comentarios	**glaciares**	**moderna**	**construcciones**	**habitantes**	**montañas**

You can use cognates to help you understand the overall meaning of Spanish sentences. To practice this strategy, read the captions under the following photographs.

En la Ciudad de México hay *(there are)* más de 20 millones de habitantes. Es la ciudad más poblada del mundo.

Chile y Argentina comparten *(share)* la Patagonia, donde hay glaciares e inmensas montañas.

En Puerto Rico, el contraste entre la arquitectura moderna y la arquitectura colonial es visible.

La Avenida 9 de Julio en Buenos Aires, Argentina, es enorme. Buenos Aires se considera el París de América.

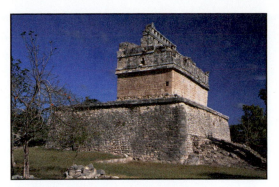

Los mayas habitaron parte de México y de Centroamérica.

Las impresionantes murallas de Ávila fueron *(were)* construidas para proteger la ciudad después de expulsar a los árabes del territorio español.

El pueblo inca construyó Machu Picchu en las montañas de los Andes.

D. Latinoamérica. Examina las fotografías para *(in order to)* indicar si los comentarios son **ciertos** o **falsos**.

D. You may assign **Práctica D** for homework.

	Cierto	Falso
1. En la Ciudad de México hay más de 20 millones de personas.	✓	☐
2. Puerto Rico tiene *(has)* muchas construcciones antiguas y modernas.	✓	☐
3. Los aztecas construyeron Machu Picchu.	☐	✓
4. El clima de Chile es tropical.	☐	✓
5. La Avenida 9 de Julio es enorme.	✓	☐
6. Los incas eran *(were)* habitantes de México y Guatemala.	☐	✓
7. Los árabes fueron expulsados de España.	✓	☐

Learning Strategy: How to be a successful language-learner

Learning to speak another language can be fun and exciting. Many successful language-learners share certain basic characteristics. Read the following statements to determine why these particular traits are useful in language learning.

1. Students who are excited about learning Spanish do better than students who are indifferent.
   Why do you think a positive attitude is important?

2. Students who are not afraid of speaking Spanish learn more than students who are reluctant to speak.
   Why do you think being willing to speak is important?

3. Students who take risks progress more rapidly than students who are inhibited.
   Why do you think taking risks is important?

4. Students who accept that uncertainty and inconsistency are part of learning a language learn at a faster rate.
   Why do you think that tolerance of ambiguity is important?

Whether or not you possess these traits, you can learn to communicate well in Spanish. Throughout this book, you will encounter **Learning Strategy** sections designed to improve your study skills. Here are a few for starters.

Listen

Listen carefully in class. At first, you will not be able to understand everything you hear, but you will absorb a lot of Spanish without realizing it.

Speak

Speak as much Spanish as you can. Talk to your instructor and to your classmates in Spanish. Don't be afraid to make mistakes, as they will help you to identify things you need to learn.

Take Notes

Take notes in class. Your memory is going to get a workout, so write things down. Be sure to ask questions in class. Remember, there are no silly questions.

Practice

You will need to practice every day. Learning Spanish is like learning to swim or to play the guitar—the more you practice, the better you become. Cramming the night before an exam is a recipe for disaster!

Take Charge

The key element in shaping your success is you. Look for opportunities to practice Spanish outside of class: watch television in Spanish and listen to Spanish radio, talk to your neighbors, use the Internet. Take charge of your own learning!

Have Fun

You are going to learn Spanish, but it will take time. After all, you didn't learn to speak English overnight! Your worktext is designed to make your learning enjoyable. Have fun and relax. If you do, you will learn faster and more easily.

Episodio

1

Escenas de la vida: El primer día de clases

Video
CD-ROM

A. ¡Mira cuánto puedes entender! *(See how much you can understand!)* As you watch the video or listen to your Audio CD-ROM, fill in the blanks with the characters' names.

Audio
CD-ROM

Instructor's Resources
- Overheads
- VHS Video
- Worktext CD
- Website
- IRM: Videoscript, Comprehensible input

Sofía, Adriana, Manolo

Cultura a lo vivo
Did you notice how, when the characters greet each other, there is always some kind of physical contact? Hispanics like to touch each other (a kiss, a pat on the back, or simply a handshake) to demonstrate openness and warmth.

El   profesor López

Escenas de la vida.
The purpose of this section is to set the stage for the entire lesson. Comprehensible input provided by you, the instructor, prepares students to watch the video and complete the activities that follow. In the event that you cannot or do not wish to show the video in class, students may access the conversations in the video on their Audio CD-ROM, or entire video on the Video CD-ROM; both of these components are packaged with each new Student Worktext. The images on this page are available on the overhead transparencies. See the **Instructor's Resource Manual** or the Website for sample comprehensible input to use with this section and for more detailed information about language to pre-teach.

Video Synopsis. Sofía meets Adriana in calculus class. Manolo greets Prof. López. He tells Manolo to study more if he wants to pass. Sofía introduces Manolo to Ana Mari.

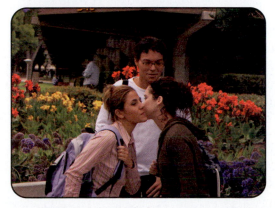

Ana Mari, Sofía, Manolo

5

Video
CD-ROM

Audio
CD-ROM

B. ¿Te diste cuenta? *(Did you realize?)* Escucha las conversaciones otra vez para indicar si los comentarios son **ciertos** o **falsos.**

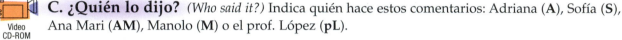

	Cierto	Falso
1. Adriana es de México.	☐	☑
2. Manolo necesita estudiar más.	☑	☐
3. Ana Mari es amiga de Manolo.	☐	☑
4. Manolo toma una clase de inglés.	☐	☑
5. Ana Mari no tiene novio *(doesn't have a boyfriend).*	☑	☐

Video
CD-ROM

Audio
CD-ROM

C. ¿Quién lo dijo? *(Who said it?)* Indica quién hace estos comentarios: Adriana (**A**), Sofía (**S**), Ana Mari (**AM**), Manolo (**M**) o el prof. López (**pL**).

_A_	1.	Soy de Puerto Rico.
_M_	2.	Buenos días, profesor López.
_pL_	3.	Este semestre necesitas estudiar más.
_S_	4.	Te presento a Ana Mari.
_AM_	5.	Encantada.
_AM_	6.	Tengo clase de inglés ahora.
_AM_	7.	Mucho gusto de conocerte.
_pL, S_	8.	¡Que te vaya bien!

Práctica adicional

| Cuaderno de tareas WB pp.21–22, A–C | Video CD-ROM Episodio 1 |

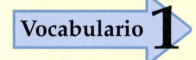

Para comunicarnos mejor

Vocabulario 1 ▷ **Greeting and saying good-bye to others**
• **Greetings and good-byes**

Use these informal expressions when speaking to someone with whom you have a close relationship, such as a family member, friend, or someone your age or younger.

Para hablar con amigos	
¿Cómo estás?	*How are you?*
¿Y tú?	*And you?*
¿Cómo te llamas?	*What's your name?*
¡Que te vaya bien!	*Have a nice day!*
Te presento a...	*I'd like you to meet...*

¡Fíjate!
Be aware that you are responsible for learning all words and structures presented in the **Vocabulario** and **Gramática** sections of your book. They will be practiced in activities that follow and will appear on tests.

When speaking to someone with whom you do not have a close relationship, someone you would address with a title and a last name, or an older or higher–ranking person, use these formal expressions to show respect:

Para hablar con respeto

¿Cómo está?	*How are you?*	señor (Sr.)	*Mr., sir*
¿Y usted?	*And you?*	señora (Sra.)	*Mrs., ma'am*
¿Cómo se llama?	*What's your name?*	señorita (Srta.)	*Miss*
¡Que le vaya bien!	*Have a nice day!*	doctor(a) (Dr(a).)	*Doctor*
Le presento a...	*I'd like you to meet...*	profesor(a) (Prof(a).)	*Professor*

¡Fíjate!

When in doubt about whether you should use **tú** or **usted**, use the formal **usted** forms to show respect.

Más saludos, despedidas y expresiones de cortesía

Hola.	*Hi.*
Buenos días.	*Good morning.* (from dawn until noon)
Buenas tardes.	*Good afternoon.* (from noon until dusk)
Buenas noches.	*Good evening/Good night.* (from dusk until dawn)
Hasta luego.	*See you later.*
Hasta mañana.	*See you tomorrow.*
Nos vemos mañana.	*See you tomorrow.* (you have arranged to meet tomorrow)
Adiós.	*Good-bye.*
Mucho gusto.	*Nice to meet you.*
Encantado.	*Pleased to meet you.* (said by a man)
Encantada.	*Pleased to meet you.* (said by a woman)
Igualmente.	*Nice to meet you, too.*
Gracias.	*Thank you.*
De nada.	*You're welcome.*
Bien.	*Fine.*
Muy bien.	*Very well.*
Más o menos.	*So-so.*

Additional Activity.
You may want to distribute different pairs of questions and answers on index cards to the class, for students to match together. Each student should have one card. To check their answers, have pairs of students read their cards. For example: Student 1 matches **Hola, ¿cómo estás?** with Student 2's **Bien, gracias, ¿y tú?**

Learning Strategy: Avoid word-for-word translation

Because English and Spanish are independent languages that often express the same thought in different ways, you should avoid translating word-for-word. For example, **¡Que te vaya bien!** might be translated as *May it go well with you.* The idea Spanish speakers mean to convey, however, is *Have a nice day!* So, learn the meaning of language "chunks," and avoid word-for-word translations.

PRÁCTICA

A. ¡A actuar! With a classmate, act out the following conversations.

Después de la clase

Manolo	**Buenos días**, profesor López. **¿Cómo está usted?**
Profesor	¿Otra vez aquí? *((You) here again?)*
Manolo	Sí, necesito pasar esta clase.
Profesor	Este semestre necesitas estudiar más.
Manolo	Sí, ya sé. **Hasta mañana**.
Profesor	**¡Que te vaya bien!**
Manolo	**Gracias. Igualmente.**

Te presento a Ana Mari

Sofía	**Hola**, Ana Mari. **¿Cómo estás?**
Ana Mari	**Muy bien. ¿Y tú?**
Sofía	**Bien, gracias.**
Sofía	Mira, Manolo, **te presento** a Ana Mari. Es mi mejor amiga. Y no tiene novio.
Ana Mari	¡Sofía!
Manolo	**Mucho gusto.**
Ana Mari	**Encantada.** Bueno, tengo clase de inglés ahora. **Hasta luego.** Y **mucho gusto** de conocerte.
Manolo	**Gracias. Igualmente.**
Sofía	**Adiós**, Ana Mari. **¡Que te vaya bien!**

B. ¿Qué respondes? Imagina que conversas con Sofía. Responde apropiadamente.

1. Hola, ¿cómo te llamas? _____ Me llamo… _____
2. Te presento a Manolo. _____ Mucho gusto/Encantado/a. _____
3. Hasta luego. _____ Hasta luego/¡Que te vaya bien! _____
4. ¡Buenos días! _____ Hola/¡Buenos días! _____
5. Gracias. _____ De nada. _____
6. Adiós. _____ Adiós/¡Que te vaya bien! _____

C. Buenos días, profesor. Imagina que conversas con el profesor López. Responde apropiadamente.

1. Buenas tardes. _____ Hola/Buenas tardes. _____
2. ¿Cómo estás? _____ Bien, gracias, ¿y usted? _____
3. Mucho gusto. _____ Igualmente/Encantado/a. _____
4. Hasta mañana. _____ Hasta mañana/¡Que le vaya bien! _____
5. ¡Que te vaya bien! _____ Gracias. Igualmente. _____
6. Buenas noches. _____ Buenas noches. _____

D. ¿Saludo o despedida? Escucha las frases para indicar si cada una *(each one)* es un **saludo** o una **despedida**.

Instructor's Resources
• Worktext CD
• IRM: Tapescript

	Saludo	Despedida
1.	☐	✓
2.	✓	☐
3.	☐	✓
4.	✓	☐
5.	✓	☐
6.	☐	✓

Script. Escucha las frases para indicar si cada una es un saludo o una despedida.
1. *Adiós.*
2. *Buenos días.*
3. *Hasta mañana.*
4. *Hola.*
5. *Buenas tardes.*
6. *Hasta luego.*

E. ¿Cómo respondes? *(How do you answer?)* Escucha las frases para seleccionar la respuesta apropiada.

1. a. Más o menos.   (b.) Mucho gusto.   c. Gracias.
2. (a.) Igualmente.   b. ¡Que le vaya bien!   c. Buenos días.
3. a. Igualmente.   b. ¿Y usted?   (c.) ¡Que te vaya bien!
4. a. ¿Y tú?   b. ¿Cómo se llama?   (c.) Muy bien, gracias.
5. a. Sí, gracias.   (b.) Me llamo...   c. Hasta luego.

Script. Escucha las frases para seleccionar la respuesta apropiada.
1. *Te presento a Ana.*
2. *Mucho gusto.*
3. *Hasta luego.*
4. *¿Cómo está?*
5. *¿Cómo te llamas?*

F. ¡A conversar! Con un(a) compañero/a, usa las expresiones necesarias para inventar una conversación para cada *(each)* situación. Answers will vary.

1. You see your instructor at ten in the morning. Extend a greeting, ask how they are, then say good-bye.

2. A new student has just joined the class. Greet the student and find out their name.

3. Your friend wants to meet the new student. Introduce them.

4. Class is over. Say good-bye to your friend and wish them a good day.

5. Your roommate returns home at four in the afternoon. Greet each other and ask each other how you are.

F. Ask students to create the dialogues for homework. In pairs, students practice and act the dialogues out in class the next day.

Práctica adicional

Cuaderno de tareas
WB pp.22–23, D–H

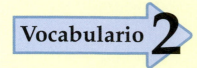

Vocabulario 2

Saying which classes you take
- **The alphabet**
- **Class subjects**

You have probably noticed that, in Spanish, there is a very close relationship between the way words are written and the way they are pronounced. This feature facilitates the learning of spelling and pronunciation. Spanish sounds, however, do not have exact equivalents in English. For this reason, do not rely on English sounds to pronounce Spanish words.

A	**Be** (grande)	**Ce**	**CHe**	**De**
alfabeto	bandera	cuaderno	mochila	diccionario
E	**eFe**	**Ge**	**Hache**	**I**
escritorio	fotocopias	geografía	hombre	inglés
Jota	**Ka**	**eLe**	**eLLe**	**eMe**
mujer	kiosko	libro	silla	mapa
eNe	**eÑe**	**O**	**Pe**	**Q** (cu)
números	baño	oficina	pluma	química
eRe	**eRRe**	**eSe**	**Te**	USC UNIVERSITY OF SOUTHERN CALIFORNIA
librería	carro	salón de clases	tenis	universidad
Ve (chica)	**W** doble u	**X** equis	**Y** (i griega)	**Zeta**
video	Washington	examen	playa	lápiz

(In the "I" cell: adiós / good bye / au revoir / ciao)

¡Fíjate!

Because the letters **b** and **v** have the same pronunciation in Spanish, Spanish speakers distinguish between the two by calling **b** "**Be grande**" and **v** "**Ve chica.**"

¡Fíjate!

To *say uppercase* and *lowercase*, use the terms **mayúscula** and **minúscula**, respectively. To indicate that a letter takes an accent, say **con acento** after the letter.

1. As of 1994, **ch** and **ll** are no longer regarded as letters in the Spanish alphabet. Even though these letters can no longer be found in separate sections of the dictionary, people continue to use them when spelling names or difficult words. You should use them when spelling your name to Spanish speakers.

2. The letter **ñ** does not exist in English. However, the [ñ] sound does exist in words like *onion* and *canyon*.

3. The Spanish vowels **a, e, i, o,** and **u** are short and tense. Do not move your tongue, lips, or jaws when pronouncing them, to avoid the glide sound of English vowels.

PRÁCTICA

G. Pronunciación. Repeat the letters and the words in the alphabet box on page 10 after your instructor. Which words are cognates (words that are the same or almost the same in the both languages)?

alfabeto, diccionario, fotocopias, geografía, kiosko, mapa, números, oficina, química, carro, universidad, video, examen

H. ¿Tienes buena memoria? Write the words in Spanish.

1. pen ___pluma___
2. bookstore ___librería___
3. notebook ___cuaderno___
4. pencil ___lápiz___
5. dictionary ___diccionario___
6. English ___inglés___
7. book ___libro___
8. classroom ___salón de clases___
9. office ___oficina___

I. Dictado. You will hear eight famous last names. Write the names in the spaces provided.

Audio CD-ROM

Instructor's Resources
• Worktext CD
• IRM: Tapescript

1. ___Olmos___
2. ___Banderas___
3. ___Sosa___
4. ___Cruz___
5. ___Leguizamo___
6. ___Hayek___
7. ___López___
8. ___De la Hoya___

Script. *You will hear the spelling of eight famous last names. Write the names in the spaces provided.*
1. Olmos. O-ele-eme-o-ese
2. Banderas. Be-a-ene-de-e-ere-a-ese
3. Sosa. Ese-o-ese-a
4. Cruz. Ce-ere-u-zeta.
5. Leguizamo. Ele-e-ge-u-i-zeta-a-eme-o
6. Hayek. Hache-a-i griega-e-ka
7. López. Ele-o-(con acento)-pe-e-zeta
8. De la Hoya. De (mayúscula)-e; Ele-a; Hache (mayúscula)-o-i griega-a

J. ¿Quiénes son? *(Who are they?)* Match the last names from **Práctica I** with the first names below to describe eight Spanish-speaking celebrities.

John	Jennifer	Edward	Celia
Sammy	Óscar	Antonio	Salma

1. ___John Leguizamo___ es un actor colombiano.
2. ___Jennifer López___ es una actriz de origen puertorriqueño.
3. ___Edward Olmos___ es un actor mexicoamericano.
4. ___Salma Hayek___ es una actriz mexicana.
5. ___Sammy Sosa___ es un beisbolista dominicano.
6. ___Celia Cruz___ es una cantante cubana.
7. ___Antonio Banderas___ es un actor español.
8. ___Óscar De La Hoya___ es un boxeador mexicoamericano.

• Class subjects

Listen carefully as your instructor pronounces the names of following class subjects **(las materias)**. Repeat each word after them, reproducing the Spanish sounds as closely as you can.

Las materias			
antropología	economía	geografía	matemáticas
astronomía	(educación) física	historia	música
biología	español	inglés	química
drama	filosofía	literatura	sicología

Vocabulario 2. Have students read the class subjects and emphasize that these words are active vocabulary. Model the pronunciation, having students repeat after you.

K. Personas famosas. Empareja las personas famosas con las materias.

_f_	1. antropología	a. Shakespeare
_e_	2. astronomía	b. Sócrates
_c_	3. economía	c. Adam Smith
_b_	4. filosofía	d. Barbara Tuchman
_a_	5. drama	e. Galileo
_d_	6. historia	f. Jane Goodall

L. Asociaciones. ¿Qué materia(s) asocias con estas (*these*) personas?

1. Charles Darwin _____antropologia/biologia_____

2. Pitágoras (*Pythagoras*) _____matemáticas_____

3. Toni Morrison _____literatura_____

4. Gabriel García Márquez _____literatura/español_____

5. Wolfgang Amadeus Mozart _____música_____

6. Sigmund Freud _____sicología_____

M. ¿Tomas una clase de...? (*Are you taking a...class?*) Use the list of classes from page 11 to find out which classes your partner is currently taking. Answers will vary.

Modelo	—¿Tomas (*are you taking*) una clase de historia?
—Sí, ¿Y tú?	—No, ¿Y tú?
—Yo también (*Me too*). or Yo no.	—Yo tampoco (*Me neither*). or Yo sí.

Now write the classes your partner is taking.

Las clases de mi compañero/a son: _____

N. Mis clases. Escribe las clases que tomas (*you take*) este (*this*) semestre/trimestre y las clases que necesitas tomar (*you need to take*) el próximo (*next*) semestre/trimestre. Answers will vary.

N. Encourage students to write down the names of their classes. They will want to know many that are not on page 11. They will be expected to tell you the classes they are taking. Ask them to use the **Vocabulario personal** section on page 20 to write their personal vocabulary.

Este semestre/trimestre	El próximo semestre/trimestre
_____	_____
_____	_____
_____	_____
_____	_____
_____	_____

 Ñ. Tus clases. Talk to a classmate to find out which classes they are currently taking and which classes they need to take next semester/trimester. *Answers will vary.*

> **Modelo**
> —¿Qué clases tomas este semestre/trimestre (*which classes are you taking this semester/trimester*)?
> —Historia, matemáticas y español.
> —¿Qué clases necesitas tomar el próximo semestre/trimestre (*which classes do you need to take next semester/trimester*)?
> —Física, antropología y español. ¿Y tú, qué clases tomas este semestre?

Práctica adicional

Cuaderno de tareas
WB p.23, I–J

Vocabulario 3

Saying how many credits/units you take and how many hours you work
• Numbers 0–40

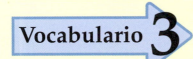

Los números del 0 al 40			
0 **cero**			
1 **uno**	11 **once**	21 **veintiuno**	31 **treinta y uno**
2 **dos**	12 **doce**	22 **veintidós**	32 **treinta y dos**
3 **tres**	13 **trece**	23 **veintitrés**	33 **treinta y tres**
4 **cuatro**	14 **catorce**	24 **veinticuatro**	34 **treinta y cuatro**
5 **cinco**	15 **quince**	25 **veinticinco**	35 **treinta y cinco**
6 **seis**	16 **dieciséis**	26 **veintiséis**	36 **treinta y seis**
7 **siete**	17 **diecisiete**	27 **veintisiete**	37 **treinta y siete**
8 **ocho**	18 **dieciocho**	28 **veintiocho**	38 **treinta y ocho**
9 **nueve**	19 **diecinueve**	29 **veintinueve**	39 **treinta y nueve**
10 **diez**	20 **veinte**	30 **treinta**	40 **cuarenta**

1. In some countries, the numbers from 16 through 19 and 21 through 29 are written as three separate words: **diez y seis, veinte y tres.**
2. The number *one* has three forms: **uno** (used when counting: **treinta y uno, treinta y dos...**), **un** (used before masculine nouns: **un libro, veintiún cuadernos**), and **una** (used before feminine nouns: **una pluma, treinta y una señoras**).
3. To ask and say how many classes you take and how many hours you work, use the following expressions.

¿Cuántas clases tomas? Tomo... *How many classes are you taking? I take...*
¿Cuántas horas trabajas? Trabajo... *How many hours do you work? I work...*

Vocabulario 3.
Have students repeat the numbers after you. You may wish to play a counting game.

Additional Activity.
Papas game:
Students form a circle and call out numbers: first multiples of of 2 (2, 4, 6, 8, etc.), then of 3 (3, 6, 9, 12, etc.), then of 4, and finally of 5. Students have to say **papas** instead of the actual number or its multiples (i.e., for 3, students would say **uno, dos**, *papas*, **cuatro, cinco**, *papas…*). Students who make a mistake must leave the circle and return to their seats.

PRÁCTICA

O. Asociaciones. What number do you associate with...?

1. a week   *siete*
2. the month of May   *cinco*
3. a triangle   *tres*

4. all of your fingers   *diez*
5. a square   *cuatro*
6. the lives of a cat   *nueve*

7. an octopus   *ocho*
8. your eyes   *dos*
9. your head   *uno*

P. Sumas y restas. *(Additions and subtractions.)* Imagine you are a teacher **(maestro/a)** tutoring a first-grade student in math. Ask the student to give you the answers to the following problems.

Modelo	$2 + 5 = ?$	$25 - 12 = ?$
	Maestro: **Dos más (*plus*) cinco son...**	Maestro: **Veinticinco menos (*minus*) doce son...**
	Estudiante: **Siete.**	Estudiante: **Trece.**

1. $8 + 6 = ?$ catorce
2. $11 + 9 = ?$ veinte
3. $23 - 12 = ?$ once
4. $12 + 13 = ?$ veinticinco

5. $30 - 18 = ?$ doce
6. $28 - 7 = ?$ veintiuno
7. $18 + 4 = ?$ veintidós
8. $20 - 1 = ?$ diecinueve

9. $47 - 14 = ?$ treinta y tres
10. $15 + 17 = ?$ treinta y dos
11. $45 - 7 = ?$ treinta y ocho
12. $26 - 16 = ?$ diez

Q. Trabajas demasiado. *(You work too much.)*

Parte 1. Find out from four of your classmates how many academic units/credits they are taking and how many hours per week they work. Fill out the chart below. Answers will vary.

Modelo	—¿Cuántos créditos tomas este semestre?	—¿Cuántas horas trabajas?
	—12. ¿Y tú?	—25. ¿Y tú?
	—18.	—No trabajo.

Nombre	Créditos este semestre	Horas de trabajo a la semana
1. _____	_____	_____
2. _____	_____	_____
3. _____	_____	_____
4. _____	_____	_____

¡Fíjate!

You are not responsible for learning the words in the **Banco de palabras**, although you may be responsible for learning these words and structures in later episodes. Currently, they appear to help you complete the activity at hand.

Parte 2. Now check the chart to see if your classmates follow the recommended work/study ratio. Comment on the results. You may use expressions from the **Banco de palabras**. Answers will vary.

Si trabajas...	Debes tomar sólo...	Necesitas estudiar...
40 hrs.	6 créditos	12 horas por semana
30 hrs.	9 créditos	18 horas por semana
20 hrs.	12 créditos	24 horas por semana
10 hrs.	15 créditos	30 horas por semana
0 hrs.	18 créditos	36 horas por semana

Banco de palabras

Trabajas demasiado.
You work too much.

...horas (hrs.) por semana
...hours per week

Necesitas tomar menos clases.
You need to take fewer classes.

Vas a salir bien.
You're going to do well.

R. Juego de lotería. You are going to play the lottery. First write six numbers between ten and forty on the lines in your worktext. Then listen to the three sets of winning numbers, write them down, and circle the ones that match your selections.

Juego # 1	11	14	17	23	25	31
Juego # 2	12	13	16	27	34	38
Juego # 3	15	18	21	29	32	40

Invitación a **Estados Unidos**

Del álbum de
Sofía

La comunidad hispana más grande *(biggest)* en Estados Unidos es la mexicoamericana. Su influencia en la cultura estadounidense es obvia en la comida *(food)*, la música y el arte. La fiesta del 5 de mayo *se* celebra en muchas ciudades y prácticamente en todos los estados del suroeste del país *(southwest of the country)*. Los mariachis y grupos folclóricos son espectáculos comunes en muchos eventos norteamericanos.

Práctica adicional

| Cuaderno de tareas WB p.24, K–M LM pp.29–30, A–B, Pron. | Audio CD-ROM Episodio 1 | Website vistahigher learning.com |

Script. *You are going to play the lottery. First, write six numbers between ten and forty on the lines in your worktext. Then listen to the three sets of winning numbers, write them down, and circle the ones that match your selections. Juego 1: 11, 14, 17, 23, 25, 31. Juego 2: 12, 13, 16, 27, 34, 38. Juego 3: 15, 18, 21, 29, 32, 40.*

Actividades comunicativas

In this activity, you will interact with another student. Before you begin, decide who will take the role of **Estudiante 1,** and who will take the role of **Estudiante 2. Estudiante 1** follows one set of instructions, while **Estudiante 2** follows another set found on the following page. Neither you nor your partner should look at the other's instructions or information.

> ## ¡Fíjate!
> The **Actividades comunicativas** require you to use all the Spanish you have learned to accomplish the task at hand. Do not be afraid of making mistakes. The purpose of these activities is to provide practice communicating in Spanish.

A. Las agendas.

Instrucciones para **Estudiante 1**

You took home your co-worker's list of clients and left your own list at the office. By telephone, ask your co-worker to give you the names and phone numbers of your clients. Ask your partner to spell out the names. When asked, be ready to tell your co-worker the names and numbers of their clients. Alternate asking and answering questions. Use questions like the ones below.

A. You may wish to review the task with students before they begin to interact. It is crucial to explain to students the importance of this section for developing fluency in Spanish. Insist that they do not speak English to accomplish the tasks at hand. This activity should take from 8 to 10 minutes. Review some of the answers with the whole class.

> **Banco de palabras**
>
> **¿Cómo se llama el cliente número uno?**
> *What is the first client's name?*
>
> **¿Cómo se escribe su nombre?**
> *How do you spell their name?*
>
> **¿Cuál es su teléfono?**
> *What is their phone number?*

> ## ¡Fíjate!
> Review **El alfabeto** on page 10 to prepare for this activity. Notice that telephone numbers are given in sets of two, except for the first number (4-21-05-25).

Mis clientes:

	Nombre	Teléfono
1.	Dr. Prathimano, G.	4-11-16-19
2.	Sra. Vasconcelos, X.	6-20-14-03
3.	Prof. Babayants, Q.	7-27-12-28
4.	Sra. Corrella, J.	2-10-15-23

Instructor's Resource
• IRM: Additional Activities

Los clientes de tu compañero/a:

1. Dr. Lyrintzis, C. 8-26-40-14
2. Sra. Bishara, W. 3-15-22-06
3. Srta. Palchefsky, J. 9-31-12-18
4. Sr. Cedeña, U. 5-37-13-11

Additional Activity. See the IRM for materials for this activity. Take the five different dialogues and cut them into individual phrases. Place them in an envelope and divide the class into groups. Have students reorganize the cards into a logical dialogue. Rotate the envelopes so all groups have an opportunity to recreate all dialogues.

Los clientes de tu compañero/a:

	Nombre	Teléfono
1.	Dr. Pratithmano, G.	4-11-16-19
2.	Sra. Vasconselos, X.	6-20-14-03
3.	Prof. Babayants, Q.	7-27-12-28
4.	Sra. Corrella, J.	2-10-15-23

Mis clientes:

	Nombre	Teléfono
1.	Dr. Lyritzis, C.	8-26-40-14
2.	Sra. Bishara, W.	3-15-22-06
3.	Srta. Palchetsky, J.	9-31-12-18
4.	Sr. Cedeña, U.	5-37-13-11

Banco de palabras

¿Cómo se llama el cliente número uno?
What is the first client's name?

¿Cómo se escribe su nombre?
How do you spell their name?

¿Cuál es su teléfono?
What is their phone number?

¡Fíjate!

Review **El alfabeto** on page 10 to prepare for this activity. Notice that telephone numbers are given in sets of two, except for the first number (4-21-05-25).

Instrucciones para Estudiante 2

You took home your co-worker's list of clients and left your own list at the office. By telephone, ask your co-worker to give you the names and phone numbers of your clients. Ask your partner to spell out the names. When asked, be ready to tell your co-worker the names and numbers of their clients. Alternate asking and answering questions. Use questions like the ones below.

A. Las agendas.

La correspondencia

El correo: La Universidad Autónoma de Guadalajara.

Parte 1. You received a brochure in the mail from the Universidad Autónoma de Guadalajara, but it has been damaged and you cannot read all of the information. Call the university and listen to their automated message to fill out the missing information.

UNIVERSIDAD AUTÓNOMA DE GUADALAJARA

ÚNICO. Universidad en la comunidad ofrece las siguientes carreras:

- Fisioterapia
- _Nutrición_
- Prótesis Dental
- _Decoración_
- Diseño y _ornamentación_ de parques y _jardines_
- Electromecánica industrial

- Comercialización y ventas
- _Relaciones públicas_
- Mercado de valores
- Fotografía
- _Publicidad_

VEN A FORMAR PARTE DE UNA UNIVERSIDAD

¡Con un estilo ÚNICO!

ÚNICO

UNIVERSIDAD EN LA COMUNIDAD

Parte 2. Read the complete brochure and answer the following questions. Answer in English.
Answers will vary.

1. Which area of study look the most interesting to you? Why?

_____

2. Which areas appeal you the least? Why?

_____

En papel: Presentación. Introduce yourself to your instructor! Fill out the card your instructor will give you with your personal information.

¡A ver de nuevo! Watch or listen to the **Escena** again to match the elements from the two columns.

I.
_c_	1. Adriana	a. es amiga de Ana Mari.
_a_	2. Sofía	b. necesita pasar la clase de cálculo.
_b_	3. Manolo	c. es de Puerto Rico.

II.
_b_	1. El Prof. López	a. tiene una clase de inglés.
_c_	2. Manolo	b. es profesor.
_a_	3. Ana Mari	c. necesita estudiar más *(needs to study more)*.

III.
_b_	1. Sofía	a. no tiene novio *(doesn't have a boyfriend)*.
_a_	2. Ana Mari	b. es de México.
_c_	3. El Prof. López	c. dice *(says)* "Manolo, ¿otra vez aquí?"

En papel. This is an activity is an opportunity for you to collect some background on your students. Copy the materials from the **Instructor's Resource Manual** and hand them out to your class, or write the following text onto the board for students to copy on a separate sheet of paper and hand in. You may want to refer to this information as the course continues.

Nombre… Télefono…Tomo … Trabajo…

Experiencia con el español: a. Estudié *(I studied)* en la prepa *(high school)* b. Es la primera vez *(first time)* que estudio español c. Necesito aprender *(to learn)* español d. Quiero *(I want to)* aprender español

Vocabulario del Episodio 1

Para hablar con amigos *To speak to friends*

¿Cómo estás?	*How are you?*
¿Y tú?	*And you?*
¿Cómo te llamas?	*What's your name?*
¡Que te vaya bien!	*Have a nice day!*
Te presento a...	*I'd like you to meet...*

Para hablar con respeto *To speak with respect*

¿Cómo está?	*How are you?*	**señor (Sr.)**	*Mr., sir*
¿Y usted?	*And you?*	**señora (Sra.)**	*Mrs., ma'am*
¿Cómo se llama?	*What's your name?*	**señorita (Srta.)**	*Miss*
¡Que le vaya bien!	*Have a nice day!*	**doctor(a) (Dr(a).)**	*Doctor*
Le presento a...	*I'd like you to meet...*	**profesor(a) (Prof(a).)**	*Professor*

Más saludos y despedidas *More greetings and good-byes*

Hola.	*Hi.*
Buenos días.	*Good morning.* (from dawn until noon)
Buenas tardes.	*Good afternoon.* (from noon until dusk)
Buenas noches.	*Good evening/Good night.* (from dusk until dawn)
Hasta luego.	*See you later.*
Hasta mañana.	*See you tomorrow.*
Nos vemos mañana.	*See you tomorrow.* (you have arranged to meet tomorrow)
Adiós.	*Good-bye.*
Mucho gusto.	*Nice to meet you.*
Encantado.	*Pleased to meet you.* (said by a man)
Encantada.	*Pleased to meet you.* (said by a woman)
Igualmente.	*Nice to meet you, too.*
Gracias.	*Thank you.*
De nada.	*You're welcome.*
Bien.	*Fine.*
Muy bien.	*Very well.*
Más o menos.	*So-so.*

Las materias *Class subjects*

antropología	economía	geografía	matemáticas
astronomía	(educación) física	historia	música
biología	español	inglés	química
drama	filosofía	literatura	sicología

Los números del 0 al 40

0 **cero**			
1 **uno**	11 **once**	21 **veintiuno**	31 **treinta y uno**
2 **dos**	12 **doce**	22 **veintidós**	32 **treinta y dos**
3 **tres**	13 **trece**	23 **veintitrés**	33 **treinta y tres**
4 **cuatro**	14 **catorce**	24 **veinticuatro**	34 **treinta y cuatro**
5 **cinco**	15 **quince**	25 **veinticinco**	35 **treinta y cinco**
6 **seis**	16 **dieciséis**	26 **veintiséis**	36 **treinta y seis**
7 **siete**	17 **diecisiete**	27 **veintisiete**	37 **treinta y siete**
8 **ocho**	18 **dieciocho**	28 **veintiocho**	38 **treinta y ocho**
9 **nueve**	19 **diecinueve**	29 **veintinueve**	39 **treinta y nueve**
10 **diez**	20 **veinte**	30 **treinta**	40 **cuarenta**

¿Cuántas clases tomas? Tomo...　　*How many classes are you taking? I take...*
¿Cuántas horas trabajas? Trabajo...　　*How many hours do you work? I work...*

¡Fíjate!

This section is the place where you can write down and easily reference the vocabulary that applies to your own life and interests.

Vocabulario personal

Write the words that you need to know to talk about yourself in Spanish.

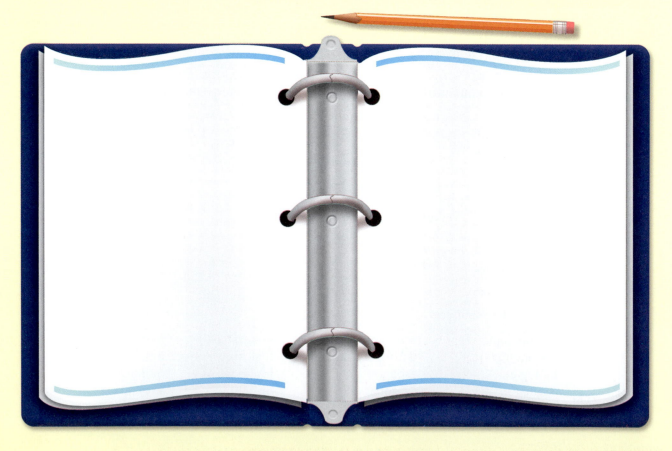

Episodio

¡A escribir!

Escenas de la vida: El primer día de clases

A. ¡Mira cuánto entendiste! See how much of the **Escena** you understood by matching the Spanish sentences with their English equivalents.

1. En la clase de cálculo

_f_ 1. Mucho gusto.   a. And you?

_c_ 2. ¿Hablas español?   b. Nice to meet you, too.

_b_ 3. Igualmente.   c. Do you speak Spanish?

_e_ 4. ¿Cómo te llamas?   d. I'm from...

_d_ 5. Soy de...   e. What's your name?

_a_ 6. ¿Y usted?   f. Nice to meet you.

2. Después de la clase

_f_ 1. Hasta mañana.   a. I'd like you to meet...

_d_ 2. ¡Que te vaya bien!   b. See you later.

_c_ 3. Necesito pasar esta clase. c. I need to pass this class.

_e_ 4. Es mi mejor amiga.   d. Have a nice day!

_b_ 5. Hasta luego.   e. She's my best friend.

_a_ 6. Te presento a...   f. See you tomorrow.

B. ¡Hola! Use the words from the list to complete the conversations between Adriana and Pilar, a counselor.

Adriana	**mucho**
cómo	**soy de**
español	**usted**
igualmente	**vaya**

Adriana   ¿Habla (1) _____español_____?

Pilar   Sí, (2) _____soy de_____ España.

Adriana   ¿(3) _____Cómo_____ se llama?

Pilar   Pilar. ¿Y (4) _____usted_____?

Adriana   Me llamo (5) _____Adriana_____.

Pilar   (6) _____Mucho_____ gusto.

Adriana   (7) _____Igualmente_____.

Video
CD-ROM

C. Te presento a Ana Mari. Order the statements in the dialogue, so that it makes sense.

__6__ a. Igualmente.

__1__ b. Hola, Ana Mari. ¿Cómo estás?

__5__ c. Mucho gusto.

__4__ d. Pilar, te presento a Ana Mari.

__2__ e. Muy bien. ¿Y tú?

__3__ f. Bien, gracias.

__8__ g. Adiós, Ana Mari. ¡Que te vaya bien!

__7__ h. Bueno, hasta luego. Tengo clase ahora.

Vocabulario 1 Greeting and saying good-bye to others
• Greetings and good-byes

D. Saludos. Match each statement with the appropriate response.

__b__ 1. Hola. ¿Cómo te llamas?

__d__ 2. Te presento a Roberto.

__c__ 3. Hasta luego.

__a__ 4. ¿Cómo está usted?

a. Bien, ¿y usted?

b. Martha.

c. Adiós.

d. Mucho gusto.

E. ¿Formal o informal? Write the expressions that you would use when talking to Manolo and those you would use when talking to Professor López in the appropiate column.

¿Cómo estás?   **¿Cómo se llama?**   **¿Y tú?**   **¿Y usted?**

Te presento a...   **¿Cómo está?**   **¿Cómo te llamas?**   **¡Que le vaya bien!**

Manolo	Profesor López
¿Cómo estas?	¿Cómo se llama?
Te presento a ...	¿Cómo está?
¿Y tú?	¿Y usted?
¿Cómo te llamas?	¡Que le vaya bien!

F. Para saludar. Select the appropriate greeting, according to the time of the day:
Buenos días, Buenas tardes, or **Buenas noches.**

1. 1:45 pm ___Buenas tardes___.   3. 6:30 am ___Buenos días___.   5. 11:00 am ___Buenos días___.

2. 8:00 pm ___Buenas noches___.   4. 10:30 pm ___Buenas noches___.   6. 3:30 pm ___Buenas tardes___.

G. Hablas con Sofía. Complete the conversation.

Sofía ¡Hola! ¿Cómo estás?

Tú (1) ___Bien/Muy bien, ¿y tú?___

Sofía Bien, gracias. Mira, te presento a Manolo.

Tú (2) ___Mucho gusto___.

Manolo Igualmente. Bueno, adiós.

Tú (3) ___Hasta luego___.

H. Una conversación con tu profesor(a). Complete the conversation.

Profesor(a)   Buenas tardes, (1) ¿ <u>Cómo se llama</u> _____?
Tú   (2) Me llamo <u>Answers will vary.</u>
Profesor(a)   Mucho gusto. ¿Cómo está hoy?
Tú   (3) <u>Bien, gracias, ¿y usted?</u>
Profesor(a)   Bien, también. Hasta mañana.
Tú   (4) <u>¡Que le vaya bien!</u>
Profesor(a)   Gracias. Igualmente.

Vocabulario 2

Saying which classes you take
• **The alphabet**
• **Class subjects**

I. Ésa me gusta. *(I like that one.)* Indicate which subjects you like **(me gusta)** and which ones you do not like **(no me gusta).** Answers will vary.

antropología _____   economía _____
drama _____   filosofía _____
literatura _____   educación física _____
astronomía _____   geografía _____
sicología _____   química _____
biología _____   historia _____
música _____   español _____
botánica _____   inglés _____

J. El alfabeto. Write the names of the underlined letters in the following words. Then write their English equivalents.

> **Modelo**   **Mi<u>ll</u>ones** se escribe con **elle** y significa *millions*.

1. **<u>G</u>eografía** se escribe con ___ge___ y significa ___geography___.
2. **E<u>x</u>amen** se escribe con ___equis___ y significa ___exam___.
3. **Ba<u>ñ</u>o** se escribe con ___eñe___ y significa ___bathroom___.
4. **Mu<u>j</u>er** se escribe con ___jota___ y significa ___woman___.
5. **<u>D</u>iccionario** se escribe con ___de___ y significa ___dictionary___.
6. **Ca<u>rr</u>o** se escribe con ___erre___ y significa ___car___.
7. **Lápi<u>z</u>** se escribe con ___zeta___ y significa ___pencil___.
8. **<u>M</u>ochila** se escribe con ___eme___ y significa ___backpack___.
9. **Fo<u>t</u>ocopia** se escribe con ___te___ y significa ___photocopy___.
10. **Uni<u>v</u>ersidad** se escribe con ___ve___ y significa ___university___.

Vocabulario 3

Saying how many credits/units you take and how many hours you work
• Numbers 0–40

K. Los números. Match each number with its Spanish equivalent. Draw a line to link them.

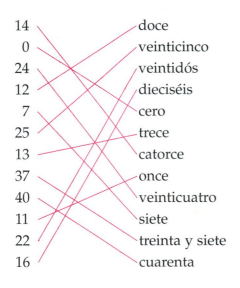

14   doce
0   veinticinco
24   veintidós
12   dieciséis
7   cero
25   trece
13   catorce
37   once
40   veinticuatro
11   siete
22   treinta y siete
16   cuarenta

L. ¿Qué sigue? *(What's next?)* Write out the numbers that precede and follow the given numbers.

#	(precede)	(given)	(follow)
1.	cuatro	cinco	seis
2.	catorce	quince	dieciséis
3.	diecisiete	dieciocho	diecinueve
4	veintisiete	veintiocho	veintinueve
5.	treinta y dos	treinta y tres	treinta y cuatro
6.	treinta y cinco	treinta y seis	treinta y siete
7.	treinta y ocho	treinta y nueve	cuarenta

M. Preguntas personales. Answer the following questions. Answers will vary.

1. ¿Qué *(which)* clases tomas este semestre? _____

2. ¿Cuántas unidades *(units/credits)* son? _____

3. ¿Cuántas horas trabajas? _____

4. ¿Cuántas horas estudias? _____

5. ¿Qué clases necesitas tomar *(do you need to take)* el próximo *(next)* semestre?

_____

Para terminar

N. Una invitación de boda. *(A wedding invitation)* Examine the Mexican wedding invitation below in order to answer the following questions. You will also need to read the explanation that follows.

1. What is the name of the bride's father?
   Jesús Moreno Olivarria.

2. What is the name of the groom's mother?
   Ada González de Hauter.

3. What will be the traditional married name of the bride?
   Minerva Guadalupe Olivarria de Hauter.

4. What is the groom's full name? (first name and last names)
   Arturo Hauter González.

Minerva Guadalupe y Arturo

Ante Dios y con la bendición de nuestros padres

Jesús Moreno Olivarria	*Arturo Hauter Salazar*
Minerva Ibarra de Moreno	*Ada González de Hauter*

*Nos uniremos en matrimonio y les invitamos
a la ceremonia religiosa el sábado
veintidós de octubre a las diecinueve horas
en la Iglesia del Espíritu Santo,
Fraccionamiento Chapultepec.*

*Impartiendo la Bendición
el Reverendo Alfonso González Quevedo S. E.*

Tijuana, Baja California

Cultura a lo vivo

You may have noticed that Spanish speakers often have long names. Most Spanish speakers have two first names, both of which they may or may not use. Some double names, however, are common, such as Ana Mari and José Luis. In addition, Spanish speakers use two last names—their father's family name (which goes first), and their mother's family name (which goes second). For example, a brother and a sister, both single, might be called Ramón Robledo Suárez and Ana María Robledo Suárez (informally, they would be Ramón Robledo and Ana Mari Robledo). If Ana Mari marries, she will not change her last name; traditionally, her husband's last name will be added, using **de,** and replacing her mother's last name. So, if Ana María Robledo Suárez marries Manolo Báez Rodríguez, her name would be Ana María Robledo de Báez. Today many Hispanic women keep their maiden name; in this case, Mrs. Báez would be Ana María Robledo.

Ñ. Los personajes de Escenas de la vida. In **Escenas de la vida**, you will follow the lives of several Spanish speakers who live and study in the United States. As you learn about them, you will learn to communicate in Spanish, and you will get a glimpse into the rich and diverse culture of the Spanish-speaking world. Read the information for each character and answer the questions in **Práctica O**.

Sofía Blasio Salas

mexicana

20 años

arquitectura

extrovertida

Nombre
Nacionalidad
Edad
Carrera
Personalidad

Manolo Báez Rodríguez

cubano

25 años

no ha decidido[1]

bohemio

Wayne Andrew Reilly

norteamericano

23 años

computación

aventurero

Nombre
Nacionalidad
Edad
Carrera
Personalidad

Adriana Ferreira de Barrón

puertorriqueña

45 años

contabilidad[2]

reservada

Ana María Robledo Suárez

mexicoamericana

20 años

leyes[3]

sociable

Nombre
Nacionalidad
Edad
Carrera
Personalidad

Emilio Andrés Pradillo Salas

español

30 años

publicidad

serio

[1]*undecided*   [2]*accounting*   [3]*law*

O. ¡Mucho gusto! Based on the information about the characters, answer the following questions.

1. What is Sofía's mother's last name?
   _____ Salas _____

2. Which of the female characters is married?
   _____ Adriana _____

3. Who has a double name?
   _____ Wayne Andrew, Ana María, and Emilio Andrés _____

4. What is Manolo's father's last name?
   _____ Báez _____

5. If Sofía married Wayne Reilly, what would be her traditional married name?
   _____ Sofía Blasio de Reilly _____

6. Where is Sofía from?
   _____ Mexico _____

7. What is Manolo studying?
   _____ Undecided _____

8. What is Wayne studying?
   _____ Computer Science _____

9. How old is Adriana?
   _____ 45 _____

10. Where is Emilio from?
    _____ Spain _____

11. How do you say *serious* in Spanish?
    _____ Serio _____

12. What is the English equivalent of
    a. **aventurero?** _____ adventurous _____
    b. **arquitectura?** _____ architecture _____

Nombre ______________________ Fecha ____________

P. ¿Y tú? Now write your information. Answers will vary.

Your picture goes here!

Apellido: ______________________

Nacionalidad: ______________________

Edad: ______________________

Carrera: ______________________

Personalidad: ______________________

Episodio 1

Comprensión

 A. Las clases.

Audio CD-ROM

Parte 1. You are going to listen to Ana Mari and some of her classmates say which classes they are taking this semester. First, listen to the list of classes and repeat each one after the speaker.

economía	inglés	sicología	matemáticas	filosofía
astronomía	química	tenis	historia	

Now, listen to Ana Mari and her friends and check off the classes each person is taking.

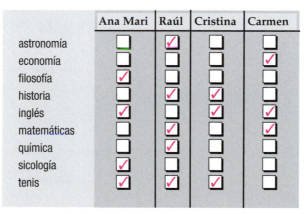

	Ana Mari	Raúl	Cristina	Carmen
astronomía		✓		
economía				✓
filosofía	✓			
historia		✓	✓	
inglés	✓		✓	✓
matemáticas		✓		✓
química		✓		
sicología	✓			
tenis	✓	✓	✓	

Parte 2. You will now hear four questions. Look at the list of classes in **Parte 1** and answer the questions that you hear. Then repeat the correct answer after the speaker.

Modelo	You hear:	**¿Cuántos estudiantes toman tenis?**
	You say:	**Tres estudiantes: Ana Mari, Raúl y Cristina toman tenis.**

 B. ¿Cuántos? How many are there of the following items? Listen and write the numerals for the numbers that you hear.

Audio CD-ROM

1. _20_ sillas
2. _7_ banderas
3. _35_ lápices
4. _11_ plumas
5. _40_ diccionarios

6. _2_ escritorios
7. _15_ cuadernos
8. _19_ libros
9. _26_ profesores
10. _8_ mapas

Pronunciación

Las vocales. The vowels in Spanish, **a, e, i, o,** and **u,** are important sounds to master. Unlike English, each vowel in Spanish has only one pronunciation. In addition, the vowel sounds are shorter and crisper than the vowel sounds in English. Repeat these letters, words, and sentences after the speaker.

a

Ana	lápiz	habilidad	Ana camina a la casa.
Adán	papa	América	Adán habla con las amigas de Ana.

e

Pepe	me	septiembre	Pelé bebe leche.
te	le	televisión	Héctor lee lentamente.

i

Ignacio	igual	importante	Allí está mi diccionario de inglés.
Víctor	química	librería	Perdí el lápiz de Lilí.

o

Octavio	kiosko	oportunidad	Manolo dejó las fotocopias.
poco	hombre	fotocopias	El pobre hombre come poco.

u

Humberto	número	universidad	Lupe usa la computadora.
Lupe	mujer	unidad	La mujer usa su pluma.

Más escenas de la vida

A. ¿Quién lo dijo? Wayne is calling Ramón, and Ramón's mother answers. Listen to their conversation, and indicate who said each statement: Wayne **(W)** or Ramón **(R)**. You will hear the conversation twice.

_W_ 1. Buenos días, señora.

_W_ 2. Bien gracias, ¿y usted?

_R_ 3. ¿Qué pasó, Wayne?

_R_ 4. Más o menos. Estoy un poco enfermo.

_W_ 5. Hasta luego.

_R_ 6. Gracias. Hasta mañana.

B. ¿Cierto o falso? Sofía and Ana Mari run into Adriana at school. Indicate whether the following statements are **cierto** or **falso**, according to their conversation. You will hear the conversation twice.

	Cierto	Falso
1. Adriana runs into Ana Mari and Sofía in the afternoon.	✓	
2. Adriana has met Ana Mari before.		✓
3. Sofía wishes Adriana a good day.	✓	
4. Ana Mari and Sofía are going to work.	✓	
5. Adriana will see Sofía again tomorrow.	✓	

Escenas de la vida: En la librería

Video
CD-ROM

A. ¡Mira cuánto puedes entender!

Audio
CD-ROM

Instructor's Resources
- Overheads
- VHS Video
- Worktext CD
- Website
- IRM: Videoscript, Comprehensible input

1. Watch or listen to the **Escena** to indicate who needs to buy the following items: Manolo (**M**), or Sofía (**S**). Place an **X** next to the items no one mentions.

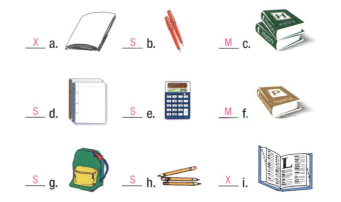

X a.   S b.   M c.

S d.   S e.   M f.

S g.   S h.   X i.

2. First, place a check next to the classes Manolo has tomorrow. Then, write the time when the classes begin.

miércoles	
7:45	Cálculo
9:20	Geología
12:15	Física

lunes/miércoles/ viernes	
✔ Cálculo	7:45
✔ Sicología	1:30
martes/jueves	
☐ Computación	8:45
☐ Historia	10:00
☐ Sociología	5:15

Cultura a lo vivo

In the Spanish-speaking world, a student must complete all general education requirements in high school in order to enter the university. The specifics vary from country to country, but before entering a university, a student must declare a major and frequently take an admissions exam to determine whether they qualify for admission. Upon entering the university, a student begins a specific field of study; there are no undeclared majors.

Video Synopsis. Sofía and Manolo are shopping for school supplies. They cannot believe how much they spend on books. They discuss their schedules, and complain about some of their classes and their heavy load. They agree to meet the next day.

B. ¿Te diste cuenta? Listen to or watch the **Escena** again to match the following sentence fragments.

_____d_____ 1. Manolo gasta más de...

_____a_____ 2. Sofía necesita comprar...

_____e_____ 3. Los libros cuestan...

_____c_____ 4. La clase favorita de Manolo...

_____b_____ 5. Manolo y Sofía van...

a. dos cuadernos.

b. al café mañana.

c. es sicología.

d. 200 dólares en libros.

e. mucho dinero.

B and C. Have students read activities **B** and **C,** then play the video again. Have students respond orally to the prompts.

C. ¿Quién lo dijo? Review the **Escena** and indicate whether the following phrases describe Sofía (**S**), Manolo (**M**), or both.

_____S_____ 1. Necesita novio.

_____M_____ 2. Necesita libros.

_____SM_____ 3. Gasta mucho en libros.

_____M_____ 4. Toma cinco clases.

_____S_____ 5. Necesita ir a la biblioteca.

_____SM_____ 6. Va al café mañana.

Práctica adicional	
Cuaderno de tareas	Video CD-ROM
WB pp.51–52, A–C	Episodio 2

Para comunicarnos mejor

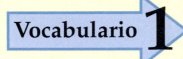

Vocabulario 1

Identifying university-related objects, places, and people
• University-related vocabulary

Vocabulario 1. Model the pronunciation of the university-related vocabulary. Have students repeat after you. Give them time to read the translations so they understand what they are repeating. Use the classroom for visual support.

Las cosas, los lugares y las personas en la universidad

Cosas	Things	Lugares	Places
la bandera	flag	el auditorio	auditorium
la calculadora	calculator	el baño	bathroom
el cuaderno	notebook	la biblioteca	library
el diccionario	dictionary	la cafetería	cafeteria
el escritorio	desk (teacher's)	la cancha de tenis	tennis court
el lápiz	pencil	de vóleibol	volleyball court
el libro	book	el edificio	building
el mapa	map	la enfermería	health center; infirmary
la mochila	backpack	el estacionamiento	parking lot
el papel	paper	el estadio	stadium
la papelera	wastebasket	el gimnasio	gym
el pizarrón	chalkboard	la librería	bookstore
la pluma	pen	la oficina	office
la prueba	quiz	la piscina	swimming pool
la puerta	door	la residencia estudiantil	dormitory
el pupitre	desk (student's)	el salón de clase	classroom

Instructor's Resource
• Overheads

el reloj	clock		
la silla	chair		
la tele(visión)	TV		
la ventana	window		
la videocasetera	VCR		

Personas	People		
el compañero	la compañera	los/las compañeros/as	classmate(s)
el consejero	la consejera	los/las consejeros/as	counselor(s)
el estudiante	la estudiante	los/las estudiantes	student(s)

También se dice...

el estudiante	→ el alumno
la papelera	→ el basurero, el bote/cubo/latón de basura
el pizarrón	→ la pizarra
la pluma	→ el bolígrafo
el profesor	→ el maestro
el salón	→ el aula, la sala

Learning Strategy: Make your own tape

Record the words or phrases you need to learn and their English equivalents on a cassette. Listen to them as often as you can, perhaps even while you drive or jog. When preparing the tape, be sure to pause before recording the English translation in order to allow yourself time to say the word/phrase.

¡Fíjate!

You will see **También se dice** boxes throughout the text. Because Spanish is spoken in many countries, many times there are five or six different words for the same item. You do not need to learn all the variations; learn the ones your professor tells you or the ones you hear in your community.

Additional Activity. Organize a scavenger hunt. See the **IRM** for materials for this activity, or create your own to suit your class. Write six different lists of the names and quantities of seven classroom items on each of six index cards (e.g., **dos cuadernos, tres lápices, una pluma, una calculadora, un diccionario, un libro de texto y una mochila**). Divide the class into six groups and have each group collect the items on their card. The first group to bring you all of the items wins.

PRÁCTICA

A. ¿Qué es? Identifica las cosas, los lugares y las personas en las ilustraciones.

Instructor's Resource
• IRM: Additional Activities

a
1. el escritorio
2. los pupitres
3. la profesora
4. la estudiante
5. el pizarrón
6. la ventana
7. la puerta
8. las mochilas
9. el mapa
10. el reloj

b
1. el estadio
2. el estacionamiento
3. el edificio
4. la cancha de tenis
5. el gimnasio
6. la piscina

B. ¿Qué compraste? *(What did you buy?)* Write down the items you bought this semester for your classes. Answers will vary.

Este semestre compré *(I bought)...*_____

_____

_____

C. ¿Adónde vas *(Where do you go)* con más frecuencia?

Parte 1. How often do you go to the following places? Write **0** next to places you never go to, **1** next to places you almost never go to, **2** next to places you sometimes go to, **3** next to places you often go to, and **4** next to places you go to every day. Answers will vary.

¡Fíjate!

The words in **Banco de palabras** are presented to enable you to carry out specific classroom activities. You are not expected to memorize them or use them without support. However, begin to familiarize yourself with the words, since they may become part of your active vocabulary in later episodes.

Banco de palabras

Voy	(2) **a veces**
I go	*sometimes*
(4) **todos los días**	(1) **casi nunca**
every day	*almost never*
(3) **con frecuencia**	(0) **nunca**
often	*never*

¿Con qué frecuencia vas...?

_____ 1. al auditorio   _____ 6. a la cafetería

_____ 2. al gimnasio   _____ 7. a la biblioteca

_____ 3. a la piscina   _____ 8. a la oficina de los profesores

_____ 4. a la librería   _____ 9. a la enfermería

_____ 5. al estadio   _____ 10. a las canchas

Parte 2. Now interview a partner to find out how often they go to these places. Use the expressions from the **Banco de palabras.**

Modelo —¿Con qué frecuencia vas al auditorio?
—Casi nunca voy. ¿Y tú?
—Yo voy todos los días.

¡Fíjate!

Use **nunca** and **casi nunca** before the verb **voy;** use the other expressions after it.

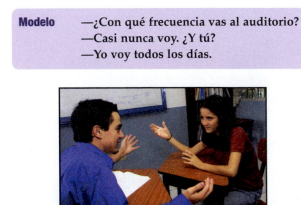

Práctica adicional

Cuaderno de tareas
WB pp.52–53, D–G

Gramática 1

Talking about university-related objects, places, and people
- **Gender of nouns**
- **Plural of nouns**
- <u>Hay</u>

In the dialogue, Manolo mentioned **el libro de sicología** and **unos libros de historia.** They also mentioned **una mochila** and **la biblioteca. Libro, mochila,** and **biblioteca** are nouns. A noun is a word that names a person, a place, an animal, an object, or an idea. The articles **(los artículos)** *the* **(el, la)** or *a(n)* **(un, una)** usually accompany nouns.

• Gender of nouns

Every noun in Spanish has a gender (feminine or masculine) and number (singular or plural). When you learn a new word, you must also learn whether that word is feminine or masculine, since the gender of nouns is arbitrary. See if you can make some helpful generalizations.

Analizar y descubrir

1. Look at the following feminine words:

la plum**a**	una televisi**ón**	la universid**ad**
la sill**a**	una conversaci**ón**	la libert**ad**

Using these words, what observations can you make about the endings of feminine nouns? Most words that end in the letters ___-a___ , ___-ión___, and ___-ad___ are feminine. Use **la** or **una** with feminine words.

2. Look at the following masculine words:

un libr**o**   un pupitr**e**   el pizarr**ón**   el inglé**s**   un profeso**r**   el pape**l**

Using these words, what observations can you make about the endings of masculine nouns? Most words that end in the vowels ___-o___ and ___-e___, or in a ___consonant___ are masculine. Use **el** or **un** with masculine nouns.

3. Although most words that end in **-e** are masculine, some words that end in **-e** are feminine. Therefore, it is best to learn the word along with its article:

(feminine)	**la clase**	**la noche**
(masculine)	**el pupitre**	**el coche** *(car)*

4. Most words that end in **-a** are feminine, but a few words (of Greek origin) that end in **-ma** are masculine. Notice that these words are cognates.

(masculine)	**el** proble**ma**	**el** progra**ma**	**el** siste**ma**

Los artículos				
	Singular		**Plural**	
Definidos	**el, la**	*the*	**los, las**	*the*
Indefinidos	**un, una**	*a(n)*	**unos, unas**	*some*

PRÁCTICA

D. ¿Masculino o femenino? Escribe el o la.

1. __el__ estacionamiento
2. __el__ pizarrón
3. __la__ bandera
4. __el__ drama
5. __la__ oficina
6. __la__ piscina
7. __el__ teatro
8. __el__ inglés
9. __la__ cancha
10. __la__ biblioteca
11. __la__ computación
12. __el__ pupitre

E. Artículos indefinidos. Escribe un o una.

1. __un__ auditorio
2. __un__ reloj
3. __una__ silla
4. __un__ libro
5. __un__ profesor
6. __una__ clase
7. __una__ pluma
8. __una__ ventana
9. __un__ diccionario
10. __un__ lápiz
11. __un__ juego de béisbol
12. __una__ comunidad

• Plural of nouns

Analizar y descubrir

In a conversation with Adriana, Sofía said:

Las universidades aquí son muy diferentes... | *The universities here are quite different...*
Aquí **los salones** están muy bien equipados. | *Here the classrooms are very well-equipped.*
¿En Puerto Rico hay **consejeros...?** | *Are there counselors in Puerto Rico...?*
Hablando de **profesores...** | *Speaking of professors...*

1. Examine the above examples to complete the following:

    a. What is added to the word **universidad** to make it plural? __-es__

    b. What is added to **salón** to make it plural? __-es__

    c. What is added to **consejero** to make it plural? __-s__

    d. What is added to **profesor** to make it plural? __-es__

2. Based on your answers, what observations can you make about how plural nouns are formed in Spanish?

Pluralizing rule:

    a. When a word ends in a consonant, add __-es__ to make it plural.

    b. When a word ends in a vowel, add __-s__ to make it plural.

Spelling rule: lápiz → lápices

    c. When a word ends in __-z__, change the **-z** to __-c__ in the plural form.

Accent marks: pizarrón → pizarrones

    d. When a word has an accent mark on the last syllable and it ends in a consonant, it loses __the accent mark__ in the plural form.

PRÁCTICA

F. En la universidad. Escribe la forma plural de estos sustantivos.

1. el profesor   los profesores
2. la silla   las sillas
3. un estadio   unos estadios
4. la biblioteca   las bibliotecas
5. una cancha   unas canchas
6. un baño   unos baños

G. Personas y cosas. Escribe la forma singular de estos sustantivos.

1. los consejeros   el consejero
2. las compañeras   la compañera
3. unos mapas   un mapa
4. los pizarrones   el pizarrón
5. unos relojes   un reloj
6. los cuadernos   el cuaderno
7. unos lápices   un lápiz
8. las bibliotecas   la biblioteca

• Hay

Use **hay** + [*indefinite article*] to express the English equivalent of *there is/are* and to describe what you see. Use **unos/as** to say *some*.

Hay un diccionario en la mochila.   *There is a dictionary in the backpack.*
Hay unos estudiantes en la oficina.   *There are some students in the office.*

PRÁCTICA

H. ¿Qué hay en el escritorio? Escribe los nombres (*names*) de las cosas que hay en el escritorio.

Modelo

Hay una mochila.

1. _____Hay unos cuadernos._____
2. _____Hay una pluma._____
3. _____Hay un lápiz._____
4. _____Hay una calculadora._____
5. _____Hay un diccionario._____
6. _____Hay un libro._____

I. ¿Qué hay en tu mochila? Escribe los nombres de cuatro cosas.   Answers will vary.

1. _____
2. _____
3. _____
4. _____

J. ¿Está bien equipado tu salón? Describe what your classroom does and doesn't have, using the vocabulary on pages 32–33. Write your answers in your notebook.

Answers will vary.

Modelo	En el salón de... hay...
	En el salón de... no hay...

Práctica adicional

Cuaderno de tareas
WB pp.53–54, H–K

Gramática 2

Asking and telling when an event takes place
- **Time of events**

You heard the following statements and questions when Sofía and Manolo were discussing the times their classes meet.

¿A qué hora es tu clase de sicología?   (At) What time is your psychology class?
Es a la una y media.   It's at one-thirty.
¿Nos vemos mañana **a las doce?**   See you tomorrow at twelve?
...mi clase de física es **a las doce y cuarto.**   ...my physics class is at twelve-fifteen.

Spanish, like English, depends on a few routine phrases to express clock time. One formula with **a** is used to say when events happen. Look at Ana Mari's weekly agenda to answer the following questions.

¿A qué hora?

¿A qué hora es...
   la clase de horticultura?   **A la** una **de la tarde.**
   la clase de inglés?   **A las** once y cuarto **de la mañana.**
   la clase de biología?   **A las** siete y media **de la noche.**
   el concierto?   **A las** cinco menos veinte **de la tarde.**
   la fiesta?   **A las** diez menos cuarto **de la noche.**

Instructor's Resource
• Overheads

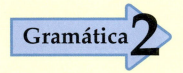

AGOSTO/SEPTIEMBRE

semana 36

31 lunes
1 horticultura

1 martes
11 :15 inglés
7 :30 biología

2 miércoles

3 jueves

4 viernes
9:45 ¡fiesta!

5 sábado
4:40 concierto

6 domingo

Notice that **a la** is used with *one o'clock* and that **a las** is used for the rest of the hours.

PRÁCTICA

K. ¿A qué hora...? When does Professor López teach this semester? Look at his schedule and write out when the calculus class meets. Note that the 24-hour clock (military time) is used.

Modelo	16:40
	El profesor tiene una clase a las cinco menos veinte de la tarde.

Cálculo

a. 7:30   El profesor tiene una clase a las siete y media de la mañana.

b. 10:00   El profesor tiene una clase a las diez de la mañana.

c. 14:15   El profesor tiene una clase a las dos y cuarto de la tarde.

d. 15:00   El profesor tiene una clase a las tres de la tarde.

e. 17:20   El profesor tiene una clase a las cinco y veinte de la tarde.

f. 19:45   El profesor tiene una clase a las siete cuarenta y cinco/a las ocho menos cuarto de la noche.

¡Fíjate!
The 24-hour clock is generally used in newspapers, and in TV, train, flight, and class schedules throughout the Spanish-speaking world. To convert between a 24-hour and a 12-hour clock, subtract twelve from times after 12:00 p.m. (15:00-12 = 3:00 p.m.).

L. Vamos al cine. *(Let's go to the movies.)* Tienes planes para ir al cine con un amigo. Pregúntale a qué hora son las funciones *(screenings)*. Túrnense. Answers will vary.

Modelo	*Fresa y chocolate:* 11:30 / 18:20 / 21:55
	—**¿A qué hora es** *Fresa y chocolate*?
	—**Es a las once y media de la mañana, a las seis y veinte de la tarde y a las diez menos cinco de la noche.**

★	1. Frida	14:45-16:30-18:05
★	2. El crimen del padre Amaro	11:15-17:40-22:25
★	3. Como agua para chocolate	14:30-16:15-19:10
★	4. Hable con ella	10:50-12:15-21:20
★	5. Chasing papi	17:25-19:35-20:17

¡Fíjate!
These films are highly acclaimed and are available in most video stores. Check them out!

M. Hoy y mañana. Dile a tu compañero/a a qué hora son tus clases hoy *(today)* y mañana *(tomorrow)*. Answers will vary.

Modelo	
Hoy tengo clases a las ocho, a las nueve, a las once y media y a las cuatro. Mañana tengo clases a las ocho y a la una. ¿Y tú?	

N. ¿A qué hora...? Conversa con tres compañeros para saber quién sale de casa más temprano *(leaves home earliest)* y quién llega más tarde *(gets home latest)*. Answers will vary.

N. You may wish to review the task with students before they begin to interact. Have students report when classmates leave and return home. You may ask: ¿A qué hora llega Juan a casa? ¿A qué hora sale Raquel de casa? ¿Y tú, a qué hora llegas a casa?

Instructor's Resources
• Worktext CD
• IRM: Tapescript

Modelo
—¿A qué hora sales de casa por la mañana?
—A las siete y media. ¿Y tú?
—A las seis y cuarto. ¿A qué hora llegas a casa?
—A la una y media de la tarde. ¿Y tú?
—A las ocho de la noche.

nombre *(name)*	sale de casa	llega a casa
1. _____	_____	_____
2. _____	_____	_____
3. _____	_____	_____

Ñ. El horario. *(The schedule)* Listen to find out when the following classes are being offered. Write each time in the space provided.

Audio CD-ROM

1. inglés   __8:10__   4. arte moderno   __17:30__

2. historia de Estados Unidos   __10:15__   5. física   __20:00__

3. biología   __12:45__

O. ¡A hablar! In pairs, discuss your schedules. Fill in the agenda with the times your partner has classes, which classes they are, and the times your partner works. Answers will vary.

Estudiante					Semestre Nº 1
	lunes	martes	miércoles	jueves	viernes
AM					
PM					

Práctica adicional

Cuaderno de tareas
WB p.55, L–N
LM pp.57–58, A–B, Pron.

Audio CD-ROM
Episodio 2

Script. *Listen to find out when the following classes are being offered. Write each time in the space provided.*
1. La clase de inglés es a las ocho y diez de la mañana. 2. La clase de historia de Estados Unidos es a las diez y cuarto de la mañana. 3. La clase de biología uno es a la una menos cuarto de la tarde. 4. La clase de arte moderno es a las cinco y media de la tarde. 5. La clase de física es a las ocho de la noche.

Actividades comunicativas

A. El horario de clases.

Instrucciones para **Estudiante 1**

It is time to plan your class schedule for next semester. The chart shows the hours you will be at work **(trabajo)**. Before you graduate, you need to complete six courses:

antropología	**biología**	**historia**
álgebra	**español**	**sicología**

You will not be able to take all these classes this semester. Call your peer advisor for information and choose the four courses that best meet your needs. Use expressions like the ones below. Answers will vary.

días

¿A qué hora es la clase de...?	*When is... class?*
¿Qué día es...?	*What day is...?*
Los lunes trabajo de... a...	*On Mondays I work from... to...*
¿Hay una clase de... a las...?	*Is there a... class at...?*
A esa hora no puedo.	*I can't do that time.*
¿Hay otra clase de...?	*Is there another... class?*

Banco de palabras:
Los días de la semana

los lunes
on Mondays

los martes
on Tuesdays

los miércoles
on Wednesdays

los jueves
on Thursdays

los viernes
on Fridays

los sábados
on Saturdays

los domingos
on Sundays

	Lunes	Martes	Miércoles	Jueves	Viernes
8:00–9:00					
9:00–10:00					
10:00–11:00					
11:00–12:00		Trabajo		Trabajo	
12:00–1:00		Trabajo		Trabajo	
1:00–4:00					
4:00–6:00	Trabajo		Trabajo		
6:00–8:00	Trabajo		Trabajo		

A. El horario de clases.

Instrucciones para Estudiante 2

You are a peer advisor. By phone, help a student prepare a class schedule for next semester. Use expressions like the ones below. Answers will vary.

¿Por qué no tomas...?   *Why don't you take...?*
Hay una clase de...a...   *There's a class from... to...*
¿Puedes tomar...?   *Can you take...?*
No hay clase de... a esa hora.   *There is no... class at that time.*
La clase de... es de... a...   *The class is from... to...*
Hay dos secciones de...   *There are two sections of...*

Banco de palabras:
Los días de la semana

los lunes
on Mondays

los martes
on Tuesdays

los miércoles
on Wednesdays

los jueves
on Thursdays

los viernes
on Fridays

los sábados
on Saturdays

los domingos
on Sundays

Clase/hora	Clase/hora
álgebra	**antropología**
lun. mar. miér. juev. vier. 9:00–10:00	lun. mar. miér. juev. 8:00–9:00
lun. mar. miér. juev. vier. 10:00–11:00	mar. juev. 16:00–17:30
biología	**español**
lun. mar. miér. juev. 8:00–9:00	lun. mar. miér. juev. vier. 8:00–9:00
mar. juev. 10:00–12:00	lun. mar. miér. juev. vier. 10:00–11:00
miér. 16:00–20:00	mar. juev. 12:00–14:30
historia	**sicología**
mar. juev. 11:00–12:15	lun. miér. vier. 10:00–11:00
lun. miér. vier. 17:00–19:30	lun. miér. vier. 16:00–18:15
	mar. juev. 10:00–11:15

B. Los precios.

Instrucciones para **Estudiante 1**

You and a friend are tired of spending so much for school supplies. This semester you are shopping for the best prices. The prices you found in **Papelería Las Rosas** are shown in the drawing. Your partner found different prices in **Papelería El Trópico.** Share your information to determine the best price. Circle the items you decide to buy at your store. Follow the model. Answers will vary.

> **Modelo** —**¿Cuánto cuesta** (*how much is*) **una calculadora ahí** (*there*)?
> —**Aquí** (*here*) **cuesta veinte dólares y diecinueve centavos. ¿Y ahí?**
> —**Aquí cuesta veinte dólares y veintinueve centavos.**
> —**Ah, pues aquí es más barato** (*cheaper*).

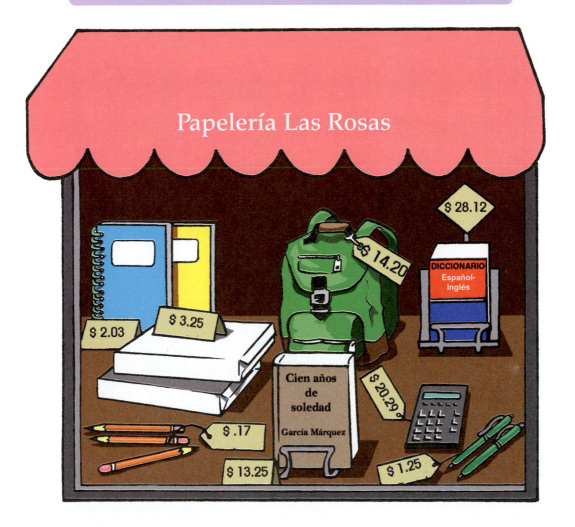

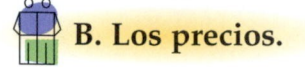

B. Los precios.

Instrucciones para **Estudiante 2**

You and a friend are tired of spending so much for school supplies. This semester you are shopping for the best prices. The prices you found in **Papelería El Trópico** are shown in the drawing. Your partner found different prices in **Papelería Las Rosas.** Share your information to determine the best price. Circle the items you decide to buy at your store. Follow the model. Answers will vary.

Modelo	—**¿Cuánto cuesta** (*how much is*) **una calculadora ahí** (*there*)**?**
	—**Aquí** (*here*) **cuesta veinte dólares y diecinueve centavos. ¿Y ahí?**
	—**Aquí cuesta veinte dólares y veintinueve centavos.**
	—**Ah, pues aquí es más barato** (*cheaper*)**.**

Papelería El Trópico

$ 23.15

DICCIONARIO
Español-
Inglés

$ 3.25

$ 2.11

Cien años
de
soledad

García Márquez

$13.29

$20.19

$ .21

$ 14.10

$ 1.25

C. Diferencias.

Instrucciones para **Estudiante 1**

The picture of the classroom below differs in several ways from your partner's picture. You and your partner will take turns saying what you see until you find seven differences. Check off the seven differences. Follow the model. *Answers will vary.*

Modelo	—**Hay una profesora en el salón.**
	—**Aquí también.**
	or
	—**Aquí no hay una profesora. Hay un profesor.**

C. Diferencias.

Instrucciones para **Estudiante 2**

The picture of the classroom below differs in several ways from your partner's picture. You and your partner will take turns saying what you see until you find seven differences. Check off the seven differences. Follow the model. Answers will vary.

Modelo
—Hay una profesora en el salón.
—Aquí también.
or
—Aquí no hay una profesora. Hay un profesor.

La correspondencia

El correo: El catálogo. Look over the following brochure in order to answer the
questions below. **El correo.** This activity may be assigned for homework. If there is time in class, have students read the
questions in class. Afterwards, they may work with a partner to take turns reading the **Plan de estudios.**

Reading Strategy: Determining the purpose for reading

Successful readers first determine a purpose for reading, which guides the way they approach a selection. You should
develop this strategy as you read in Spanish, where a purpose for reading is even more important, since here, at the
beginning of your study, you will not understand large amounts of the text. For this reason, limit your purpose to
understanding words and phrases—those you have learned and those you can understand based on their similarity
to English.

You will read an entry from the catalog of the **Universidad Autónoma de Guadalajara.** First look at the following
questions (1–4) to determine your purpose for reading. Then, after you have read the selection, answer the questions.

Plan de estudios

1. What is the English equivalent of **Fisioterapia?** _____Physical therapy_____

2. How many **quarters** are necessary to complete a degree? _____eight_____

3. Indicate in which quarter students take the following courses:

   a. Human Anatomy _____first quarter_____   c. Introduction to Pathology _____third quarter_____

   b. Nutrition _____seventh quarter_____   d. Pharmacology _____eighth quarter_____

Mercado de trabajo

4. Where may a person with this degree work? Answers will vary.

   a. _____   b. _____   c. _____   d. _____

COLEGIO DE CIENCIAS ASOCIADAS A LA SALUD

Fisioterapia

Perfil del egresado

El profesional en Fisioterapia
estará capacitado para distinguir,
en una evaluación física, los
estados de normalidad e
implementar, en su caso, el
tratamiento de rehabilitación
indicado, así como la aplicación
del mismo, manejando el
material y equipo necesarios
en un área de medicina física y
rehabilitación. Podrá participar
conjuntamente con el médico
fisiatra en la rehabilitación de
casos especiales y en medicina
del deporte.

Mercado de trabajo

El campo de trabajo del fisioterapeuta es amplio considerando
su participación en programas dirigidos a personas sanas o
enfermas y en el deporte. Escuelas de Educación Física, Clubes
Deportivos, Gimnasios, Hospitales y Clínicas del Sector Público
y Privado, Departamentos de Medicina del Deporte y Atención
a pacientes particulares.

PLAN DE ESTUDIOS

PRIMER TRIMESTRE
- Introducción a la Fisioterapia.
- Anatomía Humana.
- Fisiología General.

SEGUNDO TRIMESTRE
- Principios para el Cuidado del Paciente.
- Primeros Auxilios.
- Fisiología Especial.

TERCER TRIMESTRE
- Sicología Aplicada a la Fisioterapia.
- Física Aplicada a la Fisioterapia.
- Introducción a la Patología.

CUARTO TRIMESTRE
- Instrumentación a la Fisioterapia.
- Técnicas de Evaluación del Estado Físico Normal.
- Ejercicio Físico.

QUINTO TRIMESTRE
- Técnicas de Evaluación de Escuelas Patológicas.
- Medios en la Fisioterapia.
- Deontología.

SEXTO TRIMESTRE
- Rehabilitación Músculo-Esquelética.
- Técnicas de Rehabilitación Pediátrica.
- Técnicas de Rehabilitación Geriátrica.

SÉPTIMO TRIMESTRE
- El Deporte y la Fisioterapia.
- Nutriología.
- Terapia y Kinesiología.

OCTAVO TRIMESTRE
- Rehabilitación del Paciente Cardíaco.
- Rehabilitación del Paciente Neurológico.
- Farmacología.

En papel: ¿Qué hay en tu universidad? Write sentences describing what there is and what there is not at your school, using the vocabulary on pages 32–33. Also indicate what classes you are taking and when they meet. Answers will vary.

> **Modelo** En mi universidad hay una piscina, pero *(but)* no hay auditorios.
> Mi clase de matemática es a las ocho de la mañana.

¡A ver de nuevo! Contesta las preguntas. **¡A ver de nuevo!** Play the videotape again and have students respond to the questions.

Video
CD-ROM

Audio
CD-ROM

Instructor's Resources
• VHS Video
• Worktext CD
• IRM: Videoscript

1. ¿Qué necesita comprar Sofía? Sofía necesita comprar una mochila, una calculadora, dos cuadernos, lápices, plumas.

2. ¿Cuántas clases toma Manolo? Manolo toma cinco clases.

3. ¿Qué clases tiene Manolo mañana? Cálculo y sicología.

4. ¿Adónde va Sofía antes *(before)* de su clase de física? A la biblioteca.

5. ¿A qué hora es su clase de física? A las doce y cuarto.

6. ¿Adónde van mañana después de la clase de cálculo? A la cafetería.

Invitación a **Honduras**

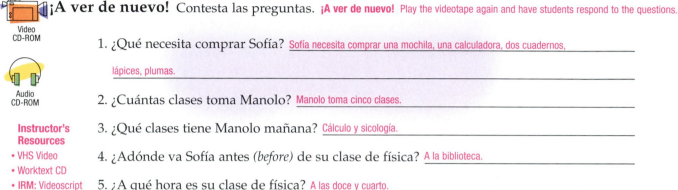

> Del álbum de
> *Ana Marí*

Honduras es un país pequeño *(small country)*; es un poco más grande que *(slightly larger than)* el estado de Tenessee. Copán es una bella ciudad maya *(beautiful Mayan city)* en Honduras. Durante más de un milenio, Copán fue *(was)* el centro cultural y educativo más importante para los Mayas.

Práctica adicional

| Cuaderno de tareas WB p.56, Ñ LM p.58, A–B | Audio CD-ROM Episodio 2 | Website vistahigher learning.com |

Vocabulario del Episodio 2

¿A qué hora es...?	*(At) What time is...?*
Es a las once y cuarto de la mañana.	*It's at eleven-fifteen in the morning.*
Es a la una y media de la tarde.	*It's at one-thirty in the afternoon.*
Es a las diez menos veinte de la noche.	*It's at twenty till ten in the evening.*
Hay...	*There is/are...*

En la universidad *At the university*

Cosas	*Things*	**Lugares**	*Places*
la bandera	*flag*	el auditorio	*auditorium*
la calculadora	*calculator*	el baño	*bathroom*
el cuaderno	*notebook*	la biblioteca	*library*
el diccionario	*dictionary*	la cafetería	*cafeteria*
el escritorio	*desk* (teacher's)	la cancha de tenis	*tennis court*
el lápiz	*pencil*	de vóleibol	*volleyball court*
el libro	*book*	el edificio	*building*
el mapa	*map*	la enfermería	*health center; infirmary*
la mochila	*backpack*	el estacionamiento	*parking lot*
el papel	*paper*	el estadio	*stadium*
la papelera	*wastebasket*	el gimnasio	*gym*
el pizarrón	*chalkboard*	la librería	*bookstore*
la pluma	*pen*	la oficina	*office*
la prueba	*the quiz*	la piscina	*swimming pool*
la puerta	*door*	la residencia estudiantil	*dormitory*
el pupitre	*desk* (student's)	el salón de clase	*classroom*
el reloj	*clock*		
la silla	*chair*		
la tele(visión)	*TV*		
la ventana	*window*		
la videocasetera	*VCR*		

Personas *People*

el compañero	la compañera	los/las compañeros/as	*classmate(s)*
el consejero	la consejera	los/las consejeros/as	*counselor(s)*
el estudiante	la estudiante	los/las estudiantes	*student(s)*

Artículos definidos *Definite articles*

el	*the* (for masculine singular nouns)
la	*the* (for feminine singular nouns)
los	*the* (for masculine plural nouns)
las	*the* (for feminine plural nouns)

Artículos indefinidos *Indefinite articles*

un	*a/an* (for masculine singular nouns)
una	*a/an* (for feminine singular nouns)
unos	*some* (for masculine plural nouns)
unas	*some* (for feminine plural nouns)

Vocabulario personal

Write the words that you need to know to talk about your class schedule and academic life in Spanish.

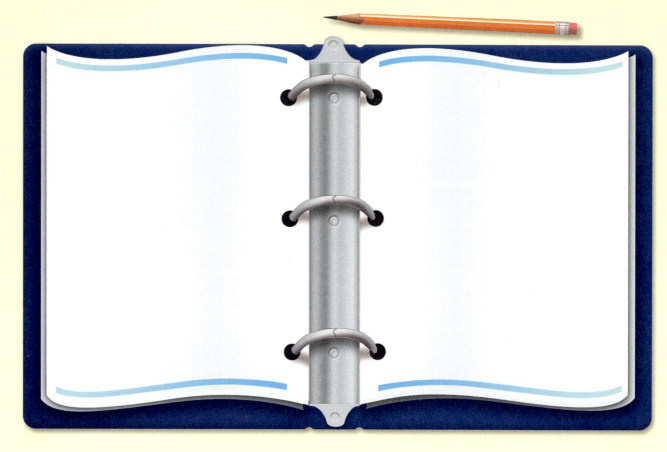

¡A escribir!

Episodio

2

Escenas de la vida: En la librería

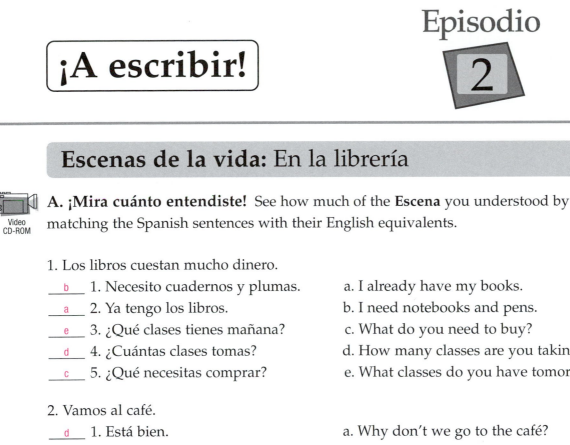

Video
CD-ROM

A. ¡Mira cuánto entendiste! See how much of the **Escena** you understood by matching the Spanish sentences with their English equivalents.

1. Los libros cuestan mucho dinero.

_b_	1. Necesito cuadernos y plumas.	a. I already have my books.
_a_	2. Ya tengo los libros.	b. I need notebooks and pens.
_e_	3. ¿Qué clases tienes mañana?	c. What do you need to buy?
_d_	4. ¿Cuántas clases tomas?	d. How many classes are you taking?
_c_	5. ¿Qué necesitas comprar?	e. What classes do you have tomorrow?

2. Vamos al café.

_d_	1. Está bien.	a. Why don't we go to the café?
_e_	2. Necesito ir a la biblioteca.	b. Let's go after class.
_b_	3. Vamos después de clase.	c. Should I invite Ana Mari?
_f_	4. Nos vemos mañana.	d. That's fine.
_c_	5. ¿Invito a Ana Mari?	e. I need to go to the library.
_a_	6. ¿Por qué no vamos al café?	f. See you tomorrow.

Video
CD-ROM

B. En la librería. Use the words below to complete the conversation.

comprar	cuadernos	historia	mochila
crimen	dinero	libros	plumas

Sofía   ¿Qué necesitas (1) _____comprar_____?

Manolo   Unos libros de (2) _____historia_____. ¿Y tú?

Sofía   Necesito lápices, (3) _____plumas_____, (4) _____cuadernos_____ y una
(5) _____mochila_____.

Manolo   Cada semestre gasto mucho (6)_____dinero_____ en libros.

Sofía   No entiendo por qué los (7) _____libros_____ cuestan tanto.

Manolo   Es un (8) _____crimen_____.

C. Después de clase. Order the statements in the dialogue so that it makes sense.

___3___ a. ¡Qué horror! Cinco clases, pobrecito. Oye, ¿qué clases tienes mañana?

___5___ b. ¿A qué hora es tu clase de sicología?

___2___ c. Cinco, y tres son horribles.

___1___ d. ¿Cuántas clases tomas este semestre?

___6___ e. Es a la una y media.

___4___ f. Cálculo y sicología.

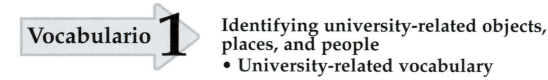

Vocabulario 1 Identifying university-related objects, places, and people
• University-related vocabulary

D. En el salón de clase. Identify the items in the illustration.

1. _____ la puerta _____
2. _____ las ventanas _____
3. _____ el escritorio _____
4. _____ la profesora _____
5. _____ el pizarrón _____
6. _____ la videocasetera _____
7. _____ la televisión _____
8. _____ el cuaderno _____
9. _____ la calculadora _____
10. _____ la mochila _____
11. _____ los pupitres _____
12. _____ los estudiantes _____

E. En la papelería. Identify the items in the illustration.

1. _____ el diccionario _____
2. _____ el cuaderno _____
3. _____ el libro _____
4. _____ la mochila _____
5. _____ el papel _____
6. _____ los lápices _____
7. _____ las plumas _____
8. _____ la calculadora _____

Papelería El Trópico

F. ¿Qué son? Examine the following words to determine whether they are **una cosa, un lugar,** or **una persona.** Write them in the appropriate column.

el auditorio	el consejero	la consejera
la bandera	el edificio	el reloj
el compañero	el mapa	la residencia estudiantil
la prueba	la piscina	las sillas

una cosa	un lugar	una persona
el mapa	el auditorio	el compañero
las sillas	la piscina	la consejera
la bandera	el edificio	el consejero
el reloj	la residencia estudiantil	
la prueba		

G. ¿Adónde vas? Say where you would go in each case.

Modelo	to swim	la piscina

1. to buy a book	la librería
2. to exercise	el gimnasio
3. to eat something while at the university	la cafetería
4. to park your car	el estacionamiento
5. to watch a football game	el estadio
6. to play tennis	la cancha de tenis
7. to study while on campus	la biblioteca
8. to wash your hands	el baño

Gramática 1

Talking about university-related objects, places, and people
• **Gender of nouns**
• **Plural of nouns**
• **Hay**

H. ¿Qué necesitas comprar? To express what you need to buy in Spanish, use indefinite articles, just as in English (*I need to buy* a *pen*). Fill in the missing articles.

Necesito comprar...

1. _un_ libro
2. _un_ reloj
3. _una_ mochila
4. _unos_ mapas de Latinoamérica

5. _unos_ lápices
6. _un_ cuaderno
7. _una_ pluma
8. _unas_ videocaseteras

I. ¿Masculino o femenino?
Examine the following words to determine whether they are masculine or feminine. Write them in the appropriate column. Use the definite articles.

auditorio	comunidad	inglés	química	televisión
compañera	consejero	pizarrón	salón	ventana

Masculino	Femenino
1. el inglés	6. la compañera
2. el auditorio	7. la comunidad
3. el consejero	8. la televisión
4. el salón	9. la química
5. el pizarrón	10. la ventana

J. El plural.
Make each statement plural.

> **Modelo**   Hay <u>un lápiz</u> en la mochila.
> **Hay unos lápices en la mochila.**

1. Hay <u>un estudiante</u> en el salón.

Hay unos estudiantes en el salón.

2. Hay <u>una piscina</u> en el gimnasio.

Hay unas piscinas en el gimnasio.

3. Hay <u>una calculadora</u> en el pupitre.

Hay unas calculadoras en el pupitre.

4. Hay <u>un edificio</u> en la universidad.

Hay unos edificios en la universidad.

5. Hay <u>un compañero</u> en la cafetería.

Hay unos compañeros en la cafetería.

K. Las opiniones.
In Spanish, when a general statement is made about something (a noun) the definite article is needed. In English, the article is not needed (i.e., *Books cost too much.* **Los libros cuestan demasiado dinero**). Provide the necessary article and state whether you agree (**estoy de acuerdo**) or disagree (**no estoy de acuerdo**).

1. _Los_ relojes son indispensables.   Answers will vary.

2. _Las_ clases son difíciles.   _____

3. _Las_ universidades son instituciones importantes.   _____

4. _Los_ profesores no ganan mucho dinero.   _____

5. _Los_ papeles necesitan reciclarse siempre.   _____

6. _Las_ papeleras están llenas (*full*).   _____

7. _Las_ cafeterías en las universidades son caras (*expensive*).   _____

Gramática 2 — Asking and telling when an event takes place
• Time of events

L. ¡Pon la hora! Set the clocks to the correct time.

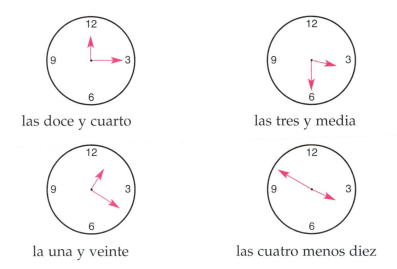

las doce y cuarto

las tres y media

la una y veinte

las cuatro menos diez

M. Los eventos universitarios. A Spanish-speaking friend has asked you to find out when the following events will take place. Write down what you would say in Spanish. Remember: **a las tres de la tarde**, but **a la una de la tarde**.

¿A qué hora es...

1. el concierto de música clásica? (9:00 pm) _____A las nueve de la noche._____

2. el programa sobre literatura moderna? (8:15 pm) _____A las ocho y cuarto de la noche._____

3. el partido de fútbol? (5:45 pm) _____A las cinco cuarenta y cinco/seis menos cuarto de la tarde._____

4. la reunión del club latino? (10:30 am) _____A las diez y media de la mañana._____

5. la conferencia sobre el arte prehispánico? (1:30 pm) _____A la una y media de la tarde._____

6. la excursión al Museo de Ciencia y Tecnología? (8:10 am) _____A las ocho y diez de la mañana._____

N. Preguntas personales. Answer the following questions with the times requested; you do not need to use full sentences. Answers will vary.

1. ¿A qué hora sales *(leave)* de casa por la mañana? _____

2. ¿A qué hora regresas *(return)*? _____

3. ¿A qué hora llegas a la universidad? _____

4. ¿A qué hora es tu primera *(first)* clase los lunes? _____

5. ¿A qué hora miras la tele *(watch TV)*? _____

Para terminar

Ñ. La Universidad en la Comunidad-Único. Read the following brochure for the **Universidad en la Comunidad** and answer the following questions.

Plan de estudios

1. What is the English word for **Nutrición**? _____ Nutrition _____

2. How many quarters are necessary to complete a degree? _____ eight _____

3. Indicate in which quarter students take the following courses:

       a. Epidemology   __third__

       b. Thesis Seminar   __seventh__

       c. Human Physiology __first__

       d. Pediatric Nutrition __sixth__

Mercado de trabajo

4. Where may a person with this degree work?   Answers will vary.

     a. _____

     b. _____

     c. _____

     d. _____

COLEGIO DE CIENCIAS ASOCIADAS A LA SALUD

Perfil del esgresado

El profesional en Nutrición tendrá los conocimientos necesarios para colaborar en la solución de los problemas de nutrición y alimentación de México, ofreciendo apoyo nutricional, orientación y asesoría a todo individuo sano o enfermo.

Nutrición

Mercado de trabajo

El campo de trabajo del nutriólogo es amplio, ya que podrá prestar asesoría y desempeñar funciones de apoyo nutricional en hospitales y clínicas del sector público y privado, así como en otras disciplinas de interés: Salud Pública, epidemiología, saneamiento ambiental e industria del alimento.

PLAN DE ESTUDIOS

PRIMER TRIMESTRE
- Bioquímica de la Nutrición.
- Morfología Humana.
- Fisiología Humana.

SEGUNDO TRIMESTRE
- Introducción a la Fisiopatología.
- Nutrición Básica.
- Salud Pública y Nutrición.

TERCER TRIMESTRE
- Química de los alimentos.
- Epidemiología.
- Métodos de la Investigación.

CUARTO TRIMESTRE
- Bioestadística.
- Principios de Dietocálculo.
- Principios Básicos de Administración.

QUINTO TRIMESTRE
- Nutrición Clínica en Adultos.
- Saneamiento Ambiental.
- Dietoterapia en Salud y Enfermedad.

SEXTO TRIMESTRE
- Apoyo Nutricional Especial.
- Nutrición Pediátrica.
- Salud Materno Infantil.

SÉPTIMO TRIMESTRE
- Sicología y Nutrición.
- Nutrición Comunitaria.
- Seminario de Tesis.

OCTAVO TRIMESTRE
- Tecnología Educativa en Nutrición.
- Administración de los Servicios de Alimentación y Nutrición.
- Nutrición Clínica Intrahospitalaria.

<table>
<tr><td colspan="2">

¡A escuchar!
</td><td>

Episodio

2
</td></tr>
</table>

Comprensión

Audio
CD-ROM

A. Los planes de tres amigos.

Parte 1. Ana Mari and two classmates from her English class want to get together to study for a test. They need to compare their schedules to determine at what time all three are free. As Carmen and Ana Mari speak, fill in the schedule. You will hear the conversation twice.

	9:00	10:00	11:00	12:00	1:00	2:00
Carmen	matemáticas	economía				inglés
Ana Mari		sicología		tenis		inglés
Cristina				tenis	historia	inglés

Parte 2. Now, look at the schedule you completed in **Parte 1** and, in Spanish, answer the questions that you hear. There will be six questions.

Modelo	You hear:	**¿A qué hora tiene Ana Mari la clase de sicología?**
	You say:	**A las diez.**

B. Asociaciones. You are going to hear nine words. For each word, select the word you associate with it from the choices provided.

Modelo	You hear:	**el tenis**		
	You see:	**la librería**	**la cancha**	**la mochila**
	You say:	**la cancha**		

1. el estadio ✓	el edificio	el baño
2. la calculadora	el diccionario	el cuaderno ✓
3. el auditorio	el consejero	el pupitre ✓
4. el cálculo ✓	la literatura	el libro
5. la piscina	la pluma ✓	el pizarrón
6. la mochila ✓	la bandera	la cafetería
7. la puerta	el reloj ✓	la silla
8. la antropología	la geografía ✓	la filosofía
9. la enfermería	el estacionamiento	la oficina ✓

Audio CD-ROM

Pronunciación

Los diptongos. Spanish has five vowels: **a, e, i, o,** and **u.** Every syllable has a vowel: a-ni-mal, e-le-fan-te. The vowels **i** and **u,** when unstressed, can combine with another vowel in the same syllable (**suel-do, sie-te**) to form a diphthong: **ai, ia, ou, ue,** and so on.

Here are possible combinations of **i** and **u** with other vowels and with each other. As you repeat these diphthongs and words after the speaker, notice that the stressed syllable of each word is in bold type.

ia	**dia**-rio	ai	Rai-**mun**-do
ie	**sie**-te	ei	**seis**
io	dic-cio-**na**-rio	oi	**oi**-go
iu	ciu-**dad**	ui	cui-**da**-do
ua	i-**gual**	au	nau-**fra**-gio
ue	**bue**-no	eu	**deu**-da
uo	**cuo**-ta	ou	**Sou**-za

Más escenas de la vida

Audio CD-ROM

A. ¿Entendiste? Sofía and Ana Mari are looking at the newspaper. They call Manolo to make plans for a movie. Listen to their conversation and then answer the questions. You will hear the conversation twice.

1. What times is the movie showing today? _4:30, 6:15, and 8:40_
2. When are Sofía, Ana Mari, and Manolo going to the movies? _at 6:15_
3. Where does Ana Mari have to go? _She has to go to the bookstore._
4. What does Ana Mari think about Manolo? _She thinks he's attractive._
5. When does Manolo get off work? _He gets off work at five._
6. Where will they meet to go to the movies? _They will meet at Sofía's house._

Audio CD-ROM

B. ¿Cierto o falso? Adriana is at home, talking to her children, Viviana and Santiaguito. Indicate whether the statements are **cierto** or **falso**, according to their conversation. You will hear the conversation twice.

	Cierto	Falso
1. Adriana desea comprar los materiales de la escuela para sus hijos.	✓	☐
2. Viviana necesita un escritorio.	☐	✓
3. Viviana necesita una computadora más grande.	☐	✓
4. Santiaguito necesita cuatro cuadernos.	☐	✓
5. Santiaguito necesita unas plumas y una calculadora.	✓	☐
6. Viviana necesita una mochila nueva.	☐	✓

Episodio 3

Escenas de la vida: Los profesores y las clases

A. ¡Mira cuánto puedes entender! As you listen to or watch the **Escena**, indicate the correct characteristic.

Video CD-ROM

Audio CD-ROM

1. ¿Cómo es el profesor de cálculo?

☐ arrogante   ☐ competente
☐ atractivo   ☐ reservado
☑ estricto   ☐ flexible

2. A Adriana le gusta la clase de composición porque el profesor es...

☐ extrovertido   ☐ interesante
☑ paciente   ☐ serio
☐ excelente   ☐ flexible

3. A Adriana no le gusta la clase de contabilidad porque la profesora es...

☑ impaciente   ☐ seria
☐ reservada   ☑ arrogante
☐ pesimista   ☐ tímida

Sofía   Adriana

4. Indica qué características aplican a Sofía (**S**) y cuáles a Adriana (**A**)

S sociable   S activa
A tímida   A responsable
A madura   S inteligente

Cultura a lo vivo

In the Spanish-speaking world, the concept of the nuclear family versus the extended family does not exist. The boundaries of the family extend beyond the immediate family to include grandparents, aunts and uncles, cousins, and others. Spanish speakers are widely assumed to have large families. However, Latin American families come in just as many sizes and varieties as families in the U.S. Many countries in Latin America have launched TV, radio, and billboard campaigns to promote smaller families— **"La familia pequeña vive mejor"** (*Smaller families live better*) is a popular slogan in Mexico.

Video Synopsis. Sofía and Adriana discuss their professors and their classes. Sofía learns that Adriana is shy and that her husband is a bit impatient. Adriana learns that Sofía is very active, both in and outside of school.

Video
CD-ROM

Audio
CD-ROM

B. ¿Te diste cuenta? Indica si los comentarios son **ciertos** o **falsos**.

	Cierto	Falso
1. En las universidades de México hay televisiones y videocaseteras en todos los salones.	☐	☑
2. En Puerto Rico, las universidades tienen un gimnasio, un auditorio y una biblioteca.	☑	☐
3. En México no hay consejeros.	☑	☐
4. A Adriana le gusta mucho la clase de composición.	☑	☐
5. El profesor de la clase de diseño es increíble.	☑	☐
6. La clase de geología es aburrida *(boring)*.	☐	☑
7. El esposo de Adriana es impaciente.	☑	☐

B and C. Have students read exercises **B** and **C**, then play the video again. Have students respond orally to the prompts.

C. ¿Quién lo dijo? ¿Quién dijo las siguientes frases, Sofía (**S**) o Adriana (**A**)?

Video
CD-ROM

Audio
CD-ROM

_____S_____ 1. ¿Le gusta la clase de cálculo?

_____A_____ 2. El cálculo es difícil.

_____S_____ 3. A mí me gusta mucho la clase.

_____A_____ 4. No me gusta la clase, pero la necesito porque es mi carrera.

_____A_____ 5. ¿Cuál te gusta más?

Práctica adicional	

Cuaderno de tareas	Video CD-ROM
WB p.73, A–C	Episodio 3

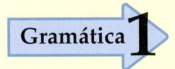
Para comunicarnos mejor

Gramática 1

Expressing likes and dislikes
• Me gusta, te gusta, le gusta

In their conversation, Sofía and Adriana made the following statements.

La clase de composición **me gusta** mucho.
¿**Le gusta** la clase de cálculo?
A mí **me gusta** mucho la clase.
¿Cuál **te gusta** más?

I like composition class a lot.
Do you like calculus class?
I like the class a lot.
Which one do you like better?

1. Notice that you need to use the definite article after **gusta** when it is followed by a noun.

   ¿Le gusta **la** clase de cálculo?

2. When Sofía asks Adriana about her preferences, she does not use **¿te gusta?**; she uses **¿le gusta?** instead. Adriana is older, and Sofía just met her, so she wants to be polite. When you ask or tell a friend whether they like something, use **te gusta**. Use **le gusta** with your instructor, and **me gusta** when referring to your own preferences.

PRÁCTICA

A. ¿Qué clases te gustan? Use the list of class subjects on page 11 to interview a partner and find out your classmate's preferences. Remember, you need to use **el** or **la** before a noun.

Answers will vary.

> **Modelo**
> —¿Te gusta el drama?
> —Sí, me gusta. ¿Y a ti?
> —A mí también.   or   —A mí no.
>
> —¿Te gusta la biología?
> —No, no me gusta. ¿Y a ti?
> —A mí tampoco.   or   —A mí sí.

¡Fíjate!

Look at the ending of the class subjects to determine whether they are masculine or feminine.

B. Tus preferencias. Find out whether your classmate likes the activities listed below. Each activity begins with a verb. You can guess what the verbs mean from the context. For example, in **¿Te gusta jugar fútbol?** you can safely guess that **jugar** means *to play*.

Answers will vary.

> **Modelo**
> —¿Te gusta jugar fútbol?
> —No, no me gusta. ¿Y a ti?
> —A mí tampoco.   or   —A mí sí.
>
> —¿Te gusta comer ensaladas?
> —Sí, me gusta. ¿Y a ti?
> —A mí también.   or   —A mí no.

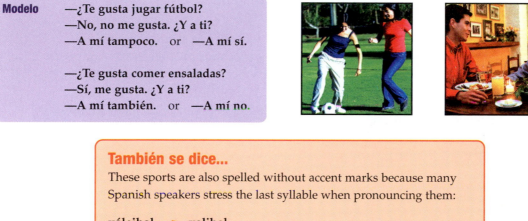

También se dice...

These sports are also spelled without accent marks because many Spanish speakers stress the last syllable when pronouncing them:

vóleibol ➝ volibol

béisbol ➝ beisbol

fútbol ➝ futbol

fútbol americano ➝ futbol americano

1. jugar (vóleibol, béisbol, fútbol americano, fútbol *(soccer)*, tenis)
2. comer (pizza, tacos, enchiladas, hamburguesas, frutas, ensaladas)
3. estudiar (en casa, en la biblioteca, con compañeros de clase)
4. escuchar música (clásica, alternativa, rap, latina, moderna)
5. leer (novelas, poemas, el periódico *(newspaper)*, el horóscopo)
6. mirar programas (cómicos, policíacos, de suspenso)

C. Las preferencias de tu profesor(a). As a class, find out whether your instructor likes some of the same activities.   Answers will vary.

> **Modelo**   —Profesor(a), ¿le gusta escuchar música rap?

D. Una entrevista. Find out whether your classmate has similar preferences. Write down your own preferences before you begin the interview. Answers will vary.

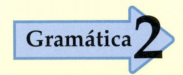
Modelo
—A mí me gusta Britney Spears. ¿Y a ti?
—No me gusta. Christina Aguilera me gusta más. ¿Te gusta el programa *Friends*?
—Sí, me gusta mucho.

Mis cantantes (*singers*) favoritos	Mis actores favoritos	Mis programas favoritos
_____	_____	_____
_____	_____	_____
_____	_____	_____

Práctica adicional

Cuaderno de tareas
WB p.74, D–E

Gramática 2

Describing yourself and others
- **Ser** + [*adjectives*] (cognates)
- **Subject pronouns**

In the dialogue, Adriana says **soy un poco tímida** when describing herself and **el profesor es muy estricto** when describing her calculus instructor. **Soy** and **es** are forms of the verb **ser** (*to be*). Use the following forms to describe yourself and others.

Ser		
yo	**Soy** un poco tímida.	*I'm a little shy.*
tú	**Eres** muy pesimista.	*You are very pessimistic.* (informal)
usted (Ud.)	**Es** creativo/a.	*You are creative.* (formal)
él	**Es** ambicioso.	*He is ambitious.*
ella	**Es** seria.	*She is serious.*
nosotros nosotras	**Somos** inteligentes.	*We are intelligent.*
ustedes (Uds.)	**Son** impacientes.	
vosotros* vosotras	**Sois** impacientes.	*You are impatient.* (plural)
ellos ellas	**Son** muy sociables.	*They are easy-going.*

*Spain is the only country that uses **vosotros/as** for *you* (plural, informal) and **ustedes** for *you* (plural, formal). All other Spanish-speaking countries use **ustedes** for both formal and informal second-person plural.

¡Fíjate!
The **vosotros** forms are provided for your reference only; you are not responsible for learning them.

1. Notice that **nosotros, vosotros,** and **ellos** may refer to a group of men or to a mixed group, whereas **nosotras, vosotras,** and **ellas** refer only to women.

2. Notice that there is no pronoun for *it*. Use **es** to convey the idea *it is*.

Es mi libro.   *It is my book.*   **Son mis libros.**   *They are my books.*

• Subject pronouns

In their conversation, Sofía and Adriana said:

Soy de Puerto Rico.   *I'm from Puerto Rico.*
Es mi mejor amiga.   *She is my best friend.*

Notice that the characters do not say *yo* **soy** or *ella* **es**. In Spanish, the verb form itself and/or the context indicates the person we are talking about *(I, you, he, she, we, they)*. Therefore, it is not necessary to use subject pronouns. The subject pronouns (**yo, tú, usted, él, ella, nosotros/as, vosotros/as, ustedes, ellos/as**) are used only when:

a. you want to establish contrast or emphasis.   **Tú no eres responsable, yo sí.**
b. there is no verb.   **Yo también, nosotros tampoco, tú no.**
c. you are answering a "who" question.   **¿Quién es romántico? Yo soy.**

Read the following descriptive adjectives. They are all cognates. Can you understand what they mean? The spelling of these adjectives stays the same whether they describe a man or a woman.

Para describir la personalidad I		
arrogante	increíble	pesimista
competente	interesante	(ir)responsable
excelente	materialista	sentimental
flexible	optimista	sociable
idealista	(im)paciente	terrible

The following adjectives end in **-o** when they refer to a man and in **-a** when they refer to a woman.

Para describir la personalidad II			
activo/a	discreto/a	(des)honesto/a	romántico/a
ambicioso/a	estudioso/a	(in)maduro/a	serio/a
atractivo/a	extrovertido/a	nervioso/a	tímido/a
creativo/a	generoso/a	reservado/a	tranquilo/a

To ask what someone is like, use the expression ¿**Cómo es/son...**?
¿**Cómo es la profesora de composición**?   *What is your composition professor like?*

PRÁCTICA

E. Los amigos de Sofía. Complete Sofía's description and answer her questions using **ser**. Answers will vary.

1. Mi mamá ___es___ extrovertida y sociable. ¿Y tú mamá?
   Mi mamá _____
2. Ana Mari y Ramón ___son___ responsables y maduros.
   ¿Cómo son tus amigos?
   Mis amigos _____
3. Manolo y yo ___somos___ amigos; ___somos___ muy diferentes.
4. ¿Cómo es tu mejor amigo? _____
5. ¿Cómo eres tú? _____
6. Mi mejor amigo y yo _____

Sofía

F. Características. Escucha los comentarios para indicar si las características mencionadas son **positivas** o **negativas**.

Audio
CD-ROM

Instructor's Resources
• Worktext CD
• Website
• IRM: Tapescript

	Positiva	Negativa
1.	✓	☐
2.	✓	☐
3.	☐	✓

	Positiva	Negativa
4.	✓	☐
5.	☐	✓
6.	☐	✓

G. ¿Cómo eres? Chat with a partner about each other's characteristics. Ask questions like:

Modelo —¿Eres responsable?   —¿Eres reservado?
—Sí, soy responsable. ¿Y tú?   —No, no soy reservado ¿Y tú?
—Yo también.   or   —Yo no.   —Yo tampoco.   or   —Yo sí.

Additional Activity. Bring or ask students to bring pictures of famous people, including both very popular people and people that nobody likes. Hold up the pictures in front of the class, and have students describe the person in question. Emphasize the meaning of **¿Cómo es...?** to ask for people's characteristics.

Script. *Escucha los comentarios de los estudiantes para indicar si las características mencionadas son positivas o negativas.*
1. El profesor y yo somos muy optimistas. 2. La profesora es muy activa. 3. A veces soy arrogante. 4. Eres tranquila, ¿verdad? 5. Las señoritas son terribles. 6. Es muy deshonesto.

H. ¿Cómo es tu profesor(a)? With your partner, try to determine the three characteristics that best describe your instructor. Then ask your instructor to tell whether your guesses are correct. Answers will vary.

Modelo   Profesor(a), ¿usted es romántico/a?

Práctica adicional

Cuaderno de tareas
WB pp.75–76, F–I

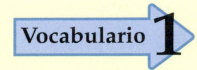

Vocabulario 1   Identifying Spanish-speaking countries

Study the map below to learn the positions, names, and capitals of the Spanish-speaking countries.

Los países de habla hispana y sus capitales

España, Madrid

Estados Unidos, Washington D.C.

Océano Atlántico

Cuba, La Habana

República Dominicana, Santo Domingo

México, Ciudad de México

Puerto Rico, San Juan

Honduras, Tegucigalpa

Guatemala, Ciudad de Guatemala

Colombia, Bogotá

Venezuela, Caracas

El Salvador, San Salvador

Nicaragua, Managua

Costa Rica, San José

Panamá, Ciudad de Panamá

Ecuador, Quito

Perú, Lima

Paraguay, Asunción

Bolivia, La Paz y Sucre

Uruguay, Montevideo

Océano Pacífico

Argentina, Buenos Aires

Chile, Santiago

PRÁCTICA

I. El mundo hispano. Examina el mapa para completar las frases.

1. ¿En cuántos países (countries) se habla español? En ___21 países___.
2. Los países hispanos de Centroamérica son: ___Guatemala___, ___El Salvador___, ___Nicaragua___, ___Costa Rica___, ___Panamá___ y ___Honduras___.
3. En el Caribe, se habla español en ___Cuba___, ___República Dominicana___ y ___Puerto Rico___.
4. ¿Qué países de Sudamérica no tienen (do not have) acceso al océano? ___Bolivia___ y ___Paraguay___.
5. En Europa, un país de habla hispana es ___España___.

¡Fíjate!

Bolivia has two capitals: La Paz, the administrative capital and the center of government, and Sucre, the constitutional capital and judicial center.

J. Capitales. Escribe los países o las capitales necesarias para completar la lista.

Países	Capitales
1. Argentina	Buenos Aires
2. Chile	_Santiago_
3. _Colombia_	Bogotá
4. Cuba	_La Habana_
5. _Ecuador_	Quito
6. El Salvador	_San Salvador_
7. _España_	Madrid
8. _Nicaragua_	Managua
9. _Uruguay_	Montevideo
10. Perú	_Lima_
11. _Venezuela_	Caracas
12. Costa Rica	_San José_
13. _Bolivia_	La Paz y Sucre
14. Puerto Rico	_San Juan_

Invitación a **Bolivia**

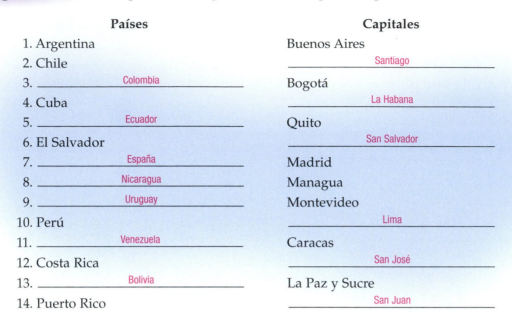

Del álbum de
Sofía

Bolivia es aproximadamente tres veces el tamaño (size) de Montana y su población es de 9.1 millones de habitantes. Es el país más alto y aislado (isolated) de América. La influencia indígena es palpable; hay estaciones de radio en Qechua (lengua inca) y Aymará (lengua pre-inca) y en la televisión se pueden escuchar las noticias en Qechua.

Práctica adicional

Cuaderno de tareas WB p.76, J–K LM pp.79–80, A–C, Pron.	Audio CD-ROM Episodio 3	Website vistahigher learning.com

Actividades comunicativas

A. Los habitantes en Latinoamérica.

Instrucciones para Estudiante 1

You have half of the information on populations in Latin America, and your partner has the other half. First, write the names of the countries you are missing, then ask your partner to give you the number of inhabitants for each one. Take turns and use the following model.

> **Modelo**
> —**Cuántos habitantes hay en México?**
> —**En México hay ciento uno punto ocho millones de habitantes.**

¡Fíjate!

The numbers next to each country represent the number of people in millions. They are read as follows:

El Salvador, seis punto ocho millones de habitantes.

En Estados Unidos hay más de 30 millones de hispanohablantes.

Cuba, 11.3

República Dominicana, 8.9

México, 101.8

Puerto Rico, 4

Guatemala, 12.6

Honduras, 7

Nicaragua, 5.6

El Salvador, 6.8

Venezuela, 26

Costa Rica, 4.3

Panama, 3

Ecuador, 13.6

Colombia, 44.9

Perú, 27.4

Paraguay, 6

Bolivia, 9.1

Uruguay, 3.4

Chile, 16

Argentina, 38.8

A. Review the instructions with students to be sure that they know how to complete the activity. Review the **¡Fíjate!** note with them.

Sources: US Census Bureau and the Population Division, UN Secretariat.

A. Los habitantes en Latinoamérica.

You have half of the information on populations in Latin America, and your partner has the other half. First, write the names of the countries you are missing, then ask your partner to give you the number of inhabitants for each one. Take turns and use the following model.

> **Modelo** —**Cuántos habitantes hay en México?**
> —**En México hay ciento uno punto ocho millones de habitantes.**

¡Fíjate!

The numbers next to each country represent the number of people in millions. They are read as follows:

Honduras, siete millones de habitantes.

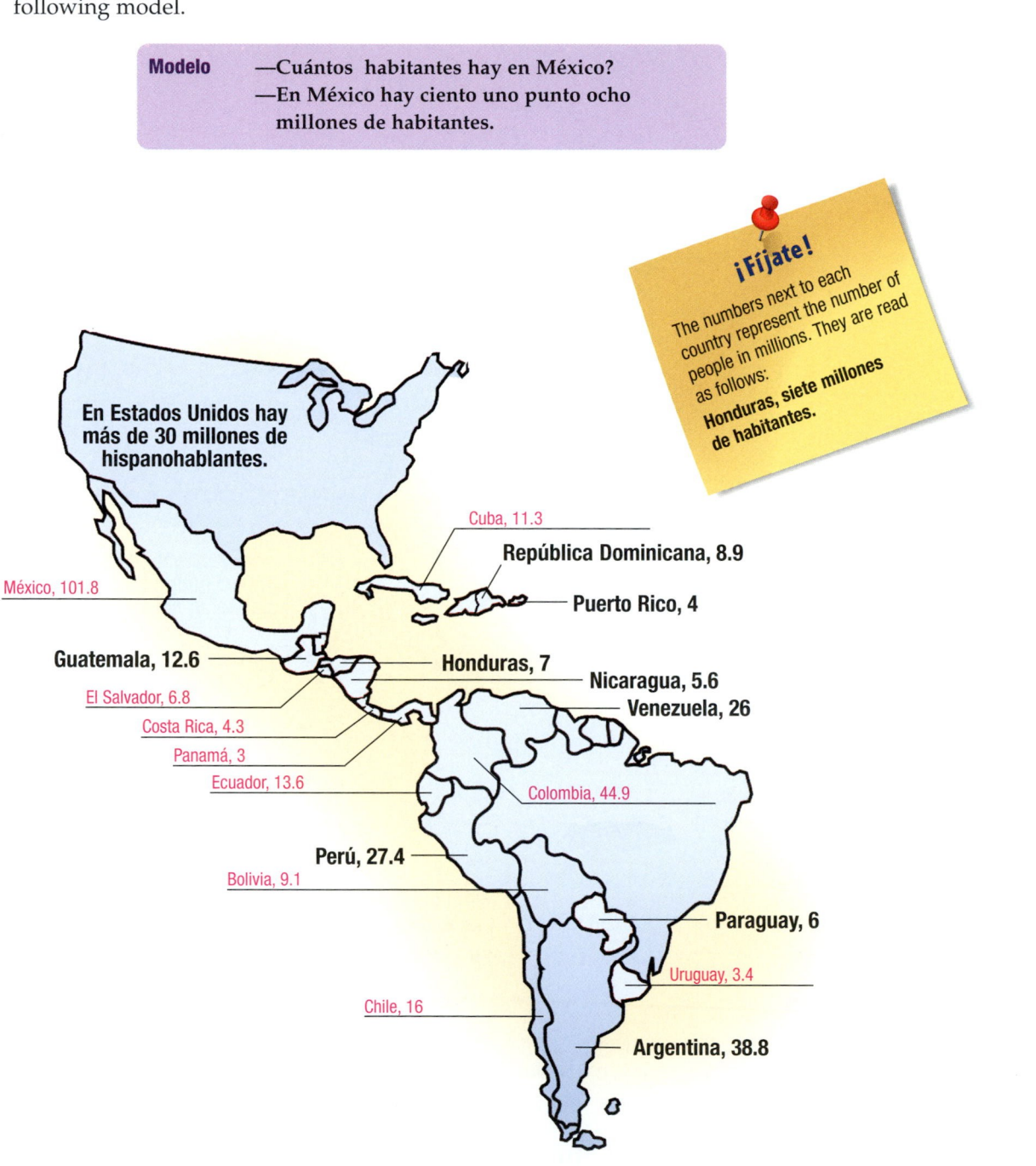

En Estados Unidos hay más de 30 millones de hispanohablantes.

México, 101.8

Cuba, 11.3

República Dominicana, 8.9

Puerto Rico, 4

Guatemala, 12.6

El Salvador, 6.8

Costa Rica, 4.3

Panamá, 3

Ecuador, 13.6

Honduras, 7

Nicaragua, 5.6

Venezuela, 26

Colombia, 44.9

Perú, 27.4

Bolivia, 9.1

Paraguay, 6

Uruguay, 3.4

Chile, 16

Argentina, 38.8

*Sources: US Census Bureau and the Population Division, UN Secretariat.

B. ¡A hablar! Interview a classmate. Find out your classmate's name, how many classes they are taking, which ones, at what time, which classes they like or dislike, whether they work, and how many hours. Ask them to describe themself and two of their teachers.

B. Assign this activity for homework the day before, so students are ready to ask and answer their partner's questions.

La correspondencia

El correo: Una carta para Odette. Read Sofia's letter to her friend Odette and answer the questions.

1. ¿Cuántas clases toma Sofía? Sofía toma cuatro clases.
2. ¿Cómo son las clases de Sofía? Cálculo y geología son fáciles. Cálculo es divertida.
3. ¿Quién *(who)* es Manolo? Manolo es un amigo de Sofía.
4. Describe a Lalo. Lalo es irresponsable e inmaduro.

Reading Strategy: Understanding the overall meaning

When reading, you do not have to understand every word. To understand the overall meaning of Sofía's letter, read the first paragraph and underline all the words you understand. Then use those words to determine the main idea of the paragraph. Read the other paragraphs, repeating the process. Read the questions first to find out what you need to know.

Querida Odette:

¿Cómo estás? Yo estoy muy contenta porque ya comenzamos las clases en la universidad. Este semestre tomo cuatro clases. Creo que van a ser fáciles,[1] especialmente cálculo y geología. Lo único[2] diferente es que son en inglés. La clase de cálculo es divertida[3], porque mi amigo Manolo está en la clase, y a veces es cómico.

Mis papás están muy bien; están planeando unas vacaciones en Cancún y están muy emocionados[4]. Lalo me preocupa un poco. Es bastante[5] irresponsable e inmaduro, y ya casi tiene dieciséis años. No es diligente en la escuela y solamente le interesa ir a fiestas y estar con sus amigos. Espero que cuando se gradúe de la preparatoria madure un poco.

Bueno querida Odette, un beso[6] para ti y toda tu familia. Escríbeme pronto.

Tu amiga que te quiere,
Sofía

[1]*easy* [2]*the only thing* [3]*fun* [4]*excited* [5]*rather* [6]*kiss*

En papel: Una notita para Sofía. Complete the following e-mail to Sofía telling her about yourself. Answers will vary.

En papel. Ask students to read their note to Sofia out loud. That way, students can check their own answers.

> **Writing Strategy: Identifying the content of a note**
> Successful writers identify the information they wish to communicate before they begin to write. In the early stages of learning Spanish, this information will be lists of words and phrases. Later you can incorporate these lists into brief notes you write to Spanish speakers. Pay close attention to spelling, so that your early written communication will be understandable.

From: _____
To: Sofía. <Blasio@sol.red>
Re: Saludos

Date: Lunes, 19 de feb. 12:07 EST
_____

Hola Sofía,

Me llamo _____. Soy de _____.
Mi universidad se llama _____.
Este semestre tomo _____ clases. Son: _____.
Me gusta mucho la clase de _____ porque
el/la profesor(a) es _____.
Este semestre trabajo _____ horas a la semana. ¿Y tú? ¿Cuántas clases tomas?
¿Trabajas? ¿Cuántas horas? ¡Escríbeme pronto! Buena suerte este semestre.

                                        Saludos,

                                        _____

Video
CD-ROM

Audio
CD-ROM

Instructor's Resources
• VHS Video
• Worktext CD
• IRM: Videoscript

¡A ver de nuevo! Escucha la conversación o mira el video de **Escenas de la vida** para completar cada frase con la palabra apropiada.

¡A ver de nuevo! Play the video again and have students complete the sentences logically.

1. Los salones de clase en Puerto Rico no tienen tantas _____cosas_____.
2. La mayoría de las universidades tienen un _____gimnasio_____, un _____auditorio_____ y una _____biblioteca_____.
3. En Puerto Rico y en Estados Unidos hay _____consejeros_____, pero en México no.
4. El profesor de cálculo es _____estricto_____ y _____atractivo_____.
5. Adriana es un poco _____tímida_____.
6. A Sofía le gustan las clases de _____diseño_____, _____geología_____ y _____vóleibol_____.

Práctica adicional

Cuaderno de tareas
WB pp.77–78, L–M
LM p.80, A–B

Audio
CD-ROM
Episodio 3

Website
vistahigher
learning.com

Vocabulario del Episodio 3

Los gustos *Likes and dislikes*

Instructor's Resources
• Testing program
• Website

¿Te gusta...?	*Do you like… (informal)*
Sí, me gusta.	*Yes, I like it.*
No, no me gusta.	*No, I don't like it.*
¿Le gusta...?	*Do you like...? (formal)*

Los pronombres personales y el verbo <u>ser</u>

yo **soy**	*I am*
tú **eres**	*you are (informal)*
usted (Ud.) **es**	*you are (formal)*
él **es**	*he is*
ella **es**	*she is*
nosotros/as **somos**	*we are*
ustedes (Uds.) **son**	
vosotros/as **sois**	*you are* (plural)
ellos/as **son**	*they are*

Adjetivos

activo/a	excelente	(in)maduro/a	romántico/a
ambicioso/a	extrovertido/a	materialista	sentimental
arrogante	flexible	nervioso/a	serio/a
atractivo/a	generoso/a	optimista	sociable
competente	(des)honesto/a	(im)paciente	terrible
creativo/a	idealista	pesimista	tímido/a
discreto/a	increíble	reservado/a	tranquilo/a
estudioso/a	interesante	(ir)responsable	

Los países de habla hispana y sus capitales

Argentina, Buenos Aires	Honduras, Tegucigalpa
Bolivia, La Paz y Sucre	México, Ciudad de México
Chile, Santiago	Nicaragua, Managua
Colombia, Bogotá	Panamá, Ciudad de Panamá
Costa Rica, San José	Paraguay, Asunción
Cuba, La Habana	Perú, Lima
Ecuador, Quito	Puerto Rico, San Juan
El Salvador, San Salvador	República Dominicana, Santo Domingo
España, Madrid	Uruguay, Montevideo
Guatemala, Ciudad de Guatemala	Venezuela, Caracas

Vocabulario personal

Write the words that you need to know to describe yourself and express your likes and dislikes in Spanish.

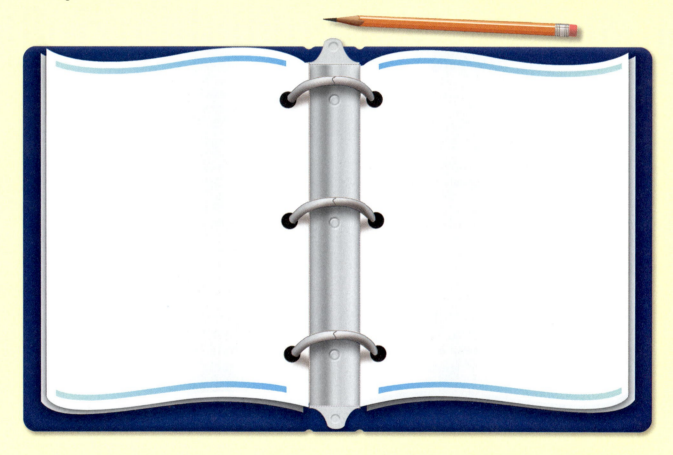

¡A escribir!

Episodio 3

Escenas de la vida: Los profesores y las clases

A. ¡Mira cuánto entendiste! See how much of the **Escena** you understood by matching the Spanish sentences with their English equivalents.

En la universidad

_c_	1. ¿Hay consejeros?	a. It's my major.
_d_	2. ¡Qué mala suerte!	b. The professor gives good explanations.
_b_	3. El profesor explica bien.	c. Are there counselors?
_a_	4. Es mi carrera.	d. Too bad!
_f_	5. Me gusta hacer ejercicio.	e. I play tennis with my husband.
_e_	6. Juego tenis con mi esposo.	f. I like to exercise.

B. Los profesores y las clases. Use the words in the box to complete the conversation.

atractivo	consejeros	excelentes	le gusta
difícil	diferentes	salones	auditorio

Sofía   Las universidades aquí son muy (1) _____ diferentes _____. ¿En Puerto Rico hay (2) _____ consejeros _____ como en Estados Unidos?

Adriana   Sí, y los profesores son (3) _____ excelentes _____.

Sofía   ¿(4) _____ Le gusta _____ la clase de cálculo?

Adriana   Más o menos. Es (5) _____ difícil _____ y el profesor es muy estricto.

Sofía   Pero es muy (6) _____ atractivo _____.

C. ¿Qué clase te gusta? Order the statements in the dialogue so that it makes sense.

  _5_   a. A mí me gusta mucho la clase. La de vóleibol también. Me gusta mucho hacer ejercicio. ¿Y a usted?

  _2_   b. En Puerto Rico, sí. Y los profesores son excelentes.

  _4_   c. Pues, más o menos. El cálculo es difícil. ¿Y a ti?

  _1_   d. ¿En Puerto Rico hay consejeros como en Estados Unidos? En México no hay.

  _6_   e. A veces juego tenis con mi esposo, pero no me gusta.

  _3_   f. Hablando de profesores, ¿le gusta la clase de cálculo?

Nombre _____ Fecha _____

 **Gramática 1**   **Expressing likes and dislikes**
•<u>**Me gusta, te gusta, le gusta**</u>

D. ¿Qué materias te gustan? Indicate which subjects you like and which ones you do not like. You may use the subjects on the list below, or any subjects you wrote in your **Vocabulario personal** section. Remember to use the definite article after **gusta**. Answers will vary.

cálculo	geología	inglés	contabilidad
economía	español	música	drama

1. Me gusta el arte. _____   No me gusta la astronomía. _____
2. _____   _____
3. _____   _____
4. _____   _____
5. _____   _____

E. ¿Qué te gusta hacer? Indicate six activities you like to do and six activities you do not like to do. Answers will vary.

a. jugar (vóleibol, béisbol, fútbol americano, fútbol, tenis)

b. comer (pizza, tacos, enchiladas, hamburguesas, frutas, ensaladas)

c. estudiar (en casa, en la biblioteca, con compañeros de clase)

d. escuchar música (clásica, alternativa, rap, latina, moderna)

e. leer (novelas, poemas, el periódico, el horóscopo)

f. mirar programas (cómicos, policíacos, de suspenso)

1. Me gusta estudiar en la biblioteca. _____
2. _____
3. _____
4. _____
5. _____
6. _____
7. _____
8. No me gusta escuchar música clásica. _____
9. _____
10. _____
11. _____
12. _____
13. _____
14. _____

Nombre _____ Fecha _____

Gramática 2 〉 Describing yourself and others
• <u>Ser</u> + [*adjective*] (cognates)
• **Subject pronouns**

F. Descríbelos. Describe yourself, your family members, your friends, and your Spanish instructor. Use at least three adjectives per person. Answers will vary.

| **Modelo** | Mis hermanos son activos, irresponsables y sociables. |

arrogante	idealista	optimista	sentimental
competente	increíble	(im)paciente	sociable
excelente	interesante	pesimista	terrible
flexible	materialista	(ir)responsable	tranquilo/a
activo/a	discreto/a	(des)honesto/a	romántico/a
ambicioso/a	estudioso/a	estricto/a	serio/a
atractivo/a	extrovertido/a	nervioso/a	tímido/a
creativo/a	generoso/a	reservado/a	inmaduro/a

1. (Yo) _____
2. Mi mamá _____
3. Mi papá _____
4. Mis compañeros _____
5. Mi profesor(a) de español _____

G. Mis amigos y yo: una descripción. Fill in the appropriate forms of **ser**.

(Yo) (1)____soy____ estudioso y ambicioso, pero no (2)____soy____ muy creativo.
Y tú, ¿cómo (3)____eres____ ? (4) Tú ____eres____ un poco nerviosa, ¿no?
Sofía (5)____es____ muy sociable y Manolo (6)____es____ tímido. Ellos
(7)____son____ buenos amigos. Ramón y yo (8)____somos____ inteligentes, pero también
(9)____somos____ materialistas. Y tus amigos, ¿cómo (10)____son____?

H. ¿Cómo es… ? Describe the famous people below. To ask someone to describe a person/people, you ask **¿Cómo es/son… ?** Answers will vary.

| **Modelo** | Mike Tyson |
| | **¿Cómo es Mike Tyson? Es irresponsable y arrogante.** |

1. Christina Aguilera _____
2. La Sra. Clinton _____
3. Bill Gates _____
4. Tiger Woods _____
5. Eminem _____

I. Un poco sobre mí. *(A little about me.)* Write a paragraph with the following information: your name, the classes you take (**tomo...**), a description of your instructors (**Mi profesor de... es...**), the number of hours a week you work (**trabajo...**) and study (**estudio...**), and something you like to do. Answers will vary.

_____

_____

_____

_____

_____

Vocabulario 1 ▷ Identifying Spanish-speaking countries

J. Capitales. Write the capitals of the following countries.

País	Capital
México	Ciudad de México
Guatemala	Ciudad de Guatemala
Costa Rica	San José
Panamá	Ciudad de Panamá
Chile	Santiago
España	Madrid
República Dominicana	Santo Domingo
Puerto Rico	San Juan
Uruguay	Montevideo

K. Los países. Look at the map in order to identify the countries.

1. México
2. Cuba
3. República Dominicana
4. Puerto Rico
5. Guatemala
6. Honduras
7. El Salvador
8. Nicaragua
9. Costa Rica
10. Panamá
11. Venezuela
12. Colombia
13. Ecuador
14. Perú
15. Bolivia
16. Chile
17. Argentina
18. Paraguay

Para terminar

L. La Universidad Estatal de San Marcos en California.

Parte 1. Read the description of the university and answer the questions.

> La universidad está en la ciudad de San Marcos, localizada a unas cuarenta millas al norte de San Diego. Es la última universidad (la número vientiuno) construída en California por el sistema californiano de universidades estatales. California State University San Marcos es una universidad nueva y todavía es pequeña. La universidad no está totalmente terminada aún. Los salones son nuevos y modernos. Uno de los edificios es muy moderno, los salones tienen televisiones, computadoras, videocaseteras, pupitres y pizarrones nuevos, pero no hay piscinas ni gimnasios. La cafetería y la biblioteca son muy bonitas y modernas. Además hay un *Centro para el estudio de libros en español* que tiene una de las colecciones de libros infantiles y juveniles más grandes en español. Asisten aproximadamente seis mil estudiantes, pero no hay residencias estudiantiles para ellos todavía. Hay estacionamiento porque casi todos los estudiantes llegan a la universidad en coche.

1. Describe the university, its size, and its facilities.

   _____ It's new and small. _____

2. Describe the classrooms. _____

   _____ They have TVs, computers, VCRs, desks, and boards. _____

3. Why is this a good place to study? _____

   _____ The library and the cafeteria are new and there is a **Centro para el estudio de libros en español**. _____

4. How many students are there? How many live on campus? How is parking?

   _____ There are 6,000 students, but there are no dorms. There is a lot of parking. _____

   _____

Parte 2. Use the reading above as a model to write about your own university or college.   Answers will vary.

_____
_____
_____
_____
_____
_____

Nombre ______________________________ Fecha _______________

M. Una miniprueba. Complete the following communicative tasks to test your knowledge of the content of this chapter. Answers will vary.

1. Ask Sofía:	a. how many classes she is taking.
	b. if she likes the calculus class.
2. Ask Adriana:	c. when her composition class is.
	d. to describe her instructor.
3. Tell Manolo:	e. the classes you take.
	f. which ones you like and why.
4. Describe:	g. yourself.
	h. your favorite instructor.

a. ¿Cuántas clases tomas?

b. ¿Te gusta la clase de cálculo?

c. ¿A qué hora es la clase de composición?

d. ¿Cómo es el profesor?

e. ______________________________

f. ______________________________

g. ______________________________

h. ______________________________

Nombre _____ Fecha _____

¡A escuchar!

Episodio

Comprensión

A. La clase de Ana Mari. Listen to Ana Mari talk about her classmates and one of her classes, and then fill in the missing information. **¡Atención!** Pay attention to the gender and number of the adjectives. You will hear Ana Mari's narration twice.

La clase de _____inglés_____

La clase es _____interesante_____ . El profesor es un hombre _____estricto_____ y _____serio_____ .
Hoy los estudiantes están _____nerviosos_____ porque hay un examen. Natalia es _____inmadura_____
y _____extrovertida_____ . Pete no está _____nervioso_____ porque está bien _____preparado_____ . Él es un
estudiante _____competente_____ y _____responsable_____ .

B. Descripciones. The following adjectives are listed in the masculine singular form. You will hear a cue for each one (masculine or feminine, singular or plural). Aloud, match the adjective to each cue with **es** or **son**. Repeat the correct answer after the speaker.

Modelo	You see:	**generoso**	You see:	**estricto**
	You hear:	**Adriana**	You hear:	**los profesores**
	You say:	**Adriana <u>es</u> generos<u>a</u>.**	You say:	**Los profesores <u>son</u> estrict<u>os</u>.**

1. honesto	3. optimista	5. extrovertido	7. difícil	9. romántico
2. inmaduro	4. interesante	6. sentimental	8. estudioso	10. sociable

C. La mejor respuesta. You will hear ten questions or statements. Select the best response for each one. You will hear each question or statement twice.

1. a. Bien, gracias.   b. La clase de química.   (c.) Ana Mari.
2. (a.) Igualmente.   b. Más o menos.   c. Que le vaya bien.
3. a. Adiós.   b. A mí tampoco.   (c.) Mucho gusto.
4. a. Buenos días.   (b.) Que te vaya bien.   c. Regular.
5. a. Con frecuencia.   (b.) A las diez.   c. Hay dos clases.
6. (a.) Sí, me gusta.   b. No le gusta.   c. Mucho gusto.
7. a. Sí, señorita.   b. Hasta mañana.   (c.) Bien, ¿y tú?
8. (a.) Es arrogante.   b. Es optimista.   c. Es paciente.
9. a. A las nueve.   b. A veces.   (c.) Los martes y los jueves.
10. a. Hay cinco.   (b.) Dos dólares.   c. Necesito uno.

Audio
CD-ROM

Pronunciación

La h y la ch. **H (hache)** is completely silent in Spanish. Repeat these words and sentences after the speaker. Pay close attention to the vowels **a, e, i, o,** and **u**, as well.

hambre	humo	almohada	Hasta ahora no tengo hambre.
honor	hielo	alcohol	Humberto es de Honduras.

Ch (che) is pronounced just like the English *ch*. In Spanish, **ch** was a separate letter of the alphabet until 1994. You may still see it treated as a separate letter, following **c**, in texts published before that date. Repeat these words and sentences after the speaker.

chico	chile	muchacha	El chico sale con la muchacha.
hacha	concha	choca	Me choca usar el hacha.

Más escenas de la vida

Sofía, Ana Mari, and Manolo are coming out of the movies. Listen to their conversation, and then complete activities **A** and **B**. You will hear the conversation twice.

A. ¿Cierto o falso? Indicate whether the following statements are **cierto** or **falso**, according to the conversation.

	Cierto	Falso
1. Ramón es el hermano de Ana Mari.	✓	☐
2. Ramón es impaciente.	✓	☐
3. Ramón es irresponsable e inmaduro.	☐	✓
4. Ana Mari y Sofía son perfectas.	☐	✓
5. Ramón es un controlador.	✓	☐
6. A Manolo le gusta la música latina.	✓	☐
7. Ana Mari quiere ir a un concierto de música latina.	✓	☐
8. Los artistas favoritos de Ana Mari son Jennifer López y Christina Aguilera.	☐	✓

Audio
CD-ROM

B. Responde. Write the answers to the following questions.

1. ¿Cómo es Ramón, según Ana Mari? _____ Es arrogante, impaciente e inflexible. _____

2. ¿Cómo es Ramón, según Sofía? _____ Es responsable y maduro. _____

3. ¿Cómo es Ramón, según Sofía y Ana Mari? _____ Es controlador. _____

4. ¿Qué cantantes *(singers)* le gustan a Manolo? _____ Le gustan Maná, Mark Anthony y Shakira. _____

Objetivos comunicativos

In this episode, you will practice:

✓ talking about your family

✓ telling and asking for someone's age

✓ saying and asking where someone is from

✓ asking for and giving phone numbers

Escenas de la vida: ¡Qué internacionales!

Video
CD-ROM

A. ¡Mira cuánto puedes entender!

1. Indicate where the following people are from.

Audio
CD-ROM

Instructor's Resources
• Overheads
• VHS Video
• Worktext CD
• Website
• IRM: Videoscript, Comprehensible input

2. Indicate who prefers to speak English and who prefers to speak Spanish.

Los papás y los hermanos de Ramón.

Cultura a lo vivo

Educational politics, where schools actively discourage the use of any language other than English, has intensified the problem of language loss within the Hispanic family. Because of educational politics, many Hispanic children have stopped speaking Spanish and so will be unable to pass it on to their children.

This trend has led many Spanish-speaking Americans to use Spanish in their homes as a way of preserving the links to their native countries. These families maintain their native language in order to enjoy the cultural and economic benefits of being bilingual and bicultural.

Video Synopsis. Sofía introduces her friend Ramón to Adriana and Manolo. Ramón is surprised to learn that Sofía's friends are from all over the Spanish-speaking world. They discuss the fact that it is a struggle to keep Spanish alive in their families.

Video
CD-ROM

Audio
CD-ROM

B. ¿Te diste cuenta? Escucha las conversaciones otra vez para indicar si los comentarios son **ciertos** o **falsos**.

B and C. Have students read activities **B** and **C**, and then play the video again. Have students respond orally to the prompts.

	Cierto	Falso
1. A la hija de Adriana no le gusta hablar español.	✓	☐
2. Manolo está en la clase de cálculo.	✓	☐
3. Adriana y Sofía toman geología juntas.	☐	✓
4. Ana Mari habla español muy bien.	✓	☐
5. Ramón y Sofía tienen una clase a las nueve.	✓	☐

Video
CD-ROM

Audio
CD-ROM

C. Completa las oraciones. Complete the following sentences, according to what you heard in the **Escena.**

1. _____ Ana Mari _____ es la hermana de Ramón.
2. Los padres de Manolo viven en _____ la Florida _____ .
3. Adriana _____ tiene _____ tres hijos.
4. Los _____ hermanos _____ menores de Ramón no hablan español, pero lo entienden.
5. Manolo escribe _____ poemas _____ en español.

Práctica adicional	
Cuaderno de tareas WB pp.101–102, A–D	Video CD-ROM Episodio 4

Para comunicarnos mejor

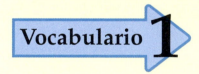

Vocabulario 1

Identifying family members and friends
- **The family**
- **Expressing possession**

When Ramón and Adriana talked about their families, they made the following statements.

Mi **mamá** es de México.	*My mom is from Mexico.*
Mi **papá** es de Honduras.	*My dad is from Honduras.*
Mis **hijos** mayores hablan español.	*My older children speak Spanish.*
Mis **hermanos** menores lo entienden todo.	*My younger brothers understand everything.*

Vocabulario 1. Use the family tree on page 85 in order to teach family-related vocabulary. While pointing, you may say: **Adriana tiene tres hijos: Carlos, Santiaguito y Viviana. Carlos es el mayor; tiene veinticinco años. Viviana es la menor; tiene once años. Adriana también tiene dos hermanos... una hermana que se llama Cristina y un hermano que se llama José Luis...,** etc.

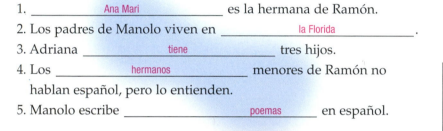

Learning Strategy: Make associations

Think of English words that sound similar to Spanish words you are trying to learn. Then associate them with each other in some creative way. For example, the name *Sabrina* sounds a lot like the Spanish **sobrina** *(niece).* Create a mental link: **Mi amiga Sabrina tiene una sobrina.** Recognize the relationships that exist in the two languages. For example, look at the words *apprentice (student)* and **aprender** *(to learn);* to remember the Spanish, visualize an apprentice that must **aprender mucho.**

The following table contains the terms you use to identify the members of your family and your friends.

La familia, los familiares y más			
los abuelos	grandparents	el abuelo	la abuela
los amigos	friends	el amigo	la amiga
los chicos	adolescents, teenagers	el chico	la chica
los cuñados	brother(s)-in-law and sister(s)-in-law	el cuñado	la cuñada
los esposos	husband and wife	el esposo	la esposa
los familiares	relatives	el familiar	
los hermanos	brother(s) and sister(s)	el hermano	la hermana
los hijos	children (one's own): son(s) and daughter(s)	el hijo	la hija
los nietos	grandchildren	el nieto	la nieta
los niños	children: boy(s) and girl(s)	el niño	la niña
los novios	boyfriend and girlfriend; bride and groom; fiancés	el novio	la novia
los padres	parents	el padre	la madre
los primos	cousins	el primo	la prima
los sobrinos	nephew(s) and niece(s)	el sobrino	la sobrina
los suegros	father-in-law and mother-in-law	el suegro	la suegra
los tíos	uncle(s) and aunt(s)	el tío	la tía

Las mascotas *pets*

el gato	cat
el pájaro	bird
el perro	dog
el pez	fish

Vocabulario 1. You may ask personalized questions such as: ¿Tienes hermanos? ¿Cuántos? ¿Tienes mascotas?

También se dice...
los padres → los papás (el papá, la mamá)
los familiares → los parientes
los chicos → los muchachos

¡Fíjate! Ask your instructor for other family relationships you may need to describe your family. Write them in the **Vocabulario personal** at the end of **Episodio 4**.

• Expressing possession

1. Notice how Spanish uses the construction **el esposo de Adriana** to say *Adriana's husband*. Where English uses *'s* to express possession, Spanish uses [*article*] + [*noun*] + **de** + [*noun*].

la hermana de Ramón *Ramón's sister*
los hijos de Adriana *Adriana's children*
el gato de Manolo *Manolo's cat*

Ana Mari es la hermana de Ramón.

2. Another way of indicating possession or relationship is to use possessive adjectives. Read the following examples:

Mis padres son de México.	*My parents are from Mexico.*
¿De dónde son **tus** padres?	*Where are your parents from?*
Sus abuelos son de Irlanda.	*His/Her grandparents are from Ireland.*
Éstos son **nuestros** hijos.	*These are our children.*
No me gusta **su** gata. ⎫	*I don't like your cat.*
No me gusta **vuestra** gata. ⎭	
Su perro es un chihuahueño.	*Their dog is a chihuahua.*

3. Notice that the possessive adjectives agree in number with the noun possessed, not with the possessor. **Nuestro/a** and **vuestro/a** also agree in gender.

Los adjetivos posesivos			
mi, mis	*my*	**nuestro, nuestros** ⎫	*our*
tu, tus	*your* (informal)	**nuestra, nuestros** ⎭	
su, sus	*his, her, your* (formal)	**vuestro, vuestros** ⎫	*your* (informal)
	their, your (plural)	**vuestra, vuestras** ⎭	

PRÁCTICA

A. La familia de Adriana. Indicate if the following statements are **cierto** (*true*) or **falso** (*false*), according to Adriana's family tree. Correct the false statements by replacing the incorrect word.

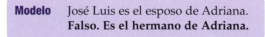

	Modelo	José Luis es el esposo de Adriana.
		Falso. Es el hermano de Adriana.

	Cierto	Falso
1. Doña Cristina es la esposa de don José Luis.	✓	☐
2. Beto y Esther son primos.	☐	✓
Falso. Son hermanos.		
3. Roberto es el papá de Santiaguito.	☐	✓
Falso. Es el tío de Santiaguito.		
4. Las sobrinas de José Luis son Tina, Esther y Viviana.	✓	☐
5. El abuelo de Beto se llama Roberto.	☐	✓
Falso. El padre de Beto se llama Roberto.		
6. Don José Luis y doña Cristina tienen tres nietas.	✓	☐
7. Roberto es el tío de Santiaguito y Viviana.	✓	☐
8. Beto, Tina y Esther son hermanos.	✓	☐

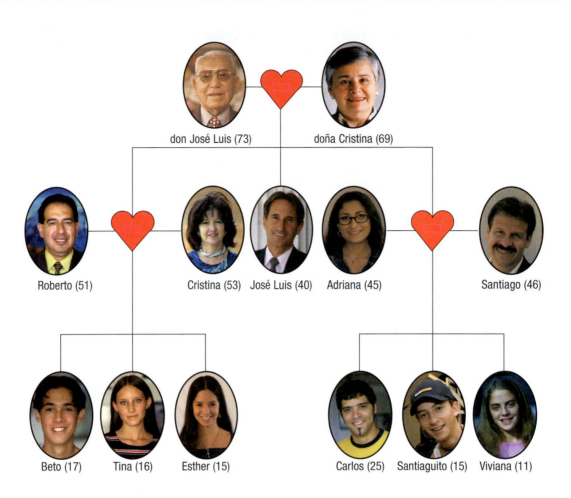

don José Luis (73)   doña Cristina (69)

Roberto (51)   Cristina (53)   José Luis (40)   Adriana (45)   Santiago (46)

Beto (17)   Tina (16)   Esther (15)   Carlos (25)   Santiaguito (15)   Viviana (11)

B. Relaciones familiares. ¿Cuál es la relación entre estas personas en la familia de Adriana?

> **Modelo**   Adriana y Santiago son **esposos.**

1. Santiaguito y Viviana son _____ hermanos _____ .

2. Esther y Viviana son _____ primas _____ .

3. Roberto y Cristina son los _____ padres/papás _____ de Esther.

4. Carlos, Santiaguito y Viviana son los _____ hijos _____ de Adriana.

5. Santiaguito y Beto son _____ nietos _____ de doña Cristina.

6. José Luis es _____ tío _____ de Santiaguito.

7. Don José Luis y doña Cristina son los _____ abuelos _____ de Tina, Esther, Viviana, Beto, Carlos y Santiaguito.

8. Doña Cristina es la _____ suegra _____ de Roberto y Santiago.

C. ¿Quiénes son? *(Who are they?)* Completa las frases lógicamente.

¡Fíjate!
Be sure to use the appropriate forms of the possessive adjectives: **mi** and **tu** are singular, while **mis** and **tus** are plural.

Modelo	La hija de mi mamá es **mi hermana.**
	Los papás de tus primas son **tus tíos.**

1. La madre de mi madre es _____mi abuela_____.

2. Los hijos de mi hermana son _____mis sobrinos_____.

3. La esposa de tu hermano es _____tu cuñada_____.

4. Las hijas de tus hijas son _____tus nietas_____.

5. El hijo de mis tíos es _____mi primo_____.

6. El padre de tu esposa es _____tu suegro_____.

D. ¿Y tus parientes? Who **(quién)** do the following questions describe? Answer them yourself, and then interview a partner. Answers will vary.

1. ¿Con qué familiares vives *(do you live)*? _____

2. ¿Qué *(which)* familiares viven lejos *(far)*? _____

3. ¿Qué familiares ves *(do you see)* con frecuencia? _____

4. ¿Con quién celebras las fiestas del fin del año *(the holidays)*? _____

Práctica adicional

Cuaderno de tareas
WB pp.102–104, E–I

Gramática 1

Expressing age
- **The verb tener**
- **Numbers 41–100**

In the conversation, you heard the following statements.

Yo **tengo** tres hijos.	*I have three children.*
¿Y **tienes** familia en Cuba?	*And do you have family in Cuba?*
En mi casa también **tenemos** ese problema.	*We also have that problem at home.*

Tengo, tienes, and **tenemos** are forms of the verb **tener** *(to have)*. You will use these forms, and the other forms of **tener,** to talk about the members of your family and to tell how old they are. Observe the conjugation of **tener** below.

Tener	
No **tengo** hijos.	*I don't have children.*
¿**Tienes** hermanos?	*Do you have brothers and sisters?*
Sofía **tiene** un hermano.	*Sofía has a brother.*
Tenemos mucha tarea.	*We have a lot of homework.*
¿Uds. **tienen** familia en España?	*Do you have family in Spain?*
¿**Tenéis** familia en España?	
Ellos no **tienen** gatos, ¿verdad?	*They don't have cats, right?*
Tener is also used to indicate age.	
¿**Cuántos años tienes?**	*How old are you?*
Tengo treinta y seis **años.**	*I'm thirty-six years old.*
¿**Cuántos años tienen** tus papás?	*How old are your parents?*
Mi papá **tiene** sesenta y tres **años**	*My dad is sixty-three years old*
y mi mamá **tiene** cincuenta y nueve.	*and my mom is fifty-nine.*

PRÁCTICA

E. ¿Cierto o falso? Completa cada frase con la forma apropiada del verbo **tener**. Después decide si la frase es **cierta** o **falsa**.   Answers will vary.

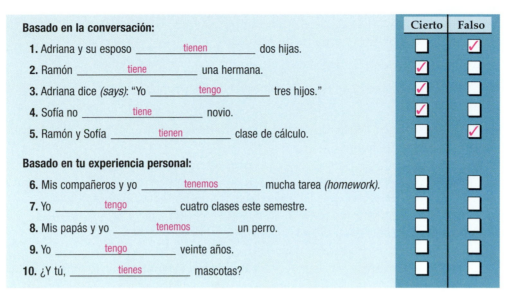

Basado en la conversación:	Cierto	Falso
1. Adriana y su esposo _____tienen_____ dos hijas.	☐	☑
2. Ramón _____tiene_____ una hermana.	☑	☐
3. Adriana dice *(says)*: "Yo _____tengo_____ tres hijos."	☑	☐
4. Sofía no _____tiene_____ novio.	☑	☐
5. Ramón y Sofía _____tienen_____ clase de cálculo.	☐	☑
Basado en tu experiencia personal:		
6. Mis compañeros y yo _____tenemos_____ mucha tarea *(homework)*.	☐	☐
7. Yo _____tengo_____ cuatro clases este semestre.	☐	☐
8. Mis papás y yo _____tenemos_____ un perro.	☐	☐
9. Yo _____tengo_____ veinte años.	☐	☐
10. ¿Y tú, _____tienes_____ mascotas?	☐	☐

• Numbers 41–100

Más números		
41	cuarenta y uno	42, 43 . . . cuarenta y dos, cuarenta y tres…
50	cincuenta	53, 54 . . . cincuenta y tres, cincuenta y cuatro…
60	sesenta	64, 65 . . . sesenta y cuatro, sesenta y cinco…
70	setenta	75, 76 . . . setenta y cinco, setenta y seis…
80	ochenta	86, 87 . . . ochenta y seis, ochenta y siete…
90	noventa	97, 98 . . . noventa y siete, noventa y ocho…
100	cien	

Gramática 1. Model the pronunciation of the numbers, and have students repeat them after you. Write a few numbers on the board and ask students to tell you what numbers they are.

PRÁCTICA

F. El inventario. You work in the bookstore at your university. Here is this week's inventory. Inform your co-worker of how many of the following articles are in stock. When you are done, your co-worker will repeat them back to you.

> **Modelo**   48 calculadoras ⟶ **Hay cuarenta y ocho calculadoras.**

1. 86 libros de historia
2. 79 cuadernos
3. 100 mochilas
4. 65 calculadoras

5. 92 plumas
6. 43 diccionarios
7. 58 lápices
8. 74 libros de cálculo

Additional Activity. Play a Bingo game with the students to practice listening comprehension of the numbers they have just learned.

G. ¿Cuántos años tiene...? Usa el árbol genealógico de la página 85 para contestar las preguntas.

1. ¿Quién *(who)* es la persona que tiene sesenta y nueve años? <u>Doña Cristina tiene sesenta y nueve años.</u>

2. ¿Quién tiene cuarenta y cinco años? <u>Adriana tiene cuarenta y cinco años.</u>

3. ¿Cuántos años tiene la hermana de Adriana? <u>Tiene cincuenta y tres años.</u>

4. ¿Cuántos años tiene el suegro de Santiago? <u>Tiene setenta y tres años.</u>

5. ¿Cuántos años tiene el menor *(the youngest)* de los primos? <u>Tiene once años.</u>

H. ¿Cuál es tu teléfono? Write down the phone numbers of three of your classmates, and ask them when they are home. Answers will vary.

¡Fíjate!
Pay attention to the way Spanish speakers give phone numbers. Look at the model.

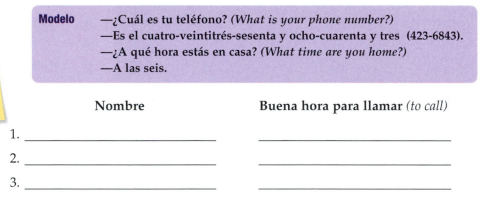

Modelo	—¿Cuál es tu teléfono? *(What is your phone number?)*
	—Es el cuatro-veintitrés-sesenta y ocho-cuarenta y tres (423-6843).
	—¿A qué hora estás en casa? *(What time are you home?)*
	—A las seis.

Nombre	**Buena hora para llamar** *(to call)*
1. _____	_____
2. _____	_____
3. _____	_____

I. Preguntas personales. Answer the following questions about your family, your classes, and your social life. Afterwards, interview a partner. Answers will vary.

1. **Acerca de *(concerning)* tu familia:** ¿Tienes una familia grande *(large)*? ¿Cuántos hermanos tienes? ¿Cuántos años tienen? ¿Cuántos años tienen tus papás? ¿Tienes mascotas?

_____

_____

_____

2. **Acerca de tus clases:** ¿Cuántas clases tienes este semestre? ¿Cuáles *(which ones)* son? ¿Cómo son tus clases: interesantes o aburridas *(boring)*? ¿Qué clase te gusta más?

_____

_____

_____

3. **Acerca de ti:** ¿Tienes novio/a o esposo/a? ¿Cómo se llama? ¿Cuántos años tiene? ¿Cómo es: romántico/a o reservado/a?

_____

_____

_____

Práctica adicional

Cuaderno de tareas
WB pp.104–106, J–L

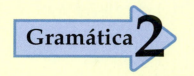 **Gramática 2**

Saying where someone is from
• Ser de

In the conversation, you heard the following statements.

¿Y tú, **de dónde eres**?	*Where are you from?*
Soy de aquí.	*I'm from here.*
Mi papá **es de** Honduras.	*My dad is from Honduras.*

When asking and telling where someone is from, use the verb **ser**, plus the preposition **de**.

–**De** dónde **son** tus abuelos?	–*Where are your grandparents from?*
–Mis abuelos **son de** España.	–*My grandparents are from Spain.*

Notice that when asking where someone is from, the Spanish **de** (*from*) is always at the beginning of the question.

PRÁCTICA

J. Personas famosas. With a classmate, match these famous people with their country of origin by asking each other questions. Be prepared to report to the class.

> **Modelo** —¿De dónde es Julio Iglesias?
> —Es de España.

¿De dónde es/son...

___c___	1. Nelson Mandela?	a. Colombia
___d___	2. Luciano Pavarotti y Sophia Loren?	b. Israel
___h___	3. Rigoberta Menchú?	c. Sudáfrica
___f___	4. Tony Blair?	d. Italia
___a___	5. Gabriel García Márquez?	e. España
___e___	6. Enrique Iglesias?	f. Inglaterra
___b___	7. Shimon Peres y Benjamín Netanyahu?	g. Japón
___g___	8. el emperador Akihito y su esposa?	h. Guatemala

K. ¿De dónde son? Complete each description with the appropriate form of **ser**.

1. Adriana _____es_____ de Puerto Rico.
2. Sofía y Lalo _____son_____ de México.
3. Manolo _____es_____ de Cuba.
4. ¿De dónde _____eres_____ tú?
5. Yo _____soy_____ de aquí.
6. ¿De dónde _____son_____ ustedes?
7. Nosotros _____somos_____ de Estados Unidos.
8. Emilio y su esposa _____son_____ de España, ¿verdad?

¡Fíjate!

You may want to review the conjugation of **ser** on page 62 before completing this activity.

L. ¿De dónde es tu familia? Interview three classmates to find out where their parents and grandparents are from (**de dónde son**). Write down their answers. Answers will vary.

Modelo
—¿De dónde eres?
—Soy de...
—¿Y tus abuelos?
—Mi abuela materna es de... Mis abuelos paternos son de...
—¿De dónde son tus padres?
—Mi papá es de..., y mi mamá es de...

Banco de palabras

Soy adoptado/a.
I'm adopted.

No sé de dónde es/son.
I don't know where they are from.

Mi abuela murió.
My grandmother died.

Mis padres murieron.
My parents died.

Lo siento.
I'm sorry.

L. Students will need to know the names of some countries in order to tell where their relatives are from. Remind them to use the **Vocabulario personal** section on page 100 to personalize their learning.

Nombre	Padres	Abuelos
_____	_____	_____
_____	_____	_____
_____	_____	_____

M. Una familia internacional. Escucha la narración de Ana Mari para completar la información.

Ana Mari

Nombre	Relación	Edad	Origen
Ramón	abuelo	75	España
Carmen	abuela	72	Cuba
Pilar	mamá	48	México
Alejandro	papá	46	Honduras
Álex, Luis y Ramón	hermanos	12, 13 y 23	Estados Unidos

Script: *Escucha la narración de Ana Mari para completar la información.*
Te voy a hablar de mi familia. La historia de mi familia es muy interesante porque tengo familia en muchos países hispanos. Mi abuelo Ramón es de España. Tiene setenta y cinco años y trabaja. Es propietario de un restaurante. Mi abuela se llama Carmen y es de Cuba. Ella no trabaja. Es ama de casa y tiene ochenta años. Mi mamá es de México. Se llama Pilar. Tiene cuarenta y ocho años y es intérprete. Mi papá, Alejandro, no es de México como mi mamá; él es de Honduras. Tiene cuarenta y seis años y es ingeniero. También tengo tres hermanos. Son de Estados Unidos. Se llaman Álex, Luis y Ramón. Tienen doce, trece y veintitrés años.

Práctica adicional

Cuaderno de tareas
WB p.106, M
LM pp.107–108, A–C, Pron.

Audio
CD-ROM
Episodio 4

Actividades comunicativas

A. Árbol genealógico: la familia de Ramón y Ana Mari Robledo.

Instrucciones para **Estudiante 1**

Parte 1. With a partner, complete Ramón and Ana Mari's family tree. You have half of the information; your partner has the other half. Use the following expressions.

—¿Cuántos años tiene Luis?

—Tiene... años.

—¿De dónde es?

—Es de...

—¿Cuál es la profesión de Pilar?

—Es...

—¿Cómo se llama el papá de Ana Mari?

—Se llama...

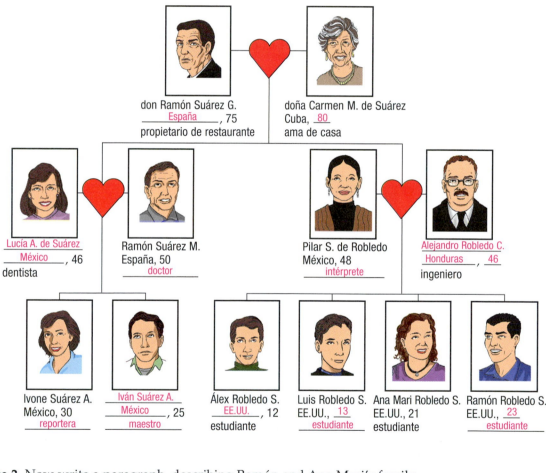

don Ramón Suárez G.
España, 75
propietario de restaurante

doña Carmen M. de Suárez
Cuba, 80
ama de casa

Lucía A. de Suárez
México, 46
dentista

Ramón Suárez M.
España, 50
doctor

Pilar S. de Robledo
México, 48
intérprete

Alejandro Robledo C.
Honduras, 46
ingeniero

Ivone Suárez A.
México, 30
reportera

Iván Suárez A.
México, 25
maestro

Álex Robledo S.
EE.UU., 12
estudiante

Luis Robledo S.
EE.UU., 13
estudiante

Ana Mari Robledo S.
EE.UU., 21
estudiante

Ramón Robledo S.
EE.UU., 23
estudiante

Parte 2. Now write a paragraph, describing Ramón and Ana Mari's family.
Answers will vary.

> **Modelo**   Ramón tiene... hermanos. Sus hermanos son... Su papá se llama... Tiene... años. etc.

A. Árbol genealógico: la familia de Ramón y Ana Mari Robledo.

Instrucciones para Estudiante 2

Parte 1. With a partner, complete Ramón and Ana Mari's family tree. You have half of the information; your partner has the other half. Use the following expressions.

—¿Cómo se llama la mamá de Ana Mari? —¿Cuál es la profesión de Alejandro?
—Se llama... —Es...
—¿De dónde es? —¿Cuántos años tiene Álex?
—Es de... —Tiene... años.

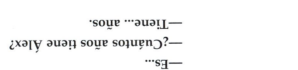

don Ramón Suárez G.
España, 75
propietario de restaurante

doña Carmen M. de Suárez
Cuba, 80
ama de casa

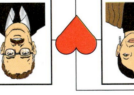

Alejandro Robledo C.
Honduras, 46
ingeniero

Pilar S. de Robledo
México, 48
intérprete

Ramón Suárez M.
España, 50
doctor

Lucía A. de Suárez
México, 46
dentista

Ramón Robledo S.
EE.UU., 23
estudiante

Ana Mari Robledo S.
EE.UU., 21
estudiante

Luis Robledo S.
EE.UU., 13
estudiante

Álex Robledo S.
EE.UU., 12
estudiante

Iván Suárez A.
México, 25
maestro

Ivone Suárez A.
México, 30
reportera

Parte 2. Now write a paragraph, describing Ramón and Ana Mari's family.
Answers will vary.

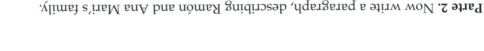

B. Los números de emergencia.

Instrucciones para **Estudiante 1**

Imagine you are going to Guadalajara, Mexico, with Sofía and her friends. As a precaution, you want the telephone numbers of various emergency services, and other important numbers. You were able to locate only a few. Ask your partner for the numbers you need and fill them in.

Modelo —¿Tienes el número de teléfono de los bomberos (*firefighters*)?

NOMBRE	TELÉFONO
La Cruz Roja	6-13-15-50 y 6-14-27-07
Los Ángeles Verdes (problemas mecánicos)	5-13-26-64
La casa de Odette	5-82-99-24
La policía federal	6-21-91-74 y 6-22-88-37
La casa de los abuelos de Ramón	5-54-13-90
Los bomberos	6-19-52-41 y 6-23-08-33
La policía municipal	6-17-60-60 y 6-18-02-06
La defensa del consumidor	6-14-94-16 y 6-14-94-01

B. Los números de emergencia.

▲ Instrucciones para Estudiante 2

Imagine you are going to Guadalajara, Mexico, with Sofía and her friends. As a precaution, you want the telephone numbers of various emergency services, and other important numbers. You were able to locate only a few. Ask your partner for the numbers you need and fill them in.

Modelo —¿Tienes el número de teléfono de la policía federal?

NOMBRE	TELÉFONO
La Cruz Roja	6-13-15-50 y 6-14-27-07
Los Ángeles Verdes (problemas mecánicos)	5-13-26-64
La casa de Odette	5-82-99-24
La policía federal	6-21-91-74 y 6-22-88-37
La casa de los abuelos de Ramón	5-54-13-90
Los bomberos (firefighters)	6-19-52-41 y 6-23-08-33
La policía municipal	6-17-60-60 y 6-18-02-06
La defensa del consumidor	6-14-94-16 y 6-14-94-01

 **C. En imágenes.**

Instrucciones para **Estudiante 1**

Use the following words and the drawings to create logical sentences. When you know what your sentences are, read them to your partner, who will check the answer key to see if your sentences are correct. Take turns.

C. Review the task with students before they begin to interact. The activities on pages 95 and 96 recycle the vocabulary from **Episodio 2**, page 49; you may ask students to review it for homework or before they begin to interact.

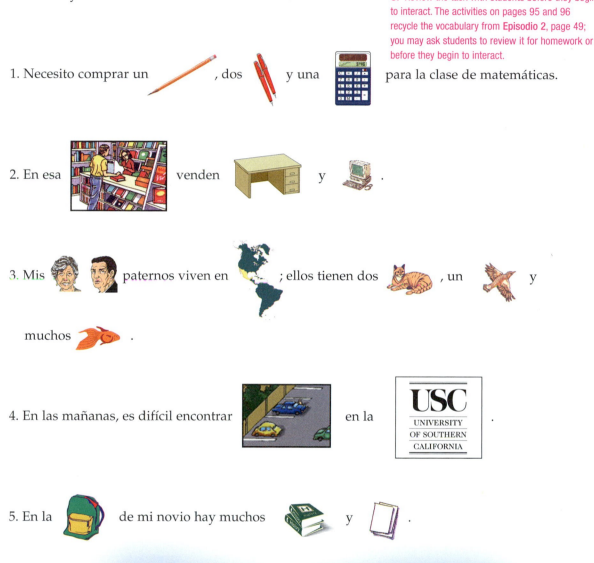

Las respuestas de tu compañero/a:

1. En nuestro **salón de clases** hay treinta y ocho **pupitres**, tres **pizarrones**, una **bandera** y un **reloj**.
2. En la **escuela** de mi prima no hay **canchas de tenis**, **piscina** ni **gimnasio**.
3. Necesito ir al **baño** antes de mi clase de **química** porque hoy tenemos un **examen** difícil.
4. Mi **profesor** de **matemáticas** tiene cuarenta **chicos/estudiantes** en su clase.
5. Tengo una **familia** pequeña: mis **padres**, una **hermana** y un **perro**.

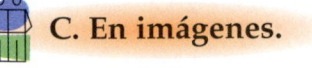

C. En imágenes.

Instrucciones para **Estudiante 2**

Use the following words and the drawings to create logical sentences. When you know what your sentences are, read them to your partner, who will check the answer key to see if your sentences are correct. Take turns.

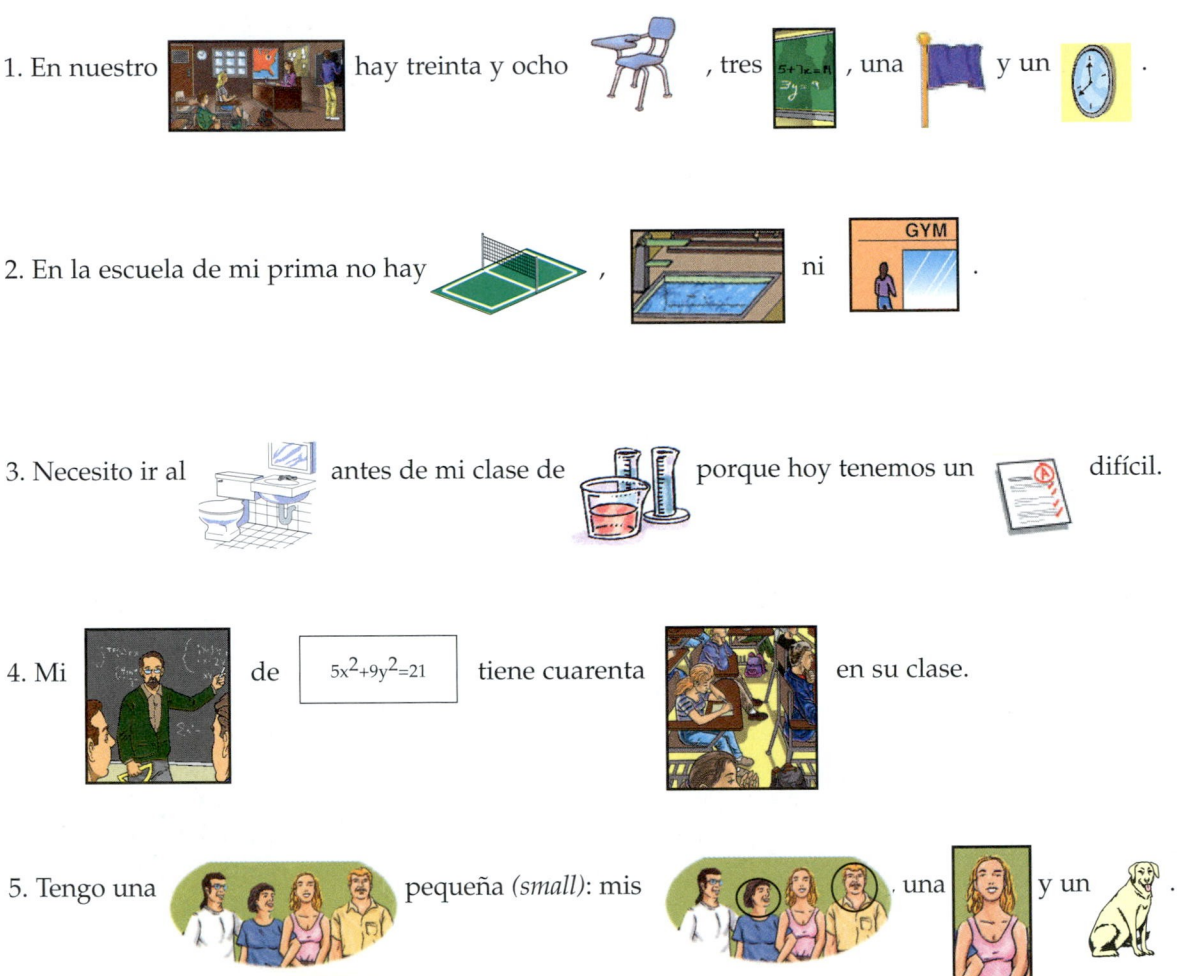

1. En nuestro [imagen] hay treinta y ocho [imagen], tres [imagen], una [imagen] y un [imagen].

2. En la escuela de mi prima no hay [imagen], [imagen] ni [imagen].

3. Necesito ir al [imagen] antes de mi clase de [imagen] porque hoy tenemos un [imagen] difícil.

4. Mi [imagen] de $5x^2+9y^2=21$ tiene cuarenta [imagen] en su clase.

5. Tengo una [imagen] pequeña (*small*): mis [imagen], una [imagen] y un [imagen].

Las respuestas de tu compañero/a:

1. Necesito comprar un **lápiz**, dos **plumas** y una **calculadora** para la clase de matemáticas.
2. En esa **librería** venden **escritorios** y **computadoras**.
3. Mis **abuelos** paternos viven en **México**; ellos tienen dos **gatos**, un **pájaro** y muchos **peces**.
4. En las mañanas, es difícil encontrar **estacionamiento** en la **universidad**.
5. En la **mochila** de mi novio hay muchos **libros** y **papeles**.

La correspondencia

El correo: Sofía te escribe. *(Sofía writes to you)*. Read the questions and Sofía's letter to you. Then answer the questions.

1. ¿Cuántas personas hay en la familia de Sofía? <u>Hay seis personas en la familia de Sofía.</u>
2. ¿Por qué la abuela de Sofía es más generosa con Lalo? <u>Es más generosa con Lalo por que él es su nieto favorito.</u>
3. ¿Qué profesión tienen los padres de Sofía? <u>Su padre es banquero y su madre es supervisora de créditos comerciales.</u>
4. ¿Cómo es Lalo? ¿Conoces *(do you know)* a una persona similar? ¿Quién *(who)*?
   <u>Answers will vary.</u>
5. ¿La relación de Sofía y Lalo es buena *(good)* o mala *(bad)*? <u>Answers will vary.</u>

Querido/a estudiante:

Tengo una familia pequeña: mis abuelos, mis padres, un hermano y un perro. Mi abuela es mexicana y mi abuelo es español. Viven seis meses en Guadalajara y seis meses en Estados Unidos con nosotros. Mi abuela es muy generosa, especialmente con Lalo porque es su nieto favorito.

Mis padres son jóvenes. Mi papá se llama Rubén. Tiene cuarenta y cuatro años. Es banquero; trabaja mucho y es muy estricto con nosotros. Mi mamá se llama Diana. Es una señora muy elegante e inteligente. Trabaja en un banco también, donde es supervisora de créditos comerciales.

Lalo, mi hermano, tiene quince años. Es estudiante. Es un poco irresponsable e inmaduro, pero es muy buen hermano. Le gustan los deportes y la música alternativa.

Con cariño,
tu amiga Sofía

En papel: Una carta para Sofía. Sofía wants to know what your family is like. Use her letter as a model to write a description of your own family. Answers will vary.

Modelo	Tengo una familia...: mi..., mi... y... Mi... se llama..., tiene... años. Es de... Le gusta... (actividades). Etc.

¡Fíjate!

Try to express yourself simply with the language you know. Although you may be tempted, avoid writing your letter in English and translating it into Spanish. At this point, your ability to write in English far exceeds your ability to communicate in Spanish... as time goes on, this will change!

¡A ver de nuevo! Review this episode's **Escena** to complete the summary that follows.

Adriana y Manolo están en la clase de (1)_____cálculo_____ con Sofía. Manolo es

(2)_____amigo_____ de Sofía. En este episodio, conocemos *(we meet)* a Ramón, el

(3)_____hermano_____ de Ana Mari. Él es de (4)_____Estados Unidos_____, pero su papá es

de (5)_____Honduras_____ y su (6)_____mamá_____ es de México. Adriana no es de

México; es de (7)_____Puerto Rico_____. Tiene (8)_____tres_____ hijos. Sus hijos

mayores hablan español, pero a su (9)_____hija_____ no le gusta hablarlo. En la

familia de Ramón (10)_____tienen_____ el mismo problema. (11)_____Sus_____

hermanos (12)_____sí_____ entienden español, pero no lo hablan.

Video
CD-ROM

Audio
CD-ROM

Instructor's Resources
• VHS Video
• Worktext CD
• IRM: Tapescript

¡A ver de nuevo! Play the video again and have students complete the summary. Explain to students that, after this episode, they will be writing the summaries themselves in short paragraphs.

Invitación a **Cuba**

Del álbum de
Manolo

Cuba es una isla grande; es un poco más grande que *(slightly larger than)* el estado de Pennsylvania. Hay aproximadamente 11.2 millones de habitantes. La mitad de los cubanos es de descendencia afro-española; el 11% es de descendencia africana; el 37% es blanco y un pequeño porcentaje es de origen chino.

Un restaurante famoso, La Bodeguita del Medio, está en una calle típica de la parte vieja de la ciudad de La Habana, Cuba. El escritor norteamericano Ernest Hemingway visitaba ese restaurante con frecuencia.

Práctica adicional

Cuaderno de tareas	Audio	Website
WB p. 106, N LM p. 108, A–B	CD-ROM Episodio 4	vistahigher learning.com

Vocabulario del Episodio 4

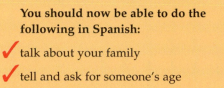

Objetivos comunicativos

You should now be able to do the following in Spanish:

✓ talk about your family

✓ tell and ask for someone's age

✓ say and ask where someone is from

✓ ask for and give phone numbers

La familia, los familiares y más

los abuelos	*grandparents*	el abuelo	la abuela
los amigos	*friends*	el amigo	la amiga
los chicos	*adolescents, teenagers*	el chico	la chica
los cuñados	*brother(s)-in-law and sister(s)-in-law*	el cuñado	la cuñada
los esposos	*husband and wife*	el esposo	la esposa
los familiares	*relatives*	el familiar	
los hermanos	*brother(s) and sister(s)*	el hermano	la hermana
los hijos	*children (one's own): son(s) and daughter(s)*	el hijo	la hija
los nietos	*grandchildren*	el nieto	la nieta
los niños	*children: boy(s) and girl(s)*	el niño	la niña
los novios	*boyfriend and girlfriend; bride and groom; fiancés*	el novio	la novia
los padres	*parents*	el padre	la madre
los primos	*cousins*	el primo	la prima
los sobrinos	*nephew(s) and niece(s)*	el sobrino	la sobrina
los suegros	*father-in-law and mother-in-law*	el suegro	la suegra
los tíos	*uncle(s) and aunt(s)*	el tío	la tía

Las mascotas *pets*

el gato	*cat*
el pájaro	*bird*
el perro	*dog*
el pez	*fish*

Posesivos

mi, mis	*my*
tu, tus	*your*
su, sus	*his; her; their*
nuestro/a(s)	*our*
la hija de Adriana	*Adriana's daughter*

Verbs

tener	*to have*
ser de	*to be from*
tener... años	*to be... years old*
¿Cuántos años tienes? Tengo... años.	*How old are you? I'm... years old.*
¿De dónde eres? Soy de...	*Where are you from? I'm from...*

Más números

41	**cuarenta y uno**	42, 43...	**cuarenta y dos, cuarenta y tres…**
50	**cincuenta**	53, 54...	**cincuenta y tres, cincuenta y cuatro…**
60	**sesenta**	64, 65...	**sesenta y cuatro, sesenta y cinco…**
70	**setenta**	75, 76...	**setenta y cinco, setenta y seis…**
80	**ochenta**	86, 87...	**ochenta y seis, ochenta y siete…**
90	**noventa**	97, 98...	**noventa y siete, noventa y ocho…**
100	**cien**		

Vocabulario personal

Write the words that you need to know to talk about yourself and your family in Spanish.

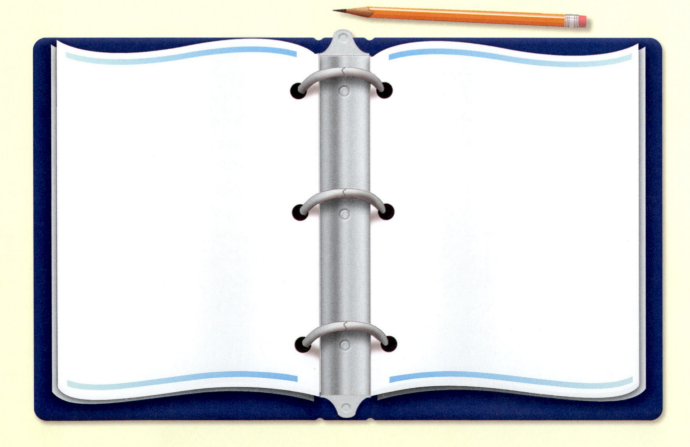

Nombre _____ Fecha _____

Cuaderno de tareas

Episodio 4

¡A escribir!

Escenas de la vida: ¡Qué internacionales!

A. ¡A ver cuánto entendiste! See how much of the **Escena** you understood by matching the Spanish sentences with their English equivalents.

___c___ 1. ¡Qué bueno que hablas español!

___a___ 2. Los dos mayores hablan español muy bien.

___d___ 3. A mi hija no le gusta hablar español.

___b___ 4. También tenemos ese problema.

___e___ 5. Mis hermanos menores lo entienden todo, pero no lo hablan.

a. The two older ones speak Spanish well.

b. We also have that problem.

c. That's great that you speak Spanish!

d. My daughter doesn't like to speak Spanish.

e. My younger brothers understand everything, but they do not speak it.

B. ¿Quién lo dijo? Write the initial of the person who made each statement: Adriana **(A)**, Ramón **(R)**, or Sofía **(S)**.

___S___ 1. Manolo es escritor; escribe poemas.

___R___ 2. Vamos a llegar tarde.

___A___ 3. Yo tengo tres hijos.

___R___ 4. Ya son las nueve menos cinco.

___S___ 5. Tomamos geología juntos.

C. ¡Qué internacionales! Complete the conversation, based on what you saw in the video.

Manolo   Ramón, ¿tú, de dónde (1)____eres____?

Ramón   Soy de (2) ___Estados Unidos___. Mi mamá (3) ____es de____ México y (4) ___mi papá___ es de Honduras. ¿Y tú?

Manolo   (5) ___Soy de___ Cuba. Tengo algunos parientes en Cuba, pero (6) ___mis papás___ viven en la Florida.

Ramón   Señora, ¿usted también es de Cuba?

Adriana   No. Soy de (7) ___Puerto Rico___.

Ramón   ¡Qué (8) ___internacionales___!

Video CD-ROM

101

Video
CD-ROM

D. ¿Quién habla español? Use the following words to complete the conversation.

entienden	hija	menos cinco
tener	hijos	mis hermanos menores
habla	mayores	tarde

Adriana　　Tengo tres (1) ___hijos___. Los dos (2) ___mayores___ hablan español, pero a mi (3) ___hija___ no le gusta hablarlo.

Ramón　　(4) ___Mis hermanos menores___ lo (5) ___entienden___ todo, pero no lo hablan.

Sofía　　Ana Mari (6) ___habla___ español perfectamente.

Ramón　　¡Ya son las nueve (7) ___menos cinco___! Vamos a llegar (8) ___tarde___ a clase.

Vocabulario 1

Identifying family members and friends
- The family
- Expressing possession

E. ¿De quién son las cosas? Tell Adriana to whom the following objects belong.

> **Modelo**　calculadoras/Manolo
> **Son las calculadoras de Manolo.**

1. mochila/Sofía ___Es la mochila de Sofía.___
2. lápices/Santiaguito ___Son los lápices de Santiaguito.___
3. reloj/Santiago ___Es el reloj de Santiago.___
4. cuadernos/Viviana ___Son los cuadernos de Viviana.___
5. diccionario/Manolo ___Es el diccionario de Manolo.___
6. plumas/Ana Mari ___Son las plumas de Ana Mari.___

F. La familia de Manolo.

Parte 1. Read Manolo's description of his family. Then answer the questions.

> Hola, soy Manolo Báez Rodríguez. Soy estudiante y me gusta mucho tocar la guitarra. Tengo una familia relativamente pequeña. Solamente somos mi hermana y yo. Mi hermana es dos años menor que yo. Se llama Nancy. Mis papás son cubanos y ahora viven en Miami. Mi papá es doctor y mi mamá es profesora. Mi papá se llama Manuel Báez y mi mamá es Isabel Rodríguez de Báez. Los padres de mi papá son Arturo y Carlota. Ellos todavía viven en La Habana. Tengo un tío y una tía. Son los hermanos de mi papá. Mi tío Francisco es soltero, tiene 50 años; mi tía Perla es viuda[1] y tiene tres hijos: dos hombres y una mujer. Mi prima tiene 25 años, como yo; por eso, somos muy buenos amigos. Ahora ella tiene novio, y creo que van a casarse[2] pronto. Mis dos primos son menores que[3] nosotros. Yo no tengo novia, pero hay una chica que me gusta.

[1]widowed　[2]get married　[3]younger than

1. ¿Cuántos hermanos tiene Manolo? Tiene una hermana. _____

2. ¿Dónde viven sus padres? ¿Como se llaman? Viven en Miami. Su papá se llama Manuel Báez y su
mamá se llama Isabel Rodríguez de Báez. _____

3. ¿Qué profesión tiene su papá? ¿Y su mamá? Su papá es doctor y su mamá es profesora. _____

4. ¿Cómo se llaman los abuelos de Manolo? ¿Dónde viven?
Se llaman Arturo y Carlota. Viven en La Habana. _____

5. ¿De quién (whose) son hermanos los tíos de Manolo? Son los hermanos de su papá. _____

6. ¿Cuántos años tiene Manolo? Tiene veinticinco años. _____

7. ¿Cuántos primos tiene? Tiene tres primos. _____

Parte 2. Use Manolo's letter as a model to write about your own family. Be as thorough as you can with the Spanish you have. Remember: keep it simple! Answers will vary.

_____

_____

_____

_____

_____

G. Crucigrama. You've been asked to create the clues for the crossword puzzle (**crucigrama**) in this week's school newspaper. Write a description or definition of the words in the puzzle. Answers will vary.

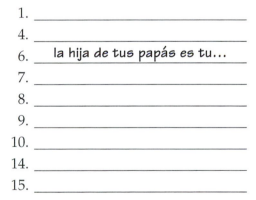

horizontales

1. _____

4. _____

6. la hija de tus papás es tu...

7. _____

8. _____

9. _____

10. _____

14. _____

15. _____

verticales

1. _____

2. _____

3. _____

5. _____

11. un animal como Pluto

12. _____

13. _____

H. El primo Emilio. Lalo and Sofía talk about their cousin Emilio. Complete their description with the appropriate forms of the possessive adjectives.

Él es (1) ____nuestro____ (nuestro/tu) primo. Se llama Emilio y tiene treinta años. (2) ____Su____ (su/mi) esposa está en España. (3) ____Sus____ (Su/Sus) padres viven *(live)* en Madrid. (4) ____Nuestros____ (nuestro/nuestros) tíos, los padres de Emilio, se llaman Laura y Emilio. Son muy buenos. Emilio es (5) ____mi____ (mis/mi) primo favorito. ¿Quién es (6) ____tu____ (tu/tus) primo favorito?

Emilio

I. Tu familia. You are showing a family picture to a friend. Answer their questions using the appropriate forms of the possessive adjectives.

Modelo	¿Ella es la hermana de tu mamá?
	Sí, es **su** hermana.

1. ¿Éste es tu hermano?

   No, es ____mi____ primo.
2. ¿Él es tu papá?

   Sí, es ____mi____ papá.
3. Ah, y ellos son los papás de tus primos.

   Sí, son *(their)* ____sus____ papás.
4. ¿Ellos son tus abuelos?

   Sí, son ____mis____ abuelos paternos.
5. ¿De quién son estos perritos?

   Son *(our)* ____nuestras____ mascotas.
6. ¿Los chicos son tus hermanos?

   No, él es ____mi____ amigo y ella es *(his)* ____su____ novia. ____Mis____ hermanos no están en la foto.

Gramática 1

Expressing age
- **The verb <u>tener</u>**
- **Numbers 41–100**

J. ¿Cuántos años tienen tus familiares? Complete the followig information with the ages of different people in your own family, or an imaginary family.
Answers will vary.

1. Mi papá _____ años.
2. Mi mamá _____ años.
3. Mi hermano/a menor _____ años.
4. Mi _____ tiene _____ años.
5. Yo _____ años.

K. ¿Qué tiene? Create true statements or questions using an element from each column.   Answers will vary.

Manolo		mucha tarea
Sofía		cinco clases este semestre
Las universidades		novio/a
Mis amigos y yo	(no) tener	veintitrés años
Mis compañeros		una clase de español
Tú		coche
Ana Mari		un hermano
Yo		biblioteca y gimnasio

1. _____ .
2. _____ .
3. _____ .
4. _____ .
5. _____ .
6. _____ .
7. _____ .
8. _____ .

L. ¡Cuánto dinero! (*So much money!*) As the bookkeeper at your university bookstore, you have to pay the distributor of foreign books and movies. Complete the checks according to the invoices. Remember to make note of the items you are paying for (under *Memo*).   Answers will vary.

Libro/Video	Cantidad	Total
Relato de un náufrago	23 libros	$98.35
Pedro Páramo	15 libros	$64.73
Fresa y chocolate	1 video	$51.69
¡Ay, Carmela!	1 video	$42.80

Tienda Universitaria   5322

Fecha _____

Páguese a la orden de ___*Distribuidora Internacional*___ $ _____

La cantidad de _____ dólares

Memo _____   _____

|00231334: 232443 ||2343243434

Tienda Universitaria   5323

Fecha _____

Páguese a la orden de ___*Distribuidora Internacional*___ $ _____

La cantidad de _____ dólares

Memo _____   _____

| 00231334: 232443 | | 2343243434

Tienda Universitaria   5324

Fecha _____

Páguese a la orden de ___*Distribuidora Internacional*___ $ _____

La cantidad de _____ dólares

Memo _____   _____

| 00231334: 232443 | | 2343243434

Tienda Universitaria   5325

Fecha _____

Páguese a la orden de ___*Distribuidora Internacional*___ $ _____

La cantidad de _____ dólares

Memo _____   _____

| 00231334: 232443 | | 2343243434

Gramática 2 ➤ Saying where someone is from
• **Ser de**

M. ¿De dónde son? Complete the sentences based on what you know about the characters.

1. Sofía ____es____ mexicana. ____Es de____ la Ciudad de México.
2. Ramón y Ana Mari ____son____ mexicoamericanos. ____Son de____ Estados Unidos.
3. El papá de Ramón ____es de____ Honduras. Su mamá es mexicana; es de ____México____.
4. Adriana y su familia ____son de____ Puerto Rico.
5. Manolo es cubano. Él ____es de____ Cuba.

Para terminar

N. Mi árbol genealógico. To preserve your heritage, you have decided to record the name, place of origin, and age of as many relatives as you can. Create your family tree. If you prefer not to do your own, you may want to interview a friend. Answers will vary.

Episodio

Comprensión

A. Los familiares. You will hear six statements about family. Listen and say whether each statement is true (**cierto**) or false (**falso**). If it is false, change the last word in the statement to make it true. Repeat the correct answer after the speaker.

Modelo	You hear:	**El esposo de mi tía es mi hermano.**
	You say:	**Falso. El esposo de mi tía es mi tío.**

B. Los nuevos estudiantes internacionales. You have a telephone message from the president of the Club Latino. She needs you to go to the airport to pick up four students who are arriving on various flights (**vuelos**). Listen to her message and fill in the form with the necessary information. You will hear the message twice.

Nombre	Hora	Aerolínea	Vuelo	De
Rosa Orozco	1:15	Mexicana	2642	México
Diego Méndez	2:05	Delta	1590	Argentina
Fernando Robles	2:30	Viasa	3117	Venezuela
Graciela Ruiz	3:00	Iberia	4273	España

C. La nueva compañera de cuarto. Listen as Mónica describes her new roommate. Then select the best completion for each sentence. You will hear the description twice.

1. Mónica y su compañera de cuarto viven en...
   a. un apartamento.   b. una casa.   (c.) una residencia estudiantil.

2. La compañera se llama...
   a. Mariquita.   (b.) Silvia.   c. Miguela.

3. La compañera es de...
   a. Costa Rica.   (b.) Perú.   c. México.

4. Aquí en la universidad, ella...
   a. no tiene familia.   b. tiene una prima.   (c.) tiene un hermano.

5. La nueva compañera no tiene...
   (a.) novio.   b. dinero.   c. amigos.

Pronunciación

La *n* y la *ñ*. The **n (ene)** is pronounced much like the English pronunciation of the same letter. Repeat these words and sentences after the speaker.

nuevo	moreno	**Nicaragua**	**Gana el número nueve.**
nieto	interesante	**Norteamérica**	**Buenas noches, Nena.**
nombre	grande	**Noruega**	**Nicolás no necesita nada.**

The **ñ (eñe)** is pronounced as English *ny*, as in the words *canyon* and *onion*.

año	señora	compañero	**Son niños de nueve años.**
mañana	señor	cuñado	**Es una señorita española.**

Más escenas de la vida

Ramón and Wayne run into Manolo in the cafeteria. Listen to their conversation, and then complete activities **A** and **B**. You will hear the conversation twice.

A. ¿Entendiste? Rearrange the following statements in the order they occur in the conversation.

___5___ a. No. ¡Yo estoy muy contento!

___1___ b. Hola, Manolo. Te presento a Wayne.

___4___ c. ¿No quieres vivir allá con tu familia?

___3___ d. Igualmente.

___2___ e. Mucho gusto.

B. ¿Cierto o falso? Indicate whether the following statements are **cierto** or **falso**, according to the conversation.

	Cierto	Falso
1. Wayne no tiene familia aquí.	✓	
2. Su familia es de Wisconsin.	✓	
3. Sus padres son de Manhattan.		✓
4. Wayne quiere vivir con su familia.		✓
5. Wayne tiene veinticuatro años.		✓
6. Manolo necesita su independencia.		✓
7. Manolo no habla muy bien español.		✓
8. Wayne vivió en Chile.	✓	

Episodio 5

Escenas de la vida: ¿Estudiamos el sábado?

Video
CD-ROM

Audio
CD-ROM

A. ¡Mira cuánto puedes entender! Listen to the conversation or watch the **Escena** to complete the tasks below.

Instructor's Resources

• Overheads
• VHS Video
• Worktext CD
• Website
• IRM: Videoscript, Comprehensible input

1. ¿Qué días están libres *(are free)* Manolo y Adriana para estudiar?

	lunes	martes	miércoles	jueves	viernes	sábado	domingo
Manolo		✓		✓		✓	✓
Adriana						✓	

2. Adriana dice que nunca descansa; ¿por qué? ¿Qué hace Adriana los martes y jueves?

Compra la comida.

Trabaja en una oficina.

Llega tarde a casa.

3. ¿Qué hace la hija de Adriana los lunes?

Baila en un grupo.

Lava su ropa.

Limpia su cuarto.

Video Synopsis. Sofía, Manolo, and Adriana make plans to study for their calculus exam. Adriana is concerned that she may be too old to learn. As they discuss a time to meet, Sofía and Manolo find out how busy Adriana is and decide not to complain about their own schedules.

...

...

4. ¿Qué hacen su hijo y sus amigos?

Miran la tele.

Visitan a los abuelos.

Tocan la guitarra.

Video
CD-ROM

B. ¿Te diste cuenta? Escucha la conversación o mira la **Escena** otra vez para indicar a quién se refieren los siguientes comentarios: Manolo **(M)**, Adriana **(A)**, Sofía **(S)** o todos **(T)** *(everybody)*.

Audio
CD-ROM

_M_ 1. No es pesimista.
_A_ 2. Está libre los sábados por la tarde.
_T_ 3. Necesitan estudiar para el examen.
_A_ 4. Nunca tiene tiempo para descansar.
_A_ 5. Está muy preocupada.

Cultura a lo vivo
In Spanish-speaking countries, most young adults do not move out to become "independent." It is common for them to stay home until they get married, or relocate to another city to work or pursue their studies.

Video
CD-ROM

C. Responde. Contesta las siguientes preguntas.

Audio
CD-ROM

1. ¿Qué día toca la guitarra el hijo de Adriana?
Los miércoles.

2. ¿A qué hora trabaja Adriana?
De dos a siete.

3. ¿Dónde tocan la guitarra el hijo de Adriana y sus amigos?
En casa de Adriana.

4. ¿Por qué Adriana nunca descansa?
No tiene tiempo.

5. ¿Dónde y cuándo van a estudiar?
En casa de Adriana, el sábado a las dos.

Práctica adicional

Cuaderno de tareas
WB pp.123–124, A–C

Video
CD-ROM
Episodio 5

B and C. Have students read activities B and C, then play the video again.
Have students respond orally to the prompts.

Para comunicarnos mejor

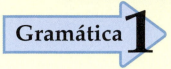

Gramática 1

Talking about activities at school and at home
- **-ar verbs**
- **Days of the week**
- **Infinitive constructions**

In their conversation, you heard the following statements:

Trabajo en una oficina.	*I work in an office.*
Mi hija **baila** en un grupo folclórico.	*My daughter dances in a folk group.*
Mi hijo **toca** la guitarra.	*My son plays the guitar.*
Estudiamos el sábado a las dos, ¿de acuerdo?	*We'll study on Saturday at two, okay?*

To talk about the activities of her friends and family, Adriana uses different verb endings, which change depending on whom she is describing. In Spanish, verb forms consist of two parts: the stem **(la raíz)**, and the ending **(la terminación)**. For example, the verb form **trabajo** *(I work)* is made up of the stem **trabaj-** and the ending **-o**. Different endings are attached to the stem to indicate who does the action *(I, you, he, she, it, we, they)*, when the action occurs *(today, yesterday, tomorrow)*, and how the action is carried out *(right now, only once, all the time)*. Attaching different endings to verb stems is called *conjugating the verb* **(conjugar el verbo)**. Study the following conjugation and use it to conjugate regular **-ar** verbs.

El presente de los verbos del grupo -ar		
yo	**Trabajo** en una oficina.	*I work in an office.*
tú	**Trabajas** mucho.	*You work a lot.* (informal)
usted	**Trabaja** por la mañana.	*You work in the morning.* (formal)
él/ella	**Trabaja** en un hospital.	*He/She works in a hospital.*
nosotros/as	**Trabajamos** juntos/as.	*We work together.*
ustedes	**Trabajan** de noche, ¿no?	*You work at night, right?* (plural)
vosotros/as	**Trabajáis** de noche, ¿no?	
ellos/as	**Trabajan** en un banco.	*They work in a bank.*

1. When the ending of the verb is **-ar** (as in **trabajar**), **-er**, or **-ir**, the verb has not been conjugated; that is, we do not know who is doing the action. This verb form is called the *infinitive* **(el infinitivo)**. In English, the infinitive is indicated by the word *to*, as in *to work*.

2. As a form of the present tense, **trabajo** may mean *I work* or *I am working*.

Trabajo en una oficina en Nueva York.	*I work in an office in New York.*
Trabajo en una oficina este semestre.	*I'm working in an office this semester.*

3. Every Spanish verb belongs to one of three groups, according to its infinitive ending.

- Verbs that end in **-ar** **trabajar** *to work*
- Verbs that end in **-er** **comer** *to eat*
- Verbs that end in **-ir** **vivir** *to live*

4. Remember that the **vosotros** form is used only in Spain.

5. The following verbs use the same endings as **trabajar**.

Gramática 1. Model the pronunciation of the words and phrases and have students repeat them after you. Ask personalized questions emphasizing the verbs that were not used in the Escena. You may sequence questions as follows: yes/no (¿Bailas bien? ¿Sacas buenas notas? ¿Usas la computadora con frecuencia?), either/or (¿Qué te gusta más: escuchar música o mirar la tele?), and short answers (¿Qué días estudias? ¿A qué hora llegas a casa los viernes? ¿Dónde trabajas? ¿Cuántas clases tomas este semestre?).

Instructor's Resource
• Overheads

Actividades frecuentes	
En la escuela	
buscar información en Internet	*to look for information on the Internet*
estudiar mucho/poco	*to study a lot/a little*
llegar a tiempo	*to arrive (get somewhere) on time*
necesitar libros	*to need books*
sacar buenas notas	*to get good grades*
tomar clases	*to take classes*
café	*to drink coffee*
usar la computadora	*to use the computer*
Los fines de semana	
bailar (bien)	*to dance (well)*
comprar cosas	*to buy things*
comida	*food*
ropa	*clothes*
descansar	*to rest*
llegar tarde/temprano/a tiempo a casa	*to get home late/early/on time*
trabajar en una tienda	*to work at a store*
visitar a los abuelos	*to visit one's grandparents*
En la casa	
escuchar música	*to listen to music*
hablar por teléfono	*to talk on the phone*
lavar el coche	*to wash the car*
la ropa	*to do the laundry*
limpiar la casa	*to clean the house*
el cuarto	*the (one's) room*
mirar la tele	*to watch TV*
tocar la guitarra	*to play the guitar*

También se dice...

el coche → el carro, el auto

mirar la tele → ver la tele

las notas → las calificaciones

Learning Strategy: Create flash cards
On one side, write the word in Spanish; on the other, write its English equivalent. If possible, draw a picture of the item and write a sentence where you use the word in a meaningful way. Study the words in both directions: from English to Spanish, and vice versa.

PRÁCTICA

A. ¿Qué hacen? Empareja las ilustraciones de la página siguiente con las oraciones apropiadas.

<u>c</u> 1. Trabajo en una oficina.

<u>d</u> 2. Los chicos siempre buscan información en Internet.

<u>b</u> 3. Sofía escucha música alternativa.

<u>f</u> 4. A veces tomamos el autobús a la escuela.

<u>a</u> 5. Me gusta mucho comprar ropa.

<u>e</u> 6. Los chicos sacan buenas notas.

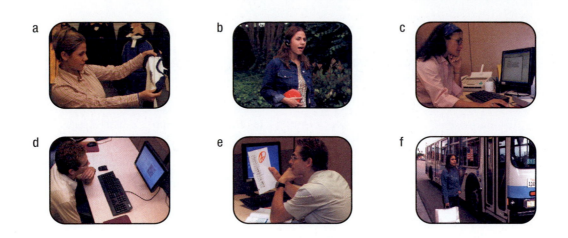

B. ¿Cuáles son tus actividades? Indica si las frases son **ciertas** o **falsas** para ti. Answers will vary.

B. Give students time to respond to the questions, or assign it for homework. When completed, check answers by asking students the questions: **Peter, tus amigos y tú necesitan dinero, ¿verdad?** or **Sue, ¿tu mamá usa la computadora en casa?** Encourage students to respond to you in complete sentences: **Sí, mis amigos y yo necesitamos dinero.**

	Cierto	Falso
1. Mis amigos y yo necesitamos dinero.	☐	☐
2. Nunca lavo mi coche.	☐	☐
3. Mi mamá usa la computadora en casa.	☐	☐
4. Mi papá descansa por la noche.	☐	☐
5. Siempre llego a tiempo a la clase de español.	☐	☐
6. No trabajo este semestre.	☐	☐
7. Mis compañeros de clase estudian mucho.	☐	☐
8. Mi novio/a busca mucha información en Internet.	☐	☐

C. Las actividades de la familia de Adriana.

Parte 1. Adriana habla de sus actividades y de las actividades de su familia los sábados. Usa estos verbos para completar sus comentarios.

llegar	escuchar	trabajar	hablar	estudiar
lavar	mirar	descansar	necesitar	tomar

Los sábados por la mañana, mi esposo (1) ____lava____ su coche. Yo (2) ____necesito____ preparar la comida para toda la semana. Mis hijos (3) ____llegan____ de la escuela a las tres de la tarde. Por la tarde, mi hija (4) ____toma____ lecciones de baile. Mi hijo (5) ____habla____ con sus amigos por teléfono. Yo (6) ____estudio____ para mis clases por lo menos *(at least)* dos horas todos los días. Por la noche, nosotros no (7) ____miramos____ la televisión; hablamos y (8) ____escuchamos____ música.

Parte 2. Usa las oraciones como modelo para escribir sobre tu familia. Haz los cambios necesarios.
Answers will vary.

Modelo	Los sábados por la mañana mi **papá** lava su coche.

• Days of the week

Los días de la semana y más			
los lunes	on Mondays	entre semana	on weekdays
los martes	on Tuesdays	los fines de semana	on weekends
los miércoles	on Wednesdays	por la mañana	in the morning
los jueves	on Thursdays	por la tarde	in the afternoon
los viernes	on Fridays	por la noche	in the evening
los sábados	on Saturdays	todos los días	every day
los domingos	on Sundays		

Note: In Spanish, the days of the week are not capitalized. **Los lunes** means on *Mondays*, but **el lunes** means *on Monday*.

PRÁCTICA

D. Mis actividades. Escribe en tu cuaderno una de tus actividades para cada día de la semana. Answers will vary.

Modelo   **Los lunes lavo la ropa. Los martes trabajo cinco horas. Los miércoles…**

E. Lotería. Find out who does the following things. Write the name of a different classmate who responds **sí** to your question in each box. Ask appropriate questions, according to the model. The first student to form three straight lines wins the game.   Answers will vary.

Modelo   _____ visita a sus abuelos los domingos
—José, ¿visitas a tus abuelos los domingos?
—Sí, visito a mis abuelos los domingos.
(Write "José" on the corresponding line)

E. Give students at least seven minutes to interact with their classmates. You may want to participate in the activity, as your participation provides students with an opportunity to use the **usted** form of the verbs they are learning. Remind them to use the **tú** form of the verbs when speaking with their classmates.

_____ lava la ropa los viernes.	_____ saca buenas notas en la clase de español.	_____ no trabaja.	_____ necesita comprar una computadora.
_____ escucha música alternativa.	_____ habla otro idioma *(another language)* con sus padres.	_____ toma cuatro clases este semestre.	_____ siempre llega tarde a clase.
_____ toca bien el piano.	_____ no es de aquí.	_____ no estudia en la biblioteca.	_____ visita a sus abuelos los domingos.
_____ le gusta bailar los fines de semana.	_____ descansa los lunes por la tarde.	_____ busca información para las clases en Internet.	_____ no tiene hermanos.

Instructor's Resource
• IRM: Additional Activities

Additional Activity. Have students play a concentration game (see directions and sample in the IRM). Allow ten to twelve minutes. The student with most pairs wins. Insist that they read the descriptions aloud, and, if it is an image, that they indicate the verb. Monitor students to make sure they speak only Spanish. Remind students to use **Español al instante**, on the inside back cover of their worktext, in order to carry out all the interactions in Spanish.

• Infinitive constructions

In the conversation, Adriana said:

Necesito repasar todo.   *I need to review everything.*
Necesito estar presente, porque si no...   *I need to be there, otherwise...*

1. In both English and Spanish, some verbs may be used in combination with other verbs in the infinitive. Notice that Adriana uses a combination of two verbs: the main verb, which is conjugated, and a second verb, which is in the infinitive form (the **-r** form). These combined verbs are called *infinitive constructions*, as in the following examples.

No **me gusta llegar** tarde a clase.   *I don't like to be late for class.*
Necesitamos buscar información en Internet.   *We need to look for information on the Internet.*
No **quiero sacar** F.   *I don't want to get an F.*

PRÁCTICA

F. Las actividades de Sofía. Sofía nos habla de sus actividades y las de *(those of)* su familia. Completa las frases.

1. Los sábados me gusta _____descansar_____; por eso *(because of that)*, no trabajo por las tardes.
2. Los domingos necesito _____lavar_____ la ropa y _____estudiar_____ para mis clases.
3. Mi hermano nunca _____estudia_____; por eso, no _____saca_____ buenas notas.
4. Mis papás _____necesitan_____ trabajar mucho para vivir *(to live)* bien.
5. Hoy no quiero lavar ropa porque necesito_____estudiar_____ para el examen.

G. Los fines de semana. Escribe cuatro cosas que **necesitas, te gusta** o **no te gusta** hacer *(to do)* durante los fines de semana. Comparte tus comentarios con un(a) compañero/a.
Answers will vary.

> **Modelo**   Los viernes por la noche no me gusta estudiar.

1. _____
2. _____
3. _____
4. _____

¡Fíjate!

Remember to use **los viernes** for *on Fridays* and **el viernes** for *on Friday.*

H. Personas importantes. Describe las actividades de cuatro personas importantes en tu vida. Comparte tus respuestas con un(a) compañero/a.
Answers will vary.

> **Modelo**   Mi novio no baila bien.

H. This activity may be assigned as homework or done in class. Ask each student to write one sentence on the board.

1. _____
2. _____
3. _____
4. _____

Práctica adicional

Cuaderno de tareas
WB pp.124–125, D–F

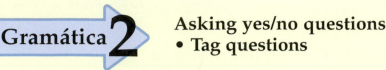

Gramática 2

Asking yes/no questions
• Tag questions

Adding **¿no?** at the end of a statement is one of two ways of asking a yes/no question in Spanish. When asking a question that requires a yes/no answer, use the following two patterns.

1. **Tag questions.** Add **¿no?** or **¿verdad?** *(right?)* at the end.

Sus hijos podrían hacernos un show, **¿no?**	*Your kids could put on a show for us, right?*
Tus padres trabajan en un banco, **¿verdad?**	*Your parents work at a bank, right?*

2. **Intonation.** Raise your voice in a questioning tone at the end.

Me gusta bailar *La macarena.*	*I like dancing La Macarena.*
¿Te gusta bailar *La macarena?*	*Do you like dancing La Macarena?*
Este semestre no trabajo.	*I don't work this semester.*
¿Este semestre no trabajas?	*You don't work this semester?*

PRÁCTICA

I. Una entrevista. Convierte las frases de la **Práctica B** (página 113) a preguntas. Después entrevista a un(a) compañero/a. Answers will vary.

> **Modelo**   Mis amigos y yo necesitamos dinero.
> —**¿Tus amigos y tú necesitan dinero?**
> or
> **Tus amigos y tú necesitan dinero, ¿no?/¿verdad?**

J. ¡A hablar! In groups of four, try to set a date and time to study Spanish together **(juntos)**. Indicate which days and times you can't meet, and why **(no puedo porque...)**. Use expressions like **Estoy libre los..., Ese día no puedo..., ¿Estudiamos el...?, ¿Quién puede a las...?,** etc.
Answers will vary.

Actividades comunicativas

A. Las actividades de mis compañeros.

Parte 1. First, answer the questions by writing **yo** in column **B** after any question to which you can respond *yes.* Then, ask these questions to your classmates and fill in the empty spaces in both columns with the names of those who answer *yes.*

	A	B
1. ¿Limpias la casa los sábados?	_____	_____
2. ¿Usas una computadora Macintosh?	_____	_____
3. ¿Trabajas en un restaurante?	_____	_____
4. ¿Miras mucho la tele?	_____	_____
5. ¿Necesitas dinero?	_____	_____
6. ¿Hablas mucho por teléfono?	_____	_____

Instructor's Resource
• IRM: Additional Activities

Additional Activity. See the Instructor's Resource Manual for materials for **Las actividades de los chicos**, to practice -ar verbs and tag questions.

Práctica adicional	
Cuaderno de tareas WB pp.126–127, G–H LM pp.129–130, A–B, Pron.	Audio CD-ROM Episodio 5

A. Give students at least seven minutes to interact. You may want to participate in the activity, so as to provide students with an opportunity to use the **usted** form of the verbs. For **Parte 1,** students must attempt to fill both columns, yeilding the conjugations in all forms except the **tú** form. For **Parte 2,** have students report their findings to the class, or write their reports for homework.

Parte 2. Now, write a brief report using the information you have uncovered. Include at least six sentences in your report. Be prepared to share your findings with the class.

Modelo	Akiko y Jenny usan una computadora Macintosh.
	Nadie (*nobody*) trabaja en un restaurante.

B. Submarino. The object of this game, played like Battleship, is to find the location of your classmate's submarines. First, draw submarines in any five of the boxes on your grid. Do not let your partner see your grid. Then take turns asking each other yes/no questions, matching an action pictured at the top of the grid with one of the subjects on the side. If you have a submarine in the box that corresponds to your partner's question, give an affirmative answer, and vice-versa; if there is no submarine in the box that corresponds to the question, give a negative answer.

B. Model the process using the grid on this page. Have students form pairs. If there is an odd number of individuals, form one group of three. Allow enough time for three pairs to win.

Modelo	—¿Trabajas en una oficina?
	—Sí, trabajo en una oficina. (*If there is a submarine in that box.*)
	or
	—No, no trabajo en una oficina. (*If there is no submarine in that box.*)

Depending on your classmate's answer, write **sí** or **no** in that box. If you answer **sí** to your classmate's question, put an **X** through your submarine. It's been found! The first player to find all five submarines wins.

Tú				
Tus primos				
Adriana				
Ustedes				

C. La fotonovela.

Audio
CD-ROM

Parte 1. As you listen to Sofía's weekend routine, indicate which pictures were used to tell her story.

Pictures: I, B, K, J, and L.

Instructor's Resources
• Worktext CD
• IRM: Tapescript

Script. *As you listen to Sofía's weekend routine, indicate which pictures were used to tell the story.*

Los sábados por la mañana Sofía toma una clase. Después de su clase toma el autobús al centro comercial. Ahí, busca ropa en oferta y luego come algo ligero. Generalmente llega temprano a su casa, y por la noche mira la televisión con sus papás.

C. Parte 2: Allow enough time for students to write their story in groups. When they have finished their stories, have one member of each group read it, while the rest of the class listens and writes the letters of the illustrations that correspond to the events in the story.

Parte 2. In groups, use five of the drawings to write a short paragraph describing what Sofía does on weekends. Your pictures do not have to reflect what you heard on the recording. Use connectors like **primero,** *(first),* **luego...** *(then),* **después...** *(later, afterward),* **por la tarde...,** **por la noche....** Begin with **Por la mañana, Sofía....** When you have finished, be prepared to read your story to the class. Your classmates will guess which pictures you used. Answers will vary.

La correspondencia

El correo: Los problemas de Manolo. Lee las siguientes preguntas. Después lee la carta que Manolo le escribe a un amigo. Contesta las preguntas.

1. ¿Cuál es el peor *(what is the worst)* defecto del compañero de cuarto de Manolo?

   Es muy desordenado./Casi nunca lava su ropa./No limpia su cuarto./Escucha música horrible.

2. ¿Qué cualidades tiene su compañero?

   Es muy generoso, compra todo para la casa y cocina muy rico.

3. ¿Qué cosas tienen en común?

   Los dos son cubanos y tienen conversaciones muy interesantes.

4. ¿Cuál es la rutina de Manolo?

   Estudia por las mañanas y luego trabaja varias horas. Por la noche, lava su ropa, y los fines de semana estudia y limpia la casa.

From: mbaez@casa.mía.red
To: Amigo@dayton.fla.red
Re: ¡Hola!

En cuanto a mi nuevo compañero de cuarto, tenemos algunos problemas. Es muy desordenado. Casi nunca lava la ropa y no limpia su cuarto; siempre está sucio[1]. Le gustan mucho las fiestas; con frecuencia invita a sus amigos y bailan y cantan toda la noche... ¡La música es horrible! Bueno, no todo es malo; él es muy generoso, compra todo para la casa y cocina muy rico. También tenemos varias cosas en común: los dos somos cubanos y tenemos conversaciones muy interesantes porque él es súper inteligente. A veces pasamos toda la noche conversando.

Yo sigo con la misma rutina; estudio por las mañanas y luego trabajo varias horas. Por la noche, lavo mi ropa, y los fines de semana estudio y limpio la casa. Nada nuevo.

[1]*dirty*

Invitación a **Estados Unidos**

Del álbum de
Manolo

De los 35 millones de hispanos en Estados Unidos, casi 2 millones son cubanos. La mayor concentración de cubanos está en Miami y el condado de Dade, en la Florida, pero hay comunidades cubanas en todos los estados. La Pequeña Habana, en Miami, es el centro cultural de los cubanoamericanos. Muchas personalidades de la música y el cine son de origen cubano, como Gloria y Emilio Estefan, Andy García, Celia Cruz, Daisy Fuentes, Jon Secada y Cameron Díaz, entre otros.

Práctica adicional

Website
vistahigher
learning.com

En papel: Mi vida diaria. *(My daily life)* In his e-mail, Manolo described his living situation. Use his letter as a model to write about your own situation. Write about your weekly activities and the activities of the people you live with. Answers will vary.

Video
CD-ROM

¡A ver de nuevo!

¡Fíjate!
Express yourself simply with the Spanish you know. Do not write your summary in English.

Audio
CD-ROM

Parte 1. Escucha la conversación de **Escenas de la vida** o mira el video para escribir un resumen del episodio. Answers will vary.

Instructor's Resources
• VHS Video
• Worktext CD
• IRM: Videoscript

Adriana está preocupada porque tiene un examen de cálculo y quiere sacar A...

Parte 2. Now, compare your summary with a classmate's and add any information you might have left out.

Práctica adicional

| Cuaderno de tareas WB pp.127–128, I–J LM p.130, A–B | Audio CD-ROM Episodio 5 | Website vistahigher learning.com |

Vocabulario del Episodio 5

Verbos

bailar (bien)	*to dance (well)*
buscar información en Internet	*to look for information on the Internet*
comprar cosas	*to buy things*
comida	*food*
ropa	*clothes*
descansar	*to rest*
escuchar música	*to listen to music*
estudiar mucho/poco	*to study a lot/a little*
hablar por teléfono	*to talk on the phone*
lavar el coche	*to wash the car*
la ropa	*to do the laundry*
limpiar la casa	*to clean the house*
el cuarto	*the (one's) room*
llegar a tiempo a casa	*to get home on time*
tarde	*late*
temprano	*early*
mirar la tele	*to watch TV*
necesitar libros	*to need books*
sacar buenas notas	*to get good grades*
tocar la guitarra	*to play the guitar*
tomar clases	*to take classes*
café	*to drink coffee*
el autobús	*to take the bus*
trabajar en casa	*to work at home*
usar la computadora	*to use the computer*
visitar a los abuelos	*to visit one's grandparents*

Los días de la semana y más

los lunes	*on Mondays*	todos los días	*every day*
los martes	*on Tuesdays*	entre semana	*on weekdays*
los miércoles	*on Wednesdays*	los fines de semana	*on weekends*
los jueves	*on Thursdays*	por la mañana	*in the morning*
los viernes	*on Fridays*	por la tarde	*in the afternoon*
los sábados	*on Saturdays*	por la noche	*in the evening*
los domingos	*on Sundays*		

Vocabulario personal

In this section write all the words that you want to know in Spanish so that you can better talk about your activities and the activities of those you know.

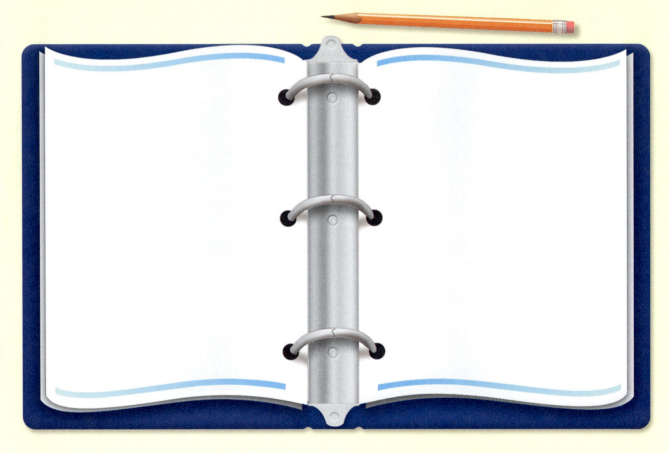

¡A escribir!

Episodio 5

Escenas de la vida: ¿Estudiamos el sábado?

A. ¡A ver cuánto entendiste! See how much of the **Escena** you understood by matching the Spanish sentences with their English equivalents.

¿Dónde estudiamos?

__d__	1. ¿Está libre algún otro día?	a. Let's study on Saturday.
__g__	2. ¿A qué hora descansa?	b. What do you do on Saturdays and
__a__	3. Estudiamos el sábado.	Sundays?
__f__	4. ¿En casa de quién?	c. Your kids could sing and dance for us.
__e__	5. ¿Cuándo estudiamos?	d. Are you free any other day?
__b__	6. ¿Qué hace los sábados y domingos?	e. When are we going to study?
__h__	7. Estoy muy preocupada.	f. At whose house?
__c__	8. Sus hijos podrían cantar y bailar	g. When do you rest?
	para nosotros.	h. I'm very worried.

B. ¿Estudiamos el sábado? Use the expressions to complete the activities below, according to the **Escena**.

descansar	preocupada	por la mañana
estoy libre	los lunes	necesito
qué	los martes y los jueves	estudiamos
vieja	cuándo	por la tarde

Adriana ¿(1) _____Cuándo_____ estudiamos para el examen?

(2) _____Necesito_____ repasar *(to review)* todo. Estoy muy

(3) _____preocupada_____.

Sofía ¡No se preocupe! No es tan complicado.

Adriana Ay, chica, pero yo ya soy (4) _____vieja_____. Bueno,

(5) _____estoy libre_____ solamente los sábados (6) _____por la tarde_____.

Sofía ¿(7) _____Qué_____ hace los otros días?

Adriana (8) _____Los martes y los jueves_____ trabajo en una oficina y los otros días estoy muy

ocupada con las actividades de mis hijos. Bueno, ¿a qué hora

(9) _____estudiamos_____ el sábado?

C. La vida de Adriana. Use what you know about Adriana to answer Sofia's question.

¿Qué hace Adriana los otros días? (de lunes a viernes)

Answers will vary. Possible answer: Los martes y los jueves trabaja en una oficina de dos a siete. Los lunes su hija baila en un grupo

folclórico puertorriqueño. Los miércoles su hijo toca guitarra con sus amigos en casa.

_____

_____

Gramática 1

Talking about activities at school and home
- **-ar verbs**
- **Days of the week**
- **Infinitive constructions**

D. ¿Qué hacen? Say what these people do at the places mentioned. Fill in the blanks with the appropriate forms of the verbs.

1. En la universidad

tomar	hablar	llegar	sacar	estudiar

Los lunes yo (1) _____llego_____ a la universidad a las 8:00 de la mañana.
(2) _____Tomo_____ una clase de español. Normalmente (3) _____saco_____ buenas
notas cuando (4) _____estudio_____ el vocabulario. Después de clase, me gusta
(5) _____hablar_____ con mis amigos. A veces, tomamos café y nos quedamos (stay)
hablando en la cafetería.

2. En un café

escuchar	bailar	tocar	cantar (to sing)

Los viernes mi amigo y yo (6) _____tocamos_____ la guitarra y la flauta en un grupo de
jazz. También (7) _____cantamos_____ karaoke cuando sabemos (we know) la letra de las
canciones. A veces (8) _____bailamos_____ y otras veces solamente (only) nos gusta
(9) _____escuchar_____ la música.

3. En mi casa

visitar	usar	lavar	mirar	necesitar	limpiar	trabajar

Los domingos mis hermanitos (10) _____lavan_____ mi coche cuando ellos
(11) _____necesitan_____ dinero. Mi papá (12) _____limpia_____ el garaje, mientras (while)
mi mamá (13) _____trabaja_____ en su jardín (garden). Yo normalmente necesito
(14) _____usar_____ la computadora por la mañana. Por la tarde, mis papás y mis
hermanos (15) _____visitan_____ a mis abuelos y yo visito a mis amigos. Por la noche,
todos (16) _____miramos_____ una película.

E. Las actividades de los estudiantes. Describe what the characters are doing in the illustrations. Use the verbs from **Episodio 5** page 112 of your textbook. Use **porque** to justify the first part of your sentence. Keep the statements simple (e.g., *They study a lot **because** they have an exam*). Answers will vary.

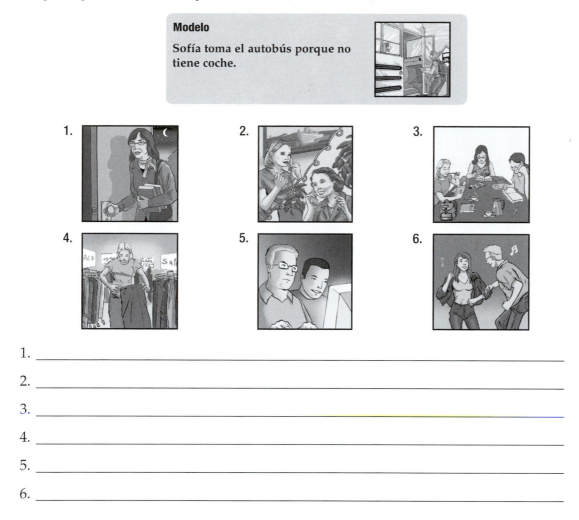

Modelo

Sofía toma el autobús porque no tiene coche.

1. _____

2. _____

3. _____

4. _____

5. _____

6. _____

F. Los días de la semana. Complete the following statements with the appropriate word.

1. En español, el primer día de la semana es el ____el lunes____.

2. Si hoy es miércoles, mañana es ____jueves____.

3. Hay siete días en una ____semana____.

4. Mi día favorito es el ____Answers will vary.____.

5. El Día de la Madre es el segundo (*second*) ____domingo____ de mayo.

6. Un día de mala suerte (*bad luck*) en Estados Unidos es el ____viernes____ trece.

7. El día preferido para hacer (*throw*) fiestas es el ____viernes/sábado____.

Gramática 2

Asking yes/no questions
• **Tag questions**

G. ¡Preguntas! Imagine you and a classmate are talking about the characters in the video. Use the elements below to form questions. Then answer each question.

> **Modelo**   la hija de Adriana / tocar la guitarra / ¿no? (bailar)
> —La hija de Adriana toca la guitarra, ¿no?
> —No, ella baila en un grupo folclórico puertorriqueño.

1. tú / estudiar italiano / ¿no? (español)

   Q. Tú estudias italiano, ¿no?   A. No, yo estudio español.

2. Adriana / trabajar en un restaurante (oficina)

   Q. ¿Adriana trabaja en un restaurante?   A. No, ella trabaja en una oficina.

3. los hermanos de Ramón / hablar español / ¿verdad? (inglés)

   Q. Los hermanos de Ramón hablan español, ¿verdad?   A. No, ellos hablan inglés.

4. Manolo / ser de Puerto Rico / ¿no? (Cuba)

   Q. Manolo es de Puerto Rico, ¿no?   A. No, él es de Cuba.

5. Sofía y Ana Mari / tener hermanas / ¿verdad? (no)

   Q. Sofía y Ana Mari tienen hermanas, ¿verdad?   A. No, ellas no tienen hermanas.

6. Ana Mari / tomar la clase de cálculo con Sofía y Manolo (Adriana)

   Q. ¿Ana Mari toma la clase de cálculo con Sofía y Manolo?   A. No, Adriana toma la clase de cálculo con Sofía y Manolo.

H. Sofía y Adriana. You want to know more about Sofía and Adriana. Ask them questions using the cues. In each case, write an answer according to the drawing.

> **Modelo**
>
> if they study geology
> —¿Ustedes estudian geología?
> —No, estudiamos cálculo.

1. if they speak English

   ¿Ustedes hablan inglés?

   No, nosotras hablamos español.

2. if she uses the computer Friday nights

   Sofía, ¿tú usas la computadora los viernes por la noche?

   No, yo miro la televisión con mis papás.

3. if she always gets home late

Adriana, ¿usted siempre llega tarde a casa? _____

Sí, siempre llego tarde a casa. _____

4. if her mother does the laundry

Sofía, ¿tu mamá lava la ropa? _____

No, yo lavo la ropa. _____

Para terminar

I. Preguntas personales. Answer the following questions. Answers will vary.

1. ¿Qué clases tomas? ¿Estudias todos los días?

_____

_____

2. ¿Te gusta bailar? ¿Dónde?

_____

_____

3. ¿Qué te gusta hacer *(do)* los domingos?

_____

_____

4. ¿Cuántos años tienes? ¿Cuántos años tienen tus padres? ¿Cuántos años tiene tu novio/a /esposo/a? _____

_____

5. ¿Qué programas miras en la tele?

_____

6. ¿Trabajas? ¿Dónde? ¿Qué días trabajas?

_____

_____

7. ¿Qué días de la semana descansas?

_____

8. ¿A qué hora llegas a tu casa los sábados?

_____

_____

9. ¿A qué hora llegas a la universidad los lunes?

_____

_____

10. ¿Sacas buenas notas en todas tus clases? ¿En qué clases sacas A y B? ¿Por qué?

_____

_____

J. La vida de Lorena. First read the questions, then read the following description of Lorena's activities, and then answer the questions.

1. ¿De dónde es Lorena?

   Es de Tijuana, Baja California.

2. ¿Qué estudia? ¿Qué quiere estudiar en el futuro?

   Estudia en un programa internacional. Quiere estudiar biología.

3. ¿Cuáles son sus actividades favoritas?

   Sus actividades favoritas son mirar películas y escuchar música.

4. ¿Qué días tiene clase por la noche? ¿Qué clase es?

   Tiene clase por la noche los martes; es una clase de actuación.

5. ¿Qué hace (does) los fines de semana? ¿Con quién?

   Va a bailar con sus amigas y amigos.

Hola, me llamo Lorena; tengo 16 años. Soy de Tijuana, Baja California. Tengo un hermano mayor; se llama Iván y tiene 24 años. También tengo una gata y un hámster; ¡adoro a los animales! Estudio en una preparatoria que tiene un programa internacional; con ese programa puedo estudiar en cualquier universidad del mundo[1]. Quiero estudiar biología en San Diego. Algunas de mis clases me gustan mucho, otras no me gustan, pero tengo que tomarlas. Aquí no tenemos muchas clases opcionales.

Durante las vacaciones trabajé en una tienda de helados[2]. Ahora no trabajo, pero siempre tengo actividades. Por ejemplo, por las tardes, estudio o preparo mi tarea. Los martes por la noche, tomo una clase de actuación. Me gusta mucho la clase, pero llego a las 10 de la noche a mi casa, y el miércoles por la mañana no me puedo levantar[3]. Los jueves tengo mi clase de baile. Me gusta el jazz y el tap. Me gusta mirar películas y escuchar música, especialmente el rock mexicano y la música alternativa. La música pop no me gusta mucho. Los viernes o los sábados voy a bailar con mis amigas (y amigos). Nos gusta bailar en una discoteca donde no hay bebidas alcohólicas. Tengo muchas amigas, algunas son amigas de la escuela y otras son amigas del barrio[4]. También estudio piano con mi mamá porque ella es maestra de música en una escuela primaria y en la Normal[5].

Todavía no tengo licencia de manejar[6]. Mi papá dice que soy muy joven; ¡yo no opino lo mismo! Los domingos normalmente es día de descanso, pero a veces visito a mi abuela o a mis tías.

[1]world   [2]ice cream   [3]I can't get up   [4]neighborhood   [5]school that prepares teachers   [6]driving license

¡A escuchar!

Episodio

5

Comprensión

A. Los sábados en casa de Ana Mari. Listen as Ana Mari describes what she and her family normally do on Saturdays, and indicate who does each activity. **¡Atención!** Some of the activities may be done by more than one person. The people are: Ana Mari **(AM),** Ramón **(R),** her mother **(M),** her father **(P),** and Ana Mari's younger brothers, Alex and Luis **(AL).** You will hear Ana Mari's description twice.

___AM___ 1. Descansa y escucha música.

___AL___ 2. Miran la tele.

___P___ 3. Trabaja en la oficina.

___P, R, AL___ 4. Lavan el coche.

___AM, M___ 5. Compran la comida.

___AM, R, AL___ 6. Limpian sus cuartos.

___M, P___ 7. Miran el fútbol en la tele.

___M, P___ 8. Visitan a unos amigos.

B. El calendario de Wayne. You will hear Wayne tell Carlos what he does in a normal week. Listen and fill in the calendar with the words and phrases provided to indicate what Wayne does each day. Then answer the question at the end of this activity. You will hear the conversation twice.

Wayne

trabaja   toma clases   estudia   sale con sus amigos   descansa

	lunes	martes	miércoles	jueves	viernes	sábado	domingo
mañana							
noche							

Wayne necesita lavar la ropa y limpiar su cuarto. ¿Cuándo hay tiempo? Escríbelo en el calendario.   sábado por la mañana

Pronunciación

La *r* y la *rr*. **R (ere)** and **rr (erre)** are two separate letters of the Spanish alphabet; they are not interchangeable. For example, **pero** means *but*, and **perro** means *dog*. The most similar sound to the Spanish **r** in English is the double *tt* or double *dd*, as in *butter* and *ladder*. The tip of the tongue taps once on the ridge behind the upper front teeth. Repeat these words and sentences after the speaker.

cero   serio   cafetería   Ana Mari es cariñosa.

When the single **r** is combined with a consonant, you may hear a slight trill.

tres   drama   puerta   Mi madre es agradable.

When **r** occurs at the beginning of a word, it becomes a trill. To produce a trill, the tip of the tongue taps in rapid succession on the ridge behind the upper front teeth. If you find it difficult to produce the sound, try imitating a motor sound, or the purr of a cat.

Ramón   rubio   romántico   Ricardo corre rápido.

The letter **rr** is always trilled. Repeat these words and sentence after the speaker.

arrogante   aburrido   irregular   los verbos irregulares.

Más escenas de la vida

Sofía arrives at Manolo's apartment. Listen to their conversation and then complete activities **A** and **B.** You will hear the conversation twice.

A. ¿Quién? Indicate to whom the following descriptions refer: Manolo's roommate Jorge **(J),** Manolo **(M),** Lalo **(L)** or Sofía **(S).**

__J__ 1. Es un desordenado.

__M__ 2. Necesita buscar otro compañero de cuarto.

__J__ 3. No limpia nada.

__L__ 4. Es desordenado como Jorge.

__M__ 5. Cree que nadie es perfecto.

__J__ 6. Es generoso e inteligente.

__M, S__ 7. Van a casa de Adriana.

B. ¿Entendiste? Write the answers to the following questions.

1. ¿Qué hace Jorge cuando está en casa? Mira la tele o escucha música horrible.

2. ¿Cómo es Lalo? Es como Jorge y es inmaduro.

3. ¿Por qué en perspectiva, la situación de Manolo no es mala?
   Jorge tiene sus cosas buenas. Compra comida y es generoso e inteligente.

4. ¿Qué necesitan a hacer a casa de Adriana? Necesitan estudiar.

Objetivos comunicativos

In this episode, you will practice:

✓ describing people and things

✓ asking for information

Episodio

6

Escenas de la vida: ¡Qué guapos!

A. ¡Mira cuánto puedes entender! Use the spaces provided to describe Adriana and Sofía: what classes they take, what their families are like, where they are from, etc. Then select the statements that apply to the characters. *Answers will vary.*

Video CD-ROM

Audio CD-ROM

Instructor's Resources
• Overheads
• VHS Video
• Worktext CD
• Website
• **IRM:** Videoscript, Comprehensible input

Adriana

_____
_____
_____
_____
_____

Sofía

_____
_____
_____
_____
_____

1. ¿Cómo es Adriana?

☐ Es baja.   ☑ Es alta.
☑ Es morena.   ☐ Es rubia.
☑ Es casada.   ☐ Es soltera.
☑ Es agradable.   ☐ Es antipática.
☐ Es perezosa.   ☑ Es trabajadora.

2. ¿Cómo es Sofía?

☑ Es delgada.   ☐ Es gorda.
☐ Es antipática.   ☑ Es agradable.
☑ Es joven.   ☐ Es vieja.
☑ Es bonita.   ☐ Es fea.
☑ Es graciosa.   ☐ Es seria.

3. ¿Qué le gusta a Adriana?

☑ Preparar comida puertorriqueña.
☐ Comer comida mexicana.

4. ¿Quién le gusta a Sofía?

☐ Le gusta Manolo.
☑ Le gusta Carlos.

B. ¿Te diste cuenta? Contesta las siguientes preguntas.

1. ¿En cuánto tiempo prepara Adriana el flan? En media hora.
2. ¿Cómo se llaman los hijos de Adriana? Santiago, Viviana y Carlos.
3. ¿Cuántos años tienen? 15, 11 y 25.
4. ¿Cómo se llama el hermano de Sofía? ¿Cuántos años tiene? Se llama Lalo y tiene 15 años.
5. ¿Cuántas personas hay en la familia de Manolo? Cuatro.

C. ¿Cómo son? Selecciona las características de cada uno.

1. **Carlos**	alto	guapo	moreno	casado	joven	soltero
2. **La hermana de Manolo**	rubia	vieja	casada	alta	bonita	gorda
3. **Manolo**	bajo	feo	moreno	bueno	amable	guapo

Video Synopsis. Manolo and Sofía meet at Ariana's house to study. Adriana has prepared a *flan de queso*. While looking at family pictures, the three discuss their families. Sofía is attracted to Adriana's older son, and asks whether he is married.

D. Emparejar. Empareja las personas con las frases.

Video
CD-ROM

_c_ 1. Santiaguito   a. tiene un hermano.

_b_ 2. Carlos   b. es el mayor.

_d_ 3. Manolo   c. tiene quince años.

_a_ 4. Sofía   d. tiene una hermana.

Audio
CD-ROM

Práctica adicional	
Cuaderno de tareas WB pp.147–148, A–C	Video CD-ROM Episodio 6

> **Cultura a lo vivo**
>
> When Spanish speakers are successful in the United States, they are viewed as examples of how dreams can come true by both those who have remained in the home country, as well as by those who have immigrated to the United States. A notable example is Chicago Cubs home-run hitter Sammy Sosa, hailed as a national hero in his native Dominican Republic, for his success on the playing field.

Para comunicarnos mejor

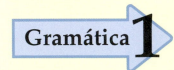

Gramática 1

Describing people and things
- **Descriptive adjectives**
- **Placement of adjectives**

Analizar y descubrir

In the conversation, you heard the following statements.

¡Qué **guapos** son sus hijos!	*Your children are so good-looking!*
Tú eres **alto** y muy **guapo**.	*You're tall and very handsome.*
Tu hermana es **alta** y **rubia**.	*Your sister is tall and blonde.*

1. Notice that the adjectives **guapo** and **alto** have more than one form. Study the previous statements and answer these questions:

     a. Which word was used to describe Adriana's children? _____guapos_____

     b. Which words were used to describe Manolo? _____alto_____ and _____guapo_____

     c. Which words were used to describe Manolo's sister? _____alta_____ and _____rubia_____

Circle the correct answer in items **d-f**, and answer **g**.

     d. **Guapos** is used in **(a)** because it matches **hijas /(hijos.)**

     e. **Alto** and **guapo** are used in **(b)** because they match **(Manolo)/ Sofía.**

     f. **Alta** and **rubia** are used in **(c)** because they match **él /(ella.)**

     g. Which form of **guapo** would be used to describe Sofía and Viviana? _____guapas_____

2. Unlike English, Spanish adjectives change their form to match the gender (masculine or feminine) and number (singular or plural) of the nouns they describe.

La clase es divertid**a**.	*The class is fun.*
Manolo es alt**o**; **él y Carlos** son moren**os**.	*Manolo is tall; he and Carlos are dark-haired.*
Las amigas de Sofía son gracios**as**.	*Sofía's friends are funny.*

3. Some adjectives (ending in **-e** or in some consonants) do not change form to indicate gender. All, however, change form to indicate number.

La casa es grand**e**; **el estadio** es grand**e**.	*The house is big; the stadium is big.*
Los salones no son grand**es**.	*The classrooms are not big.*

Here are some adjectives used to describe physical appearance.

Gramática 1. Model the pronunciation of the words and have students repeat after you. You may want to bring in pictures of famous people, and have the students use the vocabulary to describe them.

Adjetivos descriptivos: La apariencia física

guapo/a	*handsome, good-looking*	**joven**	*young*
bonito/a	*good-looking, pretty*	**viejo/a***	*old*
feo/a	*ugly, plain*	**grande**	*large, big*
alto/a	*tall*	**pequeño/a**	*small*
bajo/a	*short (height)*	**rubio/a**	*blond(e)*
gordo/a	*fat*	**moreno/a**	*dark*
delgado/a	*thin*		

*In some Spanish-speaking countries, it is impolite to describe an older person as **viejo** or **vieja**. It is better to say **Es una persona mayor**.

Below are some adjectives used to describe character and personality.

También se dice...

delgado ⟶ flaco

perezoso ⟶ flojo

gracioso ⟶ chistoso

rubio ⟶ güero

Adjetivos descriptivos: El carácter y la personalidad

agradable	*pleasant, nice*	**grosero/a**	*rude*
antipático/a	*unpleasant, nasty*	**amable**	*kind, friendly*
bueno/a	*good, nice*	**cariñoso/a**	*affecionate*
malo/a	*bad*	**reservado/a**	*reserved*
gracioso/a	*funny*	**listo/a**	*smart*
serio/a	*serious*	**tonto/a**	*dumb, silly*
trabajador(a)	*hard-working*	**perezoso/a**	*lazy*

Learning Strategy: Focus on word clusters and word families

You will understand more if you are able to relate words with similar roots: for example, **persona, personal,** and **personalidad** or **arte, artista,** and **artístico.** Use the words you know to figure out what other words mean: knowing **perezoso,** what could **pereza** mean? It means *laziness.* Try to guess the meaning of **grosería, amabilidad, aburrimiento,** and **cariño.**

Here are some words and expressions used to describe people and things.

Descripciones: Las personas y las cosas

nuevo/a	*new*	**fácil**	*easy*	**mayor**	*older*
viejo/a	*old*	**difícil**	*hard, difficult*	**menor**	*younger*
aburrido/a	*boring*	**rico/a**	*rich; tasty*	**hijo/a único/a**	*only child*
divertido/a	*fun*	**pobre**	*poor*	**soltero/a**	*single*
diferente	*different*	**casado/a**	*married*	**similar**	*similar*

PRÁCTICA

A. ¿Cómo son? Selecciona la característica que mejor describe a los personajes.

Sofía   Adriana   Manolo

¡Fíjate!

Be sure to look at the ending of the adjectives to select the one that matches the character in gender and in number.

1. Manolo es (bajas / gordos / <u>moreno</u> / rubia).
2. Sofía es (vieja / <u>joven</u> / feo / bonitas).
3. Los hijos de Adriana son (soltera / diferente / <u>guapos</u> / cariñosas).
4. Adriana es (rubios / moreno / mexicanas / <u>trabajadora</u>).
5. Manolo y su compañero de cuarto son (argentinas / cubano / <u>jóvenes</u> / casado).

B. Los opuestos. Completa cada frase con el adjetivo contrario.

> **Modelo**   Sofía no es seria: es **graciosa**.

1. La abuela de Sofía no es joven: es _____ vieja _____.
2. Lalo no es responsable: es _____ irresponsable _____.
3. Sofía no es tonta: es _____ inteligente/lista _____.
4. Los hijos de Adriana no son gordos: son _____ delgados _____.
5. Manolo no es serio: es _____ gracioso _____.
6. Sofía no es casada: es _____ soltera _____.
7. Ramón no es grosero: es _____ amable _____.

C. Tu familia. Usa adjetivos para describir a tu familia.   Answers will vary.

> **Modelo**
>
> **Mis hermanas son cariñosas y graciosas.**

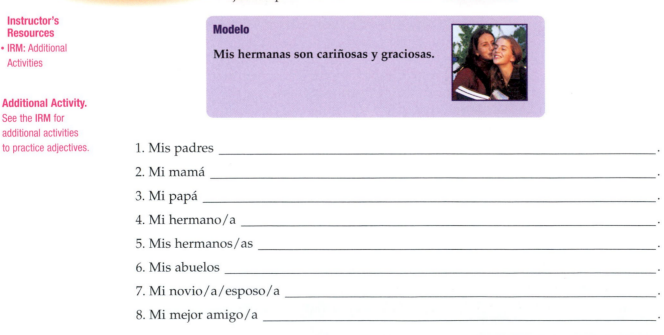

1. Mis padres _____.
2. Mi mamá _____.
3. Mi papá _____.
4. Mi hermano/a _____.
5. Mis hermanos/as _____.
6. Mis abuelos _____.
7. Mi novio/a/esposo/a _____.
8. Mi mejor amigo/a _____.

• Placement of adjectives

An important difference between English and Spanish is the order of adjectives and nouns in a sentence. In English, the adjective comes *before* the noun *(I have a boring class)*, whereas in Spanish, most adjectives go *after* the noun (**Tengo una clase** *aburrida*).

A few adjectives in Spanish do precede the noun.

1. Adjectives of quantity (**mucho, poco,** etc.) always come before the noun.

Hay **pocos** estudiantes en la clase.   *There are few students in class.*
Hoy tengo **mucha** tarea.   *I have a lot of homework today.*

2. Demonstrative adjectives also precede nouns.

Necesito **este** libro.   *I need this book.*
Sofía desea comprar **esa** mochila.   *Sofía wants to buy that backpack.*

Los adjetivos demostrativos			
este, esta	*this*	ese, esa	*that*
estos, estas	*these*	esos, esas	*those*

3. The adjectives **bueno** and **malo** may be used before the noun for emphasis. In this case, you must drop the **-o** from the masculine singular form.

Tengo un **buen** coche.   *I have a good car.*
¿Tienes **buenos** profesores?   *Do you have good teachers?*
No es un **mal** estudiante.   *He isn't a bad student.*

PRÁCTICA

D. ¿Qué tienen? Termina las frases usando adjetivos para describir cómo son las cosas que tienen las siguientes personas. Answers will vary.

Modelo	Este semestre Adriana tiene compañeros **agradables**.

1. Sofía tiene un coche _____.
2. Adriana tiene una casa _____.
3. Carlos, Santiaguito y Viviana tienen dos perros _____.
4. Manolo tiene un compañero de cuarto _____.
5. Este semestre tengo una clase _____.

E. La tarea de Johnny. Imagine you are helping Johnny, your eight year-old neighbor, with his Spanish homework. He wants to write the following things about his family. Teach him how to do it in Spanish.

1. The blonde girl is my sister.

   La chica rubia es mi hermana.

2. She has a pretty friend, Lulú.

   Ella tiene una amiga bonita, Lulú.

3. Lulú is very funny.

   Lulú es muy graciosa.

4. I have a married brother.

   Tengo un hermano casado.

5. He buys a lot of cars and all of them (**todos**) are ugly.

   Él compra muchos coches y todos son feos.

6. I also have three pets: a big dog, a fat cat, and a dumb bird!

   También tengo tres mascotas: un perro grande, un gato gordo y ¡un pájaro tonto!

7. This year I have a very good math teacher.

   Este año tengo un maestro de matemáticas muy bueno.

F. Anuncios. Read the ads, which appeared in the Spanish-language newspaper *Diario del Club Latino*, in order to answer the questions that follow. First, read the questions so you can determine the purpose of the reading.

> **Reading Strategy:** **Using cognates and content to determine meaning**
> You can read Spanish with far greater ease if you guess at the meaning of cognates—words that look similar to English words. Before you read the personal ads below, consider these cognates: **americano, ingeniero, económicamente estable, español, inteligente, ejercicio, computadoras, atractiva, matrimonio, tel., bilingüe, sensual, educada, elegante, cine, responder**, and **electrónico**. The content of a text will provide clues to the meaning as well. Think about what you would expect to find in a personal ad and use this knowledge to help you understand the reading.

1. ¿Cómo es la persona del anuncio?

   Es inteligente, cariñoso y trabajador.

2. ¿Qué le gusta a esta persona?

   Le gusta hacer ejercicio, cocinar y trabajar con computadoras.

3. ¿Qué tipo de persona busca?

   Busca una mujer atractiva, flaca y de 20 a 30 años de edad.

AMERICANO

Ingeniero económicamente estable, hablo español. Soy inteligente, cariñoso y trabajador. Me gusta hacer ejercicio, cocinar y trabajar con computadoras. Busco mujer atractiva, flaca. 20-30 años. ¿Amistad? ¿Matrimonio? Niño ok. Tel. 434-4444

4. ¿Cómo es la persona de este anuncio?

Es sensual, educada, elegante y simpática.

5. ¿Cuántos años tiene?

Tiene 30 años.

6. ¿Qué le gusta hacer?

Le gusta viajar, bailar e ir al cine.

ATRACTIVA

Bilingüe, 30 años, sensual, educada, elegante y simpática. Me gusta viajar, bailar e ir al cine. Busco amigo para diversiones sanas.[1] Favor de responder vía correo electrónico. Atractiva@homemail.loc

[1]*healthy fun*

G. ¡Un anuncio gratis! A local Spanish newspaper is offering free personal ads as a promotion for their weekend edition. Write an ad that will appeal to your ideal mate. Use the ads from **Práctica F** as models. *Answers will vary.*

Writing Strategy: **Using a text as a model for writing**

To write successfully in Spanish, you will need to examine samples so you can identify the information you need to include when you write your own texts. Prepare to write your own personal ad. First, reread the personal ads from the previous section and identify the information they provide, such as physical characteristics, personality traits, and hobbies. Then, list the information you want to communicate in each of these categories in the space provided. Finally, write your ad.

Características físicas	Personalidad	Actividades

H. Las personas importantes en mi vida. Bring three or four photos of family members or friends to class. In groups of three, introduce the people in your photos and tell as much as you can about them, such as their age, their personality, and your relationship to them. Make sure you ask each classmate at least three questions about their family. *Answers will vary.*

Modelo   **¿Dónde trabaja tu hermano mayor?**
           ¿Cuántos años tiene?
           ¿Es casado?

Práctica adicional

Cuaderno de tareas
WB pp.148–150, D–H

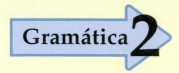

Asking for information
• Interrogative words

Spanish, like English, uses inversion (placing the verb before the subject) to ask information questions. To change a statement into a *wh*-question *(who, what, where, when, why)*, place the conjugated verb in front of the subject, and add the appropriate interrogative word.

Statement		Question	
subject	verb		verb subject
Adriana trabaja en una oficina.	→	¿Dónde trabaja Adriana?	
subject verb			verb subject
Manolo es alto y moreno.	→	¿Cómo es Manolo?	
subject verb			verb subject
Sofía toma cálculo y vóleibol.	→	¿Qué clases toma Sofía?	

¡Fíjate!

Cuál and **Qué** may be confusing. Do not use **Cuál** + [*noun*]; use **Cuál** + [*verb to be*].
¿Cuál es tu mochila?
Use **Qué** + [*nouns*].
¿Qué libro lees? ¿Qué coche te gusta?

Here is a summary of all the interrogative words you have been using.

Palabras interrogativas	
¿**Cómo** es Manolo?	*What is Manolo like?*
¿**Cuál** es tu clase favorita?	*Which class is your favorite?*
¿**Cuándo** descansa Adriana?	*When does Adriana rest?*
¿**Cuántos** hijos tiene?	*How many children does she have?*
¿**Cuántas** clases toma Manolo?	*How many clases does Manolo take?*
¿**Dónde** trabaja Adriana?	*Where does Adriana work?*
¿**Por qué** te gusta la clase?	*Why do you like the class?*
¿**Qué** clases toma Manolo?	*What/which classes is Manolo taking?*
¿**Quién** es Carlos?	*Who is Carlos?*

PRÁCTICA

I. Las respuestas. Empareja las preguntas de arriba *(above)* con las respuestas.

1. ¿ Quién es Carlos _____? Es el hijo de Adriana.

2. ¿ Cuál es tu clase favorita _____? La clase de español.

3. ¿ Cuántos hijos tiene _____? Tiene tres hijos.

4. ¿ Cómo es Manolo _____? Es alto y moreno.

5. ¿ Cuántas clases toma Manolo _____? Toma cuatro clases.

6. ¿ Por qué te gusta la clase _____? Porque es muy divertida.

7. ¿ Dónde trabaja Adriana _____? En una oficina.

8. ¿ Cuándo descansa Adriana _____? Nunca.

9. ¿ Qué clases toma Manolo _____? Cálculo, sicología e historia.

J. Preguntas. Completa las preguntas sobre Adriana.

1. ¿ <u>Dónde</u> estudia Adriana? En la biblioteca.
2. ¿ <u>Cuántos</u> días a la semana trabaja? Dos días.
3. ¿ <u>Qué</u> días? Martes y jueves.
4. ¿ <u>Cuándo</u> descansa? Nunca.
5. ¿ <u>Cómo</u> es el profesor? Es agradable.
6. ¿ <u>Quién</u> es Santiago? Es su esposo.

Additional Activity. You may want to write sets of questions and answers on separate pieces of paper (or index cards), then distribute them to the students and have them find their match. To check answers, have pairs of students read their card. For example, card one, **¿Qué clases tomas este semestre?**, matches with card two, **Tomo español, historia, matemáticas e inglés.**

K. Preguntas personales. Responde apropiadamente a las preguntas. Después entrevista a un(a) compañero/a.   Answers will vary.

K. Ask students to prepare for the interview by writing their answers for homework. When interviewing their partner, do not allow them to read their answers.

1. ¿Qué clases tomas este semestre?
2. ¿Cuál es tu clase favorita? ¿Por qué?
3. ¿Qué clase no te gusta? ¿Por qué?
4. ¿Cómo es tu profesor/a de español? ¿Es divertida la clase?
5. ¿Dónde trabajas? ¿Cuántas horas a la semana trabajas? ¿Cuándo descansas?
6. ¿Cuándo estudias? ¿Dónde? ¿Con quién?
7. ¿A qué hora regresas a casa generalmente? ¿Qué haces (do you do) cuando llegas?
8. ¿Qué haces los fines de semana? ¿Lavas la ropa? ¿Limpias la casa? ¿Estudias? ¿Trabajas?

Audio
CD-ROM

L. La pareja perfecta. The individuals below are participants on a radio program called "La pareja perfecta." Listen to determine why the participants feel they are the ideal partner. After sharing your opinion about their comments, write a brief description of your ideal partner on a separate sheet of paper.   Answers will vary.

Instructor's Resources
• Worktext CD
• IRM: Tapescript

	características	mi opinión
participante 1	alto, guapo, gana mucho dinero, trabaja todo el día, así que ella va de compras cuando lo desea.	
participante 2	muy inteligente y bonita, usa ropa muy atractiva y elegante, prepara una comida deliciosa, le gusta mirar los deportes en la televisión.	
participante 3	muy bueno con toda la familia, prepara la comida y lava la ropa si es necesario.	

Script. For the script to this activity, consult the **Instructor's Resource Manual.**

M. La entrevista. Imagine you can meet with anyone in the world: your favorite actor, musician, or politician. Use the **Palabras interrogativas** box on the previous page to write five questions. Keep it simple!   Answers will vary.

Modelo	Preguntas para Gabriel García Márquez
	¿De dónde es usted?
	¿Cuál es su novela favorita?
	¿Cuántas novelas tiene?

Práctica adicional

Cuaderno de tareas
WB pp.150–151, I–J
LM pp.153–154, A–B, Pron.

Audio
CD-ROM
Episodio 6

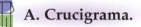

Actividades comunicativas

A. Crucigrama.

Instrucciones para **Estudiante 1**

You and your partner have a copy of the same partially completed crossword puzzle. The words missing on your copy of the puzzle are filled in on your partner's copy. Give each other clues to complete the puzzle. Do not say the word your partner needs; instead, use definitions, examples, and incomplete sentences that provide a context for the missing word. Here are some examples:

Modelo	*17 vertical:* **La hija de mi hija es mi...**
	15 horizontal: **Un niño no es viejo; es...**

¡Fíjate!

Find simple but creative ways of communicating the meaning of the words to your partner.

A. Encourage students to find creative ways to communicate the meaning of the words in the puzzle. Expand the examples in the **modelo** and/or create new ones to show students how to prompt an answer **(las modelos son muy...)**. Emphasize that they may not use **guapo** to elicit **guapa**. They can not use the target words in any form to elicit a response. Allow eight to ten minutes.

[Crucigrama / Crossword puzzle]

Across/down answers shown in grid:
- 1 D
- 2 G / 3 F E A
- GUA / L
- A / G — 4 A 5 L T 6 A S
- 7 P R I M A S — I / G
- O / D — 8 G — S / R
- A — 9 T — R — T / A
- 10 G 11 R O S E R O — 12 M A M Á — O / D
- U — O — N — N — A
- B — T — D — B
- I — 13 S O L T E R O — 14 M A L O
- 15 J O 16 V E N — 17 N — E
- S — 18 C A R I Ñ O S O
- 19 P A P Á — U — E
- 20 V I E J O — Ñ — 21 T Í A S
- 22 S O B R I N A S — A
- O — D
- 23 H I J A S

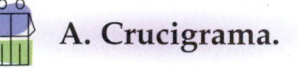 **A. Crucigrama.**

Instrucciones para Estudiante 2

You and your partner have a copy of the same partially completed crossword puzzle. The words missing on your copy of the puzzle are filled in on your partner's copy. Give each other clues to complete the puzzle. Do not say the word your partner needs; instead, use definitions, examples, and incomplete sentences that provide a context for the missing word. Here are some examples:

| Modelo | *17 vertical:* **La hija de mi hija es mi...** |
| | *15 horizontal:* **Un niño no es viejo; es...** |

¡Fíjate!

Find simple but creative ways of communicating the meaning of the words to your partner.

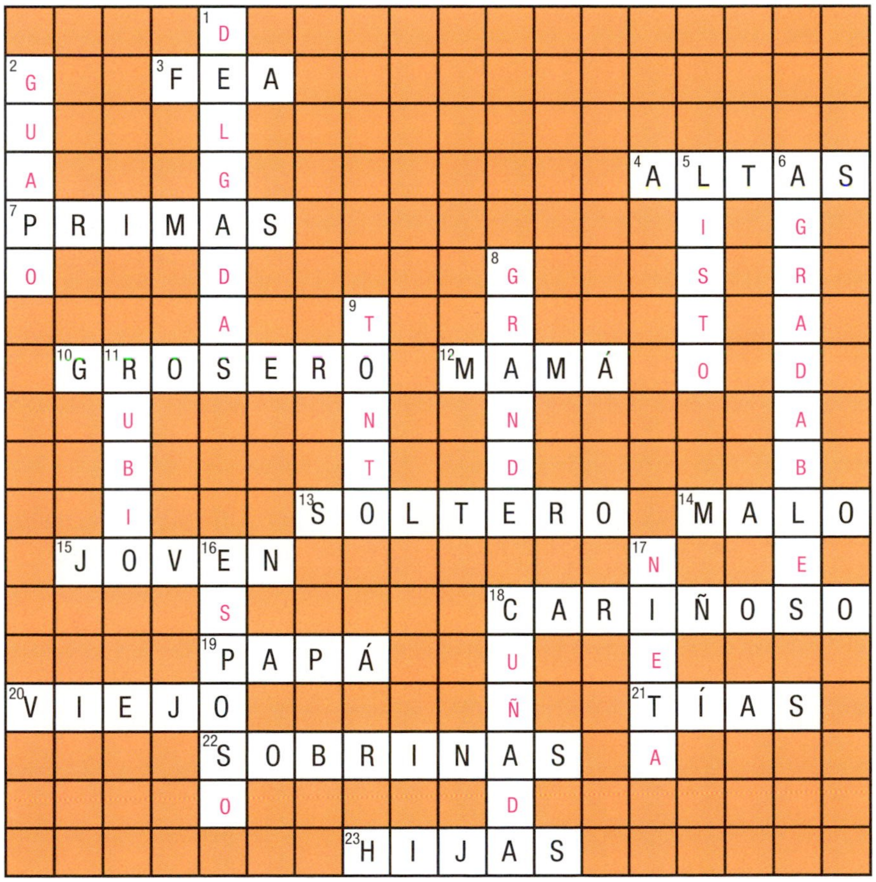

The crossword grid contains the following filled answers:

- 3 horizontal: FEA
- 4 horizontal: ALTAS
- 7 horizontal: PRIMAS
- 10 horizontal: GROSERO
- 12 horizontal: MAMÁ
- 13 horizontal: SOLTERO
- 14 horizontal: MALO
- 15 horizontal: JOVEN
- 18 horizontal: CARIÑOSO
- 19 horizontal: PAPÁ
- 20 horizontal: VIEJO
- 21 horizontal: TÍAS
- 22 horizontal: SOBRINAS
- 23 horizontal: HIJAS
- 2 vertical: GUAPO
- 1 vertical: D / FLGDA (FEA column)
- 5 vertical: LISTO
- 6 vertical: AGRADABLE
- 8 vertical: GRANDE
- 9 vertical: TANTI (TNT)
- 11 vertical: RUBI
- 16 vertical: ENS
- 17 vertical: NETA

B. Actividades en común. First answer the questions in the column labeled **Yo**. Then look for classmates whose answers are the same as yours and write their names in the column labeled **Compañero/a**. Be prepared to share your findings with the class.   *Answers will vary.*

> **Modelo** —¿Dónde trabajas?
> —Trabajo en un banco. ¿Y tú?
> —Yo también.   *or*   Yo trabajo en una tienda.
> —Mary y yo trabajamos en un supermercado.

B. You may ask students to fill in the **Yo** column prior to class. Students will need at least six minutes to interact with their classmates. You may participate in the activity to enable students to use the **usted** form of the verbs they are learning. Select students to report their findings, or assign a written report for homework.

	Compañero/a	Yo
1. ¿Dónde trabajas?	_____	_____
2. ¿Cuántas clases tomas este semestre?	_____	_____
3. ¿Qué programa miras en la televisión?	_____	_____
4. ¿A qué hora llegas a casa los lunes?	_____	_____
5. ¿Cuántos idiomas hablas bien?	_____	_____
6. ¿Qué computadora usas?	_____	_____
7. ¿Dónde compras tu ropa?	_____	_____
8. ¿Qué estación de radio escuchas?	_____	_____
9. ¿Dónde estudias para los exámenes?	_____	_____
10. ¿Cuántas hermanas tienes?	_____	_____

C. Veinte preguntas. Think of three famous people, but do not reveal their names to your partner. Your partner will ask you yes/no questions as they try to guess the names of each person. You get a point for every question your partner has to ask you before they find out who you are thinking of. Take turns.

> **Modelo** ¿Es hombre? ¿Es actor? ¿Es alto?

Invitación a **Estados Unidos**

Del álbum de
Adriana

Después de los mexicanos, los puertorriqueños son la comunidad de hispanos más grande del país. Cada verano (*each summer*) se celebra en Nueva York el desfile (*parade*) puertorriqueño al que asisten (*attend*) más de un millón de personas. Muchas personalidades famosas son de origen puertorriqueño, como Jennifer López, John Leguizamo, Ricky Martin y Marc Anthony, entre otros.

Práctica adicional

Website
vistahigher
learning.com

La correspondencia

El correo: Otra carta para Odette. Lee la carta que Sofía le escribe a su amiga Odette en Guadalajara, México. Primero lee las preguntas para después contestarlas.

1. ¿Cómo es el hijo de Adriana, según *(according to)* Sofía? Es guapísimo y superatractivo.

2. ¿Cómo es Lalo? Regresa tardísimo a casa, escucha música horrorosa, nunca saca buenas notas en sus clases y siempre necesita dinero.

3. ¿Cómo es el ex novio de Odette? Es grosero y flojo.

4. ¿Cuándo van a Guadalajara? Van a Guadalajara en diciembre.

Querida Odette:

Me da tanta alegría[1] recibir tus cartas. Estoy bien. Mis clases me gustan mucho. En mi clase de cálculo, tengo una compañera puertorriqueña. Se llama Adriana y es una señora muy agradable. Aunque ya es mayor, somos buenas amigas. Además, ¡tiene un hijo guapísimo! Bueno, no lo conozco[2] en persona, pero en las fotos es superatractivo. Es piloto y ahora está en Chicago. ¿Te imaginas, poder visitar todo el mundo gratis?[3] Lalo, como siempre, regresa tardísimo a casa, escucha una música horrorosa, nunca saca buenas notas en sus clases y siempre necesita dinero.

¡Qué bueno que terminaste con tu ex novio! Era grosero y flojo. Tú mereces[4] una persona buena y cariñosa como tú. No te preocupes, hay muchos muchachos. Yo no tengo novio, pero tengo muchos amigos.

Bueno, querida amiga, sí voy a visitarte en diciembre. Ramón y Ana Mari van a visitar a sus abuelos en Guadalajara. ¡Tal vez vamos juntos! Escríbeme pronto.

Tu amiga que te quiere,
Sofía

[1]*It makes me so happy* [2]*know* [3]*free* [4]*deserve*

En papel: Una notita para Odette. Write a letter to Odette telling her about your family, friends, instructors, classmates, and other important people in your life. Include their name, their relationship to you, their physical description, their personality, and one or two interesting things about them. Answers will vary.

¡Fíjate!

Create a simple outline, in Spanish, of the information you want to include in your letter before you begin to write.

Video
CD-ROM

Audio
CD-ROM

¡A ver de nuevo!

Parte 1. Listen to or watch the **Escena** again and write as much as you can about Manolo, Sofía, and Adriana: age, description, family, activities, etc.   Answers will vary.

Parte 2. Now compare your summary with a classmate's, and add any information you may have left out.

Práctica adicional		
Cuaderno de tareas WB pp.151–152, K–M LM p.154, A-B	Audio CD-ROM Episodio 6	Website vistahigher learning.com

Vocabulario del Episodio 6

Objetivos comunicativos

You should now be able to do the following in Spanish:

✓ describe people and things

✓ ask for information

Para describir a las personas y las cosas

aburrido/a	boring	hijo/a único/a	only child
agradable	pleasant, nice	joven	young
alto/a	tall	listo/a	smart
amable	kind, friendly	malo/a	bad
antipático/a	unpleasant, nasty	mayor	older
bajo/a	short (height)	menor	younger
bonito/a	good-looking, pretty	moreno/a	dark
bueno/a	good , nice	nuevo/a	new
cariñoso/a	affectionate	pequeño/a	small
casado/a	married	perezoso/a	lazy
delgado/a	thin	pobre	poor
diferente	different	reservado/a	reserved
difícil	hard, difficult	rico/a	rich; tasty
divertido/a	fun	rubio/a	blond(e)
fácil	easy	serio/a	serious
feo/a	ugly, plain	similar	similar
gordo/a	fat	soltero/a	single
gracioso/a	funny	tonto/a	dumb, silly
grande	large, big	trabajador(a)	hard-working
grosero/a	rude	viejo/a	old
guapo/a	handsome, good-looking		

Los adjetivos demostrativos

este, esta	this	ese, esa	that
estos, estas	these	esos, esas	those

Palabras interrogativas

¿Cómo...?	How...?
¿Cuál...?	Which...?
¿Cuándo...?	When...?
¿Cuántos/as..?	How many...?
¿Dónde...?	Where...?
¿Por qué...?	Why...?
¿Qué...?	What...?
¿Quién...?	Who...?

Vocabulario personal

In this section, write all the words that you want to know how to say in Spanish so that you can better talk about yourself, family, friends, and, your activities.

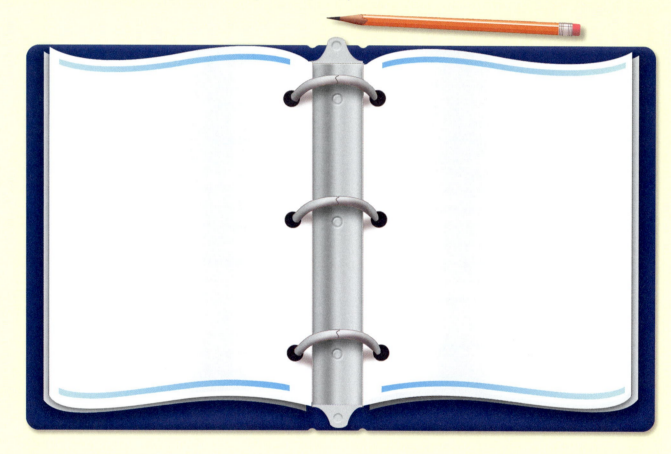

¡A escribir!

Episodio 6

Escenas de la vida: ¡Qué guapos!

A. ¡A ver cuánto entendiste! See how much of the **Escena** you understood by matching the Spanish sentences with their English equivalents.

1. El flan de queso

_b_ 1. ¿Es difícil prepararlo?	a. It's easy to make.
_d_ 2. ¡Qué rico!	b. Is it hard to make?
_e_ 3. Lo preparo en media hora.	c. I like to cook a lot.
_a_ 4. Es fácil prepararlo.	d. How delicious!
_c_ 5. Me gusta mucho cocinar.	e. I make it in half an hour.

2. Los hermanos

_f_ 1. Tu hermana es alta y rubia.	a. You're tall and very good-looking.
_d_ 2. ¿Cuántos años tiene?	b. You're so different!
_b_ 3. ¡Qué diferentes son!	c. I have her picture.
_a_ 4. Tú eres alto y muy guapo.	d. How old is she?
_e_ 5. Soy moreno y feo.	e. I have dark hair and I'm ugly.
_c_ 6. Tengo su foto.	f. Your sister is tall and blonde.

B. El flan de queso. Use the expressions below to complete the following conversation.

fácil	seria	similar	rico	difícil
está	me encanta	media hora	joven	preparar comida

Manolo ¡Qué (1) ___rico___! (2) ___Me encanta___ el flan de queso.

Sofía   Es muy (3) ___similar___ al flan mexicano. ¿Es (4) ___difícil___ prepararlo?

Adriana No, es muy (5) ___fácil___. Lo preparo en (6) ___media hora___. Me gusta (7) ___preparar comida___ puertorriqueña.

Sofía   ¡ (8) ___Está___ delicioso!

Video CD-ROM

C. ¡Qué guapos! Answer the questions based on what you know about the **Escena**.

1. ¿Cuántos hijos tiene Adriana? Tiene tres hijos.

2. ¿Quién es el mayor? ¿Es casado? Carlos es el mayor. No, no es casado.

3. ¿Cuántos hermanos tiene Manolo? Tiene una hermana.

4. ¿Cómo es la hermana de Manolo? Es rubia y muy bonita.

5. ¿Y cómo es Manolo? Es alto y muy guapo.

Gramática 1 Describing people and things
• **Descriptive adjectives**
• **Placement of adjectives**

D. ¿Cómo son? Describe the characters of the book. Mention their physical appearance and their personality. Answers will vary.

1. Sofía es _____
_____
_____

2. Manolo es _____
_____
_____

3. Ana Mari es _____
_____
_____

4. Adriana es _____
_____
_____

E. Las descripciones. Write sentences using all the elements.

> **Modelo**   Hay / poco / **coches** / bueno / bonito / barato (*inexpensive*)
> Hay pocos coches buenos, bonitos y baratos.

¡Fíjate!

Remember to use the appropriate articles, to match adjectives to the nouns, and to conjugate the verbs.

1. Ramón / tener / un / **trabajo** / fácil / bueno
   Ramón tiene un trabajo fácil y bueno.

2. El **compañero** de cuarto de Manolo / ser / antipático / grosero
   El compañero de cuarto de Manolo es antipático y grosero.

3. La / **universidades** públicas en Latinoamérica / ser / muy / grande
   Las universidades públicas en Latinoamérica son muy grandes.

4. Este semestre / yo / tener / bueno / **profesores**
   Este semestre yo tengo buenos profesores.

5. La **gata** de Manolo / ser / viejo / malo
   La gata de Manolo es vieja y mala.

6. Sofía / tener / mucho / **amigas** / joven / soltero / guapo
   Sofía tiene muchas amigas jóvenes, solteras y guapas.

F. Mi familia. Adriana's adolescent daughter likes to talk about her own family. Use her family tree and the adjectives provided to describe her family.

> **Modelo**   Mi hermano menor es tímido.

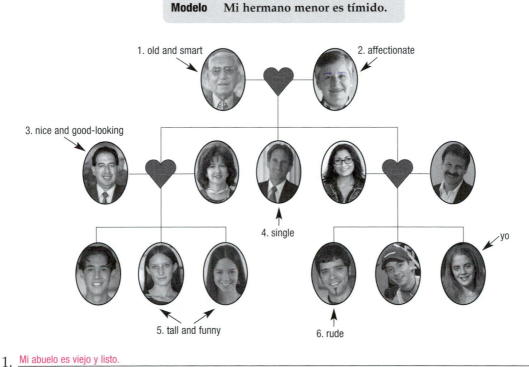

1. old and smart
2. affectionate
3. nice and good-looking
4. single
5. tall and funny
6. rude
yo

1. Mi abuelo es viejo y listo.
2. Mi abuela es cariñosa.
3. Mi tío es simpático y guapo.
4. Mi tío es soltero.
5. Mis primas son altas y graciosas.
6. Mi hermano mayor es grosero.

G. ¡Qué caro! *(How expensive!)* Sofía and Ana Mari are at the bookstore gathering supplies for Sofía's design class. Complete the conversation with the appropriate forms of the demonstrative adjectives.

este	ese	estos	esos
esta	esa	estas	esas

Sofía   ¡Mira cuánto cuestan (1) _____estos_____ *(these)* lápices de grafito!

Ana Mari   ¡Qué horror! (2) _____Esos_____ *(Those)* lápices son más caros *(expensive)* que los libros. Bueno, (3) _____este_____ *(this)* libro de diseño es carísimo también.

Sofía   A ver… ¡Ah! Por suerte ya tengo (4) _____ese_____ *(that)* libro.

Ana Mari   ¿Y (5) _____estas_____ *(these)* plumas de colores?

Sofía   Ay, de (6) _____esas_____ *(those)* plumas necesito dos paquetes.

H. Voy a comprar… Sofía is shopping for school supplies. Fill in her list with the appropriate forms of the demonstrative adjectives for each column.

Voy a comprar…

1. ___este___ libro de dibujo
2. ___estos___ lápices
3. ___estas___ plumas
4. ___esta___ mochila
5. ___este___ diccionario

No necesito…

6. ___esos___ papeles
7. ___ese___ mapa
8. ___esas___ banderitas
9. ___esa___ calculadora
10. ___esos___ cuadernos

Gramática 2   **Asking for information**
                • Interrogative words

I. Preguntas y respuestas. Provide the appropriate interrogative expressions and answer the questions.   Answers will vary.

1. ¿ ___Cómo___ te llamas?   Me llamo _____.
2. ¿ ___De dónde___ eres?   Soy de _____.
3. ¿ ___Dónde___ estudias?   En la universidad de _____.
4. ¿ ___Qué materias___ estudias?   Español y _____.
5. ¿ ___Cuántos___ hermanos tienes?   Tengo _____.
6. ¿ ___Cómo___ es tu profesor(a)?   Es muy _____.
7. ¿ ___Quiénes___ son tus amigos?   Mis amigos son _____.
8. ¿ ___Cuál___ es tu teléfono?   Es el _____.
9. ¿ ___Por qué___ estudias español?   Porque _____.
10. ¿ ___A qué hora___ es tu clase de español?   Es a las _____ de la _____.

J. Una entrevista. You would like to know more about one of your classmates. Write four questions you might ask if you were to interview them. Answers will vary.

1. _____
2. _____
3. _____
4. _____

Para terminar

K. Mi persona favorita. On a separate piece of paper, write a diary entry describing the person you like/admire the most. Explain why he/she is your favorite person: **Es mi persona favorita porque** *(because)*…. Include the following information. Answers will vary.

- name
- age
- favorite activities

- where he/she is from
- physical appearance and personality
- occupation

Start like this: **Querido diario: Mi persona favorita se llama...**

L. El talento latino. Read the questions, then read the following articles and answer the questions.

Jennifer López: Una estrella puertorriqueña

1. ¿De dónde son los padres de Jennifer? Son de Puerto Rico. _____

2. ¿Cuántas hermanas tiene? ¿Qué profesiones tienen sus hermanas? _____
   Tiene dos hermanas. Su hermana menor es D.J. y su hermana mayor es maestra de música.

3. ¿Cómo es Jennifer? Answers will vary. _____

4. ¿En qué idioma canta? Canta en inglés y en español. _____

> Jennifer López nació en el Bronx, Nueva York. Sus padres son puertorriqueños, originarios de la ciudad de Ponce. Jennifer tiene una hermana menor, que es D. J. en una radiodifusora en Nueva York, y una hermana mayor, que es maestra de música, es casada y tiene un hijo. Jennifer tomó clases de baile desde los seis años. Ella y sus hermanas hacían presentaciones "artísticas" para la familia en su apartamento de Nueva York. La carrera artística de Jennifer se establece cuando hace la película *Selena*. Su belleza física, típicamente latina, su talento artístico y su ritmo musical latino la hacen famosa. Poco tiempo después graba un disco que llega a tener ventas de más de un millón. Ella ahora canta en español y en inglés. Por el momento, es la actriz y cantante latina más conocida y mejor pagada *(highest–paid)* en Estados Unidos. Dos de sus películas son *Enough* y *Maid in Manhattan*.

Salma Hayek: Una estrella mexicana

1. ¿De dónde es Salma? <u>Es de México.</u>
2. ¿Cómo es? <u>Es morena, tiene grandes ojos cafés y mide 5'2".</u>
3. ¿De dónde son sus abuelos? <u>Sus abuelos paternos son del Líbano.</u>
4. Según Salma, ¿qué es lo más importante para estar guapa? <u>La felicidad.</u>
5. ¿Cuál es su mejor película? <u>Su mejor película es *Frida*.</u>

Lo más importante en una relación es aceptar a la gente como es.
                                                                    –Salma Hayek

Esta bella actriz mexicana tiene 33 años, es morena, tiene unos grandes ojos cafés y mide solamente 5' 2". Sus abuelos paternos son del Líbano y su mamá es mexicana. Sus más recientes películas en Estados Unidos incluyen *The Hunchback of Notre Dame* para la televisión, *Fools Rush In* con Matthew Perry, *54*, de la famosa discoteca neoyorquina, *Studio 54* y *Dogma*. En una entrevista reciente, Hayek dijo: "Uno de los ingredientes imprescindibles para estar guapa es la felicidad." La mejor actuación de Salma es en la película *Frida*. La actriz trabajó siete años para lograr[1] que filmaran la película.

[1]*to achieve*

M. Una miniprueba para terminar. Complete the following communicative tasks to test your knowledge of the content of the chapter.

1. Ask Sofía:
   - a. to describe her family.
   - b. how old her brother is.
   - c. where her grandparents are from.

2. Ask Adriana:
   - d. when she works.
   - e. if her children clean their rooms.
   - f. when she usually gets home.

3. Ask Wayne and Ramón:
   - g. if they get goods grades.
   - h. who does the laundry in their house.
   - i. if they use the computer.

4. Tell the characters:
   - j. what your typical day is like.
   - k. something you do on the weekends.
   - l. something about your family.

a. <u>¿Cómo es tu familia?</u>

b. <u>¿Cuántos años tiene tu hermano?</u>

c. <u>¿De dónde son tus abuelos?</u>

d. <u>¿A qué hora trabaja?</u>

e. <u>¿Sus hijos limpian su cuarto?</u>

f. <u>¿A qué hora llega generalmente a su casa?</u>

g. <u>¿Sacan buenas notas?</u>

h. <u>¿Quién lava la ropa en su casa?</u>

i. <u>¿Usan la computadora?</u>

j. <u>Answers will vary.</u>

k. <u>Answers will vary.</u>

l. <u>Answers will vary.</u>

Episodio

Comprensión

A. Perrolandia.

Audio CD-ROM

Parte 1. You will hear a radio ad. Listen and mark the statements as **cierto** or **falso**.

Banco de palabras			
blanco	negro	peludo	raza
white	black	furry	breed

	Cierto	Falso
1. Perrolandia tiene una gran selección de perros, gatos y pájaros para toda la familia.	☐	☑
2. Para las madres, se sugiere *(they suggest)* un perro pequeño, cariñoso y obediente.	☑	☐
3. Para los padres, se sugiere un perro tonto, perezoso, gordo y grande.	☐	☑
4. Para los niños, se sugiere un perro pequeño, bonito y blanco.	☐	☑

Parte 2. All of the adjectives in the list can be used to describe dogs. First, repeat the adjectives after the speaker to practice their pronunciation. You will then hear the radio ad from **Parte 1** again. As you listen, check off the adjectives you hear in the ad.

✓ adorables   ____ gordos   ✓ peludos

✓ blancos   ✓ grandes   ✓ pequeños

____ bonitos   ✓ listos   ____ perezosos

✓ cariñosos   ✓ negros   ✓ trabajadores

✓ divertidos   ✓ obedientes   ____ tontos

B. Una respuesta lógica. You will hear six questions. Look over the possible answers provided, and select the most logical response for each question. You will hear each question twice.

Audio CD-ROM

1. a. Soy inteligente.   b. Estoy en mi casa.   ⓒ Muy bien, gracias.
2. ⓐ Soy de Los Ángeles.   b. Estoy en la clase.   c. Soy estudiante.
3. ⓐ Es bajo y chistoso.   b. Está muy bien.   c. Está en su oficina.
4. a. Tengo muchos amigos.   ⓑ Tengo veinte años.   c. No tengo dinero.
5. a. Es un cuaderno.   b. Es casado.   ⓒ Es mi tío.
6. a. Me gusta más la biología. ⓑ Tomo cinco clases.   c. Son muy difíciles.

Pronunciación

La *l*, la *ll* y la *y*. The Spanish **l** (ele) is generally a lighter sound than the English *l*. Repeat these words and sentences after the speaker.

lunes	**biología**	**biblioteca**	**papel**	**Luis lee el libro.**

The Spanish **ll** (elle) sounds very much like an English *y* in most dialects.

llevar	**silla**	**pollo**	**llegar**	**ella**

The Spanish **y** (i griega) has the same sound as *i* when it stands alone or at the end of a word.

y	**hoy**	**hay**	**soy**	**estoy**

When preceding a vowel, the Spanish **y** sounds like English *y*.

yo	**ya**	**yerno**	**yoga**

In some areas, **y** and **ll** are pronounced like the *s* in *measure*.

yo	**ya**	**llover**	**llegar**

In many Latin American regions, when **y** and **ll** begin a word, they have the sound of the English *j* in *jam* and *jelly*.

yo	**ya**	**llover**	**llegar**

Más escenas de la vida

You will hear a conversation among Sofía, Manolo, and Carlos. Listen and then complete activities **A** and **B**. You will hear the conversation twice.

A. ¿Quién? Indicate who the following statements describe: Carlos **(C)**, Manolo **(M)**, or Sofía **(S).**

_M, S_ 1. Son compañeros de Adriana.

_C_ 2. Es moreno y guapo.

_M_ 3. Cree que Carlos es serio y reservado.

_C_ 4. No quiere hablar con Sofía.

_C_ 5. Es grosero y antipático.

_S_ 6. Hace muchas preguntas.

B. Responde. Write the answers to the following questions.

1. ¿Cómo es Carlos? _Es alto, moreno, joven y guapo._

2. ¿Qué clase toman con Adriana? _Toman una clase de cálculo con Adriana._

3. ¿Qué trabajo tiene Carlos? _Es piloto._

4. ¿Qué le gusta a Sofía? _Le gusta viajar._

5. ¿Por qué Carlos no habla con Sofía? _No habla con Sofía porque es antipático y grosero._

Episodio 7

Escenas de la vida: ¿Qué van a hacer el sábado?

Video
CD-ROM

A. ¡Mira cuánto puedes entender! Listen to the conversation or watch the video to complete the tasks that correspond to each picture.

Audio
CD-ROM

1. Indica qué nota creen que van a sacar en el primer examen de cálculo.

F   pasar   A

2. Indica qué tiene ganas de hacer Ramón el sábado y por qué Sofía no puede hacer nada el sábado con Ramón. ¿Qué tiene que hacer Sofía?

☑ **Tiene ganas de hacer un picnic.**

☑ **Tiene que trabajar.**
☐ **Tiene que limpiar su cuarto.**
☑ **Tiene que hacer una presentación.**
☐ **Tiene que estudiar.**

☐ **Tiene ganas de ir a la biblioteca.**

Video Synopsis. After the test, Sofía, Adriana, and Manolo talk about the calculus exam. Ramón wants to plan a picnic to celebrate Wayne's birthday; Sofía suggests Sunday. Adriana tells Ramón that she spends Sunday with her family and will not be able to attend.

3. Mira los planes de Manolo; completa la hora o la actividad necesaria.

sábado	domingo
12:00 aeropuerto	¡nada!
después llevar a la	
gata al veterinario	
en la tarde trabaja	

4. ¿Qué va a hacer Adriana el domingo?

Cultura a lo vivo

Throughout the Spanish-speaking world, Sunday is considered a day to be spent with the family. Some families attend religious services and then go to a restaurant; other families visit parents and/or grandparents; still others go on outings—a picnic, a visit to a nearby town, a day at a swimming pool, a trip to the mountains, to a river, or to a park. These gatherings include family members of all ages, as well as close friends whose families may live elsewhere. Some parents feel so strongly about reserving Sunday for the family that teenage children are not allowed to go out with friends that day.

B. ¿Te diste cuenta? Escucha la conversación o mira el video otra vez para indicar quién hace estos comentarios: Sofía **(S),** Adriana **(A),** Ramón **(R)** o Manolo **(M).**

_____S_____ 1. El examen fue muy fácil.

_____A_____ 2. Para mí fue muy difícil.

_____M_____ 3. Tenemos que hacer algo divertido.

_____S_____ 4. No tengo nada que hacer el domingo.

_____A_____ 5. Los domingos paso el día con la familia.

_____R_____ 6. Todos están invitados.

B and C. Have students read activities **B** and **C;** then play the video again. Have students respond orally to the prompts.

C. ¡A responder! Contesta las preguntas.

1. ¿Quién tiene ganas de celebrar? ¿Por qué? _____

Sofía tiene ganas de celebrar porque cree que va a sacar A en el examen.

2. ¿Qué quiere organizar Ramón? ¿Por qué? _____

Ramón quiere organizar un picnic porque es el cumpleaños de Wayne.

3. ¿Qué tiene que hacer Sofía el sábado por la tarde? _____

Sofía tiene que hacer una presentación en el Club Latino.

4. ¿Qué hace Adriana los domingos? _____

Adriana pasa el día con la familia y visita a los abuelos.

Práctica adicional
Cuaderno de tareas   Video
WB pp.171–172, A–C   CD-ROM
Episodio 7

Para comunicarnos mejor

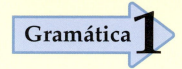 **Gramática 1**

Talking about weekend plans
- **Ir a** + [*infinitive*]
- **The personal a**

In the conversation, you heard Sofía, Ramón, and Adriana say the following:

Creo que **voy a sacar** A.   *I think I'm going to get an A.*
¿Qué **van a hacer** el sábado?   *What are you (all) going to do on Saturday?*
Vamos a visitar a los abuelos.   *We're going to visit our grandparents.*

Voy, van, and **vamos** are forms of the verb **ir** *(to go).* To talk about things and activities that are going to happen in the future, Spanish uses a form of **ir** followed by **a** and the infinitive (**-r** form) of a verb. In another conversation, the characters said the following about the things they are *going to do.*

Gramática 1. You may ask personalized questions such as ¿Vas a trabajar este fin de semana? ¿Qué programa vas a mirar hoy por la noche? ¿Cuándo vas a estudiar para el examen?

Ir a + [*infinitive*]	
Hoy **voy a llevar** a Viviana a su clase de baile.	*Today I'm going to take Viviana to her dance class.*
¿**Vas a trabajar** el domingo?	*Are you going to work on Sunday?*
Sofía **va a comprar** un regalo.	*Sofía is going to buy a present.*
El próximo domingo **vamos a celebrar** el cumpleaños de Wayne.	*Next Sunday we're going to celebrate Wayne's birthday.*
¿Qué **van a hacer** mañana? ¿Qué **vais a hacer** mañana? }	*What are you going to do tomorrow?* (pl.)
Todos **van a ir** al parque.	*They are all going to go to the park.*

1. Notice that the verb **llevar** *(to take something or someone somewhere)* is followed by **a** (**llevar a Viviana**). This is called the personal **a** (la *a* personal), and it has no English equivalent. You need to include **a** after verbs that have a person or a pet as direct object.

   La familia de Adriana siempre visita **a** los abuelos los domingos.
   Los lunes Adriana **lleva a** su hija a la clase de baile folclórico.
   El sábado Manolo **lleva a** la gata al veterinario, ¿verdad?
   Escucho **a** mis padres.

2. To talk about your plans, use these expressions:

Expresiones de tiempo			
esta noche	*tonight*	**el próximo sábado**	*next Saturday*
hoy	*today*	**la próxima semana**	*next week*
mañana	*tomorrow*	**el año que viene**	*next year*

PRÁCTICA

A. ¿Qué vas a hacer el próximo fin de semana?

Parte 1. Indica si vas a hacer *(to do)* las siguientes actividades. Answers will vary.

	Sí	No
1. El sábado por la mañana voy a estudiar.	☐	☐
2. Voy a trabajar todo el fin de semana.	☐	☐
3. Voy a lavar mi coche.	☐	☐
4. Voy a visitar a mi abuela.	☐	☐
5. Mi papá y yo vamos a jugar golf.	☐	☐
6. Mi compañero/a y yo vamos a ir al supermercado.	☐	☐
7. El domingo voy a mirar la televisión todo el día.	☐	☐
8. Voy a escribir *(to write)* una composición.	☐	☐

> **Learning Strategy: Getting the most out of class time**
> Class time is invaluable. To maximize your learning, you must actively participate during class sessions. Try to speak only Spanish during class activities.

Parte 2. Convierte las frases de la **Parte 1** en preguntas. Después entrevista a tu compañero/a.

> **Modelo** El sábado por la mañana voy a estudiar.
> **¿Vas a estudiar el sábado por la mañana?**

B. ¿Qué van a hacer? Usa las fotos para escribir lo que *(what)* van a hacer los personajes la próxima semana.

1. Sofía y Manolo...

van a ir a la librería.

2. Adriana...

va a trabajar.

3. Nosotros...

vamos a estudiar.

4. Manolo...

va a bailar con Sofía.

5. Sofía...

va a lavar la ropa.

6. Ellos...

van a tocar la guitarra.

C. Una entrevista. ¿Qué van a hacer tus compañeros esta noche, mañana por la mañana y el fin de semana? Escribe los nombres y las actividades. Answers will vary.

C. Allow five minutes for students to interview two different classmates. Check results with the class. ¿Qué va a hacer… esta noche? ¿Y tú?, etc.

| Modelo | —¿Qué vas a hacer esta noche? |
| | —Voy a estudiar. |

Práctica adicional

Cuaderno de tareas
WB pp.172–174, D–G

Gramática 2 — Expressing obligations and desires
• Tener que, tener ganas de

You have used the verb **tener** to express ownership and possession.

Tenemos muy poco dinero.	*We have very little money.*
Tengo cuatro perros.	*I have four dogs.*
¿Tienes coche?	*Do you have a car?*

In every language, many common verb phrases have meanings independent of the verbs that comprise them. In English, these combinations are called *verb constructions*; in Spanish, they are called **construcciones verbales.** For example, when you use *have* as an independent verb, as in *I have a new car, have* means *to own* or *to possess.* When you use *have* in combination with an infinitive, as in *I have to buy a new car, have* does not mean *to possess.* The combination *have* + [*infinitive*] expresses an obligation, something you must do.

1. In Spanish, obligation is expressed by the verb construction **tener que** + [*infinitive*]. In this episode, you heard these statements containing **tener que**:

| **Tengo que trabajar** por la mañana. | *I have to work in the morning.* |
| **Tenemos que hacer** algo divertido. | *We have to do something fun.* |

2. Another verb construction you heard is **tener ganas de** + [*infinitive*]. Use this construction to express what you feel or don't feel like doing.

| **Tengo ganas de celebrar.** | *I feel like celebrating.* |
| **No tenemos ganas de estudiar.** | *We don't feel like studying.* |

¡Fíjate!

Tener que + [*infinitive*] expresses an obligation or duty.
Tener ganas de + [*infinitive*] expresses a desire to do something.

PRÁCTICA

D. ¿Obligación, deseo o acción? Escucha los comentarios para indicar si son obligaciones, deseos o acciones futuras.

Audio CD-ROM

	Obligación	Deseo	Acción
1.	☐	✓	☐
2.	✓	☐	☐
3.	☐	☐	✓

	Obligación	Deseo	Acción
4.	☐	☐	✓
5.	☐	✓	☐
6.	✓	☐	☐

Instructor's Resources
• Worktext CD
• IRM: Tapescript

Script: See the **Instructor's Resource Manual** for the script to this activity.

E. ¿Y ustedes, qué tienen que hacer? Completa las frases lógicamente. Answers will vary.

> **Modelo** Los jueves mi hermana tiene que **lavar la ropa.**

1. Los lunes tengo que _____

2. En la clase de español todos tenemos que _____

3. Los sábados mis amigos y yo tenemos ganas de _____

4. Los domingos no tengo ganas de _____

5. Yo (no) _____ hacer la tarea.

6. Mi mejor amigo _____

F. Las actividades de nuestros amigos. Escribe la expresión necesaria para completar los comentarios. Después indica si son **ciertos** o **falsos.** Usa **tener que, tener ganas (de)** o **tener.** Answers will vary.

	Cierto	Falso
1. Sofía dice: "Yo _____tengo que_____ hacer una presentación en el Club Latino."	✔	☐
2. Adriana _____tiene_____ mucho trabajo en casa.	☐	✔
3. Manolo _____tiene que_____ llevar a Jorge al aeropuerto.	✔	☐
4. Los chicos _____tienen ganas_____ de ir al parque después de la clase.	✔	☐
5. Y tú, ¿_____tienes ganas_____ de ir a una fiesta este fin de semana?	☐	☐
6. Sí, pero (yo) _____tengo que_____ trabajar el domingo.	☐	☐

G. ¿Por qué no quieres ir? Explícale a un(a) compañero/a por qué no quieres ir *(want to go)* a esos lugares. Usa **no tengo ganas de** con los siguientes verbos. Answers will vary.

nadar	hacer ejercicio	estudiar	comprar nada
correr	jugar tenis	leer libros	escribir correo electrónico *(e-mail)*

> **Modelo** a las canchas de tenis
> —¿Quieres ir a las canchas de tenis?
> —No, porque hoy no tengo ganas de jugar tenis.

1. al gimnasio
2. a la biblioteca
3. al laboratorio de computadoras

4. al centro comercial
5. al parque
6. a la piscina

Banco de palabras

Quiero...	**nadar**
I want...	*to swim*
Quieres...	**correr**
You want...	*to run*

H. Lo siento, pero no puedo. Imagina que un(a) amigo/a te invita a salir, pero tú no tienes ganas de salir. ¡Inventa excusas! Answers will vary.

> **Modelo** ir al cine/trabajar
> —¿Quieres ir al cine el próximo sábado?
> —Lo siento, pero no puedo porque tengo que trabajar el próximo sábado.

1. ir al parque/hacer la tarea
2. ir al centro comercial/lavar la ropa
3. ir al concierto de Maná/estudiar para un examen
4. ir a la cafetería/regresar a casa temprano
5. ir a un restaurante a comer/llevar a mi hermano al doctor
6. mirar una película en mi casa/leer un libro para mi clase de historia

> **Banco de palabras**
>
> **No puedo**
> *I can't*
>
> **¿Puedes...**
> *Can you...?*
>
> **Lo siento**
> *I'm sorry*

 I. Preguntas personales. Contesta las preguntas. Después entrevista a un(a) compañero/a. Answers will vary.

1. ¿Qué tienes que hacer después de las clases?
2. ¿Qué tienes que hacer los fines de semana?
3. ¿Cuándo tienes ganas de estudiar? ¿Vas a estudiar esta noche? ¿Vas a mirar la tele?
4. ¿Qué tienes ganas de hacer este fin de semana?

Práctica adicional		
Cuaderno de tareas WB pp.174–175, H–J LM pp.177–178, A–B, Pron.	Audio CD-ROM Episodio 7	Website vistahigher learning.com

Invitación a **Colombia**

Del álbum de
Sofía

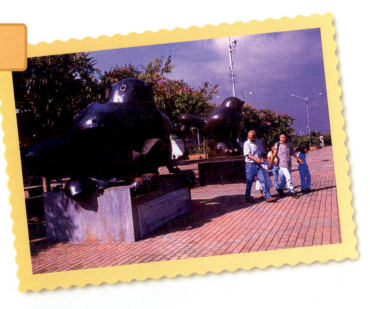

Colombia tiene casi tres veces el tamaño de California y tiene aproximadamente 41 millones de habitantes. Es un bello país que ha dado (*has given*) al mundo renombradas personalidades de fama mundial, como Gabriel García Márquez (Premio Nobel de Literatura) y Francisco Botero (pintor, escultor). Además de artistas e intelectuales, produce el mejor café del mundo, y por supuesto, a la cantautora (*singer-songwriter*) Shakira.

Actividades comunicativas

A. Los planes para el fin de semana.

Instrucciones para **Estudiante 1**

First, fill in the column marked **Yo** to indicate what you are going to do the days and times indicated on the grid. Then talk to your partner in order to fill in the column marked **Mi compañero/a.** Finally, interview each other in order to fill in the empty boxes in the last two columns; you each have the information that the other needs.   *Answers will vary.*

A. Review the instructions with students to be sure they know how to complete the activity. Have pairs who finish early switch roles. Allow five to eight minutes.

Modelo   **¿Qué va a hacer Sofía el sábado por la tarde?**

¡Fíjate!

Remember not to conjugate the verbs that follow **ir a**. Always use the infinitive **(-r)** form.

	Yo	Mi compañero/a	Sofía	Ramón y su familia
El viernes por la noche				
El sábado por la mañana				
El sábado por la tarde				
El domingo				

A. Los planes para el fin de semana.

Instrucciones para **Estudiante 2**

First, fill in the column marked **Yo** to indicate what you are going to do the days and times indicated on the grid. Then talk to your partner in order to fill in the column marked **Mi compañero/a**. Finally, interview each other in order to fill in the empty boxes in the last two columns; you each will have the information that the other needs. Answers will vary.

Modelo ¿Qué va a hacer Sofía el sábado por la tarde?

	Yo	Mi compañero/a	Sofía	Ramón y su familia
El viernes por la noche				
El sábado por la mañana				
El sábado por la tarde				
El domingo				

B. En imágenes.

Instrucciones para **Estudiante 1**

Use the first letter of the verb and the drawings to create logical sentences stating what you and the characters are going to do, have to do, or feel like doing during the weekend. Concentrate on the actions in the drawings. When you know what your sentences are, read them to your partner, who will check the answer key to see if your sentences are correct. Take turns. Answers are in the book.

¡Fíjate!

Try to interpret the whole sentence before attempting to give your partner the answer.

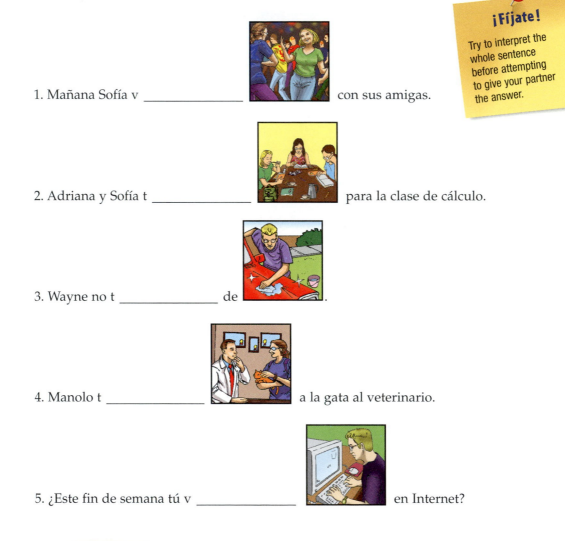

1. Mañana Sofía v _____ con sus amigas.

2. Adriana y Sofía t _____ para la clase de cálculo.

3. Wayne no t _____ de .

4. Manolo t _____ a la gata al veterinario.

5. ¿Este fin de semana tú v _____ en Internet?

Las respuestas de tu compañero/a:

1. Adriana **tiene que trabajar** todo el día.
2. Los hermanos de Ramón **tienen ganas de** ir a la **piscina** con sus amigos.
3. Sofía **va a tomar el autobús** porque su coche no funciona.
4. Ana Mari y yo **vamos a mirar** un programa de terror.
5. ¿Tú **tienes que comprar** muchos libros para tus clases como Manolo y Sofía?

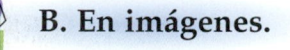

B. En imágenes.

Instrucciones para **Estudiante 2**

Use the first letter of the verb and the drawings to create logical sentences stating what you and the characters are going to do, have to do, or feel like doing during the weekend. Concentrate on the actions in the drawings. When you know what your sentences are, read them to your partner, who will check the answer key to see if your sentences are correct. Take turns. *Answers are in the book.*

¡Fíjate! Try to interpret the whole sentence before attempting to give your partner the answer.

1. Adriana t_____ todo el día.

2. Los hermanos de Ramón t_____ ir a la _____ con sus amigos.

3. Sofía v_____ porque su coche no funciona.

4. Ana Mari y yo v_____ un programa de terror.

5. ¿Tú t_____ muchos libros para tus clases como Manolo y Sofía?

Las respuestas de tu compañero/a:
1. Mañana Sofía **va a bailar** con sus amigas.
2. Adriana y Sofía **tienen que estudiar** para la clase de cálculo.
3. Wayne no **tiene ganas de lavar el coche.**
4. Manolo **tiene que llevar** a la gata al veterinario.
5. ¿Este fin de semana tú **vas a buscar información** en Internet?

 **C. ¡Mucho gusto!**

Instrucciones para **Estudiante 1**

Interview a classmate that you have not had the opportunity to get to know. Find out:

C. You may want to ask students to prepare the questions the day before, as homework.

- your partner's name
- if your partner has brothers and sisters; their names, ages, and physical descriptions
- if they work; where, what days
- if they use a computer; what type **(tipo)**
- if they like to watch TV; what programs
- what your partner usually feels like doing on weekends

You will need to report some of the information you learned about your partner to the rest of the class. Take notes.   Answers will vary.

C. ¡Mucho gusto!

Instrucciones para **Estudiante 2**

Interview a classmate that you have not had the opportunity to get to know. Find out:

- your partner's name
- if your partner has a special friend; their name, age, physical description
- how many classes they take, which ones, what days
- if your partner likes to listen to music; what kind
- what they have to do after school
- what they are going to do this weekend

You will need to report some of the information you learned about your partner to the rest of the class. Take notes.   Answers will vary.

La correspondencia

El correo: Una invitación para Wayne. Lee las preguntas, luego lee el correo electrónico que recibe Wayne y después contesta las preguntas.

1. ¿Quién invita a Wayne? Lupita invita a Wayne.
2. ¿Qué va a hacer Wayne el sábado por la mañana? Va a/tiene que reparar el coche de un amigo.
3. ¿Adónde va a llevar a su sobrino? Va a llevar a su sobrino a un juego de hockey.
4. ¿Qué planes tiene Wayne para el próximo sábado? Wayne no tiene planes para el próximo sábado.

From: Wayne Reilly <wreilly@micorreo.com>
To: "Guadalupe Amaré" <gamare@micorreo.com>
Re: Invitación para el sábado

Hola Lupita,

Gracias por la invitación. Me gustaría ir pero no puedo. ¡Tengo muchísimas cosas que hacer! Por la mañana tengo que reparar el coche de un amigo, porque no puede ir a trabajar sin[1] coche. Por la tarde necesito estudiar, porque el lunes tengo un examen de física que va a ser muy difícil y tengo que sacar A. A las siete de la tarde, voy a llevar a mi sobrino a un juego de hockey. Así que muchas gracias de todas maneras[2].

No tengo planes para el próximo fin de semana. ¿Podemos organizar algo[3]? ¡Que te diviertas mucho!

Wayne

[1]*without* [2]**de todas...** *anyway* [3]*something*

En papel: Lo siento, pero no puedo. A friend sends you an e-mail message inviting you to a crafts fair (**una feria**) this weekend. You have a lot to do and cannot go. Write a reply explaining your weekend plans. Use Wayne's letter as a model, paying special attention to the way that Wayne politely declines the invitation. Answers will vary.

Video
CD-ROM

¡A ver de nuevo!

Parte 1. Escribe de lo que se trató este episodio en tus propias palabras.

Answers will vary.

Audio
CD-ROM

Instructor's Resources
• VHS Video
• Worktext CD
• IRM: Videoscript

¡Fíjate!

Your summary must include everybody's plans for the weekend. Be as specific as you can.

Ramón quiere organizar un picnic para Wayne porque...

Parte 2. Now compare your summary with a classmate's and add any information you may have left out.

Práctica adicional

Cuaderno de tareas	Audio CD-ROM	Website
WB pp.175–176, K–L LM p.178, A–B	Episodio 7	vistahigher learning.com

Vocabulario del Episodio 7

Instructor's Resources
• Testing program
• Website

Ir a + [*infinitive*]	*to be going to +* [*infinitive*]
Tener ganas de + [*infinitive*]	*to feel like...*
Tener que + [*infinitive*]	*to have to...*
Llevar a + [*person*]	*to bring* (someone or an animal)
Llevar + [*object*]	*to bring* (something inanimate)

Expresiones de tiempo

esta noche	*tonight*	**el próximo sábado**	*next Saturday*
hoy	*today*	**la próxima semana**	*next week*
mañana	*tomorrow*	**el año que viene**	*next year*

▼ Vocabulario personal

Write all the words that you need to know in Spanish so that you can better talk about your own obligations and weekend plans.

170

¡A escribir!

Episodio 7

Escenas de la vida: ¿Qué van a hacer el sábado?

Video CD-ROM

A. ¡A ver cuánto entendiste! See how much of the **Escena** you understood by matching the Spanish sentences with their English equivalents.

Después del examen

__c__	1. ¿Qué les parece a las dos?	a. I spend the day with my family.
__f__	2. Está solo y es su cumpleaños.	b. I don't have to do anything on Sunday.
__h__	3. ¡Todos están invitados!	c. How does two o'clock sound to you?
__a__	4. Paso el día con la familia.	d. We have to do something fun this weekend, ok?
__g__	5. Y usted, ¿puede ir?	e. I want to organize a picnic in the park.
__d__	6. Tenemos que hacer algo divertido este fin de semana, ¿no?	f. He's alone and it's his birthday.
__e__	7. Quiero organizar un picnic en el parque.	g. Can you go?
__b__	8. No tengo nada que hacer el domingo.	h. Everyone is invited!

Video CD-ROM

B. ¿Qué van a hacer el sábado? Use the expressions to complete the conversation.

van a	vamos	picnic
divertido	fácil	cumpleaños
tengo ganas	voy a	difícil

Sofía   ¡El examen fue muy (1) _____fácil_____, ¿verdad? Creo que

(2) _____voy a_____ sacar A. (3)_____Tengo ganas_____ de celebrar.

Adriana   Para mí fue muy (4) _____difícil_____. Tengo que estudiar mucho más.

Manolo   No hay que ser pesimistas. Tenemos que hacer algo (5) _____divertido_____

este fin de semana, ¿no?

Ramón   ¿Qué (6)_____van a_____ hacer el sábado? Quiero organizar un

(7)_____picnic_____ en el parque para Wayne. Es su

(8) _____cumpleaños_____.

C. ¿A quién se refieren? Indicate whether the statements refer to Manolo (**M**), Sofía (**S**), Adriana (**A**), or Ramón (**R**).

<u>M</u> 1. Tiene que llevar a Jorge al aeropuerto.

<u>A</u> 2. Pasa el domingo con la familia.

<u>R</u> 3. Quiere organizar un picnic para Wayne.

<u>M</u> 4. Tiene que llevar a la gata al veterinario.

<u>M, S</u> 5. Tienen que trabajar el sábado.

<u>R</u> 6. Invita a todos al parque.

<u>S</u> 7. Tiene ganas de celebrar.

<u>A</u> 8. Tiene que estudiar más.

Gramática 1

Talking about weekend plans
- **ir a** + [*infinitive*]
- **The personal a**

D. Las actividades de la próxima semana. Describe what Sofía, her friends, and you are going to do next week.

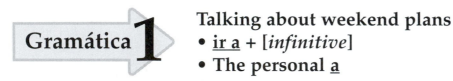

Modelo   Mis hijos y yo

Mis hijos y yo vamos a visitar a los abuelos el domingo.

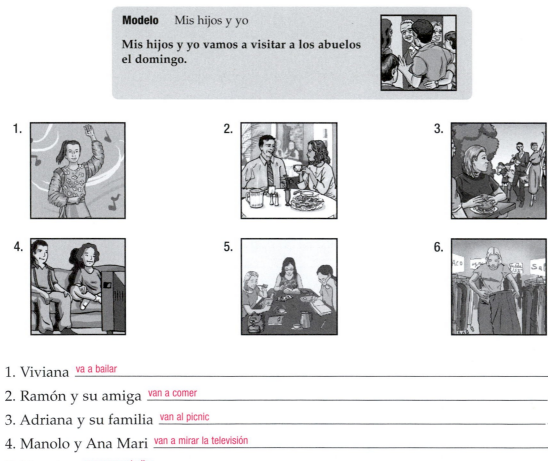

1. Viviana _va a bailar_____.

2. Ramón y su amiga _van a comer_____.

3. Adriana y su familia _van al picnic_____.

4. Manolo y Ana Mari _van a mirar la televisión_____.

5. Nosotros _vamos a estudiar_____.

6. Y tú, ¿ _vas a comprar ropa_____?

E. **Los planes de Sofía y Manolo.** Sofía and Manolo are making plans for the weekend. Look at the illustrations and describe what they are going to do on Saturday and Sunday. Sequence their activities in a cohesive paragraph. Use phrases like **por la mañana/tarde/noche, después, más tarde, también,** etc.

Answers will vary.

_____

_____

_____

_____

_____

_____

_____

_____

F. **¿Y tus planes?** Now describe your own weekend plans. Be specific and thorough.

Answers will vary.

_____

_____

_____

_____

_____

_____

_____

_____

G. ¡En español! How would you say the following in Spanish?

1. Are you going to work next weekend?
   ¿Vas a trabajar el próximo fin de semana?

2. No, I am going to study for (**para**) a test.
   No, voy a estudiar para un examen.

3. I am going to visit my grandmother in Utah next week, so (**entonces**) I am not going to be (**estar**) in class.
   Voy a visitar a mi abuela en Utah la próxima semana, entonces no voy a estar en clase.

4. But (**pero**) you are going to get an F.
   Pero vas a sacar F.

5. No, I am going to talk to the teacher tonight.
   No, voy a hablar con el/la profesor(a) esta noche.

Gramática 2　**Expressing obligations and desires**
• Tener que, tener ganas de

H. Las obligaciones. Describe the activities that you and the people you know usually have to do during the weekend. Answers will vary.

> **Modelo**　Mi hijo **tiene que lavar su ropa**.

1. Yo _____.
2. Mi papá _____.
3. Mi mamá _____.
4. Mis hermanos/as _____.
5. Mi mejor amigo/a _____.

I. ¿Qué (no) tienen ganas de hacer? Indicate what the people feel like or don't feel like doing, according to the place or activity indicated. Answers will vary.

> **Modelo**　Mi novia va a ir a la biblioteca.　**Tiene ganas de estudiar.**
> Yo voy a quedarme (*stay*) en casa.　**No tengo ganas de visitar a mis amigos.**

1. Voy a ir al centro comercial (*mall*). _____
2. Mis amigos y yo vamos a poner (*turn on*) el radio. _____
3. Tú no vas a salir (*go out*) esta noche. _____
4. Mis padres van a ir a la tienda de videos. _____
5. Sofía y Ana Mari van a ir a una discoteca. _____
6. Ramón va a usar la computadora. _____

J. ¿Por qué no pueden salir? *(Why can't they go out?)* Explain why Ana Mari's brothers cannot go out to play on the days and at the times indicated.

> **Modelo** lunes
> **El lunes a las doce tienen que ir a la biblioteca.**

semana 36 — **AGOSTO/SEPTIEMBRE**

31 lunes	1 martes	2 miércoles
8	8	8
9	9	9
10	10	10
11	11	11
12 biblioteca	12	12
1	1	1
2	2	2
3	3	3
4	4	4
5	5	5
6 lavar el coche	6	6
7 de Ramón	7 estudiar	7
8	8	8

3 jueves	4 viernes	5 sábado
8	8	lavar la ropa
9	9	
10	10	
11	11	
12	12	**6 domingo**
1	1	
2	2 comprar	visitar a los
3	3 libros	abuelos
4	4	
5	5	
6	6	
7 limpiar el cuarto	7	
8	8	

1. El lunes a las seis de la tarde/en la tarde tienen que lavar el coche de Ramón.

2. El martes a las siete de la noche/en la noche tienen que estudiar.

3. El jueves a las siete de la noche/en la noche tienen que limpiar el cuarto.

4. El viernes a las dos de la tarde/en la tarde tienen que comprar libros.

5. El sábado tienen que lavar la ropa.

6. El domingo tienen que visitar a los abuelos.

Para terminar

K. Una invitación. Read the e-mail message Sofía's mother sent to her friend Liz. Then answer the questions.

From: Diana Blasio
To: Liz Margolis
Re: Invitación al teatro

Hola, Liz:

Gracias por tu invitación al teatro esta noche, pero no voy a poder acompañarte. Tengo que trabajar hasta las cinco de la tarde y después voy a llevar a Lalo al doctor. No está bien. No tiene ganas de comer nada desde hace varios días y también tiene un poco de fiebre. Vamos a ver qué dice el doctor.

Tengo muchas ganas de hablar contigo. ¿Tienes planes mañana por la noche? Llámame.

Diana

1. Who is inviting Diana? Liz invita a Diana. _____

2. Where is she invited? Al teatro. _____

3. Why can't she go? Tiene que trabajar hasta las cinco de la tarde y después tiene que llevar a Lalo al doctor. _____

4. What is wrong with Lalo? No quiere comer nada y tiene un poco de fiebre. _____

L. Para resumir la historia. Answer the questions about the **Escena**, based on the images.

1. ¿Quién va a sacar A en el examen?

   Sofía va a sacar A en el examen. _____

2. ¿Quién tiene que estudiar mucho más?

   Adriana tiene que estudiar más. _____

3. ¿Qué tiene ganas de hacer Ramón? ¿Por qué?

   Tiene ganas de hacer un picnic en el parque para Wayne, porque es su cumpleaños. _____

4. ¿Por qué Adriana no puede *(can't)* ir al parque?

   Los domingos los pasa con la familia y van a visitar a los abuelos. _____

5. ¿Qué tiene que hacer Manolo el sábado?

   Tiene que llevar a Jorge al aeropuerto, tiene que llevar a la gata al veterinario y tiene que trabajar. _____

6. ¿Quiénes van a ir al picnic?

   Wayne, Ramón, Sofía y Manolo van al picnic. _____

¡A escuchar!

Episodio **7**

Comprensión

Audio CD-ROM

A. ¿Qué van a hacer?

Parte 1. Repeat the activities in the list after the speaker to practice their pronunciation and to familiarize yourself with them.

bailar	escuchar música	limpiar la casa	sacar malas notas
comprar comida	estudiar	llegar tarde	visitar a...
descansar	hablar por teléfono	mirar la tele	

Parte 2. You will now hear ten statements. React to them by saying or asking what the people are going to do, using the cues provided and activities from the list in **Parte 1.** Repeat the correct answers after the speaker.

Modelo	You hear:	**Ramón tiene un examen de geología mañana.**
	You say:	**Ramón va a estudiar.**

1. Adriana...
2. Sofía y sus amigos...
3. Yo...
4. (Nosotras)...
5. Manolo...
6. ¿(Tú)...?
7. (Nosotros)...
8. ¿(Tú)...?
9. Lalo...
10. Sofía y su mamá...

B. ¡Vamos al aeropuerto! You will hear a conversation between Manolo and his roommate Jorge as they prepare to leave for the airport. Listen and choose the best options to summarize the conversation. **¡Atención!** Items 2 and 5 have multiple responses. You will hear the conversation twice.

1. Jorge va a visitar a su familia en…
   (a.) Miami   b. Los Ángeles   c. Nueva York

Banco de palabras

llamar	maletas	poner	escribir
to call	suitcases	to put, place	to write
el vuelo sale	**pesado**	**regalos**	
the flight leaves	heavy	gifts	

2. Jorge tiene mucha familia allí. Los parientes que menciona son sus…
   (a.) hermanas   b. nietos   (c.) padres   (d.) primos   e. sobrinos   (f.) tíos

3. El vuelo sale…
   a. temprano   b. tarde   (c.) a tiempo

4. Jorge tiene que…
   (a.) empacar las maletas   b. llamar por teléfono a sus padres   c. comprar un boleto

5. En la maleta, Jorge lleva…
   (a.) computadora   b. libros   c. guitarra   (d.) regalos   (e.) ropa

Pronunciación

La *t* y la *d*. To pronounce the Spanish **t (te)**, touch the tip of the tongue to the back of your upper front teeth and do not emit a puff of air. Repeat these words and sentences after the speaker.

Tito	treinta	patata	**Tomás te prestó el motor a ti.**
total	tomar	motor	**Hay treinta y tres técnicos en total.**

When **d (de)** occurs as an initial sound, or after **n (ene)** or **l (ele)**, it is similar to English *d*, except that the tip of the tongue rests against the back of the upper front teeth. Repeat these words after the speaker.

Donaldo	doce	Andrés	el dinero
Daniel	dos	donde	falda

When **d** follows a sound that is not **n** or **l**, in other words most of the time, it sounds similar to the *th* sound in English *father*. Repeat these words and sentences after the speaker.

padre	mi doctor	**Los sábados y domingos no estudio.**
cuaderno	su dinero	**Si me das tu cuaderno, te doy dos dólares.**

Más escenas de la vida

Ramón first chats with Ana Mari and then phones Manolo. Listen and then complete activities **A** and **B**. You will hear the conversation twice.

A. ¿Quién? Match the people to the activity they have to or (don't) want to do.

___d___ 1. Manolo   a. Tiene que lavar ropa.

___a___ 2. Ana Mari   b. Tiene ganas de jugar vóleibol.

___b___ 3. Ramón   c. Tienen ganas de comer y hablar.

___c___ 4. Ana Mari y Manolo   d. No tiene ganas de hacer ejercicio.

B. Responde. Write the answers to the following questions.

1. ¿Qué quiere llevar Ramón al parque?
   Quiere llevar la pelota de vóleibol al parque.

2. ¿Qué tiene Ana Mari de todas sus clases?
   Tiene tarea de todas sus clases.

3. ¿Quién tiene ganas de ver una película? (*see a movie?*)
   Ana Mari tiene ganas de ver la última película de Salma Hayek.

4. ¿Qué van a hacer en el picnic?
   Van a comer y a hablar.

Episodio 8

Escenas de la vida: Vamos al parque

Video
CD-ROM

A. ¡Mira cuánto puedes entender! Check the activities that you hear mentioned in the **Escena**.

Audio
CD-ROM

Instructor's Resources

• Overhoadc
• VHS Video
• Worktext CD
• Website
• IRM: Videoscript, Comprehensible input

Sofía y mi hermana corren en el parque.

Hace la tarea.

Después comemos en El Huarache Veloz.

No recibe regalos el día de su cumpleaños.

Lee el periódico y su correo electrónico.

Hacen ejercicio.

Salen a cenar.

Ve películas en la computadora.

Ana Mari quiere salir con Wayne.

Video Synopsis. While out with Sofía and Ana Mari, Ramón calls Wayne. He invites Wayne to go jogging in the park on Sunday, in order to get Wayne to come to his surprise party. Wayne promises to go, as long as they have lunch with Ana Mari and Sofía afterwards.

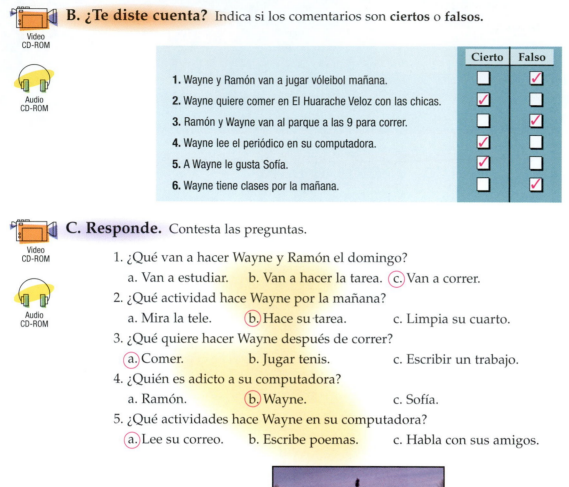

Video CD-ROM

Audio CD-ROM

B. ¿Te diste cuenta? Indica si los comentarios son **ciertos** o **falsos**.

	Cierto	Falso
1. Wayne y Ramón van a jugar vóleibol mañana.		✓
2. Wayne quiere comer en El Huarache Veloz con las chicas.	✓	
3. Ramón y Wayne van al parque a las 9 para correr.		✓
4. Wayne lee el periódico en su computadora.	✓	
5. A Wayne le gusta Sofía.	✓	
6. Wayne tiene clases por la mañana.		✓

Video CD-ROM

Audio CD-ROM

C. Responde. Contesta las preguntas.

1. ¿Qué van a hacer Wayne y Ramón el domingo?
   a. Van a estudiar.   b. Van a hacer la tarea.   (c.) Van a correr.

2. ¿Qué actividad hace Wayne por la mañana?
   a. Mira la tele.   (b.) Hace su tarea.   c. Limpia su cuarto.

3. ¿Qué quiere hacer Wayne después de correr?
   (a.) Comer.   b. Jugar tenis.   c. Escribir un trabajo.

4. ¿Quién es adicto a su computadora?
   a. Ramón.   (b.) Wayne.   c. Sofía.

5. ¿Qué actividades hace Wayne en su computadora?
   (a.) Lee su correo.   b. Escribe poemas.   c. Habla con sus amigos.

El Retiro

Cultura a lo vivo. You may ask students to use the Internet to search for additional information to share with the class about the parks mentioned here.

Cultura a lo vivo

Large public parks in major Hispanic cities provide an important place for inexpensive recreational activities. For example, in Mexico City, **El Parque de Chapultepec** is the oldest, most important, and largest park in the city. There are museums, a lake, rides, an area for picnics, a zoo, restaurants, outdoor cafés, and other activities. In Madrid, Spain, **El Retiro** has just as much variety. From spectacles like street performers, puppet shows, jugglers, mimes, and musical performances, to quick acupuncture sessions or yoga classes, this park offers much more than just a simple stroll or boat ride along its central lake. In Caracas, Venezuela, **Los Caobos** is one of the oldest parks in the city. People go to the park to relax, walk among the beautiful mahogany trees, go bird watching, and enjoy children's activities on weekends. These parks serve an important social function, since families may celebrate birthdays, anniversaries, or any family event at the park.

Práctica adicional	
Cuaderno de tareas WB p.197, A–B	Video CD-ROM Episodio 8

Para comunicarnos mejor

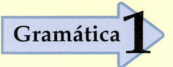 **1**
Talking about common daily activities
• **Regular -er and -ir verbs**

You have used many regular **-ar** verbs, such as **trabajar** and **descansar**, to talk about some of your activities. When Ramón and Wayne talked, they used verbs ending in **-er** and **-ir** to talk about their activities. You will discover that the endings of these verbs are similar to the verbs you already know.

Analizar y descubrir

1. Complete these statements.

-ar verbs

a. invitar   Yo _____invito_____ a mis amigos al picnic.

b. descansar   ¿Tú ____descansas____ los fines de semana?

c. trabajar   Sofía _____trabaja_____ los sábados; por eso, no estudia.

d. celebrar   Nosotros ____celebramos____ el cumpleaños de Wayne el domingo.

e. hablar   Los papás de Wayne _____hablan_____ con él por teléfono.

2. Compare the verb endings you provided with the endings of the verb **comer** *(to eat)*.

Comer	
Yo **como** hamburguesas con frecuencia.	*I often eat hamburgers.*
¿Tú, qué **comes**?	*What do you eat?*
Sofía no **come** grasa.	*Sofía doesn't eat fat.*
Mi papá y yo no **comemos** carne.	*My dad and I don't eat meat.*
¿Ustedes también **comen** tortillas? ¿Vosotros también **coméis** tortillas? }	*Do you also eat tortillas?*
En Cuba no **comen** tacos.	*They don't eat tacos in Cuba.*

3. Now examine the endings of the verb **vivir** *(to live)*.

Vivir	
Yo **vivo** en San Diego.	*I live in San Diego.*
¿Tú, dónde **vives**?	*Where do you live?*
Sofía **vive** cerca de la universidad.	*Sofía lives near the university.*
Mis hermanas y yo **vivimos** con mis papás.	*My sisters and I live with my parents.*
¿Dónde **viven** ustedes? ¿Dónde **vivís** vosotros? }	*Where do you live?*
Los abuelos de Ramón **viven** en México.	*Ramón's grandparents live in Mexico.*

4. In the following chart, fill in the endings of the **-ar (trabajar)**, **-er (comer)**, and **-ir (vivir)** verbs.

	-ar verbs	-er verbs	-ir verbs
yo	trabaj _____o_____	com _____o_____	viv _____o_____
tú	trabaj _____as_____	com _____es_____	viv _____es_____
usted/él/ella	trabaj _____a_____	com _____e_____	viv _____e_____
nosotros/as	trabaj _____amos_____	com _____emos_____	viv _____imos_____
ustedes/ellos/as	trabaj _____an_____	com _____en_____	viv _____en_____

5. Compare the endings of the **-ar** and **-er** verbs in the present tense. Where the **-ar** verbs have an **a**, the **-er** verbs have an _____e_____ .

6. Compare the endings of the **-er** and **-ir** verbs. All endings of the **-er** and **-ir** verbs are the same except for the _____nosotros_____ and the _____vosotros_____ forms.

Here are some common **-er** and **-ir** verbs you may use to talk about your activities.

Más actividades: verbos **-er** e **-ir**			
abrir	*to open*	**leer el periódico**	*to read the newspaper*
beber	*to drink*	**recibir correo electrónico**	*to receive (get) e-mail*
comer hamburguesas	*to eat hamburgers*	**regalos**	*gifts*
correr	*to run, jog*	**salir a cenar***	*to go out to dinner*
discutir (de/con)	*to discuss,*	**con los amigos***	*with friends*
	argue (about/with)	**vender comida**	*to sell food*
escribir cartas	*to write letters*	**ver una película en casa**	*to watch a movie at home*
un trabajo	*a paper*	**vivir en/con**	*to live in/with*
hacer la tarea*	*to do homework*		
ejercicio*	*to excercise*		

***hacer** and **salir** have a g in the **yo** person — **Yo hago** la tarea y **salgo** con mi novio.

7. Use these expressions to tell how often you do something.

¿Con qué frecuencia…?	
todos los días	*every day*
con frecuencia	*often*
a veces	*sometimes*
una vez a la semana	*once a week*
dos veces al mes	*twice a month*
tres (cuatro…) veces al año	*three (four…) times a year*
siempre	*always*
(casi) nunca	*(almost) never*

Gramática 1. Ask personalized questions emphasizing the verbs not included in the narration. You may sequence the questions as follows: yes/no (¿Lees el periódico todos los días?); either/or (¿Qué te gusta más: recibir regalos o recibir dinero?); and short answers (¿Con quién vives? ¿Con quién discutes más?).

Gramática 1. Ask personalized questions with ¿Con qué frecuencia…? For example: Yo voy al cine una o dos veces al mes. ¿Y tú, con qué frecuencia vas?

PRÁCTICA

Instructor's Resource
• IRM: Additional Activities

Additional Activity. You may want to play a concentration game with these verbs; see the IRM for a sample.

A. ¿Con qué frecuencia?

Parte 1. Indica con qué frecuencia tú o los miembros de tu familia hacen las siguientes cosas.
Answers will vary.

1. Leo el periódico. _____
2. Mi papá bebe café. _____
3. Mi hermana/o va a correr al parque. _____
4. Mis abuelos comen en mi casa. _____
5. Discuto con mi papá. _____

6. Vendo mis libros viejos. _____
7. Abro mi libro de español. _____
8. Escribo mis trabajos en la computadora. _____
9. Vemos películas en casa. _____

Parte 2. Convierte las oraciones de **Parte 1** en preguntas para entrevistar a tu compañero/a.

Modelo	Leo el periódico.
	—¿Con qué frecuencia lees el periódico?
	—Casi nunca. ¿Y tú?
	—Yo leo la sección deportiva todos los días.

> **¡Fíjate!**
> Remember that **nunca** and **casi nunca** go before the verb. The other expressions of frequency may go before or after the verb.

B. En casa de Ramón. Termina la descripción usando las ilustraciones.

1.   2.   3.

En la casa de Ramón tienen la misma rutina casi todos los sábados. Por la mañana, el papá de Ramón (1) ____lee el periódico____, mientras que su mamá (2) ____escribe____ los cheques para pagar las cuentas *(pay the bills)*. Los hermanos menores siempre (3) ____abren____ el refrigerador para buscar bebidas; generalmente (4) ____beben____ Coca-Cola. A las dos de la tarde, toda la familia (5) ____come____ en su restaurante favorito: El Huarache Veloz. Después de comer, con frecuencia van a una tienda donde (6)____venden____ todo a muy buen precio. Los niños siempre quieren comprar juguetes *(toys)*.

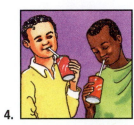

4.   5.   6.

C. Manolo y su compañero de cuarto.

Parte 1. Escribe los verbos necesarios de la página 182 para completar el texto acerca de la vida de Manolo y su compañero de cuarto.

Manolo, el amigo cubano de Sofía, no (1) _____vive_____ con su familia. Sus padres (2) _____viven_____ en Miami, y él (3) _____vive_____ en California con un amigo. Manolo les (4) _____escribe_____ correos electrónicos a sus padres con frecuencia, pues es más barato[1] que llamarlos por teléfono. Él también (5) _____recibe_____ muchos correos electrónicos de sus padres y de sus familiares de Cuba.

Manolo y Jorge, su compañero de cuarto, a veces (6) _____discuten_____ de política cubana. Pero en general, ellos tienen muchas cosas en común; por ejemplo, la comida y el gusto por los libros.

A Jorge le gusta estar siempre en buena condición física[2]; por eso, él (7) _____corre_____ dos millas todos los días. A Manolo no le gusta (8) _____correr_____, pero le gusta jugar fútbol. Tanto Manolo como Jorge desean estar saludables[3]; por eso, ellos siempre (9) _____comen_____ comida nutritiva y (10) _____beben_____ mucha agua[4].

[1]*cheaper* [2]**en...** *in good shape* [3]*healthy* [4]*water*

Parte 2. Ahora contesta las preguntas.

1. ¿Por qué Manolo escribe y recibe muchas cartas?
   Escribe y recibe muchas cartas porque vive lejos de su familia.

2. ¿Qué es importante para Manolo y Jorge?
   Es importante estar saludables.

3. ¿Qué hacen para estar en buena condición física?
   Comen comida nutritiva y beben mucha agua.

Práctica adicional

Cuaderno de tareas
WB pp.198–200, C–G

Gramática 2

Identifying places to go and places to be
• <u>Ir a</u> + [*place*] and <u>estar en</u> + [*place*]

You have used the verbs **ir** and **estar** already. We praticed **ir a** to express the future (**Mañana voy a bailar con mis amigos**). **Ir** is also used to indicate where someone is going: **Siempre voy al Museo de Historia los jueves.** We used **estar** to find out how someone is, as in **¿Cómo estás? Estar** is also used to indicate where someone or something is located, as in **¿Dónde estás? Estoy en la escuela.** Notice that you need the preposition **en**.

Read the following examples to examine the present tense forms of **estar.**

Estar en	
Estoy en el Museo del Oro.	*I'm at the Museo del Oro.*
Estás en casa, ¿verdad?	*You're at home, right?*
El lago **está en** el centro del parque.	*The lake is in the center of the park.*
¿En qué museo **estamos**?	*What museum are we at?*
Uds. **están en** el Museo del Prado. Vosotros **estáis en** el Museo del Prado. }	*You are at the Prado Museum.*
Algunos cuadros de Picasso **están en** el Museo Nacional Reina Sofía.	*Some of Picasso's paintings are at the Reina Sofía National Museum.*

The verb **ir** usually requires the preposition **a.** Read the following examples.

Las personas van...	*People go...*
al parque	*to the park*
a los museos	*to the museums*
a la discoteca	*to the nightclub (disco)*
a las exhibiciones de arte	*to art exhibitions*

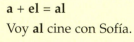

¡Fíjate!

Notice that **al** *(to the)* is used instead of **"a el"** before a masculine singular noun.

There are two contractions in Spanish: **al** and **del** *(from/of the)*, both used before masculine singular nouns.

Wayne

a + el = al
Voy **al** cine con Sofía.

Manolo

de + el = del
Voy a la oficina **del** profesor López.

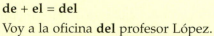

You have already learned the names of many places at the university or college. Here are some places where people can go in the city.

Más lugares en la ciudad	
(No) Voy...	I (don't) go...
al aeropuerto	to the airport
al boliche	to the bowling alley
al café	to the café
a la casa de mi novio/a	to my boyfriend's/girlfriend's house
a la casa de mis amigos /padres	to my friends'/parents' house
al centro comercial	to the mall
al cine	to the movie theater
a la discoteca	to the nightclub (disco)
al/a la doctor(a)	to the doctor
a la escuela	to school
a la exhibición de arte	to the art exhibition
a la iglesia /a misa	to church/Mass
al museo	to the museum
a ninguna parte	nowhere
al partido de fútbol	to the soccer game
a la playa	to the beach
a un restaurante	to a restaurant
al supermercado	to the supermarket
a la tienda	to the store
al trabajo	to work

¡Fíjate!

Do you remember the present tense of **ir**?
Voy a la escuela.
Vas a la cafetería.
Va al baño.
Vamos al salón.
Van al trabajo.

PRÁCTICA

D. Una llamada telefónica. Llama por teléfono a tu compañero/a para saber (to find out) dónde está y qué va a hacer allí. Empareja los lugares con las actividades. Answers will vary.

Modelo parque ⟶ correr dos millas
—¿Dónde estás ahora?
—Estoy en el parque.
—¿Qué vas a hacer allí?
—Voy a correr dos millas.

1. librería
2. casa de mi novio/a
3. supermercado
4. biblioteca
5. casa
6. cine
7. restaurante

a. mirar una película española
b. estudiar para un examen
c. comer con una amiga
d. comprar unos libros
e. leer el periódico
f. mirar la tele y descansar un rato
g. comprar la comida para la fiesta

E. ¿Es fácil localizarte? Indica dónde estás en los días y a las horas mencionadas. Después compara tus respuestas con las de tu compañero/a. Answers will vary.

¿Dónde estás...   _____Estoy en mi casa._____

1. los lunes a las siete de la mañana?   _____

2. los miércoles a las diez de la mañana?   _____

3. los jueves a las dos de la tarde?   _____

4. los viernes por la noche?   _____

5. los sábados por la mañana?   _____

6. los domingos al mediodía?   _____

F. ¿Cuántas veces? *(How often?)*

Parte 1. En grupos de tres personas, contesten las preguntas para decidir quién es la persona **más activa** o **más tranquila**. Answers will vary.

Nombres   _____   _____   _____

En el transcurso *(course)* de un mes, ¿con qué frecuencia…

1. vas al cine?   _____   _____   _____

2. comes en un restaurante?   _____   _____   _____

3. vas a las discotecas?   _____   _____   _____

4. vas al centro comercial?   _____   _____   _____

5. vas al parque?   _____   _____   _____

6. vas a casa de tus amigos?   _____   _____   _____

7. vas al boliche?   _____   _____   _____

Parte 2. Ahora comparte la información con el resto de la clase. Usa expresiones como:
Answers will vary.

Modelo	Nancy es la más activa porque va a las discotecas tres veces al mes. Larry es el más tranquilo porque nunca va al cine ni a las discotecas.

¡Fíjate!

When using **a ninguna parte** *(nowhere)*, place **no** before the verb.
Los domigos no voy a ninguna parte.

G. ¿Adónde vas? Indica adónde vas en cada situación. Usa **voy**. Answers will vary.

¿Adónde vas...

1. cuando tienes ganas de beber algo? _____

2. cuando tienes que estudiar? _____

3. cuando tienes ganas de comer comida italiana? _____

4. cuando estás enfermo/a *(sick)*? _____

5. después de tus clases? _____

6. cuando no tienes ganas de hablar con nadie *(anybody)*? _____

7. cuando estás aburrido/a? _____

H. ¿Dónde estás ahora y adónde vas después? Usa las ilustraciones para indicar a tu compañero/a dónde están las personas ahora, adónde van después y por qué. Usa **tener ganas de, tener que** u otros verbos. Answers will vary.

Mis hermanos   pero después   porque...

> **Modelo**   Mis hermanos están en casa ahora, pero después van al aeropuerto porque tienen ganas de ver a sus abuelos de México.

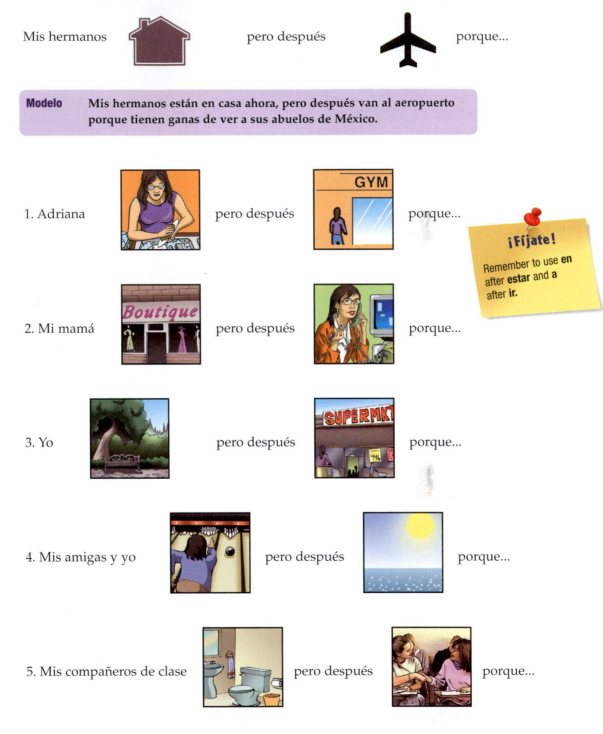

1. Adriana   pero después   porque...

2. Mi mamá   pero después   porque...

3. Yo   pero después   porque...

4. Mis amigas y yo   pero después   porque...

5. Mis compañeros de clase   pero después   porque...

¡Fíjate!

Remember to use **en** after **estar** and **a** after **ir.**

Práctica adicional	
Cuaderno de tareas WB pp.201–204, H–N LM pp.205–206, A–B, Pron.	Audio CD-ROM Episodio 8

Actividades comunicativas

Audio
CD-ROM

A. La historia va así.

Parte 1. Look carefully at each of the eight drawings. Then, as you listen to Wayne's plans for Saturday, identify the sequence of events by placing the numbers one through eight next to the appropriate image. Check your answers when you listen to Wayne's plans the second time.

Instructor's Resources
- Worktext CD
- IRM: Tapescript

2 ___

6 ___

8 ___

1 ___

5 ___

7 ___

4 ___

3 ___

 Parte 2. En grupos de tres escriban la historia en diferente orden.

B. Submarino. First draw a submarine in five of the boxes on your grid. Then take turns asking your partner yes/no questions, matching an action pictured at the top of the grid with one of the subjects on the side. *Answers will vary.*

Modelo	—¿Adriana lee el periódico todos los días?
	—**Sí, lee el periódico.** *(If there is a submarine in that box.)*
	or
	—**No, no lee el periódico.** *(If there is not a submarine in that box.)*

Depending on your partner's answer, write **sí** or **no** in that box. If you answer **sí** to you partner's question, put an **X** through your submarine. It's been located! The first player to locate all five submarines wins.

B. You may want to use the grid to model the process again.

¡Fíjate!

Be as creative as you can in your questions, using the frequency expressions on page 182. Don't just ask *do you drink?*, try *do you drink coffee frequently?* Put all the Spanish you know to use!!

Tú				
Tus primos				
Adriana				
Ustedes				

C. Cosas en común.

Parte 1. First answer the questions in the column labeled **Yo**. Then look for classmates whose answers are the same as yours and write their names in the column labeled **Compañero/a**. Answers will vary.

Modelo	—¿Qué bebes en las fiestas?
	—Coca–Cola. ¿Y tú?
	—Yo también. or —Yo bebo agua.

	Compañero/a	Yo
1. Generalmente, ¿qué bebes en las fiestas?	_____	_____
2. ¿Con quién discutes más?	_____	_____
3. ¿Dónde vives?	_____	_____
4. ¿A qué hora comes los sábados?	_____	_____
5. ¿Qué vas a hacer hoy después de clase?	_____	_____
6. ¿A qué hora llegas a la escuela los martes?	_____	_____
7. ¿Recibes regalos el día de San Valentín?	_____	_____
8. ¿Dónde estás los lunes a las 8:00 de la mañana?	_____	_____
9. ¿Con quién sales los fines de semana?	_____	_____
10. ¿Con qué frecuencia haces ejercicio?	_____	_____

C. You may have students fill in the **Yo** column prior to class. Allow at least six minutes to interact with classmates and to find the necessary responses. You may take part in the activity to give students an opportunity to use the **usted** form of the verbs they are learning. Select students to report their findings to the class.

Parte 2. Be prepared to share your findings with the class.

Modelo	—Lupe y yo bebemos Coca–Cola en las fiestas.

D. ¡A hablar! In groups of four, find out who does the following activites at least three times a week: exercise, use the computer, read novels, sing or dance in a group, go out at night. Write the activity and the name(s) of the person/people in the appropriate columns.

Actividad	Persona(s)
_____	_____
_____	_____
_____	_____
_____	_____
_____	_____
_____	_____

La correspondencia

 El correo: El regreso a la escuela. Lee las preguntas, luego lee la carta que Adriana le escribe a su hermana en Puerto Rico. Después contesta las preguntas.

1. ¿Cómo está Adriana?

Está muy bien, pero está muy nerviosa.

2. ¿Cómo son los compañeros según (*according to*) Adriana?

Son muy buenos y muy jóvenes.

3. ¿Por qué Adriana no tiene tiempo para cocinar ni limpiar?

No tiene tiempo para cocinar y limpiar porque tiene muchas actividades.

4. ¿Ahora quién tiene que lavar y cocinar?

Santiago tiene que lavar y cocinar.

5. ¿Quién apoya y ayuda a Adriana?

Viviana, Santiaguito y Carlos apoyan y ayudan a Adriana.

Querida hermana,   15 de octubre

¿Cómo estás? Yo estoy muy bien. Estudiar en la universidad es una experiencia fabulosa.

Éste es el segundo mes de clases y todavía[1] estoy muy nerviosa. Tengo clases muy interesantes, pero tengo que dedicar mucho tiempo a leer y estudiar.

Por suerte tengo unos compañeros de clase muy buenos y siempre me invitan a estudiar con ellos. Aunque[2] son muy jóvenes (tienen la edad de Carlos, ¿te imaginas?), son responsables e inteligentes, y siempre me incluyen en sus actividades.

Desafortunadamente para Santiago, ahora él tiene que cocinar y lavar, pues yo no tengo tiempo (ni ganas) para cocinar, limpiar y lavar. No le gusta mucho la situación. También creo que está un poco celoso[3] de mis actividades y mis nuevos amigos. Por suerte, a Viviana, Santiaguito y Carlos les gusta mucho que yo estudie, y por eso me apoyan y me ayudan[4] en la casa. Escríbeme pronto.

Tu hermana que te quiere,
Adriana

[1]*still* [2]*although* [3]*jealous* [4]***me...*** *support me and help me*

En papel: Los fines de semana. Write to Adriana about how you and your family and friends spend your weekends. Describe where you go, what you do at home, and how you prepare for school.   Answers will vary.

Invitación a **México**

Del álbum de
Sofía

Con más de 20 millones de habitantes, la Ciudad de México tiene muchos lugares que visitar los fines de semana. Puedes ir al Bosque de Chapultepec; también puedes visitar el Museo de Antropología, ver exposiciones o ir a la feria. Aquí se ve el Castillo de Chapultepec, la residencia presidencial hasta 1939. Ahora es el Museo Nacional de Historia.

Práctica adicional

Website
vistahigher
learning.com

Video
CD-ROM

Audio
CD-ROM

¡A ver de nuevo!

Parte 1. In your own words, write a description of what Ramón wants to do with Wayne at the park. Explain why he wants Wayne to go.   Answers will vary.

Instructor's Resources

• VHS Video

• Worktext CD

• IRM: Videoscript

Ramón llama a Wayne por teléfono…

Parte 2. Now work with a partner to add any information you may have left out.

Práctica adicional

| Cuaderno de tareas WB p. 204, Ñ LM p. 206, A–B | Audio CD-ROM Episodio 8 | Website vistahigher learning.com |

Vocabulario del Episodio 8

Instructor's Resources

• Testing program
• Website

Expresiones verbales

estar en	*to be (at)*
ir a + [*place*]	*to go to*
al	*to the*
a la (los, las)	*to the*

Más actividades: verbos **-er** e **-ir**

abrir	*to open*
beber	*to drink*
comer hamburguesas	*to eat hamburgers*
correr	*to run, jog*
discutir (de/con)	*to discuss, argue (about/with)*
escribir un trabajo	*to write a paper*
cartas	*letters*
hacer ejercicio	*to excercise*
la tarea	*to do homework*
leer el periódico	*to read the newspaper*
recibir correo electrónico	*to receive (get) e-mail*
regalos	*gifts*
salir a cenar	*to go out to dinner*
con los amigos	*with friends*
vender comida	*to sell food*
ver una película en casa	*to watch a movie at home*
vivir en/con	*to live in/with*

¿Con qué frecuencia...? *How often…?*

todos los días	*every day*
con frecuencia	*often*
a veces	*sometimes*
una vez a la semana	*once a week*
dos veces al mes	*twice a month*
tres (cuatro...) veces al año	*three (four...) times a year*
siempre	*always*
(casi) nunca	*(almost) never*

Los lugares en la ciudad *Places in the city*

el aeropuerto	*airport*
el boliche	*bowling alley*
el café	*café*
la casa de mi novio/a	*my boyfriend's/girlfriend's house*
la casa de mis amigos/padres	*my friends'/parents' house*

el centro comercial	*mall*
el cine	*movie theater*
la discoteca	*nightclub (disco)*
el/la doctor(a)	*doctor*
la escuela	*school*
la exhibición de arte	*art exhibition*
la iglesia/misa	*church/Mass*
el museo	*museum*
ninguna parte, (a)	*nowhere*
el parque	*park*
el partido de fútbol	*soccer game*
la playa	*beach*
el restaurante	*restaurant*
el supermercado	*supermarket*
la tienda	*store*
el trabajo	*work*

Vocabulario personal

Write the words you need to know to talk about the places you like to go to and the activities you like to do.

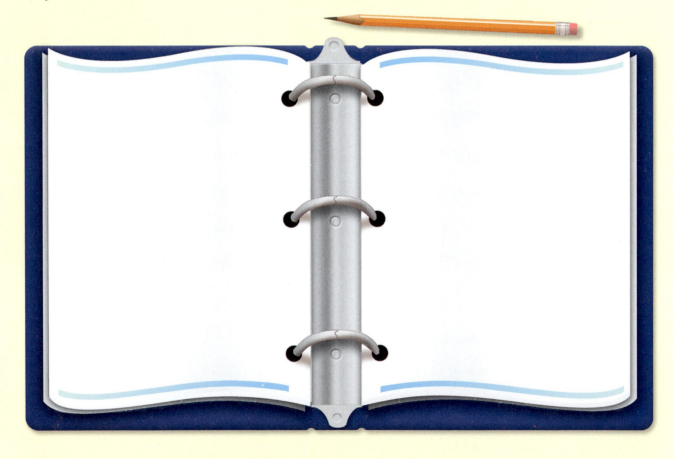

Nombre _____ Fecha _____

¡A escribir!

Episodio 8

Escenas de la vida: Vamos al parque

A. ¡A ver cuánto entendiste! See how much of the **Escena** you understood by matching the Spanish sentences with their English equivalents.

_d_ 1. Hace mucho que no hacemos ejercicio juntos.

_c_ 2. Además, ¿no quieres ver a Sofía?

_e_ 3. Todo listo. Ya convencí a Wayne de ir al parque mañana.

_a_ 4. ¿Qué, la usa mucho?

_f_ 5. Bueno, ¿y cómo lo convenciste?

_b_ 6. Le dije que Sofía muere por salir con él.

a. What, does he use it a lot?

b. I told him that Sofía is dying to go out with him.

c. Besides, don't you want to see Sofía?

d. We haven't exercised together for a while.

e. All done! I convinced Wayne to come to the park tomorrow.

f. Good, and how did you convince him?

B. Para el domingo. Use the expressions to complete Ramón and Wayne's conversation.

| hago | comemos | corremos | vamos a |
| leo | corren | hacemos | ver |

Wayne   Hello?

Ramón   Hey, Wayne. ¿ (1) ___Vamos a___ correr un par de millas al parque mañana? Hace mucho que no (2) ___hacemos___ ejercicio juntos.

Wayne   No gracias. Por la mañana siempre (3) ___hago___ mi tarea y (4) ___leo___ mis correos tranquilamente, porque tengo clases toda la tarde y por la noche trabajo.

Ramón   Wayne, ¡mañana es domingo! Además…¿no quieres (5) ___ver___ a Sofía? Ella y mi hermana (6) ___corren___ todos los domingos.

Wayne   Hummm, ella es muy bonita.

Ramón   Sí, y no tiene novio.

Wayne   Está bien, pero con una condición…después, (7) ___comemos___ con las chicas en El Huarache Veloz.

Ramón   Perfecto.

Gramática 1

Taking about common daily activities
• **Regular -er and ir verbs**

C. Actividades para todos. Use the expressions to complete the description of the park.

venden	restaurantes	leer	familias	celebrar
ejercicio	comer	museos	correr	discutir

Muchas personas van al parque de Chapultepec en la Ciudad de México a hacer
(1) ___ejercicio___ o van a (2) ___correr___ alrededor del lago. Otros simplemente
van a descansar, estudiar, (3) ___leer___, escribir o conversar bajo los árboles. Los
domingos muchas (4) ___familias___ hacen picnics para (5) ___celebrar___ cumpleaños
y aniversarios. Alrededor del lago (*lake*) hay bares, cafés y (6) ___restaurantes___ donde la
gente va a (7) ___comer___, a beber y a escuchar música. Hay centros culturales
donde (8) ___venden___ artesanía mexicana y recuerdos. Hay conciertos de música al
aire libre, exhibiciones en los (9) ___museos___ y clases de pintura y teatro.

D. Más actividades. Sofía habla de las actividades de los fines de semana.
Escribe frases lógicas.

Sofía

¡Fíjate!
Remember to conjugate the verbs appropriately!

1. mis padres / leer / periódico / la mañana
   Mis padres leen el periódico en la mañana.

2. mi mamá / escribir / cartas
   Mi mamá escribe cartas.

3. yo / ver / películas / con Ana Mari / viernes
   Yo veo películas con Ana Mari los viernes.

4. Lalo nunca / abrir / libros / fines de semana
   Lalo nunca abre sus libros los fines de semana.

5. Lalo y mi papá / discutir / porque / Lalo / ser / irresponsable
   Lalo y mi papá discuten porque Lalo es irresponsable.

6. por la noche nosotros / hacer / ejercicio / o escuchar / música
   Por la noche nosotros hacemos ejercicio o escuchamos música.

E. Actividades frecuentes. Write a complete sentence describing each illustration. Include how often the activity takes place. Answers will vary.

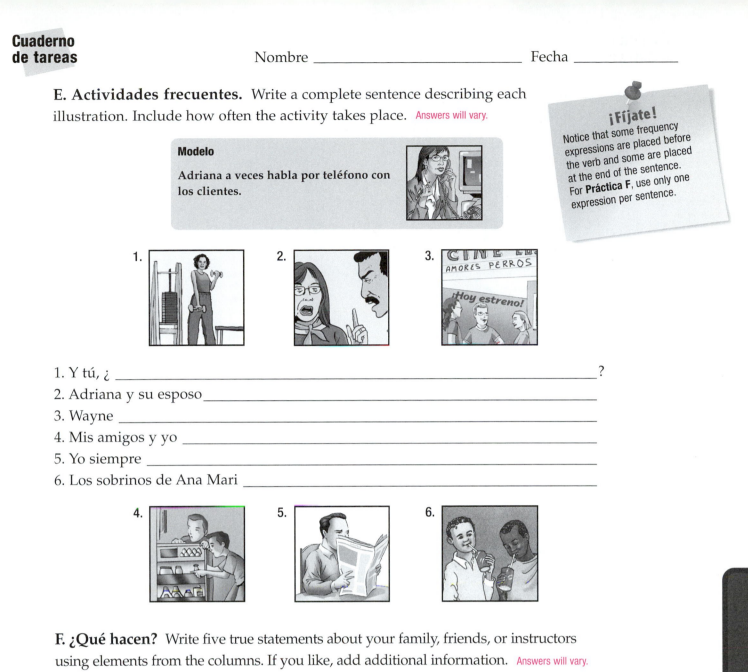

Modelo

Adriana a veces habla por teléfono con los clientes.

¡Fíjate!

Notice that some frequency expressions are placed before the verb and some are placed at the end of the sentence. For **Práctica F**, use only one expression per sentence.

1.
2.
3. AMORES PERROS ¡Hoy estreno!

1. Y tú, ¿ _____ ?

2. Adriana y su esposo _____

3. Wayne _____

4. Mis amigos y yo _____

5. Yo siempre _____

6. Los sobrinos de Ana Mari _____

4.
5.
6.

F. ¿Qué hacen? Write five true statements about your family, friends, or instructors using elements from the columns. If you like, add additional information. Answers will vary.

Modelo   Mi amiga Angie come hamburguesas una vez a la semana.

	comer		
siempre	hacer la tarea	en la casa	una vez a la semana
a veces	salir con	hamburguesas	con frecuencia
casi nunca	leer novelas	amigos	todos los días
nunca	vivir con	novio/a	por la noche

1. _____

2. _____

3. _____

4. _____

5. _____

G. Las obligaciones y los deseos. Explain what the characters and you feel like doing but can't and why. Answers will vary.

> **Modelo**   Adriana tiene ganas de descansar, pero no puede porque tiene que trabajar.

1. Wayne _____

_____

_____

_____

2. Ana Mari y Ramón _____

_____

_____

_____

3. Manolo y yo _____

_____

_____

_____

 **Gramática 2**   Identifying places to go and places to be
• <u>ir a</u> + [*place*] and <u>estar en</u> + [*place*]

H. ¿Adónde vas? Indicate where you go when you want to do the following things.   Answers will vary.

> **Modelo**   Voy **a la biblioteca** cuando tengo ganas de estudiar.

1. Voy _____ cuando tengo ganas de correr.

2. Voy _____ cuando tengo ganas de escuchar música.

3. Voy _____ cuando necesito hablar con un profesor.

4. Voy _____ cuando necesito comprar un regalo.

5. Voy _____ cuando llegan por avión mis familiares.

6. Voy _____ cuando necesito comprar la comida para toda la semana.

7. Voy _____ cuando tengo que trabajar.

8. Voy _____ cuando no tengo ganas de comer en mi casa.   Answers will vary.

I. ¿Cuándo vas? Write how often you go to the following places and explain why.

cine	casa de mis abuelos	iglesia (a misa)
trabajo	centro comercial	tienda de videos

> **Modelo**   aeropuerto
> **Nunca voy al aeropuerto porque toda mi familia vive aquí.**

1. _____

_____

2. _____

_____

3. _____

_____

4. _____

_____

5. _____

_____

6. _____

_____

J. ¿De quién son las cosas? Say to whom the following things belong. Use an element from each column. Answers will vary.

| Modelo | Estos pacientes son del Dr. Pérez. |

			profesor
gato			profesor
mochilas		del	estudiante de literatura
oficina	es	de la	jugadores/as (*players*)
novela	son	de los	Sr. López
video		de las	niño

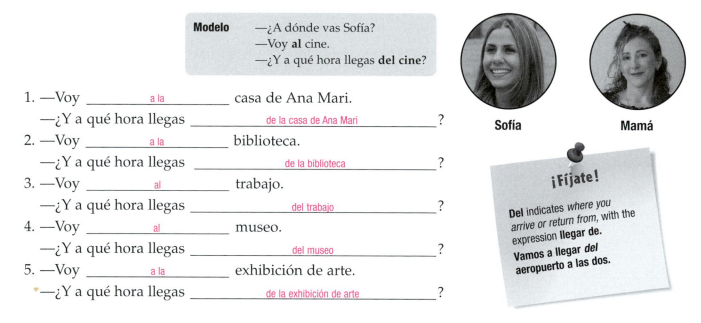

¡Fíjate!

de + el = del

Del is used to express *to whom something belongs*, often with the expression **ser de.**

¿Este coche nuevo es *del* hijo de Adriana?

1. _____
2. _____
3. _____
4. _____
5. _____

K. ¿Y a qué hora, Sofía? Sofía's mother always wants to know where her daughter is going and when she will come back. Complete the mother's questions and Sofía's answers, using contractions where necessary.

| Modelo | —¿A dónde vas Sofía?
—Voy **al** cine.
—¿Y a qué hora llegas **del** cine? |

Sofía   Mamá

1. —Voy _____ a la _____ casa de Ana Mari.

   —¿Y a qué hora llegas _____ de la casa de Ana Mari _____?

2. —Voy _____ a la _____ biblioteca.

   —¿Y a qué hora llegas _____ de la biblioteca _____?

3. —Voy _____ al _____ trabajo.

   —¿Y a qué hora llegas _____ del trabajo _____?

4. —Voy _____ al _____ museo.

   —¿Y a qué hora llegas _____ del museo _____?

5. —Voy _____ a la _____ exhibición de arte.

   —¿Y a qué hora llegas _____ de la exhibición de arte _____?

¡Fíjate!

Del indicates *where you arrive or return from*, with the expression **llegar de.**

Vamos a llegar *del* aeropuerto a las dos.

L. ¿Dónde están? Sofía reveals where she and her friends are on different days and at different times. Complete her statements with the appropriate forms of **estar.**

1. Los lunes por la mañana, mis amigos y yo _____ estamos _____ en la clase de cálculo.

2. Los martes a las seis, la Sra. Barrón _____ está _____ en el trabajo.

3. Los miércoles por la tarde, generalmente Ramón y Wayne _____ están _____ en casa.

4. Los jueves a las doce, (yo) _____ estoy _____ en la clase de geología.

5. Y tú, ¿dónde _____ estás _____ a esa hora?

M. ¡Adivina! *(guess)* Look at the images and write where the characters are now.

> **Modelo**
>
> Manolo va a hablar con el doctor.
> **Está en la clínica veterinaria.**

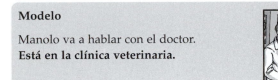

1. Sofía va a lavar su ropa.

Está en su casa.

2. Ramón y yo vamos a mirar una película.

Estamos en el cine.

3. Yo voy a hacer un poco de ejercicio.

Estoy en el parque.

4. ¿Tú vas a ver a tus amigos?

Estás en el boliche.

5. Adriana va a comprar la comida.

Está en el supermercado.

6. Ana Mari va a comprar ropa nueva.

Está en la tienda.

7. Adriana va a comprar libros para sus hijos.

Está en la librería.

8. Wayne y Ramón van a tomar el sol.

Están en la playa.

N. ¿Qué tienes que hacer? Explain what you have to do at each place using **tengo ganas de** or **tengo que**. Answers will vary.

> **Modelo** ¿Estás en el aeropuerto?
> **Sí porque tengo que llevar a Jorge; va a Miami.**

1. ¿Estás en la discoteca? _____
_____

2. ¿Estás en el parque? _____
_____

3. ¿Estás en la librería? _____
_____

4. ¿Estás en el supermercado? _____
_____

5. ¿Estás en la casa de tus padres? _____
_____

6. ¿Estás en un restaurante? _____
_____

Para terminar

Ñ. Una miniprueba para terminar. Complete the following communicative tasks to test your knowledge of the content of the episode.

1. Ask Sofía and Ana Mari:
    a. if they watch TVprograms in Spanish.
    b. how many times a week they run.
    c. if they argue with their parents.
    d. where they live.

2. Ask Adriana:
    e. if she sells her books at the end of the (**al final del**) semester.
    f. what she feels like doing this weekend.
    g. what her kids have to do on Sundays.

1.
  a. ¿Ven programas de televisión en español? _____
  b. ¿Cuántas veces a la semana corren? _____
  c. ¿Discuten con sus padres? _____
  d. ¿Dónde viven? _____

2.
  e. ¿Vende sus libros al final del semestre? _____
  f. ¿Qué tiene ganas de hacer este fin de semana? _____
  g. ¿Qué tienen que hacer sus hijos los domingos? _____

¡A escuchar!

Episodio **8**

Comprensión

 A. Una sorpresa para Wayne. You are going to hear a phone conversation between Wayne and his former host family in Chile, where he went to study Spanish. Listen and select the best completion for each sentence. You will hear the conversation twice.

Wayne

1. Los Señores Iturbe llaman de Chile para…

   a. desearle a Wayne un feliz cumpleaños. b. invitar a Wayne a regresar a Chile.

2. El Señor Iturbe le pregunta a Wayne…

   a. ¿qué hacen sus padres?   b. ¿cómo están sus padres?

3. Ahora, Wayne tiene…

   a. 21 años.   b. 24 años.

4. La Sra. Iturbe desea…

   a. recibir una carta de Wayne.   b. ir a Estados Unidos a estudiar.

5. Wayne no escribe cartas porque…

   a. trabaja y estudia mucho.   b. no le gusta escribir cartas.

6. Si es posible, Wayne promete que…

   a. va a escribirles muchas cartas.   b. va a visitar Chile el año que viene.

 B. ¿Dónde están? You will hear cues indicating the locations of these people and things. Say where they are and then repeat each correct response after the speaker.

Modelo	You see:	**libros**
	You hear:	**librería**
	You say:	**Los libros están en la librería.**

1. computadora   5. Manolo

2. niños   6. Mis amigos y yo

3. Sofía y Ana Mari   7. Yo

4. Wayne y su amiga   8. Tú

Pronunciación

La *p*, la *b* y la *v*. The letters **p (pe), b (be grande),** and **v (ve chica)** are produced with both lips. The Spanish **p** sounds like English *p*, except that the lips are tighter and no puff of air is released. Hold your hand in front of your lips and say the English words *pat* and *puff*. You can feel the puff of air on your hand. Now, repeat these words and sentences after the speaker, being careful to hold your lips more tensely and not to release a puff of air.

Pablo	**lápiz**	**Pablo pone el lápiz en el pupitre.**
Perú	**pluma**	**Paco Pérez practica el polo en Panamá.**

The letters **b** and **v** in the Spanish alphabet have the same pronunciation. When they are the initial sound in a word, they sound like the English *b*. The lips touch and then release the sound.

boca	**vestido**
blusa	**Venezuela**
bikini	**visitar**

When Spanish **b** and **v** are not the initial sound in a word or phrase, they are pronounced with the lips touching lightly, allowing air to escape through.

abuelo	**huevos**	**Vamos a visitar a la abuela.**
rubio	**avión**	**Su novia, Verónica, es rubia y bonita.**

Más escenas de la vida

Adriana and her husband are arguing again. Listen to their conversation, then complete activities **A** and **B**. You will hear the conversation twice.

A. ¿Cómo ocurre? Organize these statements in chronological order, according to what you heard in the conversation.

_5_ 1. Van a la tienda de videos y ya está.   _1_ 4. ¿Adriana, vamos a correr?

_2_ 2. No tengo ganas de ir a correr.   _6_ 5. Vamos a salir a comer con papá.

_4_ 3. Necesitas hacer ejercicio.   _3_ 6. Tengo que escribir una composición.

B. Responde. Write the answers to the following questions.

1. ¿Adónde quiere ir Santiago? _____Quiere ir a correr._____

2. ¿Por qué Adriana no puede? _____Tiene que escribir una composición._____

3. ¿Adónde ya no va Adriana? _____No va al gimnasio._____

4. ¿Qué tiene ganas de hacer Adriana por la noche? _____Tiene ganas de ver una película en casa._____

5. ¿Qué tienen que comprar en el supermercado? _____Tienen que comprar comida._____

Episodio 9

Escenas de la vida: ¡Qué rica comida!

Video
CD-ROM

A. ¡Mira cuánto puedes entender! Mira el video o escucha la **Escena** para contestar las preguntas.

1. ¿Qué comida llevan los chicos al parque?

Audio
CD-ROM

sándwiches	carne para asar
salsa	pasteles puertorriqueños
refrescos	pastel
helado	flan
frutas	tortillas
verduras	arroz
guacamole	papas

A. If students are watching the video in class, they may notice additional food items on the table that are not explicitly mentioned in the conversation: **refrescos, pastel, arroz,** and **tortillas.**

Cultura a lo vivo

In the Spanish-speaking world, meals are important social events. **La comida,** the principal meal, usually begins at one and lasts until three in the afternoon. People generally go home to eat with family members and rest before returning to work for a few more hours. In Spain, for example, most small stores are closed between one and three so people can return home.

Since Spanish speakers like to relax and to enjoy the food and conversation, a meal in a restaurant may last as long as three hours. For this reason, it would be extremely rude for the server to bring the check after the meal has been served. Servers wait until the customer asks for the check.

Instructor's Resources
• Overheads
• VHS Video
• Worktext CD
• Website
• IRM: Videoscript, Comprehensible input

2. ¿Cómo se prepara la carne en casa de Ramón? Selecciona los ingredientes.

3. ¿Qué comida pide Wayne cuando sale a comer?

Video Synopsis. Wayne goes to the park to meet Ramón, and is surprised to learn that a party has been planned for him. The friends discuss the food they eat, and Wayne burns his mouth with the salsa. They talk about a Caribbean restaurant nearby.

4. ¿Qué comida sirven en El Rincón Caribeño?

a. mexicana   c. china
b. cubana   d. puertorriqueña

Video
CD-ROM

Audio
CD-ROM

B. ¿Te diste cuenta? Indica si los comentarios son **ciertos** o **falsos**.

	Cierto	Falso
1. No es necesario ser puntual para las fiestas.	✓	
2. A Wayne le gusta mucho la comida puertorriqueña.		✓
3. En México no hay chili.	✓	
4. Los pasteles puertorriqueños tienen plátano verde y carne.	✓	
5. El plato favorito de Manolo es arroz con carne de cerdo.		✓
6. Los chicos están en el café.		✓

B and C. Have students read exercises B and C, then play the video again. Have students respond out loud.

C. El picnic. Contesta las preguntas.

Video
CD-ROM

Audio
CD-ROM

1. ¿Por qué llegan tarde Ana Mari y Sofía? _____ Porque para las fiestas no es necesario ser puntual. _____

2. ¿Quién sabe *(knows)* el secreto para preparar carne? _____ El papá de Ramón. _____

3. ¿Qué llevó Manolo al picnic? _____ Pasteles puertorriqueños. _____

4. ¿Qué pide Manolo en El Rincón Caribeño? _____ Pollo con arroz. _____

5. ¿Pica la salsa? _____ Answers will vary. _____

Práctica adicional

Cuaderno de tareas WB p.227, A–B	Video CD-ROM Episodio 9

Para comunicarnos mejor

Vocabulario **1**   **Talking about food**
     • **Food and meals**

Instructor's Resource
• Overheads

Vocabulario 1. Use the images on the overhead transparencies and pages 208, 209, and 210 to teach the rest of the food and meal-related vocabulary. Ask personalized questions that emphasize the verbs introduced in the box: Generalmente, ¿desayunas? ¿Qué desayunas? ¿Qué comes en la cafetería de la escuela? ¿Es buena la comida? ¿Qué cenas? ¿A qué hora cenas entre semana? ¿Qué te gusta comer cuando tienes mucha hambre?... Introduce pedir and servir.

El desayuno

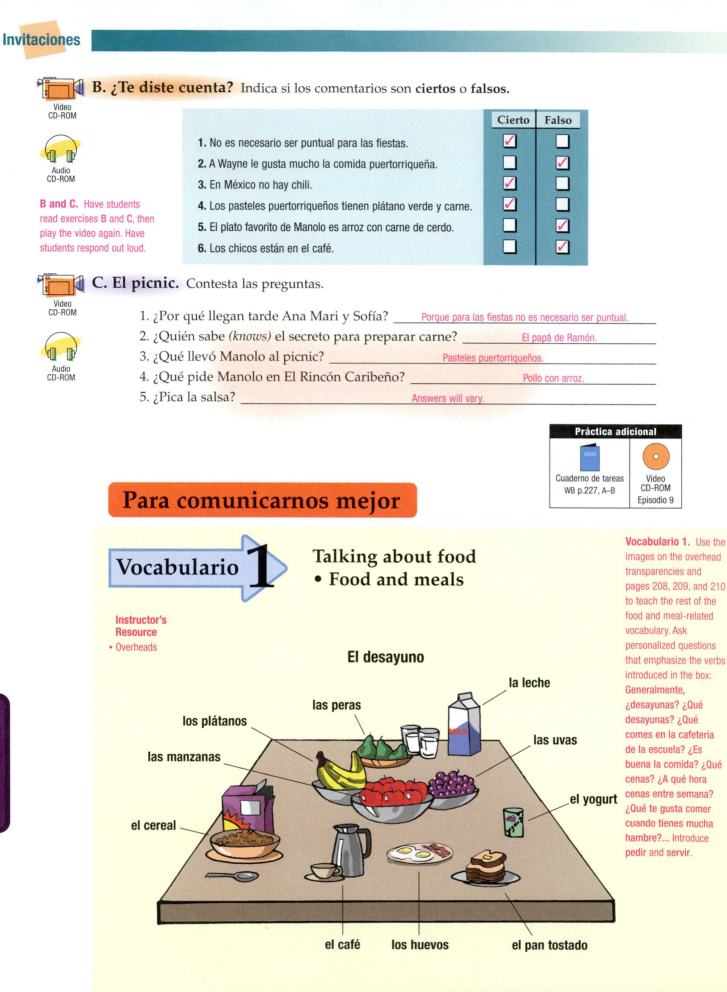

la leche
las peras
los plátanos
las manzanas
las uvas
el yogurt
el cereal
el café   los huevos   el pan tostado

El almuerzo

los refrescos

la sopa

la limonada

el jamón

los sándwiches de atún

la ensalada
de lechuga y tomate

las papas fritas

el espagueti

el pavo

el pollo

la sal y la pimienta

las hamburguesas

También se dice...

refrescos ⟶ gaseosas

papas ⟶ patatas

plátanos ⟶ bananas, guineos

Cultura a lo vivo

In the Spanish-speaking world, table manners are important. It is disrespectful to start eating before everyone has been served, to put your elbows on the table, to speak with your mouth full, or to leave the table before everyone has finished eating. When leaving the table, Spanish speakers usually say **Con permiso, buen provecho** (*Excuse me,* and *bon appétit*).

Although the morning and evening meals vary from country to country, breakfast **(el desayuno)** and dinner **(la cena)** are generally light and less formal. Dinner or supper takes place between eight and ten in the evening, and often consists of leftovers from **la comida,** or coffee and bread.

Para hablar de las comidas en un restaurante

desayunar	*to have breakfast*	**el plato/platillo**	*dish*
comer	*to eat; to have lunch*	**el/la mesero/a**	*waiter/waitress*
cenar	*to have dinner/supper*	**la cuenta**	*bill*
tener hambre	*to be hungry*		
tener sed	*to be thirsty*		

La cena

el vino tinto

la cerveza

el agua

los dulces

las galletas

los camarones

el arroz

los frijoles

el pescado

el pastel

el helado

la carne de cerdo

las zanahorias

el brócoli

las papas al horno

el bistec de res

la langosta

Otro vocabulario

la bebida	*drink*	la fruta	*fruit*
la carne	*meat*	el jugo de naranja	*orange juice*
la carne de res	*beef*	los mariscos	*seafood*
la dona	*donut*	el postre	*dessert*
la ensalada de	*lettuce and tomato*	el queso	*cheese*
lechuga y tomate	*salad*	el té	*tea*
el flan	*flan*	la verdura	*vegetable*

PRÁCTICA

A. Asociaciones. ¿Qué platos y bebidas asocias con las siguientes comidas?   Answers will vary.

1. la comida china
2. la comida italiana
3. la comida mexicana
4. la comida norteamericana
5. la comida japonesa
6. la comida vegetariana

B. ¿Tienes una dieta saludable *(healthy)*? Marca con un círculo la mejor *(best)*
respuesta según tus hábitos de comida.   Answers will vary.

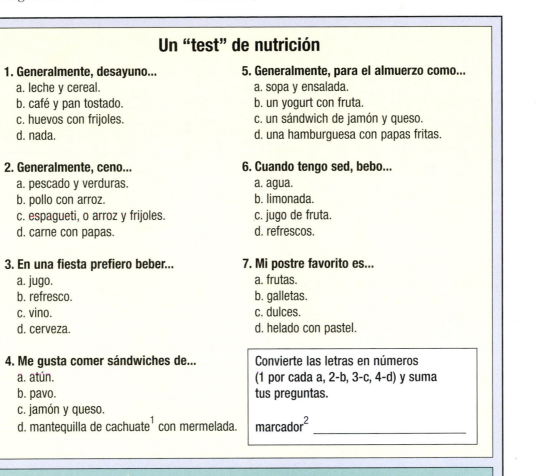

Un "test" de nutrición

1. Generalmente, desayuno...
   a. leche y cereal.
   b. café y pan tostado.
   c. huevos con frijoles.
   d. nada.

2. Generalmente, ceno...
   a. pescado y verduras.
   b. pollo con arroz.
   c. espagueti, o arroz y frijoles.
   d. carne con papas.

3. En una fiesta prefiero beber...
   a. jugo.
   b. refresco.
   c. vino.
   d. cerveza.

4. Me gusta comer sándwiches de...
   a. atún.
   b. pavo.
   c. jamón y queso.
   d. mantequilla de cachuate[1] con mermelada.

5. Generalmente, para el almuerzo como...
   a. sopa y ensalada.
   b. un yogurt con fruta.
   c. un sándwich de jamón y queso.
   d. una hamburguesa con papas fritas.

6. Cuando tengo sed, bebo...
   a. agua.
   b. limonada.
   c. jugo de fruta.
   d. refrescos.

7. Mi postre favorito es...
   a. frutas.
   b. galletas.
   c. dulces.
   d. helado con pastel.

Convierte las letras en números
(1 por cada a, 2-b, 3-c, 4-d) y suma
tus preguntas.

marcador[2] _____

Interpreta tus resultados

De 7 a 14. ¡Bravo! Seguramente eres una persona consciente de la salud[3]. Tienes buenos hábitos de comida. Probablemente eres muy organizado/a y haces ejercicio regularmente.

De 15 a 22. ¡Muy bien! Probablemente eres una persona consciente de la salud, pero a veces sucumbes a la tentación de comer cosas con muchas calorías o grasas. Seguramente haces ejercicio para compensar.

De 23 a 28. ¡Qué barbaridad! Seguramente no tienes tiempo de preparar comidas saludables. Tienes que incluir en tu dieta más frutas y verduras. Debes evitar las cosas dulces y grasosas.

[1]*peanut butter* [2]*score* [3]*health*

C. Una entrevista. Entrevista a tu compañero/a para saber qué le gusta comer y beber.
Usa el vocabulario de las páginas anteriores.   Answers will vary.

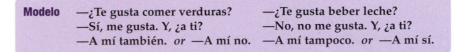

Modelo	—¿Te gusta comer verduras?	—¿Te gusta beber leche?
	—Sí, me gusta. Y, ¿a ti?	—No, no me gusta. Y, ¿a ti?
	—A mí también. *or* —A mí no.	—A mí tampoco. *or* —A mí sí.

D. La pirámide de la salud. Primero indica cuántas porciones comes de las siguientes categorías. Luego lee *La pirámide de la salud* para completar la información y determinar si llevas una dieta saludable.   Answers will vary.

Generalmente como…

1. _____ porciones de frutas.

2. _____ porciones de carnes.

3. _____ porciones de verduras.

4. _____ porciones de panes y cereales.

5. _____ porciones de productos lácteos.

6. _____ porciones de dulces y grasas.

La pirámide de la salud

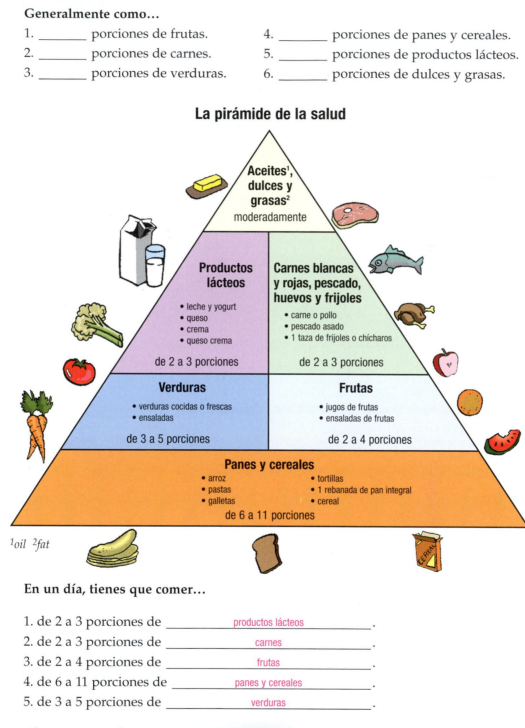

En un día, tienes que comer…

1. de 2 a 3 porciones de _____productos lácteos_____ .

2. de 2 a 3 porciones de _____carnes_____ .

3. de 2 a 4 porciones de _____frutas_____ .

4. de 6 a 11 porciones de _____panes y cereales_____ .

5. de 3 a 5 porciones de _____verduras_____ .

Ahora compara lo que tienes que comer con lo que generalmente comes para completar la información.

6. Necesito comer más _____ .

7. Necesito comer menos _____ .

8. En general, tengo una dieta balanceada/deficiente.

E. Un menú saludable. You have realized that you are not eating a balanced diet. Using the food pyramid on page 212, write out a balanced menu that includes breakfast, lunch, dinner, and beverages.   *Answers will vary.*

E. This is a good activity for posting. Students should share the menus they create with the class. Discuss the best/healthiest ones.

Banco de palabras

un vaso de
a glass of

un taza de
a cup of

un pedazo de
a piece of

una rebanada de
a slice of

¡Fíjate!

Write your menu on card stock so your instructor can share it with the class.

 F. Los hábitos alimenticios del grupo. En grupos de tres, contesten las preguntas para hacer un resumen de los hábitos alimenticios de sus compañeros.   *Answers will vary.*

1. ¿Qué desayunan generalmente? _____

2. ¿Qué cenan? _____

3. ¿Qué beben cuando tienen sed? _____

4. ¿Qué comen cuando tienen mucha hambre? _____

5. ¿Con qué frecuencia comen comida chatarra (*junk food*)? _____

6. ¿Cuáles son sus frutas y verduras favoritas? _____

7. ¿Qué tipo de comida prefieren? ¿Cuál es su plato favorito? _____

_____

 G. Una madre preocupada. The mother of a six-year-old boy is concerned that her son may not have a balanced diet. Listen to the conversation between the doctor and the mother. As you listen, use the food pyramid to place a check next to the food group the mother mentions as part of her son's diet. Then decide whether her son's diet is healthy or not; formulate recommendations for them. Discuss your opinion with a classmate.

Audio CD-ROM

Instructor's Resources
• Worktext CD
• IRM: Tapescript

Script: See the Instructor's Resource Manual for the script to this activity.

¿Come/bebe suficiente(s)...	Sí	No
1. frutas?	✓	☐
2. verduras?	☐	✓
3. carnes?	✓	☐
4. productos lácteos?	✓	☐
5. agua?	✓	☐
6. pan y cereales?	✓	☐

Recomendaciones para la madre:

*Answers will vary.*_____

_____

_____

Práctica adicional

Cuaderno de tareas
WB pp.228–230, C–F

Gramática 1

Ordering a meal
• <u>Pedir</u> and <u>servir</u>

Analizar y descubrir

In the conversation, you heard the following:

¿Por qué siempre **pides** chili?	*Why do you always order chili?*
Ahí siempre **pido** arroz con pollo.	*I always order chicken with rice there.*
También **sirven** comida cubana.	*They also serve Cuban food.*

Pides, pido, and **sirven** are forms of the stem-changing verbs **pedir** *(to ask for, order a meal)* and **servir** *(to serve).*

1. Read the following examples to complete the conjugation of the verb **pedir.**

Pedir	
¿Desea **pedir** algo más?	*Do you want to order something else?*
Nunca **pido** el plato más caro del menú.	*I never order the most expensive dish on the menu.*
¿Qué **pides** cuando cenas aquí?	*What do you order when you eat dinner here?*
Ana Mari a veces **pide** postre.	*Ana Mari sometimes orders dessert.*
¿**Pedimos** vino para todos?	*Should we order wine for everyone?*
Ustedes siempre **piden** lo mismo. Vosotros siempre **pedís** lo mismo.	*You always order the same thing.*
Ellos siempre **piden** la cuenta primero.	*They always ask for the bill first.*

2. Read the following examples to complete the conjugation of the verb **servir.**

Servir	
¿Qué van a **servir?**	*What are you going to serve?*
Casi nunca **sirvo** nada tan tarde.	*I almost never serve anything so late.*
Y tú, ¿qué **sirves?**	*And what do you serve?*
Mi mamá siempre nos **sirve** un desayuno grande.	*My mom always serves us a big breakfast.*
En casa **servimos** tamales para las fiestas.	*At home we serve tamales for parties.*
Y ustedes, ¿qué **sirven?** Y vosotros, ¿qué **servís?**	*And what do you serve?*
¿Con qué **sirven** el bistec aquí?	*What do they serve the steak with here?*

3. Now complete the conjugations of **pedir** and **servir**.

	Pedir	Servir
yo	pido	sirvo
tú	pides	sirves
usted/él/ella	pide	sirve
nosotros/as	pedimos	servimos
vosotros/as	pedís	servís
ustedes/ellos/as	piden	sirven

4. In which forms of **pedir** and **servir** does the **-e-** of the infinitive change to an **-i-**?
yo, tú, usted, él, ella, ustedes, ellos/as.

5. In which forms does the **-e-** remain unchanged? vosotros/as, nosotros/as.

PRÁCTICA

H. Recomendaciones. En grupos de tres personas, hagan (make) recomendaciones sobre los mejores lugares de la ciudad para comer. Incluye muchos detalles. Después comparte tu opinión con tus compañeros. Answers will vary.

> **Modelo** comida italiana
> **Si tienes ganas de comer comida italiana, tienes que ir al Mamma Lucia. El restaurante está en la calle/avenida…. Generalmente pido la pizza vegetariana. También sirven un espagueti delicioso.**

1. comida mexicana (cubana, china, japonesa, etc.)
2. hamburguesas
3. espagueti
4. pastel de chocolate

5. desayunos
6. café
7. helados
8. ensaladas

I. Adriana y Santiago van a cenar. Usa las siguientes palabras para completar el diálogo entre el mesero, Adriana y Santiago.

ensalada	mariscos	pides	cerveza	pido
servir	vino	pedir	pescado	sirven

Mesero   Buenas tardes, señores. ¿Están listos para (1) _____pedir_____?

Adriana   Pues más o menos. ¿Qué nos recomienda?

Mesero   Bueno, la especialidad de la casa es el pescado y los (2) _____mariscos_____.

Santiago   ¿Con qué (3) _____sirven_____ el filete de pescado?

Mesero   Lo servimos con arroz y verduras. Tenemos un pescado excelente.

Adriana   Yo no tengo ganas de comer (4) _____pescado_____ hoy. Voy a pedir carne.

Santiago   ¿Por qué no pedimos una (5) _____ensalada_____ César para los dos?
Tú (6) _____pides_____ un filete miñón y yo (7) _____pido_____ el filete de pescado.

Adriana   También queremos una botella de (8) _____vino_____ tinto. Gracias.

J. ¿Qué te gusta hacer? En grupos de tres personas, hablen de las cosas que comen en algunas ocasiones especiales (cumpleaños, aniversarios, graduaciones, etc.). Incluyan en su conversación: Answers will vary.

- qué hacen, adónde van, con quién, qué sirven en casa
- cuando van a restaurantes, qué piden, cuál es su plato favorito
- si van al parque, a qué parque van, qué hacen allí

J. Ask the students to prepare their own answers to this activity for homework, to discuss in groups in class. Point out that the construction *to have* + [*food*] in English cannot be transferred into Spanish.

K. En el restaurante. En grupos de tres personas, escriban las conversaciones entre las personas; inventen todos los detalles. Después actúen los diálogos para el resto de la clase. Answers will vary.

Primera conversación

_____
_____
_____
_____

Segunda conversación

_____
_____
_____
_____

K. Allow at least eight minutes for students to prepare their dialogues. Ask them to act them out in front of the rest of the class. As students make mistakes, jot them down. When they have all presented, reconvene the class in order to discuss the mistakes.

Invitación a **Argentina**

Del álbum de
Sofía

Argentina tiene aproximadamente 38 millones de habitantes y es famosa por su carne, el mate y el tango. La carne de res es uno de los platos principales de la comida argentina. El mate (un té verde) es la bebida argentina por excelencia, aunque se bebe en Uruguay y otros países también. Para beber mate, se necesita una taza (cup) especial y un popote (straw) metálico.

Práctica adicional		
Cuaderno de tareas WB p.230, G–H LM pp.233–234, A–B, Pron.	Audio CD-ROM Episodio 9	Website vistahigher learning.com

Actividades comunicativas

 **A. Crucigrama.**

Instrucciones para Estudiante 1

Complete the crossword puzzle by testing your partner's knowledge of foods and drinks. You each have a different half of the puzzle. Read the definitions so that your partner can guess the missing words. Take turns until the puzzle is complete.

[Crossword puzzle grid with the following entries:]

- 1 vertical: J U G (JUGO)
- 2 vertical: F R I J O L E S
- 3 vertical: H U E V O S
- 4 vertical: J A M Ó N
- 5 vertical: A L M U E R Z O
- 6 horizontal: M A R I S C O S
- 7 vertical: C O M I D A
- 8 horizontal: L E C H E
- 9 vertical: C E R E A L
- 10 horizontal/vertical: P A N — P O L L O
- 11 horizontal: A R R O Z
- 12 vertical: C A F É
- 13 vertical: D E S A Y U N O
- 14 horizontal/vertical: C A M A R O N E S — C A R N E
- 15 vertical: R E F R E S C O S
- 16 horizontal: P E S C A D O
- 17 horizontal: Y O G U R T
- 18 horizontal: C E N A
- 19 horizontal: V E R D U R A S

Definiciones

Verticales:

1. Una bebida de fruta común para el desayuno.
2. Se sirven con la comida mexicana; son pequeños y negros o cafés.
3. Se comen fritos o en omelet; son ricos en colesterol.
4. Es común hacer sándwiches de _____ y queso.
5. La comida del mediodía.
7. Todo lo que comemos; los alimentos.
9. Se come en el desayuno con leche; tiene fibra.
10. Lo que se come en KFC.
12. Una bebida similar al té.
13. La primera comida del día.
14. Los vegetarianos nunca comen _____.
15. La Coca-Cola y el 7-UP son _____.

A. Crucigrama.

Instrucciones para Estudiante 2

Complete the crossword puzzle by testing your partner's knowledge of foods and drinks. You each have a different half of the puzzle. Read the definitions so that your partner can guess the missing words. Take turns until the puzzle is complete.

Definiciones

Horizontales:

6. Los camarones y la langosta son _____.
8. Una bebida blanca; tiene calcio.
10. Se necesita para hacer un sándwich.
11. Se usa mucho en la comida china; es blanco.
14. Un marisco pequeño y caro (en la forma plural).
16. Vive en el agua; se come en filetes.
17. Un producto lácteo; se come con o sin frutas.
18. La última comida del día.
19. Tienen vitaminas; no son dulces; generalmente son verdes.

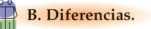 **B. Diferencias.**

Instrucciones para **Estudiante 1**

Hay varias diferencias entre tu restaurante y el restaurante de tu compañero/a. Para encontrar las diferencias, necesitas describir qué hay en el restaurante, qué comen o beben las personas, qué piden o qué sirven los meseros; anota siete diferencias.

Modelo   Hoy hay helado de chocolate en las especiales del día.

1. Camarones a la diabla: $29.45/$19.45
2. Filete de pescado/Langosta termidor
3. Cerveza/Coca-Cola
4. Menú: helados/hamburguesa, papas fritas
5. Ensalada/Sándwich
6. Pastel/Galletas
7. Café/Té

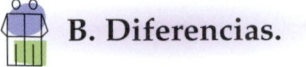

B. Diferencias.

Hay varias diferencias entre tu restaurante y el restaurante de tu compañero/a. Para encontrar las diferencias, necesitas describir qué hay en el restaurante, qué comen o beben las personas, qué piden o qué sirven los meseros; anota siete diferencias.

| Modelo | Hoy hay helado de chocolate en las especiales del día. |

1. Camarones a la diabla: $29.45/$19.45
2. Filete de pescado/Langosta termidor
3. Cerveza/Coca-Cola
4. Menú: helados/hamburguesa, papas fritas
5. Ensalada/Sándwich
6. Pastel/Galletas
7. Café/Té

C. Un programa de intercambio.

Instrucciones para Estudiante 1

You are considering becoming a host family for an international student. Interview the student applying to stay at your home for a summer immersion program. Based on their responses, decide if you wish to accept this student. Answers will vary.

Find out about the student's:

- activities
- eating habits and dietary requirements
- family and hometown or country
- personality traits

C. Give students time to prepare written questions before they complete this activity. Provide appropriate examples.

¡Fíjate!

You may take time to prepare written questions for your partner before you begin this activity, i.e. **¿Te gusta bailar? ¿Qué te gusta comer? ¿Haces ejercicio?**, etc.

C. Un programa de intercambio.

▲ Instrucciones para Estudiante 2

You are applying for an exchange program and are being interviewed by a prospective host. Based on this interview, you will decide if you will stay with this family or look for another one. Answer all the questions you are asked, and ask a few of your own. Answers will vary.

Ask about:
- the members of the host family
- their activities
- their eating habits
- anything else you think may be important

¡Fíjate! You may take time to prepare written questions for your partner before you begin this activity, i.e. ¿Cuántas personas viven en la casa? ¿Cuántos años tienen? ¿Salen con frecuencia?, etc.

La correspondencia

 El correo: La Estancia Santa Gertrudis. A friend of yours wants to go to a place to relax, eat a healthy diet, and relieve stress. She found this brochure in Spanish. First, read the questions. Then read the brochure for her and answer the questions in English.

1. Where is the resort? The resort is in Chascomús, Argentina.

2. What is the spa like? Answers will vary. Sample answer: The spa is large, tranquil, and healthy.

3. What is the food like? The food is natural and homemade.

4. What are the daily activities? Describe them. The daily activities include walks around the lake, swimming, soccer, horseback riding, biking, and yoga.

5. What do you think are some special features of this spa? Would it be a place for relaxation and meditation? Why? Answers will vary.

Reading Strategy: Scanning for specific information

When reading a Spanish text for specific information, you can disregard information that does not correspond to your purpose for reading. Be content with understanding the overall meaning. *Scan* the text—that is, locate and read carefully only the information you are looking for. For example, in the following article, you need to know where **la Estancia Santa Gertrudis** is. *Scan* the first paragraph to locate the country or state. Be sure to read the questions first so you know what specific information you are looking for. Remember to look for cognates to help you understand the text.

Lo último en salud y descanso:

Un fin de semana en la Estancia Santa Gertrudis

La Estancia Santa Gertrudis es un spa ecológico de 1.660 hectáreas, con enormes arboledas,[1] un lago de 200 hectáreas y actividades para todos los gustos. Está localizada en el partido[2] de Chascomús, a 165 kilómetros de la capital, en Argentina. La estancia recibe un máximo de diez personas cada fin de semana: seis en la casa principal y cuatro en la casa de huéspedes.[3]

En un oasis de tranquilidad, comida saludable, ejercicio diario, safaris fotográficos, observación de varias clases de animales silvestres, la Estancia Santa Gertrudis es una "opción ideal para un fin de semana saludable y activo".

Las actividades del día incluyen caminatas alrededor del lago, fútbol, natación, caballos, bicicletas y, la especialidad de la casa, clases de yoga (método Iyengar).

La comida es natural y casera, elaborada con harinas integrales, verduras cultivadas en la estancia y, para quienes lo deseen, carne ecológica de producción propia. Por la tarde, usted puede descansar en la vieja arboleda que rodea la casa, leer, conversar con los otros huéspedes, remar[4] en el lago o simplemente relajarse.

Un fin de semana de dieta saludable, ejercicio diario, descanso total y cuidados especiales hacen que usted se sienta[5] extraordinariamente bien y feliz.

Para recibir más información, llame a Darío Sarachaga, teléfono (0242) 3-21-33, fax 8-06-14.

[1]*forests* [2]*state or province* [3]*guests* [4]*row* [5]*you feel*

En papel: Una visita por la ciudad. A good friend of yours from high school is coming to visit you for a week next month. Write a letter telling your friend what you have planned during their stay—places you will visit, activities you have planned, new restaurants you will go to, and so on. Answers will vary.

> ### Writing Strategy: Recombining learned material
> As your ability to communicate in Spanish increases, you will be able to link the words and phrases you know to express more complex messages. When responding to a writing task—in this case, a letter to a friend, you should devise an appropriate plan to organize your ideas effectively. First, determine the information that needs to be included in the letter. Then identify the places you want to go. Organize your letter by linking those places with activities you plan to do. Finally, write your letter.

En papel. This activity may be assigned as homework. Focus on only the vocabulary and grammatical structures practiced in **Episodio 9**: food and meal-related vocabulary and structures. Group students for them to share their plans and compare the places they chose to take their friends.

Video
CD-ROM

¡A ver de nuevo!

Parte 1. Escribe un resumen del episodio. Incluye la comida que llevan al parque y las cosas que les gusta comer. Answers will vary.

Audio
CD-ROM

Instructor's Resources
• VHS Video
• Worktext CD
• IRM: Videoscript

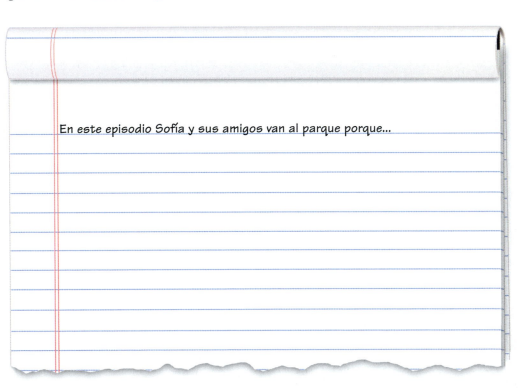

En este episodio Sofía y sus amigos van al parque porque...

Parte 2. Después trabaja con un(a) compañero/a para añadir más información.

Práctica adicional		
Cuaderno de tareas WB pp.231–232, I–J LM p.234, A–B	Audio CD-ROM Episodio 9	Website vistahigher learning.com

Vocabulario del Episodio 9

Instructor's Resources
• Testing program
• Website

Objetivos comunicativos

You should now be able to do the following in Spanish:

✔ talk about food

✔ discuss healthy eating habits

✔ order a meal

Para hablar de las comidas

desayunar	*to have breakfast*	el almuerzo	*lunch*
comer	*to eat; to have lunch*	la cuenta	*bill, check*
cenar	*to have dinner/supper*	el/la mesero/a	*waiter/waitress*
pedir (e → i)	*to ask (for), order* (a meal)	el plato/platillo	*dish*
servir (e → i)	*to serve*		
tener hambre	*to be hungry*		
tener sed	*to be thirsty*		

La comida

Un desayuno internacional *An international breakfast*

el cereal	*cereal*	la fruta	*fruit*
la dona	*donut*	la manzana	*apple*
el huevo	*egg*	la pera	*pear*
el pan tostado	*toast*	el plátano	*banana*
el yogurt	*yogurt*	la uva	*grape*

Un almuerzo norteamericano *An American lunch*

la ensalada de lechuga y tomate	*lettuce and tomato salad*
el espagueti	*spaghetti*
la hamburguesa	*hamburger*
el jamón	*ham*
las papas fritas	*French fries*
el pavo	*turkey*
la pimienta	*pepper*
el pollo	*chicken*
el queso	*cheese*
la sal	*salt*
el sándwich de atún	*tuna sandwich*
la sopa	*soup*

La cena *Dinner*

el arroz	*rice*	la carne de res	*beef*
el bistec de res	*roast beef*	la langosta	*lobster*
los camarones	*shrimp*	los mariscos	*seafood*
la carne de cerdo	*pork*	el pescado	*fish*

Las verduras *Vegetables*

el brócoli	*broccoli*
los frijoles	*beans*
la papa al horno	*baked potato*
la zanahoria	*carrot*

Postres *Desserts*

los dulces	*candy, sweets*
el flan	*flan*
las galletas	*cookies*
el helado	*ice cream*
el pastel	*cake*

Las bebidas *Drinks*

el agua	*water*
el café	*coffee*
la cerveza	*beer*
el jugo de naranja	*orange juice*
la leche	*milk*
la limonada	*lemonade*
los refrescos	*sodas*
el té	*tea*
el vino tinto	*red wine*

Vocabulario personal

Write all the words you need to know in Spanish so that you can better talk about your eating habits and the foods you like/dislike.

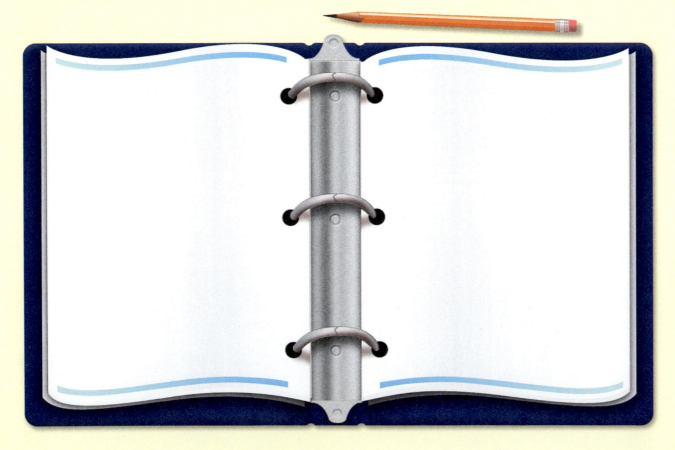

¡A escribir!

Episodio 9

Escenas de la vida: ¡Qué rica comida!

Video
CD-ROM

A. ¡A ver cuánto entendiste! See how much of the **Escena** you understood by matching the Spanish sentences with their English equivalents.

_g_	1. Es hora latina.	a. For parties, it's not necessary to be punctual.
_e_	2. La carne está muy buena.	
_a_	3. Para fiestas no es necesario ser puntual.	b. The secret is to prepare it the night before.
_b_	4. El secreto es prepararla la noche anterior.	c. It's about time!
		d. But it's not work.
_d_	5. Si no es el trabajo.	e. The meat is very good.
_c_	6. ¡Ya era hora!	f. The sauce isn't at all hot.
_h_	7. Eso dice mi papá.	g. It's Latin time.
_f_	8. La salsa no pica nada.	h. That's what my dad says.

Video
CD-ROM

B. Todos en el parque. Order the statements so that the dialogue makes sense.

_2_ a. El secreto para que la carne esté perfecta es prepararla la noche anterior con cerveza, sal y limón. Bueno, eso dice mi papá.

_6_ b. Ana Mari, ¿pica la salsa?

_1_ c. La carne está muy buena.

_3_ d. Tu papá tiene razón. Me gusta mucho la comida mexicana.

_7_ e. No, no pica nada.

_4_ f. ¿Entonces por qué siempre pides chili? En México no hay chili.

_5_ g. *No way!*

Vocabulario **1**

Talking about food
• **Food and meals**

C. Las categorías. Your ten-year-old niece has asked you to help her with her school project on food groups in Spanish. Fill in each of the categories with the names of foods in Spanish. Answers will vary.

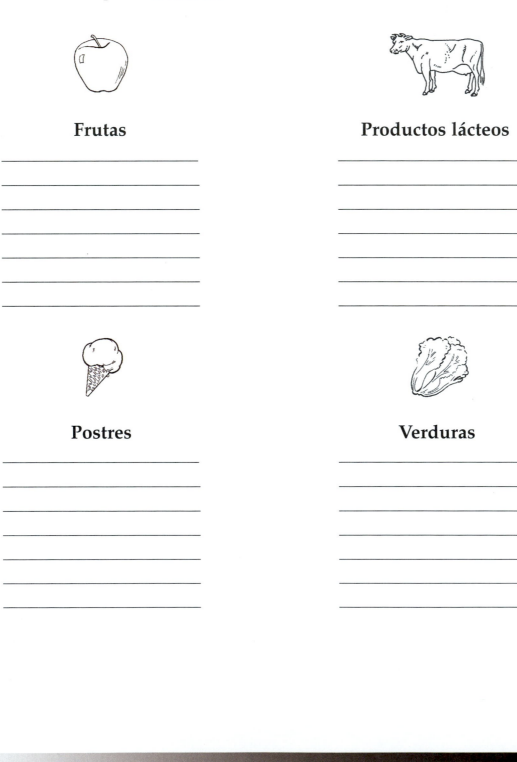

Frutas

_____

_____

_____

_____

_____

_____

Productos lácteos

_____

_____

_____

_____

_____

_____

Postres

_____

_____

_____

_____

_____

_____

Verduras

_____

_____

_____

_____

_____

_____

D. Cuerpo sano, mente sana. *(Healthy body, healthy mind.)* Look at the foods in the illustrations. Then write the foods you consider healthy under **Saludable** and write the reason why each is considered good: vitamins **(vitaminas)**, proteins **(proteínas)**, calcium **(calcio)**, or low in fat **(poca grasa)**. Under **No muy saludable,** list the foods and beverages that are high in fat **(grasa),** sugar **(azúcar),** salt **(sal),** or cholesterol **(colesterol)**.
Answers will vary.

Saludable	No muy saludable
leche (tiene calcio)	jamón (tiene grasa y sal)

E. Tres menús. You are planning three different breakfasts for the restaurant where you work. Write down the appropriate foods and beverages. Answers will vary.

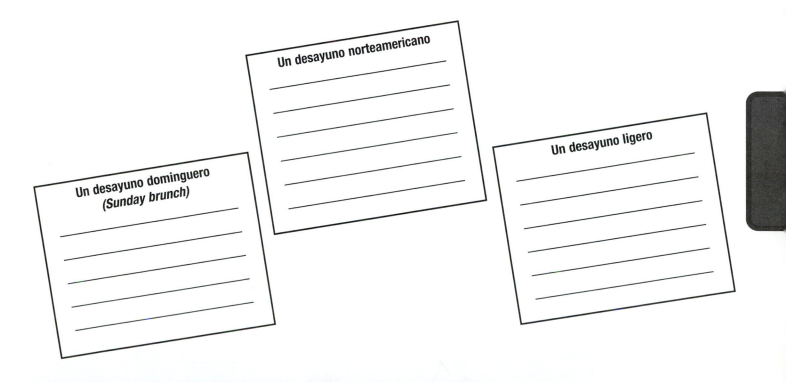

Un desayuno norteamericano

Un desayuno dominguero (Sunday brunch)

Un desayuno ligero

F. Las definiciones. Write the food item that best fits the description.

> **Modelo** La comida favorita de los chimpancés. **Los plátanos.**

1. Una bebida anaranjada *(orange)*, no tiene alcohol. _____ El jugo de naranja.
2. Son unas verduras anaranjadas. A Bugs Bunny le gustan. _____ Las zanahorias.
3. Es un marisco rojo muy caro. _____ La langosta.
4. Un pescado que se usa para hacer sándwiches. _____ El atún.
5. Tienes que beber ocho vasos de este líquido al día. _____ El agua.
6. A los niños les gusta mucho; es frío, de chocolate o vainilla. _____ El helado.
7. Escribe dos ejemplos de carne. _____ Answers will vary.
8. Es la comida más popular para *Thanksgiving*. _____ El pavo.
9. Un plato de verduras frescas. _____ La ensalada.
10. De esta bebida, hay tinto, blanco y rosado. _____ El vino.

 **Gramática 1**

Ordering a meal
• Pedir and servir

G. ¡Qué desastre! Lalo and Santiaguito are working at a cafeteria during their vacation. Since they are both easily distracted, they bring the wrong things to Sofía and her friends. Describe this disaster by completing the sentences with the appropriate forms of **pedir** and **servir.** (Note: **me** means *[to] me,* **te** means *[to] you,* **le** means *[to] him/her,* and **les** means *[to] them.*).

> **Modelo** Los niños **piden** una pizza de queso, pero Lalo les **sirve** una pizza vegetariana.

1. Sofía _____ pide _____ un café, pero Santiaguito le _____ sirve _____ un té.
2. Adriana y Ana Mari _____ piden _____ frutas, pero los chicos les _____ sirven _____ pastel.
3. Yo _____ pido _____ pastel, pero ellos me _____ sirven _____ yogurt.
4. Nosotras _____ pedimos _____ limonadas para todas, pero Lalo nos _____ sirve _____ refrescos.
5. ¿Tú _____ pides _____ helado de fresa? ¡De seguro *(for sure),* Lalo y Santiaguito te van a _____ servir _____ helado de vainilla!

H. ¡Vamos a cenar! Imagine you are at an Argentinian restaurant. Answer the waiter's questions. Answers will vary.

1. Buenas noches, ¿está listo para pedir? _____
2. ¿Y quiere pedir algo *(something)* antes del plato principal? _____
3. ¿Quiere beber un café o un refresco? _____
4. ¿Va a pedir postre? _____

Nombre _____ Fecha _____

Para terminar

I. ¡ Vivir bien con poca grasa[1]! Lee las preguntas, después lee el anuncio de libro *Vivir bien con poca grasa* y responde a las preguntas.

1. ¿Qué beneficios puede tener el comer con poca grasa? _Tener mejor humor y más energía._
_____

2. ¿Qué ayuda a que la grasa se queme más rápidamente? _Tomar agua._

3. ¿Qué actividad hace que engordemos *(makes us get fat)*? _Mirar la televisión._

¡Disfrute[2] de la mejor salud de toda su vida!
Una vez que usted viva con poca grasa, su calidad de vida va a mejorar inmediatamente. Va a tener mejor humor y más energía. Va a dejar de[3] preocuparse por su peso y va a comenzar a disfrutar de los beneficios de un cuerpo más delgado y sano, sin los peligros propios[4] de las dietas. ¡No se tarde más! Envíe el **Certificado de Inspección GRATUITA ¡hoy mismo!**

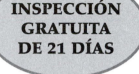

INSPECCIÓN GRATUITA DE 21 DÍAS

Secreto para controlar la  GRASA automáticamente

Nº 1

Tomar agua puede ayudar a reducir los depósitos de grasa. Cuando usted está totalmente hidratada su cuerpo transporta más rápidamente la grasa a los músculos para ser quemada[5] allí. En la PÁGINA 107 de VIVIR BIEN CON POCA GRASA, descubra cómo el AGUA HELADA puede servir durante todo el día como ¡SÚPER estimulante de la combustión de grasa!

Secreto para controlar la GRASA automáticamente

Nº 2

La TV hace aumentar de peso: Increíble, pero es ¡la pura verdad! Estar sentada[6] delante del televisor la hace engordar más que el estar solamente sentada. Además, si usted mira TV por 4 horas o más, es DOS VECES más probable que sufra[7] de sobrepeso. Antes de prender[8] el "control de producción de grasa" de su televisor, lea la PÁGINA 71 para saber cuántas horas de televisión puede usted mirar.

---

[1]*fat*　[2]*enjoy*　[3]**dejar**... *stop*　[4]**peligros**... *inherent risks*　[5]*burned*　[6]*sitting*　[7]*suffer*　[8]*turn on*

J. Una miniprueba para terminar. Give Ramón the following information about yourself. Write it in the form of a paragraph. Then write how you would ask him for the information in **2**. Remember that you have to create the questions that would ellicit the information you need.

1. Tell Ramón: a. about your eating habits.

                             b. the places you usually go after school.

                             c. who you live with.

                             d. everything you are going to do tomorrow.

2. Ask Ramón: e. what they serve at his home for dinner.

                             f. what his favorite dish is.

                             g. what he usually eats between meals (**entre comidas**).

                             h. where he goes when he feels like eating his favorite food.

                             i. if he has to work on Sundays.

1. _____ Answers will vary. _____

_____

_____

_____

_____

_____

_____

_____

_____

_____

2. e. _____ ¿Qué sirven en tu casa para la cena? _____

    f. _____ ¿Cuál es tu plato favorito? _____

    g. _____ ¿Qué comes generalmente entre comidas? _____

    h. _____ ¿Adónde vas cuando quieres comer tu comida favorita? _____

    i. _____ ¿Tienes que trabajar los domingos? _____

Episodio

¡A escuchar!

9

Comprensión

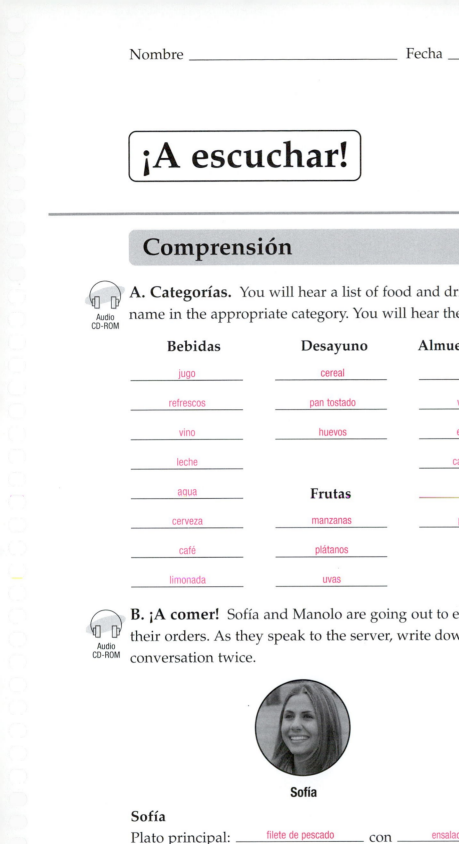

A. Categorías. You will hear a list of food and drinks. As you hear each item, write its name in the appropriate category. You will hear the list twice.

Bebidas	Desayuno	Almuerzo o cena	Postres
jugo	cereal	sopa	pastel
refrescos	pan tostado	verduras	galletas
vino	huevos	ensalada	helado
leche		camarones	dulces
agua	**Frutas**	pollo	
cerveza	manzanas	pescado	
café	plátanos		
limonada	uvas		

B. ¡A comer! Sofía and Manolo are going out to eat. You are going to hear them place their orders. As they speak to the server, write down their orders. You will hear the conversation twice.

Sofía

Manolo

Sofía

Plato principal: _____filete de pescado_____ con _____ensalada mixta_____ y _____arroz_____

Bebida: _____café_____ Postre: _____nada_____

Manolo

Plato principal: _____carne asada_____ con _____sopa de verduras_____ y _____frijoles negros_____

Bebida: _____agua_____ Postre: _____flan y pastel_____

Pronunciación

Audio CD-ROM

La *c*, la *z*, *que* y *qui*. The letter **c (ce)** has three sounds. **C** followed by **a, o, u,** or any consonant is pronounced as *k*. When **c** is followed by **e** or **i,** it is pronounced as *s* in Latin America and *th* in most parts of Spain. Listen and repeat these words, phrases, and sentences after the speaker as a Latin American would.

Cuba	**calculadora**	**ciencia**	**a veces**
Compro cinco cuadernos para la clase.		**Carmen come cereal con calcio.**	

The letter **z (zeta)** always has the sound of *s* in Latin American Spanish, and always has the sound of *th* in Spanish from Spain.

zanahorias	**almorzar**	**Venezuela**	**lápiz**	**perezoso**
No como zanahorias.			**Almorzamos y tomamos una cerveza.**	

Now, listen to the same words and sentences spoken by a speaker from Spain.

In Spanish, the sounds **ke** and **ki** are represented in writing by **que** and **qui** respectively.

¿qué?	**química**	**máquina**	**aquí**	**chaqueta**
¿Por qué quiere esquiar aquí?			**¿De quién es la chaqueta?**	

Más escenas de la vida

Sofía, Ana Mari, Manolo, and Wayne are eating at a Caribbean restaurant. Listen to their conversation, and complete activities **A** and **B**. You will hear the conversation twice.

A. Definiciones. Describe the following dishes based on the conversation.

Audio CD-ROM

1. El lechón es... _____ carne de cerdo. _____

2. El congrí es... _____ frijoles negros cocinados con arroz. _____

3. La ropa vieja es... _____ carne de res desmenuzada con verduras. _____

4. Un postre cubano es... _____ guayaba con queso. _____

B. Responde. Write the answers to the following questions.

Audio CD-ROM

1. ¿Qué plato sirven que es espectacular?
_____ El lechón asado con papas. _____

2. ¿Qué va a pedir Sofía? _____ Va a pedir sopa de pescado y ensalada. _____

3. ¿Qué va a pedir Ana Mari?
_____ Va a pedir camarones fritos, congrí, plátanos maduros y guayaba con queso. _____

4. ¿Qué plato es similar a la machaca mexicana?
_____ La ropa vieja. _____

5. ¿Qué va a pedir Wayne? _____ Va a pedir ropa vieja. _____

Episodio 10

Escenas de la vida: Una invitación confusa

Video
CD-ROM

A. ¡Mira cuánto puedes entender! As you listen, indicate who makes the following statements: Wayne (**W**), Sofía (**S**), or Ana Mari (**AM**).

Audio
CD-ROM

Instructor's Resources
- Overheads
- VHS Video
- Worktext CD
- Website
- IRM: Videoscript, Comprehensible input

La película **empieza** a las 8:30. ___W___

Podemos tomar café antes de la película. ___W___

¿Ana Mari, **puedes venir conmigo** al cine? ___S___

Bueno, **voy contigo**, pero mi coche no funciona. ___AM___

Wayne no **viene por mí** a mi casa. ___S___

Es difícil **encontrar** estacionamiento. ___W___

Prefiero no manejar de noche. ___S___

Cultura a lo vivo

In many Latin American countries, when a young man invites a girl out on a date, he is expected to pick her up at home. This custom provides an opportunity for the parents of the girl to meet the young man.

Video Synopsis. Wayne asks Sofía out and asks her to meet him at the café. Sofía is irritated that Wayne is not planning to pick her up, and asks Ana Mari to go with her. Ana Mari says they will have to invite Ramón to drive them. Sofía says Wayne will pick her up next time; Ana Mari isn't certain that there will be a next time.

Video
CD-ROM

B. ¿Te diste cuenta? Escucha las conversaciones o mira el video otra vez para indicar el orden cronológico, del uno al seis, de las siguientes acciones.

Audio
CD-ROM

_____2_____ a. Wayne invita a Sofía al cine.

_____5_____ b. Sofía habla con Ana Mari.

_____1_____ c. Wayne llama a Sofía por teléfono.

_____6_____ d. Ana Mari acepta ir con Sofía al cine.

_____3_____ e. Sofía acepta la invitación de Wayne.

_____4_____ f. Wayne y Sofía deciden encontrarse en el café.

Video
CD-ROM

C. Los hechos. Selecciona la respuesta correcta.

Audio
CD-ROM

Sofía

Wayne

Ana Mari

1. Wayne dice (_says_)...
   a. Voy por ti.
   b. ¿Dónde dan la película?
   c. ¿Quieres ir al cine el sábado?

2. Wayne dice...
   a. ¿Quieres visitar el Centro Cultural de la universidad?
   b. ¿Puedes llegar a las 7:30?
   c. Mi coche no funciona.

3. Ana Mari...
   a. no entiende a Sofía.
   b. cree que Sofía es muy moderna.
   c. puede ir en su coche.

4. Sofía...
   a. sale sola por la noche con frecuencia.
   b. va al cine en el coche de Ramón.
   c. no cree que Wayne la invite a salir otra vez.

Learning Strategy: Making an educated guess

To understand the general meaning of a message, you do not have to understand every word you hear or read. In most situations, you can use the context, your knowledge of the world and of how people communicate, and also visual cues such as facial expressions, gestures, and body language to make an educated guess about meaning. Use the context to derive meaning. More often than not, you can guess correctly at the meaning of a word by focusing on the words that precede and follow it. For example, when Wayne said to Sofía, "**quiero llegar temprano porque es difícil encontrar estacionamiento,**" you had not seen **encontrar** before, but you know that **quiero llegar temprano** means _I want to arrive early_ and that **estacionamiento** means _parking_. Therefore, using the context, you can easily guess that **encontrar** means _to find_.

Práctica adicional

Cuaderno de tareas
WB pp.251–252, A–C

Video
CD-ROM
Episodio 10

Learning Strategy. Highlight the importance of using context to derive meaning. Encourage students to always guess at the meaning of words, using their knowledge of the context.

Gramática 1

Accepting and declining invitations
• **Stem-changing verbs (e → ie)**
and (**o → ue**)

In the conversation, Wayne said **¿Quieres ir al cine el sábado?** to ask Sofía if she wanted to go to the movies. Sofía responded **Sí, puedo. Quieres** and **puedo** are forms of the verbs **querer** and **poder**.

Analizar y descubrir

1. Study the following exchanges:

Querer y poder	
—¿**Quieres** tomar un café?	*Do you want some coffee?*
—Sí, **quiero**, pero no **puedo** tomar cafeína.	*Yes, I want some, but I can't have any caffeine.*
—¿Ana Mari **quiere** llevar su coche?	*Does Ana Mari want to take her car?*
—No **puede**, porque no funciona.	*She can't, because it doesn't work.*
—¿Sofía y Ana Mari **quieren** ir al cine?	*Do Sofía and Ana Mari want to go to the movies?*
—Sí, **quieren**, pero no **pueden**.	*Yes, they want to, but they can't.*
—¿**Quieren** ustedes ir al cine? —¿**Queréis** ir al cine?	*Do you want to go to the movies?*
—**Queremos** ir pero no **podemos**, porque tenemos que trabajar.	*We want to go but we can't, because we have to work.*

2. Write the forms of **querer** and **poder**.

Gramática 1. Students may work with a partner to complete the activity. Lead students through this activity to help them learn the rules governing stem-changing verbs.

	Querer	Poder
yo	quiero	puedo
tú	quieres	puedes
usted/él/ella	quiere	puede
nosotros/as	queremos	podemos
vosotros/as	queréis	podéis
ustedes/ellos/as	quieren	pueden

3. Look at the endings of **querer** and **poder**. Are they the same as other **-er** verbs you know, such as **comer** and **beber**? __yes__

4. Look at the stems of the two verbs (**quer-, pod-**) and answer the questions.

    a. What happens to the **-e-** of **querer**? It becomes _____-ie-_____.

    b. What happens to the **-o-** of **poder**? It becomes _____-ue-_____.

    c. Does the **-e-** of **querer** change in all the verb forms? _____no_____.

    d. Does the **-o-** of **poder** change in all the verb forms? _____no_____.

5. Complete these rules for stem-changing verbs.

    a. In stem-changing verbs like **querer**, **-e-** changes to __-ie-__ in all forms except the _____nosotros/as_____ and _____vosotros/as_____ forms.

    b. In stem-changing verbs like **poder**, **-o-** changes to __-ue-__ in all forms except the _____nosotros/as_____ and _____vosotros/as_____ forms.

6. The following expressions contain other common stem-changing verbs:

Para hacer planes con los amigos			
e ⟶ ie		**o/u ⟶ ue**	
empezar a…	*to start . . .*	**almorzar**	*to have lunch*
entender el problema	*to understand the problem*	**dormir bien/mal**	*to sleep well/poorly*
pensar en	*to think about* (someone)	**encontrar**	*to find*
pensar que	*to think that* (phrase)	**jugar (al) tenis**	*to play tennis*
preferir no manejar	*to prefer not to drive*	**(no) poder ir**	*(not) to be able to go*
querer	*to want; to love*	**recordar**	*to remember*
venir por mí	*to pick me up*		

*__venir__ has a **g** in the **yo** person—**yo vengo.**

Note that **jugar** is the only verb that has the **u ⟶ ue** stem change.

PRÁCTICA

A. Hombres y mujeres.

Parte 1. Indica si estás de acuerdo *(if you agree)* con los siguientes estereotipos sobre los hombres y las mujeres.   Answers will vary.

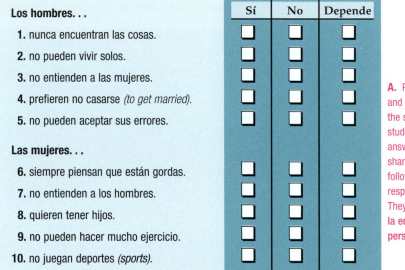

Los hombres. . .	Sí	No	Depende
1. nunca encuentran las cosas.	☐	☐	☐
2. no pueden vivir solos.	☐	☐	☐
3. no entienden a las mujeres.	☐	☐	☐
4. prefieren no casarse *(to get married).*	☐	☐	☐
5. no pueden aceptar sus errores.	☐	☐	☐
Las mujeres. . .			
6. siempre piensan que están gordas.	☐	☐	☐
7. no entienden a los hombres.	☐	☐	☐
8. quieren tener hijos.	☐	☐	☐
9. no pueden hacer mucho ejercicio.	☐	☐	☐
10. no juegan deportes *(sports).*	☐	☐	☐

A. Read the instructions and have volunteers read the sentences while students select their answers. Have students share their opinions, and follow up when they respond with **depende.…** They may use **depende de la edad, depende de la persona,** etc.

Parte 2. En grupos de tres personas, compartan sus respuestas y discutan sus ideas.

> **Modelo**   **No estoy de acuerdo con el comentario número dos.**
> **Mis amigos y yo vivimos solos y estamos muy bien.**
> **No necesitamos a las mujeres.**

B. Lotería. Find a classmate who fits the following descriptions. Write their name in the space provided; the first student with two lines of four in a row wins. Answers will vary.

| Modelo | —¿Haces ejercicios tres veces a la semana?
—Sí, hago ejercicios tres veces a la semana. ¿Y tú?
—Yo no. |

_____ casi nunca almuerza en la cafetería.	_____ juega vóleibol una vez a la semana.	_____ prefiere no manejar por la noche.	_____ empieza a estudiar tres días antes del examen.
_____ hace ejercicio tres veces a la semana.	_____ a veces no entiende la tarea.	_____ quiere ir al cine este fin de semana.	_____ no tiene ganas de hacer la tarea hoy.
_____ ve videos en casa de su novio/a.	_____ no duerme ocho horas por noche.	_____ recuerda a su primer(a) maestro/a.	_____ vive en casa de sus abuelos.
_____ encuentra estacionamiento cuando llega.	_____ sirve tamales en Navidad.	_____ no puede tomar clases por las noches.	_____ piensa que esta clase es muy fácil.

Instructor's Resources
• IRM: Additional Activities

Additional Activities. You may want to play a concentration game, or make up a dialogue and cut it up into pieces for the class to reconstruct. See the **Instructor's Resource Manual** for samples.

Invitación a **España**

Práctica adicional

Website
vistahigher
learning.com

Del álbum de
Sofía

España tiene aproximadamente 40 millones de habitantes y es dos veces el tamaño del estado de Oregon. Salamanca, en España, es una ciudad con una larga tradición intelectual y cultural. La Universidad de Salamanca se fundó en 1218 y es la más antigua del país. Hoy en día, la ciudad tiene innumerables academias, institutos, escuelas, colegios y universidades, por lo que estudian ahí miles de estudiantes nacionales e internacionales.

C. Problemas de familia. Completa la conversación entre Adriana y su esposo con los verbos de la lista. Después contesta las preguntas.

empiezas	almuerzas	quieres
puedes	duermes	prefiero
encontrar	jugar	vienes

Santiago   Adriana, no entiendo por qué (1) ____quieres____ trabajar y estudiar. Si quieres estudiar para contadora, es mejor que no trabajes hasta que termines.

Adriana   Si no tengo experiencia, no voy a poder (2) ____encontrar____ trabajo cuando termine.

Santiago   Es cierto, pero tú (3) ____puedes____ adquirir *(acquire)* experiencia más adelante. Recuerda que tienes esposo, casa e hijos. No tienes tiempo para nada. La casa es un desastre.

Adriana   Ay, Santiago, limpiar la casa es muy aburrido. (4) ____Prefiero____ trabajar y estudiar. Con el dinero que gano le puedo pagar a una empleada.

Santiago   No es sólo la casa; últimamente tú no (5) ____duermes____ suficiente, a veces sólo cinco o seis horas por noche. Además (6) ____almuerzas____ mal, porque no tienes tiempo ni para ir al supermercado. Casi nunca hay comida en el refrigerador.

Adriana   Santiago, (7) ____empiezas____ a hablar como esos hombres que no quieren que sus esposas progresen.

Santiago   No es verdad. Quiero que tú progreses, pero...

1. ¿Por qué quiere trabajar Adriana?

   Quiere trabajar porque quiere tener experiencia.

   _____

2. ¿Qué piensa Santiago que Adriana debe *(should)* hacer?

   Piensa que debe estudiar ahora y trabajar más adelante.

   _____

3. En tu opinión, ¿quién tiene razón *(is right)*?

   Answers will vary.

   _____

D. Un anuncio de periódico.

Parte 1. Adriana siempre lee el periódico para estar bien informada. Hoy encuentra este anuncio de un restaurante nuevo cerca de su casa. Completa el anuncio con las formas apropiadas de los verbos.

Restaurante El Huarache Veloz

Calle Rancho del Rey 345   Tel. 2-A-COMER

Si usted (1) _____quiere_____ (querer) almorzar bien y sin trabajo, venga a nuestro restaurante, El Huarache Veloz. Nosotros (2) ____entendemos____ (entender) las necesidades de la mujer moderna que trabaja y que no (3) _____tiene_____ (tener) tiempo para cocinar. Ud. y sus compañeros de trabajo (4) _____pueden_____ (poder) comunicarse con nosotros por teléfono al número 2-A-COMER. Es muy fácil (5) ____recordar____ (recordar) nuestro número. Si usted (6) _____prefiere_____ (preferir), comuníquese por correo electrónico al hv@acomer.com. Nuestro restaurante se (7) ____encuentra____ (encontrar) en las calles de Rancho del Rey y Paseo Ladera. Nosotros (8) ____empezamos____ (empezar) a tomar órdenes desde las ocho de la mañana.

Parte 2. Encuentra un restaurante en Internet que acepte las órdenes por correo electrónico para compartir con la clase. Después hablen de la comida que sirven y los precios. *Answers will vary.*

E. Preguntas personales. Contesta las preguntas en tu cuaderno y después entrevista a tu compañero/a y escribe sus respuestas aquí. *Answers will vary.*

En la universidad

1. ¿Qué quieres estudiar? ¿Por qué?

_____

2. ¿Vas bien en tus clases? ¿Cuáles son más difíciles?

_____

3. ¿Empiezas a estudiar con tiempo para un examen? ¿Qué cosas haces para prepararte?

_____

4. ¿Dónde prefieres estudiar? ¿Por qué te gusta estudiar ahí?

_____

E. Have students answer the questions in writing (as homework), and then share their answers out loud with a partner, in groups, or as a class.

Los fines de semana

5. ¿En qué ocasiones prefieres estar con tus amigos? ¿Y con tu familia?

_____

6. ¿Puedes hacer todas las cosas que quieres? Si no, ¿por qué no?

_____

7. ¿Cuántas horas duermes? ¿Piensas que es importante dormir suficiente? ¿Por qué o por qué no?

_____

8. ¿Almuerzas en casa? ¿Qué almuerzas generalmente? ¿Con quién?

_____

9. ¿Qué deportes (*sports*) practicas? ¿Juegas béisbol?, ¿tenis?, ¿fútbol americano?

_____

10. ¿Sales mucho? ¿Con quién? ¿Qué hacen?

_____

11. Cuando sales con alguien por primera vez, ¿piensas que el chico tiene que ir por la chica a su casa? ¿En qué casos sí y en qué casos no? Explica.

_____

_____

Banco de palabras:
Para hablar del trabajo

el horario flexible/fijo
flexible/fixed schedule

el sueldo alto/bajo
high/low salary

tiempo completo/parcial
full-time/part-time

el tiempo libre
spare time

el turno de la mañana /tarde/noche
morning/afternoon/evening (night) shift

¡Fíjate!

You will need these words to answer the questions. Familiarize yourself with them, since they will become active in the next episode.

En el trabajo

12. ¿Es fácil encontrar trabajo en tu ciudad? ¿Qué tipo de trabajos hay? ¿Te gusta tu trabajo? ¿Por qué?

_____

13. ¿Trabajas tiempo completo o tiempo parcial? ¿Recibes buen sueldo o quieres ganar más (*earn more*)?

_____

14. ¿Cuántas horas a la semana puedes trabajar? ¿Qué días no puedes trabajar?

_____

_____

15. ¿Prefieres trabajar el turno de la tarde o el de la mañana? ¿Tienes un horario flexible?

_____

_____

16. ¿Quieres encontrar otro trabajo este semestre? ¿Por qué?

_____

_____

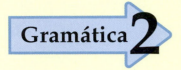

Gramática 2

Extending invitations
• Prepositional pronouns

In other conversations, the characters said the following statements.

Pronombres preposicionales	
¿Quieres ir **conmigo** al cine?	*Do you want to go to the movies with me?*
Bueno, voy **contigo** si vienes **por mí**.	*Fine, I'll go with you if you pick me up.*
Wayne siempre habla **de ti**.	*Wayne always talks about you.*
¿Y Sofía? ¿Piensa **en él**?	*And Sofía? Does she think about him?*
Ramón va a jugar **con nosotros**.	*Ramón is going to play with us.*
¿Wayne vive **con ustedes**? ¿Wayne vive **con vosotros**?	*Does Wayne live with you?*
No, él vive **con ellos**.	*No, he lives with them.*

1. Notice that the subject pronouns (**yo, tú, usted, él, ella, nosotros/as, ustedes, vosotros/as,** and **ellos/as**) and pronouns that follow prepositions (**a, de, con, para, por**) are the same, with two exceptions: **yo/mí** (**Vienes** *por mí*) and **tú/ti** (**Lo siento, no puedo ir** *por ti.*)
2. Notice that **conmigo** means *with me* and **contigo** means *with you.*
3. Some verbs you already know may be followed by prepositions: **hablar de, discutir con, vivir con, jugar con, ir por,** and **venir por.**

PRÁCTICA

F. ¿De quién habla? Sofía hizo *(made)* los siguientes comentarios. ¿A quién(es) se refiere(n) los pronombres preposicionales? Empareja las dos columnas.

___e___ 1. Necesito hablar *con ella*.   a. amigos

___a___ 2. Lalo va a jugar fútbol *con ellos*.   b. Lalo

___d___ 3. Mi abuela vive *con nosotros*.   c. Ana Mari y Sofía

___f___ 4. Quiero hablar *contigo*.   d. Mis padres y yo

___c___ 5. No comparte *(share)* sus cosas *con ellas*.   e. la profesora

___b___ 6. Es un irresponsable; por eso, discuto   f. tú
       mucho *con él*.

G. Un poco de lógica. Empareja cada pregunta o declaración con la respuesta lógica.

___c___ 1. ¿Está Sofía en casa?   a. Lo siento, pero no puedo.

___a___ 2. ¿Quieres ir conmigo al cine?   b. Claro que puedes venir conmigo.

___d___ 3. Su hijo es muy considerado, ¿no?   c. Sí. ¿Quieres hablar con ella?

___b___ 4. ¿Puedo ir contigo?   d. Sí. Siempre piensa en

___e___ 5. Estas flores son para ti.   nosotros primero.

            e. Gracias. Siempre piensas en mí.

H. Traducción. Escribe las siguientes frases en español.

1. I have tickets for the game tonight—do you want to go? Manolo and Jorge are also coming with us. We can go in Jorge's car.

Tengo boletos para el juego de esta noche— ¿quieres ir? Manolo y Jorge también vienen

con nosotros. Podemos ir en el carro de Jorge.

_____

¡Fíjate!

Remember not to translate word-for-word; translate ideas.

2. Sure I want to go, but I'd rather take my own car. I don't understand why you always invite Jorge—he's silly!

Claro que quiero ir, pero prefiero manejar mi (propio) coche. No entiendo porque siempre

invitas a Jorge—¡es un tonto!

_____

I. Escribe sobre las personas queridas. Contesta todas las preguntas en forma de párrafo. Después comparte tus respuestas con un(a) compañero/a. Answers will vary.

Modelo	Tu hermano/a: ¿Ves a tu hermano/a? ¿Qué haces con él/ella? ¿Vives con él/ella? **Veo a mi hermana casi todos los días. Tomo café con ella por las mañanas. A veces salgo con ella a cenar. Nunca discuto con ella. Y tampoco voy por ella con frecuencia. Prefiere manejar su coche. No vivo con ella, vivo con mi hija.**

1. Tus abuelos: ¿Ves a tus abuelos? ¿Sales con ellos? ¿Qué actividades haces con ellos?

_____
_____

2. Tu novio/a/mejor amigo/a: ¿Hablas mucho con él/ella? ¿Discutes con él/ella?

_____
_____
_____

3. Tus compañeros de clase: ¿Qué actividades haces con ellos? ¿Estudias con ellos? ¿Dónde y cuándo?

_____
_____
_____

4. Tu mamá o tu papá: ¿Vives con él/ella? ¿Discuten con frecuencia? ¿Por qué? ¿Qué actividades hacen juntos (together)?

_____
_____
_____
_____

Práctica adicional	
Cuaderno de tareas WB pp.254–255, H–L LM pp.257–258, A–B, Pron.	Audio CD-ROM Episodio 10

Actividades comunicativas

Audio
CD-ROM

A. La historia va así.

Parte 1. Mira las ilustraciones y escucha los comentarios de Manolo con respecto a su trabajo. Indica el orden cronológico en el que menciona las actividades. Después escucha los comentarios otra vez para verificar tus respuestas.

Instructor's Resources
• Worktext CD
• IRM: Tapescript

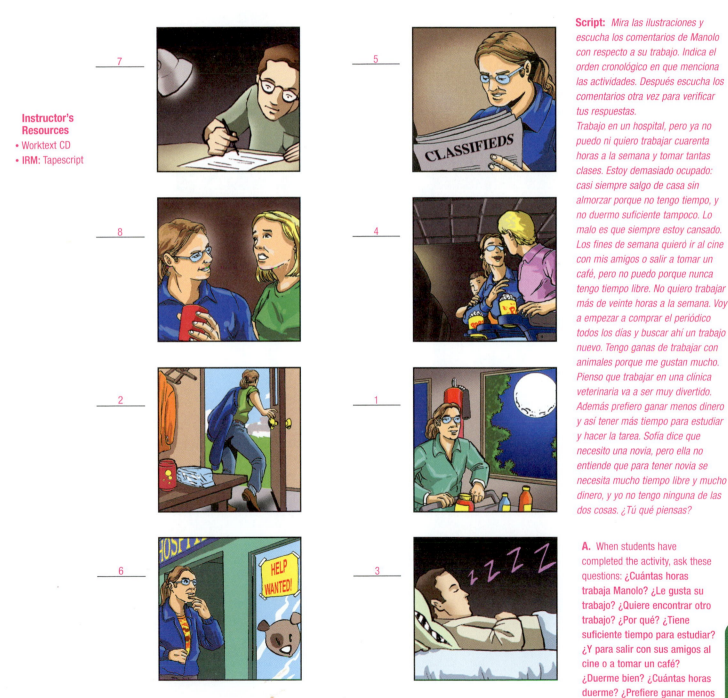

Script: *Mira las ilustraciones y escucha los comentarios de Manolo con respecto a su trabajo. Indica el orden cronológico en que menciona las actividades. Después escucha los comentarios otra vez para verificar tus respuestas.*

Trabajo en un hospital, pero ya no puedo ni quiero trabajar cuarenta horas a la semana y tomar tantas clases. Estoy demasiado ocupado: casi siempre salgo de casa sin almorzar porque no tengo tiempo, y no duermo suficiente tampoco. Lo malo es que siempre estoy cansado. Los fines de semana quieró ir al cine con mis amigos o salir a tomar un café, pero no puedo porque nunca tengo tiempo libre. No quiero trabajar más de veinte horas a la semana. Voy a empezar a comprar el periódico todos los días y buscar ahí un trabajo nuevo. Tengo ganas de trabajar con animales porque me gustan mucho. Pienso que trabajar en una clínica veterinaria va a ser muy divertido. Además prefiero ganar menos dinero y así tener más tiempo para estudiar y hacer la tarea. Sofía dice que necesito una novia, pero ella no entiende que para tener novia se necesita mucho tiempo libre y mucho dinero, y yo no tengo ninguna de las dos cosas. ¿Tú qué piensas?

A. When students have completed the activity, ask these questions: ¿Cuántas horas trabaja Manolo? ¿Le gusta su trabajo? ¿Quiere encontrar otro trabajo? ¿Por qué? ¿Tiene suficiente tiempo para estudiar? ¿Y para salir con sus amigos al cine o a tomar un café? ¿Duerme bien? ¿Cuántas horas duerme? ¿Prefiere ganar menos dinero o tener más tiempo libre? ¿Piensas que es necesario tener tiempo y dinero para tener novia o novio? ¿Por qué?

Parte 2. En grupos de tres, escriban la historia en diferente orden.

B. ¿Qué hace Manolo los sábados?

Instrucciones para **Estudiante 1**

 Parte 1. Tú tienes la mitad *(half)* de las ilustraciones, y tu compañero/a tiene la otra mitad. Juntos tienen que descubrir *(find out)* cómo es la rutina de Manolo los sábados. Describe tus ilustraciones y haz preguntas para completar el cuadro. Tu compañero/a empieza.

Answers will vary.

Modelo	Manolo limpia su cuarto por la mañana. ¿Qué hace después?

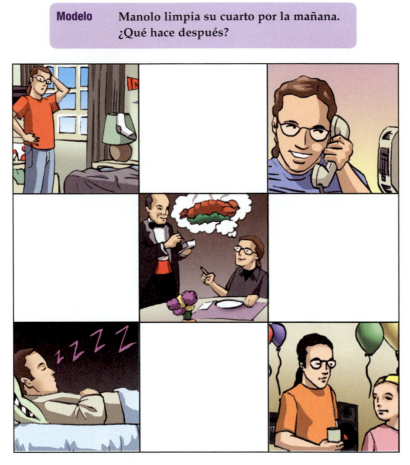

Parte 2. Ahora escribe un párrafo con los eventos. Inventa los detalles.

Modelo	Los sábados por la mañana Manolo generalmente…

_____

_____

_____

_____

_____

_____

_____

_____

_____

B. ¿Qué hace Manolo los sábados?

Instrucciones para Estudiante 2

Parte 1. Tú tienes la mitad *(half)* de las ilustraciones, y tu compañero/a tiene la otra mitad. Juntos tienen que descubrir *(find out)* cómo es la rutina de Manolo los sábados. Describe tus ilustraciones y haz preguntas para completar el cuadro. Tú empiezas. Answers will vary.

Modelo ¿Qué hace Manolo primero?

Parte 2. Ahora escribe un párrafo con los eventos. Inventa los detalles.

Modelo Los sábados por la mañana Manolo generalmente...

_____

_____

_____

_____

_____

_____

_____

_____

_____

C. Te invito a salir. Vas a salir con tu compañero/a. Selecciona una cartera *(wallet)* para saber cuánto dinero pueden gastar. Inventen una conversación que incluya (1) adónde van a ir, (2) cuándo y a qué hora van y (3) cómo van a gastar todo el dinero. Estén listos para actuar su diálogo en clase. *Answers will vary.*

20

50

200

500

1000

La correspondencia

El correo: ¡Los hombres! Primero, lee las siguientes preguntas. Después, lee la página del diario de Sofía y contesta las preguntas.

1. ¿Por qué invita Sofía a sus amigos al cine?

   Wayne no se ofreció a ir a su casa por ella.

2. ¿Por qué cree Sofía que Wayne va a pensar que está loca?

   Va a llegar a su primera cita con Ana Mari y Ramón.

3. ¿Crees que es interesante salir con una persona de otra cultura? ¿Por qué?

   Answers will vary.

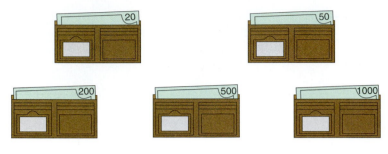

Querido diario,   9 de octubre

Hoy me llamó Wayne para invitarme al cine, pero pienso que acabo de[1] tener un malentendido cultural con él. Creo que Wayne quiere salir conmigo, y yo quiero salir con él, pero como no conoce[2] mis costumbres, no se ofreció a venir a la casa por mí. Creo que él no entiende que tiene que venir por mí a mi casa; así mis papás pueden conocerlo. Wayne va a pensar que no quiero salir con él, o que estoy loca. ¡Llegar con Ana Mari y Ramón a nuestra primera cita! ¡Qué problema! Bueno, los dos tenemos que recordar que tenemos culturas y costumbres diferentes. ¡Así es más interesante. ¡A ver qué pasa el sábado!

[1]*I have just* [2]*he doesn't know*

En papel: ¡Un viaje a Salamanca! Vas a ir a Salamanca a estudiar el próximo verano *(next summer)*. Escríbele una carta a la familia con quien vas a vivir para presentarte *(introduce yourself)*. Incluye la siguiente información: Answers will vary.

- tu nombre, tu edad y una descripción de tu familia
- tu rutina diaria y cosas que quieres hacer en Salamanca
- los platos que te gusta comer y los que no puedes comer
- las actividades que te gusta hacer después de las clases y los fines de semana

Video
CD-ROM

¡A ver de nuevo!   Answers will vary.

Parte 1. Escucha **Escenas de la vida** otra vez para escribir un resumen del episodio.

Audio
CD-ROM

Instructor's Resources
- VHS Video
- Worktext CD
- IRM: Videoscript

En este episodio Wayne habla con Sofía para invitarla al cine...

Parte 2. Ahora trabaja con un(a) compañero/a para comparar la información y añadir lo que te haya faltado.

Práctica adicional		
Cuaderno de tareas WB p.256, M LM p.258, A–B	Audio CD-ROM Episodio 10	Website vistahigher learning.com

Vocabulario del Episodio 10

Verbos

Instructor's Resources
• Testing program
• Website

almorzar (o → ue)	to have lunch	pensar (e → i) en	to think about (someone)
dormir (o → ue) bien/mal	to sleep well/poorly	pensar (e → i) que	to think that (phrase)
empezar a... (e → ie)	to start...	poder (o → ue)	to be able to, can
encontrar (o → ue)	to find	(no) poder (o → ue) ir	(not) to be able to go
entender	to understand	preferir (e → ie)	to prefer
el problema (e → ie)	the problem	querer (e → ie)	to want; to love
invitar a	to invite	recordar (o → ue)	to remember
jugar (u → ue) (al) tenis	to play tennis	venir por mí	to pick me up
manejar	to drive		

Las preposiciones y los pronombres preposicionales

a mí	for me	por él	for him	de ellos/as	from them
para ti	for you	de nosotros/as	from us	conmigo	with me
con ella	with her	de ustedes	from you (pl.)	contigo	with you

Vocabulario personal

Write all the words you need to know in Spanish so that you can better talk about your dates and your weekend plans.

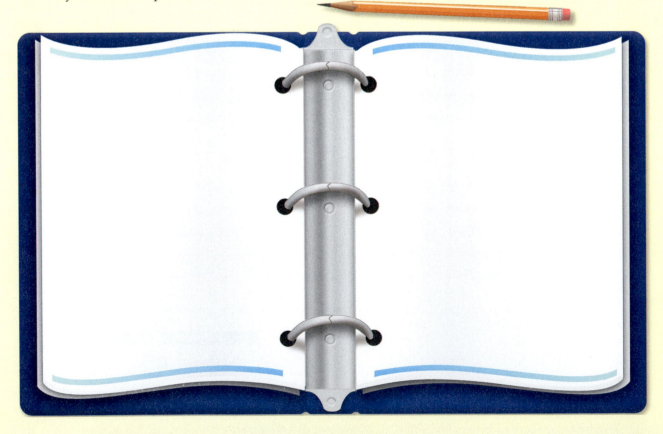

250

Episodio

10

Escenas de la vida: Una invitación confusa

A. ¡A ver cuánto entendiste! See how much of the **Escena** you understood by matching the Spanish sentences with their English equivalents.

Sofía

Wayne

Ana Mari

_d_ 1. No viene por mí.	a. The movie starts early.
_e_ 2. Es normal hacer eso en una cita.	b. Next time I bet you he comes to pick me up.
_f_ 3. Vamos a encontrarnos ahí.	c. Can you go with me?
_a_ 4. La película empieza temprano.	d. He's not going to pick me up.
_g_ 5. Voy contigo.	e. It's normal to do that on a date.
_c_ 6. ¿Puedes ir conmigo?	f. We're going to meet there.
_b_ 7. La próxima vez te apuesto que viene por mí.	g. I'll go with you.

B. ¡Vamos al cine! Match the questions or statements in column **A** with the appropriate responses in column **B**. Then identify the speakers.

A	B
_c_ 1. ¿Quieres ir al cine el sábado?	a. Pues... sí puedo.
_e_ 2. ¿A qué hora?	b. En el Centro Cultural de la universidad.
_a_ 3. ¿Puedes llegar a las siete y media?	c. Sí, claro.
_d_ 4. Bueno, entonces nos vemos el sábado a las siete y media.	d. Está bien.
_b_ 5. ¿Dónde dan la película?	e. La película empieza a las ocho y media.

¿Quiénes conversan?

_____ Sofía _____ y _____ Wayne _____

Video
CD-ROM

C. La conversación de Sofía con Ana Mari. Put the following statements in chronological order.

___7___ a. ¿Podemos ir en tu coche? Prefiero no manejar de noche.

___1___ b. ¿Puedes ir conmigo al cine el sábado? No quiero ir sola con Wayne.

___4___ c. Es normal aquí hacer eso en una cita.

___2___ d. No entiendo. ¿Por qué?

___3___ e. ¿Puedes creer que Wayne me invita al cine, pero no viene por mí a la casa? Eso no es una cita.

___5___ f. Pues, a mí no me gusta.

___6___ g. Bueno voy contigo, pero necesitas modernizarte.

___8___ h. Mi coche no funciona.

Gramática 1

Accepting and declining invitations
• **Stem-changing verbs (e → ie) and (o → ue)**

D. Una invitación a jugar. Ramón wants Wayne to play soccer with him this evening. Use the verbs to complete the conversation.

quieres	puedo	empieza	encuentro
venir	prefiero	preferir	puedes

Ramón   Hola, Wayne, ¿(1) ____quieres____ ir a jugar fútbol esta tarde?

Wayne   Me gustaría, pero no (2) ____puedo____ porque no (3) ____encuentro____ mis tenis (*sneakers*) de fútbol.

Ramón   ¡Qué raro! Tengo dos pares de tenis. Si quieres, (4) ____puedes____ usar los míos.

Wayne   Gracias, pero (5) ____prefiero____ buscar bien mis tenis o ir a comprar otros.

Ramón   ¡Como quieras (*As you wish*)! El juego (6) ____empieza____ a las seis. Si decides ir conmigo, puedes (7) ____venir____ a mi casa.

E. ¿Qué hacen? Write a complete sentence with each illustration. Answers will vary.

1.   2.   3.   4.

1. Wayne y su amiga/almorzar _____

2. Adriana/(no) entender _____

3. Manolo/encontrar trabajo _____

4. ¿Tú?/venir por mí _____

F. ¡Ay, Lalo!

Parte 1. Use the verbs to complete the description. Fill in the appropriate forms.

tener	entender	llegar	preferir
recordar	querer	empezar	jugar

¡Lalo es tremendo! Sus clases (1) _____empiezan_____ a las siete y media de la mañana; por eso, (2) _____tiene_____ que salir de casa a las seis y cuarto a más tardar *(at the latest)*. Pues nunca lo hace. Siempre (3) _____llega_____ tarde a sus clases. No (4) _____entiende_____ que es muy importante ser puntual y responsable. Pero cuando (5) _____quiere_____ salir con una chica, entonces sí (6) _____recuerda_____ que ser puntual es importante. Le dice a mi mamá: "Mami, (7) _____prefiero_____ salir temprano de casa porque a las chicas no les gusta que llegue tarde." ¡Vaya inconsistencia!

Parte 2. What is the inconsistency in Lalo's behavior? Explain in your own words. Answers will vary.

_____

_____

_____

_____

G. Las actividades. Make up six true statements using an element from each column. Answers will vary.

> **Modelo**
>
> Mi amigo Roberto piensa que su trabajo es aburrido.

Yo	dormir	los libros
Mi novio/a	entender	los problemas de matemáticas
Mis profesores	jugar	(a) los estudiantes
Mi hermano/a…	encontrar	la tarea
Mi amigo/a…	pensar en/que	en comer
		bien
		hasta tarde los domingos

1. _____

2. _____

3. _____

4. _____

5. _____

6. _____

Gramática 2

Extending invitations
• Prepositional pronouns

H. ¡Ramón está celoso (jealous)! Use five of these words to complete the conversation.

ti	usted	conmigo	mí	contigo	ella	él	nosotros

Laura   Ramón, ¿quién va a ir (1) _____contigo_____ a la fiesta?

Ramón   Nadie. ¿Quieres ir (2) _____conmigo_____?

Laura   Lo siento, pero voy a ir con Jorge.

Ramón   ¿¡Con quién!? ¿Por qué vas con (3) _____él_____? Es un antipático.

Laura   Pues sí, un poco, pero viene por (4) _____mí_____ a mi casa, me paga todo y me lleva a lugares elegantes.

Ramón   A (5) _____ti_____ sólo te interesa lo material y eso no está bien.

I. Hablando de Wayne. Choose the appropriate words to complete the conversation.

contigo	ella	nosotros	ustedes
ti	ellos	él	mí

Ramón   Sofía, Wayne habla mucho de (1) _____ti_____.

Sofía   ¿Ah sí? ¿Y qué cosas dice de (2) _____mí_____?

Ramón   Pues… que quiere salir (3) _____contigo_____.

Sofía   Él es muy agradable. ¿Por qué no lo invitas a salir con (4) _____nosotros_____ con más frecuencia? Así puedo conocerlo mejor.

Ramón   Creo que tú debes salir sola con (5) _____él_____.

J. Preguntas personales. Answer the questions using prepositional pronouns. Answers will vary.

> **Modelo**   ¿Discutes mucho con tus hermanos?
> **Sí, a veces discuto con ellos.**

1. ¿Vives con tus padres?

_____

2. ¿Piensas mucho en tu novio/a?

_____

3. ¿Qué deporte juegas con tus amigos?

_____

4. ¿Hablas con tus profesores con frecuencia?

_____

5. ¿Vas por tu mejor amigo/a a su casa cuando salen?

_____

K. Traducción. Write the following sentences in Spanish.

1. —Do you want to go out with me on Friday or Saturday?
   —I prefer Saturday, because Friday I can't.

   – ¿Quieres salir conmigo el viernes o el sábado?

   – Prefiero el sábado, porque el viernes no puedo.

2. —I am going to have lunch with him, and then watch a movie.
   —Is he going to pick you up?

   – Voy a almorzar con él, y después vamos a ver una película.

   – ¿Va a ir por ti?

3. —Are you going to start going out with him?
   —Yes, I think he is a nice guy.

   – ¿Vas a empezar a salir con él?

   – Sí, pienso que es un buen chico.

L. ¿Quieres salir? Manolo finally calls Ana Mari to go out. However, they have very different ideas about what kind of date it is. Write their conversation using the illustrations; take either Manolo's or Ana Mari's role. Make sure you use **poder, preferir,** and **querer** to express your preferences and desires. Finish up by agreeing to meet at a time and place. Answers will vary.

Manolo	Hola, Ana Mari. ¿Cómo estás? Habla Manolo.
Ana Mari	¡Hola, qué milagro!
Manolo	_____
Ana Mari	_____
Manolo	_____
Ana Mari	_____
Manolo	_____
Ana Mari	_____
Manolo	_____
Ana Mari	_____

Para terminar

M. Los problemas de Laura y Alfredo.

Parte 1. Read the description of Laura and Alfredo's marital problems.

> Laura y Alfredo son diferentes en casi todo. Alfredo tiene 48 años y es muy conservador; Laura tiene 30 y es bastante liberal. Laura piensa que la mujer puede trabajar y desenvolverse[1] profesionalmente, pero Alfredo piensa que una esposa tiene que quedarse en casa, cuidar a los hijos y atender a su esposo. Ella quiere tener sólo dos hijos y él quiere seis. Ella no entiende por qué.
>
> En cuanto a sus actividades, tampoco tienen muchas cosas en común. A Laura le gusta salir con sus amigas a los centros comerciales y al cine. Es muy activa; juega tenis con frecuencia y toma una clase de yoga. Alfredo nunca quiere salir; prefiere estar en casa, ver la televisión, trabajar en el jardín o dormir. Con frecuencia duerme doce horas, porque dice que trabaja mucho entre semana. No le gusta hacer ejercicio; de hecho[2], se pone celoso[3] porque piensa que Laura quiere estar delgada y guapa para coquetear[4] con otros hombres. Lo único que hace es jugar cartas toda la noche cuando sus amigos vienen a visitarlo una vez al mes.
>
> En fin, Laura está aburrida; por eso, va a empezar a trabajar la próxima semana. Ella cree que si no empieza a trabajar pronto se va a volver loca. Él no sabe que va a empezar a trabajar y seguramente no le va a gustar nada.

[1]develop [2]in fact [3]gets jealous [4]to flirt

Parte 2. Indicate whether the following statements are **cierto** or **falso**.

	Cierto	Falso
1. Alfredo tiene 48 años.	✓	☐
2. Laura tiene dos hijos.	☐	✓
3. Alfredo duerme mucho.	✓	☐
4. Alfredo no es muy moderno.	✓	☐
5. A Laura no le gustan los niños.	☐	✓
6. Alfredo juega a las cartas con sus amigos.	✓	☐

Parte 3. Answer the following questions.

1. ¿Cómo es Laura? ¿Cómo es Alfredo? _____ Laura es liberal y activa. Alfredo es conservador. _____

2. ¿En qué cosas son diferentes? _____ Answers will vary. _____

3. ¿Qué no entiende Laura? _____ Laura no entiende por qué Alfredo quiere tener tantos hijos. _____

4. ¿Qué va a hacer Laura pronto? _____ Va a empezar a trabajar. _____

5. ¿Por qué va a hacer eso? _____ Está aburrida en su casa y con su vida. _____

6. ¿Crees que ellos van a divorciarse? _____ Answers will vary. _____

7. ¿Cómo piensas tú que Laura tiene que solucionar su problema? _____ Answers will vary. _____
_____

¡A escuchar!

Episodio 10

Comprensión

Audio CD-ROM

A. En el café.

Parte 1. Listen to Ramón and a classmate, Rosalía, as they have a cup of coffee in the cafeteria. Then, select the best answer to the question.

What is the main topic of Ramón's and Rosalía's conversation?

a. Rosalía's literature class   (b.) plans for the weekend

c. the cafeteria menu   d. a tennis match

Parte 2. You will hear the conversation between Ramón and Rosalía again, followed by four questions. Select the answers to the questions. **¡Atención!** There may be more than one answer to each question.

1. (a.) viernes   b. sábado   c. domingo

2. a. trabajar   c. leer una novela   (e.) escribir una composición
   b. dormir todo el día   d. descansar   (f.) estudiar para un examen

3. a. ir al cine   c. ir al parque   (e.) comer en un restaurante
   (b.) jugar al tenis   d. mirar la televisión   f. estudiar

4. a. Rosalía va por Ramón a las ocho.   (c.) Ramón va por Rosalía a las nueve.
   b. Los dos van a encontrarse en las canchas de tenis a las diez.

Audio CD-ROM

B. ¿Estudias conmigo?
You are going to hear eight questions. Answer each one aloud in the affirmative, using a prepositional pronoun and the written cues provided, and write the appropriate prepositional pronoun in the space provided. Repeat the correct answer after the speaker.

| mí (conmigo) | él | nosotros | ellos | usted |
| ti (contigo) | ella | vosotros | ellas | ustedes |

> **Modelo**   You hear: ¿Estudias conmigo?
>   You say/write: **Sí, estudio contigo.**

1. Sí, paso ____por ti____.   5. Sí, vivo ____con él____.

2. Sí, voy ____contigo____.   6. Sí, hablamos ____de ellos____.

3. Sí, pienso ____en ella____.   7. Sí, Ana Mari va ____con nosotros____.

4. Sí, Wayne viene ____por mí____.   8. Sí, discuto ____con ellas____.

Pronunciación

La _j_ y la _g_. The Spanish letter **j (jota)** sounds similar to the English _h_. Repeat these words and sentences after the speaker.

Juan	Jalisco	reloj	**Juan es de Jalisco.**
José	junio	consejero	**El hijo de José lleva un traje.**

The letter **g (ge)** has a sound similar to the English _g_ in _gap_ before consonants and **a, o, u** and a sound similar to the English _h_ or the Spanish **j** before **e** and **i**.

g + consonant, ga, go, gu   **ge, gi**

gracias	yogurt	general	geografía
galletas	langosta	gimnasio	biología

El general Gustavo Gutiérrez es generoso.   **Mis amigos juegan en el gimnasio.**

In order to retain the sound of _g_ in _gap_ before the vowels **e** and **i**, a silent **u** is placed after the **g**: **gue, gui.** Repeat these words after the speaker.

pague   **espagueti**   **guisado**

Más escenas de la vida

Holding a tennis racket, Santiago enters the room where Adriana is studying. Listen and then complete activities **A** and **B**. You will hear the conversation twice.

A. ¿Quién lo dijo? Indicate who made the following statements in the conversation: Adriana **(A),** or Santiago **(S).**

_S_ 1. ¿Quieres ir con nosotros?

_A_ 2. ¿Por qué no me ayudan a limpiar?

_S_ 3. Te ayudamos a limpiar si vienes con nosotros.

_S_ 4. Y esta noche te dedicas a tus hijos y a tu esposo.

_A_ 5. Ya vas a empezar con eso.

B. Responde. Write the answers to the following questions.

1. ¿Adónde va Santiago con sus hijos? _Van a jugar tenis._

2. ¿Por qué Adriana no puede ir con ellos? _Tiene que limpiar la casa._

3. ¿Por qué no tiene tiempo libre entre semana? _Tiene tarea y trabaja._

4. ¿Cuándo juegan tenis? _Juegan tenis los sábados._

5. Si ayudan a Adriana a limpiar, ¿qué cosas no puede hacer Adriana esta noche?

No puede estudiar o abrir los libros.

Objetivos comunicativos

In this episode, you will practice:
✔ talking about your job
✔ saying what people do for you
✔ sharing your talents

Episodio 11

Escenas de la vida: ¡A ganarse la vida!¹

Video
CD-ROM

A. ¡Mira cuánto puedes entender! Indica qué dicen *(what they say)* sobre sus trabajos.

Audio
CD-ROM

Wayne:
☐ Me pagan bien.   ✔ Me pagan mal.
✔ Salgo tarde.   ☐ Salgo temprano.
☐ Mi jefe es agradable.   ✔ Mi jefe es antipático.
✔ No me gusta mi trabajo.   ☐ Me gusta mucho.
✔ Me dan propinas.   ☐ No me dan propinas.
☐ No busco otro trabajo.   ✔ Necesito encontrar otro trabajo.

Instructor's Resources
• Overheads
• VHS Video
• Worktext CD
• Website
• IRM: Videoscript, Comprehensible input

Sofía: " A mí sólo me dan problemas… los niños que cuido por las tardes y los fines de semana.
_____
_____
_____ "

Video Synopsis. Wayne is surprised to see Ana Mari and Ramón with Sofía in the café. Ana Mari tries to distract Wayne by asking about his job; the other characters join in and discuss their own jobs. Wayne says goodbye to Ana Mari and Ramón, not realizing that they are going out with Sofía and him on their date.

Ana Mari: " A mí tampoco me gusta mi trabajo, pero me pagan bien y mis compañeros son muy buenos. Me invitan a salir y me ayudan cuando necesito algo.
_____
_____ "

Ramón: " Por suerte mi trabajo es bueno. Soy chofer de limusinas. Tengo muchos clientes latinoamericanos y, como hablo español, son muy generosos conmigo. Siempre me dan buenas propinas.
_____ "

¹*Making a living*

B. ¿Te diste cuenta? Indica quién hace los siguientes comentarios: Sofía **(S)**, Ramón **(R)**, Ana Mari **(AM)** o Wayne **(W)**.

   AM   1. Mis compañeros me invitan a salir.

   W   2. ¿Quién te da problemas?

   R   3. Por suerte, mi trabajo es bueno.

   S   4. A ti te dan propinas; a mí me dan problemas.

   AM   5. Sabemos que son trabajos de tiempo parcial.

   W   6. Ramón y Ana Mari, adiós, que les vaya bien.

   S   7. Ellos van al cine con nosotros.

> **Cultura a lo vivo**
> Traditionally in the Spanish-speaking world, students don't always work while going to school. However, depending on the family's economic situation, many students help out in the family business and/or work during the summer.

C. ¿En qué trabajan? Completa las frases.

1. Los compañeros de Ana Mari son _____ muy buenos _____.
2. Sofía trabaja con _____ niños _____.
3. Ramón es _____ chofer _____ de limusinas, sus clientes son _____ muy generosos _____ con él.
4. Ana Mari y Ramón van _____ al cine _____ con Sofía y Wayne.
5. Wayne le dice a Sofía: "Ya vámonos. Vamos a _____ llegar tarde _____ al cine."

Práctica adicional

Cuaderno de tareas WB pp.277–278, A–C   Video CD-ROM Episodio 11

Para comunicarnos mejor

Gramática 1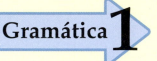

Talking about your job
• <u>Saber</u>, <u>salir</u>, <u>poner</u>, and job-related vocabulary

Para hablar del trabajo	
el ama de casa (m, f)	homemaker
atender (e→ie) a los clientes	to attend the customers/clients
el/la chofer	driver
el/la empleado/a	clerk, employee
el horario flexible/fijo	flexible/fixed schedule
el/la jefe/a	boss
el/la mesero/a	waiter/waitress
el/la niñero/a	baby-sitter
poner las cosas en su lugar	to put/place things in their place
las prestaciones	fringe benefits
el puesto	position
saber + [verb]	to know how (to do something)
salir temprano/tarde	to get off, to leave early/late
el sueldo alto/bajo	high/low salary
el tiempo completo/parcial/libre	full-time/part-time/free time
el turno de la mañana/tarde/noche	morning/afternoon/night shift
las vacaciones	vacation
la ventaja/desventaja	advantage/disadvantage

Read the following examples:

¿**Saben** usar la computadora?	*Do they know how to use a computer?*
No **sé** si **saben** usarla.	*I don't know if they know how to use it.*
Mi jefe **pone** los documentos en el archivador.	*My boss puts the documents in the file cabinet.*
Yo **pongo** las cosas en su lugar.	*I put everything in its place.*
No **salgo** con mis amigos entre semana.	*I don't go out with my friends during the week.*

1. Note that *only* the **yo** forms of the verbs have a spelling change. The rest of the forms are conjugated as regular **-er** or **-ir** verbs.

Instructor's Resource
• IRM: Additional Activities

Verbos con irregularidades en la primera persona (yo)

saber	Yo **sé**…	usar la computadora.	*I know how to use the computer.*
	¿Tú **sabes**…	cocinar?	*Do you know how to cook?*
	Sofía **sabe**…	cuidar niños.	*Sofía knows how to take care of children.*
poner	Yo **pongo**…	las cosas en su lugar.	*I put things in their place.*
	Tú no **pones**…	la mesa.	*You don't set the table.*
salir	Yo **salgo**…	temprano/tarde.	*I get off (leave) early/late.*
	Él **sale**…	bien/mal en sus clases.	*He does well/badly in class.*

Additional Activity.
Play Lotería with students; see the sample in the Instructor's Resource Manual.

Learning Strategy: Advanced organizers

To maximize your learning before class, take a few minutes to look at the material that will be presented that day. Read the titles of the sections in the episode and look at the illustrations, to get an idea of the story and to find out what vocabulary and grammatical structures you will encounter. When you organize in advance, you will understand better and retain more information.

PRÁCTICA

A. Las personas y sus trabajos. Empareja la(s) persona(s) con el trabajo que sabe(n) hacer.

_d_	1. Una secretaria		a. hacer experimentos.
_g_	2. Una doctora		b. entender los problemas de las personas.
_b_	3. Los sicólogos		c. reparar coches.
_c_	4. Un mecánico		d. usar la computadora.
_i_	5. Una veterinaria	sé	e. diseñar casas y edificios.
_e_	6. Los arquitectos	sabe	f. combinar colores y formas.
_a_	7. Los científicos	saben	g. hacer operaciones médicas.
_f_	8. Un diseñador		h. crear literatura.
_h_	9. Los poetas		i. trabajar con animales.
_j_	10. Yo		j. hablar inglés.
			k. cocinar *(to cook).*

B. ¡Cuánto sabes de Latinoamérica! En grupos de tres personas, contesten las preguntas. Decidan quién sabe más de Latinoamérica.

1. ¿Sabes dónde están las pirámides mayas?
   Están en el sureste de México, Guatemala, Belice, El Salvador y el oeste de Honduras.

2. ¿Sabes quién es el presidente de México?
   El presidente de México es Vicente Fox.

3. ¿Sabes cuál es la capital de Argentina?
   La capital de Argentina es Buenos Aires.

4. ¿Sabes cuándo se celebra el Día de los Muertos *(The Day of the Dead)*?
   Se celebra el Día de los Muertos el 2 de noviembre.

5. ¿Sabes a qué hora se comen las uvas el 31 de diciembre?
   Se comen las uvas a las 12 de la noche.

6. ¿Sabes cómo se dice *"I love you"* en español?
   "Te quiero."

7. ¿Sabes cuántos países hay en Centroamérica?
   Hay seis países en Centroamérica.

8. ¿Sabes en cuántos países se habla español?
   Se habla español en veintiún países.

C. Ana Mari y Sofía hablan de sus trabajos. Completa las descripciones.

Ana Mari:

1. Me gusta mi trabajo porque me pagan bien. Tengo un ____sueldo____ alto.
2. Trabajo tiempo ____parcial____, sólo 24 horas a la semana.
3. Tengo el ____turno____ de la tarde: empiezo a las 2:30 y termino a las 7:30 de la tarde.
4. No me dan ____vacaciones____; tengo que trabajar todo el año.
5. Desafortunadamente, no tengo ____prestaciones____: no tengo seguro médico, pensión ni vacaciones.

Sofía:

6. Soy ____niñera____; por las tardes y los fines de semana cuido niñas y niños. Me gusta mi trabajo porque tiene muchas ____ventajas____: es flexible, trabajo las horas que yo quiero y es divertido estar con los niños pequeños. Con frecuencia los padres me dan regalos.

7. Las ____desventajas____ son que no me pagan muy bien, tengo que poner todas las cosas en su lugar y a veces los niños son groseros conmigo.

Práctica adicional
Cuaderno de tareas
WB pp.278–279, D–G

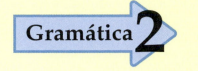 **Saying what people do for you**
• The object pronouns <u>me</u> and <u>te</u>

Analizar y descubrir

In the conversation, you heard the following statements. Study the examples and answer the questions below.

Me pagan bien.	*They pay me well.*
Mis compañeros **me invitan** a salir y **me ayudan.**	*My co-workers invite me out and help me.*
Por lo menos a ti **te dan** propinas; a mí sólo **me dan** problemas.	*At least they give you tips; they only give me problems.*

1. Where are **me** and **te** placed in relation to the verb **(pagan, invitan, ayudan, dan)** in Spanish? _____before_____
Where are *me* and *you* placed in relation to the verb in English? _____after_____

2. Notice the phrases **a ti** and **a mí** in the third example. Use them for emphasis or contrast.

A mí me pagan mal, pero **a ti te pagan** una fortuna. ¡No es justo!	*They pay me poorly, but they pay you a fortune. It's not fair!*

Here are some common verbs used with **me** and **te.**

	Las cosas que mi familia y amigos hacen	
ayudar	*to help*	Mi mamá **me ayuda** mucho.
contar (o → ue) los problemas	*to tell your problems*	Mis hermanos no **me cuentan** sus problemas.
dar consejos	*to give advice*	Mi abuela **me da** buenos consejos.
dejar usar su coche	*to let someone use one's car*	Mi novio **me deja** usar su coche.
invitar a salir	*to ask someone out*	Tus compañeros, ¿**te invitan** a salir?
llamar	*to call*	Mi profesora no **me llama** a la casa.
mandar un regalo	*to send a present*	Mis abuelos siempre **me mandan** regalos.
pagar	*to pay*	¿**Te pagan** bien en el trabajo?
pedir (e → i) cosas prestadas	*to borrow things*	Mi sobrina **me pide** ropa *(clothes)* prestada.
prestar dinero	*to lend money*	¿Quién **te presta** dinero cuando necesitas?

3. Now observe where **me** (or **te**) is placed in expressions with multiple verbs.

Me tienes que ayudar. Tienes que ayudar**me.** }	*You have to help me.*
No va a invitar**me** a salir otra vez. No **me** va a invitar a salir otra vez. }	*He's not going to ask me out again.*

¡Fíjate!

The verb **contar** is conjugated like **recordar**.
¿**Recuerdas?**
¿**Me cuentas** ese **problema?**

4. In an expression with a conjugated verb and an unconjugated verb, you may place **me** and **te** _____before_____ the first verb or attach it to the _____second verb_____ .

PRÁCTICA

D. Otra cita. Después de dos semanas, Wayne llama a Sofía para invitarla a salir otra vez. Lee la conversación y escribe la forma apropiada de los verbos de la lista. Después contesta las preguntas con un(a) compañero/a.

saber	salir	estar	querer
ver	invitar	poder	hablar

¡**Fíjate!**
Remember that some verbs have irregular **yo** forms.

Sofía	¿Bueno?
Wayne	¿Sofía? Habla Wayne.
Sofía	¡Hola, Wayne! ¿Cómo (1) ____estás____?
Wayne	Bien, gracias. Oye, te (2) ____invito____ al cine mañana por la noche.
Sofía	Gracias, pero por la noche no (3) ____puedo____. Voy a (4)____ver____ a mis abuelos porque mañana es su aniversario. Pero si quieres, podemos (5) ____salir____ a almorzar.
Wayne	Bueno, ¿a qué hora voy por ti?
Sofía	A las doce, ¿te parece? Esta vez (tú) no (6) ____quieres____ que invite a todos mis amigos, ¿verdad?
Wayne	¡No, por favor! Ya (7) ____sé____ cuál fue *(was)* mi error.
Sofía	No te preocupes. Fue un malentendido. Yo tampoco quiero ir con ellos esta vez.

1. ¿Adónde quiere ir Wayne mañana?
   Quiere ir al cine.

2. ¿Qué tiene que hacer Sofía por la noche?
   Va a ver a sus abuelos.

3. ¿Adónde van a ir Sofía y Wayne?
   Van a salir a almorzar.

4. ¿Sabes cuál fue el error de Wayne?
   No pasar por Sofía a su casa.

E. ¡Tengo buenos amigos! Escribe el nombre de la(s) persona(s) que hace(n) estas cosas por ti. Answers will vary.

> **Modelo**   **Mis primos** me hablan por teléfono el día de mi cumpleaños *(birthday).*

1. _____ me sirve la comida.

2. _____ me habla(n) por teléfono el día de mi cumpleaños.

3. _____ me escribe(n) cartas.

4. _____ me invita(n) a salir los fines de semana.

5. _____ me ayuda(n) con la tarea.

6. _____ me lleva a la doctora cuando estoy enfermo/a *(sick).*

F. ¡Qué consentido! (*How spoiled!*) Indica si los siguientes comentarios son **ciertos** o **falsos**.

Answers will vary.

	Cierto	Falso
1. Mi mamá me prepara el desayuno, el almuerzo y la cena.	☐	☐
2. Mi compañero/a de cuarto me ayuda en todo.	☐	☐
3. Mi familia siempre me escucha cuando tengo problemas.	☐	☐
4. Mis profesores no me dan mucha tarea.	☐	☐
5. Todos me quieren mucho.	☐	☐
6. Mis amigas siempre me prestan dinero.	☐	☐
7. Mi jefe me deja salir temprano.	☐	☐
8. Mis abuelos me dan muchos regalos.	☐	☐
9. Mis amigos vienen por mí cuando vamos a las fiestas.	☐	☐

G. ¿Quién? Contesta las siguientes preguntas. Después entrevista a tu compañero/a para ver (*see*) si tienen algo en común. Answers will vary.

> **Modelo** ¿Quién te manda correos electrónicos con frecuencia?
> **Mi amiga Irene me manda correos electrónicos casi todos los días.**

1. ¿Quién te presta dinero? _____

2. ¿Quién te escribe cartas de amor? _____

3. ¿Quién te da buenos consejos? _____

4. ¿Quién te manda regalos? _____

5. ¿Quién te visita cuando estás enfermo/a? _____

6. ¿Quién te lava la ropa? _____

7. ¿Quién te necesita más? _____

8. ¿Quién te escucha cuando tienes problemas? _____

¡Fíjate!
Remember to place **me** before the conjugated verb.

H. Una entrevista. Convierte a preguntas las oraciones de la **Práctica F** para entrevistar a tu compañero/a. Haz los cambios necesarios. Después decide si tu compañero/a es un(a) consentido/a (*spoiled*) o no. Answers will vary.

> **Modelo** Mi mamá me prepara el desayuno, el almuerzo y la cena.
> **¿Tu mamá te prepara el desayuno, el almuerzo y la cena?**

I. Una persona especial. Habla con un(a) compañero/a de una persona importante en tu vida. Explica las cosas que esta persona hace por ti. Answers will vary.

> **Modelo** **Mi hermana es muy importante para mí. Siempre me ayuda cuando tengo problemas. Hablo mucho con ella porque siempre me da buenos consejos. Nunca me presta dinero; no tiene porque compra mucha ropa. Pero me deja usar su coche y su computadora.**

J. El trabajo de Adriana.

Audio CD-ROM

Instructor's Resources
• Worktext CD
• IRM: Tapescript

Parte 1. Escucha la narración de Adriana para completar el párrafo.

(1) _____Sé_____ que tengo algunos problemas con mi esposo porque trabajo y también (2) _____estudio_____, pero para mí es importante adquirir experiencia y aprender cosas relacionadas con mi carrera. Mi jefe es muy bueno. (3) _____Me ayuda_____ mucho y me explica (4) _____cuando_____ no sé hacer algo que él desea. (5) _____Hago_____ muchas cosas interesantes en la oficina. Llamo por teléfono a (6) _____nuestros_____ clientes para saber si todo está bien con nuestros productos. Analizo muchos expedientes *(files)* y (7) _____pongo_____ los documentos importantes en orden. Mi jefe también (8) _____me presta_____ su computadora cuando necesito (9) _____escribir_____ mis trabajos de la universidad. Además, (10) _____me deja_____ salir temprano cuando termino todo el trabajo a tiempo.

Adriana

Script.
See the **Instructor's Resource Manual** for the script to this activity.

Parte 2. Ahora escribe una descripción de tu trabajo para tu profesor(a).   Answers will vary.

_____

_____

_____

_____

_____

_____

K. El trabajo. Primero contesta las preguntas. Después entrevista a tu compañero/a para determinar quién tiene el mejor *(the best)* trabajo.

1. ¿Qué días trabajas? ¿Trabajas tiempo parcial o completo?

_____

2. ¿Tienes buen sueldo?

_____

3. ¿Qué prestaciones tienes? ¿Cuándo te dan vacaciones? ¿Cuántos días?

_____

4. ¿Cómo es tu jefe/a?

_____

5. ¿Por qué trabajas ahí? ¿Qué ventajas/desventajas tienes?

_____

K. Encourage students to have a real conversation by using tag questions such as ¿y tú?.

6. ¿Te dejan hablar por teléfono? ¿Qué cosas no te dejan hacer?

_____

L. Preguntas indiscretas. Usa las siguientes preguntas para conversar con tu compañero/a. *Answers will vary.*

> **Modelo** ¿Hace ejercicios ¿Dónde? ¿Con qué frecuencia?
> **Hago ejercicio tres veces a la semana.**
> **Voy con mi amigo Mark al gimnasio. ¿Y tú?**

1. ¿Haces ejercicio? ¿Dónde? ¿Con qué frecuencia?

_____

_____

2. ¿Sabes cocinar? ¿Qué platos sabes hacer? ¿Con qué frecuencia cocinas? ¿Te gusta cocinar?

_____

_____

3. ¿Sales temprano del trabajo? ¿A qué hora? ¿Qué días sales tarde?

_____

_____

4. ¿Ves a tus familiares con frecuencia? ¿Cuándo ves a tus tíos y primos? ¿Qué actividades haces con ellos?

_____

_____

5. ¿Pones tu ropa en el clóset o en el suelo (*floor*) cuando llegas tarde a casa? ¿Dónde pones tu mochila? ¿Y tus libros?

_____

_____

6. Generalmente, ¿sales bien en todas tus clases? ¿A veces sales mal en algunas clases? ¿En qué clase? ¿Por qué?

_____

_____

_____

Práctica adicional

Cuaderno de tareas	Audio
WB pp.280–281, H–K	CD-ROM
LM pp.285–286, A–B, Pron.	Episodio 11

Actividades comunicativas

A. La fotonovela. En grupos de cuatro personas, seleccionen cinco de las siguientes actividades para escribir una descripción de lo que hace Adriana entre semana. Después tu grupo va a leer la descripción a la clase y tus compañeros deben adivinar (*guess*) las letras de las actividades que usaron en la descripción. Usen expresiones como **generalmente, con frecuencia, casi siempre** y **muchas veces.** Answers will vary.

Modelo Hay semanas que son terribles para mí. A veces…

B. Sopa de palabras.

Instrucciones para Estudiante 1

First, create logical sentences out of the scrambled words (the first and last words of each sentence are already in place). Then read your sentences to your partner, who will tell you whether they are correct. You have your partner's unscrambled sentences. Do not tell your partner the right word order immediately; let them try to correct any mistakes.

> **Modelo**
>
> **Mis** a compañeros invitan me **salir.**
> **Mis compañeros me invitan a salir.**

En mi trabajo.

1. **Mi** hace horas a la supervisora me trabajar veinte más de **semana.**

   _____

   _____

2. **Mis** salen me cuando amigos escriben de no **vacaciones.**

   _____

   _____

3. **Mis** cuando soy clientes me dan buenas con propinas amable **ellos.**

   _____

   _____

4. ¿**Tu** cuando ayuda problemas jefe te tienes **económicos**?

   _____

   _____

5. **Mis** con agradables; compañeros con son muy ellos salgo **frecuencia.**

   _____

   _____

Las respuestas de mi compañero/a

1. Mis papás no me dan suficiente dinero; por eso, trabajo.
2. Mis abuelos siempre me mandan chocolates el día de mi cumpleaños.
3. Mi hermano me llama por teléfono cuando necesita algo.
4. ¿Tus amigos te visitan cuando estás enfermo?
5. Mi prima estudia conmigo; por eso, voy por ella todos los días.

> **¡Fíjate!**
> Remember to place **me** and **te** before the conjugated verb.

> **B.** Pair students and allow four minutes for them to unscramble their sentences before they begin to interact. Students check their answers with their classmate.

Las respuestas de mi compañero/a

1. Mi supervisora me hace trabajar más de veinte horas a la semana.
2. Mis amigos no me escriben cuando salen de vacaciones.
3. Mis clientes me dan buenas propinas cuando soy amable con ellos.
4. ¿Tu jefe te ayuda cuando tienes problemas económicos?
5. Mis compañeros son muy agradables; salgo con ellos con frecuencia.

_____

_____

5. **Mi** conmigo; los por eso, estudia por ella todos prima voy **días**.

_____

4. **¿Tus** te cuando amigos visitan estás **enfermo?**

_____

3. **Mi** teléfono necesita me por hermano llama cuando **algo**.

_____

¡Fíjate!
Remember to place **me** and **te** before the conjugated verb.

2. **Mis** chocolates el día me siempre abuelos mandan mi de **cumpleaños**.

_____

1. **Mis** dinero; no me por suficiente eso, papás dan **trabajo**.

En mi casa.

Modelo

Mi ayuda primo me a la limpiar casa.
Mi primo me ayuda a limpiar la casa.

First, create logical sentences out of the scrambled words (the first and last words of each sentence are already in place). Then read your sentences to your partner, who will tell you whether they are correct. You have your partner's unscrambled sentences. Do not tell your partner the right word order immediately; let them try to correct any mistakes.

Instrucciones para **Estudiante 2**

B. Sopa de palabras.

C. Dos familias diferentes.

Instrucciones para Estudiante 1

You and a friend are spending the summer in Ecuador as exchange students. Call your friend to find out how things are going with their Ecuadorian family. You will start by finding out if:

- they take them to school
- they prepare good food for them
- they let them use the computer
- they help them with homework
- your friend's parents call them often

¡Fíjate!

Review the verbs in **Las cosas que mi familia y amigos hacen** on page 263.

Modelo   ¿Te preparan buena comida? ¿Te llevan a...?

Then, read about your own situation at home, so you can answer your partner's questions.
Answers will vary.

C. When finished, discuss which student has a better situation (the one who gets presents, or the one who gets attention), and why.

> This is your situation at home:
>
> Your host family is nice, but they are all very busy. They do not have time to cook for you, so you prepare your own meals. About three times a week, they take you out to dinner and do not let you pay for anything. They are generous, and buy you many small presents. They do not take you to school, nor do they pick you up from school; you have to take the bus. They are very busy people, and they have little time to help you with your Spanish homework. You do your own laundry and clean your own room.

Decide who is the luckiest! Be ready to explain your reasoning to the class; take notes in the space provided.

_____

_____

_____

C. Dos familias diferentes.

Instrucciones para **Estudiante 2**

You and a friend are spending the summer in Ecuador as exchange students. Your friend calls you to find out how things are going with your Ecuadorian family. Read about your own situation at home so you can answer your partner's questions:

Answers will vary.

> This is your situation at home:
>
> Your host family is nice. They take you to school every morning and they pick you up. Your Ecuadorian mother prepares all your meals for you, does your laundry, and makes your bed. Your sister helps you with your homework and lets you use her computer. Your host family does not take you out much, nor do they give you gifts. Your parents back home do not call you, but they write e-mails to you every day.

Now find out how your friend is doing.

Find out if:
- they take them out to dinner
- they do your friend's laundry and clean their room
- they pick your friend up from school
- they help them with homework
- they buy things for your friend

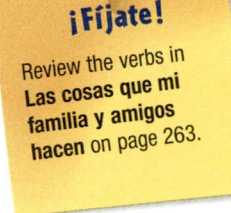

¡Fíjate!

Review the verbs in **Las cosas que mi familia y amigos hacen** on page 263.

Modelo   ¿Te invitan a cenar? ¿Te llevan a… ?

Decide who is the luckiest! Be ready to explain your reasoning to the class; take notes in the space provided.

_____

_____

_____

_____

_____

_____

_____

_____

_____

_____

La correspondencia

El correo: El club de corazones solitarios. *(Lonely Hearts Club.)* Acabas de recibir esta carta. Lee las preguntas y luego la carta; contesta las preguntas.

1. ¿Qué hace **El club de corazones solitarios**? _____ Te encuentran la pareja perfecta. _____
2. ¿Qué ofrece el club para ayudarte? _____ Me hacen un video y me preparan para la primera cita. _____
3. ¿Cómo te preparan para la primera cita? _____ Me dan consejos prácticos. _____

El correo. As a class project, you may have students write a script for a personal video to send to **El club de corazones solitarios**. Tape them in class, or ask them to turn in their tape. Have students describe their own personalities: routine, activities they do for fun, favorite foods, favorite places to go, sports they play, and what they want for the future. They should also mention the qualities they are looking for in a partner.

Querido corazón solitario:

¿No tienes pareja[1]? No te preocupes: nosotros te encontramos la pareja perfecta. No es necesario ir a bares de solteros para encontrar la pareja ideal. Nosotros te encontramos pareja sin ningún peligro[2]. Te hacemos un video donde puedes hablar de tus gustos, tus preferencias, tus actividades, tu personalidad y las características que deseas encontrar en tu pareja ideal. También te preparamos para la primera cita: te damos consejos prácticos en cuanto a la ropa, los temas[3] de conversación, los mejores restaurantes y las actividades culturales de la ciudad ese día. Solamente tienes que contestar las preguntas del cuestionario, y nosotros hacemos el resto.

[1]*partner* [2]**sin...** *safely* [3]*topics*

Invitación a **Ecuador**

Del álbum de
Sofía

Ecuador tiene unos 14 millones de habitantes y es un poco más pequeño que Nevada. En la pequeña ciudad de Otavalo, a unas horas de Quito, vemos un excelente ejemplo de cómo los indígenas ecuatorianos han logrado una prosperidad inigualable *(unequaled)*. Esta industriosa comunidad de indígenas otavalenses ha logrado establecer contactos comerciales en Europa para la venta de sus productos artesanales y textiles, sin necesidad de intermediarios.

Práctica adicional

Website
vistahigher
learning.com

En papel: El club de corazones solitarios. Completa el cuestionario. Answers will vary.

Club de corazones solitarios

1. **Nombre** _____ 2. **Edad** _____ 3. **Sexo:** ☐ hombre ☐ mujer

4. **Estatura (en pies)**   5. **Peso (en libras)**

☐ entre 4' y 5'   ☐ entre 6'7" y 7'   ☐ 100–125   ☐ 190–205
☐ entre 5' y 5'6"   ☐ más de 7'   ☐ 126–140   ☐ 206–225
☐ entre 5'7" y 6'   ☐ 141–165   ☐ 225+
☐ entre 6' y 6'6"   ☐ 166–190

6. **Color de pelo**   7. **Profesión u ocupación** _____

☐ negro   ☐ rubio
☐ castaño   ☐ pelirrojo

8. **Sueldo (en dólares):**

☐ 5,000–15,000   ☐ 25,000–35,000   ☐ 45,000–55,000
☐ 16,000–25,000   ☐ 35,000–45,000   ☐ 55,000+

9. **Marca sí o no según tus preferencias.**

Sí   No   Sí   No

☐ ☐ ¿Fumas?   ☐ ☐ ¿Viajas?
☐ ☐ ¿Haces ejercicio?   ☐ ☐ ¿Te interesa el matrimonio?
☐ ☐ ¿Cocinas?   ☐ ☐ ¿Prefieres sólo una amistad?
☐ ☐ ¿Lees?   ☐ ☐ ¿Quieres tener hijos?

10. **¿Qué deportes haces/practicas?** _____

11. **¿Tienes mascotas? ¿Cuáles?** _____

12. **¿Cómo es tu personalidad?** _____

13. **¿Cuáles son tus actividades favoritas?** _____

14. **¿Qué características de la personalidad son importantes en tu pareja?**

_____

15. **¿Qué características físicas prefieres en tu pareja?** _____

_____

¡Fíjate!

To convert meters to feet **(pies)**:
meters x 3.2808

To convert kilos to pounds **(libras)**:
kilos x 2.2046

Instructor's Resources
• VHS Video
• Worktext CD
• IRM: Videoscript

¡A ver de nuevo! Escribe un resumen del episodio. Incluye detalles que describen los trabajos de los amigos. Después, trabaja con un(a) compañero/a para añadir más información.

Video
CD-ROM

Práctica adicional

Cuaderno de tareas
WB pp.281–284, L–M
LM p.286, A–B

Audio
CD-ROM
Episodio 11

Website
vistahigher
learning.com

Vocabulario del Episodio 11

Instructor's Resources
• Testing program
• Website

Objetivos comunicativos

You should now be able to do the following in Spanish:

✓ talk about your job

✓ say what people do for you

✓ share your talents

Las cosas que mi familia y amigos hacen

ayudar	*to help*
contar (o → ue) los problemas	*to tell your problems*
dar consejos	*to give advice*
dejar usar su coche	*to let someone use one's car*
invitar a salir	*to ask someone out*
llamar	*to call*
mandar un regalo	*to send a present*
pagar	*to pay*
pedir (e → i) cosas prestadas	*to borrow things*
prestar dinero	*to lend money*

Para hablar del trabajo

el ama de casa (m, f)	*homemaker*
atender (e → ie) a los clientes	*to attend the customers/clients*
el/la chofer	*driver*
el/la empleado/a	*clerk, employee*
el horario flexible/fijo	*flexible/fixed schedule*
el/la jefe/a	*boss*
el/la mesero/a	*waiter/waitress*
el/la niñero/a	*baby-sitter*
poner las cosas en su lugar	*to put/place things in their place*
las prestaciones	*fringe benefits*
el puesto	*position*
saber + [verb]	*to know how (to do something)*
salir temprano/tarde	*to get off, to leave early/late*
el sueldo alto/bajo	*high/low salary*
el tiempo completo/parcial/libre	*full-time/part-time/free time*
el turno de la mañana/tarde/noche	*morning/afternoon/night shift*
las vacaciones	*vacation*
la ventaja/desventaja	*advantage/disadvantage*

Vocabulario personal

In this section, write all the words you want to know in Spanish so you can talk about your own job.

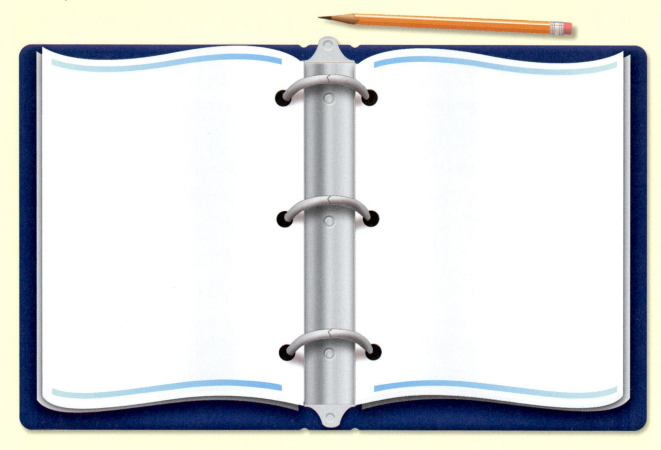

¡A escribir!

Episodio 11

Escenas de la vida: ¡A ganarse la vida!

A. ¡A ver cuánto entendiste! See how much of the **Escena** you understood by matching the Spanish sentences with their English equivalents.

___c___ 1. Cuido niños por la tarde.   a. They invite me out.

___e___ 2. A ti te dan propinas.   b. How's your job?

___a___ 3. Me invitan a salir.   c. I baby-sit children in the afternoons.

___b___ 4. ¿Qué tal el trabajo?   d. Do they pay you well?

___f___ 5. La verdad es que no sé qué hacer.   e. They give you tips.

___d___ 6. ¿Te pagan bien?   f. The truth is, I don't know what to do.

___g___ 7. Sabemos que son trabajos de   g. We know that they're part-time jobs
tiempo parcial.

B. ¡Tenemos que trabajar! Complete each phrase in column **A** with the appropriate element from column **B**. Then identify the speaker.

1. ¿Quién lo dijo? *(Who said it?)*

A	B
___b___ 1. Soy mesero…	a. mal.
___d___ 2. Tengo que trabajar de…	b. en un restaurante.
___a___ 3. Me pagan…	c. tarde.
___c___ 4. Salgo…	d. noche.

_____Wayne_____ **lo dijo.**

2. ¿Quién lo dijo?

A	B
___c___ 1. Sabemos que son…	a. a salir.
___d___ 2. Me ayudan…	b. son muy buenos.
___b___ 3. Mis compañeros…	c. trabajos de tiempo parcial.
___a___ 4. Me invitan…	d. cuando necesito algo.

_____Ana Mari_____ **lo dijo.**

C. Los trabajos de Ramón y Sofía. Indicate whether the statements are **cierto** or **falso**.

	Cierto	Falso
1. Sofía trabaja durante las tardes y los fines de semana.	☑	☐
2. A Sofía le dan buenas propinas.	☐	☑
3. Ramón es chofer de autobuses.	☐	☑
4. A Ramón le dan buenas propinas.	☑	☐
5. Ramón practica el español en su trabajo.	☑	☐
6. A Sofía le gustan los niños, pero le dan problemas.	☑	☐

Gramática 1

Talking about your job
• **Saber, salir, poner, and job-related vocabulary**

D. Manolo va a una agencia de colocación *(employment agency).* Use the expressions to complete Manolo's conversation with his counselor.

ventajas	tiempo parcial	sueldo	el puesto	el turno de la tarde
tiempo libre	vacaciones	desventajas	horario fijo	el empleado

Consejero   Bueno, Manolo, ¿qué tipo de trabajo deseas encontrar?

Manolo   Pues, no sé. Quiero un trabajo que me permita tener un poco de

(1) _____tiempo libre_____ para poder continuar con mi poesía y mi música.

Consejero   ¿Cuántas horas quieres trabajar y qué días?

Manolo   Pues, unas veinte o veinticinco horas a la semana. Puedo trabajar

cualquier día de la semana.

Consejero   Creo que tengo (2) _____el puesto_____ perfecto para ti: asistente de maestro.

Este trabajo tiene muchas (3) _____ventajas_____: sólo son veinte horas de

trabajo a la semana, por las mañanas; tienes (4) _____vacaciones_____ con

frecuencia. Además *(besides)*, te da la oportunidad de ver si te gustaría ser

maestro en el futuro. Y el (5) _____sueldo_____ es bastante bueno, diez

dólares la hora.

Manolo   ¡Qué lástima! *(what a pity!)*, pero por las mañanas no puedo. Sólo puedo

trabajar (6) _____el turno de la tarde_____. Definitivamente no puedo trabajar el turno

de la mañana.

Consejero   Bueno, hay muchos trabajos de (7) _____tiempo parcial_____ en restaurantes. El

sueldo no es malo, pero una de las (8) _____desventajas_____ es que no te dan

muchas vacaciones.

Manolo   ¿Y el horario?

Consejero   Bueno, no es un (9) _____horario fijo_____. Ellos te informan cuál es tu horario

para cada semana.

Manolo   Gracias por su ayuda, pero creo que por ahora voy a quedarme con *(keep)*

mi trabajo.

E. ¿Qué sabes hacer? Indicate whether you (or the people you know) know how to do the following things, using the verb **saber**. If you do not know anyone, use **nadie** (*nobody*). Answers will vary.

jugar tenis	**esquiar**	**usar las computadoras**
patinar en línea (*rollerblade*)	**cocinar**	**hablar bien español**

> **Modelo**   **Mis primos Mark y Jim saben patinar en línea.**

1. _____
2. _____
3. _____
4. _____
5. _____
6. _____

F. ¿Qué quiere saber Wayne? Sofía and Wayne are talking on the phone. Judging from Sofía's answers, write down what Wayne asks her.

1. Wayne   ¿Dónde haces la tarea? _____

    Sofía   Hago la tarea en la biblioteca.

2. Wayne   ¿Qué haces los sábados? _____

    Sofía   Los sábados salgo con Ana Mari y Ramón o con Manolo.

3. Wayne   ¿Ves mucho la tele? _____

    Sofía   No, no veo mucho la tele. Prefiero leer o usar Internet.

4. Wayne   ¿Te gusta ver películas extranjeras? _____

    Sofía   Sí, me gusta mucho ver películas extranjeras.

5. Wayne   ¿Por qué sales bien en tus clases? _____

    Sofía   Pues, pongo atención en clase y por eso salgo bien.

6. Wayne   ¿Sabes cocinar? _____

    Sofía   No, no sé cocinar, pero quiero aprender.

G. Justificaciones. Complete the sentences logically. Answers will vary.

> **Modelo**   No sé tocar el piano porque **no tengo tiempo para aprender.**

1. No hago la tarea cuando _____.
2. A veces no pongo atención en clase porque _____.
3. Mis amigos y yo vemos películas en casa cuando _____.
4. Hago ejercicio porque _____.
5. Salgo con mis amigos cuando _____.
6. Voy a salir bien en esta clase porque _____.
7. No pongo mi ropa en el clóset cuando _____.
8. No sé jugar fútbol porque _____.

Gramática 2 | Saying what people do for you
• The object pronouns <u>me</u> and <u>te</u>

H. Adriana está muy ocupada. Everybody wants Adriana's help today. Use the expressions to complete the questions her family asks her.

me lees	ayudarme	me llamas
me prestas	me cuentas	comprarme
pagarme	invitarme	me dejas

Viviana   Mami, ¿vas a (1) _____*ayudarme*_____ con la tarea esta noche?

Santiago   Cariño, ¿vas a (2) _____*invitarme*_____ a salir esta noche?

Carlos   Mami, ¿(3) _____*me dejas*_____ usar tu coche esta noche?

Viviana   Mami, ¿(4) _____*me lees*_____ la carta de tía Cristina?

Santiaguito   Mami, ¿(5) _____*me prestas*_____ veinte dólares?

Viviana   Mami, ¿vas a (6) _____*comprarme*_____ un uniforme nuevo?

I. Mi mejor amiga.

Parte 1. Ana Mari explains why Sofía is her best friend. Complete the description, using verbs and object pronouns from this episode. *Answers will vary.*

> Sofía es mi mejor amiga. Ella (1) _____*me ayuda*_____ con mis problemas. Hay mucha confianza *(trust)* entre nosotras. Ella (2) _____*me cuenta*_____ sus problemas y secretos también. Además, (3) _____*me da*_____ consejos cuando los necesito. Si mi coche no funciona, ella (4) _____*me deja*_____ usar el suyo *(hers)*. Los fines de semana, (5) _____*me invita*_____ a salir al cine o a cenar. A veces vamos a tomar café o a visitar a Adriana. Una amiga así *(like her)* no es fácil de encontrar.

Parte 2. Now write what *your* best friend does for you. *Answers will vary.*

_____

_____

_____

_____

_____

_____

J. Mi profesor(a) favorito/a. Answer the questions in a paragraph to describe your favorite teacher. *Answers will vary.*

¿Quién es tu profesor(a) favorito/a? ¿Qué clase enseña? ¿Te da mucha tarea? ¿Te deja entregar *(turn in)* la tarea tarde? ¿Te ayuda cuando no entiendes? ¿Te deja salir temprano? ¿Te escucha cuando haces una pregunta? ¿Necesitas estudiar mucho?

_____

_____

_____

_____

_____

K. Las personas que (no) me ayudan. Make up true statements about the people who do/not do the following things for you. *Answers will vary.*

mandarte flores	prestarte dinero	llamarte con frecuencia
dejarte usar su computadora	darte consejos	invitarte a salir

> **Modelo** Mi hermano Rubén nunca me presta dinero.

1. _____
2. _____
3. _____
4. _____
5. _____
6. _____

Para terminar

L. La curiosa de Ana Mari. Ana Mari wants to know more about Manolo, so she is asking Sofía many questions. How would Ana Mari ask the following?

1. Do you know where he works? ¿Sabes dónde trabaja?

2. Do you know who lives with him? ¿Sabes quién vive con él?

3. Do you know which days he works? ¿Sabes qué días trabaja?

4. Do you know how many classes he takes? ¿Sabes cuántas clases toma?

5. Does he know how to play volleyball? ¿Sabe jugar vóleibol?

6. Does he know how to cook? ¿Sabe cocinar?

7. Do you know if he has a girfriend? ¿Sabes si tiene novia?

8. Do you know if he is going to ask me out? ¿Sabes si va a invitarme a salir?

M. Gustos y aptitudes. Read and complete the following survey to find out if your chosen career suits your talents and interests. Do not spend time thinking about your responses; instead, select the first answer that comes to mind. Answers will vary.

Parte 1. Ocupaciones y profesiones. Para cada ocupación, selecciona la posibilidad de hacer ese trabajo: **(S) Sí:** me gustaría; **(I) Indiferente:** ni me gusta ni me disgusta; **(N) No:** no me gustaría.

	S	I	N				S	I	N	
1.	☐	☐	☐	Abogado/a		13.	☐	☐	☐	Ingeniero/a
2.	☐	☐	☐	Director(a) de ventas		14.	☐	☐	☐	Contador(a)
3.	☐	☐	☐	Político/a		15.	☐	☐	☐	Gerente
4.	☐	☐	☐	Ejecutivo/a internacional		16.	☐	☐	☐	Analista de sistemas
5.	☐	☐	☐	Educador(a)		17.	☐	☐	☐	Guardia de seguridad[1]
6.	☐	☐	☐	Maestro/a		18.	☐	☐	☐	Mecánico/a
7.	☐	☐	☐	Líder religioso		19.	☐	☐	☐	Guardabosques[2]
8.	☐	☐	☐	Sicólogo/a		20.	☐	☐	☐	Ingeniero/a mecánico/a
9.	☐	☐	☐	Farmacéutico/a		21.	☐	☐	☐	Fotógrafo/a
10.	☐	☐	☐	Cirujano/a		22.	☐	☐	☐	Músico/a
11.	☐	☐	☐	Asistente dental		23.	☐	☐	☐	Dibujante o Diseñador(a)
12.	☐	☐	☐	Investigador(a) científico/a		24.	☐	☐	☐	Escritor(a) de libros para niños

Parte 2. Materias de la escuela. Para cada materia, selecciona la mejor opción, aunque nunca hayas estudiado esa materia. *(It does not matter if you have never taken a class in that subject.)* **(S) Sí:** me interesa; **(I) Indiferente:** ni me gusta ni me disgusta; **(N) No:** no me interesa.

	S	I	N				S	I	N	
1.	☐	☐	☐	Leyes		13.	☐	☐	☐	Ley de impuestos
2.	☐	☐	☐	Administración		14.	☐	☐	☐	Administración laboral
3.	☐	☐	☐	Ciencias políticas		15.	☐	☐	☐	Computación
4.	☐	☐	☐	Idiomas		16.	☐	☐	☐	Composición
5.	☐	☐	☐	Salud		17.	☐	☐	☐	Educación física
6.	☐	☐	☐	Sicología infantil		18.	☐	☐	☐	Geología
7.	☐	☐	☐	Pedagogía		19.	☐	☐	☐	Reparación automotriz
8.	☐	☐	☐	Sicología		20.	☐	☐	☐	Electricidad
9.	☐	☐	☐	Filosofía		21.	☐	☐	☐	Arte visual
10.	☐	☐	☐	Química		22.	☐	☐	☐	Historia de la música
11.	☐	☐	☐	Matemáticas		23.	☐	☐	☐	Diseño gráfico/dibujo
12.	☐	☐	☐	Estadística		24.	☐	☐	☐	Literatura

[1] *Security guard* [2] *Park ranger*

Parte 3. Actividades. Selecciona las actividades que te gustan o te interesan.

	S	I	N			S	I	N	
1.	☐	☐	☐	Hablar en público	13.	☐	☐	☐	Preparar tus propios impuestos
2.	☐	☐	☐	Entrevistar personas	14.	☐	☐	☐	Trabajar en la computadora
3.	☐	☐	☐	Discutir de política	15.	☐	☐	☐	Escribir tus gastos del mes
4.	☐	☐	☐	Ver las noticias de otros países	16.	☐	☐	☐	Organizar tus documentos
5.	☐	☐	☐	Ayudar a personas con problemas	17.	☐	☐	☐	Ir a exposiciones de armas
6.	☐	☐	☐	Cuidar niños	18.	☐	☐	☐	Ir de campamento
7.	☐	☐	☐	Ser voluntario en tu comunidad	19.	☐	☐	☐	Limpiar el motor de tu coche
8.	☐	☐	☐	Organizar actividades en grupo	20.	☐	☐	☐	Participar en actividades deportivas
9.	☐	☐	☐	Hablar del significado de la vida	21.	☐	☐	☐	Ir a conciertos/galerías de arte
10.	☐	☐	☐	Hacer experimentos químicos	22.	☐	☐	☐	Hacer trabajos manuales/dibujar
11.	☐	☐	☐	Ver una operación de corazón	23.	☐	☐	☐	Ir a desfiles de modas[1]
12.	☐	☐	☐	Leer artículos de medicina	24.	☐	☐	☐	Escribir historias

Parte 4. Tipo de personas. Piensa si te interesa socializar con personas con las siguientes características.

	S	I	N			S	I	N	
1.	☐	☐	☐	Personas ricas	8.	☐	☐	☐	Personas estables y tranquilas
2.	☐	☐	☐	Personas de distintas culturas	9.	☐	☐	☐	Personas deportistas
3.	☐	☐	☐	Bebés/Ancianos	10.	☐	☐	☐	Personas a las que les gusta
4.	☐	☐	☐	Personas con problemas de salud					el peligro[2]
5.	☐	☐	☐	Científicos	11.	☐	☐	☐	Genios musicales
6.	☐	☐	☐	Personas famosas o importantes	12.	☐	☐	☐	Personas con talentos artísticos
7.	☐	☐	☐	Personas que tienen tus mismos intereses					

Parte 5. Tus características Selecciona las respuestas que describan el tipo *(kind)* de persona que eres. **(S) Sí:** me describe; **(D) Depende:** depende de la situación: a veces sí, a veces no; **(N) No:** no me describe.

	S	D	N			S	D	N	
1.	☐	☐	☐	Puedes resolver problemas entre dos personas.	7.	☐	☐	☐	Prefieres trabajar horas regulares.
2.	☐	☐	☐	Te comunicas fácilmente con personas de otras culturas.	8.	☐	☐	☐	Prefieres trabajar solo/a que en comités.
3.	☐	☐	☐	Te gusta organizar actividades en tu grupo.	9.	☐	☐	☐	Tienes habilidades mecánicas.
4.	☐	☐	☐	Tienes paciencia para enseñar.	10.	☐	☐	☐	Prefieres estar al aire libre que en una oficina.
5.	☐	☐	☐	Te gusta aprender cosas nuevas.	11.	☐	☐	☐	Prefieres trabajar sin horario fijo.
6.	☐	☐	☐	Sabes escribir bien; de forma clara y concisa.	12.	☐	☐	☐	Te gusta crear cosas originales.

[1]**desfiles**...*fashion shows*   [2]*danger*

Parte 6. Interpretación de resultados. Basado en el exámen *STRONG: Strong Interest Inventory* (publicado por *Consulting Psychologists Press, Inc.*), el inventario de preferencias, gustos e intereses puede dividirse en seis áreas principales:

Mecánica:	construcción, reparación, trabajar al aire libre
Investigativa:	investigación y análisis
Artística:	crear y disfrutar el arte, drama, música, escribir
Social:	ayudar, enseñar y cuidar a otros
Comercial:	ventas, administración, persuasión
Tradicional:	contabilidad, organizar, procesamiento de datos

Para saber en qué área están tus intereses, sigue los siguientes pasos:

1. Primero examina las **Partes 1**, **2** y **3** escribe el número total de veces en las que marcaste la columna **(Sí)** de las preguntas:

Preguntas	1–4	5–8	9–12	13–16	17–20	21–24
	____	____	____	____	____	____

2. Ahora determina el área de interés predominante. Por ejemplo, si en las preguntas 13–16 tienes el número más alto, entonces quiere decir que tus intereses están en el área tradicional. Busca arriba las carreras y profesiones del área tradicional.

Partes 1, 2 y 3

1–4: Comercial	13–16: Tradicional
5–8: Social	17–20: Mecánica
9–12: Investigativa	21–24: Artística

3. Ahora examina las **Partes 4** y **5** y haz lo mismo: escribe el número total de veces en las que marcaste la columna **(Sí)** de las preguntas.

Preguntas	1–2	3–4	5–6	7–8	9–10	11–12
	____	____	____	____	____	____

4. Ahora determina el área de interés predominante. Luego busca las carreras o profesiones de esa área.

Partes 4 y 5

1–2: Comercial	7–8: Tradicional
3–4: Social	9–10: Mecánica
5–6: Investigativa	11–12: Artística

Resultado final: Mi área de interés es _____ y las carreras que podría (*I could*) estudiar son: _____

¡A escuchar!

Episodio 11

Comprensión

Audio CD-ROM

A. ¿Qué hacen por ti?

Parte 1. You are going to hear six questions about what people do for you. Answer the questions aloud using the written cues provided. Then repeat the correct answer after the speaker.

Modelo	You see:	cien dólares
	You hear:	¿Cuánto te pagan por semana?
	You say:	Me pagan cien dólares.

1. un regalo   2. un secreto   3. consejos   4. mi compañero   5. mi hermano   6. bien

Parte 2. A friend is telling you who does things for her, but you cannot hear her very well in the noisy cafeteria where you are having a cup of coffee together. Each time she finishes a sentence, you have to ask her about what she said. Formulate your questions, using the written cues provided and an indirect object pronoun. Then repeat the correct question after the speaker.

Modelo	You see:	invitar al cine
	You hear:	Mi hermana me invita al cine.
	You say:	¿Quién te invita al cine?

1. escuchar en clase   3. conocer bien   5. prometer cosas
2. ayudar en casa   4. escribir cartas   6. dar dinero

Audio CD-ROM

B. El horario de Wayne.
You are going to hear Wayne describe a normal Tuesday in his weekly schedule. Listen and write down his schedule on the daily planner. ¡Atención! Remember to change the verbs to the **él** form. You will hear Wayne's description twice.

El martes			
Hora		**Hora**	
8:00	Hace ejercicio.	1:00	Tiene tiempo libre.
9:00	Sale para la universidad.	2:00	Tiene tiempo libre.
10:00	Tiene clase de computación.	3:00	Tiene tiempo libre.
11:00	Hace tarea en la biblioteca.	4:00	Tiene tiempo libre.
12:00	Almuerza con Ramón en la cafetería.	5:00	Tiene tiempo libre.
		6:00	Va a trabajar al restaurante.

Pronunciación

Audio
CD-ROM

La x. The letter **x (equis)** most often represents the combination of the English sounds *ks*. Repeat these words after the speaker.

explicar	**examen**	**existir**	**taxi**
excelente	**mixta**	**expresar**	**sexto**

Spoken with certain accents, the letter **x (equis)** sometimes represents the sound of the English *s*. Many native Mexican words and names have this sound. Repeat these words after the speaker.

exacto	**exquisito**	**Taxco**	**Xochimilco**

The letter **x** also sounds somewhat similar to English *h* and Spanish **j** in some native Mexican words and names. Repeat these words after the speaker.

México	**Oaxaca**	**Xoco**

Más escenas de la vida

Ramón, Ana Mari, Wayne, and Sofía are leaving the theater and going home. Listen to their conversation, and then complete activities **A** and **B**. You will hear the conversation twice.

A. Emparejar. Match the following phrases with the correct responses, according to what you heard in the conversation.

__c__ 1. ¿Llevas a Sofía a su casa?

__d__ 2. ¿Te gusta vivir en el dormitorio?

__e__ 3. Debe ser horrible vivir solo.

__b__ 4. No sé cómo puedes vivir con tus padres.

__a__ 5. No entiendo cómo tú puedes vivir
　　　sin tu familia.

a. Para nosotros la independencia
　 es primero.

b. En mi casa tengo todo.

c. Claro.

d. Sí, mucho.

e. No, estoy contento.

B. Responde. Write the answers to the following questions.

1. ¿Cómo está Wayne en el dormitorio? _____ Wayne está contento en el dormitorio. _____

2. ¿Quién está triste? ¿Qué hace ella? _____ Su mamá está triste; lo llama casi todos los días. _____

3. ¿Por qué a Wayne le gusta vivir solo? _____ Nadie lo molesta y tiene su independencia. _____

4. ¿Por qué le gusta a Sofía vivir con su familia? ¿Qué dice (*says*) de su mamá?
_____ En su casa tiene todo. Su mamá la ayuda y le da buenos consejos. _____

5. ¿Qué dice (*says*) de su papá? _____ Dice que su papá la deja usar su coche y le presta dinero cuando lo necesita. _____

Objetivos comunicativos

In this episode, you will practice:

✔ discussing professional plans

✔ talking about people and places you know

✔ talking about salaries

✔ avoiding repetition when answering questions

Episodio 12

Escenas de la vida: Los planes profesionales

A. ¡Mira cuánto puedes entender! Escucha a los personajes expresar sus planes para saber...

a. ¿Qué quiere ser Sofía?

☐ **contadora**   ✔ **arquitecta**

Sofía dice que...

☐ quiere trabajar con números.

✔ quiere diseñar edificios modernos.

✔ conoce a un arquitecto que gana más de $80.000.

☐ conoce a un contador que gana más de $8.000.

b. ¿Qué quiere ser Wayne?

☐ **periodista**   ✔ **analista de sistemas**

Wayne dice que...

☐ entiende mejor a las personas.

✔ entiende mejor las computadoras.

☐ va a empezar con un sueldo bajo.

✔ va a ganar $45.000.

c. ¿Qué quiere ser Ana Mari?

✔ **abogada**   ☐ **maestra**

1. ¿A quién quiere ayudar?

   Quiere ayudar a las personas de la comunidad.

   _____

2. ¿A quién admira, y por qué?

   Admira a Janet Reno, porque es una abogada trabajadora y honesta.

Video Synopsis. Manolo interviews his friends about their career plans. Sofía wants to be an architect, while Wayne is interested in computers, since he understands them better than people. Ana Mari wants to be a lawyer and help the Spanish-speaking community, and Ramón wants to go into international business. Manolo is undecided.

d. ¿Qué quiere ser Ramón?

oficial de prisión

 ✓

hombre de negocios

1. ¿Qué quiere estudiar?

Quiere estudiar negocios internacionales.

2. ¿Qué necesitan los profesionales del siglo XXI?

Necesitan saber dos o tres idiomas.

3. ¿Cuántos idiomas sabe hablar?

Sabe hablar dos idiomas.

e. ¿Qué debe ser Manolo? Answers will vary.

artista

veterinario

1. ¿Qué quiere ser Manolo?

No sabe.

2. ¿Qué cosas le gusta hacer?

Le gusta escribir poesía, escuchar música, pintar, cuidar a los animales.

3. ¿Qué debería (should he) estudiar?

Answers will vary.

Video
CD-ROM

Audio
CD-ROM

B. ¿Te diste cuenta? Escucha los comentarios otra vez para indicar si las oraciones son **ciertas** o **falsas**.

	Cierto	Falso
1. Sofía toma una clase de diseño de circuitos.	✓	
2. Ana Mari no va a defender criminales.	✓	
3. Ana Mari es idealista.	✓	
4. Muchos trabajos requieren comunicación en tres idiomas.	✓	
5. Manolo va a ser maestro de primaria.		✓

Video
CD-ROM

Audio
CD-ROM

C. ¿Quién? Escucha para indicar a quién se refieren estos comentarios: Ana Mari (**AM**), Manolo (**M**), Ramón (**R**) o Wayne (**W**).

___R___ 1. Habla japonés, pero no lo sabe escribir.

___W___ 2. Va a empezar con 40.000 o 45.000 dólares de sueldo.

___AM___ 3. Dice que hay pocos abogados bilingües.

___M___ 4. Tiene muchos talentos artísticos.

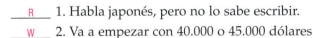

Práctica adicional	

Cuaderno de tareas WB pp.311–312, A–C	Video CD-ROM Episodio 12

Cultura a lo vivo

In both Hispanic and Anglo cultures, most people are creative and productive; they take pride in their work and strive to support their families and improve their communities. Spanish speakers, however, do not generally define themselves by their work; they rather tend to place greater value on their relationships with family and friends. Spanish speakers do not find personal self-esteem in the amount of money they earn; far more important is the knowledge and level of education they acquire. Although in Latin America, for example, teachers do not earn a lot of money, they are greatly respected and appreciated by the community.

Para comunicarnos mejor

Vocabulario 1

Discussing professional plans
• Careers and professions

Carreras y ocupaciones con futuro

Agente de bienes raíces
Título: licencia
Sueldo promedio: variable

Bombero
Título: licencia
Sueldo promedio: $722 a la semana

Enfermero/a
Título: universitario
Sueldo promedio: $4.934 al mes

Carreras y profesiones

el/la abogado/a	*lawyer*	**el/la ingeniero/a en computación**	*computer engineer*
el/la administrador(a) de empresas	*business administrator*	**el/la investigador(a)**	*investigator*
el/la agente de bienes raíces	*real estate agent*	**el/la maestro/a**	*teacher*
el/la analista de sistemas	*systems analyst*	**el/la médico/a**	*physician*
el/la bombero	*firefighter*	**el/la oficial de prisión**	*prison guard/officer*
el/la contador(a)	*accountant*	**el/la periodista**	*journalist*
el/la diseñador(a) gráfico/a	*graphic designer*	**el/la policía**	*police officer*
el/la educador(a)	*educator*	**el/la profesor(a) de idiomas**	*language professor*
el/la enfermero(a)	*nurse*	**el/la programador(a)**	*computer programmer*
el/la fisioterapeuta	*physical therapist*	**el/la sicólogo/a**	*phychologist*
ganar	*to earn*		
el/la gerente de ventas y mercadeo	*sales and marketing manager*	**el/la técnico/a en computación**	*computer technician*
el/la higienista dental	*dental hygienist*	**el/la veterinario/a**	*veterinarian*

PRÁCTICA

A. Los profesionales. Empareja la descripción con la profesión.

_h_	1. Defiende a los criminales y a los inocentes.	a. arquitecta
_a_	2. Diseña casas o edificios.	b. enfermero
_e_	3. Escribe artículos para periódicos.	c. maestro
_b_	4. Cuida a los pacientes.	d. programadora
_c_	5. Enseña en las escuelas.	e. periodista
_j_	6. Repara las computadoras.	f. técnico veterinario
_i_	7. Administra compañías y programas internacionales.	g. policía
_g_	8. Protege a la comunidad.	h. abogado
_f_	9. Ayuda al veterinario.	i. ejecutiva internacional
_d_	10. Programa computadoras.	j. técnico en computación

B. Estereotipos sobre las profesiones. Completa las frases lógicamente. Algunas frases pueden tener varias respuestas. *Answers will vary.*

1. Los _____ ganan mucho dinero.
2. Las _____ analizan a todas las personas con quienes hablan.
3. Las _____ son dulces y pacientes con los niños.
4. Los _____ saben hablar muchos idiomas.
5. Los _____ son estrictos y muy ordenados.

C. Adivina quién lo hace. Identifica la profesión que corresponde a cada descripción.

1. Este profesional le ayuda al dentista. También les limpia los dientes a los pacientes.
   Higienista dental

2. Diseña sistemas de computación específicos a las necesidades de las compañías.
   Programador

3. Toma las decisiones importantes de una empresa. Diseña e implementa planes económicos y de trabajo.
   Administrador de empresas

4. Representa a la organización; resuelve problemas entre personas y grupos.
   Abogado

5. Vende casas, condominios y edificios.
   Agente de bienes raíces

D. Aspectos personales. Contesta las preguntas y comparte la información con tu compañero/a para ver si tienen cosas en común.   Answers will vary.

D. After students interview a partner, you may have them share their answers with the class.

1. ¿Qué ocupación o profesión tienen tus familiares y amigos?

_____

2. ¿Y tú, qué quieres ser?

_____

3. ¿Por qué quieres estudiar esa carrera *(major)*?

_____

4. ¿Cuáles son algunas ventajas de tu carrera?

_____

5. ¿Cuáles son algunas desventajas?

_____

6. ¿Cuántos años de preparación necesitas?

_____

7. ¿Dónde quieres trabajar?

_____

8. ¿Qué sueldo vas a ganar?

_____

9. ¿Qué prestaciones vas a tener?

_____

Práctica adicional

Cuaderno de tareas
WB pp.312–313, D–E

Gramática 1

Talking about people and places you know
• The verb <u>conocer</u>

Analizar y descubrir

Study the examples and answer the questions.

Conocer	
¿Quieres **conocer a** Wayne?	*Do you want to meet Wayne?*
Conozco a un arquitecto que gana mucho.	*I know an arquitect who earns a lot.*
¿**Conoces** Guadalajara?	*Do you know (Have you been to) Guadalajara?*
Ramón no **conoce a** mi abogado.	*Ramón doesn't know my lawyer.*
Mi hija y yo **conocemos a** una diseñadora excelente.	*My daughter and I know an excellent designer.*
¿Ustedes **conocen** Miami? ¿**Conocéis** Miami? }	*Do you know (Have you been to) Miami?*
Ellos no **conocen a** Emilio.	*They don't know Emilio.*

1. What do you need to place after **conocer** when referring to a *specific* person?

_____An **a.**_____

2. Do you do the same when you are talking about a place? _____No._____

291

PRÁCTICA

E. Personas y lugares. Busca entre tus compañeros una persona que te pueda dar la siguiente información. Usa el verbo **conocer.** Answers will vary.

E. Give students time to interact and then ask volunteers to share their findings.

> **Modelo**   un buen dentista
> —¿Conoces un buen dentista?
> —Pues no. ¿Y tú?
> —Yo sí. Conozco a la doctora Villalba.

	Nombre	**¿Dónde?**
1. un buen dentista	Dra. Villalba	Chula Vista
2. una buena manicurista	_____	_____
3. un buen restaurante chino	_____	_____
4. un buen veterinario	_____	_____
5. una buena discoteca	_____	_____
6. un buen café	_____	_____
7. un buen mecánico	_____	_____

F. La familia de Sofía. La familia de Sofía viaja mucho y conoce muchos lugares famosos. Completa las frases para saber qué han visitado.

> **Modelo**   Sofía _____ los Andes porque _____ Ecuador.
> **Sofía conoce los Andes porque visitó Ecuador.**

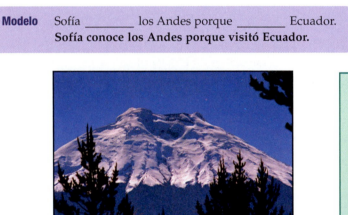

Banco de palabras

visité
I visited

visitaste
you visited

visitó
he/she visited

visitamos
we visited

visitaron
they/you visited

1. Mi hermano y yo _____conocemos_____ la Torre Eiffel porque _____visitamos_____ París el verano pasado.

2. Mis padres _____conocen_____ las Pirámides de Chichen-Itzá porque _____visitaron_____ México en 1999.

3. Mis primos _____conocen_____ la Estatua de la Libertad porque _____visitaron_____ Nueva York.

4. Mi abuelo _____conoce_____ el Vaticano porque _____visitó_____ Italia.

5. La profesora _____conoce_____ Machu Picchu porque _____visitó_____ Perú hace tres años *(three years ago)*.

6. ¿Tú _____conoces_____ Chicago?

7. Yo _____Answers will vary._____ .

Práctica adicional

Cuaderno de tareas
WB pp.313–314, F–G

Talking about salaries
• Numbers 101–100,000

When Wayne was thinking about his future career, he predicted that his entry-level salary would be between **cuarenta** and **cuarenta y cinco mil dólares.** Sofía said that she knows an architect who earns **más de ochenta mil dólares.** When talking about salaries, you will need to use numbers such as the following:

Más números			
101 **ciento uno**	120 **ciento veinte**	700 **setecientos**	20.000 **veinte mil**
102 **ciento dos**	200 **doscientos**	800 **ochocientos**	30.000 **treinta mil**
103 **ciento tres**	300 **trescientos**	900 **novecientos**	80.000 **ochenta mil**
104 **ciento cuatro**	400 **cuatrocientos**	1.000 **mil**	100.000 **cien mil**
105 **ciento cinco**	500 **quinientos**	2.000 **dos mil**	
110 **ciento diez**	600 **seiscientos**	10.000 **diez mil**	

1. The numbers from **doscientos** to **novecientos**, when followed by nouns, are adjectives and agree in gender with those nouns. Observe these masculine/feminine distinctions.

> Necesito quinient**os** pes**os**.
>
> Mi primo trabaja en Londres y gana seiscient**as** lib**ras** *(pounds)* a la semana.

2. In some Latin American countries and in Spain, a period is used instead of a comma to indicate thousands, and a comma is used instead of a period to indicate decimals.

> En España: **2.367,00** euros   En México: **2,367.00** pesos

PRÁCTICA

G. Los cheques de la señora Blasio. Ayuda a la abuela de Sofía a pagar sus cuentas. Escribe la cantidad que falta en cada cheque.

1.

> **Banco Santander Mexicano**
>
> *8 de noviembre del 2003*
> Fecha
>
> Páguese por este cheque a:
>
> *Dr. Fernández*
>
> $ *27.742,00*
> Moneda nacional
>
> 2810-2182-4-12-2000
>
> Veintisiete mil setecientos cuarenta y dos.
> La cantidad de
>
> *Sara Blasio*
>
> Cuenta personal
> SARA BLASIO
> Firma
>
> Cuenta   Cheque
> **7406-:11991715:·0011307993·-·0030·** Santander S.A. Institución de Banca Múltiple

2.

Banco Santander Mexicano

8 de noviembre del 2003
Fecha

Páguese por este cheque a:

Automotriz Salas

$ 97.845,00
Moneda nacional

Noventa y siete mil ochocientos cuarenta y cinco.

La cantidad de

Cuenta personal
SARA BLASIO

Sara Blasio

Firma

2810-2182-4-12-2000

Cuenta   Cheque

7406-:11991715:0011307993-0031   Santander S.A. Institución de Banca Múltiple

3.

Banco Santander Mexicano

8 de noviembre del 2003
Fecha

Páguese por este cheque a:

Palacio de Gobierno

$ 18.538,00
Moneda nacional

Dieciocho mil quinientos treinta y ocho.

La cantidad de

Cuenta personal
SARA BLASIO

Sara Blasio

Firma

2810-2182-4-12-2000

Cuenta   Cheque

7406-:11991715:0011307993-0032   Santander S.A. Institución de Banca Múltiple

4.

Banco Santander Mexicano

8 de noviembre del 2003
Fecha

Páguese por este cheque a:

Cablevisión

$ 15.269,00
Moneda nacional

Quince mil doscientos sesenta y nueve.

La cantidad de

Cuenta personal
SARA BLASIO

Sara Blasio

Firma

2810-2182-4-12-2000

Cuenta   Cheque

7406-:11991715:0011307993-0033   Santander S.A. Institución de Banca Múltiple

H. ¿Cuánto cuesta? You are helping an administrator with the budget for a new university classroom. Tell them the price of the items you have selected. Take turns with your partner.

> **Modelo**   10 calculadoras / $135.25
> **Diez calculadoras cuestan ciento treinta y cinco dólares con veinticinco centavos** (cents).

1. 1 televisión /$326.64
2. 1 videocasetera / $213.00
3. 1 pizarrón / $111.99
4. 2 escritorios / $449.83
5. 2 sillas ergonómicas / $755.30

6. 6 programas de multimedia / $508.22
7. 15 diccionarios bilingües / $126.40
8. 1 computadora / $970.68
9. 1 cámara digital / $664.00
10. La Enciclopedia Hispánica / $843.10

1. Una televisión cuesta trescientos veintiséis dólares con sesenta y cuatro centavos. 2. Una videocasetera cuesta doscientos trece dólares. 3. Un pizarrón cuesta ciento once dólares con noventa y nueve centavos. 4. Dos escritorios cuestan cuatrocientos cuarenta y nueve dólares con ochenta y tres centavos. 5. Dos sillas ergonómicas cuestan setecientos cincuenta y cinco dólares con treinta centavos. 6. Seis programas de multimedia cuestan quinientos ocho dólares con veintidós centavos. 7. Quince diccionarios bilingües cuestan ciento veintiséis dólares con cuarenta centavos. 8. Una computadora cuesta novecientos setenta dólares con sesenta y ocho centavos. 9. Una cámara digital cuesta seiscientos sesenta y cuatro dólares. 10. La Enciclopedia Hispánica cuesta ochocientos cuarenta y tres dólares con diez centavos.

I. Eventos históricos. Empareja las fechas con los eventos. Compara tus respuestas con las de tu compañero/a.

1. La conquista de México ocurre en __b__ .
2. El hombre va a la luna (moon) por primera vez en __f__ .
3. El muro de Berlín fue destruido en __g__ .
4. La Guerra Civil de Estados Unidos empieza en __d__ .
5. Estamos en el año de __h__ .
6. La Segunda Guerra Mundial empieza en __e__ .
7. La independencia de Estados Unidos es en __c__ .
8. Cristóbal Colón llega a América en __a__ .

a. 1492
b. 1521
c. 1776
d. 1860
e. 1939
f. 1969
g. 1989
h. _____

J. ¿Cuánto ganan estos profesionales? Cada dos años la Oficina de Estadística Laboral proyecta los sueldos promedio de las profesiones con más futuro. Escucha el informe (report) para completar la información.

Audio
CD-ROM

A la semana…
1. Un diseñador gana ___$737___ a la semana.
2. Un doctor gana ___$2.568___ a la semana.

Al mes (month)…
3. Un policía gana ___$4.508___ al mes.
4. Un piloto gana ___$8.190___ al mes.

Al año…
5. Un administrador de empresas gana ___$101.240___ al año.
6. Un técnico en computación gana ___$39.910___ al año.
7. Un fisioterapeuta gana ___$58.350___ al año.
8. Un bombero gana ___$49.100___ al año.

Instructor's Resources
• Worktext CD
• IRM: Tapescript

J. Give students time to write their responses, then ask volunteers to share their answers.

Script. *Cada dos años la Oficina de Estadística Laboral proyecta los sueldos promedio de las profesiones con más futuro. Escucha el informe para completar la información.*
1. El sueldo promedio para un diseñador es de $737 a la semana. 2. El sueldo promedio para un doctor es de $2.568 a la semana. 3. El sueldo promedio para un policía es de $4.508 al mes. 4. El sueldo promedio para un piloto es de $8.190 al mes. 5. El sueldo promedio para un administrador de empresas es de $101.240 al año. 6. El sueldo promedio para un técnico en computación es de $39.910 al año. 7. El sueldo promedio para un fisioterapeuta es de $58.350 al año. 8. El sueldo promedio para un bombero es de $49.100 al año.

Instructor's Resources
• Worktext CD
• IRM: Tapescript

K. Los profesionales hablan. Escucha los comentarios que hacen José Martínez, un sicólogo, y Josefina López, una policía, sobre las ventajas y desventajas de sus trabajos. Después contesta las preguntas.

José Martínez

1. ¿Qué hace la compañía Electromex? <u>Vende, compra, importa y exporta productos electrónicos.</u>
2. ¿Qué trabajo tiene José en esa compañía? <u>Trabaja con la directora de personal, la ayuda a entrevistar y contratar nuevos empleados.</u>
3. ¿Cuáles son las ventajas de su trabajo? <u>Conoce a muchas personas, tiene seguro médico, plan de retiro y viaja varias veces al año.</u>
4. ¿Cuáles son las desventajas? <u>Tiene que despedir a los empleados, sólo tiene 2 semanas de vacaciones al año y el sueldo no es muy bueno.</u>
5. ¿Cuánto gana? <u>Gana treinta y cinco mil dólares al año.</u>
6. ¿Crees que la carrera de José tiene futuro? <u>Answers will vary.</u>

Script. For the script to this activity, see the Instructor's Resource Manual.

Josefina López

1. ¿Qué hace Josefina y quién es Daisy? <u>Josefina es policía y Daisy es una perra policía.</u>
2. ¿Qué hacen antes de empezar su turno? <u>Van al gimnasio y salen a correr.</u>
3. ¿Por qué le gusta su trabajo? <u>Puede ayudar a muchas personas de su comunidad, ayudar a combatir el crimen, trabajar con Daisy y el sueldo es bueno.</u>
4. ¿Cuáles son las desventajas de ser policía? <u>Tienen turnos muy largos; el horario no es fijo.</u>
5. ¿Por qué quiere ser detective? <u>Los detectives ganan más y es más interesante que ser policía.</u>
6. ¿Crees que la carrera de policía es buena? <u>Answers will vary.</u>

L. Infórmate sobre tu carrera.

Parte 1. Busca información en Internet sobre tus planes profesionales y prepara un reporte escrito. <u>Answers will vary.</u>

L. Students should go to their university's career center or look up the information in the Internet. Have students share their findings. They may create a poster with the information for posting.

a. Prepara la información en español para compartir con tus compañeros.
b. Compara tus respuestas con las de la **Práctica D** en la página 291.

¡Fíjate!

Incluye la siguiente información: el sueldo, las prestaciones, el mercado de trabajo y los estudios necesarios.

> **Writing Strategy: Creating a simple plan**
>
> Planning to respond to a writing task in Spanish requires several steps:
> 1. First, you must be sure you understand what is being asked of you. To do this, you should read the task several times and make a brief outline of what is required. In this section, you are asked to use what you know about yourself—your interests, your abilities, the activities you enjoy—to explain why you have selected a certain career path. Perhaps you will focus on your personality as a key aspect of your choice.
> 2. Next, you need to determine the ideas you want to communicate. These must be simple enough to be communicated with the language you have learned: descriptive adjectives, verbs, and connecting words such as **por eso** and **porque.**
> 3. Finally, you need to organize your sentences in such a way that your meaning is clearly communicated. Use the outline you prepared to organize your writing.

Parte 2. En grupos de tres, hablen de sus planes profesionales, dónde hay trabajos en sus especialidades, qué sueldo van a ganar, qué prestaciones hay en sus campos (*fields*) y otra información interesante.

Práctica adicional

Cuaderno de tareas
WB p.314, H

Gramática 2

Avoiding repetition when answering questions
• The direct object pronouns <u>lo</u>, <u>la</u>, <u>los</u>, and <u>las</u>

Analizar y descubrir

In their remarks, the characters used the words **lo**, **la**, **los**, and **las** to avoid repeating words already mentioned. Study the following examples and answer the questions.

Voy a trabajar con computadoras.
   Las entiendo mucho mejor que a las personas.
Admiro mucho a Janet Reno.
   ¿**La** recuerdan?
También hablo japonés. Bueno, en realidad no **lo** hablo bien y no **lo** sé escribir.
Todos mis amigos ya saben qué quieren ser.
   Los envidio.

I'm going to work with computers.
   I understand them much better than people.
I admire Janet Reno a lot.
   Do you remember her?
I also speak Japanese. Well, actually I don't speak it well, and I don't know how to write it.
All my friends already know what they want to be. I envy them.

1. In the first example, what word does **las** replace? <u>Computadoras.</u>

2. In the second example, what words does **la** replace? <u>Janet Reno.</u>

3. In the third example, what word does **lo** replace? <u>Japonés.</u>

4. In the fourth example, what words does **los** replace? <u>Todos mis amigos.</u>

5. Where, with respect to the verb, are **lo, la, los,** and **las** placed? <u>Before.</u>

6. Which other pronouns that you know are also placed before the verb?

   <u>**me** and **te.**</u>

7. In a construction with multiple verbs **(En poco tiempo voy a hablar*lo* bien. / En poco tiempo *lo* voy a hablar bien.),** where may the object pronoun be placed?

   <u>It may be attached to the second verb or placed before the first verb.</u>

In summary, direct object pronouns match in gender (masculine or feminine) and number (singular or plural) with the nouns they replace, and are placed in the same position as the object pronouns **me** and **te**—that is, before conjugated verbs or attached to infinitives.

PRÁCTICA

M. ¿Dónde está? Como ya sabes, el compañero de cuarto de Manolo es muy desordenado; él nunca sabe dónde están sus cosas. ¿Qué cosas busca ahora? Completa los diálogos con la(s) palabra(s) apropiada(s) de la lista.

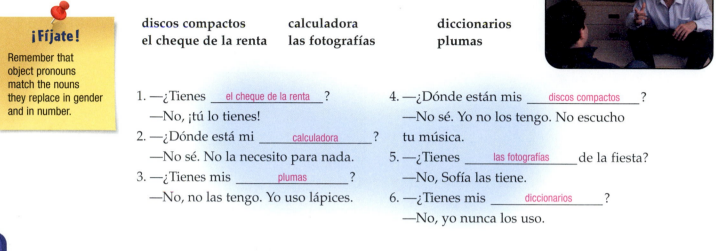

¡Fíjate!

Remember that object pronouns match the nouns they replace in gender and in number.

discos compactos	calculadora	diccionarios
el cheque de la renta	las fotografías	plumas

1. —¿Tienes ___el cheque de la renta___?
   —No, ¡tú lo tienes!

2. —¿Dónde está mi ___calculadora___?
   —No sé. No la necesito para nada.

3. —¿Tienes mis ___plumas___?
   —No, no las tengo. Yo uso lápices.

4. —¿Dónde están mis ___discos compactos___?
   —No sé. Yo no los tengo. No escucho tu música.

5. —¿Tienes ___las fotografías___ de la fiesta?
   —No, Sofía las tiene.

6. —¿Tienes mis ___diccionarios___?
   —No, yo nunca los uso.

N. La comida. Contesta las preguntas acerca de lo que te gusta comer y beber. *Answers will vary.*

> **Modelo** ¿Prefieres las hamburguesas con queso o sin queso?
> **Las prefiero sin queso.**

1. ¿Cómo sirven el pollo en tu casa, frito o asado? _____

2. ¿Cómo bebes el café, negro o con leche? _____

3. ¿Bebes la leche fría o caliente? _____

4. ¿Prefieres los huevos fritos o en *omelette*? _____

5. ¿Vas a pedir las quesadillas con jamón o sin jamón? _____

6. ¿Cómo sirven el espagueti, con carne o con mantequilla? _____

Ñ. ¡Cuánta repetición! The following comments are too repetitive. Use **lo, la, los,** and **las** to make the exchanges less repetitive. Then, practice the dialogue with a classmate.

> **Modelo** —¿Adónde va **tu novio**?
> —Va a San Francisco. Mañana tengo que llevar a **mi novio** al aeropuerto y no voy a ver a **mi novio** hasta el domingo.
>
> **Sin repetición**
> —Va a San Francisco. Mañana **lo** tengo que llevar al aeropuerto y no **lo** voy a ver hasta el domingo.
>   or
> —Va a San Francisco. Mañana tengo que llevar**lo** al aeropuerto y no voy a ver**lo** hasta el domingo.

1. — ¡Qué bonita **pluma**!

   — Gracias. ¿Quieres **la pluma**? Tengo muchas.

   — ¿Puedo usar **la pluma?**

   — Sí, es tuya *(it's yours)*.

Sin repetición

   — ¡Qué bonita pluma!

   — Gracias. ¿La quieres? Tengo muchas.

   — ¿La puedo usar?/¿Puedo usarla?

   — Sí, es tuya.

¡Fíjate!

Remember that object pronouns are placed before a conjugated verb or attached to an infinitive.

2. — ¿Ves **a tus padres** con frecuencia?

   — No mucho, veo **a mis padres** dos o tres veces al año.

   — ¿Tú visitas **a tus padres** en Miami o ellos te visitan aquí?

   — Yo visito **a mis padres**. Ellos no pueden viajar.

Sin repetición

   — ¿Ves a tus padres con frecuencia?

   — No mucho, los veo dos o tres veces al año.

   — ¿Tú los visitas en Miami o ellos te visitan aquí?

   — Yo los visito. Ellos no pueden viajar.

3. — Mamá, **tu coche** siempre está limpio.

   — Por supuesto, lavo **mi coche** con mucha frecuencia. También pongo **mi coche** en el garaje. Además, cuido mucho **mi coche.**

Sin repetición

   — Mamá, tu coche siempre está limpio.

   — Por supuesto, lo lavo con mucha frecuencia. También lo pongo en el garaje. Además, lo cuido mucho.

Invitación a **Perú**

Del álbum de
Ana Marí

Perú es la tierra de los incas. Su cultura, ropa, idioma, comida y costumbres continúan influenciando al peruano moderno. Esta antigua y avanzada cultura construyó *(built)* increíbles ciudades fortaleza en remotos lugares de los Andes.

Práctica adicional

Website
vistahigher
learning.com

O. Preguntas personales. Usa las preguntas como guía para hablar con tu compañero/a; escribe sus respuestas. Usa **lo, la, los** y **las** para evitar la repetición cuando sea posible. Answers will vary.

> **Modelo** — ¿Tienes muchos amigos? ¿Cuándo los ves? ¿Los visitas con frecuencia?
> — Me gusta tener amigos; por eso, tengo muchos. Los veo en la escuela todos los días, pero también los veo los fines de semana. Estudio con ellos con frecuencia. Casi nunca los visito porque ellos prefieren venir a mi casa.

¡Fíjate!

Be as creative as you can with your answers. Put all the Spanish you have acquired to work!

1. ¿Tienes muchos amigos? ¿Cuándo los ves? ¿Los visitas con frecuencia?

_____

_____

_____

2. ¿Qué computadora usas? ¿La usas con mucha frecuencia? ¿Dónde la tienes?

_____

_____

_____

3. ¿Siempre haces tu tarea? ¿A qué hora prefieres hacerla? ¿Dónde?

_____

_____

_____

4. ¿Tienes novio/a? ¿Cómo se llama? ¿Lo/La ves todos los días? ¿Tus padres lo/la conocen? ¿Qué piensan de él/ella?

_____

_____

_____

5. ¿Vives con tus padres? ¿Los ayudas en la casa? Si no vives con ellos, ¿los invitas a tu casa? ¿Los llamas por teléfono con frecuencia?

_____

_____

_____

Práctica adicional	
Cuaderno de tareas WB p.315, I–J LM pp.317–318, A–B, Pron.	Audio CD-ROM Episodio 12

Actividades comunicativas

A. Larga distancia.

Instrucciones para Estudiante 1

Trabajas para la compañía de teléfonos más grande de Estados Unidos. Hay un problema con tu computadora y no puedes obtener el área telefónica de las siguientes regiones. Llama a tu compañero/a y pídele *(ask them for)* la información que necesitas. Él/Ella también te va a hacer preguntas; lee las respuestas como un solo número (617 = seiscientos diecisiete).

Modelo	—¿Me puedes dar el área telefónica de Illinois? —Es setecientos setenta y tres.

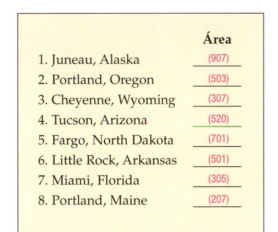

	Área
1. Juneau, Alaska	(907)
2. Portland, Oregon	(503)
3. Cheyenne, Wyoming	(307)
4. Tucson, Arizona	(520)
5. Fargo, North Dakota	(701)
6. Little Rock, Arkansas	(501)
7. Miami, Florida	(305)
8. Portland, Maine	(207)

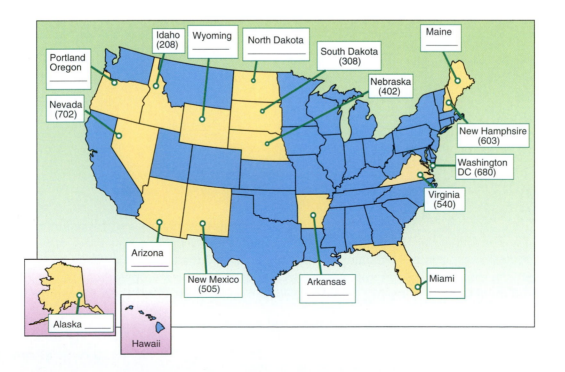

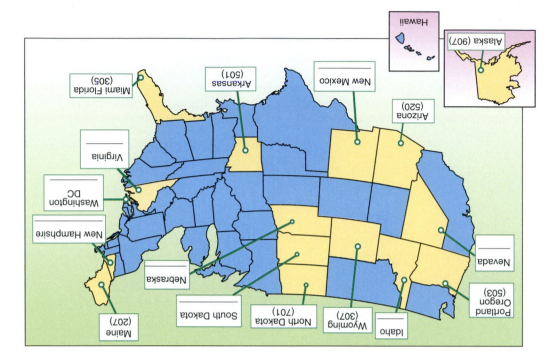

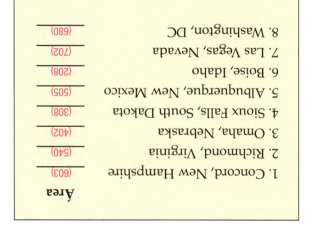

Área	
1. Concord, New Hampshire	(603)
2. Richmond, Virginia	(540)
3. Omaha, Nebraska	(402)
4. Sioux Falls, South Dakota	(308)
5. Albuquerque, New Mexico	(505)
6. Boise, Idaho	(208)
7. Las Vegas, Nevada	(702)
8. Washington, DC	(680)

Modelo —¿Me puedes dar el área telefónica de Illinois?
—Es setecientos setenta y tres.

número (617 = seiscientos diecisiete).

compañero/a te llama para pedirte las áreas de teléfono que necesita. Dáselas (give them to
them) y pídele (ask them for) la información que tú necesitas; lee las respuestas como un solo

Trabajas para la compañía de teléfonos más grande de Estados Unidos. Hay un problema
con tu computadora y no puedes obtener el área telefónica de las siguientes regiones. Tu

Instrucciones para **Estudiante 2**

A. Larga distancia.

B. Crucigrama.

Instrucciones para Estudiante 1

Tu compañero/a y tú tienen el mismo crucigrama, pero tú tienes las respuestas que él/ella no tiene, y viceversa. Necesitas explicarle las palabras usando definiciones, sinónimos, antónimos o frases incompletas.

Modelo	11 vertical:	**Janet Reno es una...**
	5 horizontal:	**Esta persona trabaja en una escuela y da clases.**

El crucigrama contiene las siguientes palabras:

1. S
2. INGENIERO / ICÓROGO
3. POLICÍA / PROFESO
4. AGENTE
5. MAESTRA
6. GERENTE / DUCU
7. EDUCADOR
8. ENFERMERA
9. VETERINARIO
10. TÉCNICO
11. ABOGADA
12. PROGRAMADORA
13. BOMBERO
14. CONTADORA

B. Crucigrama.

Instrucciones para **Estudiante 2**

Tu compañero/a y tú tienen el mismo crucigrama, pero tú tienes las respuestas que él/ella no tiene, y viceversa. Necesitas explicarle las palabras usando definiciones, sinónimos, antónimos o frases incompletas.

Modelo 11 vertical: **Janet Reno es una...**
5 horizontal: **Esta persona trabaja en una escuela y da clases.**

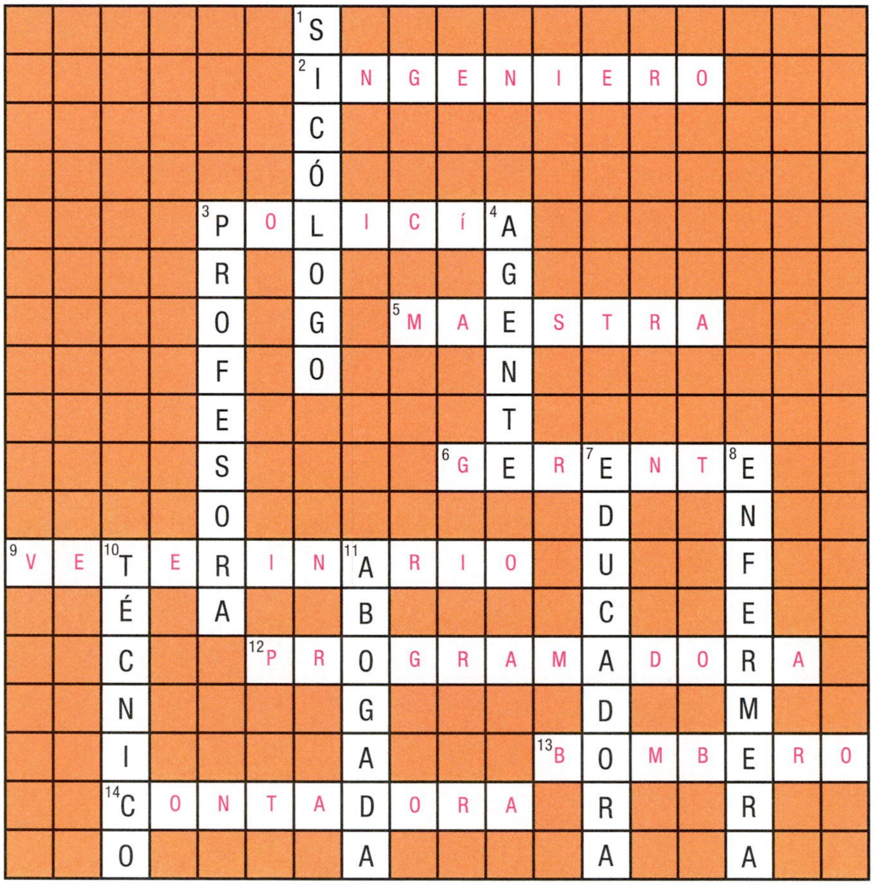
1 SICÓLOGO
2 INGENIERO
3 PROFESORA
3 POLICÍA
4 AGENTE
5 MAESTRA
6 GERENTE
7 EDUCADORA
8 ENFERMERA
9 VETERINARIO
10 TÉCNICO
11 ABOGADA
12 PROGRAMADORA
13 BOMBERO
14 CONTADORA

C. La encuesta dice... Esta actividad es similar al programa *Family Feud*. En grupos de tres, escriban las cinco respuestas que ustedes creen que son las más comunes. Tu profesor(a) tiene las respuestas correctas.

1. ¿Qué hacen los estudiantes con el libro de español?

> **Modelo**   Lo compran en la librería.

a. Lo leen.
b. Lo ponen en su mochila.
c. Lo abren todos los días.
d. Lo usan en la clase.
e. Lo venden.

C. Divide the class into teams of four or five. Have each team write their answers on the board without looking at the answers of the other teams. The team with the largest number of correct answers wins. Put the answers on a transparency and uncover them one by one.

2. ¿Cómo debe comportarse *(should behave)* un buen hijo con su mamá?

> **Modelo**   Un buen hijo debe invitarla a comer o al cine.

Un buen hijo debe...
a. Ayudarla en la casa.
b. Escucharla cuando habla.
c. Invitarla a salir.
d. Llevarla al supermercado o al doctor.
e. Quererla mucho.

3. ¿Qué hacen las personas con sus coches?

> **Modelo**   Las personas los manejan con cuidado.

a. Los lavan.
b. Los compran.
c. Los usan todos los días.
d. Los venden.
e. Los limpian.

La correspondencia

El correo: Premio escolar "Espíritu de Superación". Acabas de recibir este artículo por correo. Lee las preguntas, y después lee el artículo para contestarlas.

1. ¿Quién otorga los premios? El fabricante norteamericano de autos Ford.

2. ¿Cuántos estudiantes solicitaron *(applied for)* este premio? Treinta y cinco mil estudiantes.

3. ¿Cuál es el estado con mayor número de ganadores *(winners)*? California.

4. ¿Cuánto dinero van a recibir los estudiantes ganadores? Van a recibir mil doscientos dólares.

5. ¿A quién admira la ganadora Silvia Posada? Admira a su hermana.

Cien estudiantes ganaron el premio
"Espíritu de Superación"

Cien estudiantes en su último año de estudios pre-universitarios ganaron el premio escolar "Espíritu de Superación," otorgado por el fabricante norteamericano de autos Ford. El objetivo del premio es apoyar y motivar a los estudiantes para continuar sus estudios universitarios y ayudarlos a alcanzar sus metas.

En colaboración con la cadena televisiva Univisión, un panel de jueces seleccionó a los cien mejores estudiantes de entre 35.000 participantes. Los requisitos eran: escribir una composición que hablara de la persona que más admiran y cómo esta persona se ha superado, estar en el último año de estudios secundarios y tener un promedio mínimo de 3,0. La selección de los ganadores se basó en la originalidad, creatividad, relevancia del tema y uso correcto del idioma.

Los ganadores van a recibir $1.200 cada uno y representan varios grupos étnicos de todas partes de la nación; el 88% de los ganadores son hispanos. El estado con mayor número de ganadores es California con un 38%; después vienen Texas con 16%, Nueva York y Nueva Jersey con 13%, Illinois con 11% y Florida con 6%.

"Para nosotros es un honor premiar a estudiantes que han demostrado esfuerzo y dedicación en sus estudios. Su espíritu de superación nos inspira," declaró Ross Roberts, Vicepresidente y Gerente General de la División Ford.

La ganadora Silvia Posada de Los Ángeles, California, escribe: "Yo admiro [a mi hermana] por todos sus logros en la escuela y por nunca dudar de sí misma. La seguridad y confianza que ella tiene en sus habilidades es la misma que tiene para mí y ése es el mejor regalo que me pueden ofrecer."

En papel: Mi futuro. Escribe una carta a la Ford, basándote en la lectura de **El correo**, en la que describas: Answers will vary.

• tus estudios, tus notas y tus planes profesionales
• por qué necesitas $1.200 dólares y qué vas a hacer con el dinero

Video
CD-ROM

Audio
CD-ROM

¡A ver de nuevo!

Parte 1. Escucha la conversación de **Escenas de la vida** o mira el video para hacer un resumen de los planes profesionales de cada personaje. Answers will vary.

Parte 2. Ahora trabaja con un(a) compañero/a para comparar la información y añadir lo que te haya faltado.

Práctica adicional		
Cuaderno de tareas WB p.316, K LM p.318, A–B	Audio CD-ROM Episodio 12	Website vistahigher learning.com

Vocabulario del Episodio 12

Instructor's Resources
• Testing program
• Website

Las profesiones y las ocupaciones

el/la abogado/a	*lawyer*
el/la administrador(a) de empresas	*business administrator*
el/la agente de bienes raíces	*real estate agent*
el/la analista de sistemas	*systems analyst*
el/la bombero	*firefighter*
el/la contador(a)	*accountant*
el/la diseñador(a) gráfico/a	*graphic designer*
el/la educador(a)	*educator*
el/la enfermero/a	*nurse*
el/la fisioterapeuta	*physical therapist*
el/la gerente de ventas y mercadeo	*sales and marketing manager*
el/la higienista dental	*dental hygienist*
el/la ingeniero/a en computación	*computer engineer*
el/la investigador(a)	*investigator*
el/la maestro/a	*teacher*
el/la médico/a	*physician*
el/la oficial de prisión	*prison guard/officer*
el/la periodista	*journalist*
el/la policía	*police officer*
el/la profesor(a) de idiomas	*language professor*
el/la programador(a)	*computer programmer*
el/la sicólogo/a	*psychologist*
el/la técnico/a en computación	*computer technician*
el/la veterinario/a	*veterinarian*

Verbos

conocer	*to know; to meet someone*
ganar	*to earn (money); to win*

Pronombres de complemento directo

¿Me ayudas?	*Will you help **me**?*
Sí, te ayudo.	*Yes, I'll help **you**.*
Lo sé.	*I know **it**.*
La veo, Lo veo.	*I see **her**, I see **him**.*
Los conozco.	*I know **them**. (m)*
Las ayudo.	*I help **them**. (f)*

Más números

101	**ciento uno**	600	**seiscientos**
102	**ciento dos**	700	**setecientos**
103	**ciento tres**	800	**ochocientos**
104	**ciento cuatro**	900	**novecientos**
105	**ciento cinco**	1.000	**mil**
110	**ciento diez**	2.000	**dos mil**
120	**ciento veinte**	10.000	**diez mil**
200	**doscientos**	20.000	**veinte mil**
300	**trescientos**	30.000	**treinta mil**
400	**cuatrocientos**	80.000	**ochenta mil**
500	**quinientos**	100.000	**cien mil**

Vocabulario personal

In this section, write the words you want to know in Spanish so you can talk about your professional plans.

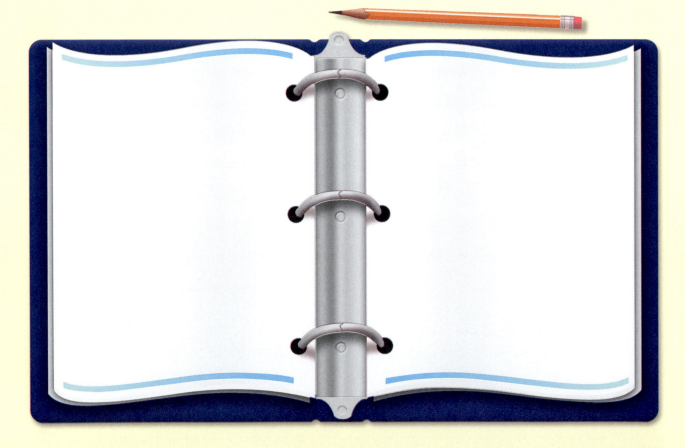

¡A escribir!

Episodio

12

Escenas de la vida: Los planes profesionales

Video CD-ROM

A. ¡A ver cuánto entendiste! See how much of the **Escena** you understood by matching the Spanish sentences with their English equivalents. Then identify the speakers.

___g___ 1. Conozco a un arquitecto que gana más de ochenta mil dólares al año.

___e___ 2. Si no me electrocuto antes de terminar la clase de diseño de circuitos.

___c___ 3. Los envidio.

___d___ 4. Tengo que ganarme la vida.

___a___ 5. Me gusta cuidar a los animales.

___b___ 6. Las entiendo mucho mejor que a las personas.

___f___ 7. Me gustaría diseñar edificios modernos.

a. I like to take care of animals.

b. I understand them much better than people.

c. I envy them.

d. I have to earn a living.

e. If I don't electrocute myself before I finish my circuit design class.

f. I would like to design modern buildings.

g. I know an architect that earns more than eighty thousand dollars a year.

Video CD-ROM

B. Los planes profesionales de Sofía y Wayne. Use the words from the list to complete the monologues.

casa	arquitecta	diseñar	sueldo	computadoras
suerte	las	ochenta mil	abogada	edificios

Sofía Quiero ser (1) _____arquitecta_____ porque me gusta diseñar

(2) _____edificios_____ modernos. Algún día voy a

(3) _____diseñar_____ mi propia (4) _____casa_____.

Conozco a un arquitecto que gana más de (5) _____ochenta mil_____ dólares al año.

Wayne Voy a trabajar con (6) _____computadoras_____. (7) _____Las_____ entiendo mucho mejor que a las personas. Sé que voy a empezar con

(8) _____sueldo_____ bueno, y con un poco de suerte...

Video CD-ROM

C. Los planes profesionales de Ana Mari y Ramón. Answer the questions.

1. ¿Qué quiere ser Ana Mari? ¿A quién quiere ayudar? ¿A quién admira, por qué? ¿A quién nunca va a defender?

Quiere ser abogada. Quiere ayudar a las personas de la comunidad. Admira a Janet Reno porque es

trabajadora y honesta. Nunca va a defender a criminales.

_____

2. ¿Por qué estudia Ramón negocios internacionales? ¿Qué dice *(says)* el artículo de periódico? ¿Qué idiomas habla? ¿Qué pasa con el japonés? ¿Cuándo lo va a hablar perfectamente?

Quiere ganar mucho dinero. Los profesionales hoy tienen que saber dos o tres idiomas. Habla español,

japonés e inglés. No lo habla bien y no lo sabe escribir. Lo va a hablar perfectamente después de

tomar unos cursos intensivos.

Vocabulario 1

Discussing professional plans
• Careers and professions

D. ¿Qué profesión tienen? Match the definitions with the illustrations; then, write the correct profession.

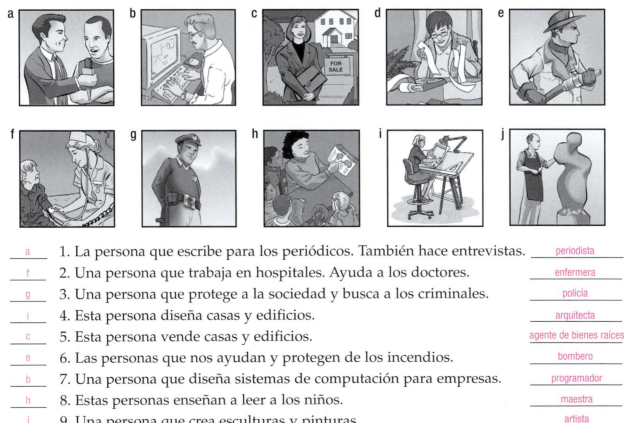

_a_	1. La persona que escribe para los periódicos. También hace entrevistas.	periodista
_f_	2. Una persona que trabaja en hospitales. Ayuda a los doctores.	enfermera
_g_	3. Una persona que protege a la sociedad y busca a los criminales.	policía
_i_	4. Esta persona diseña casas y edificios.	arquitecta
_c_	5. Esta persona vende casas y edificios.	agente de bienes raíces
_e_	6. Las personas que nos ayudan y protegen de los incendios.	bombero
_b_	7. Una persona que diseña sistemas de computación para empresas.	programador
_h_	8. Estas personas enseñan a leer a los niños.	maestra
_j_	9. Una persona que crea esculturas y pinturas.	artista
_d_	10. Las personas que llevan la contabilidad de una empresa.	contadora

E. Ventajas y desventajas. Based on what you know about the following professions, list the advantages, disadvantages, and rate the salary. Answers will vary.

Carrera	Ventajas	Desventajas	Sueldo
policía	• prestaciones buenas • poder ayudar a las personas	• muchas horas de trabajo • horario de noche • peligroso	• bajo al empezar • buen sueldo con los años
gerente de ventas y mercadeo			
niñero/a			
escritor(a) de novelas (como Stephen King)			
sicólogo			

 **Gramática 1**

Talking about people and places you know
• The verb <u>conocer</u>

F. Las grandes ciudades norteamericanas. You are talking to Sofía, who is interested in traveling in the United States. Tell her about cities you know.
Answers will vary.

> **Modelo** ¿Conoces la ciudad de Chicago?
> **No, no la conozco, pero sé que es muy grande, interesante y que hay muchos mexicanos.**

¿Conoces la ciudad de...

1. Nueva York? _____
_____

2. Miami? _____
_____

3. San Francisco? _____

4. Atlanta? _____
_____

5. Seattle? _____
_____

6. Washington, DC? _____

_____

7. San Antonio? _____

_____

G. ¿A quién conocemos? Complete Manolo and Ana Mari's conversation using **conocer**.

Ana Mari   Manolo, ¿tú (1) ____conoces____ a alguien famoso?

Manolo   Pues no, pero mi hermana que vive en Miami (2) ____conoce____ al hermano de Julio Iglesias.

Ana Mari   Huy, ¡qué interesante! Yo tampoco (3) ____conozco____ a nadie famoso, pero mis papás (4) ____conocen____ a varios actores mexicanos.

Manolo   Wayne y yo (5) ____conocemos____ la casa de alguien famoso.

Ana Mari   ¿De veras? ¿De quién?

Manolo   El castillo de Hurst.

Ana Mari   ¿El castillo de Hurst? ¡Ay Manolo, pero si eso es un museo!

Manolo   Bueno, pero era su casa, ¿no?

Vocabulario 2   **Talking about salaries**
• **Numbers 101–100,000**

H. ¿Cuánto?

Parte 1. Match each number with its written equivalent.

__d__ 1. 54.641   a. cincuenta y cuatro mil setecientos cuarenta y uno

__e__ 2. 183.835   b. dieciséis mil cuatrocientos noventa y seis

__b__ 3. 16.496   c. veinte mil trescientos sesenta y tres

__a__ 4. 54.741   d. cincuenta y cuatro mil seiscientos cuarenta y uno

__c__ 5. 20.363   e. ciento ochenta y tres mil ochocientos treinta y cinco

Parte 2. Fill in the missing parts of the numbers.

1. 92.517   ____noventa____ y dos ____mil____ ____quinientos____ diecisiete

2. 75.409   ____setenta____ y cinco mil ____cuatrocientos____ nueve

3. 39.212   treinta y ____nueve____ mil ____doscientos____ doce

4. 116.578   ____ciento____ dieciséis ____mil____ ____quinientos____ ____setenta____ y ocho

5. 48.024   cuarenta ____y____ ocho mil ____veinticuatro____

Gramática 2 — Avoiding repetition when answering questions
• The direct object pronouns <u>lo</u>, <u>la</u>, <u>los</u>, and <u>las</u>

I. El primer día de clases. Ana Mari's little brothers are preparing for their first day of school. Answer their questions using direct object pronouns.

> **Modelo** ¿Tengo que llevar la calculadora?
> No, **no la tienes que llevar./no tienes que llevarla.**

1. ¿Necesito el papel?
   Sí, lo necesitas. _____.

2. ¿Podemos llevar al perro a la escuela?
   No, no lo pueden llevar./no pueden llevarlo. _____.

3. ¿Voy a usar mis lápices de colores?
   No, no los vas a usar./no vas a usarlos. _____.

4. ¿Tengo que llevar las plumas?
   Sí, las tienes que llevar./tienes que llevarlas. _____.

5. ¿Necesitamos los libros de texto?
   Sí, los necesitan. _____.

J. ¡Qué ocupados! Answer the questions about the characters, using direct object pronouns. You may make up some answers.

> **Modelo**
>
> ¿Con quién hace Sofía la tarea?
> **La hace con Adriana y Manolo.**

4. 1:00 pm   5. Los sábados

1. ¿Con quién mira Sofía la tele? La mira con sus papás. _____

2. ¿Qué va a hacer con la ropa? La va a lavar./Va a lavarla. _____

3. ¿Adónde va a llevar a Manolo? Lo va a llevar a una fiesta./Va a llevarlo a una fiesta. _____

4. ¿A qué hora va a hacer Adriana el flan? Lo va a hacer a la una de la tarde./Va a hacerlo a la una de la tarde.

5. ¿Visitan a los abuelos entre semana? No, los visitan los sábados. _____

Para terminar

K. La CIA: Agencia Central de Inteligencia. Read the article on the CIA, taken from *Hispanic Business* magazine. Then answer the questions.

1. ¿Qué características personales necesita tener un agente de la CIA?
   Necesita tener espíritu aventurero, personalidad bien definida, habilidad intelectual superior, fuerza mental y alto grado de integridad.

2. ¿Qué preparación académica necesitas para hacer una carrera en la CIA?
   Necesitas un título universitario con excelente historial académico.

3. ¿Qué tipo de experiencia o habilidades especiales son deseables?
   Estudios de posgrado, viajes al extranjero, hablar otros idiomas, haber vivido en otros países o tener experiencia militar.

4. ¿Te parece interesante trabajar para la CIA? ¿Por qué sí o por qué no?
   Answers will vary.

Lo máximo en carreras internacionales

Para el individuo que quiere más que un simple trabajo, ésta es una carrera única; un estilo de vida que prueba[1] los límites de la inteligencia, la autosuficiencia[2] y la responsabilidad. Requiere un espíritu aventurero, una personalidad bien definida, una habilidad intelectual superior, fuerza[3] mental y un alto grado de integridad. Se necesitan habilidades especiales y disciplina profesional para producir resultados. Usted debe resolver situaciones volátiles, ambiguas y poco estructuradas que prueban al máximo su ingenio[4].

El Programa de Entrenamiento de la CIA es la puerta de entrada a una carrera internacional. Para calificar, usted debe poseer calificaciones de primera: título universitario con excelente historial académico, sólidas habilidades interpersonales, la habilidad de escribir clara y precisamente, y un inagotable interés en asuntos internacionales.

Las personas con estudios de posgrado, viajes al extranjero, que hablen otros idiomas, que hayan vivido en otros países, o con experiencia militar tienen ya cierta ventaja.

El sueldo va de $31.459 a $48.222 dependiendo de la experiencia y preparación. Los solicitantes deben someterse a un riguroso examen psicológico y médico, una entrevista poligráfica y una investigación extensa de antecedentes. La edad máxima para ingresar a la agencia es de 35 años, se requiere la ciudadanía[5] norteamericana para usted y su pareja. La CIA busca hombres y mujeres de todas las razas y de todos los sectores culturales de la población. La CIA representa a Estados Unidos y el personal debe ser representativo de la diversidad cultural del país. Para solicitar empleo, mande su currículum[6] (incluya promedio académico) y una carta que explique sus destrezas[7] y habilidades. En treinta días nos pondremos en contacto con los solicitantes mejor calificados.

---

[1]*tests* [2]*self-sufficiency* [3]*strength* [4] **prueban...** *test your resourcefulness to the limit* [5]*citizenship* [6]*résumé* [7]*skills*

Episodio

Comprensión

 A. ¿Cuántos hay? Imagine that you and a classmate are working in a bookstore taking inventory. You are going to hear your co-worker call out eight items and ask how many there are. Consult the inventory list and report the quantities aloud. Your co-worker will then repeat the number to make sure she heard correctly. Repeat the number after her.

Modelo	You hear:	¿Cuántas plumas hay?
	You see:	2.759 plumas
	You say:	**Hay dos mil setecientas cincuenta y nueve plumas.**

Inventario

2.759	plumas	987	discos compactos
343	borradores	2.525	discos para la computadora
438	libros de consulta	1.896	lápices
662	cuadernos de composición	520	paquetes de papel
114	diccionarios		

B. Las personas y sus trabajos. You are going to hear five people describe their careers and professions. Listen and select the correct job title of each person.

1. Carmen es...
   a. ingeniera   b. enfermera   c. profesora

2. Enrique es...
   a. mesero   b. arquitecto   c. científico

3. Marta es...
   a. abogada   b. periodista   c. maestra

4. Jesús es...
   a. sicólogo   b. escritor   c. policía

5. Miguel es...
   a. programador   b. veterinario   c. médico

Pronunciación

Audio
CD-ROM

El enlace. In Spanish, in natural speech, words are linked together without regard to word boundaries, producing a smooth flow of articulation. This linking is called **enlace**. Repeat these questions and statements after the speaker.

¿Qué puedes hacer?	[ke-pue-de-sa-ser]
¿Me das una invitación?	[me-da-su-nain-bi-ta-sion]
Viven en la ciudad de Miami.	[bi-be-nen-la-siu-da-de-mia-mi]
¡Vamos a un restaurante italiano!	[ba-mo-saun-res-tau-ran-tei-ta-lia-no]

Más escenas de la vida

Adriana and Santiago are talking about Santiago's job. Listen to their conversation and then complete activities **A** and **B**. You will hear the conversation twice.

Adriana

Santiago

Audio
CD-ROM

A. Emparejar. Match up these phrases based on what you heard in the conversation.

__c__ 1. ¿Crees que no es suficiente?   a. Ay, Santiago, contigo no se puede hablar.

__a__ 2. ¿Ahora eres sicóloga también?   b. A veces me preocupo mucho por ti.

__d__ 3. ¿Ves por qué discutimos?   c. No es por el sueldo.

__b__ 4. Sé que ganas bien pero...   d. Como tú ahora vas a la escuela…

Audio
CD-ROM

B. Responde. Write the answers to the following questions.

1. ¿Por qué se preocupa Adriana por Santiago?

Se preocupa porque ahora hay más criminales que antes.

2. ¿Por qué Adriana quiere que Santiago sea detective?

Piensa que ser detective es más interesante y menos peligroso.

3. ¿Santiago quiere seguir estudiando *(keep studying)*?

No, Santiago no quiere seguir estudiando.

4. ¿Por qué no quiere seguir estudiando?

No quiere seguir estudiando porque le gusta su trabajo.

Episodio 13

Escenas de la vida: Las vacaciones

A. ¡Mira cuánto puedes entender! Escucha la conversación o mira el video para seleccionar la información correcta.

Video
CD-ROM

Audio
CD-ROM

Instructor's Resources
- Overheads
- VHS Video
- Worktext CD
- Website
- IRM: Videoscript, Comprehensible input

☐ **Necesitamos pasaporte y visa para ir a México.**

☑ **Ya tenemos las reservaciones de avión.**

☑ **El boleto de ida y vuelta cuesta $390.00.**

☑ **Hace calor durante el día.**

☐ **Llueve mucho en el invierno.**

☑ **Hace frío por la noche.**

☑ **Manolo va a ayudar a Sofía con sus maletas.**

Cultura a lo vivo

In both Hispanic and Anglo cultures, the climate, the weather, and the formality of the occasion determine the appropriateness of a particular outfit. Although it varies from country to country, in general, Spanish speakers dress more formally than people in the U.S.

Spanish speakers tend to dress formally for parties and social events. Depending on the country, Spanish speakers may not wear shorts or sandals unless they are at the beach. Even in the most informal situations, they do not go barefoot or shirtless.

Video Synopsis. The characters make plans to spend winter break in Guadalajara, Mexico. Manolo asks Sofía to lend him money for the plane ticket. They discuss the weather, whether they will go to the beach, and what to pack.

B. ¿Te diste cuenta? Escucha la conversación otra vez para indicar si las oraciones son **ciertas** o **falsas**.

Audio
CD-ROM

	Cierto	Falso
1. Los chicos no necesitan pasaporte para ir a México.	✓	
2. Ana Mari conoce Guadalajara.		✓
3. Manolo paga su boleto con tarjeta de crédito.		✓
4. En Guadalajara siempre hace calor.		✓
5. Los chicos quieren ir a la playa.	✓	

Video
CD-ROM

C. No es cierto. Escucha la conversación de nuevo para seleccionar la respuesta falsa.

Audio
CD-ROM

1. Los chicos…
   a. salen el 18 de diciembre para Guadalajara y regresan el primero de enero.
   b. dicen que en Guadalajara nieva en invierno.
   c. tienen que pagar los boletos antes del 10 de diciembre.

2. Manolo…
   a. ya tiene un pasaporte nuevo.
   b. no tiene dinero para pagar el boleto.
   c. va a ayudar a Sofía con sus maletas.

3. Sofía…
   a. va a llevar un traje de baño a Puerto Vallarta.
   b. le va a cobrar a Manolo el 50% de interés.
   c. va a pagar el boleto de Manolo.

4. Manolo dice…
   a. si tú me pagas mi boleto, yo te ayudo con tus maletas.
   b. ¿me puedes pagar mi boleto con tu tarjeta?
   c. no tengo ganas de ir a Puerto Vallarta.

Invitación a Costa Rica

Del álbum de
Sofía

Costa Rica es un paraíso para los amantes (lovers) de la naturaleza y del turismo de aventura. Los numerosos parques ecológicos del país ofrecen actividades para todos los gustos: desde caminatas en las selvas (jungles), exploración de volcanes (activos e inactivos), 'canopy' y surfeo, hasta paseos en balsas (rafts) por rápidos.

Práctica adicional		
Cuaderno de tareas WB p.337, A–B	Video CD-ROM Episodio 13	Website vistahigher learning.com

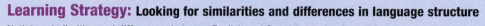

Learning Strategy: Looking for similarities and differences in language structure

Noticing similarities and differences between English and Spanish word order will help you understand and learn Spanish. For instance, look at the placement of adverbs in the following examples:

¡Tú **nunca** vas al gimnasio!	You **never** go to the gym!
Yo hago ejercicio **todos los días.**	I exercise **every day.**

Notice that the placement of *never* (**nunca**) and *every day* (**todos los días**) is the same in English and in Spanish. You do not have to learn a different word order when using these words.

Differences in word order however, should be learned. These include:
- the placement of the direct object pronouns **me, te, lo, la, los,** and **las.**

Te doy un cheque la próxima semana.	I'll give **you** a check next week.

In Spanish, these pronouns are placed before a conjugated verb, whereas in English, they are placed after the verb.
- the placement of descriptive adjectives

Lleva ropa **ligera** para el día...	Take **light** clothing for daytime...

In Spanish, most descriptive adjectives are placed after the noun, whereas in English, they come before the noun.

When you study, concentrate on the differences and just make a mental note of the similarities.

Para comunicarnos mejor

Vocabulario 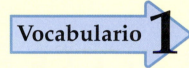 **Talking about dates and the weather**
• **Seasons, months, and the weather**

In the conversation, you heard the following statements.

Salimos **el 18 de diciembre.**	*We're leaving on the 18th of December.*
Regresamos **el primero de enero.**	*We're returning on the first of January.*
Durante el día **hace calor...**	*During the day it's hot...*
Por la noche... **hace** bastante **frío.**	*At night... it's rather cold.*
Llueve durante el verano.	*It rains during the summer.*

1. Use **el** + [*number*] + **de** + [*month*] to talk about dates.
2. Use **el primero** to say *the first of* [*month*].
3. Notice that months are not capitalized in Spanish.

Instructor's Resource
• Overheads

Vocabulario 1. Review the vocabulary with the students. Using the pictures on the following page, discuss the temperature in Celsius and the fact that some countries in South America have winter in July and summer in January.

• **Seasons, months, and the weather**

¡Fíjate!

In Latin America, like in most of the world, Celcius degrees are used instead of Fahrenheit degrees. You will practice converting from Celcius to Fahrenheit using the following formula: F = (C x 1.8) + 32.

¿Qué tiempo hace?	La temperatura	Los meses
el invierno Hace frío. Llueve o nieva. Hace mal tiempo.	-15° – 10°	diciembre enero febrero
la primavera Hace fresco. Llueve. Hace viento.	10° – 18°	marzo abril mayo
el verano Hace calor. Hace sol. Hace buen tiempo.	20° – 30°	junio julio agosto
el otoño Hace viento. Está nublado. Hace fresco.	10° – 22°	septiembre octubre noviembre

Additional Activity. Ask students to form a line in order of their birthdates—from January to December. They need to ask each other ¿Cuándo es tu cumpleaños? and arrange themselves in the order that their birthdays occur in the course of a calendar year.

PRÁCTICA

A. ¿Cuándo se celebra? Escribe la fecha de estas celebraciones.

> **Modelo**   El Día de los Muertos es **el dos de noviembre.**

1. El Día de San Valentín es _el catorce de febrero_.
2. El Día de la Independencia de Estados Unidos es _el cuatro de julio_.
3. La Navidad es _el veinticinco de diciembre_.
4. El Día de los Inocentes (*April Fool's Day*) es _el primero de abril_.
5. El Día de Año Nuevo es _el primero de enero_.
6. El día de mi cumpleaños es _Answers will vary_.

B. Fechas importantes. Escribe cinco fechas importantes para ti. Incluye dos cumpleaños, un aniversario y dos días festivos (*holidays*). Después comparte con tu compañero/a las actividades que haces en esos días.   _Answers will vary._

B. You may assign this activity for homework. When students return to class, ask volunteers to share their answers with the class or have students work in groups to share what they wrote.

> **Modelo**   **El 9 de octubre es importante para mí porque es el cumpleaños de mi mamá. Mi familia y yo salimos a cenar con ella. Generalmente vamos a un restaurante elegante.**

1. _____
   _____
2. _____
   _____
3. _____
   _____
4. _____
   _____
5. _____
   _____

C. ¿Dónde? Indica en qué ciudades de Estados Unidos existen estas condiciones climatológicas.

Tampa	Seattle	Chicago	Buffalo

1. En esta ciudad llueve todo el año. Hace fresco. La temperatura promedio durante la primavera es de 60°F.   _Seattle_
2. En esta ciudad hace mucho frío durante el invierno. Nieva mucho. La temperatura promedio es de 5°F bajo cero.   _Buffalo_
3. En esta ciudad el clima es húmedo y hace mucho calor en el verano.   _Tampa_
4. En esta ciudad hace viento. El clima es extremo: hace calor en el verano y hace frío en el invierno.   _Chicago_

C. You may select students to read the weather descriptions. Ask volunteers to provide the answers.

Audio
CD-ROM

D. El mes de enero. Escucha la narración acerca del clima de Guayaquil, en Ecuador, y de Madrid, en España. Indica el clima de cada lugar.

Clima en enero	Guayaquil, Ecuador	Madrid, España
1. Hace frío.		✓
2. Hace calor.	✓	
3. Hace buen tiempo.		
4. Hace sol.		✓
5. Llueve.	✓	✓
6. Nieva.		
7. Está nublado.	✓	

Práctica adicional

Cuaderno de tareas
WB pp.338–339, C–F

Vocabulario 2

Planning your wardrobe
• Clothing and colors

La ropa que Sofía quiere llevar a Guadalajara

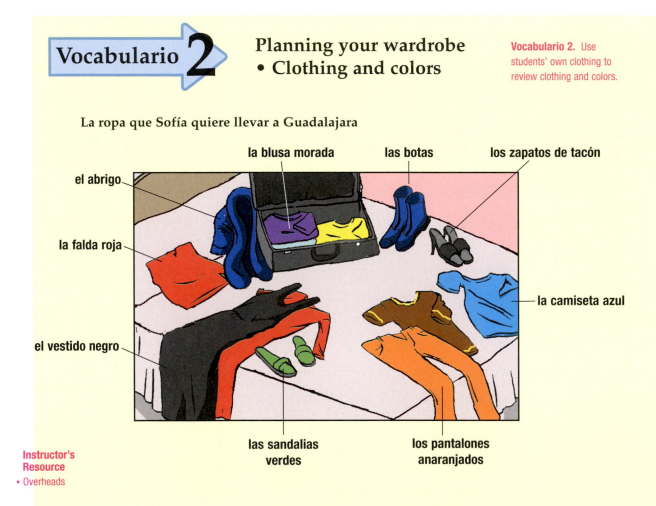

la blusa morada — las botas — los zapatos de tacón — el abrigo — la falda roja — la camiseta azul — el vestido negro — las sandalias verdes — los pantalones anaranjados

La ropa que Manolo va a llevar a Guadalajara

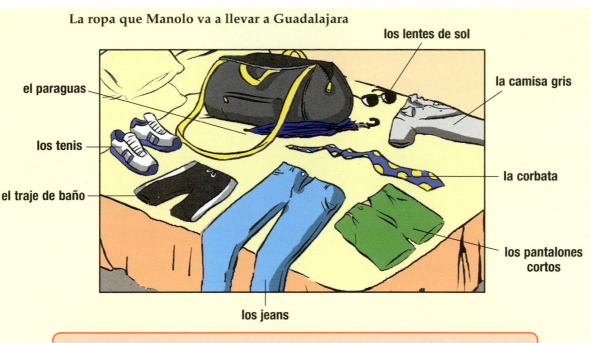

los lentes de sol

el paraguas

la camisa gris

los tenis

la corbata

el traje de baño

los pantalones cortos

los jeans

También se dice...

la chaqueta ⟶ la chamarra, el saco

color café ⟶ marrón, pardo

la falda ⟶ la pollera

la maleta ⟶ la valija, la petaca, el veliz

los jeans ⟶ los pantalones de mezclilla, los bluejeans, los mahones, los vaqueros

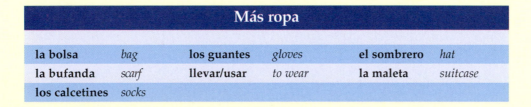

Más ropa

la bolsa	*bag*	los guantes	*gloves*	el sombrero	*hat*
la bufanda	*scarf*	llevar/usar	*to wear*	la maleta	*suitcase*
los calcetines	*socks*				

La maleta de Ana Mari

la blusa blanca

la chaqueta azul

el bikini

el suéter café

el impermeable gris

el/la pijama

el traje

la minifalda amarilla

PRÁCTICA

E. ¿Qué ropa llevan? Describe la ropa que los chicos piensan llevar a una fiesta.

1. Manolo piensa llevar <u>una camisa verde, unos jeans y unos tenis</u>

_____ .

Additional Activity. Organize a fashion show in class. Students will work with a partner. They will introduce their partner and describe what they are wearing. The show is most effective if you can bring a microphone and design a run-way **(pasarela)** with white tape or paper. One student will walk down the **pasarela** while their partner speaks: **Compañeros, les presento a Rosa, hoy Rosa lleva una falda negra, una blusa amarilla y unas botas de tacón.** Also play a **Go Fish** game with clothing items; see the **IRM** for materials.

2. Sofía quiere llevar <u>un abrigo café, un vestido morado y un sombrero</u>

_____ .

¡Fíjate!
Remember to use **un, una, unos,** and **unas** when talking about the clothes people wear.

3. Ana Mari va a llevar <u>una blusa anaranjada, una minifalda azul, una bolsa café y</u>

<u>unas sandalias cafés</u>_____ .

Additional Activity. You may create a **Juego de tablero;** see the sample in the **Instructor's Resource Manual.** You will need to provide dice and markers. Students play in groups of four or five. Also see the IRM for a **Go Fish** game.

4. Ramón quiere llevar <u>un traje gris, una camisa blanca, una corbata anaranjada, unos</u>

<u>calcetines grises y unos zapatos negros</u>_____ .

F. ¿Qué llevan? Comenta con un(a) compañero/a la ropa que llevan los chicos para salir en Guadalajara.

Manolo lleva una camiseta azul, jeans y tenis.
Sofía lleva un vestido morado y zapatos blancos.
Ana Mari lleva una blusa verde, pantalones cortos negros y sandalias negras.
Ramón lleva camisa amarilla, chaqueta café, pantalones cafés y tenis azules.

G. Las estaciones. Describe la ropa que usas en las siguientes situaciones; menciona colores cuando sea posible. Después de contestar las preguntas, comparte tus respuestas con tu compañero/a. *Answers will vary.*

1. En el invierno para ir a la universidad, uso _____
_____.

2. En la primavera para ir al trabajo, llevo _____
_____.

3. Cuando la temperatura es de 80°F, uso _____
_____.

4. Cuando la temperatura es de -10°F, llevo _____
_____.

5. Cuando voy a la playa, llevo _____
_____.

6. Cuando voy al supermercado, uso _____
_____.

7. Cuando voy a una fiesta elegante, llevo _____
_____.

8. Para ir a una entrevista de trabajo, uso _____
_____.

Additional Activity. You may ask students to create, in groups of three, outfits for different occasions (a birthday party, a job interview, a first date, etc). They may draw their outfits or bring in magazine pictures (or you may want to provide them). Teach the expression **Me pongo** and have students describe their outfits and the occasion. **Me pongo un traje, corbata y zapatos negros para ir a una entrevista de trabajo.** You may also make copies of clothes in transparencies. Have students describe the outfits and the occasion using the overhead projector (for transparencies) or in front of the class.

H. ¿Qué tiempo hace? Tú eres un(a) agente de viajes y tu trabajo es informar a tus clientes qué clima hay en diferentes ciudades de Latinoamérica. Mira el mapa para saber la información necesaria. Túrnate con un(a) compañero/a. *Answers will vary.*

F= (C x 1.8) + 32

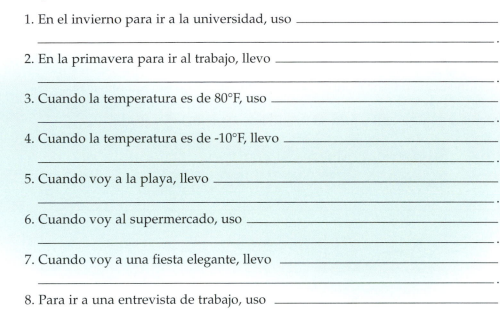

1. ¿Qué tiempo hace en Bariloche en junio? ¿Qué estación del año es? ¿Qué ropa necesita llevar?
Hace frío, la temperatura es de 37ºF y es invierno.
_____

2. ¿Qué tiempo hace en Viña del Mar en enero? ¿Qué estación del año es? ¿Qué ropa necesita llevar?
_____
Hace calor, la temperatura es de 82ºF y es verano.

3. ¿Qué tiempo hace en Cuzco en marzo? ¿Qué estación del año es? ¿Qué ropa necesita llevar?
Hace viento, la temperatura es de 50ºF y es otoño.
_____

4. ¿Qué tiempo hace en Quito en septiembre? ¿Qué estación del año es? ¿Qué ropa necesita llevar?
Llueve, la temperatura es de 68ºF y es primavera.
_____

Práctica adicional

Cuaderno de tareas
WB pp.339–341, G–J
LM pp.345–346, A–B, Pron.

Audio
CD-ROM
Episodio 13

Actividades comunicativas

A. Un viaje a México.

Instrucciones para **Estudiante 1**

You want to go to Mexico on vacation. Call your travel agent to plan your trip. Look at the map and ask about places that interest you. Your requirements: a destination that is hot and sunny, and a price of $600 or less. You want to leave on Monday, July 20, and return on Friday, July 25, at night.   *Answers will vary.*

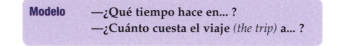

Modelo	—¿Qué tiempo hace en... ?
	—¿Cuánto cuesta el viaje *(the trip)* a... ?

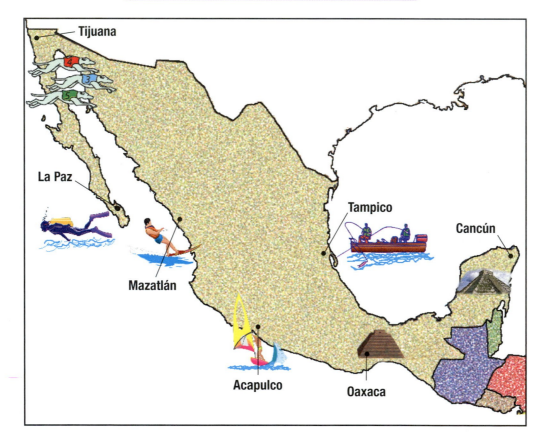

A. You may wish to review the task with students before they begin to interact. The correct place for students to select is **La Paz** or **Mazatlán.** When students complete the task, review the activity with them. Allow five to seven minutes.

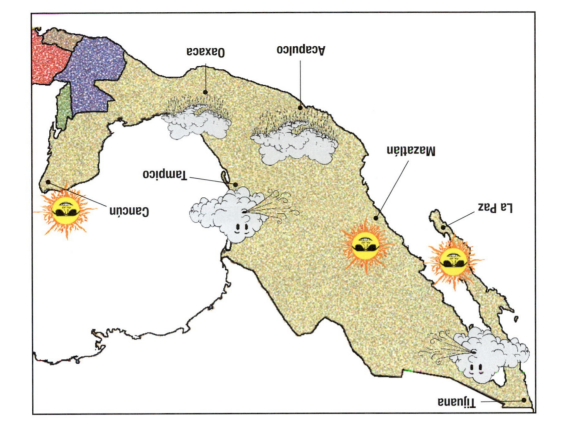

VIAJES MAJESTIC

¡Cinco días en México!

Acapulco $450   Tijuana $520   Cancún $870   Tampico $640
Mazatlán $465   La Paz $500   Oaxaca $395

| Cliente _____ Teléfono _____ |
| Viaja a _____ |
| Quiere salir el _____ |
| Quiere regresar el _____ |
| Viajan _____ personas |
| Precio _____ |

Instrucciones para **Estudiante 2**

You are a travel agent. Your job is to help your client plan a vacation. Answer your client's questions about the weather conditions of the place they would like to visit, and give prices. Once you know where your client wants to go, fill in the card.   Answers will vary.

A. **Un viaje a México.**

B. Diferencias.

Instrucciones para **Estudiante 1**

Aquí tienes un dibujo de Sofía y sus amigos en la playa de Puerto Vallarta. Hay varias diferencias entre tu dibujo y el de tu compañero/a. Para encontrarlas, describe el clima, las actividades y la ropa. Escribe siete diferencias que encontraste. Answers will vary.

| Modelo | **Manolo duerme en la hamaca. Lleva unos pantalones azules cortos, ¿no?** |

B. You may wish to review the task with students before they begin to interact. When students complete the task, review the answers with them. Allow five to seven minutes.

1. El niño lleva unos sombreros en la mano./El niño no lleva nada en las manos.
2. Ana Mari no lleva lentes./Ana Mari lleva unos lentes de sol.
3. Ramón no lleva camiseta./Ramón lleva una camiseta verde.
4. Manolo está durmiendo./Manolo está leyendo el periódico.
5. Dos chicas juegan vóleibol en la playa./Dos chicas juegan con un frisbee.
6. Hay un hombre corriendo junto a la palmera./Hay un perro junto a la palmera.
7. Hace buen tiempo/Está nublado.

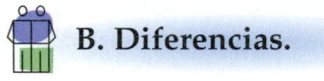

B. Diferencias.

Instrucciones para **Estudiante 2**

Aquí tienes un dibujo de Sofía y sus amigos en la playa de Puerto Vallarta. Hay varias diferencias entre tu dibujo y el de tu compañero/a. Para encontrarlas, describe el clima, las actividades y la ropa. Escribe siete diferencias que encontraste. Answers will vary.

> **Modelo**   Manolo lleva unos pantalones cortos azules, ¿no? Lee el periódico.

1. El niño lleva unos sombreros en la mano./El niño no lleva nada en las manos.
2. Ana Mari no lleva lentes./Ana Mari lleva unos lentes de sol.
3. Ramón no lleva camiseta./Ramón lleva una camiseta verde.
4. Manolo está durmiendo./Manolo está leyendo el periódico.
5. Dos chicas juegan vóleibol en la playa./Dos chicas juegan con un frisbee.
6. Hay un hombre corriendo junto a la palmera./Hay un perro junto a la palmera.
7. Hace buen tiempo/Está nublado.

C. De vacaciones. Talk to your partner about a place you like to go to when you are on vacation. Describe the season, month or date you like to go, the weather, the clothing you usually take with you, who you go with, and what you do there. Answers will vary.

Banco de palabras

la bahía *bay*	**los lagos** *lakes*	**el parque de atracciones** *amusement park*	**remar** *to row*
esquiar *to ski*	**las montañas** *mountains*	**el planetario** *planetarium*	**el zoológico** *zoo*

La correspondencia

El correo: Aprenda español en Costa Rica. Lee la información acerca de los programas para aprender español en Costa Rica. Después contesta las preguntas.

Instituto Forester

El Forester Instituto Internacional, en San José, Costa Rica, ofrece varios programas de instrucción en español. El instituto está localizado en una zona exclusiva de la ciudad, a sólo veinte minutos del centro.

Nuestros estudiantes. El Instituto recibe estudiantes de diversos países, diferentes edades y necesidades de aprendizaje:

- personas que buscan unas vacaciones diferentes y productivas
- ejecutivos de corporaciones e instituciones
- estudiantes de preparatorias y universidades
- diplomáticos
- doctores y enfermeros
- personas jubiladas[1] que desean mantenerse activas
- empleados de la líneas aéreas

Nuestros profesores. La lengua materna de todo el profesorado es el español. Además, tienen títulos universitarios y amplia experiencia en enseñar el español como segunda lengua.

Las familias anfitrionas[2]. El Instituto selecciona cuidadosamente a las familias anfitrionas. Son muy amables y abiertas, les gusta relacionarse con personas de otros países y tienen interés en ayudar a los estudiantes extranjeros. El estudiante tendrá cuarto privado, desayuno y cena. Todas las familias viven a menos de veinte minutos del Instituto, y es fácil llegar en autobús o a pie[3].

Días festivos. El Instituto está cerrado durante algunos días festivos nacionales que se celebran en Costa Rica: el primero de enero, el Jueves Santo y el Viernes Santo[4], el primero de mayo (Día del Trabajo), el 15 de agosto (la Asunción y Día de las Madres), el 15 de septiembre (Día de la Independencia) y el 25 de diciembre.

Clima. La temperatura varía muy poco durante el año. Obviamente, hace más frío en las montañas que en la costa (San José está a 4.000 pies de altura). La temporada de lluvias es de mayo a noviembre, y generalmente hace sol por las mañanas y llueve por las tardes. La temporada seca[5] es de diciembre a abril.

---

[1]*retired* [2]*host* [3]*on foot* [4]*Holy Thursday and Good Friday* [5]*dry season*

Sugerencias para la ropa. Los costarricenses usan ropa informal. Es una buena idea llevar ropa ligera y una chaqueta o un suéter. Es recomendable llevar un paraguas o un impermeable si va a visitar el país durante la temporada de lluvias. Durante la temporada seca, las noches pueden ser bastantes frías. Mujeres: jeans, camisetas, pantalones y blusas, un suéter y/o una chaqueta. Uno o dos vestidos para ocasiones especiales. Hombres: jeans, camisetas, pantalones y camisas. Se recomienda llevar un saco y una corbata para eventos especiales. Tanto las mujeres como los hombres deben llevar zapatos cómodos, tenis o sandalias. Y por supuesto, ¡los trajes de baño son indispensables!

1. ¿A qué van personas de diferentes profesiones y edades a Costa Rica?

   Van a estudiar español.

2. ¿Por qué es importante aprender un segundo idioma? ¿Qué ventajas tiene?

   Answers will vary.

3. ¿Qué características tienen las familias anfitrionas?

   Son muy amables y abiertas, les gusta relacionarse con personas de otros países y tienen interés en ayudar

   a los estudiantes extranjeros.

4. ¿Qué fiestas nacionales se celebran en Costa Rica?

   El primero de enero, el Jueves Santo y Viernes Santo, el primero de mayo, el 15 de agosto, el 15 de septiembre

   y el 25 de diciembre.

5. ¿Qué clima tiene San José? ¿Qué ropa recomiendan para viajar en Costa Rica?

   La temperatura varía muy poco durante el año... Recomiendan usar ropa informal...

6. ¿Te gustaría participar en un programa así? ¿Por qué sí o por qué no?

   Answers will vary.

En papel: ¡Ven, visita mi ciudad! Muchos costarricences tienen interés en visitar Estados Unidos. Escribe un artículo sobre tu ciudad para una revista de turismo en Costa Rica. Incluye la siguiente información: Answers will vary.

- el clima en las diferentes estaciones
- la ropa que uno debe llevar
- atracciones y lugares de interés
- actividades interesantes

¡Fíjate!
Create a simple outline of the information you want to include before you begin to write.

En papel. Ask students to write their article on posterboard for posting and reading in class.

Banco de palabras

el zoológico	**el planetario**	**las montañas**
zoo	planetarium	mountains
los lagos	**el parque de atracciones**	**la bahía**
lakes	amusement park	bay

Video
CD-ROM

Audio
CD-ROM

Instructor's Resources
• VHS Video
• Worktext CD
• IRM: Videoscript

¡A ver de nuevo!

Parte 1. Con tus propias palabras, haz un resumen del episodio. Answers will vary.

 Parte 2. Ahora trabaja con un(a) compañero/a para comparar la información y añadir lo que te haya faltado.

Práctica adicional

| Cuaderno de tareas WB pp.342–344, K–L LM pp.346, A–B | Audio CD-ROM Episodio 13 | Website vistahigher learning.com |

Vocabulario del Episodio 13

Instructor's Resources
• Testing program
• Website

Objetivos comunicativos

You should now be able to do the following in Spanish:

✔ talk about dates and the weather

✔ plan your wardrobe

Los meses *The months*

enero	*January*
febrero	*February*
marzo	*March*
abril	*April*
mayo	*May*
junio	*June*
julio	*July*
agosto	*August*
septiembre	*September*
octubre	*October*
noviembre	*November*
diciembre	*December*

Las estaciones *The seasons*

la primavera	*spring*
el verano	*summer*
el otoño	*fall*
el invierno	*winter*

¿Qué tiempo hace? *What's the weather like?*

Hace buen/mal tiempo.	*The weather is nice/bad.*
Hace (mucho) calor.	*It's (very) hot.*
Hace fresco.	*It's cool.*
Hace frío.	*It's cold.*
Hace sol.	*It's sunny.*
Hace viento.	*It's windy.*
Está nublado.	*It's cloudy.*
llover (o → ue)	*to rain*
nevar (e → ie)	*to snow*

La ropa *Clothes*

el abrigo	*coat*
el bikini	*bikini*
la blusa	*blouse*
la bolsa	*bag*
las botas	*boots*
la bufanda	*scarf*
los calcetines	*socks*
la camisa	*shirt*
la camiseta	*T-shirt*
la chaqueta	*jacket*
la corbata	*tie*
los guantes	*gloves*
el impermeable	*raincoat*
los jeans	*jeans*
los lentes de sol	*sunglasses*
llevar	*to wear*
la maleta	*suitcase*
la minifalda	*mini-skirt*

Los colores *Colors*

amarillo/a	*yellow*
anaranjado/a	*orange*
azul	*blue*
blanco/a	*white*
café	*brown*
gris	*gray*
morado/a	*purple*
negro/a	*black*
rojo/a	*red*
verde	*green*

Más vocabulario

los pantalones	*pants*
los pantalones cortos	*shorts*
el paraguas	*umbrella*
el/la pijama	*pajamas*
las sandalias	*sandals*
el sombrero	*hat*
el suéter	*sweater*
el traje	*suit*
el traje de baño	*bathing suit*
usar	*to wear*
el vestido	*dress*
los zapatos (de tacón)	*(high-heeled) shoes*
los (zapatos) tenis	*tennis shoes*

Vocabulario personal. Encourage students to personalize their vocabulary. They should write down the names of items of clothing that they wear but were not included in the episode. In addition, have them write down other words they need in order to talk about themselves, such as the places they go, their favorite season, and their wardrobe.

Vocabulario personal

Write all the words you need to know in Spanish so that you can better talk about the clothes you like to wear, the weather in your city, and important dates in your family.

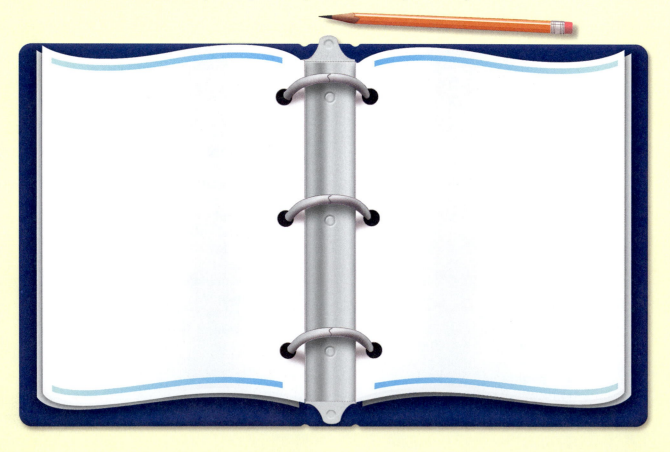

¡A escribir!

Episodio 13

Escenas de la vida: Las vacaciones

A. ¡A ver cuánto entendiste! Match the Spanish sentences with their English equivalents.

__d__ 1. Te doy un cheque la próxima semana.

__e__ 2. Tienes que pagarlo antes de diciembre.

__a__ 3. Salimos el 18 de diciembre.

__h__ 4. Cuesta trescientos noventa dólares.

__b__ 5. Ya tenemos las reservaciones de avión.

__g__ 6. No te voy a ayudar con las maletas.

__i__ 7. ¿Cuánto cuesta el boleto?

__f__ 8. Todavía no me pagan.

__c__ 9. Mi pasaporte está vencido.

a. We're leaving on the 18th of December.

b. We already have the plane reservations.

c. My passport has expired.

d. I'll give you a check next week.

e. You have to pay it before December.

f. They haven't paid me yet.

g. I'm not going to help you with your suitcases.

h. It costs three hundred and ninety dollars.

i. How much does a ticket cost?

B. Las vacaciones. Choose the correct answer.

1. El boleto cuesta…
   a. cincuenta dólares.
   b. quinientos treinta dólares.
   c. trescientos noventa dólares.

2. Para ir a México los chicos necesitan…
   a. permiso de turista.
   b. pasaporte y visa.
   c. visa.

3. ¿Puedes pagar mi boleto…
   a. con dinero?
   b. con mi tarjeta de crédito?
   c. con tu tarjeta de crédito?

4. En invierno en Guadalajara…
   a. hace frío y nieva.
   b. hace calor durante el día.
   c. hace calor por la noche.

5. Los chicos salen…
   a. el 10 de diciembre.
   b. el primero de enero.
   c. el 18 de diciembre.

6. Para usar durante el día, los chicos deben llevar…
   a. un impermeable.
   b. un abrigo.
   c. ropa ligera.

 **Vocabulario 1**

Talking about dates and the weather
• Seasons, months, and the weather

C. Algunas fechas importantes en Hispanoamérica. Write the following dates in Spanish. Do you know what holidays they are?

1. January 6 _____Seis de enero_____
2. February 14 _____Catorce de febrero_____
3. May 1 _____Primero de mayo_____

4. March 21 _____Veintiuno de marzo_____
5. July 4 _____Cuatro de julio_____
6. October 12 _____Doce de octubre_____

D. ¿Qué tiempo hace? Indicate the weather conditions and the temperature in the following places for the month in question, based on the temperature and the illustration. Remember, to convert from Celsius to Fahrenheit: **F = (C x 1.8) + 32.**

Modelo

Ciudad de México /  /17°C /septiembre

En la Ciudad de México generalmente llueve en el mes de septiembre. Hace fresco, la temperatura promedio es de sesenta y tres grados Fahrenheit.

1. Managua, Nicaragua /  / 30°C/ enero

En Managua generalmente está nublado en el mes de enero. Hace calor, la temperatura promedio es de ochenta y seis grados Fahrenheit.

2. San Juan Bautista, Paraguay /  / 37°C / febrero

En San Juan Bautista llueve y hace calor en el mes de febrero. La temperatura promedio es de noventa y ocho grados Fahrenheit.

3. Bariloche, Argentina / / 10°C / julio

En Bariloche nieva y hace frio en julio. La temperatura promedio es de cincuenta grados Fahrenheit.

4. Barcelona, España/ abril / 27°C /

En Barcelona generalmente hace viento en el mes de abril. La temperatura promedio es de ochenta grados Fahrenheit.

5. La Habana, Cuba / diciembre /  / 32°C

En La Habana hace sol en el mes de diciembre. La temperatura promedio es de ochenta y nueve grados Fahrenheit.

_____

E. El hemisferio sur. Indicate the seasons in which these holidays take place in the Southern Hemisphere. Remember that it is not the same as in the United States.

1. En Argentina las vacaciones de diciembre son en _____ verano
2. En Uruguay, en las vacaciones de julio es _____ invierno
3. En Paraguay, el 21 de marzo es el primer día de _____ otoño
4. En Perú, el 21 de septiembre es el primer día de _____ primavera

F. Odette quiere saber. Answer Odette's questions about weather in the United States. Answers will vary.

1. ¿Qué tiempo hace en Nueva York en invierno?

_____

2. ¿Qué tiempo hace en Las Vegas en verano?

_____

3. ¿Qué tiempo hace en San Francisco en primavera?

_____

4. ¿Qué tiempo hace en Minneapolis en otoño?

_____

Vocabulario 2

Planning your wardrobe
• **Clothing and colors**

G. La ropa para Guadalajara. Write the names of the items the characters are bringing to Guadalajara.

a. La ropa de Sofía

1. _____ Los zapatos de tacón
2. _____ La camisa
3. _____ Los jeans
4. _____ Las sandalias
5. _____ El vestido
6. _____ El abrigo
7. _____ La maleta

b. La ropa de Manolo

1. _____ Los tenis _____
2. _____ El traje de baño _____
3. _____ El paraguas _____
4. _____ Los lentes de sol _____
5. _____ La camisa _____
6. _____ La corbata _____
7. _____ Los pantalones cortos _____
8. _____ Los jeans _____

c. La ropa de Ana Mari

1. _____ Las camisetas _____
2. _____ La chaqueta _____
3. _____ El suéter _____
4. _____ El/la pijama _____
5. _____ La falda _____
6. _____ El traje _____
7. _____ El impermeable _____
8. _____ El bikini _____

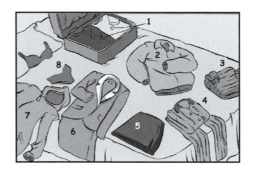

H. ¿Qué color? What color do you associate with the following foods?

1. el arroz _____ blanco _____   5. la lechuga _____ verde _____
2. las uvas _____ morado _____   6. el tomate _____ rojo _____
3. el plátano _____ amarillo _____   7. los frijoles _____ café/negro _____
4. la naranja _____ anaranjado _____ 8. el chocolate _____ café _____

I. ¿Qué no le queda? (What doesn't match?) Indicate the item that does not match. Then explain your choice.

> **Modelo** Hoy Lynn va a la playa; por eso, lleva: un traje de baño, unas sandalias blancas, un sombrero, un suéter amarillo y unos lentes de sol.
> **En la playa hace calor, no necesita llevar un suéter.**

1. Hoy hace frío, Nancy lleva: un abrigo largo, unos pantalones cortos, un suéter verde, unos zapatos verdes y un sombrero.

   Hace frío, no debe llevar pantalones cortos.

2. Esta noche Joe va a una fiesta; por eso, lleva: una corbata roja, un traje negro, una camisa blanca y unos lentes de sol.

   Es de noche, no necesita llevar lentes de sol.

3. Es verano. Para trabajar Carlos lleva: unos zapatos de tacón, unos pantalones cortos
y una camisa ligera.

Carlos es hombre; los hombres no llevan zapatos de tacón.

4. Hoy llueve; por eso, Larry lleva: un impermeable gris, una blusa anaranjada, una
chaqueta azul, pantalones grises y una camisa azul.

Larry es hombre; los hombres no llevan blusa.

5. Es otoño en Nueva York. Valerie lleva: una blusa morada, una falda negra, un traje
de baño y unos tenis morados.

En otoño en Nueva York no necesita llevar traje de baño.

6. Hoy hace sol y buen tiempo, para ir con sus amigos al parque, Joe lleva una camiseta
blanca, unos jeans, unos tenis y un paraguas café.

Hace buen tiempo, no necesita llevar paraguas.

J. ¿Qué me pongo? Imagine this is the city where you live. For each illustration,
describe the weather, the season, and the clothes you wear during each season. Answers will vary.

a

_____

_____

_____

_____

_____

_____

b

_____

_____

_____

_____

_____

_____

c

_____

_____

_____

_____

_____

_____

Para terminar

K. Cruceros Festival. Read the brochure about a boat tour in Mexico and answer the questions.

> **Reading Strategy: Looking for specific information**
>
> As you become a proficient reader in Spanish, you will learn not to be disturbed by "noise"—language you do not yet understand. Instead, you will be aware of your purpose for reading a text and will only need to use a dictionary if understanding the details is important to your purpose. Most often, you will use your background knowledge—what you know about the world—and the context of the words to guess the meaning.
>
> You are about to read a travel brochure. The information you most likely will find in a travel brochure is activities to do, interesting places to see, special events, and information about weather, costs, currency, passport, visas, and vaccinations. Your purpose in reading is to gather details about the Mexican cruise in order to answer the following questions.

1. ¿Qué día llega el barco a Cabo San Lucas? ¿Cuántas horas se queda ahí?

   Llega el martes. Se queda quince horas.

2. ¿A qué hora se va el barco de Puerto Vallarta?

   Se va a las once de la noche.

3. ¿Dónde está Cabo San Lucas?

   Está en el extremo sur de la península de Baja California.

4. ¿Qué lugares interesantes puedes visitar ahí?

   Puedes visitar playas vírgenes, montañas del desierto y rocas en forma de arco.

5. ¿Cómo es Mazatlán?

   Answers will vary.

6. ¿En qué mes hace más calor? ¿Cuál es la temperatura durante el invierno?

   En julio. La más alta es de 73 grados y la más baja de 63.

7. ¿Qué actividades puedes hacer en Mazatlán?

   Puedes hacer pesca y veleo.

8. ¿Qué característica especial tiene Puerto Vallarta?

   Conserva su aire tradicional de pequeño pueblo mexicano.

9. ¿Qué es Yelapa y cómo puedes llegar allí?

   Es una playa. Puedes llegar por barco y nadando.

10. ¿Conoces alguna de estas ciudades? ¿Cuál(es)? ¿Cuál te gustaría (would like) conocer? ¿Por qué?

    Answers will vary.

    _____

    _____

¡Descubra los tesoros[1] de México!

Ud. descubrirá tesoros: en sus playas y ciudades, en sus atardeceres[2] dorados, en la sonrisa de la gente, en la comida y en la famosa artesanía mexicana.

Itinerario

Día	Puerto	Llegada	Salida
domingo	San Diego		16:00
lunes	Travesía del Mar		
martes	Cabo San Lucas	07:00	22:00
miércoles	Mazatlán	07:00	24:00
jueves	Puerto Vallarta	07:00	23:00
viernes	San Diego	22:00	

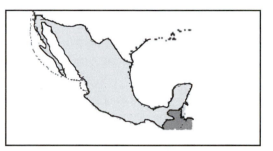

El primer tesoro: Cabo San Lucas

Cabo San Lucas está en el extremo sur de la península de Baja California, que se extiende 1.500 kilómetros al sur de la frontera con Estados Unidos. Esta pequeña ciudad, bañada por el sol los 365 días del año, tiene docenas de playas vírgenes y de aguas templadas, de arena blanca y las doradas montañas del desierto a la distancia. Cabo San Lucas es famoso por sus enormes rocas en forma de arco, donde se bañan al sol las focas[3] y los leones marinos; y donde las ballenas grises de Alaska pasan el invierno.

El segundo tesoro: Mazatlán

Mazatlán, en el estado de Sinaloa, es el puerto con la mayor flota camaronera[4] del país. Es muy popular entre los turistas mexicanos, estadounidenses y canadienses por la pesca y el veleo[5]. Esta ciudad relativamente nueva y moderna tiene playas magníficas. También hay hoteles de la mejor calidad, y la Zona Dorada, en el centro de la ciudad, tiene una gran variedad de tiendas. Pero principalmente, Mazatlán ofrece una excelente vida nocturna: restaurantes, terrazas, bares y discotecas. Es fácil y barato transportarse del puerto al centro en las famosas "pulmonías".

Temperaturas

mes	alta	baja
ene.	73	63
feb.	73	63
mar.	73	63
abr.	77	66
may.	81	72
jun.	84	77
jul.	91	79
ago.	88	79
sep.	86	77
oct.	80	76
nov.	81	70
dic.	73	64

El tercer tesoro: Puerto Vallarta

Puerto Vallarta es una pequeña ciudad de la Riviera mexicana que conserva su aire tradicional de pequeño pueblo mexicano. Tiene estrechas calles empedradas[6], una linda plaza a la orilla del mar, donde se hacen representaciones de pastorelas[7] durante la época de Navidad y donde tocan bandas musicales el resto del año. Tiene que visitar la catedral de Nuestra Señora de Guadalupe y caminar por la zona central de la ciudad. También hay pequeñas tiendas de artesanías, artículos de piel[8], cerámica y joyerías. Tiene que visitar Yelapa. Debe tomar un pequeño barco local que visita la Isla de las Rocas y la playa de Mismaloya antes de llegar a la playa de Yelapa. Ahí Ud. debe nadar hasta la playa (está muy cerca) e ir a caballo hasta el nacimiento del río.

[1]*treasures* [2]*sunsets* [3]*seals* [4]*shrimp population* [5]**pesca...** *fishing and sailing* [6]*cobblestone* [7]*humorous popular plays representing the struggle between good and evil* [8]*leather*

L. Un lugar bonito que tú conoces. Write a description of a vacation place you have visited. Talk about the weather in the season you usually go, the activities you usually do, etc. *Answers will vary.*

Writing Strategy: Using simple language to express your ideas

You may feel frustrated when you cannot communicate your ideas in written Spanish as well as you can in English. For this reason, you may make the mistake of using a dictionary and creating sentences that Spanish speakers would not be able to understand. A much more effective strategy is to limit your messages to what you are able to communicate.

You have just read a tourist brochure in Spanish. By using the illustrations, your background knowledge, and context, you were probably able to understand most of the text. But you are probably not yet able to use that level of language to communicate your own ideas. For example, in the brochure you read this about Cabo San Lucas: **Esta pequeña ciudad, bañada por el sol los 365 días del año, tiene docenas de playas vírgenes...** Although you cannot yet write a similar description, you can write something like: **Cabo San Lucas es una ciudad pequeña. Siempre hace sol y calor, y hay muchas playas bonitas,** which any Spanish speaker would understand. Using simple language enables you to express yourself effectively while you build your writing communication skills.

_____

_____

_____

_____

_____

_____

_____

_____

_____

_____

_____

_____

_____

_____

_____

_____

_____

_____

_____

Episodio

¡A escuchar!

Comprensión

Audio
CD-ROM

A. De compras con Sofía y Ana Mari. Sofía and Ana Mari are shopping for clothing that they will need in Guadalajara. Listen to their conversation and list the articles they buy, how many they buy, and the color of each article. You will hear the conversation twice.

	cantidad	artículo	color
Sofía	2	blusas	blancas
	2	faldas	azul y verde
	1	vestido	negro
	1	impermeable	gris
Ana Mari	1	traje	rojo y negro
	1	sandalias	rojas

Audio
CD-ROM

B. ¡Gran liquidación en el Almacén Franco! You are going to listen to a radio advertisement for a clothing store. Listen and select the best completion for each sentence. You will hear the advertisement twice.

Banco de palabras			
almacén	liquidación	descuento	rebajado/a
(department) store	sale	discount	reduced

1. En el Almacén Franco, se vende...
   (a.) ropa para hombres.   b. ropa para niños.   c. ropa para mujeres.

2. La liquidación es de ropa…
   a. de verano.   b. para la playa.   (c.) de invierno.

3. Hay un descuento de 50% (por ciento) en...
   (a.) las camisas.   b. los suéteres.   c. los pantalones.

4. Hay liquidación...
   a. el 4 y el 5 de enero.   b. por una semana.   (c.) por dos días.

5. Las corbatas tienen el precio de...
   a. 20% de descuento.   (b.) dos por una.   c. $25.

6. Por solamente $38 se puede comprar...
   a. una chaqueta.   b. una corbata.   (c.) un suéter.

7. Hay pantalones…
   a. de muchos colores.   (b.) rebajados.   c. por $20.

Cuaderno de tareas

Nombre _____ Fecha _____

Pronunciación

Entonación. Intonation (**entonación**) is the way in which the speaker conveys meaning by emphasizing words, pausing, and using the voice to rise and fall in pitch. The more closely you imitate a native speaker's intonation, the closer you will come to native pronunciation. Ordinary statements generally have an even pitch, dropping off on the last syllable, while *yes/no* questions rise in pitch on the last syllable. Repeat these sets of statements and questions after the speaker.

Las chicas van de compras.	**¿Las chicas van de compras?**
No saben cuánto cuestan las blusas.	**¿No saben cuánto cuestan las blusas?**

While *yes/no* questions rise in pitch on the last syllable, information questions drop in pitch on the last syllable, and the interrogative word is emphasized.

¿Dónde está el teléfono? ¿Quién es esa chica? ¿Por qué no vas conmigo?
¿Qué es eso? ¿Cuánto cuesta la bolsa? ¿Cuándo vamos a la playa?

In *either/or* questions, the pitch rises at the end of the first choice and drops at the end of the second. Repeat these questions after the speaker.

¿Quieres comprar la blusa … o la chaqueta? ¿Comemos en un restaurante … o en casa?

Más escenas de la vida

Ana Mari is chatting with Sofía, who is packing. Listen to the conversation and then complete activities **A** and **B**. You will hear the conversation twice.

A. ¿Qué ropa llevo? Indicate the clothes that Sofía says she is taking on the trip.

✓ 1. un vestido elegante ✓ 4. zapatos para caminar ___ 7. un pijama
✓ 2. tres o cinco pantalones ✓ 5. dos o tres suéteres ✓ 8. un par de faldas
___ 3. un abrigo ✓ 6. zapatos de tacón

B. Responde. Write the answers to the following questions.

1. ¿Por qué Sofía no quiere llevar mucha ropa? Nunca se pone todo lo que lleva.

2. ¿Qué consejo da la madre de Ana Mari? Saca toda la ropa que crees que necesitas llevar, pero en tu maleta sólo pon la mitad de lo que sacaste.

3. ¿Cuánto tiempo van a estar en Guadalajara? Van a estar dos semanas en Guadalajara.

4. ¿Por qué Sofía no necesita diez blusas? No necesita diez blusas porque puede lavarlas.

5. ¿Qué tiempo hace en Guadalajara? Hace buen tiempo en Guadalajara.

6. ¿Quién puede prestarle ropa a Sofía si necesita? Odette puede prestarle ropa.

7. ¿Sofía y Wayne, son novios? Sí, ellos son novios.

Episodio 14

Escenas de la vida: ¡Estás muy americanizada!

Video CD-ROM

A. ¡Mira cuánto puedes entender! Sofía y Odette hablan de sus rutinas diarias. Escucha la conversación o mira el video para indicar las actividades que mencionan.

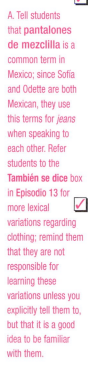
Audio CD-ROM

Instructor's Resources
• Overheads
• VHS Video
• Worktext CD
• Website
• IRM: Videoscript, Comprehensible input

A. Tell students that **pantalones de mezclilla** is a common term in Mexico; since Sofía and Odette are both Mexican, they use this terms for *jeans* when speaking to each other. Refer students to the **También se dice** box in **Episodio 13** for more lexical variations regarding clothing; remind them that they are not responsible for learning these variations unless you explicitly tell them to, but that it is a good idea to be familiar with them.

☑

Sofía **se pone** pantalones de mezclilla para ir a la universidad.

☐

Odette **se pone** ropa elegante sólo para salir.

☑

Odette no sale de casa sin **pintarse**.

☑

Odette **sale con** sus amigos entre semana.

☑

Sofía **se queda** en casa entre semana.

☐

Sofía siempre **se pinta**.

☑

Odette **se acuesta** tarde y **se levanta** temprano.

☑

Sofía y Odette **se van a divertir** en el teatro esta noche.

☐

Sofía **prefiere bañarse** por la noche.

Video Synopsis. Upon her arrival in Mexico, Sofía and her friend Odette discuss the cultural differences between Mexico and the United States. Odette teases Sofía about how much she has changed, and tells her to get enough sleep so that she will be awake at the theater.

Video
CD-ROM

Audio
CD-ROM

B. ¿Quién lo dijo? Escucha la conversación o mira el video para indicar quién hizo los siguientes comentarios: Odette (**O**) o Sofía (**S**).

_____S_____ 1. ¿Adónde vas tan elegante?

_____O_____ 2. No salgo de mi casa sin pintarme.

_____S_____ 3. En Estados Unidos hay más oportunidades profesionales para las mujeres.

_____O_____ 4. Para mí, es muy importante tener vida social.

_____S_____ 5. Casi todos salen del trabajo, van a casa, ven la tele y se acuestan.

Video
CD-ROM

Audio
CD-ROM

C. ¿Te diste cuenta? Escucha la conversación o mira el video otra vez para completar las frases.

1. No _____estoy_____ elegante; es mi _____ropa_____ normal.

2. Sofía está muy _____americanizada_____.

3. ¿Te gusta _____vivir en Estados Unidos_____?

4. El problema es que yo ya no _____puedo hacer_____ eso.

5. Odette piensa que en Estados Unidos la vida es muy _____aburrida_____ porque las personas no salen entre semana.

Cultura a lo vivo

In Spanish-speaking countries, people are used to going out regularly on weekday evenings. For Hispanics, is very important to keep in touch with their family and friends, so informal get-togethers are a constant. It's very common between Spanish speakers to improvise parties or gatherings for the pleasure of seeing each other again, regardless of the day of the week or time of day.

Práctica adicional

| Cuaderno de tareas | Video CD-ROM |
| WB p.361, A–B | Episodio 14 |

Para comunicarnos mejor

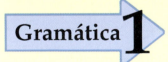

Gramática 1

Describing your daily routine
- **Reflexive pronouns**

Analizar y descubrir

In the conversation, you heard the following:

Sólo **me pongo** camisetas…	*I only wear T-shirts...*
¿Y **te pintas**?	*And do you wear makeup?*
La gente **se acuesta** temprano.	*People go to bed early.*
Nos levantamos temprano.	*We get up early.*

1. The verb forms **me pongo**, **te pintas**, **se acuesta**, and **nos levantamos** each include a reflexive pronoun. You will know that a verb is conjugated with a reflexive pronoun when **se** appears in the infinitive form: **ponerse**, **pintarse**, **acostarse**, **levantarse**. Reflexive verbs have the same endings as other **-ar**, **-er**, and **-ir** verbs.

Study the following examples and answer the questions.

Verbos con pronombres reflexivos	
Los sábados **me levanto** tarde.	*On Saturdays I get up late.*
¿A qué hora **te levantas**?	*What time do you get up?*
Usted nunca **se acuesta** temprano, ¿verdad?	*You never go to bed early, do you?*
Sofía **se quita** los lentes de contacto para dormir.	*Sofía takes off her contact lenses to sleep.*
Nosotros **nos bañamos** por la mañana.	*We take a shower/bathe in the morning.*
¿Ustedes **se divierten** en la clase ¿no? ¿Vosotros **os divertís** en la clase ¿no?	*You have fun in class, right?*
Los niños no **se lavan** las manos antes de comer.	*The kids do not wash their hands before eating.*

Gramática 1. Lead students through the activities in **Analizar y descubrir** to help them discover the rules governing the use of reflexive pronouns.

2. Which reflexive pronoun is used...

a. with the **yo** form of the verb? ___me___   e. with the **nosotros/as** form? ___nos___
b. with the **tú** form? ___te___   f. with the **ustedes** form? ___se___
c. with the **usted** form? ___se___   g. with the **ellos/as** form? ___se___
d. with the **él/ella** form? ___se___

3. Spanish uses the definite article (**el, la, los, las**) when reflexive verbs are used with parts of the body and clothing. English uses a possessive adjective (*my, your, her*). Identify the statements above that illustrate this rule.

a. Sofía se quita los lentes de contacto para dormir.

b. Los niños no se lavan las manos antes de comer.

4. Reflexive pronouns, like direct object pronouns, may be placed before a conjugated verb or attached to the infinitive.

Tengo que **levantarme** temprano porque hoy voy a trabajar.
or   **Me** tengo que **levantar** temprano porque hoy voy a trabajar.

5. Reflexive pronouns are not optional. Verbs used reflexively have different meanings than those used without reflexive pronouns; for example, while **ir** means *to go*, **irse** means *to leave*.

Para hablar de tu rutina diaria			
acostarse tarde (o → ue)	*to go to bed late*	**levantarse temprano**	*to get up early*
bañarse por la noche	*to take a bath/shower at night*	**pintarse**	*to put on makeup*
divertirse (e → ie)	*to have fun*	**ponerse la ropa**	*to put on/wear clothing*
irse (a)	*to leave*	**quedarse en casa**	*to stay home*
irse de vacaciones	*to go on vacation*	**quitarse los zapatos**	*to take off one's shoes*
juntarse	*to get together*		
lavarse las manos	*to wash one's hands*		
los dientes	*to brush one's teeth*		

Gramática 1. You may ask personalized questions like: Generalmente me acuesto tarde entre semana. Y tú, ¿a qué hora te acuestas? Me gusta levantarme temprano los fines de semana. ¿A qué hora se levantan ustedes?

También se dice...

pintarse ⟶ maquillarse

lavarse los dientes ⟶ cepillarse los dientes

Some people make a distinction between **bañarse** (*to take a bath*) and **ducharse** (*to shower*).

Learning Strategy: Quiet rehearsal

Your instructor will frequently ask students to respond before, during, or after participating in various activities. Think of how you would respond, even if you do not have a chance to speak aloud. Compare your answer with the one given by someone else. This strategy is a great way to practice and learn without being put on the spot!

PRÁCTICA

A. ¿Qué hacen? Empareja las ilustraciones con las descripciones.

a

b

c

d

e

f

_____a_____ 1. Sofía se levanta tarde los sábados.

_____c_____ 2. ¿Te pintas todos los días?

_____d_____ 3. Me baño por la noche cuando hace frío.

_____f_____ 4. Todos se divierten cuando se juntan para salir.

_____e_____ 5. Nosotros nos quedamos en casa esta noche.

_____b_____ 6. Me pongo pantalones para ir a la universidad.

B. La rutina diaria. Ordena las frases del uno al diez en una secuencia lógica.

___10___ a. Y me acuesto porque ya es tarde.

___4___ b. Luego me voy a la universidad.

___9___ c. Luego me pongo el pijama.

___2___ d. Después me baño.

___3___ e. Voy a mi cuarto a ponerme la ropa.

___8___ f. Me lavo los dientes antes de acostarme.

___5___ g. Me quedo en la universidad todo el día.

___1___ h. Me levanto temprano porque es lunes.

___6___ i. Me voy a casa porque ya estoy cansado.

___7___ j. Me divierto un rato mirando mi programa cómico favorito.

B. You may write these statements on index cards to distribute to students in groups. Each student gets one card, and the students must physically place themselves in the correct order. Groups read their cards to check the sequence.

C. Lotería.

Parte 1. Encuentra un(a) compañero/a que haga las siguientes cosas. Escribe su nombre en el cuadro indicado. La persona que llene todas las líneas sin repetir nombres gana el juego.
Answers will vary.

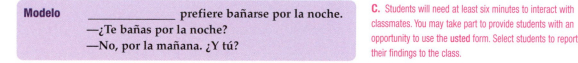

Modelo	_____ prefiere bañarse por la noche.
	—¿Te bañas por la noche?
	—No, por la mañana. ¿Y tú?

C. Students will need at least six minutes to interact with classmates. You may take part to provide students with an opportunity to use the **usted** form. Select students to report their findings to the class.

se acuesta antes de las once de la noche.	sabe jugar golf.	se levanta tarde los domingos.	no se pone pijama para dormir.
se divierte en su trabajo.	no conoce a los padres de su novio/a.	se queda en casa los sábados por la tarde.	no se pinta todos los días.
prefiere bañarse por la noche.	se va de vacaciones todos los años.	se junta con la familia el día de su cumpleaños.	ayuda a su mamá en la casa.
se quita los zapatos cuando llega a casa.	se lava los dientes con *Aquafresh*.	nunca pide postre en los restaurantes.	usa lentes de contacto.

¡Fíjate!
Remember to use reflexive pronouns only with reflexive verbs!

Parte 2. Comparte *(share)* la información con la clase.

Modelo	Estudiante 1:	**Rick se va de vacaciones todos los años.**
	Estudiante 2:	**¿Adónde vas?**
	Rick:	**Generalmente vamos a Utah a esquiar.**

D. En casa de Ramón y Ana Mari.

Parte 1. Ana Mari describe la rutina diaria de su familia. Conjuga los verbos para formar frases completas y haz los cambios necesarios.

En mi casa:

1. mis padres / levantarse / antes que todos

   Mis padres se levantan antes que todos.

2. a mí / me / gustar / acostarse temprano

   A mí me gusta acostarme temprano.

3. por eso / (yo) bañarse / por la noche

   Por eso me baño por la noche.

4. mis hermanos / preferir / bañarse / por la mañana

   Mis hermanos prefieren bañarse por la mañana.

5. mi mamá / pintarse / mientras que mi papá / preparar / el desayuno

   Mi mamá se pinta mientras que mi papá prepara el desayuno.

6. a las ocho / todos (nosotros) / desayunar / juntos

   A las ocho todos desayunamos juntos.

7. luego / todos irse / al trabajo o a la escuela

   Luego todos nos vamos al trabajo o a la escuela.

Parte 2. Ahora contesta las preguntas. Answers will vary.

1. ¿Quién se levanta primero en casa de Ramón y Ana Mari? ¿Y en tu casa?

   Sus papás se levantan primero.

2. ¿Quién se baña por la noche? Y tú, ¿cuándo te bañas?

   Ana Mari se baña por la noche.

3. ¿Quién prepara el desayuno? ¿Y en tu casa?

   Su papá prepara el desayuno.

E. ¿Cómo cambia tu rutina cuando estás de vacaciones?

Parte 1. Adriana describe cómo cambia (*changes*) su rutina cuando está de vacaciones. Lee la descripción en la siguiente página y contesta las preguntas.

1. ¿Cuáles son las diferencias principales en sus actividades?

   En las vacaciones se divierte mucho más porque hace lo que ella quiere. No tiene tantas obligaciones y se puede quedar tranquila en casa o juntarse

   con sus amigos si tiene ganas.

2. ¿Por qué se levanta temprano durante las vacaciones?

   Se levanta temprano porque su esposo siempre se levanta temprano, vacaciones o no.

3. ¿Adónde se va de vacaciones generalmente? ¿Por qué va allí? ¿Qué hacen?

   Generalmente va a Puerto Rico, porque va a ver a su hermana. Salen o se juntan con la familia para hablar, cantar y bailar hasta la madrugada.

Cuando estoy de vacaciones mi rutina de las mañanas no cambia[1] mucho. Generalmente me levanto temprano porque mi esposo siempre se levanta temprano, vacaciones o no.

La ropa que me pongo sí es diferente: para ir a trabajar me pongo vestidos, faldas o pantalones más formales. En cambio[2], cuando estoy de vacaciones me pongo jeans, camisetas y ropa muy informal. No me pinto todos los días, si no tengo que trabajar o ir a la universidad.

La diferencia más importante son las actividades que hago después de trabajar: en las vacaciones me divierto mucho más porque hago lo que yo quiero. No tengo tantas obligaciones y me puedo quedar tranquila en casa o juntarme con amigos si tengo ganas. Cuando estoy en clases siempre estudio y hago la tarea antes de acostarme.

En invierno, generalmente me voy de vacaciones a Puerto Rico a ver a mi hermana. Allá, nos acostamos muy tarde porque nos gusta mucho salir o juntarnos con la familia para hablar, cantar y bailar hasta la madrugada[3].

---

[1]*doesn't change*   [2]*on the other hand*   [3]*dawn*

Parte 2. Usa la descripción de Adriana como modelo para escribir cómo cambia tu rutina cuando estás de vacaciones.

> **¡Fíjate!**
> Notice that verbs are not conjugated after prepositions: **para hablar, cantar...,** **después de trabajar,** **antes de acostarme.**

F. ¡Qué divertido! Listen to the story Ana Mari's younger brothers tell about about when they visited their grandmother. Indicate whether their behaviors are good or bad. Share your answers with a partner.

Audio CD-ROM

Instructor's Resources
• Worktext CD
• IRM: Tapescript

Script. *Listen to the story Ana Mari's two younger brothers tell about when they visited their grandmother. Indicate whether their behaviors are good or bad. Share your answers with a partner.*

Ayer nos divertimos mucho en casa de la abuela.
1. Bañamos al gato en la piscina.
2. Después le dimos leche y lo acostamos en su cama.
3. Nos lavamos las manos antes de comer…
4. y no nos levantamos de la mesa hasta terminar toda la comida.
5. Nos pintamos la cara con el maquillaje de la abuela.
6. Nos quitamos los zapatos después de jugar en el patio.
7. Nos quedamos viendo la televisión hasta las doce de la noche…
8. y no nos lavamos los dientes antes de acostarnos. ¡Upps!

	bueno	malo			bueno	malo
1.	☐	✓		5.	☐	✓
2.	✓	☐		6.	✓	☐
3.	✓	☐		7.	☐	✓
4.	✓	☐		8.	☐	✓

G. ¡A hablar! En grupos de cuatro, hablen de sus rutinas por la mañana y por la noche, para encontrar quién en el grupo es el/la madrugador(a) (*earlybird*), quién es el/la más elegante, quién se acuesta más temprano y quién es el/la parrandero/a (*night owl*).

> **Modelo**   **Rosario es la madrugadora porque todos los días se levanta a las cinco y media.**

Práctica adicional

Cuaderno de tareas
WB pp.362–366, C–H
LM pp.369–370, A–B, Pron.

Audio
CD-ROM
Episodio 14

Actividades comunicativas

A. Submarino. First, draw a submarine in five of the boxes on your grid. Then, take turns asking your partner yes/no questions, matching an action pictured at the top of the grid with one of the people on the side. Depending on your partner's answer, write **sí** or **no** in that box. The first person to locate all five submarines wins. Answers will vary.

> **Modelo** — ¿Adriana se pinta para ir a la universidad?
> — **Sí, se pinta.** (If there is a submarine in that box)
> or — **No, no se pinta.** (If there is not a submarine there)

Tú				
Tus primos				
Adriana				
Ustedes				

Invitación a **Nicaragua**

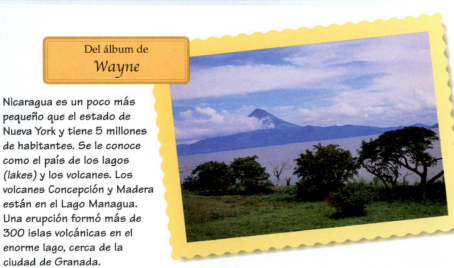

Del álbum de
Wayne

Nicaragua es un poco más pequeño que el estado de Nueva York y tiene 5 millones de habitantes. Se le conoce como el país de los lagos (lakes) y los volcanes. Los volcanes Concepción y Madera están en el Lago Managua. Una erupción formó más de 300 islas volcánicas en el enorme lago, cerca de la ciudad de Granada.

Práctica adicional

Website
vistahigher
learning.com

B. Sopa de palabras.

Instrucciones para **Estudiante 1**

Primero escribe oraciones lógicas usando todas las palabras. La primera y la última palabra ya están en su lugar. Después léele tus oraciones a tu compañero/a para verificar las respuestas. Si tiene errores, ayúdalo/la a encontrarlos, pero no le des *(don't give them)* la respuesta correcta inmediatamente. Deja que trate *(let them try)* de solucionar los problemas. Túrnense.

> **Modelo**
>
> **Sofía** pinta los se solamente **sábados.**
> **Sofía se pinta solamente los sábados.**

Los fines de semana

1. **Los** tarde, mis esposo acuestan se pero sábados, acuesta se mi hijos **temprano**.

   Los sábados, mis hijos se acuestan tarde, pero mi esposo se acuesta temprano.

2. **Me** llego cuando quitarme los a zapatos gusta **casa**.

   Me gusta quitarme los zapatos cuando llego a casa.

3. ¿**Te** para los todos ir solamente No, pintas las pinto a días? me **fiestas**.

   ¿Te pintas todos los días? No, me pinto solamente para ir a las fiestas.

4. **Es** con importante con la muy familia juntarse **frecuencia**.

   Es muy importante juntarse con la familia con frecuencia.

5. **Los** vestido pongo me domingos mi **favorito**.

   Los domingos me pongo mi vestido favorito.

Las respuestas de tu compañero/a:

1. Los lunes me levanto temprano, pero los sábados prefiero levantarme tarde.
2. Mis hijos se divierten mucho en la clase de karate.
3. No me gusta quedarme en casa los sábados; prefiero salir.
4. Mi esposo se acuesta muy tarde; yo necesito acostarme antes de las diez.
5. Siempre nos bañamos por la noche/mañana porque por la mañana/noche no tenemos tiempo.

B. Pair students and allow four minutes for them to unscramble their sentences before they begin to interact. Students check their answers with their classmate. Students may switch roles.

B. Sopa de palabras.

Primero escribe oraciones lógicas usando todas las palabras. La primera y la última palabra ya están en su lugar. Después léele tus oraciones a tu compañero/a para verificar las respuestas. Si tiene errores, ayúdalo/la a encontrarlos, pero no le des *(don't give them)* la respuesta correcta inmediatamente. Deja que trate *(let them try)* de solucionar los problemas. Túrnense.

> **Modelo**
> **Wayne** la camiseta ejercicio en se la pone hacer para **parque.**
> **Wayne se pone la camiseta para hacer ejercicio en el parque.**

Las actividades en casa

1. **Los** me temprano, lunes prefiero levanto sábados levantarme pero los **tarde.**

   Los lunes me levanto temprano, pero los sábados prefiero levantarme tarde.

2. **Mis** divierten clase en la mucho se de hijos **karate.**

   Mis hijos se divierten mucho en la clase de karate.

3. **No** me quedarme prefiero los sábados; casa gusta en **salir.**

   No me gusta quedarme en casa los sábados; prefiero salir.

4. **Mi** muy esposo tarde; se yo las acostarme antes acuesta necesito de **diez.**

   Mi esposo se acuesta muy tarde; yo necesito acostarme antes de las diez.

5. **Siempre** bañamos mañana noche nos por la tenemos no porque por la **tiempo.**

   Siempre nos bañamos por la noche/mañana porque por la mañana/noche no tenemos tiempo.

Las respuestas de tu compañero/a:

1. Los sábados, mis hijos se acuestan tarde, pero mi esposo se acuesta temprano.
2. Me gusta quitarme los zapatos cuando llego a casa.
3. ¿Te pintas todos los días? No, me pinto solamente para ir a las fiestas.
4. Es muy importante juntarse con la familia con frecuencia.
5. Los domingos me pongo mi vestido favorito.

C. La fotonovela. En grupos de cuatro personas, seleccionen cinco de las siguientes actividades para escribir una descripción de lo que hacen Sofía y sus amigos los fines de semana. Después tu grupo va a leer la descripción a la clase y tus compañeros van a adivinar (*guess*) las letras de las actividades que usaron en la descripción.

Empiecen su fotonovela así: **El viernes por la tarde, generalmente Sofía…** Answers will vary.

La correspondencia

 El correo: La gritería nicaragüense. Lee el artículo del periódico *(paper)* del Club Latino acerca de *(about)* la más famosa celebración nicaragüense. Después contesta las preguntas.

1. ¿Qué es la gritería? ¿Qué y cuándo se celebra?
   Es una fiesta dedicada a la Virgen María que se celebra el 7 de diciembre.

2. ¿Qué hacen las personas durante la gritería?
   Van de casa en casa cantando y alabando el nombre de la Virgen.

3. ¿Qué hacen ese día por la mañana? ¿A qué hora se levantan? ¿Por qué?
   Limpian toda la casa y preparan las canastas de dulces para regalar. Se levantan a las 7 de la mañana porque los preparativos empiezan muy temprano.

4. ¿Qué hacen ese día por la tarde?
   Salen a la calle y van a casa de varios vecinos, cantan, disparan cohetes, ven los fuegos artificiales y comen caña de azúcar, gofios y dulces de leche.

La gritería, celebración nacional nicaragüense

Por Wayne Reilly

Hace dos años, visité Managua, la capital de Nicaragua. Una de mis mejores experiencias fue participar en "la gritería." La gritería es una fiesta dedicada a la Virgen María que se celebra el 7 de diciembre. Las personas van de casa en casa cantando y alabando[1] el nombre de la Virgen. Cuando un grupo llega a una casa, pregunta, "¿Qué causa tanta alegría?", y las personas de la casa contestan, "¡La concepción de María!".

En la casa de mi familia adoptiva, los preparativos empezaron muy temprano. Nos levantamos a las siete de la mañana, limpiamos toda la casa (tiene que estar todo muy limpio para los visitantes) y preparamos las canastas[2] de dulces para regalar. A las cinco de la tarde, salimos a la calle y fuimos a la casa de varios vecinos. Cantamos, disparamos cohetes,[3] vimos los fuegos artificiales,[4] comimos caña de azúcar, gofios (dulces hechos de masa de maíz) y dulces de leche. Después volvimos a la casa para esperar a que llegaran otras personas del barrio. Fue una noche fabulosa; cantamos, bailamos y conversamos. Yo me acosté a las tres de la mañana y mi familia se acostó todavía más tarde.

Los nicaragüenses me dijeron que la gritería es la celebración más esperada del año. Algunos años se celebra aun[5] en medio de situaciones violentas. La gente olvida la violencia y los conflictos políticos por un día y se dedica a celebrar con alegría.

[1]*praising* [2]*baskets* [3]*firecrackers* [4]*fireworks* [5]*even*

En papel: Una celebración importante en mi país. Usa el artículo de Wayne como modelo para escribir sobre alguna celebración importante en la que tú participas con frecuencia. Recuerda que necesitas hacer un bosquejo *(outline)* primero con la información que quieres escribir. Answers will vary. **En papel.** Encourage students to include pictures in their descriptions. Students read each others celebrations and ask questions. You may also have students share their writing in groups of four. Review the ¡Fíjate! note with them.

Cultura a lo vivo.
You may ask these questions about El carnaval de La Habana: ¿Dónde se celebra el carnaval? ¿Cuánto tiempo dura? ¿Cómo se llaman los grupos de baile y música? ¿Cómo se divierte el público?

Cultura a lo vivo

En muchas ciudades de Latinoamérica se celebran carnavales que marcan el inicio de la Cuaresma[1]. El carnaval es una fiesta popular de tradición católica que celebra con alegría y excesos el período antes de la Cuaresma. El carnaval de La Habana, Cuba, es famoso en todo el mundo. Dura varios días. Incluye un desfile donde toman parte grupos de baile y música, llamados *comparsas*. El público se divierte siguiendo la música y los pasos de los grupos; bailan, beben y comen al ritmo de tambores[2], trompetas y otros instrumentos típicos de la rica tradición musical afrocubana.

[1]Lent [2]drums

¡Fíjate!

Before you write your own description, re-read the article on the previous page. Pay attention to the way Wayne orders his thoughts, his use of transition words, and how he goes from general information in the first paragraph, to specific information in the second.

Video
CD-ROM

¡A ver de nuevo! Escucha la conversación de **Escenas de la vida** o mira el video otra vez para escribir un resumen contestando las siguientes preguntas.
Answers will vary.

Audio
CD-ROM

- ¿De qué hablan Odette y Sofía?
- ¿Qué diferencias notan entre México y Estados Unidos?
- ¿Por qué dice Sofía que está americanizada?
- ¿Estás de acuerdo con el último *(last)* comentario de Odette? Explica.

Sofía   **Odette**

Instructor's Resources
- VHS Video
- Worktext CD
- **IRM:** Videoscript

Práctica adicional

Cuaderno de tareas	Audio	Website
WB pp.366–368, I–J LM p.370, A–B	CD-ROM Episodio 14	vistahigher learning.com

Objetivos comunicativos

You should now be able to do the following in Spanish:

✔ talk about your daily routine

✔ compare what you do when you are in school and when you are on vacation

✔ talk about special celebrations

Para hablar de tu rutina diaria

acostarse tarde (o → ue)	*to go to bed late*
bañarse por la noche	*to take a bath / shower at night*
divertirse (e → ie)	*to have fun*
irse (a)	*to leave*
irse de vacaciones	*to go on vacation*
juntarse	*to get together*
lavarse las manos	*to wash one's hands*
los dientes	*to brush one's teeth*
levantarse temprano	*to get up early*
pintarse	*to put on makeup*
ponerse la ropa	*to put on/wear clothing*
quedarse en casa	*to stay home*
quitarse los zapatos	*to take off one's shoes*

Instructor's Resources

• Testing Program
• Website

Vocabulario personal

Write the words you need to know to talk about your daily routine and important celebrations in your family.

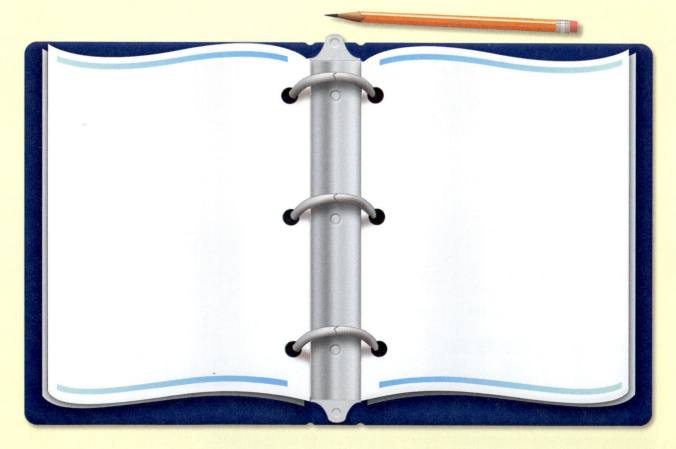

¡A escribir!

Episodio
14

Escenas de la vida: ¡Estás muy americanizada!

Video CD-ROM

A. ¡A ver cuánto entendiste! See how much of the **Escena** you understood by matching the Spanish sentences with their English equivalents. At the end, identify the speaker.

1. ¿Quién lo dijo (Who said it)?

___d___ 1. Sólo salen los fines de semana.
___a___ 2. Yo estoy tan americanizada.
___c___ 3. Me pinto cuando voy a salir.
___b___ 4. Sólo me pongo camisetas.
___e___ 5. Entre semana la gente se acuesta temprano.

a. I'm so Americanized.
b. I only wear T-shirts.
c. I put makeup on when I go out.
d. They only go out on weekends.
e. During the week, people go to bed early.

___Sofía___ **lo dijo.**

2. ¿Quién lo dijo?

___e___ 1. Es mi ropa normal.
___b___ 2. Pareces viejita.
___a___ 3. Aquí la gente sale casi todos los días.
___c___ 4. No necesitas levantarte todavía.
___d___ 5. Aquí nos acostamos tarde.

a. Here people go out almost every day.
b. You're like an old woman.
c. You don't need to get up yet.
d. Here we go to bed late.
e. These are my normal clothes.

___Odette___ **lo dijo.**

Video CD-ROM

B. Ponlo en orden, por favor. Review the **Escena** again and put the following statements in chronological order.

___5___ a. ¿Te gusta vivir en Estados Unidos?
___2___ b. No estoy elegante; es mi ropa normal.
___4___ c. Para ir a la universidad, no. Me pinto cuando voy a salir.
___3___ d. ¿Y te pintas?
___1___ e. ¿Adónde vas tan elegante?
___6___ f. Sí, me gusta porque hay más oportunidades profesionales para las mujeres.
___7___ g. Pero la vida es aburrida, ¿no?

Gramática 1

Describing your daily routine
• Reflexive pronouns

C. ¿En qué secuencia? Sequence the following activities in the order in which the people indicated do them. Use **primero**, **después**, and **por último**.

Modelo	(yo)/ ponerse el pijama, acostarse, mirar la tele
	Primero miro la tele, después me pongo el pijama y por último me acuesto.

1. (Sofía)/ bañarse, ponerse la ropa, levantarse

   Primero se levanta, después se baña y por último se pone la ropa.

   _____

2. (mi esposo y yo)/lavarse los dientes, acostarse, quitarse la ropa

   Primero nos lavamos los dientes, después nos quitamos la ropa y por último nos acostamos.

   _____

3. (yo)/ irse de vacaciones, comprar ropa, pagar mis cuentas *(bills)*

   Answers will vary.

   _____

4. (los niños)/ponerse el pijama, cenar, dormirse

   Primero cenan, después se ponen el pijama y por último se duermen.

   _____

5. (las mujeres)/peinarse, levantarse, pintarse

   Primero se levantan, después se peinan y por último se pintan.

   _____

¡Fíjate!

Notice the difference between transition words like **después** and prepositions like **después de**.

   a. Odette se pinta **después de <u>ponerse</u>** la ropa.

   b. Odette se pinta, **después <u>se pone</u>** la ropa.

In **a**, Odette first puts her clothes on; in **b**, Odette first puts makeup on. Also notice that the verb is not conjugated after the preposition **de**.

Verbs are not conjugated after prepositions: e.g., **para, antes de**, and **después de**.

Verbs are conjugated after transition words: e.g., **cuando**, and **por eso, después, antes**.

D. ¿Qué hacen? Join the actions depicted below using a preposition and a conjunction (**por eso**, **para**, **cuando**, **antes de** and **después de**) to express the order in which you do the following activities. Review the **¡Fíjate!** on conjugating verbs on the previous page. Answers will vary.

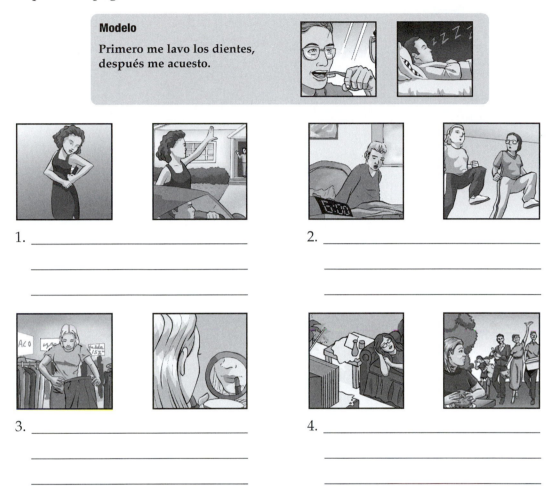

Modelo

Primero me lavo los dientes, después me acuesto.

1. _____

_____

_____

2. _____

_____

_____

3. _____

_____

_____

4. _____

_____

_____

E. La rutina de Manolo.

Parte 1. Manolo is spending a week back home with his parents. As he talks about his routine, complete the description with the appropriate forms of the verbs. Then answer the questions that follow.

Ahora estoy de vacaciones en casa de mis papás. Mi rutina aquí es un poco diferente que en mi casa. Siempre (1) ____me baño____ (bañarse) por las noches, pero en la Florida hace muchísimo calor. Por eso prefiero (2)____bañarme____ (bañarse) por las mañanas. Aquí todos (3) ____se levantan____ (levantarse) temprano. Mis papás (4) ____se levantan____ (levantarse) temprano porque trabajan, y yo también (5) ____me levanto____ (levantarse) porque voy a surfear con mis primos. Durante mi semestre regular, generalmente (6) ____me acuesto____ (acostarse) temprano porque tengo una clase de cálculo a las siete de la mañana. En casa de mis papás, (7) ____me acuesto____ (acostarse) tardísimo porque hay muchísimas cosas que hacer.

Bueno, por las noches vienen mis primos y tíos de visita (¡viven en la casa de al lado!). Jugamos cartas o Monopolio. Mis primos y yo (8) _____nos quitamos_____ (quitarse) los zapatos, (9) _____nos ponemos_____ (ponerse) cómodos y (10) _____nos quedamos_____ (quedarse) en casa toda la tarde y parte de la noche. A la una o una y media, mis primos y tíos (11) _____se van_____ (irse) a su casa. La verdad es que yo (12) _____me divierto_____ (divertirse) con ellos.

Parte 2. Answer the following questions.

1. ¿Qué cosas hace Manolo diferentes en la casa de sus papás?
   En casa de sus papás se baña por las mañanas. _____

2. ¿Por qué se acuesta tarde?
   Se acuesta tarde porque hay muchísimas cosas que hacer. _____

3. ¿Por qué todos se levantan temprano?
   Sus papás tienen que trabajar y él y sus primos van a surfear. _____

4. ¿Qué hacen Manolo y sus primos por las tardes?
   Juegan cartas o Monopolio. _____

5. ¿A qué hora se van los tíos?
   A la una o una y media. _____

F. Mi rutina de las vacaciones. Use Manolo's description as a model to write a description of your routine when you are on vacation.   Answers will vary.

_____

_____

_____

_____

_____

_____

G. ¡Pobre Carlos! In a letter to her sister in Puerto Rico, Adriana describes Carlos' life in the military. Write the appropriate forms of the verbs from the list to complete her letter. Then answer the questions.   Answers will vary.

1. ¿Por qué está contenta Adriana? _____

2. ¿Cómo es la rutina de Carlos? ¿Te gusta? ¿Por qué sí o por qué no? _____

_____

_____

3. ¿Por qué crees que se duerme inmediatamente? _____

4. ¿Por qué es buena la Fuerza Aérea para Carlos? _____

acostarse	bañarse	dormir	irse	ponerse
ser	divertirse	hacer	levantarse	verte

...por otra parte, también estoy un poco preocupada por Carlos. ¿Recuerdas que te dije que está en un entrenamiento[1] especial con la Fuerza Aérea? Pues, hoy recibí una tarjeta de él y me cuenta que está contento, pero que él y todos sus compañeros están cansados, con hambre y con sueño.

Los pobres chicos (1) _____ se levantan _____ a las cuatro de la mañana y (2) _____ se bañan _____ con agua fría. Después (3) _____ se ponen _____ la ropa, y (4) _____ hacen _____ sus camas en menos de quince minutos, pues a las cuatro y cuarto deben reportarse con el sargento en el patio. Empiezan a hacer ejercicios físicos y prácticas militares; ¡todo esto antes de desayunar! Después, toda la mañana toman clases de aviación. Por la tarde hacen sus prácticas de vuelo. Tienen que (5) _____ acostarse _____ a las ocho de la noche.

Me dice que en cuanto se acuesta, se (6) _____ duerme _____ inmediatamente. ¡Pobre de mi hijito, con lo dormilón que es! Me dice que también ha bajado de peso[2] pobrecito, con esa rutina. Lo bueno es que va a aprender a tener disciplina y a (7) _____ ser _____ ordenado.

Bueno, Cristina, escríbeme pronto y cuéntame cómo va todo por allá. ¿Cuándo vas a venir? Tengo muchas ganas de (8) _____ verte _____ .

Recibe un fuerte abrazo de tu hermana que te quiere,

Adriana

[1]training [2]has lost weight

H. Un poco de lógica. The verbs you are learning in this section use a reflexive pronoun. However, many of these same verbs may also be used without a reflexive pronoun. Compare the following models and then complete the sentences. Decide whether the reflexive pronoun is necessary or not.

¡Fíjate!

Notice that, in the first photo, **Laura lava los platos**, no reflexive pronoun is needed because Laura is washing something else. In grammatical terms, only when the subject and the object are the same person, is a reflexive pronoun necessary. In the second photo, **Laura se lava las manos**, Laura is washing her own hands, requiring the use of the reflexive pronoun.

Modelo

Laura lava los platos.

Laura se lava las manos.

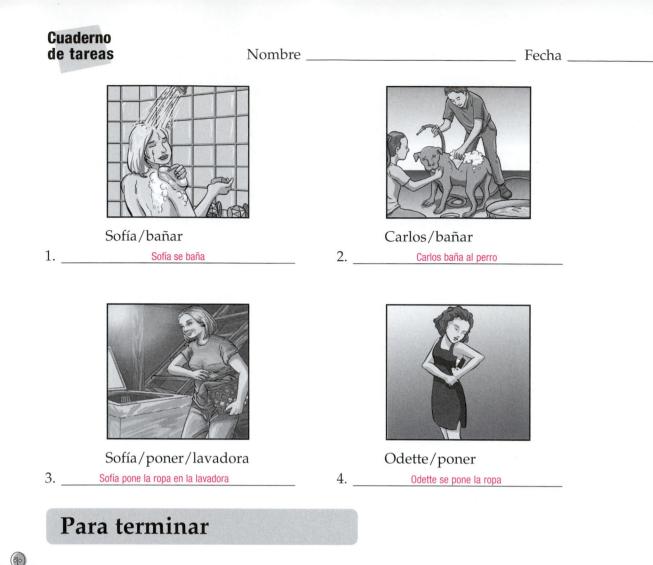

Sofía/bañar

1. _____ Sofía se baña _____

Carlos/bañar

2. _____ Carlos baña al perro _____

Sofía/poner/lavadora

3. _____ Sofía pone la ropa en la lavadora _____

Odette/poner

4. _____ Odette se pone la ropa _____

Para terminar

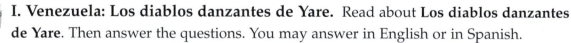

I. Venezuela: Los diablos danzantes de Yare. Read about **Los diablos danzantes de Yare**. Then answer the questions. You may answer in English or in Spanish.

1. Before you read, look at the picture of **Los diablos**. What do you think **diablos** mean? What kind of celebration might it be?

Answers will vary.

_____

2. When and where does this celebration take place?

En San Francisco de Yare en Venezuela. Empieza el miércoles de Semana Santa.

_____

3. What do participants do on the first day?

Bailan por las calles.

_____

4. What do they wear on the second day?

Llevan trajes rojos de diablos.

_____

5. What do they do after mass on the second day?

Hablan con el sacerdote.

_____

6. What do they do after the ceremony?

Salen a bailar por las calles otra vez.

_____

Los diablos danzantes de Yare

Una tradición medieval española que llega en 1619 a varias ciudades de Venezuela es la de los diablos danzantes[1]. Estos diablos celebran el Corpus Christi con ceremonias simbólicas de cómo la cruz (la religión católica) derrota el mal y los pecados[2] de la humanidad. El pueblo de San Francisco de Yare es famoso por su celebración de los diablos danzantes.

La celebración empieza el miércoles de Semana Santa[3]. Los participantes bailan por las calles del pueblo, y por la noche van al Calvario[4]. Al día siguiente, por la mañana, se ponen sus trajes rojos de diablo y van al cementerio a visitar a algunos diablos anteriores. Después van a misa. Al terminar la misa, cada diablo se acerca bailando al sacerdote[5] y le dice qué sacrificios va a hacer o no hacer. El sacerdote le pregunta cuál es el motivo del ofrecimiento y la duración de la promesa.

Al finalizar esta ceremonia, todos los diablos salen a bailar otra vez por las calles del pueblo. Este ritual combina elementos indígenas y africanos con la tradición católica romana.

Los diablos danzantes bailan por las calles de San Francisco de Yare, en Venezuela.

Los músicos, vestidos de rojo, acompañan a los diablos danzantes.

[1]*dancing devils* [2]*defeats evil and the sins* [3]*Holy Week* [4]*Calvary (symbolic of the place where Jesus was crucified)* [5]*priest*

J. Una miniprueba. Complete the following tasks in Spanish; write your answers below.

1. Ask Sofía
    a. when she gets up on Sundays
    b. if she goes to bed later on weekends
    c. what she wears to go to the gym

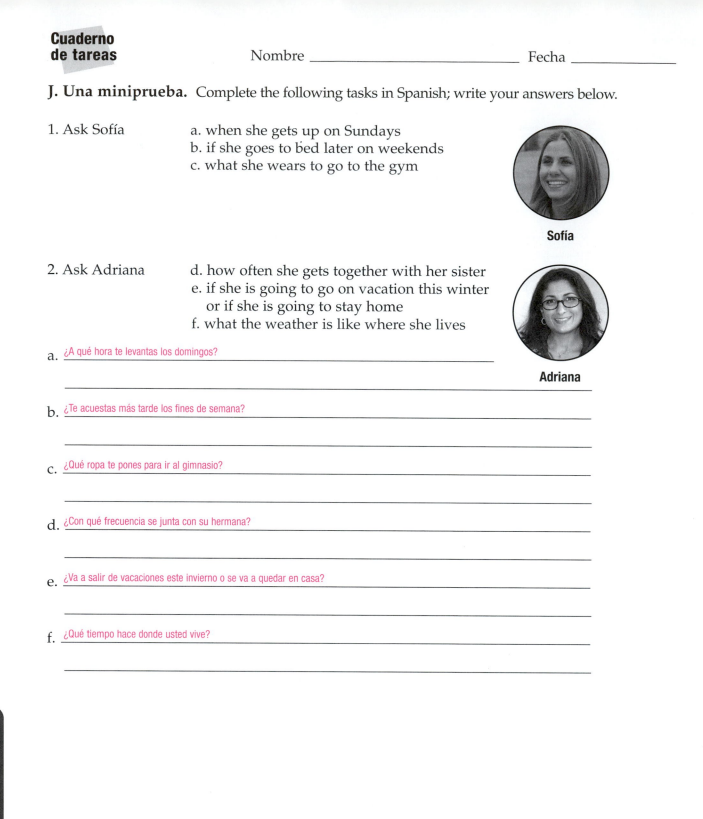

Sofía

2. Ask Adriana
    d. how often she gets together with her sister
    e. if she is going to go on vacation this winter
       or if she is going to stay home
    f. what the weather is like where she lives

Adriana

a. ¿A qué hora te levantas los domingos? _____
_____

b. ¿Te acuestas más tarde los fines de semana? _____
_____

c. ¿Qué ropa te pones para ir al gimnasio? _____
_____

d. ¿Con qué frecuencia se junta con su hermana? _____
_____

e. ¿Va a salir de vacaciones este invierno o se va a quedar en casa? _____
_____

f. ¿Qué tiempo hace donde usted vive? _____
_____

Nombre _____ Fecha _____

 **¡A escuchar!**

Episodio  **14**

Comprensión

 A. La rutina diaria. Describe the daily routines of the people mentioned, using the three verbs provided for each item. Then, repeat the correct answer after the speaker.

Modelo	You hear:	**tú**
	You see:	**lavarse las manos, peinarse y afeitarse** (*to shave*)
	You say:	**Te lavas las manos, te peinas y te afeitas.**

Por la mañana…

1. levantarse, bañarse y ponerse la ropa
2. bañarse, lavarse los dientes y afeitarse
3. peinarse, pintarse y ponerse ropa elegante

Por la noche en Guadalajara…

4. salir, divertirse y acostarse tarde

A las ocho de la noche…

5. quitarse la ropa, bañarse y acostarse

 B. Una mañana en casa de Odette. Listen to Odette as she describes the events of a morning in Guadalajara. Indicate whether the statements are **cierto** or **falso** and then correct any false statements. You will hear Odette's description twice.

	Cierto	Falso
1. Odette se levanta a las siete.	✓	
2. Sofía se baña y se peina antes que Odette. Sofía siempre se levanta más tarde.		✓
3. Sofía y Odette escuchan la radio mientras Odette se pinta. Ellas hablan de muchas cosas mientras Odette se pinta.		✓
4. Odette prepara el desayuno para todos los amigos.	✓	
5. Sofía come mucho. Sofía sólo bebe café con leche.		✓
6. Los amigos comen huevos con jamón. Ellos comen huevos con salsa.		✓
7. A los amigos les gusta el desayuno.	✓	

Pronunciación

Acentuación: Parte 1. Every syllable in Spanish has at least one vowel, which you may think of as the nucleus of the syllable. One-syllable words do not usually carry a written accent mark. Exceptions will be presented in **Acentuación: Parte 2** in **Episodio 15**. Repeat these one-syllable words:

mi   su   por   sed   sin   con   seis   pues   diez

In each word of multiple syllables, one syllable carries a spoken stress. These words do not require an accent if the stress falls on the next to the last syllable in words ending in **-n, -s,** or a vowel.

taco   gustan   amigos   muchacha   chica   hablas

Words also do not require a written accent when the stress falls on the last syllable of words ending in any consonant other than **-n** and **-s**. Repeat these words after the speaker:

ciudad   arroz   trabajar   usted   azul   universidad

Más escenas de la vida

Manolo, Ramón, Odette, Sofía and Ana Mari are planning a trip. Listen to their conversation, and then complete activities **A** and **B**. You will hear the conversation twice.

A. Unscramble. Put the words in these scrambled sentences in the correct order. The first and last words of each sentence have been put in their correct place for you.

1. Mi nos a papá llevar de estación la puede autobuses.
Mi ___papá nos puede llevar a la estación de___ autobuses.

2. Sale ahí media las siete y a estar tenemos hora que antes.
Sale ___a las siete y tenemos que estar ahí media hora___ antes.

3. Mejor al no y vamos de la dormimos nos posada autobús.
Mejor ___no dormimos y nos vamos de la posada al___ autobús.

4. Yo el dormir necesito de y antes tomar bañarme autobús.
Yo ___necesito dormir y bañarme antes de tomar el___ autobús.

5. Ana Mari la nos entonces que de la a tenemos posada ir una.
Ana Mari, ___entonces nos tenemos que ir de la posada a la___ una.

B. Responde. Write the answers to the following questions.

1. ¿A dónde se van el domingo los chicos? ___El domingo se van a Puerto Vallarta.___

2. ¿Por qué Sofía va a acostarse temprano el sábado? ___Porque el autobús sale a las siete de la mañana.___

3. ¿Qué prefiere hacer Manolo el sábado? ___Manolo prefiere no dormir.___

4. ¿Qué van a hacer en Puerto Vallarta? ___Se van a juntar con unos amigos de Odette.___

5. ¿Dónde se queda a dormir Ana Mari? ___Ana Mari se queda a dormir en casa de Odette.___

Objetivos comunicativos

In this episode, you will practice:

✓ saying how you feel and where you are

✓ talking about past activities

Escenas de la vida: La posada

Video
CD-ROM

Audio
CD-ROM

Instructor's Resources
- Overheads
- VHS Video
- Worktext CD
- Website
- IRM: Videoscript, Comprehensible input

A. ¡Mira cuánto puedes entender! Indica en qué secuencia ocurrieron las actividades de la posada, según la **Escena**.

7

Ana Mari **está feliz** porque todos quieren bailar con ella.

2

La mitad de los invitados **están en el jardín**.

6

Manolo **tocó** la guitarra.

4

Empezó a llover y los mayores **corrieron** a la casa.

9

Sofía **está en su cuarto**.

5

Los niños **se quedaron** afuera. **Están ocupados** recogiendo dulces.

3

Todos **cantaron** los versos tradicionales.

8

Ramón **está molesto** con Ana Mari.

1

Sofía **está enferma** porque **comió** demasiado pozole.

Video Synopsis. Sofía describes the **posada** from her room in Odette's house; she is sick and unable to attend. Her friends are having a good time there, but the **posada** is driven indoors when it starts to rain. Her friends visit Sofía to update her on the events.

Video
CD-ROM

B. ¿Te diste cuenta? Indica si los comentarios son **ciertos** o **falsos,** según ocurre en la **Escena**.

Audio
CD-ROM

	Cierto	Falso
1. Los niños no recogen los dulces de la piñata.	☐	☑
2. Todos los invitados llegaron a la casa de Odette.	☑	☐
3. Empezó a llover, pero los niños corrieron por sus dulces.	☑	☐
4. Las personas de afuera se quedan afuera toda la noche.	☐	☑
5. Al pedir posada, hay personas dentro y fuera de la casa.	☑	☐
6. Hay comida, bebidas y música toda la noche.	☑	☐

Video
CD-ROM

C. ¿Quién? Indica quién se siente *(feels)* así en la posada: Sofía (**S**), Ana Mari (**AM**), Manolo (**M**), Ramón (**R**), Odette (**O**) o los niños (**LN**).

Audio
CD-ROM

Sofía	Ana Mari	Manolo	Ramón	Odette

_**LN**_ 1. Están emocionados de comer dulces y jugar en la lluvia.

_**O**_ 2. Está muy contenta porque todo va muy bien.

_**AM**_ 3. Está feliz porque está de vacaciones.

_**R**_ 4. Está enojado.

_**M**_ 5. Está emocionado porque es la primera vez que va a México.

_**S**_ 6. Está en cama y solamente escucha la música y la risa *(laughter)* de los invitados.

Cultura a lo vivo

Even though Spanish speakers and English speakers, like all cultural groups, get together to enjoy each other's company, their parties differ in substantial ways. For most Spanish speakers, a party is only a **fiesta** if there is music, dancing, food, and drinks. Gatherings without dancing are called **reuniones** in Mexico and **tertulias** in Spain.

A **posada** is a special **fiesta** that takes place between December 17 and 23. Family and friends of all ages reenact the biblical story of Mary and Joseph's search for shelter before the birth of Jesus.

En esta fiesta, los niños están emocionados porque ya es hora de romper la piñata. Todos están listos con sus bolsitas para poner los dulces que van a recoger.

Práctica adicional

| Cuaderno de tareas WB p.389, A–C | Video CD-ROM Episodio 15 |

Para comunicarnos mejor

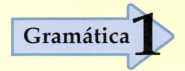

Gramática **1**

Saying how you feel and where you are
• <u>Estar</u> + [*adjective*], <u>estar</u> + [*location*]

In the **Escena**, you heard these statements:

Ahora **estoy enferma**.	*Now I'm sick.*
Odette **está** muy **contenta**.	*Odette is very happy.*
Estoy feliz; estoy de vacaciones.	*I'm happy; I'm on vacation.*
Ramón **está molesto** conmigo...	*Ramón is upset with me...*
Los niños **están emocionados** de comer dulces.	*The kids are excited about eating candies.*

1. You have used the verb **estar** to find out how someone is (**¿Cómo estás?**) and to tell where someone is (**Estoy en mi casa**). **Estar** is also used to express how you are feeling at a particular time.

2. **Enferma, contenta, molesto,** and **emocionados** are adjectives and match the gender (masculine or feminine) and number (singular or plural) of the nouns they describe.

3. Adjectives ending in **-e** or **-z,** such as **feliz,** match with nouns only in number.

Para describir cómo estás (*To describe how you feel*)

A veces estoy...	Sometimes I am...		
aburrido/a	*bored*	**libre**	*free*
borracho/a	*drunk*	**listo/a**	*ready*
cansado/a	*tired*	**molesto/a**	*upset*
contento/a	*happy*	**nervioso/a**	*nervous*
desilusionado/a	*disappointed*	**ocupado/a**	*busy*
emocionado/a	*excited*	**preocupado/a**	*worried*
enfermo/a	*sick*	**tranquilo/a**	*calm*
enojado/a	*angry*	**triste**	*sad*

4. Here are some expressions of location that are used with **estar**.

Estar + [*location*]

¿Dónde están los personajes?	*Where are the characters?*
Están de vacaciones.	*They are on vacation.*
Odette está adentro.	*Odette is inside.*
Ramón está afuera, en el jardín.	*Ramón is outside, in the garden.*
Yo estoy en cama.	*I am in bed.*
Y tú estás en la clase de español, ¿verdad?	*And you are in Spanish class, right?*

5. Use **dentro de** and **fuera de** followed by a place; use **adentro** and **afuera** when no location follows.

—¿Quién dejó la leche **fuera del** refrigerador?   —Ay, perdón, yo la dejé **afuera.**

PRÁCTICA

A. Los opuestos. Completa las descripciones de las personas en la posada.

1. Odette no está triste; está <u>contenta</u>.

2. Ramón no está contento; está <u>enojado</u>.

3. Sofía no está sana *(healthy)*; está <u>enferma</u>.

4. Los niños no están desilusionados; están <u>emocionados</u>.

5. Manolo no está preocupado; está <u>tranquilo</u>.

B. Causas. Con un(a) compañero/a empareja cada columna para formar frases lógicas en voz alta *(out loud).* Usa **porque** or **por eso** para unir las ideas.

> **Modelo**   Odette está emocionada porque su amiga Sofía va a estar en su casa dos semanas.

B. Give students a few minutes to read and compose logical sentences, then pick some students to read them aloud.

1. Odette está preocupada
porque Sofía está enferma.
2. Ramón y Ana Mari están libres
por eso van a ir a Guadalajara de vacaciones.
3. Los niños están enojados
porque llueve y no pueden salir a jugar.
4. Wayne está muy ocupado
por eso no puede ir a Guadalajara con Ramón.
5. Manolo está un poco nervioso
porque no le gusta tocar la guitarra en público.
6. Los amigos de Odette están desilusionados
porque Ana Mari no quiere bailar con ellos.

por eso

porque

a. van a ir a Guadalajara de vacaciones.

b. llueve y no pueden salir a jugar.

c. Sofía está enferma.

d. Ana Mari no quiere bailar con ellos.

e. no puede ir a Guadalajara con Ramón.

f. no le gusta tocar la guitarra en público.

C. ¿Cómo estás? Usa expresiones con **estar** para describir cómo estás en las siguientes situaciones. Answers will vary.

1. Mañana tengo un examen muy difícil; por eso, _____.

2. Los martes tengo cuatro clases y trabajo seis horas; por eso, _____.

3. Mi pareja admira a otras/os chicas/os, _____.

4. Mis padres me dan dinero, _____.

5. Mis amigos no me llaman, _____.

6. Quiero ir al parque y empieza a llover, _____.

7. Hace muchísimo calor, _____.

8. Es hora de estar en clase y no estoy listo/a, _____.

Práctica adicional

Cuaderno de tareas
WB pp.390–391, D–G

 **Gramática 2** Talking about past activities
• Introduction to the preterit tense

Analizar y descubrir

In the **Escena**, you heard these statements:

Manolo **tocó** la guitarra y **cantó...**   *Manolo played the guitar and sang...*
Comí demasiado pozole.   *I ate too much **pozole**.*
...los mayores **corrieron** a la casa.   *...the grown-ups ran into the house.*

1. **Tocó, cantó, comí,** and **corrieron** are preterit (past tense) forms of the verbs **tocar, cantar, comer,** and **correr.**

Study the examples and answer the questions.

Bailar	
Yo **bailé** toda la noche.	*I danced all night.*
Y tú, ¿**bailaste** con Manolo?	*And you, did you dance with Manolo?*
Manolo no **bailó** con Ana Mari.	*Manolo didn't dance with Ana Mari.*
Nosotras **bailamos** con Ramón.	*We danced with Ramón.*
¿Ustedes **bailaron** hasta tarde? ¿Vosotros **bailasteis** hasta tarde? }	*Did you dance until late?*
Los niños también **bailaron**.	*The kids also danced.*

2. In the preterit, the endings of **-er** verbs and **-ir** verbs are identical.

Comer	
Yo **comí** mucho.	*I ate a lot.*
Y tú, ¿**comiste** tamales?	*And you, did you eat tamales?*
Sofía **comió** demasiado pozole.	*Sofía ate too much pozole.*
Nosotros no **comimos** dulces.	*We didn't eat candy.*
¿Ustedes **comieron** pastel? ¿Vosotros **comisteis** pastel? }	*Did you eat cake?*
¡Los niños **comieron** muchos dulces!	*The kids ate a lot of candy!*

3. Now complete the conjugations of **hablar, beber,** and **escribir.**

El pretérito de los verbos regulares			
	-ar	**-er**	**-ir**
	hablar	**beber**	**escribir**
yo	hablé	bebí	escribí
tú	hablaste	bebiste	escribiste
usted/él/ella	habló	bebió	escribió
nosotros/as	hablamos	bebimos	escribimos
ustedes/ellos/as	hablaron	bebieron	escribieron

a. What are the preterit endings for regular verbs in the **yo** form? -é and -í.

b. What are the endings for the **tú** form? -aste and -iste.

c. What are the endings for the **él, ella,** and **usted** form? -ó and -ió.

d. What are the endings for regular verbs in the **nosotros/as** form? -amos and -imos.

e. How are the **-ar nosotros/as** forms different from the present tense endings?
They are identical.

f. What are the preterit endings for the **ellos, ellas,** and **ustedes** form? -aron and -ieron.

4. The following are three common irregular verbs.

El pretérito de **ir, hacer** y **tener**	
ir	fui, fuiste, fue, fuimos, fueron
hacer	hice, hiciste, hizo, hicimos, hicieron
tener	tuve, tuviste, tuvo, tuvimos, tuvieron

—¿Adónde **fue** Adriana durante las vacaciones? — *Where did Adriana go during her vacation?*

—No **fue** a ninguna parte porque **tuvo** que trabajar. — *She didn't go anywhere because she had to work.*

—Y tú, ¿qué **hiciste**? — *What did you do?*

—**Fui** a Guadalajara. — *I went to Guadalajara.*

Instructor's Resource
• IRM: Additional Activities

5. Verbs ending in **-ar** and **-er** that have stem changes (e → ie, o → ue) in the present tense will not have those changes in the preterit tense. Compare the two tenses:

Additional Activity.
See the IRM for activities to practice the new vocabulary and the preterit.

present — preterit
Ramón **juega** fútbol, pero durante las vacaciones no **jugó**.

present — preterit
El partido nunca **empieza** a tiempo, y ayer tampoco **empezó** a tiempo.

6. Verbs ending in **-gar (llegar, pagar), -car (sacar, tocar),** and **-zar (empezar, organizar)** have spelling changes in the **yo** form.

El semestre pasado lle**gué** a tiempo a todas mis clases. Pa**gué** todas mis deudas *(debts)*. También to**qué** la guitarra en la banda de la escuela. Y lo mejor es que sa**qué** buenas notas porque empe**cé** a trabajar menos y a estudiar más; hasta organi**cé** un grupo de estudio con mis compañeros.

7. The following are some of the expressions used with the preterit tense to indicate past time.

Algunas expresiones para hablar del pasado			
ayer	*yesterday*	hace dos semanas	*two weeks ago*
anoche	*last night*	hace tres meses	*three months ago*
la semana pasada	*last week*	hace cuatro años	*four years ago*
el mes pasado	*last month*	esta mañana	*this morning*
el año pasado	*last year*	durante cinco años	*for five years*

PRÁCTICA

D. ¿Por qué estás así? Une las columnas con una línea para crear oraciones lógicas usando la palabra **porque.**

> **Modelo**   **Estoy contenta porque saqué A en mi examen de inglés.**

1. Estoy nerviosa porque
2. Mi hija está triste
3. Estoy enfermo
4. Los niños están felices
5. Manolo y yo estamos cansados
6. Ramón está enojado

porque

a. recibieron mucho dinero para su cumpleaños.
b. comí demasiados mariscos.
c. jugamos fútbol toda la mañana.
d. tuvo que comprar muchos libros este semestre.
e. no encontró su bolsa.
f. no estudié para el examen que voy a tomar hoy.

E. ¿Qué hiciste ayer?

Parte 1. Indica si hiciste estas actividades la semana pasada. Después entrevista a tu compañero/a para ver si hicieron las mismas cosas.   Answers will vary.

	Sí	No
1. Me bañé muy temprano.	☐	☐
2. Lavé la ropa.	☐	☐
3. Limpié mi cuarto.	☐	☐
4. Comí en un restaurante elegante.	☐	☐
5. Visité a mis abuelos/papás.	☐	☐
6. Me quedé en casa toda la tarde.	☐	☐
7. Fui a un lugar divertido.	☐	☐
8. Tuve que trabajar.	☐	☐
9. Hice toda mi tarea.	☐	☐
10. Me acosté a las diez de la noche.	☐	☐

Parte 2. Cambia las oraciones a preguntas para entrevistar a tu compañero/a. Después escribe acerca de lo que hizo tu compañero/a.

> **Modelo**   —Jim, ¿lavaste la ropa la semana pasada?
> —Sí, la lavé. ¿Y tú?
> —Yo también.   o   —Yo no.

¡Fíjate!

Use **lo, la, los,** and **las** when you have a direct object. Remember, not all verbs take a direct object.

F. ¿Adónde fuiste?

Parte 1. Indica a qué lugares fueron las personas según lo que hicieron.   Answers will vary.

> **Modelo**   Ayer hice mucho ejercicio.
> **Fuiste al gimnasio.**

1. La semana pasada compré una blusa nueva.

   _____

2. Ana Mari y Ramón vieron una película muy interesante.

   _____

3. Ayer jugué a las cartas con Manolo.

   _____

4. Anoche Adriana estudió con sus compañeros.

   _____

5. Hace tres días comí comida china.

   _____

6. El domingo pasado hicimos un picnic para Wayne.

   _____

7. El verano pasado tomé el sol y nadé.

   _____

8. El sábado pasado Ana Mari bailó toda la noche.

   _____

 Parte 2. Ahora habla con un(a) compañero/a sobre tres cosas que hiciste la semana pasada.
Answers will vary.

G. Ana Mari escribe a casa. Escribe el pretérito de los verbos entre paréntesis para completar la carta de Ana Mari.

Queridos papá y mamá:

Ayer Ramón y yo (1) _____fuimos_____ (ir) a casa de Odette porque ella
(2) _____hizo_____ (hacer) una posada fantástica.
Yo (3) _____bailé_____ (bailar) toda la noche y (4) _____comí_____
(comer) de todo: tamales, pozole, taquitos, etc.
También (5) _____cantamos_____ (cantar; nosotros) las canciones típicas
navideñas y de posada. ¡Hacía mucho que no me divertía tanto! A la
hora de romper la piñata (6) _____empezó_____ (empezar) a llover y todos
(7) _____corrimos_____ (correr) a la casa. Los niños (8) _____comieron_____
(comer) muchos dulces y (9) _____jugaron_____ (jugar) en la lluvia. Pobre
Sofía (10) _____comió_____ (comer) tanto pozole el día anterior que se
enfermó y no (11) _____fue_____ (ir) a la posada. ¡Pobrecita!

H. ¿Qué hicieron? Usa las fotos para escribir qué hicieron Sofía y Wayne el domingo. Ordena los eventos lógicamente. Usa **por la mañana, después, a las ... de la noche,** etc. Answers will vary.

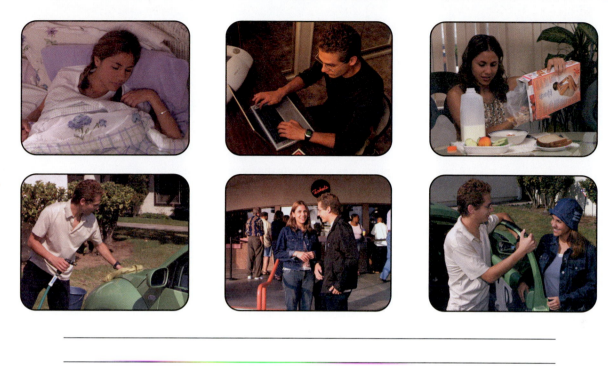

_____

_____

_____

_____

_____

_____

I. ¡A hablar! En grupos de tres personas, hablen de sus actividades de un fin de semana divertido. Por lo menos, tienen que mencionar cinco actividades.   Answers will vary.

> **Modelo**   Hace un mes fui a un juego de vóleibol. Después, mis compañeros y yo fuimos a comer. Por la noche, salí con unas amigas; vimos una película muy buena.

J. Todos a bordo. Escucha el mensaje que hay en tu correo de voz *(voicemail)* para contestar las preguntas.

Audio
CD-ROM

Instructor's Resources
• Worktext CD
• IRM: Tapescript

Script. For the script to this activity, see the Instructor's Resource Manual.

1. ¿Qué ganaste? Gané un viaje para dos personas en un crucero.

2. ¿En qué fecha lo tienes que tomar? El 27 de diciembre.

3. ¿Qué tiempo hace en invierno? Siempre hace sol y la temperatura promedio es de ochenta grados Fahrenheit.

4. ¿Cuáles son las actividades del barco? Jugar tenis y ping-pong, hacer ejercicio, tomar clases de aeróbicos o descansar.

5. ¿Qué actividades se pueden hacer en cada puerto? Visitar la ciudad, cenar, ir de compras o quedarse en el barco para ir al casino, bailar o escuchar música.

6. ¿Qué necesitas hacer para aceptar el premio? Necesito confirmar mi participación y y reservar antes del 15 de diciembre.

Práctica adicional

Cuaderno de tareas
WB pp.391–394, H–N
LM pp.397–398, A–B, Pron.

Audio
CD-ROM
Episodio 15

Actividades comunicativas

A. Un día en la guardería "El Porvenir".

Instrucciones para **Estudiante 1**

Tú eres el/la supervisor(a) en la guardería "El Porvenir". Hoy hablas con un(a) empleado/a nuevo/a. Dile cómo se llaman los niños con quienes va a trabajar. También dile lo que sabes de cada niño. Tu compañero/a empieza con una pregunta. Answers will vary.

> **Modelo** La niña que lleva la blusa rosa se llama Eliana.
> Está contenta porque es su cumpleaños y recibió muchos regalos.

Eliana
Today is her birthday and she got many presents.

Noni and Laura
They are going on vacation tomorrow.

Juan
He does not like the music.

Maggie
Mario did not play with her all day.

Iván and Rubén
They do not know anybody because it's their first day.

Concetta
She has new shoes.

Mario
He went to bed at midnight.

Tommy
He ate Maggie's crayons (**crayolas**).

Brandon
Noni and Laura do not want to talk to him.

Modelo —¿Cómo se llama la niña que lleva una blusa rosa?
—¿Por qué está contenta?

la información de cada niño. Tú empiezas.
que preguntar por qué están contentos, tristes, preocupados, enojados, etc. Escribe
supervisor(a) cómo se llaman los niños con quienes vas a trabajar. También tienes
Hoy es tu primer día de trabajo en la guardería "El Porvenir". Pregúntale a tu

Instrucciones para Estudiante 2

A. Un día en la guardería "El Porvenir".

B. La historia va así.

Audio
CD-ROM

Parte 1. Escucha lo que hizo Sofía la semana pasada y mira las ilustraciones. Identifica el orden, del uno al ocho, en que ocurrieron los eventos. Escucha una vez más para verificar tus respuestas.

Instructor's Resources
• Worktext CD
• IRM: Tapescript

B. Play the CD or read the text. Then replay/repeat the text so students can verify their answers. Have students recount the story based on the numbers. You may have students write their own stories, which they should then share in groups or with the class.

Script. *El viernes fui a estudiar cálculo con Adriana y Manolo. Hablamos de las clases que vamos a tomar el próximo semestre y conversamos de nuestras vacaciones. Después hice un poco de ejercicio con Ana Mari. Llegué a casa como a las seis, escuché un poco de música antes de irme a dormir. Al día siguiente, hablé con Manolo por la mañana, pero no salí de casa. Escribí un trabajo en la computadora y luego lavé la ropa. Por la tarde tomé el autobús para ir al centro comercial a comprar algo de ropa para mis vacaciones en Guadalajara.*

_7_ a

_6_ e

_3_ b

_1_ f

_4_ c

_5_ g

_2_ d

_8_ h

 Parte 2. Ahora en grupos escriban una historia diferente.   Answers will vary.

C. Las actividades de mis compañeros.

Parte 1. En la columna **B**, escribe **yo** junto a las actividades que sí hiciste la semana pasada. Después entrevista a tus compañeros para llenar *(to fill)* todos los espacios en las dos columnas con sus nombres. Answers will vary.

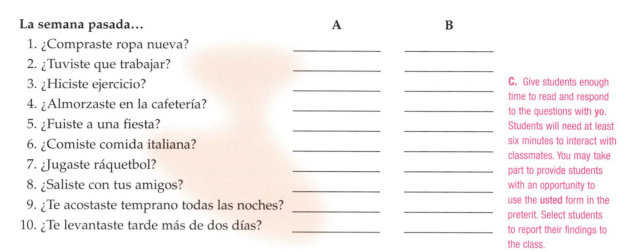

	La semana pasada…	A	B
1.	¿Compraste ropa nueva?	_____	_____
2.	¿Tuviste que trabajar?	_____	_____
3.	¿Hiciste ejercicio?	_____	_____
4.	¿Almorzaste en la cafetería?	_____	_____
5.	¿Fuiste a una fiesta?	_____	_____
6.	¿Comiste comida italiana?	_____	_____
7.	¿Jugaste ráquetbol?	_____	_____
8.	¿Saliste con tus amigos?	_____	_____
9.	¿Te acostaste temprano todas las noches?	_____	_____
10.	¿Te levantaste tarde más de dos días?	_____	_____

C. Give students enough time to read and respond to the questions with **yo**. Students will need at least six minutes to interact with classmates. You may take part to provide students with an opportunity to use the **usted** form in the preterit. Select students to report their findings to the class.

Parte 2. Escribe un informe con la información que tienes. Incluye por lo menos seis oraciones. Necesitas estar preparado/a para compartir la información con la clase.

> **Modelo**   Ana y yo compramos ropa nueva.
> Tom y Alex tuvieron que trabajar.
> Sharon almorzó en la cafetería.

Invitación a **México**

Del álbum de *Sofía*

Muchos de los elementos de la cultura mexicana conocidos en todo el mundo provienen del estado de Jalisco, cuya capital es Guadalajara. De ahí vienen los mariachis, los charros y charreadas: fiestas en rodeos donde se combinan las habilidades artísticas con el colorido y belleza de la ropa, las técnicas en el manejo del caballo y la elegancia del jinete *(rider)*; los palenques (ferias donde hay cantantes y peleas de gallos) y mucha de la "comida mexicana" es originaria de Jalisco. También, grandes escritores mexicanos como Juan Rulfo y Mariano Azuela son jaliscienses.

Práctica adicional

Website
vistahigher
learning.com

La correspondencia

 El correo: Manolo escribe desde Guadalajara. Manolo les escribe a sus padres una carta desde Guadalajara comentándoles su visita a México. Léela y contesta las preguntas.

1. ¿Qué es una posada? ¿Qué hacen los invitados en una posada? <u>Es una fiesta.</u>
   <u>Comen y se divierten.</u>

2. ¿Dónde está Manolo? ¿Qué tiempo hace allí? <u>Está en Guadalajara; hace buen tiempo.</u>
   _____

3. ¿Adónde van Manolo y sus amigos por las noches? <u>Van a cantar, bailar y escuchar música.</u>
   _____

4. ¿Adónde fueron? ¿Qué lugares conocieron? <u>Fueron al Museo Regional, Tlaquepaque, al Teatro Degollado y</u>
   <u>al Hospicio Cabañas.</u>

Queridos papás: Guadalajara, 26 de diciembre

Espero que estén bien. Yo nunca he pasado[1] mejores vacaciones. Odette y su familia son muy amables. Anteayer hicieron una posada fabulosa aquí en la casa de Odette. Comí muchos platos típicos mexicanos que no conocía. Me estoy divirtiendo como no tienen idea.

Guadalajara es una ciudad realmente bonita. Tiene zonas supermodernas y zonas coloniales; tiene árboles y flores por todas partes, pues el clima es ideal para las plantas (llueve bastante y hace calor, pero no tiene clima tropical). El lunes pasado fuimos al Museo Regional de Guadalajara, donde hay una colección de artículos de la revolución y de la independencia mexicana. También hay unas pinturas fabulosas de los mejores artistas regionales y nacionales.

Otro día visitamos el mercado de Tlaquepaque donde venden artesanía, comida típica y todo lo que se puedan imaginar. Yo no sabía que la artesanía mexicana era tan bonita y fina. Hacen una cosas de plata, cobre, latón, barro y vidrio[2], que son unas obras de arte. Compré muchas cosas y no pagué mucho.

Por las noches hay mil cosas que hacer. Una noche cantamos y bailamos en la Plaza del Mariachi, donde se pueden escuchar varios grupos de mariachis, y no se paga nada a menos que uno pida que canten algo. También fuimos a escuchar al grupo de rock Maná, unos muchachos jóvenes con mucho talento, que son de Guadalajara.

Otra noche fuimos al Teatro Degollado a ver el ballet folclórico de la Universidad de Guadalajara. Compré un video del ballet para ustedes. Les va a gustar mucho el vestuario, la música, los bailes, la alegría... ¡tienen que verlo!

En el Hospicio Cabañas están los famosos murales de Orozco. Hay unos frescos enormes, llenos de color y, lo más importante, con contenido social.

Bueno, ya tengo que irme a dormir porque mañana tenemos que madrugar[3]; salimos para Puerto Vallarta. Les mando un beso y los llamo cuando regrese a Estados Unidos.

                                        Su hijo que los quiere,
                                        Manolo

---

[1]*have spent* [2]**plata,...** *silver, copper, brass, clay, and glass* [3]*get up early (at dawn)*

En papel: Una celebración familiar. Escríbele una carta a Odette sobre un evento o una fiesta que celebraste con tu familia. Answers will vary.

Incluye la siguiente información:

- dónde fue
- cuándo fue
- qué celebraron
- qué actividades hicieron
- quiénes fueron
- qué ropa llevaste
- qué comiste

En papel. The past tense must be used in their composition. Encourage students to include pictures in their descriptions. Students should read about each others' celebrations and ask each other questions. You may also have students share their writing in groups of four. Review the ¡Fíjate! note with them.

Writing Strategy: Using simple language to express your ideas

You may feel frustrated when you cannot communicate your ideas in written Spanish as well as you can in English. For this reason, you may make the mistake of using a dictionary and creating sentences that Spanish speakers would not be able to understand. A much more effective strategy is to limit your messages to what you are able to communicate.

You have just read Manolo's letter. By using your background knowledge, and context, you were probably able to understand most of the text. But you are probably not yet able to use that level of language to communicate your own ideas.

For example, in the letter you read this about Guadalajara: **En el Hospicio Cabañas están los famosos murales de Orozco. Hay unos frescos enormes, llenos de color y ... contenido social...** Although you cannot yet write a similar description, you can write something like: **En el Hospicio Cabañas hay unos murales muy bonitos e interesantes,** which any Spanish speaker would understand. Using simple language enables you to express yourself effectively while you build your writing communication skills.

¡Fíjate!

Remember to create an outline in simple Spanish. Write a first draft with your ideas. Then use connectors to join your sentences. In the final draft, check vocabulary and grammar.

Video
CD-ROM

Audio
CD-ROM

Instructor's Resources
• VHS Video
• Worktext CD
• IRM: Videoscript

¡A ver de nuevo!

Parte 1. Escucha la narración de **Escenas de la vida** o mira el video para hacer un resumen que conteste todas las preguntas. Answers will vary.

1. ¿Qué hacen las personas a la hora de pedir posada?
2. ¿Por qué está contenta Odette?
3. ¿Por qué está feliz Ana Mari?
4. ¿Qué hizo Manolo en la posada?
5. ¿Qué pasó con Sofía? ¿Por qué no fue a la posada?

Parte 2. Ahora trabaja con un(a) compañero/a para añadir lo que te haya faltado.

Práctica adicional		
Cuaderno de tareas WB pp.394–395, Ñ LM p. 398, A–B	Audio CD-ROM Episodio 15	Website vistahigher learning.com

Vocabulario del Episodio 15

Para describir cómo estás

A veces estoy…	Sometimes I am…
aburrido/a	*bored*
borracho/a	*drunk*
cansado/a	*tired*
contento/a	*happy*
desilusionado/a	*disappointed*
emocionado/a	*excited*
enfermo/a	*sick*
enojado/a	*angry*
libre	*free*
listo/a	*ready*
molesto/a	*upset*
nervioso/a	*nervous*
ocupado/a	*busy*
preocupado/a	*worried*
tranquilo/a	*quiet, calm*
triste	*sad*

Estar + [*location*]

estar…	to be…
adentro/dentro de	*inside*
afuera/fuera de	*outside*
en cama	*in bed*
en clase	*in class*
de vacaciones	*on vacation*

Algunas expresiones para hablar del pasado

ayer	*yesterday*	**hace dos semanas**	*two weeks ago*
anoche	*last night*	**hace tres meses**	*three months ago*
la semana pasada	*last week*	**hace cuatro años**	*four years ago*
el mes pasado	*last month*	**esta mañana**	*this morning*
el año pasado	*last year*	**durante cinco años**	*for five years*

Vocabulario personal

In this section, write all the words you need to know in order to better talk about your own activities.

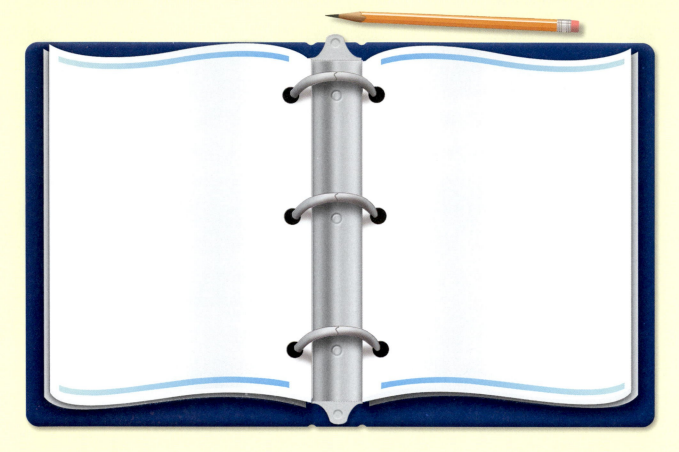

¡A escribir!

Episodio **15**

Escenas de la vida: La posada

Video
CD-ROM

A. ¡A ver cuánto entendiste! Match the sentences with their translations.

_f_ 1. La otra mitad se queda dentro de la casa.

_c_ 2. Ya es hora de pedir posada.

_e_ 3. Los niños decidieron recoger los dulces y juguetes.

_a_ 4. Están emocionados de romper la piñata.

_b_ 5. Empezó a llover.

_d_ 6. Todos tienen una vela y los versos tradicionales.

a. They're excited about breaking the piñata.

b. It began to rain.

c. It's time to ask for shelter.

d. Everyone has a candle and the traditional verses.

e. The kids decided to pick up the candies and toys.

f. The other half stays in the house.

Video
CD-ROM

B. ¿Quién se siente así? *(Who feels that way?)* Indicate who the following statements describe: Sofía (**S**), Manolo (**M**), Ramón (**R**), Ana Mari (**AM**), or Odette (**O**).

_AM_ 1. Está desilusionada porque Manolo no bailó con ella.

_S_ 2. No puede usar su vestido elegante ni sus zapatos de tacón.

_R_ 3. Está molesto porque llegaron tarde a la posada.

_AM_ 4. Está feliz porque está de vacaciones.

_M_ 5. Está emocionado porque es la primera vez que va a México.

_O_ 6. Está muy contenta porque su posada va muy bien.

Video
CD-ROM

C. La posada. Use the words to complete the description.

pozole	organizó	enferma	bailar
cuidar	cama	tocó	cantó

Todos los invitados se divierten mucho en la posada que Odette (1) ___organizó___.
Todos los muchachos quieren (2) ___bailar___ con Ana Mari. Ramón está molesto.
Cree que todavía tiene que (3) ___cuidar___ a su hermana. Manolo (4) ___tocó___
la guitarra y (5) ___cantó___. Sofía está en la (6) ___cama___. Está (7) ___enferma___.
Comió demasiado (8) ___pozole___.

Gramática 1

Saying how you feel and where you are
•<u>Estar</u> + [*adjective*], <u>estar</u> + [*location*]

D. Usa la lógica. Combine elements from the three columns to make logical sentences.

1. estoy aburrido/a		podemos irnos en este momento
2. estamos cansados/as		vamos a descansar y dormir un rato
3. estoy listo/a		comiste muchos tacos de pescado
4. mi novio/a está molesto/a	porque	todos están en casa
5. mi papá está tranquilo	por eso	sacaron F en el examen
6. los chicos están preocupados		mis amigos están ocupados y no pueden salir conmigo
7. tú estás enfermo/a		no la/o llamé por teléfono anoche

1. Mis amigos están ocupados y no pueden salir conmigo; por eso, estoy aburrido/a.

2. Vamos a descansar y dormir un rato porque estamos cansados/as.

3. Estoy listo/a; por eso, podemos irnos en este momento.

4. Mi novio/a está molesto/a porque no la/o llamé por teléfono anoche.

5. Mi papá está tranquilo porque todos están en casa.

6. Los chicos están preocupados porque sacaron F en el examen.

7. Tú estás enfermo/a porque comiste muchos tacos de pescado.

E. ¿Por qué estás así? Complete the following statements in a logical manner.   Answers will vary.

> **Modelo**   Estoy triste porque mis amigos no me invitan a sus fiestas.

1. Estoy aburrido/a porque _____.

2. Estoy cansado/a porque _____.

3. Mi mamá está enojada conmigo porque _____.

4. Estoy molesto/a porque _____.

5. Estoy tranquilo/a porque _____.

6. Estoy contento/a porque _____.

7. Estoy triste porque _____.

8. Mis padres están preocupados porque _____.

F. Un día muy interesante. Describe how people in the images feel, where they are, and the reason they feel that way using any expression with **estar.** Answers will vary.

_____

_____

_____

_____

_____

_____

G. ¿Dónde está Migdalia? Describe where Manolo's cat, Migdalia, is, using **en, dentro del,** and **afuera.**

1. Migdalia, la gata de Manolo, a veces está _____afuera_____ .

2. Otras veces está _____en_____ la cama de Manolo.

3. Pero cuando Manolo no está, a la gata le gusta estar _____dentro del_____ cajón (*drawer*) de los suéteres.

Gramática 2
Talking about past activities
• Introduction to the preterit tense

H. ¡Dime más! When Manolo mentions the things he did last week, Ramón follows every statement with a question. What does Ramón ask?

Modelo	Manolo	Hablé por teléfono con mis padres.
	Ramón	¿Y cómo están?

Manolo	**Ramón**
b 1. Salí con Ana Mari.	a. ¿Para quién?
c 2. Fui a un concierto.	b. ¿Adónde fueron?
g 3. Vi una buena película.	c. ¿A qué grupo escuchaste?

___e___ 4. Aprendí una canción nueva
 en la guitarra.

___f___ 5. Almorcé comida cubana.

___h___ 6. Llegué tarde a clase.

___d___ 7. Trabajé hasta las tres de la mañana.

___a___ 8. Escribí un poema.

d. ¿Y tienes que trabajar hoy también?

e. ¿Tuviste que practicar mucho?

f. ¿Qué comiste?

g. ¿Ah sí, cuál?

h. ¿Hablaste con la profesora?

I. Explicaciones. Complete the statements logically using verbs in the preterit. Answers will vary.

> **Modelo** Estoy cansada porque **ayer trabajé mucho.**

1. Estoy enfermo/a porque _____.
2. Estoy desilusionado/a porque _____.
3. Estoy molesto/a porque _____.
4. Estoy nervioso/a porque _____.
5. Estoy libre porque _____.
6. Estoy emocionado/a porque _____.

J. ¿Qué hicieron en la playa? Use the illustration to complete Sofía's description with the following verbs: **jugar, hacer, hablar, comer, ir, beber,** and **descansar.**

Ayer, (1) _____fui_____ a la playa con todos mis amigos. Por suerte (2) _____hizo_____ muy buen tiempo: calor y sol. Ana Mari y yo (3) _____jugamos_____ vóleibol un par de horas. Manolo no (4) _____jugó_____ con nosotras; leyó el periódico y (5) _____descansó_____ en una hamaca. Odette (6) _____habló_____ mucho con Ramón. Ellos (7) _____comieron_____ camarones y (8) _____bebieron_____ refrescos.

K. Los problemas de Adriana. Describe what happened in Adriana's house last weekend. Use the illustrations to describe what she did.

Nombre _____ Fecha _____

El sábado por la mañana Adriana (1) _____llevó_____ a Viviana a su clase de baile. Luego regresó a casa. Primero (2) _____lavó_____ los platos y luego (3) _____hizo/escribió_____ un trabajo en la computadora para su clase de composición. También (4) _____jugó tenis_____ con Santiago un par de horas. Llegó a casa muy cansada así que (5) _____descansó_____ un rato en el sofá de la sala. Por la noche Adriana y su amiga (6) _____fueron al cine_____. Vieron una película de misterio. El domingo en la mañana todos (7) _____visitaron_____ a los abuelos. Cuando llegaron a casa, ella (8) _____discutió_____ con Santiago otra vez; por eso, se fue a la biblioteca de la universidad a estudiar y no (9) _____regresó_____ hasta las diez de la noche.

L. Ahora te toca a ti. Tell what you did last weekend. Write at least six sentences. Answers will vary.

_____

_____

_____

_____

_____

_____

M. ¿Cuándo fue la última vez? Use the expressions to tell when you last did the following activities. Include direct object pronouns when possible. Answers will vary.

ayer	anoche	la semana pasada
hace tres meses	el mes pasado	hace un año

> **Modelo** ¿Cuándo hiciste la tarea?
> **La hice ayer por la mañana.**

1. ¿Cuándo lavaste tu coche?

_____

2. ¿Cuándo fuiste al supermercado?

_____

3. ¿Cuándo viste a tus padres?

_____

4. ¿Cuándo limpiaste tu cuarto?

_____

5. ¿Cuándo almorzaste con toda tu familia?

_____

Nombre ______________________________ Fecha ______________

N. El fin de semana pasado. Answer the questions with as much detail as you can. Answers will vary.

1. ¿Adónde fuiste el fin de semana pasado? ¿Con quién? ¿Qué hicieron ahí?

2. ¿Tuviste que trabajar? ¿Qué otras cosas tuviste que hacer?

3. ¿Te levantaste tarde o temprano? ¿Te bañaste por la mañana o por la noche?

4. ¿Comiste en un restaurante? ¿Qué comiste?

5. ¿Hiciste tarea o estudiaste? ¿Para qué clase? ¿Dónde?

Para terminar

Ñ. Cuba: El carnaval de La Habana. Read about the celebration of **Carnaval** in Havana, Cuba, and then answer the questions.

1. ¿Qué es un carnaval?

Es una fiesta popular de tradición católica que celebra con alegría y excesos el período antes de la Cuaresma.

_____

2. ¿Qué temas *(themes)* representan las comparsas en el desfile *(parade)*?

Temas históricos, folclóricos o literarios relacionados con Cuba o de carácter universal.

_____

3. ¿Por dónde pasa el desfile?

Pasa por las calles principales de la ciudad.

_____

4. ¿Qué comida se vende durante estas fiestas?

Yuca y congrí.

_____

5. En Estados Unidos, ¿hay celebraciones similares a los carnavales? ¿En dónde? ¿Cuáles son? ¿Cuándo?

Answers will vary.

_____

_____

_____

_____

_____

_____

6. ¿Asistes a esas celebraciones? ¿Las ves en la televisión? ¿Qué hacen las personas que participan?

Answers will vary.

_____

_____

_____

_____

_____

_____

En muchas ciudades de Latinoamérica se celebran carnavales que marcan el inicio de la Cuaresma[1]. El carnaval es una fiesta popular de tradición católica que celebra con alegría y excesos el período antes de la Cuaresma. El carnaval de La Habana es famoso en todo el mundo y dura varios días. Incluye un desfile donde toman parte grupos de baile y música, llamados *comparsas*. Estos grupos practican todo el año para presentar al público su habilidad e imaginación artística. Cada grupo se pone extravagantes trajes y adornos en la cabeza. Además llevan un estandarte[2] que identifica el barrio de procedencia y el tema de la coreografía (temas históricos, folclóricos o literarios relacionados con Cuba o de carácter universal).

La participación de las comparsas alterna con el desfile de numerosas e impresionantes carrozas[3] alegóricas. El desfile pasa por las calles principales

de la ciudad hasta llegar al palco presidencial donde hay un jurado[4] que determina el mejor grupo de danza y la mejor carroza. El público se divierte siguiendo la música y los pasos de los grupos; bailan, beben y comen al ritmo de tambores[5], trompetas y otros instrumentos típicos de la rica tradición musical afrocubana. A lo largo del malecón[6], la venta de yuca, congrí (arroz con frijoles negros), cerveza, malta, refrescos y ron deleita al público cubano y extranjero.

El carnaval ha estado varias veces en peligro[7] de desaparecer por motivos políticos y económicos. Fue suprimido en 1970 y a principios de los años 90. Afortunadamente y como resultado del descontento popular y el aumento del turismo, se vuelve a celebrar por las calles de la vieja ciudad el carnaval lleno de música y de esperanza para el porvenir[8].

[1]*Lent* [2]*banner* [3]*floats* [4]*(panel of) judges* [5]*drums* [6]*avenue closest to the ocean* [7]*danger*
[8]**esperanza...**_hope for the future_

Cuaderno de tareas

¡A escuchar!

Episodio

15

Comprensión

A. Un día especial en Tlaquepaque. You are going to hear Sofía and Ana Mari discuss Ana Mari's trip to Tlaquepaque, a Mexican city famous for its typical arts and crafts **(artesanías)**. Listen and then select the answers to the questions. **¡Atención!** Each question has more than one correct answer. You will hear the conversation twice.

Banco de palabras

barro	fábrica	latón	vajilla
clay	factory	brass	set of table ware
camión	**lámpara**	**lluvia**	
bus (in Mexico)	lamp	rain	

1. ¿Quiénes fueron a Tlaquepaque?
   a. Sofía   (b.) Ana Mari   (c.) Manolo   d. Ramón   e. Odette

2. ¿Qué tiempo hizo?
   a. Hizo calor.   (b.) Empezó a llover.   c. Hizo mal tiempo.   (e.) Hizo buen tiempo.

3. ¿Qué hicieron en Tlaquepaque?
   a. Bailaron.   (c.) Se sentaron en la plaza.   (e.) Escucharon a los mariachis.
   b. Comieron.   (d.) Bebieron aguas frescas.   f. Se perdieron.

4. ¿Qué compraron Ana Mari y Manolo?
   (a.) una bolsa y una chaqueta   c. una pintura   (e.) una vajilla de barro
   (b.) camisas típicas   (d.) una lámpara   f. unos libros

B. La respuesta más lógica. You will hear brief descriptions of six situations in the form of questions or statements. Choose the most logical response to each situation.

1. a. Compró un vestido muy bonito.   (b.) No encuentra su pasaporte.   c. Fue a la fiesta con sus amigos.

2. (a.) Está afuera.   b. Está enferma.   c. Está cansada.

3. a. Hace calor.   b. Hace sol.   (c.) Hace frío.

4. a. Voy a quitarme la ropa.   (b.) Necesito un impermeable.   c. Necesito un traje.

5. a. Van a una fiesta.   (b.) Llueve y no pueden salir a jugar.   c. Tienen una piñata con dulces y frutas.

6. a. Saliste con Ramón.   b. Voy a una fiesta.   (c.) Bailé toda la noche.

Pronunciación

Audio
CD-ROM

Acentuación: Parte 2. The written accent mark in Spanish is used for two different purposes. Accents are used for grammatical distinctions. Here are some examples of how they are used to distinguish between different parts of speech.

a. unstressed possessive article **mi** and stressed prepositional pronoun **mí**

¿Quieres usar **mi** lápiz?   Esta carta es para **mí.**

b. unstressed pronoun **te** and stressed noun **té**

Te levantas temprano.   ¿Quieres una taza de **té?**

c. unstressed conjunctions and stressed interrogative words

Estudio **cuando** hay examen.   **¿Cuándo** es el examen?

Es un chico **que** conozco.   **¿Qué** tiempo hace?

Accents also denote spoken stress in pronunciation. When a word ending in **–n, -s,** or a vowel is not stressed on the next-to-last syllable, an accent mark is placed on the vowel of the stressed syllable to indicate where the stress falls.

ca**fé**   auto**bús**   **nú**mero   pe**lí**cula   es**tás**   des**pués**

When a word ending in any consonant other than **–n** or **-s** is not stressed on the last syllable, the stressed syllable is likewise indicated by an accent mark.

suéter   di**fí**cil   **ár**bol   **fá**cil

When a stressed **i** or **u** fall next to a vowel, an accent mark is used to indicate the stress.

día   poli**cí**a   So**fí**a   le**í**a   libre**rí**a   gra**dú**a

Más escenas de la vida

Ana Mari, Sofía, and Manolo chat at the beach in Puerto Vallarta. Listen to their conversation, and then complete activities **A** and **B**. You will hear the conversation twice.

Audio
CD-ROM

A. ¿Quién lo dijo? Indicate who made each of the following statements in the conversation: Manolo **(M)**, Ana Mari **(AM)**, or Sofía **(S)**.

___M___ 1. Me impresionó la pintura de Orozco.   ___S___ 4. ¿Y se casó o tuvo hijos?

___S___ 2. Sus murales sólo reflejan injusticias sociales.   ___S___ 5. ¿Qué hicieron el viernes?

___AM___ 3. Vivió en Estados Unidos varios años.

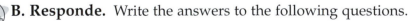

B. Responde. Write the answers to the following questions.

1. ¿Qué lugares de Estados Unidos visitó Orozco? _Visitó Nueva York y las universidades de Clairmont en California._

2. ¿A quiénes invitó la abuela a su casa? _La abuela invitó a muchos parientes a su casa._

3. ¿Después adónde los llevaron? ¿Qué hicieron ahí? _Después los llevaron a la plaza del Mariachi. Ahí_
escucharon música hasta la una de la mañana.

4. ¿Adónde fueron Sofía y Manolo? ¿Qué hicieron ahí? _Fueron al lago y comieron._

Glossary of Grammatical Terms

ADJECTIVE A word that modifies or describes a noun or pronoun.

muchos libros	un hombre **rico**
many books	*a rich man*

las mujeres **altas**
the tall women

Demonstrative adjective An adjective that points out a specific noun.

esta fiesta	**ese** chico
this party	*that boy*

aquellas flores
those flowers

Possessive adjective An adjective that indicates ownership or possession.

mi mejor vestido	Éste es **mi** hermano.
my best dress	*This is my brother*

Stressed possessive adjective A possessive adjective that emphasizes the owner or possessor.

Es un libro **mío**.
It's my book./It's a book of mine.

Es amiga **tuya**; yo no la conozco.
She's a friend of yours; I don't know her.

ADVERB A word that modifies or describes a verb, adjective, or another adverb.

Pancho escribe **rápidamente**.
Pancho writes quickly.

Este cuadro es **muy** bonito.
This picture is very pretty.

ARTICLE A word that points out either a specific (definite) noun or a non-specific (indefinite) noun.

Definite article An article that points out a specific noun.

el libro	**la** maleta
the book	*the suitcase*
los diccionarios	**las** palabras
the dictionaries	*the words*

Indefinite article An article that points out a noun in a general, non-specific way.

un lápiz	**una** computadora
a pencil	*a computer*
unos pájaros	**unas** escuelas
some birds	*some schools*

CLAUSE A group of words that contains both a conjugated verb and a subject, either expressed or implied.

Main (or Independent) clause A clause that can stand alone as a complete sentence.

Pienso ir a cenar pronto.
I plan to go to dinner soon.

Subordinate (or Dependent) clause A clause that does not express a complete thought and therefore cannot stand alone as a sentence.

Trabajo en la cafetería **porque necesito dinero para la escuela**.
I work in the cafeteria because I need money for school.

COMPARATIVE A word or construction used with an adjective or adverb to express a comparison between two people, places, or things.

Este programa es **más interesante que** el otro.
This program is more interesting than the other one.

Tomás no es **tan alto como** Alberto.
Tomás is not as tall as Alberto.

CONJUGATION A set of the forms of a verb for a specific tense or mood or the process by which these verb forms are presented.

Preterit conjugation of **cantar**

cant**é**	cant**amos**
cant**aste**	cant**asteis**
cant**ó**	cant**aron**

CONJUNCTION A word or phrase used to connect words, clauses, or phrases.

Susana es de Cuba **y** Pedro es de España.
Susana is from Cuba and Pedro is from Spain.

No quiero estudiar, **pero** tengo que hacerlo.
I don't want to study, but I have to do it.

CONTRACTION The joining of two words into one. The only contractions in Spanish are **al** and **del**.

Mi hermano fue **al** concierto ayer.
*My brother went **to the** concert yesterday.*

Saqué dinero **del** banco.
*I took money **from the** bank.*

DIRECT OBJECT A noun or pronoun that directly receives the action of the verb.

Tomás lee **el libro**.   **La** pagó ayer.
*Tomás reads **the book**.*   *She paid **it** yesterday.*

GENDER The grammatical categorizing of certain kinds of words, such as nouns and pronouns, as masculine, feminine, or neuter.

Masculine
articles **el**, un**o**
pronouns **él**, l**o**, mí**o**, ést**e**, és**e**, aquell**o**
adjective simpátic**o**

Feminine
articles **la**, un**a**
pronouns **ella**, l**a**, mí**a**, ést**a**, és**a**, aquéll**a**
adjective simpátic**a**

GERUND See Present Participle, p. 402.

IMPERSONAL EXPRESSION A third-person pl. and sing. expression with no expressed or specific subject.

Es muy importante.   **Llueve** mucho.
*It's **very important**.*   *It's **raining** hard.*

Aquí **se habla** español.   **Sirven** lasaña.
*Spanish **is spoken** here.*   *They **serve** lasagna.*

INDIRECT OBJECT A noun or pronoun that receives the action of the verb indirectly; the object, often a living being, to or for whom an action is performed.

Eduardo **le** dio un libro **a Linda**.
*Eduardo gave a book **to Linda**.*

La profesora **me** dio una C en el examen.
*The professor gave **me** a C on the test.*

INFINITIVE The basic form of a verb. Infinitives in Spanish end in **-ar**, **-er**, or **-ir**.

hablar   correr   abrir
to speak   *to run*   *to open*

INTERROGATIVE An adjective or pronoun used to ask a question.

¿**Quién** habla?   ¿**Cuántos** compraste?
***Who** is speaking?*   ***How many** did you buy?*

¿**Qué** piensas hacer hoy?
***What** do you plan to do today?*

INVERSION Changing the word order of a sentence, often to form a question.

Statement: Tu mamá vive en Boston.

Inversion: ¿(A)dónde vive tu mamá?

MOOD A grammatical distinction of verbs that indicates whether the verb is intended to make a statement or command, or to express a doubt, emotion, or condition contrary to fact.

Imperative mood Verb forms used to make commands.

Diga la verdad.   **Caminen Uds. conmigo**.
Tell the truth.   *Walk with me.*

¡**Comamos ahora**!
Let's eat now!

Indicative mood Verb forms used to state facts, actions, and states considered to be real.

Sé que **tienes** el dinero.
***I know** that **you have** the money.*

Subjunctive mood Verb forms used principally in subordinate (or dependent) clauses to express wishes, desires, emotions, doubts, and certain conditions, such as contrary-to-fact situations.

Prefieren que **hables** en español.
*They prefer that **you speak** in Spanish.*

Dudo que Luis **tenga** el dinero necesario.
*I doubt that Luis **has** the necessary money.*

NOUN A word that identifies people, animals, places, things, and ideas.

hombre   gato
man   *cat*

México   casa
Mexico   *house*

libertad
freedom

NUMBER A grammatical term that refers to singular or plural. Nouns in Spanish and English have number. Other parts of a sentence, such as adjectives, articles, and verbs, can also have number.

Singular	Plural
una cosa	**unas** cosas
a thing	*some things*
el profesor	**los** profesores
the professor	*the professors*

NUMBERS Words that represent amounts.

Cardinal numbers Words that show specific amounts.

cinco minutos
five minutes

el año **dos mil dos**
the year 2002

Ordinal numbers Words that indicate the order of a noun in a series.

el **cuarto** jugador   la **décima** hora
the fourth player   *the tenth hour*

PAST PARTICIPLE A past form of the verb used in compound tenses. The past participle may also be used as an adjective, but it must then agree in number and gender with the word it modifies.

Han **buscado** por todas partes.
They have searched everywhere.

Yo no había **estudiado** para el examen.
I hadn't studied for the exam.

Hay una **ventana rota** en la sala.
There is a broken window in the living room.

PERSON The form of the verb or pronoun that indicates the speaker, the one spoken to, or the one spoken about. In Spanish, as in English, there are three persons: first, second, and third.

Person	Singular	Plural
1st	**yo** *I*	**nosotros/as** *we*
2nd	**tú, Ud.** *you*	**vosotros/as, Uds.** *you*
3rd	**él, ella** *he/she*	**ellos, ellas** *they*

PREPOSITION A word that describes the relationship, most often in time or space, between two words.

Anita es **de** California.
Anita is from California.

La chaqueta está **en** el carro.
The jacket is in the car.

¿Quieres hablar **con** ella?
Do you want to speak to her?

PRESENT PARTICIPLE In English, a verb form that ends in *-ing*. In Spanish, the present participle ends in **–ndo**, and is often used with **estar** to form a progressive tense.

Mi hermana está **hablando** por teléfono ahora mismo.
My sister is talking on the phone right now.

PRONOUN A word that takes the place of a noun or nouns.

Demonstrative pronoun A pronoun that takes the place of a specific noun.

Quiero **ésta**.
I want this one.

¿Vas a comprar **ése**?
Are you going to buy that one?

Juan prefirió **aquéllos**.
Juan preferred those (over there).

Object pronoun A pronoun that functions as a direct or indirect object of the verb. Object pronouns may be placed before conjugated verbs or attached to an infinitive or present participle.

Te digo la verdad.
I'm telling you the truth.

Me lo trajo Juan.
Juan brought it to me.

Lo voy a llevar a la escuela.
Voy a **llevarlo** a la escuela.
I'm going to bring him to school.

Me estaba llamando por teléfono.
Estaba **llamándome** por teléfono.
She was calling me on the phone.

Reflexive pronoun A pronoun that indicates that the action of a verb is performed by the subject on itself. These pronouns are often expressed in English with -self: *myself, yourself,* etc.

Yo **me bañé** antes de salir.
*I **bathed (myself)** before going out.*

Elena **se acostó** a las once y media.
*Elena **went to bed** at eleven-thirty.*

Relative pronoun A pronoun that connects a subordinate clause to a main clause.

El chico **que** nos escribió viene a visitarnos mañana.
*The boy **who** wrote to us is coming to visit us tomorrow.*

Ya sé **lo que** tenemos que hacer.
*I already know **what** we have to do.*

Subject pronoun A pronoun that replaces the name or title of a person or thing and acts as the subject of a verb.

Tú debes estudiar más.
***You** should study more.*

Él llegó primero.
***He** arrived first.*

SUBJECT A noun or pronoun that performs the action of a verb and is often implied by the verb.

María va al supermercado.
***María** goes to the supermarket.*

(Ellos) Trabajan mucho.
***They** work hard.*

Esos **libros** son muy caros.
*Those **books** are very expensive.*

SUPERLATIVE A word or construction used with an adjective or adverb to express the highest or lowest degree of a specific quality among three or more people, places, or things.

Entre todas mis clases, ésta es la **más interesante**.
*Among all my classes, this is the **most interesting**.*

Raúl es el **menos simpático** de los chicos.
*Raúl is the **least pleasant** of the boys.*

TENSE A set of verb forms that indicates the time of an action or state: past, present, or future.

Compound tense A two-word tense made up of an auxiliary verb and a present or past participle. In Spanish, there are two auxiliary verbs: **estar** and **haber**.

En este momento, **estoy estudiando**.
*At this time, **I am studying**.*

El paquete no **ha llegado** todavía.
*The package **has** not **arrived** yet.*

Simple tense A tense expressed by a single verb form.

María **estaba** mal anoche.
*María **was** ill last night.*

Juana **hablará** con su mamá mañana.
*Juana **will** speak with her mom tomorrow.*

VERB A word that expresses actions or states-of-being.

Auxiliary verb A verb used with a present or past participle to form a compound tense. **Haber** is the most commonly used auxiliary verb in Spanish.

Los chicos **han** visto los elefantes.
*The children **have** seen the elephants.*

Espero que **hayas** comido.
*I hope you **have** eaten.*

Reflexive verb A verb that describes an action performed by the subject on itself and is always used with a reflexive pronoun.

Me compré un carro nuevo.
I bought myself *a new car.*

Pedro y Adela **se levantan** muy temprano.
*Pedro and Adela **get (themselves) up** very early.*

Spelling change verb A verb that undergoes a predictable change in spelling in order to reflect its actual pronunciation in the various conjugations.

practicar	c → qu	practico	practiqué
dirigir	g → j	dirijo	dirigí
almorzar	z → c	almorzó	almorcé

Stem-changing verb A verb whose stem vowel undergoes one or more predictable changes in the various conjugations.

entender (i → ie)	entiendo
pedir (e → i)	piden
dormir (o → ue, u)	duermo, durmieron

403

Verb conjugation tables

The verb lists

The list of verbs below and the model-verb tables that start on page 406 show you how to conjugate every verb taught in **INVITACIONES**. Each verb in the list is followed by a model verb conjugated according to the same pattern. The number in parentheses indicates where in the tables you can find the conjugated forms of the model verb. If you want to find out how to conjugate **divertirse**, for example, look up number 29, **sentir**, the model for verbs that follow the **i → ie** stem-change pattern.

How to use the verb tables

In the tables you will find the infinitive, past and present participles, and all the simple forms of each model verb. The formation of the compound tenses of any verb can be inferred from the table of compound tenses, pages 406–407, either by combining the past participle of the verb with a conjugated form of **haber** or combining the present participle with a conjugated form of **estar**.

---

abrir like vivir (3) *except* past participle is abierto
acabar de like hablar (1)
aceptar like hablar (1)
aconsejar like hablar (1)
acostarse (o→ue) like contar (21)
afeitarse like hablar (1)
ahorrar like hablar (1)
almorzar (o→ue) like contar (21) *except* (z→c)
alquilar like hablar (1)
andar like hablar (1) *except* preterit stem is anduv-
aprender like comer (2)
armar like hablar (1)
ayudar(se) like hablar (1)

bailar like hablar (1)
bañarse like hablar (1)
barrer like comer (2)
beber like comer (2)
besar(se) like hablar (1)
bucear like hablar (1)
buscar (c→qu) like tocar (35)

cambiar like hablar (1)
cantar like hablar (1)
casarse like hablar (1)
castigar like hablar (1)
cenar like hablar (1)

chocar (c→qu) like tocar (35)
colorear like hablar (1)
comer (2)
compartir like vivir (3)
comprar like hablar (1)
conocer (c→zc) (30)
contar (o→ue) (21)
correr like comer (2)
cortar like hablar (1)
costar (o→ue) like contar (21)
creer (y) (31)
cruzar (z→c) (32)
cuidar(se) like hablar (1)

dar(se) (4)
deber like comer (2)
decidir like vivir (3)
decir (e→i) (5)
dejar like hablar (1)
desayunar like hablar (1)
descansar like hablar (1)
descomponerse like poner(se) (12)
dibujar like hablar (1)
discutir like vivir (3)
disfrazar(se) like hablar (1)
divertirse (e→ie) like sentir (29)
divorciarse like hablar (1)
dormir(se) (o→ue) (22)
ducharse like hablar (1)
dudar like hablar (1)

embarazar(se) like hablar (1)
empezar (e→ie) (z→c) (23)
empujar like hablar (1)
enamorarse like hablar (1)
encantar like hablar (1)
encontrar(se) (o→ue) like contar (21)
enfermarse like hablar (1)
enseñar like hablar (1)
entender (e→ie) (24)
entrar like hablar (1)
entregar like hablar (1) *except* (g→gu)
entrenarse like hablar (1)
escribir like vivir (3) *except* past participle is escrito
escuchar like hablar (1)
esperar like hablar (1)
esquiar (esquío) (33)
estacionar(se) like hablar (1)
estar (6)
estudiar like hablar (1)
explicar (c→qu) like tocar (35)

fascinar like hablar (1)
frenar like hablar (1)
fumar like hablar (1)

ganar like hablar (1)
gastar like hablar (1)
gustar like hablar (1)

haber (hay) (7)
hablar (1)
hacer (8)

iluminar like hablar (1)
importar like hablar (1)
interesar like hablar (1)
invitar like hablar (1)
ir(se) (9)

jugar (u→ue) (g→gu) (25)
juntar(se) like hablar (1)

lastimarse like hablar (1)
lavar(se) like hablar (1)
leer (y) like creer (31)
levantar(se) like hablar (1)
limpiar like hablar (1)
llamar(se) like hablar (1)
llegar (g→gu) (34)
llenar like hablar (1)
llevar(se) like hablar (1)
mandar like hablar (1)
manejar like hablar (1)
mirar like hablar (1)
molestar like hablar (1)
montar like hablar (1)
morir (o→ue) like dormir (22)
   except past participle is muerto
mudarse like hablar (1)

necesitar like hablar (1)
nevar (e→ie) like pensar (27)

obedecer (c→zc) like conocer (30)
ofrecer (c→zc) like conocer (30)
oír (10)

pagar (g→gu) like llegar (34)
parar(se) like hablar (1)
pasar(se) like hablar (1)
pasear like hablar (1)
patinar like hablar (1)
pedir (e→i) (26)
pegar like hablar (1) *except* (g→gu)
pelearse like hablar (1)
pensar (e→ie) (27)
perder (e→ie) like entender (24)
pintar(se) like hablar (1)
planchar like hablar (1)
poder (o→ue) (11)
poner(se) (12)

ponchar(se) like hablar (1)
portar(se) like hablar (1)
practicar (c→qu) like tocar (35)
preferir (e→ie) like sentir (29)
prestar like hablar (1)
prometer like comer (2)

quedar(se) like hablar (1)
querer (e→ie) (13)
quitar(se) like hablar (1)

rasurar(se) like hablar (1)
recibir(se) like vivir (3)
recomendar (e→ie) like pensar (27)
recordar (o→ue) like contar (21)
regalar like hablar (1)
regañar like hablar (1)
romper(se) like comer (2) *except* past
   participle is roto

saber (14)
sacar (c→qu) like tocar (35)
salir(se) (15)
saltar like hablar (1)
seguir (e→i) (28)
sentir(se) (e→ie) (29)
separarse like hablar (1)
ser (16)
servir (e→i) like pedir (26)
solicitar like hablar (1)
subir(se) like vivir (3)

tener (e→ie) (17)
terminar like hablar (1)
tocar (c→qu) (35)
tomar like hablar (1)
trabajar like hablar (1)
traer (18)

usar like hablar (1)

vender like comer (2)
venir (e→ie) (19)
ver (20)
vestir(se) (e→i) (36)
viajar like hablar (1)
visitar like hablar (1)
vivir (3)

Regular verbs: simple tenses

		INDICATIVE				SUBJUNCTIVE		IMPERATIVE
Infinitive	**Present**	**Imperfect**	**Preterit**	**Future**	**Conditional**	**Present**	**Past**	
1 hablar	hablo	hablaba	hablé	hablaré	hablaría	hable	hablara	
	hablas	hablabas	hablaste	hablarás	hablarías	hables	hablaras	habla tú (no hables)
	habla	hablaba	habló	hablará	hablaría	hable	hablara	hable Ud.
Participles:	hablamos	hablábamos	hablamos	hablaremos	hablaríamos	hablemos	habláramos	hablemos
hablando	habláis	hablabais	hablasteis	hablaréis	hablaríais	habléis	hablarais	hablad (no habléis)
hablado	hablan	hablaban	hablaron	hablarán	hablarían	hablen	hablaran	hablen Uds.
2 comer	como	comía	comí	comeré	comería	coma	comiera	
	comes	comías	comiste	comerás	comerías	comas	comieras	come tú (no comas)
	come	comía	comió	comerá	comería	coma	comiera	coma Ud.
Participles:	comemos	comíamos	comimos	comeremos	comeríamos	comamos	comiéramos	comamos
comiendo	coméis	comíais	comisteis	comeréis	comeríais	comáis	comierais	comed (no comáis)
comido	comen	comían	comieron	comerán	comerían	coman	comieran	coman Uds.
3 vivir	vivo	vivía	viví	viviré	viviría	viva	viviera	
	vives	vivías	viviste	vivirás	vivirías	vivas	vivieras	vive tú (no vivas)
	vive	vivía	vivió	vivirá	viviría	viva	viviera	viva Ud.
Participles:	vivimos	vivíamos	vivimos	viviremos	viviríamos	vivamos	viviéramos	vivamos
viviendo	vivís	vivíais	vivisteis	viviréis	viviríais	viváis	vivierais	vivid (no viváis)
vivido	viven	vivían	vivieron	vivirán	vivirían	vivan	vivieran	vivan Uds.

All verbs: compound tenses

PERFECT TENSES

INDICATIVE

Present Perfect		Past Perfect		Future Perfect		Conditional Perfect	
he		había		habré		habría	
has	hablado	habías	hablado	habrás	hablado	habrías	hablado
ha	comido	había	comido	habrá	comido	habría	comido
hemos	vivido	habíamos	vivido	habremos	vivido	habríamos	vivido
habéis		habíais		habréis		habríais	
han		habían		habrán		habrían	

SUBJUNCTIVE

Present Perfect		Past Perfect	
haya		hubiera	
hayas	hablado	hubieras	hablado
haya	comido	hubiera	comido
hayamos	vivido	hubiéramos	vivido
hayáis		hubierais	
hayan		hubieran	

PROGRESSIVE TENSES

	INDICATIVE				SUBJUNCTIVE	
	Present Progressive	Past Progressive	Future Progressive	Conditional Progressive	Present Progressive	Past Progressive
	estoy	estaba	estaré	estaría	esté	estuviera
	estás	estabas	estarás	estarías	estés	estuvieras
	está hablando	estaba hablando	estará hablando	estaría hablando	esté hablando	estuviera hablando
	estamos comiendo	estábamos comiendo	estaremos comiendo	estaríamos comiendo	estemos comiendo	estuviéramos comiendo
	estáis viviendo	estabais viviendo	estaréis viviendo	estaríais viviendo	estéis viviendo	estuvierais viviendo
	estan	estaban	estarán	estarían	estén	estuvieran

Irregular verbs

	Infinitive	INDICATIVE					SUBJUNCTIVE		IMPERATIVE
		Present	Imperfect	Preterit	Future	Conditional	Present	Past	
4	dar	doy	daba	di	daré	daría	dé	diera	
		das	dabas	diste	darás	darías	des	dieras	da tú (no des)
		da	daba	dio	dará	daría	dé	diera	dé Ud.
		damos	dábamos	dimos	daremos	daríamos	demos	diéramos	demos
	Participles:	dais	dabais	disteis	daréis	daríais	deis	dierais	dad (no deis)
	dando	dan	daban	dieron	darán	darían	den	dieran	den Uds.
	dado								
5	decir (e → i)	digo	decía	dije	diré	diría	diga	dijera	
		dices	decías	dijiste	dirás	dirías	digas	dijeras	di tú (no digas)
		dice	decía	dijo	dirá	diría	diga	dijera	diga Ud.
	Participles:	decimos	decíamos	dijimos	diremos	diríamos	digamos	dijéramos	digamos
	diciendo	decís	decíais	dijisteis	diréis	diríais	digáis	dijerais	decid (no digáis)
	dicho	dicen	decían	dijeron	dirán	dirían	digan	dijeran	digan Uds.
6	estar	estoy	estaba	estuve	estaré	estaría	esté	estuviera	
		estás	estabas	estuviste	estarás	estarías	estés	estuvieras	está tú (no estés)
		está	estaba	estuvo	estará	estaría	esté	estuviera	esté Ud.
	Participles:	estamos	estábamos	estuvimos	estaremos	estaríamos	estemos	estuviéramos	estemos
	estando	estáis	estabais	estuvisteis	estaréis	estaríais	estéis	estuvierais	estad (no estéis)
	estado	están	estaban	estuvieron	estarán	estarían	estén	estuvieran	estén Uds.

	Infinitive	INDICATIVE					SUBJUNCTIVE		IMPERATIVE
		Present	Imperfect	Preterit	Future	Conditional	Present	Past	
7	haber	he	había	hube	habré	habría	haya	hubiera	
		has	habías	hubiste	habrás	habrías	hayas	hubieras	
		ha	había	hubo	habrá	habría	haya	hubiera	
	Participles:	hemos	habíamos	hubimos	habremos	habríamos	hayamos	hubiéramos	
	habiendo	habéis	habíais	hubisteis	habréis	habríais	hayáis	hubierais	
	habido	han	habían	hubieron	habrán	habrían	hayan	hubieran	
8	hacer	hago	hacía	hice	haré	haría	haga	hiciera	
		haces	hacías	hiciste	harás	harías	hagas	hicieras	haz tú (no hagas)
		hace	hacía	hizo	hará	haría	haga	hiciera	haga Ud.
	Participles:	hacemos	hacíamos	hicimos	haremos	haríamos	hagamos	hiciéramos	hagamos
	haciendo	hacéis	hacíais	hicisteis	haréis	haríais	hagáis	hicierais	haced (no hagáis)
	hecho	hacen	hacían	hicieron	harán	harían	hagan	hicieran	hagan Uds.
9	ir	voy	iba	fui	iré	iría	vaya	fuera	
		vas	ibas	fuiste	irás	irías	vayas	fueras	ve tú (no vayas)
		va	iba	fue	irá	iría	vaya	fuera	vaya Ud.
	Participles:	vamos	íbamos	fuimos	iremos	iríamos	vayamos	fuéramos	vamos
	yendo	vais	ibais	fuisteis	iréis	iríais	vayáis	fuerais	id (no vayáis)
	ido	van	iban	fueron	irán	irían	vayan	fueran	vayan Uds.
10	oír (y)	oigo	oía	oí	oiré	oiría	oiga	oyera	
		oyes	oías	oíste	oirás	oirías	oigas	oyeras	oye tú (no oigas)
		oye	oía	oyó	oirá	oiría	oiga	oyera	oiga Ud.
	Participles:	oímos	oíamos	oímos	oiremos	oiríamos	oigamos	oyéramos	oigamos
	oyendo	oís	oíais	oísteis	oiréis	oiríais	oigáis	oyerais	oíd (no oigáis)
	oído	oyen	oían	oyeron	oirán	oirían	oigan	oyeran	oigan Uds.
11	poder (o → ue)	puedo	podía	pude	podré	podría	pueda	pudiera	
		puedes	podías	pudiste	podrás	podrías	puedas	pudieras	puede tú (no puedas)
		puede	podía	pudo	podrá	podría	pueda	pudiera	pueda Ud.
	Participles:	podemos	podíamos	pudimos	podremos	podríamos	podamos	pudiéramos	podamos
	pudiendo	podéis	podíais	pudisteis	podréis	podríais	podáis	pudierais	poded (no podáis)
	podido	pueden	podían	pudieron	podrán	podrían	puedan	pudieran	puedan Uds.
12	poner	pongo	ponía	puse	pondré	pondría	ponga	pusiera	
		pones	ponías	pusiste	pondrás	pondrías	pongas	pusieras	pon tú (no pongas)
		pone	ponía	puso	pondrá	pondría	ponga	pusiera	ponga Ud.
	Participles:	ponemos	poníamos	pusimos	pondremos	pondríamos	pongamos	pusiéramos	pongamos
	poniendo	ponéis	poníais	pusisteis	pondréis	pondríais	pongáis	pusierais	poned (no pongáis)
	puesto	ponen	ponían	pusieron	pondrán	pondrían	pongan	pusieran	pongan Uds.

	Infinitive	INDICATIVE					SUBJUNCTIVE		IMPERATIVE
		Present	Imperfect	Preterit	Future	Conditional	Present	Past	
13	querer (e → ie)	quiero	quería	quise	querré	querría	quiera	quisiera	
		quieres	querías	quisiste	querrás	querrías	quieras	quisieras	quiere tú (no quieras)
		quiere	quería	quiso	querrá	querría	quiera	quisiera	quiera Ud.
		queremos	queríamos	quisimos	querremos	querríamos	queramos	quisiéramos	queramos
	Participles:	queréis	queríais	quisisteis	querréis	querríais	queráis	quisierais	quered (no queráis)
	queriendo	quieren	querían	quisieron	querrán	querrían	quieran	quisieran	quieran Uds.
	querido								
14	saber	sé	sabía	supe	sabré	sabría	sepa	supiera	
		sabes	sabías	supiste	sabrás	sabrías	sepas	supieras	sabe tú (no sepas)
		sabe	sabía	supo	sabrá	sabría	sepa	supiera	sepa Ud.
		sabemos	sabíamos	supimos	sabremos	sabríamos	sepamos	supiéramos	sepamos
	Participles:	sabéis	sabíais	supisteis	sabréis	sabríais	sepáis	supierais	sabed (no sepáis)
	sabiendo	saben	sabían	supieron	sabrán	sabrían	sepan	supieran	sepan Uds.
	sabido								
15	salir	salgo	salía	salí	saldré	saldría	salga	saliera	
		sales	salías	saliste	saldrás	saldrías	salgas	salieras	sal tú (no salgas)
		sale	salía	salió	saldrá	saldría	salga	saliera	salga Ud.
		salimos	salíamos	salimos	saldremos	saldríamos	salgamos	saliéramos	salgamos
	Participles:	salís	salíais	salisteis	saldréis	saldríais	salgáis	salierais	salid (no salgáis)
	saliendo	salen	salían	salieron	saldrán	saldrían	salgan	salieran	salgan Uds.
	salido								
16	ser	soy	era	fui	seré	sería	sea	fuera	
		eres	eras	fuiste	serás	serías	seas	fueras	sé tú (no seas)
		es	era	fue	será	sería	sea	fuera	sea Ud.
		somos	éramos	fuimos	seremos	seríamos	seamos	fuéramos	seamos
	Participles:	sois	erais	fuisteis	seréis	seríais	seáis	fuerais	sed (no seáis)
	siendo	son	eran	fueron	serán	serían	sean	fueran	sean Uds.
	sido								
17	tener (e → ie)	tengo	tenía	tuve	tendré	tendría	tenga	tuviera	
		tienes	tenías	tuviste	tendrás	tendrías	tengas	tuvieras	ten tú (no tengas)
		tiene	tenía	tuvo	tendrá	tendría	tenga	tuviera	tenga Ud.
		tenemos	teníamos	tuvimos	tendremos	tendríamos	tengamos	tuviéramos	tengamos
	Participles:	tenéis	teníais	tuvisteis	tendréis	tendríais	tengáis	tuvierais	tened (no tengáis)
	teniendo	tienen	tenían	tuvieron	tendrán	tendrían	tengan	tuvieran	tengan Uds.
	tenido								
18	traer	traigo	traía	traje	traeré	traería	traiga	trajera	
		traes	traías	trajiste	traerás	traerías	traigas	trajeras	trae tú (no traigas)
		trae	traía	trajo	traerá	traería	traiga	trajera	traiga Ud.
		traemos	traíamos	trajimos	traeremos	traeríamos	traigamos	trajéramos	traigamos
	Participles:	traéis	traíais	trajisteis	traeréis	traeríais	traigáis	trajerais	traed (no traigáis)
	trayendo	traen	traían	trajeron	traerán	traerían	traigan	trajeran	traigan Uds.
	traído								

19 — venir (e→ie)
Participles: viniendo, venido

Infinitive	Present	Imperfect	Preterit	Future	Conditional	Subjunctive Present	Subjunctive Past	Imperative
venir (e→ie)	vengo	venía	vine	vendré	vendría	venga	viniera	
	vienes	venías	viniste	vendrás	vendrías	vengas	vinieras	ven tú (no vengas)
	viene	venía	vino	vendrá	vendría	venga	viniera	venga Ud.
Participles:	venimos	veníamos	vinimos	vendremos	vendríamos	vengamos	viniéramos	vengamos
viniendo	venís	veníais	vinisteis	vendréis	vendríais	vengáis	vinierais	venid (no vengáis)
venido	vienen	venían	vinieron	vendrán	vendrían	vengan	vinieran	vengan Uds.

20 — ver
Participles: viendo, visto

Infinitive	Present	Imperfect	Preterit	Future	Conditional	Subjunctive Present	Subjunctive Past	Imperative
ver	veo	veía	vi	veré	vería	vea	viera	
	ves	veías	viste	verás	verías	veas	vieras	ve tú (no veas)
	ve	veía	vio	verá	vería	vea	viera	vea Ud.
Participles:	vemos	veíamos	vimos	veremos	veríamos	veamos	viéramos	veamos
viendo	veis	veíais	visteis	veréis	veríais	veáis	vierais	ved (no veáis)
visto	ven	veían	vieron	verán	verían	vean	vieran	vean Uds.

Stem–changing verbs

21 — contar (o→ue)
Participles: contando, contado

Infinitive	Present	Imperfect	Preterit	Future	Conditional	Subjunctive Present	Subjunctive Past	Imperative
contar (o→ue)	cuento	contaba	conté	contaré	contaría	cuente	contara	
	cuentas	contabas	contaste	contarás	contarías	cuentes	contaras	cuenta tú (no cuentes)
	cuenta	contaba	contó	contará	contaría	cuente	contara	cuente Ud.
Participles:	contamos	contábamos	contamos	contaremos	contaríamos	contemos	contáramos	contemos
contando	contáis	contabais	contasteis	contaréis	contaríais	contéis	contarais	contad (no contéis)
contado	cuentan	contaban	contaron	contarán	contarían	cuenten	contaran	cuenten Uds.

22 — dormir (o→ue)
Participles: durmiendo, dormido

Infinitive	Present	Imperfect	Preterit	Future	Conditional	Subjunctive Present	Subjunctive Past	Imperative
dormir (o→ue)	duermo	dormía	dormí	dormiré	dormiría	duerma	durmiera	
	duermes	dormías	dormiste	dormirás	dormirías	duermas	durmieras	duerme tú (no duermas)
	duerme	dormía	durmió	dormirá	dormiría	duerma	durmiera	duerma Ud.
Participles:	dormimos	dormíamos	dormimos	dormiremos	dormiríamos	durmamos	durmiéramos	durmamos
durmiendo	dormís	dormíais	dormisteis	dormiréis	dormiríais	durmáis	durmierais	dormid (no durmáis)
dormido	duermen	dormían	durmieron	dormirán	dormirían	duerman	durmieran	duerman Uds.

23 — empezar (e→ie)(c)
Participles: empezando, empezado

Infinitive	Present	Imperfect	Preterit	Future	Conditional	Subjunctive Present	Subjunctive Past	Imperative
empezar (e→ie)(c)	empiezo	empezaba	empecé	empezaré	empezaría	empiece	empezara	
	empiezas	empezabas	empezaste	empezarás	empezarías	empieces	empezaras	empieza tú (no empieces)
	empieza	empezaba	empezó	empezará	empezaría	empiece	empezara	empiece Ud.
Participles:	empezamos	empezábamos	empezamos	empezaremos	empezaríamos	empecemos	empezáramos	empecemos
empezando	empezáis	empezabais	empezasteis	empezaréis	empezaríais	empecéis	empezarais	empezad (no empecéis)
empezado	empiezan	empezaban	empezaron	empezarán	empezarían	empiecen	empezaran	empiecen Uds.

		INDICATIVE					SUBJUNCTIVE		IMPERATIVE
Infinitive	Present	Imperfect	Preterit	Future	Conditional	Present	Past	

24

Infinitive	Present	Imperfect	Preterit	Future	Conditional	Present	Past	IMPERATIVE
entender (e → ie)	**entiendo**	entendía	entendí	entenderé	entendería	**entienda**	entendiera	
	entiendes	entendías	entendiste	entenderás	entenderías	**entiendas**	entendieras	**entiende** tú (no **entiendas**)
	entiende	entendía	entendió	entenderá	entendería	**entienda**	entendiera	**entienda** Ud.
Participles:	entendemos	entendíamos	entendimos	entenderemos	entenderíamos	entendamos	entendiéramos	entendamos
entendiendo	entendéis	entendíais	entendisteis	entenderéis	entenderíais	entendáis	entendierais	entended (no entendáis)
entendido	**entienden**	entendían	entendieron	entenderán	entenderían	**entiendan**	entendieran	**entiendan** Uds.

25

Infinitive	Present	Imperfect	Preterit	Future	Conditional	Present	Past	IMPERATIVE
jugar (u → ue) (gu)	**juego**	jugaba	**jugué**	jugaré	jugaría	**juegue**	jugara	
	juegas	jugabas	jugaste	jugarás	jugarías	**juegues**	jugaras	**juega** tú (no **juegues**)
	juega	jugaba	jugó	jugará	jugaría	**juegue**	jugara	**juegue** Ud.
Participles:	jugamos	jugábamos	jugamos	jugaremos	jugaríamos	**juguemos**	jugáramos	**juguemos**
jugando	jugáis	jugabais	jugasteis	jugaréis	jugaríais	**juguéis**	jugarais	jugad (no **juguéis**)
jugado	**juegan**	jugaban	jugaron	jugarán	jugarían	**jueguen**	jugaran	**jueguen** Uds.

26

Infinitive	Present	Imperfect	Preterit	Future	Conditional	Present	Past	IMPERATIVE
pedir (e → i)	**pido**	pedía	pedí	pediré	pediría	**pida**	**pidiera**	
	pides	pedías	pediste	pedirás	pedirías	**pidas**	**pidieras**	**pide** tú (no **pidas**)
	pide	pedía	**pidió**	pedirá	pediría	**pida**	**pidiera**	**pida** Ud.
Participles:	pedimos	pedíamos	pedimos	pediremos	pediríamos	**pidamos**	**pidiéramos**	**pidamos**
pidiendo	pedís	pedíais	pedisteis	pediréis	pediríais	**pidáis**	**pidierais**	pedid (no **pidáis**)
pedido	**piden**	pedían	**pidieron**	pedirán	pedirían	**pidan**	**pidieran**	**pidan** Uds.

27

Infinitive	Present	Imperfect	Preterit	Future	Conditional	Present	Past	IMPERATIVE
pensar (e → ie)	**pienso**	pensaba	pensé	pensaré	pensaría	**piense**	pensara	
	piensas	pensabas	pensaste	pensarás	pensarías	**pienses**	pensaras	**piensa** tú (no **pienses**)
	piensa	pensaba	pensó	pensará	pensaría	**piense**	pensara	**piense** Ud.
Participles:	pensamos	pensábamos	pensamos	pensaremos	pensaríamos	pensemos	pensáramos	pensemos
pensando	pensáis	pensabais	pensasteis	pensaréis	pensaríais	penséis	pensarais	pensad (no penséis)
pensado	**piensan**	pensaban	pensaron	pensarán	pensarían	**piensen**	pensaran	**piensen** Uds.

28

Infinitive	Present	Imperfect	Preterit	Future	Conditional	Present	Past	IMPERATIVE
seguir (e → i) (gu)	**sigo**	seguía	seguí	seguiré	seguiría	**siga**	**siguiera**	
	sigues	seguías	seguiste	seguirás	seguirías	**sigas**	**siguieras**	**sigue** tú (no **sigas**)
	sigue	seguía	**siguió**	seguirá	seguiría	**siga**	**siguiera**	**siga** Ud.
Participles:	seguimos	seguíamos	seguimos	seguiremos	seguiríamos	**sigamos**	**siguiéramos**	**sigamos**
siguiendo	seguís	seguíais	seguisteis	seguiréis	seguiríais	**sigáis**	**siguierais**	seguid (no **sigáis**)
seguido	**siguen**	seguían	**siguieron**	seguirán	seguirían	**sigan**	**siguieran**	**sigan** Uds.

29

Infinitive	Present	Imperfect	Preterit	Future	Conditional	Present	Past	IMPERATIVE
sentir (e → ie)	**siento**	sentía	sentí	sentiré	sentiría	**sienta**	**sintiera**	
	sientes	sentías	sentiste	sentirás	sentirías	**sientas**	**sintieras**	**siente** tú (no **sientas**)
	siente	sentía	**sintió**	sentirá	sentiría	**sienta**	**sintiera**	**sienta** Ud.
Participles:	sentimos	sentíamos	sentimos	sentiremos	sentiríamos	**sintamos**	**sintiéramos**	**sintamos**
sintiendo	sentís	sentíais	sentisteis	sentiréis	sentiríais	**sintáis**	**sintierais**	sentid (no **sintáis**)
sentido	**sienten**	sentían	**sintieron**	sentirán	sentirían	**sientan**	**sintieran**	**sientan** Uds.

411

Reflexive verbs and verbs with spelling changes

Infinitive	INDICATIVE					SUBJUNCTIVE		IMPERATIVE
	Present	Imperfect	Preterit	Future	Conditional	Present	Past	
30 conocer (c → zc)	**conozco**	conocía	conocí	conoceré	conocería	**conozca**	conociera	
	conoces	conocías	conociste	conocerás	conocerías	**conozcas**	conocieras	conoce tú (no **conozcas**)
	conoce	conocía	conoció	conocerá	conocería	**conozca**	conociera	**conozca** Ud.
Participles:	conocemos	conocíamos	conocimos	conoceremos	conoceríamos	**conozcamos**	conociéramos	**conozcamos**
conociendo	conocéis	conocíais	conocisteis	conoceréis	conoceríais	**conozcáis**	conocierais	conoced (no **conozcáis**)
conocido	conocen	conocían	conocieron	conocerán	conocerían	**conozcan**	conocieran	**conozcan** Uds.
31 creer (y)	creo	creía	creí	creeré	creería	crea	**creyera**	
	crees	creías	**creíste**	creerás	creerías	creas	**creyeras**	cree tú (no creas)
	cree	creía	**creyó**	creerá	creería	crea	**creyera**	crea Ud.
Participles:	creemos	creíamos	**creímos**	creeremos	creeríamos	creamos	**creyéramos**	creamos
creyendo	creéis	creíais	**creísteis**	creeréis	creeríais	creáis	**creyerais**	creed (no creáis)
creído	creen	creían	**creyeron**	creerán	creerían	crean	**creyeran**	crean Uds.
32 cruzar (c)	cruzo	cruzaba	**crucé**	cruzaré	cruzaría	**cruce**	cruzara	
	cruzas	cruzabas	cruzaste	cruzarás	cruzarías	**cruces**	cruzaras	cruza tú (no **cruces**)
	cruza	cruzaba	cruzó	cruzará	cruzaría	**cruce**	cruzara	**cruce** Ud.
Participles:	cruzamos	cruzábamos	cruzamos	cruzaremos	cruzaríamos	**crucemos**	cruzáramos	**crucemos**
cruzando	cruzáis	cruzabais	cruzasteis	cruzaréis	cruzaríais	**crucéis**	cruzarais	cruzad (no **crucéis**)
cruzado	cruzan	cruzaban	cruzaron	cruzarán	cruzarían	**crucen**	cruzaran	**crucen** Uds.
33 esquiar (esquió)	**esquio**	esquiaba	esquié	esquiaré	esquiaría	**esquíe**	esquiara	
	esquias	esquiabas	esquiaste	esquiarás	esquiarías	**esquíes**	esquiaras	**esquía** tú (no **esquíes**)
	esquia	esquiaba	esquió	esquiará	esquiaría	**esquíe**	esquiara	**esquíe** Ud.
Participles:	esquiamos	esquiábamos	esquiamos	esquiaremos	esquiaríamos	**esquiemos**	esquiáramos	esquiemos
esquiando	esquiáis	esquiabais	esquiasteis	esquiaréis	esquiaríais	**esquiéis**	esquiarais	esquiad (no esquiéis)
esquiado	**esquian**	esquiaban	esquiaron	esquiarán	esquiarían	**esquien**	esquiaran	**esquien** Uds.
34 llegar (gu)	llego	llegaba	**llegué**	llegaré	llegaría	**llegue**	llegara	
	llegas	llegabas	llegaste	llegarás	llegarías	**llegues**	llegaras	llega tú (no **llegues**)
	llega	llegaba	llegó	llegará	llegaría	**llegue**	llegara	**llegue** Ud.
Participles:	llegamos	llegábamos	llegamos	llegaremos	llegaríamos	**lleguemos**	llegáramos	**lleguemos**
llegando	llegáis	llegabais	llegasteis	llegaréis	llegaríais	**lleguéis**	llegarais	llegad (no **lleguéis**)
llegado	llegan	llegaban	llegaron	llegarán	llegarían	**lleguen**	llegaran	**lleguen** Uds.

Infinitive	INDICATIVE					SUBJUNCTIVE		IMPERATIVE
	Present	Imperfect	Preterit	Future	Conditional	Present	Past	
35 tocar (qu)	toco	tocaba	**toqué**	tocaré	tocaría	**toque**	tocara	
	tocas	tocabas	tocaste	tocará	tocarías	**toques**	tocaras	toca tú (no **toques**)
	toca	tocaba	tocó	tocarás	tocaría	**toque**	tocara	**toque** Ud.
Participles:	tocamos	tocábamos	tocamos	tocaremos	tocaríamos	**toquemos**	tocáramos	**toquemos**
tocando	tocáis	tocabais	tocasteis	tocaréis	tocaríais	**toquéis**	tocarais	tocad (no **toquéis**)
tocado	tocan	tocaban	tocaron	tocarán	tocarían	**toquen**	tocaran	**toquen** Uds.
36 vestir(se) (e → i)	**me visto**	me vestía	me vestí	me vestiré	me vestiría	**me vista**	**me vistiera**	
	te vistes	te vestías	te vestiste	te vestirás	te vestirías	**te vistas**	**te vistieras**	**vístete** tú
	se viste	se vestía	**se vistió**	se vestirá	se vestiría	**se vista**	**se vistiera**	**vístase** Ud.
Participles:	nos vestimos	nos vestíamos	nos vestimos	nos vestiremos	nos vestiríamos	**nos vistamos**	**nos vistiéramos**	**vistámonos**
vistiendo	os vestís	os vestíais	os vestisteis	os vestiréis	os vestiríais	**os vistáis**	**os vistierais**	vestíos (no os **vistáis**)
vestido	**se visten**	se vestían	**se vistieron**	se vestirán	se vestirían	**se vistan**	**se vistieran**	**vístanse** Uds.

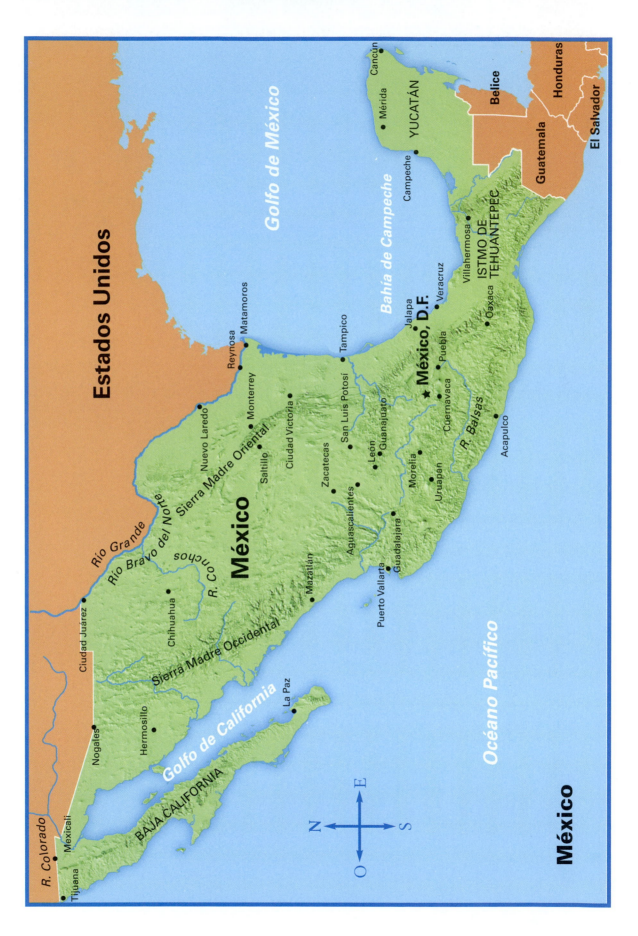

414

Andorra

Menorca

Mallorca

Palma

Islas Baleares

Ibiza

Formentera

Mar Mediterráneo

Islas Canarias

Lanzarote
Arrecife
Puerto del Rosario
Fuerteventura
Marruecos

La Palma
Santa Cruz de la Palma
Santa Cruz de Tenerife
Las Palmas
Tenerife
Gran Canaria
Gomera
Hierro

Océano Atlántico

Melilla (Esp.)

Pirineos

CATALUÑA

Gerona

Tarragona

Barcelona

Lérida

PAÍS VASCO
San Sebastián
NAVARRA
Pamplona
Bilbao
Zaragoza
LA RIOJA
ARAGÓN

COMUNIDAD VALENCIANA

Valencia

Alicante

España

CANTABRIA
Santander
ASTURIAS
Oviedo
Gijón
Avilés
Mar Cantábrico

Burgos

CASTILLA-LEÓN

Valladolid
Segovia
Ávila

Madrid

CASTILLA-LA MANCHA

Albacete

Murcia
Cartagena

Almería

Sierra Nevada

Palencia
Zamora
Salamanca

Toledo

Sierra Morena

Jaén

ANDALUCÍA
Granada

Málaga

Gibraltar (R.U.)
Ceuta (Esp.)

GALICIA
La Coruña
Pontevedra
Vigo

EXTREMADURA
Cáceres
Mérida
Badajoz

Córdoba

Sevilla

Huelva

Cádiz
Algeciras

Estrecho de Gibraltar

Marruecos

Serra da Estrela
Braga
Coimbra
Oporto

Setúbal

Portugal
Lisboa

Océano Atlántico

Islas Galápagos

Mar Caribe

Barranquilla
Maracaibo
Caracas
Puerto España
Trinidad y Tobago
Venezuela
Medellín
Colombia
Bogotá
Cali
Georgetown
Paramaribo
Cayena
Guyana
R. Orinoco
Suriname
Guayana Francesa
Pasto
Quito
Ecuador
Guayaquil
R. Magdalena
Iquitos
R. Negro
R. Amazonas
Belém
Manaus
Perú
R. Madeira
Recife
Cordillera de los Andes
Lima
Cuzco
Lago Titicaca
Arequipa
La Paz
Sucre
Bolivia
Arica
Iquique
Brasil
Brasilia
Salvador
R. Paraguay
R. Paraná
Belo Horizonte
São Paulo
Río de Janeiro
Santos
Antofagasta
Salta
Paraguay
Asunción
Chile
Córdoba
R. Paraná
R. Uruguay
Porto Alegre
Valparaíso
Mendoza
Rosario
Santiago
Buenos Aires
Uruguay
Montevideo
Concepción
Argentina
Bahía Blanca

Océano Pacífico

Océano Atlántico

Puerto Montt
Cordillera de los Andes

N
O E
S

Estrecho de Magallanes
Punta Arenas
Islas Malvinas
Tierra del Fuego

América del Sur

Islas Galápagos
Océano Pacífico
Isla Pinta
Isla Marchena
Isla Genovesa
Isla Isabela
Línea Ecuatorial
ECUADOR
Volcán Darwin
Isla Santiago (San Salvador)
Isla Fernandina
Puerto Ayora
Isla Santa Cruz
Isla San Cristóbal
Santo Tomás
Puerto Barquerizo Moreno
Isla Santa Maria
Isla Española

416

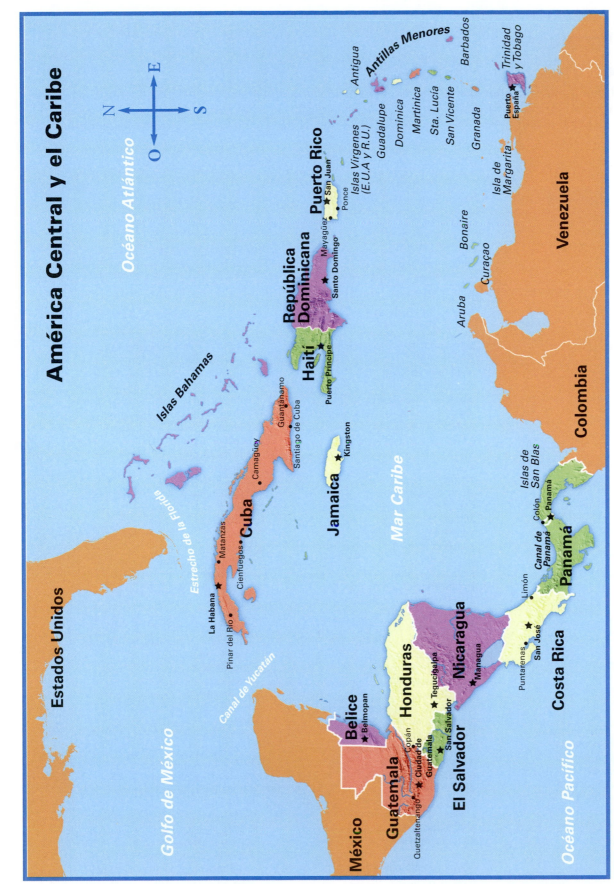

América Central y el Caribe

Estados Unidos

Océano Atlántico

Golfo de México

Islas Bahamas

Estrecho de la Florida

Canal de Yucatán

Cuba

La Habana
Pinar del Río
Matanzas
Cienfuegos
Camagüey
Santiago de Cuba
Guantánamo

México

Guatemala
Quetzaltenango
Ciudad de Guatemala
Copán

Belice
Belmopan

Honduras
Tegucigalpa
Copán

El Salvador
San Salvador

Nicaragua
Managua

Costa Rica
Puntarenas
San José
Limón

Panamá
Canal de Panamá
Colón
Panamá

Islas de San Blas

Jamaica
Kingston

Mar Caribe

Haití
Puerto Príncipe

República Dominicana
Santo Domingo

Puerto Rico
Mayagüez
San Juan
Ponce

Islas Vírgenes (E.U.A y R.U.)

Antillas Menores

Antigua
Guadalupe
Dominica
Martinica
Sta. Lucía
San Vicente
Granada
Barbados

Trinidad y Tobago
España
Puerto

Isla de Margarita

Aruba
Bonaire
Curaçao

Venezuela

Colombia

Océano Pacífico

N
E
S
O

417

Guide to Vocabulary

Note on alphabetization

Formerly, **ch**, **ll**, and **ñ** were considered separate letters in the Spanish alphabet, **ch** appearing after **c**, **ll** after **l**, and **ñ** after **n**. In current practice, for purposes of alphabetization, **ch** and **ll** are not treated as separate letters, but **ñ** still follows **n**. Therefore, in this glossary you will find that **añadir**, for example, appears after **anuncio**.

The numbers that follow the entries indicate the episode number where the words are taught; entries labelled 1–15 are found in **Primera Parte**, and entries marked 16–30 are found in **Segunda Parte**.

Abbreviations used in this glossary

adj.	adjective	*i.o.*	indirect object	*prep.*	preposition
adv.	adverb	*irr*	irregular	*pron.*	pronoun
conj.	conjunction	*m.*	masculine	*ref.*	reflexive
d.o.	direct object	*n.*	noun	*sing.*	singular
f.	feminine	*obj.*	object	*sub.*	subject
fam.	familiar	*p.p.*	past participle	*v.*	verb
form.	formal	*pl.*	plural		
interj.	interjection	*poss.*	possessive		

Spanish-English

A

a *prep.* to
abierto/a *adj.* open
abogado/a *n.* lawyer 12
abrazo *n., m* hug
abrigo *n., m* coat, jacket 13
abril *n.* April 13
abrir *v.* to open 8
abuelo/a *n.* grandfather/grandmother 4
abuelos *n., m* grandparents 4
aburrido/a *adj.* boring 6; bored 15
acabar de *v.* to have just 21
acampar *v.* to camp
aceite *n., m* oil
aceptar *v.* to accept 28
aconsejar *v.* to advise 27
acostarse (o ➤ ue) *v.* to go to bed 14
activo/a *adj.* active 3
acuario *n., m* aquarium
acuático/a *adj.* aquatic
además *adv.* besides
(a)dentro *adv.* inside 15
adiós *interj.* good-bye 1
administración *n., f* management
administrador(a) de empresas *n.* business administrator 12
adolorido/a *adj.* sore 21
aeropuerto *n., m* airport 8
afeitarse *v.* to shave 23
aficionado/a *n.* fan
(a)fuera *adv.* outside 15
agente *n., mf* agent 12
agosto *n., m* August 13
agradable *adj.* nice 6
agregar *v.* to add
agua, (el) *n., f* water 9
aguacate *n., m* avocado
ahí *adv.* there
ahora *adv.* now 28

ahorrar dinero *v.* to save money 28
aire *n., m* air
ajeno/a *n.* stranger
ajo *n., m* garlic
alberca *n., f* swimming pool
alcanzar *v.* to reach; to achieve
alcoba *n., f* bedroom
alegrarse *v.* to be happy for
alfombra *n., f* carpet 18
algo *n.* something 18
alguien *n.* somebody 18
algún, alguna *adj.* some 18
alguna vez ever 28
allí/allá *adv.* there
almohada *n., f* pillow
almorzar (o ➤ ue) *v.* to have lunch 10
almuerzo *n., m* lunch 9
alojamiento *n., m* lodging
alpinismo *n., m* mountain climbing
alquilar *v.* to rent
alrededor *adv.* around
alto *n., m* stop (sign)
alto/a *adj.* tall, high 11
alumno/a *n.* student
ama de casa, (el) *n., f* housewife, home-maker 11
amable *adj.* kind, nice, friendly 6
amante *n., mf* lover
amarillo/a *adj.* yellow 13
ambicioso/a *adj.* ambitious 3
amigo/a *n.* friend 4
amistad *n., f* friendship
amor *n., m* love
amueblar *v.* to furnish
analista *n., mf* analyst 12
anaranjado/a *adj.* orange 13
andar en bicicleta *v.* to ride bikes 18
anfitrión, anfitriona *n.* host
ángel *n., m* angel
anillo *n., m* ring 27
anoche *adv.* last night 15
anteayer *adv.* day before yesterday

antemano, (de) *adv.* beforehand
antes (de) que *adv.* before 30
antibiótico *n., m* antibiotic 21
antigüedad *n., f* antiquity; seniority
antipático/a *adj.* irritating, nasty 6
antropología *n., f* anthropology 1
anuncio *n., m* advertisement
añadir *v.* to add
año *n., m* year
Año Nuevo *n., m* New Year
aparcar *v.* to park
apartamento *n., m* apartment 18
apellido *n., m* last name
apenas *adv.* just, barely
apostar (o ➤ ue) *v.* to bet
apoyar *v.* to support
aprender *v.* to learn 19
apretado/a *adj.* tight
apuesta *n., f* wager
apuntes *n., m* notes
araña *n., f* spider
árbol *n., m* tree 20
armar (un rompecabezas) *v.* to assemble (a puzzle) 22
armario *n., m* closet
arquitecto/a *n.* architect 12
arquitectura *n., f* architecture
arrancar *v.* to start
arrecife *n., m* reef
arreglado/a *adj.* tidy 18
arreglar *v.* to tidy up, to fix
arrestar *v.* to arrest
arriba *adv.* above
arrogante *adj.* arrogant 3
arroz *n., m* rice 9
artesanía *n., f* hand-made crafts
artista *n., mf* artist 12
asador *n., m* barbecue 18
asistir *v.* to attend
aspiradora *n., f* vacuum cleaner
aspirina *n., f* aspirin 21
astronomía *n., f* astronomy 1
asunto *n., m* matter, issue
asustado/a *adj.* scared

atender a los clientes *v.* to take care of clients **11**
atento/a *adj.* kind, attentive
atractivo/a *adj.* attractive **3**
atrás *adv.* behind **25**
atún *n., m* tuna **9**
auditorio *n., m* auditorium, theater **2**
aula *n., f* classroom
aunque *conj.* although
auto *n., m* car
autobús *n., m* bus **5**
autopista *n., f* freeway, expressway **26**
autorretrato *n., m* self-portrait
autosuficiencia *n., f* self-sufficiency
avenida *n., f* avenue **26**
aventar *v.* to throw
avión *n., m* airplane **20**
ayer *adv.* yesterday **15**
ayudar *v.* to help **11**
azul *adj.* blue **13**

B

bachillerato *n., m* high school
bailar *v.* to dance **5**
bajo/a *adj.* short, low **6**
balcón *n., m* balcony
banana *n., f* banana
banco *n., m* bank
bandera *n., f* flag **2**
bañarse *v.* to shower, to take a bath **14**
bañera *n., f* bathtub
baño *n., m* bathroom **2**
bar *n., m* bar
barato/a *adj.* cheap, inexpensive
barda *n., f* fence
barrer *v.* to sweep **18**
barrio *n., m* neighborhood
bastante *adv.* quite
basura *n., f* trash **18**
bebé *n., mf* baby **8**
beber *v.* to drink
bebida *n., f* beverage
beca *n., f* scholarship
béisbol *n., m* baseball
bello/a *adj.* beautiful
berrinche *n., m* tantrum **22**
besar *v.* to kiss **20**
beso *n., m* kiss **20**
biblioteca *n., f* library **2**
bien *adv.* well, good **1**
bienes raíces *n., m* real estate **12**
bikini *n., m* bikini **13**
billetera *n., f* wallet
biología *n., f* biology **1**
bistec *n., m* steak
blanco/a *adj.* white **13**
bluejeans *n., m* jeans
blusa *n., f* blouse **13**
boca *n., f* mouth **21**
bocacalle *n., f* intersection

boda *n., f* wedding
bolera *n., f* bowling
boleto *n., m* ticket
boliche *n., m* bowling **8**
bolígrafo *n., m* pen
bolos *n., m* bowling
bolsa *n., f* bag, purse
bolsillo *n., m* pocket, purse
bombero *n., m* firefighter **12**
bonito/a *adj.* pretty **6**
borracho/a *adj.* drunk
botánica *n., f* botany
bote de basura *n., m* trash can
brazalete *n., m* bracelet
brazo *n., m* arm **21**
brincar *v.* to jump
brócoli *n., m* broccoli **9**
bronca *n., f* problem, fight
bruja *n., f* witch
bucear *v.* to scuba dive **18**
buen *adj.* good (before the noun)
buenas noches good evening, good night **1**
buenas tardes good afternoon **1**
bueno/a *adj.* good (after the noun) **6**
buenos días good morning **1**
bufanda *n., f* scarf **13**
buró *n., m* night table
buscar *v.* to look for **5**
buzón *n., m* mail box

C

caballo *n., m* horse **18**
cabeza *n., f* head **21**
cacahuate *n., m* peanut
cada *adj.* each
café *n., m* coffee, coffee shop **5**
café *adj.* brown **13**
cafetería *n., f* cafeteria **2**
caja *n., f* box, cash register
calculadora *n., f* calculator **2**
caliente *adj.* hot
calificaciones *n., f* grades
calificado/a *adj.* qualified
calle *n., f* street **26**
calor *n., m* heat, hot **13**; **hace calor** it's hot
caloría *n., f* calorie
cama *n., f* bed **15**
cámara *n., f* camera
camarero/a *n.* waiter/waitress
camarón *n., m* shrimp **9**
cambiar *v.* to change **28**
cambiarse (de casa) *v.* to move
caminata *n., f* hike
camino *n., m* way
camión *n., m* truck
camisa *n., f* shirt **13**
camiseta *n., f* T-shirt **13**
campamento *n., m* camp
cancha *n., f* court, field **2**
canción *n., f* song

canica *n., f* marble
cansado/a *adj.* tired **15**
cantar *v.* to sing **20**
capacitación *n., f* training **28**
capaz *adj.* capable
carga *n., f* freight
caricatura *n., f* cartoon
cariñoso/a *adj.* affectionate **6**
carne *n., f* meat **9**
carne de res *n., f* beef **9**
carnet (de conducir) *n., m* driver's license
caro/a *adj.* expensive
carrera *n., f* major, field of study
carretera *n., f* highway **26**
carril *n., m* lane
carro *n., m* car
carta *n., f* letter
cartas *n., f* deck of cards
cartera *n., f* wallet, purse
casa *n., f* house **8**
casado/a *adj.* married **6**
casarse *v.* to get married **27**
casero/a *adj.* homemade
casi *adv.* almost **8**
caso *n., m* case
castaño/a *adj.* brunet(te)
castigar *v.* to punish **22**
castigo *n., m* punishment
casualidad, (por) *n., f* by chance
catarro *n., m* cold **21**
católico/a *adj.* Catholic **22**
celebrar *v.* to celebrate **28**
celos *n., m* jealousy
celoso/a *adj.* jealous
cena *n., f* dinner, supper **9**
cenar *v.* to dine **9**
centavo *n., m* cent
centro *n., m* downtown; middle, center
centro comercial *n., m* mall, shopping center **8**
cepillarse los dientes *v.* to brush one's teeth
cerca *n., f* fence
cerca (de) *adv.* close, near
cercano/a *adj.* close
cerdo *n., m* pork **9**
cereal *n., m* cereal **9**
cerrar (e ➜ ie) *v.* to close
cerveza *n., f* beer **9**
césped *n., m* lawn
chamarra *n., f* jacket
chaqueta *n., f* jacket **13**
cheque *n., m* (personal) check
chico/a *n.* young person **4**
chilaquiles *n., m* Mexican dish with tortilla, salsa, and cheese
chillar *v.* to yell; to cry
chimenea *n., f* fire place
chiste *n., m* joke
chistoso/a *adj.* funny
chocar *v.* to dislike **(me choca) 19**; *v.* to hit (a car) **26**
chocolate *n., m* chocolate

chofer *n., mf* driver 11
choque *n., m* car accident (crash) 26
cierto *adj.* true, certain
cine *n., m* movies, movie theater 8
cinta *n., f* tape
cinturón (de seguridad) *n., m* seat belt 26
cirujano/a *n.* surgeon
cita *n., f* date, appointment
ciudad *n., f* city
ciudadanía *n., f* citizenship
ciudadano/a *n.* citizen
claro *interj.* of course
clase *n., f* class 2
claxon *n., m* horn
clima *n., m* weather
clóset *n., m* closet 18
cobrar *v.* to charge, collect
cobre *n., m* copper
coche *n., m* car 5
cochera *n., f* garage
cocina *n., f* kitchen 18
cocinar *v.* to cook
colar (o→ue) *v.* to strain
colegio *n., m* school 22
colgar (o→ue) *v.* to hang
colonia *n., f* neighborhood
color *n., m* color 13
colorear *v.* to color 22
comedor *n., m* dining room 18
comer *v.* to eat 8; *v.* to have lunch 9
comida *n., f* food 5
cómo *adv.* how (interrogative) 6
como *prep.* as (comparison)
cómoda *n., f* dresser 18
comodidad *n., f* comfort
cómodo/a *adj.* comfortable 20
compañero/a *n.* mate 2
compañía *n., f* company, business
compartir *v.* to share 22
competente *adj.* competent 3
completo/a *adj.* complete, full
comportamiento *n., m* behavior
comportarse *v.* to behave oneself
comprar *v.* to buy 5
comprensión *n., f* understanding
compromiso *n., m* engagement 27
computadora *n., f* computer 5
común *adj.* common
con *prep.* with
con frecuencia *adv.* frequently
conducir (yo conduzco) *v.* to drive
conductor(a) *n.* driver 26
confianza *n., f* trust
confundir *v.* to confuse
conmigo *prep. pron.* with me
conmoción *n., f* concussion
conocer *v.* to meet; *v.* to know 12
conocimiento *n., m* knowledge
consejero/a *n.* advisor 2
consejo *n., m* advice 11
consentido/a *adj.* spoiled (person) 22
consultorio *n., m* doctor's office

consumidor *n., m* consumer
contable *adj.* countable
contador(a) *n.* accountant 12
contar (o→ue) *v.* to tell 11; *v.* to count
contento/a *adj.* happy 15
contestar *v.* to answer
contigo *prep. pron.* with you
contra *prep.* against
contrario, (al) *prep.* on the contrary
conversación *n., f* conversation
conversar *v.* to talk, to chat
corbata *n., f* tie 13
coro *n., m* choir
correo *n., m* post office, mail
correo electrónico *n., m* e-mail
correr *v.* to run, to jog 8
cortar el pasto *v.* to mow the lawn 18
cortarse *v.* to cut (oneself)
corto/a *adj.* short 13
cosa *n., f* thing 2
cosecha *n., f* crops
coser *v.* to sew
costar (o→ue) *v.* to cost
crear *v.* to create
creativo/a *adj.* creative 3
crecer (yo crezco) *v.* to grow
creer *v.* to believe, to think 17
crema *n., f* cream
cruce *n., m* intersection; junction
crudo/a *adj.* raw
Cruz Roja *n., f* Red Cross
cruzadas *n., f* Crusades
cruzar *v.* to cross 26
cuaderno *n., m* notebook 2
cuadra *n., f* city block 26
cuadro *n., m* picture; square
cuál *pron.* which, what (interrogative) 6
cuando *prep., conj.* when
cuándo *adv.* when (interrogative) 6
cuánto/a(s) *adj.* how much/many (interrogative) 6
Cuaresma *n., f* Lent
cuarto *n., m* room 5
cubrir *v.* to cover
cuchara *n., f* spoon
cucharita *n., f* teaspoon
cuchillo *n., m* knife
cuello *n., m* neck 21
cuenta *n., f* bill 9
cuerda *n., f* rope 22
cuerpo *n., m* body 21
cueva *n., f* cave
cuidado *n., m* care; caution
cuidar *v.* to take care of; **cuidarse** to take care of (oneself) 21
culpa *n., f* fault 25
culpar *v.* to blame
cumpleaños *n., m* birthday
cumplido *n., m* compliment
cuñado/a *n.* brother-in-law/sister-in-law 4
cura *n., m* priest

curar *v.* to cure
curiosidades *n., f* curios
currículum *n., m* résumé 28

D

damas chinas *n., f* checkers 22
dar (yo doy) *v.* to give 11; **dar de comer** *v.* to feed 18; **dar gusto** *v.* to please; **dar un paseo** *v.* to go for a walk 18; **dar vuelta** *v.* to turn 26; **darse cuenta** *v.* to realize 25; **darse vuelta** *v.* to turn 25
de repente *adv.* suddenly, all of a sudden 25
deber *v.* must, ought to
decir (yo digo) *v.* to tell 20
dedicar *v.* to dedicate
defender (e→ie) *v.* to defend
defensa *n., f* defense
dejar *v.* to allow; to leave; to drop off 11
dejar de *v.* to stop (doing something)
delgado/a *adj.* thin 6
demasiado/a *adj.,* too much
demonio *n., m* demon
departamento *n., m* apartment
deporte *n., m* sport
derecha *n., f* right 23
derecho *n., m* law
derecho/a *adj.* straight 26
desagradable *adj.* unpleasant
desarreglado/a *adj.* messy 18
desastre *n., m* disaster
desayunar *v.* to have breakfast 9
desayuno *n., m* breakfast 9
descanso *n., m* rest 21
descansar *v.* to rest 5
descomponerse *v.* to break down
descubrimiento *n., m* discovery
descubrir *v.* to uncover; to discover
desde *prep.* since
desear *v.* to wish; to hope
desempeñar *v.* to perform
deseo *n., m* wish
desfile *n., m* parade
desierto *n., m* desert
deshonesto/a *adj.* dishonest 3
desilusionado/a *adj.* disappointed 15
desobedecer (yo desobedezco) *v.* to disobey 22
despacho *n., m* office
despedir (e→i) *v.* to fire, to lay off; **despedirse (e→i)** *v.* to say good-bye
despertador *n., m* alarm clock
después *adv.* after, later
desventaja *n., f* disadvantage 11
detalle *n., m* detail
devolver *v.* to return (merchandise) 27

día *n., m* day
diario *n., m* newspaper; diary; journal
diario/a *adj.* daily
dibujar *v.* to draw 22
dibujo *n., m* drawing
dibujo animado *n., m* cartoon 22
diccionario *n., m* dictionary 2
diciembre *n., m* December 13
dieta *n., f* diet
diferente *adj.* different 6
difícil *adj.* hard, difficult 6
dinero *n., m* money 11
dirección *n., f* address
direcciones *n., f* directions, instructions
director(a) *n.* principal, director
disco compacto (CD) *n., m* compact disc
discoteca *n., f* disco 8
discreto/a *adj.* discrete 3
disculparse *v.* to apologize
discutir *v.* to argue; to discuss 8
diseñador(a) gráfico/a *n.* graphic designer 12
diseñar *v.* to design
disfrazarse de *v.* to wear a . . . costume 20
disfrutar *v.* to enjoy
dispuesto/a *adj.* willing
divertido/a *adj.* fun 6
divertirse (e ➞ ie) *v.* to have fun 14
divorciarse *v.* to get divorced 28
doblar *v.* to turn 26
doctor(a) *n.* doctor 1
doctorado *n., m* doctorate, Ph. D. 28
dólar *n., m* dollar
doler (o ➞ ue) *v.* to hurt
dolor *n., m* pain
domingo *n., m* Sunday 5
dona *n., f* donut 9
dónde *adv.* where (interrogative) 6
dormir (o ➞ ue) *v.* to sleep 10
dormirse *v.* to fall asleep
dormitorio *n., m* bedroom
drama *n., m* drama 1
ducha *n., f* shower 18
ducharse *v.* to shower
duda *n., f* doubt
dudar *v.* to doubt
dueño/a *n.* owner
dulce *n., m* candy
dulce *adj.* sweet 9
durante *prep.* during

E

economía *n., f* economics 1
edad *n., f* age
edificio *n., m* building 2
educación física *n., f* physical education 1
educador(a) *n.* educator 12

egoísta *adj.* selfish
ejecutivo/a *n., adj.* executive
ejercicio *n., m* exercise
ejército *n., m* army
ejotes *n., m* green beans
embarazarse *v.* to get pregnant
embarazo *n., m* pregnancy
emocionado/a *adj.* excited 15
empezar (e ➞ ie) *v.* to start, to begin 10
empleado/a *n.* employee 11
empresa *n., f* company, business 12
empujar *v.* to push 25
en cuanto *adv. conj.* as soon as 30
en vez de *prep.* instead of
enamorado/a *v.* to be in love
enamorarse *v.* to fall in love 28
encantado/a *interj.* delighted 1
encantar *v.* to enchant 19
encontrar (o ➞ ue) *v.* to find 10
enero *n., m* January 13
enfermarse *v.* to get sick 21
enfermería *n., f* health center 2
enfermero/a *n.* nurse 12
enfermo/a *adj.* sick 15
enfrente *prep.* across from, in front of 26
engordar *v.* to gain weight
enojado/a *adj.* upset, mad 15
enojarse *v.* to get upset
ensalada *n., f* salad 9
ensanchar *v.* to widen
enseñar *v.* to teach; to show 24
entender (e ➞ ie) *v.* to understand 10
entonces *adv.* then
entrada *n., f* entrance 26
entrar *v.* to enter 28
entre semana *adv.* on weekdays 5
entregar *v.* to deliver; to turn in 24
entrenamiento *n., m* training
entrenar *v.* to train
entrevista *n., f* interview 28
enviar *v.* to send
envolver (o ➞ ue) *v.* to wrap
equipo *n., m* equipment; team
escandalosa/o *adj.* scandalous
escoger *v.* choose
esconderse *v.* to hide
escondidillas *n., f* hide-and-seek 22
escondite *n., m* hiding place
escondite (al) *n., m* hide-and-seek 22
escribir *v.* to write 8
escribir a máquina *v.* to type
escritor(a) *n.* writer
escritorio *n., m* desk 2
escuchar *v.* to listen 5
escuela *n., f* school 8
escuela pública *n., f* public school 22
escuela de niñas/os *n., f* all-girls/boys school 22
escultor(a) *n.* sculptor
ese/a *adj.* that 6

esencial *adj.* essential
esfuerzo *n., m* effort
esos/as *adj.* those 6
espagueti *n., m* spaghetti 9
espalda *n., f* back 21
español *n., m* Spanish 1; español(a) *adj.* Spaniard
espantoso/a *adj.* horrendous
espejo *n., m* mirror 18
esperanza *n., f* hope
esperar *v.* to wait; *v.* to hope, to expect 27
esponja *n., f* sponge
esposo/a *n.* husband/wife 4
esquiar (yo esquío) *v.* to ski 18
esquina *n., f* corner 26
esta noche *n.* tonight
estable *adj.* stable
estación *n., f* season 13
estacionamiento *n., m* parking 2
estacionar(se) *v.* to park 26
estadio *n., m* stadium 2
estancia *n., f* stay, visit
estandarte *n., m* banner
estar (yo estoy) *v.* to be 15
estar en *v.* to be at/in/on
estar listo/a *v.* to be ready 15
estar seguro *v.* to be sure
este *n., m* east 26
este/a *adj.* this 6
éste/a *n.* this one
estómago *n., m* stomach 21
estos/as *adj.* these 6
estrecho/a *adj.* narrow, close
estricto/a *adj.* strict
estudiante *n., mf* student 2
estudiar *v.* to study 5
estudios *n., m* studies
estudioso/a *adj.* studious 3
estufa *n., f* stove 18
estupendo/a *adj.* great
etapa *n., f* stage
evitar *v.* to avoid
examen *n., m* exam, test
excelente *adj.* excellent 3
exceso *n., m* excess
exhibición de arte *n., f* art exhibition 8
exigente *adj.* demanding
exigir (g ➞ j) *v.* to demand
éxito *n., m* success
experto/a *n.* expert
explicar *v.* to explain 24
extrañar *v.* to miss
extranjero/a *adj.* foreign; extranjero/a *n.* foreigner
extraño/a *adj.* strange
extrovertido/a *adj.* extroverted 3

F

fácil *adj.* easy 6
falda *n., f* skirt 13
faltar *v.* to be missing, to lack

familia *n., f* family
familiares *n., m* relatives **4**
farmaceuta *n., mf* pharmacist
fascinar *v.* to love; to be fascinated by **19**
febrero *n., m* February **13**
fecha *n., f* date (calendar)
felicidad *n., f* happiness
feliz *adj.* happy **20**
feo/a *adj.* ugly **6**
fibra *n., f* fiber
fiebre *n., f* fever **21**
fiesta *n., f* party
fijarse *v.* to pay attention
fijo/a *adj.* fixed, steady **11**
filosofía *n., f* philosophy **1**
fin de semana *n., m* weekend **5**
final *adj.* final
final *n., m* end
fino/a *adj.* fine, high quality
firma *n., f* signature
firmar *v.* to sign
flaco/a *adj.* thin
flan *n., m* flan, custard **9**
flexible *adj.* flexible **3**
flojo/a *adj.* lazy, loose
flor *n., f* flower
folleto *n., m* brochure
formal *adj.* formal **20**
fortaleza *n., f* fort
fosforescente *adj.* fluorescent
fotografía *n., f* picture
fractura *n., f* fracture
francés *n., m* French; **francés, francesa** *adj.* French
frecuencia *adv.* often, frequently
fregadero *n., m* kitchen sink **18**
frenar *v.* to break **26**
freno *n., m* brake
frente *n., f* forehead
frente a *prep.* in front of
fresco/a *adj.* fresh, cool **13**; **hace fresco** it's cool **13**
frijoles *n., m* beans **9**
frío/a *adj.* cold **13**; **hace frío** it's cold **13**
frito/a *adj.* fried
frontera *n., f* border
fruta *n., f* fruit **9**
fuente *n., f* fountain
fuerte *adj.* strong
fuerza *n., f* force
fumar *v.* to smoke **19**
funcionar *v.* to work, to function
fútbol *n., m* soccer **8**

G

galleta *n., f* cookie **9**
ganar *v.* to win **12**
ganarse *v.* to earn
garaje *n., m* garage **18**
garganta *n., f* throat **21**
gaseosa *n., f* soda

gasolina *n., f* gas **26**
gasolinera *n., f* gas station
gastar *v.* to spend **19**
gato/a *n.* cat **4**
generoso/a *adj.* generous **3**
gente *n., f* people
geografía *n., f* geography **1**
gerente *n., mf* manager **12**
gimnasio *n., m* gym **2**
gobierno *n., m* government **28**
golpe *n., m* hit **25**
goma *n., f* tire
gordo/a *adj.* fat **6**
grabado *n., m* print, carving
grabadora *n., f* tape recorder
gracias *interj.* thank you **1**
gracioso/a *adj.* funny **6**
grado *n., m* degree (temperature)
graduación *n., f* graduation **28**
graduarse *v.* to graduate **28**
grama *n., f* grass
grande *adj.* big, large **6**
grasa *n., f* fat
gratis *adj.* free (of charge)
grave *adj.* serious
gripe *n., f* flu
gris *adj.* gray **13**
gritar *v.* to shout, to yell
grosero/a *adj.* impolite, rough, rude **6**
guapo/a *adj.* handsome, good-looking **6**
guantes *n., m* gloves **13**
guardabosques *n., mf* park ranger
guayaba *n., f* guava
güero/a *adj.* blond(e)
guerra *n., f* war
guía *n., mf* tour guide (person)
guía *n., f* guide book, pamphlet
guineo *n., m* banana
guitarra *n., f* guitar **5**
gustar (me gusta) *v.* to like **3**

H

habilidad *n., f* ability
habitación *n., f* bedroom, room
hábito *n., m* habits
hablar *v.* to speak, to talk **5**
hacer (yo hago) *v.* to do, to make **8**; **hacer berrinches** *v.* to throw tantrums **22**; **hacer ejercicio** *v.* to exercise **8**; **hacer las maletas** *v.* to pack **20**; **hacer travesuras** *v.* to get into trouble **22**; **hacer un picnic** *v.* to have a picnic **18**; **hacer un viaje** *v.* to take a trip **18**; **hacer una fiesta** *v.* to throw a party **18**; **hacer una maestría** *v.* to pursue a Master's degree **28**; **hacerse daño** *v.* to hurt oneself
hambre, (el) *n., f* hunger
hamburguesa *n., f* hamburger **9**
hasta (que) *prep.* until **28**; **hasta**

ahora until now **28**; **hasta luego** see you later **1**; **hasta mañana** see you tomorrow **1**
hay *v.* there is/are
hecho, (de) *n., m* in fact
helado *n., m* ice cream **9**
herida *n., f* wound
hermano/a *n.* brother, sister **4**
hielo *n., m* ice
hierba *n., f* grass, herb
hierro *n., m* iron
higienista dental *n., mf* dental hygienist **12**
hijo/a *n.* son, daughter **4**
hijo/a único/a *n.* only child **6**
historia *n., f* history; story **1**
hola *interj.* hello, hi **1**
hombre *n., m* man
honesto/a *adj.* honest **3**
hora *n., f* hour, time (of day)
horario *n., m* schedule **11**; **horario fijo** fixed schedule **11**; **horario flexible** flexible schedule **11**
horno *n., m* oven **18**
horno, (al) *adj.* baked
horrible *adj.* horrible
hoy *n.* today
huarache *n., m* sandal
huevo *n., m* egg **9**
huir *v.* to flee
húmedo/a *adj.* humid
hundirse *v.* to sink

I

idealista *n., mf* idealist **3**
idioma *n., m* language **12**
iglesia *n., f* church **8**
igual *adj.* same, equal **21**
igualmente *adv.* likewise **1**
iluminar *v.* to color
imaginar *v.* to imagine
imaginativo/a *adj.* imaginative
impaciente *adj.* impatient **3**
impermeable *n., m* raincoat **13**
importante *adj.* important **27**
impuesto *n., m* tax
inagotable *adj.* inexhaustible
incendio *n., m* fire
incluir *v.* to include
increíble *adj.* incredible **3**
indiscreto/a *adj.* indiscreet
infección *n., f* infection **21**
información *n., f* information **5**
informal *adj.* casual **20**
ingeniero/a en computación *n.* computer engineer **12**
inglés *n., m* English; **inglés, inglesa** *adj.* English
inscripción *n., f* registration
inseguro/a *adj.* uncertain, insecure
insoportable *adj.* unbearable
inteligente *adj.* intelligent
interesante *adj.* interesting **3**

interesar (me interesa) *v.* to interest 19
intersección *n., f* intersection 26
inundación *n., f* flood
investigación *n., f* research
investigador(a) *n.* investigator 12
invierno *n., m* winter 13
invitado/a *n.* guest
invitar *v.* to invite 10
inyección *n., f* shot, injection
ir (irr.) *v.* to go 20; **ir (a exceso de velocidad)** *v.* to speed 26; **ir de campamento** *v.* to go camping 18; **ir de compras** *v.* to go shopping; **ir de excursión** *v.* to hike 18; **irse** to leave 14; **irse de vacaciones** to go on vacation 14
irreconocible *adj.* unrecognizable
irresponsable *adj.* irresponsible 3
izquierda *n., f* left 26
izquierdo/a *adj* left 23

J

jamón *n., m* ham 9
jarabe para la tos *n., m* cough syrup 21
jardín *n., m* backyard, garden 18
jeans *n. m* jeans 13
jefe/a *n.* boss
¡jolines! *interj.* Wow!
joven *n., mf* young man, woman 6
joyería *n., f* jewelry store 27
jubilado/a *adj.* retired
judío/a *adj.* Jewish; **judío/a** *n.* Jew
juego *n., m* game
jueves *n., m* Thursday 5
jugador(a) *n.* player
jugar (u ➤ ue) *v.* to play (sports, games) 10
jugo *n., m* juice 9
juguete *n., m* toy 22
julio *n., m* July 13
junio *n., m* June 13
junta *n., f* meeting
juntarse *v.* to get together 14
junto/a *adj.* together
jurado *n., m* jury (panel of judges)

L

lado *n., m* side 23
lado, (al) *prep.* next to
ladrón, ladrona *n.* thief
lago *n., m* lake
lámpara *n., f* lamp 18
langosta *n., f* lobster 9
lápiz *n., m* pencil 2
largo/a *adj.* long
lastimarse *v.* to get hurt 21
latón *n., m* brass
lavabo *n., m* bathroom sink 18
lavar *v.* to wash 5

lavar los platos *v.* to do (wash) the dishes 18
lavarse *v.* to wash (oneself)
lavarse las manos *v.* to wash one's hands 14
lavarse los dientes *v.* to brush one's teeth 14
lección *n., f* lesson
leche *n., f* milk 9
lechón *n., m* suckling pig
lechuga *n., f* lettuce 9
leer *v.* to read 8
lejos *adv.* far
lengua *n., f* tongue; language
lentes de sol *n., m* sun glasses 13
levantar pesas *v.* to lift weights 18
levantarse *v.* to get up 14
ley *n., f* law
libre *adj.* free 15
librería *n., f* bookstore 2
libro *n., m* book 2
licencia de manejar *n., f* driver's license 26
licenciatura *n., f* bachelor's degree
liceo *n., m* high school
ligero/a *adj.* light 13
límite *n., m* limit
limonada *n., f* lemonade 9
limpiar *v.* to clean 5
limpio/a *adj.* clean 18
línea *n., f* line
lío *n., m* problem
líquidos *n., m* liquids 21
listo/a (ser) *adj.* smart 6
literatura *n., f* literature 1
llamar *v.* to call 11
llanta *n., f* tire 26
llegada *n., f* arrival
llegar *v.* to arrive 5
llenar *v.* to fill 28
llevar *v.* to take someone somewhere 24; to wear 13; **llevarse bien/mal** *v.* to get along well/poorly 22
llorar *v.* to cry
llorón, llorona *adj.* crybaby 22
llover (o ➤ ue) *v.* to rain 13
lluvia *n., f* rain
loco/a *adj.* crazy, mad
logro *n., m* accomplishment, achievement
lucha *n., f* struggle
luego *adv.* later
lugar *n., m* place 11
lujo *n., m* luxury
lunes *n., m* Monday 5
luz *n., f* light

M

madre *n., f* mother 4
madrugar *v.* to get up early
maduro/a *adj.* mature 3
maestría *n., f* Master's 28

maestro/a *n.* teacher
mágico/a *adj.* magical
magisterio *n., m* teaching
mahones *n., m* jeans
majo/a *adj.* nice, cute
mal *adv.* bad, ill 21
malecón *n., m* seawall
maleducar *v.* to spoil
malentendido *n., m* misunderstanding
maleta *n., f* suitcase 13
malo/a *adj.* bad 6
malta *n., f* malt
mamá *n., f* mom
mandar *v.* to send 11
mandar un fax *v.* to fax
mandón, mandona *adj.* bossy
manejar *v.* to drive 26
manera *n., f* way
mango *n., m* mango
maní *n., m* peanut
mano *n., f* hand 14
mantequilla *n., f* butter
manzana *n., f* apple 9; city block
mañana *n., f* morning 11
mañana *adv.* tomorrow
mañanitas *n., f* birthday song 20
mapa *n., m* map 2
maquillarse *v.* to apply makeup
máquina *n., f* machine
máquina de escribir *n., f* typewriter
mareado/a *adj.* dizzy 21
mariscos *n., m* seafood 9
marrón *adj.* brown
martes *n., m* Tuesday 5
marzo *n., m* March 13
más *adv.* more; **más o menos** so-so 1; **más... que** more... than 17
masaje *n., m* massage
mascota *n., f* pet
matatena *n., f* jacks
matemáticas *n., f* math 1
materia *n., f* subject
materialista *adj.* materialistic 3
materno/a *adj.* maternal
matrimonio *n., m* marriage
mayo *n., m* May 13
mayor *adj.* older 6
mayor, (el/la) *n.* the oldest 6
mayoría *n., f* majority
mecánica *n., f* mechanics
mecánico/a *adj.* mechanic
médico/a *n.* doctor 12
medio/a *n., adj.* half, medium
mediodía *n., m* noon
mejor que *adj.* better than 17
menor *adj.* younger 6
menor, (el/la) *n.* the youngest 6
menos que, (a) *conj.* unless 30
menos... que *adv.* less... than 17
mensaje *n., m* message
mentira *n., f* lie 24
menú *n., m* menu
mercadeo *n., m* marketing
mercadotécnia *n., f* marketing 12

mermelada *n., f* marmalade
mes *n., m* month 13
mesa *n., f* table 18; **mesa de noche** *n., f* night table 18
mesero/a *n.* waiter, waitress 9
meta *n., f* goal
meterse *v.* to get involved
metro *n., m* subway; meter (measurement)
mezclilla *n., f* denim
microondas, (el) *n., f* microwave (oven) 18
miedo *n., m* fear
mientras *adv.* while
miércoles *n., m* Wednesday 5
mil *adj.* thousand
milla *n., f* mile
minifalda *n., f* mini-skirt 13
mirar *v.* to see, to watch 5
misa *n., f* mass; religious service
mismo/a *n., adj.* same; self
mochila *n., f* backpack 2
moderno/a *adj.* modern 20
moler (o→ue) *v.* to grind
molestar *v.* to bother 19
molesto/a *adj.* upset 15
momento *n., m* moment 28
moneda *n., f* coin
montaña *n., f* mountain
montar *v.* to ride 18
morado/a *adj.* purple 13
moreno/a *adj.* dark-skinned, tanned 6
morir (o→ue) *v.* to die 28
mostrar (o→ue) *v.* to show
mover (o→ue) *v.* to move
mozo/a *n.* waiter, waitress
muchacho/a *n.* young person
mucho/a *adv.* a lot 5; **mucho gusto** nice to meet you 1
muchos/as *adj.* many
mudarse *v.* to move 28
mueble *n., m* furniture 18
mujer *n., f* woman
mujeriego *n., m* womanizer
multa *n., f* fine, ticket 26
muñeco/a *n.* doll 22
muro *n., m* wall (outside)
museo *n., m* museum 8
música *n., f* music 1; **poner la música muy alta** *v.* to play loud music 23
muy *adv.* very; **muy bien** very well 1

N

nada *n.* nothing, anything 18
nadar *v.* to swim
nadie *n.* anybody, nobody, no one 18
naranja *n., f* orange 9
nariz *n., f* nose 21
Navidad *n., f* Christmas

necesario/a *adj.* necessary
necesitar *v.* to need 5
negarse (e→ie) *v.* to refuse
negocio *n., m* business
negro/a *adj.* black 13
nervioso/a *adj.* nervous 3
neumático *n., m* tire
nevar (e→ie) *v.* to snow 13
ni *conj.* neither, nor; **ni siquiera** *adv.* not even
nieto/a *n.* grandson/daughter 4
ningún, ninguna *adj.* not any 18; **ninguna parte, (a)** nowhere 8
niñero/a *n.* baby-sitter 11
niñez *n., f* childhood
niño/a *n.* child, kid 4
nivel *n., m* level
noche *n., f* evening, night 11
nombre *n., m* name
normalista *n., mf* elementary teacher
norte *n., m* north 26
nota *n., f* grades; note 5
notar *v.* to notice
noticias *n., f* news
novela *n., f* novel
noviazgo *n., m* engagement
noviembre *n., m* November 13
novio/a *n.* boy/girlfriend 4
nublado/a *adj.* cloudy 13; **está nublado** it's cloudy 13
nudo *n., m* knot
nuera *n., f* daughter-in-law
nuevo/a *adj.* new 6
número *n., m* number 1
nunca *adv.* never 8

O

obedecer (yo obedezco) *v.* to obey 22
obediente *adj.* obedient
obligación *n., f* duty
obra de arte *n., f* work of art
octubre *n., m* October 13
ocupación *n., f* occupation
ocupado/a *adj.* busy 15
odiar *v.* to hate
oeste *n., m* west 26
oficial de prisión *n., mf* prison guard 12
oficina *n., f* office 2
ofrecer (yo ofrezco) *v.* to offer 24
oído *n., m* (inner) ear 20
oír (yo oigo) *v.* to hear 17
ojalá que... *interj.* hopefully 27
ojo *n., m* eye 21
olvidar *v.* to forget
onda *n., f* wave
oportunidad *n., f* opportunity
optimista *adj.* optimistic 3
ordenado/a *adj.* tidy
ordenador *n., m* computer
organizar *v.* to organize

orgullo *n., m* pride
orgulloso/a *adj.* proud
origen *n., m* origin
ostión *n., m* oyster
otoño *n., m* fall 13
otra vez again
otro/a *adj.* another

P

paciencia *n., f* patience
paciente *n., mf* patient 3
padre *n., m* father; priest 4
padres *n., m* parents 4
paella *n., f* Spanish rice dish
pagar *v.* to pay 11
país *n., m* country
pájaro *n., m* bird 4
palabra *n., f* word
pan tostado *n., m* toast 9
pantalones *n., m* pants 13; **pantalones de mezclilla** *n., m* jeans; **pantalones cortos** *n., m* shorts 13
papa *n., f* potato 9; **papas fritas** *n., f* french fries 9
papá *n., m* dad
papás *n., m* parents
papel *n., m* paper; role 2
papelería *n., f* office supply store
par *n., m* pair, couple; even
para *prep.* for
para que *conj.* so that 30
parabrisas *n., m* windshield
paraguas *n., m* umbrella 13
pararse *v.* to stop 26
parcial *adj.* part-time; partial
pardo *adj.* brown
parecer (yo parezco) *v.* to seem; to look like
pared *n., f* wall
pareja *n., f* couple
parientes *n., m* relatives
parque (de atracciones) *n., m* (amusement) park 8
parte *n., f* part
particular *adj.* private 22
partido *n., m* match, game 8
partir *v.* to cut; to depart
pasado/a *adj.* last (year,...), past 15
pasar *v.* to pass 26
pasar la aspiradora *v.* to vacuum 18
pasarse (el alto/el semáforo en rojo) *v.* to run a red light 26
pasear *v.* to walk, to stroll
paseo *n., m* walk, stroll
pastel *n., m* cake 9
pastilla *n., f* pill 21
pasto *n., m* lawn, grass 18
patata *n., f* potato
paterno/a *adj.* paternal
patinar en línea, en hielo *v.* to skate; to rollerblade; to ice skate 18
patio *n., m* patio 18

pavo *n., m* turkey **9**
pedazo *n., m* piece
pedida *n., f* marriage proposal
pedir (e → i) *v.* to ask, to request **9**
pedir cosas prestadas *v.* to borrow things **11**
pedir la mano *v.* to propose (marriage)
pegar *v.* to hit, to glue **25**; **pegarse** *v.* to stick; to hit yourself
peinarse *v.* to comb one's hair
pelar *v.* to peel
pelearse *v.* to fight **22**
película *n., f* film
peligro *n., m* danger
peligroso/a *adj.* dangerous
pelirrojo/a *adj.* red-haired
pelota *n., f* ball
pena *n., f* pity, sorrow
pensar (e → ie) *v.* to think **10**; **pensar** + [verb] *v.* to plan
peor que *adv.* worse than **17**
pequeño/a *adj.* small **6**
pera *n., f* pear **9**
perder (e → ie) *v.* to lose; to miss **17**
perdón *interj.* sorry
perdonar *v.* to forgive; to excuse
perezoso/a *adj.* lazy **6**
perico/a *n.* parakeet
periódico *n., m* newspaper
periodista *n., mf* journalist **12**
perro/a *n.* dog **4**
persona *n., f* person
personaje *n., m* character (movie, book)
personal *n., m* personnel
pesado/a *adj.* heavy
pesar, (a) *conj.* despite
pescado *n., m* fish (food) **9**
pesimista *adj.* pessimistic **3**
peso *n., m* weight, currency
petaca *n., f* suitcase
pez *n., m* fish (live) **4**
pie *n., m* foot **21**
piel *n., f* leather; skin
pierna *n., f* leg **21**
pieza *n., f* bedroom
pijama *n., m, n., f* pajamas **13**
pincharse (una llanta) *v.* to have a flat tire
pintar *v.* to paint
pintarse *v.* to put on makeup **14**
pintor(a) *n.* painter
pintura *n., f* painting
piñata *n., f* container filled with candies **22**
pirámide *n., f* pyramid
piscina *n., f* swimming pool **2**
piso *n., m* apartment
pista *n., f* track, runway
pizarra *n., f* blackboard
pizarrón *n., m* blackboard **2**
placar *n., m* closet
plan *n., m* plan

planchar *v.* to iron **18**
plata *n., f* silver
plátano *n., m* banana **9**
platicar *v.* to chat
platillo *n., m* dish **9**
plato *n., m* dish, plate **9**
playa *n., f* beach **8**
pleito *n., m* fight
pluma *n., f* pen **2**
pobre *adj.* poor **6**
pobrecito/a *n.* poor thing
pobreza *n., f* poverty
poco/a *adj.* a little **5**
poder *n., m* power **10**
poder (o → ue) *v.* to be able to, can **20**
poema *n., m* poem
policía *n., m, n., f* police officer **12**
policía *n., f* the police force **23**
pollera *n., f* skirt
pollo *n., m* chicken **9**
poncharse (una llanta) *v.* to have a flat tire **26**
poner (yo pongo) *v.* to put, to place **11**; **poner el árbol** *v.* to decorate the tree **20**; **poner la mesa** *v.* to set the table **18**; **ponerse (irr. yo)** *v.* to wear, to put on, to become **14**
por *prep.* for, because of; **por cierto** *interj.* by the way; **por favor** please; **por lo menos** at least; **por qué** why **6**; **por supuesto** of course
porque *conj.* because
portarse bien/mal *v.* to behave, misbehave **22**
posada *n., f* shelter; a traditional Mexican pre-Christmas party
posgrado *n., m* graduate school
posible *adj.* possible
pozole *n., m* corn and meat soup
precio *n., m* price
preferir (e → ie) *v.* to prefer **10**
preguntar *v.* to ask (questions)
preocupado/a *adj.* worried **15**
preparatoria *n., f* high school **22**
prestación *n., f* fringe benefits **11**
prestar *v.* to lend **11**
pretexto *n., m* excuse, pretext
primaria *n., f* grammar school **22**
primavera *n., f* spring **13**
primero/a *adj.* first **26**
primeros auxilios *n., m* first aid
primo/a *n.* cousin **4**
principiante *n.* beginner
principio *n., m* beginning, principle
prisa *n., f* hurry
probar *v.* to taste, to try
problema *n., m* problem **11**
profesión *n., f* profession
profesor(a) *n.* professor **1**
programa *n., m* program **28**
programador(a) *n.* computer programmer **12**

promedio *n., m* average
prometer *v.* to promise **24**
propina *n., f* tip
propio *adj.* own, self
proteger *v.* to protect
protestante *n., mf* Protestant
próximo/a *adj.* next, close
prueba *n., f* test **2**
público/a *adj.* public
público *n., m* public
pueblo *n., m* town
puerta *n., f* door **2**
puesto *n., m* position, job **11**
pupitre *n., m* student desk **2**

Q

que *conj. pron.* that **27**
qué *adv. pron.* what **6**
quedar embarazada *v.* to get pregnant **28**
quedarse *v.* to stay, to remain **14**
quehacer *n., m* chore **18**
queja *n., f* complaint
quejarse *v.* to complain
quemados *n., m* dodge ball **22**
querer (e → ie) *v.* to love (a person) **10**; to want **27**
queso *n., m* cheese **9**
quién *n.* who **6**
química *n., f* chemistry **1**
quitarse *v.* to take off (clothes) **14**
quizá *adv.* maybe

R

radiador *n., m* radiator
rallar *v.* to grate
raro/a *adj.* strange
rasurarse *v.* to shave
ratito *n., m* little while
rato *n., m* while (short time)
reaccionar *v.* to react
reata *n., f* rope
rebanada *n., f* slice
rebelde *adj.* rebellious **22**
recámara *n., f* bedroom
receta *n., f* recipe
recibir *v.* to get, to receive **8**
recibirse *v.* to graduate **28**
recoger (g → j) *v.* to pick up **18**
recoger la mesa *v.* to clear the table **18**
recomendar (e → ie) *v.* to recommend **27**
recordar (o → ue) *v.* to remember **10**
recuerdo *n., m* memory
recuperación *n., f* recovery
refresco *n., m* soda **9**
refrigerador *n., m* refrigerator **18**
refrito/a *adj.* fried
regalar *v.* to give a gift **20**

regalo *n., m* gift, present **11**
regañar *v.* to scold, to reprimand **22**
regresar *v.* to come back, to return, to get back
reloj *n., m* watch, clock
remedio *n., m* remedy
reparar *v.* to repair, to mend
repartir *v.* to deliver
requisito *n., m* requirement
reservado/a *adj.* reserved **3**
resfriado *n., m* cold
residencia *n., f* residence
residencia estudiantil *n., f* dormitory **2**
resolver (o → ue) *v.* to solve **28**
respetuoso/a *adj.* respectful
respirar *v.* to breathe
responsable *adj.* responsible **3**
restaurante *n., m* restaurant **8**
revisar *v.* to check
revista *n., f* magazine
revuelto/a *adj.* scrambled
Reyes Magos *n., m* the Magi (of Catholic tradition)
rico/a *adj.* rich; tasty **6**
risa *n., f* laughter
rojo/a *adj.* red **13**
romántico/a *adj.* romantic **3**
rompecabezas *n., m* jigsaw puzzle **22**
romper *v.* to break **22; romperse** to break (a hand, an arm) **21**
ropa *n., f* clothes **5**
ropero *n., m* closet
rubio/a *adj.* blond(e) **6**
ruido *n., m* noise
ruta *n., f* route
rutina *n., f* routine

S

sábado *n., m* Saturday **5**
saber (yo sé) *v.* to know **11**
sacar *v.* to take (out) **18; sacar buenas notas** to get good grades **5; sacar al perro a pasear** to take out (walk) the dog **18**
saco *n., m* jacket
sala *n., f* living room **18;** classroom
salida *n., f* exit
salir (yo salgo) *v.* to go out, to date **8**
salirse (en) *v.* to get off (at) **26**
salón *n., m* classroom **2;** living room; **salón de belleza** *n., m* beauty salon
saltar *v.* to jump **22**
salud *n., f* health **21**
saludable *adj.* healthy
salvar *v.* to save (a life)
sandalias *n., f* sandals **13**
sándwich *n., m* sandwich **9**
sano/a *adj.* healthy

seco/a *adj.* dry
secundaria, (escuela) *n., f* high school **22**
sed *n., f* thirst; **tener sed** to be thirsty **9**
seguir (e → i) *v.* to continue, to follow **26**
según *prep.* according to
segundo *n., m* second **26**
segundo/a *adj.* second (2nd)

seguridad *n., f* safety
seguro *n., m* insurance, safe **26**
selva *n., f* jungle
semáforo *n., m* street light **25**
semana *n., f* week **15**
sentarse (e → ie) *v.* to sit
sentido contrario *n.* wrong way
sentimental *adj.* sentimental **3**
sentimiento *n., m* feeling
sentir (e → ie) *v.* to feel (sorry); **sentirse** *v.* to feel **21**
señor(a) *n.* mister, missus **1**
señorita *n., f* miss **1**
separarse *v.* to separate **28**
septiembre *n., m* September **13**
ser (irr.) *v.* to be **4**
serio/a *adj.* serious **3**
servir (e → i) *v.* to serve **9**
sicología *n., f* psychology **1**
sicólogo/a *n.* psychologist **12**
siempre *adv.* always **8**
siguiente *adj.* next, following
silla *n., f* chair **18**
sillón *n., m* armchair **18**
similar *adj.* similar **6**
simpático/a *adj.* funny
sin *prep.* without **26**
sin embargo *conj.* nevertheless
sino *conj.* but
sistema *n., m* system **12**
sobrino/a *n.* nephew, niece **4**
sociable *adj.* sociable **3**
sofá *n., m* sofa **18**
sol *n., m* sun; **hace sol** it's sunny **13**
solamente *adv.* only
solicitar empleo *v.* to request, to apply for a job **28**
solicitud *n., f* application **28**
sólo *adv.* only
solo/a *adj.* alone
soltero/a *adj.* single (unmarried) **6**
sombrero *n., m* hat **13**
sonar (o → ue) *v.* to ring (bells); to sound
sopa *n., f* soup **9**
subirse a los árboles *v.* to climb trees **22; subirse a los columpios** to go on the swings **22; subirse a los juego** to go on rides **20**
sucio/a *adj.* dirty **18**
sudor *n., m* sweat
suegro/a *n.* father/mother-in-law **4**
sueldo *n., m* salary, wage **11**
suelo *n., m* floor **18**

sueño *n., m* dream
suerte *n., f* luck
suéter *n., m* sweater **13**
suficiente *adj.* enough, sufficient
sugerir (e → ie) *v.* to suggest
superarse *v.* to better oneself
superficie *n., f* surface
supermercado *n., m* market **8**
suponer (yo supongo) *v.* to suppose
sur *n., m* south **26**
surfear *v.* to surf
susto *n., m* scare, fright

T

tacón *n., m* heel
tal vez *adv.* maybe, perhaps
tamaño *n., m* size
también *adv.* also **18**
tambor *n., m* drum
tampoco *adv.* neither **18**
tan *adj.* as; **tan** [*adjective*] **como** as [*adjective*] as **17**
tanque *n., m* tank
tanto *adv.* so much; **tanto/a** [*noun*] **como** as [*noun*] as **17**
tapas *n., f* snacks
tardar(se) *v.* to take long
tarde *adv.* late **5**
tarde *n., f* afternoon
tarea *n., f* homework
tarjeta *n., f* (credit) card
té *n., m* tea **9**
teatro *n., m* theater
técnico/a en computación *n.* computer technician **12**
telaraña *n., f* cobweb
televisión *n., f* TV **2**
televisor *n., m* TV
teléfono *n., m* telephone **5**
tema *n., m* theme
temprano *adv.* early **5**
tenedor *n., m* fork
tener (yo tengo, e → ie) *v.* to have **4; tener calor** to be hot; **tener dolor de...** to have a(n) ...ache **21; tener frío** to be cold; **tener ganas de** to feel like **7; tener hambre** to be hungry **9; tener miedo** to be afraid; **tener prisa** to be in a hurry; **tener que** to have to **20; tener razón** to be right; **tener sed** to be thirsty **9; tener sueño** to be sleepy; **tener suerte** to be lucky
tenis *n., m* tennis (sport) **2;** tennis sneakers **13**
terapeuta *n., mf* therapist
tercero/a *adj.* third
terminar *v.* to finish, to end **28**
terremoto *n., m* earthquake
terrible *adj.* terrible **3**
tiempo *n., m* time, weather; occasion **13; tiempo, (a)** on time **5; tiempo, (hace buen/mal)** the

weather is nice/bad 13; **tiempo completo/parcial** full-time, part-time 11; **tiempo libre** spare time 11

tienda *n., f* store 8; **tienda de campaña** *n., f* tent

tierra *n., f* earth, soil

tímido/a *adj.* shy 3

tina *n., f* bathtub 18

tío/a *n.* uncle, aunt 4

tipo *n., m* type, kind

tira cómica *n., f* comic strip

tirar *v.* to throw; to pull

título *n., m* degree, title

toalla *n., f* towel 18

tocar *v.* to play (instrument); to touch 5

tocino *n., m* bacon

todavía *adv.* already, yet 28

todo/a *adj.* all, everything; **todos los días** every day 5

tomar *v.* to take, to drink 5

tomate *n., m* tomato 9

tonto/a *adj.* dumb, silly 6

tortilla *n., f* tortilla

tos *n., f* cough 21

trabajador(a) *adj.* hard-working 6

trabajar *v.* to work 5

trabajo *n., m* work, job 8

traductor(a) *n.* translator

traer (yo traigo) *v.* to bring, to take 20

tráfico *n., m* traffic

traje *n., m* suit 13

traje de baño *n., m* swimming suit 13

tranquilo/a *adj.* calm, quiet 3

tranvía *n., m* trolley

trapear *v.* to mop

trapo *n., m* cloth

trastes *n., m* dishes

travesura *n., f* mischief 22

través, (a) *prep.* through

travieso/a *adj.* mischievous 22

tren *n., m* train

triste *adj.* sad 15

turno *n., m* shift, turn 11

U

últimamente *adv.* lately 28

último/a *adj.* last

único/a *adj.* unique, only

universidad *n., f* university

usar *v.* to use 5; to wear 13

útil *adj.* useful

uva *n., f* grape 9

V

vacaciones *n., f* vacation 11

vacaciones, (de) on vacation 13

vacunar *v.* to vaccinate

vajilla *n., f* dishes

valija *n., f* suitcase

vaqueros *n., m* jeans

varios/as *adj.* several

vaso *n., m* glass

veces, (a) *adv.* sometimes 8

vecino/a *adj.* neighbor 23

veliz *n., m* suitcase

velocidad *n., f* speed

veloz *adv.* quick

vencido/a *adj.* expired, defeated

vendedor(a) *n.* salesperson

vender *v.* to sell 8

venir (yo vengo, e→ie) *v.* to come 20

ventaja *n., f* advantage 11

ventana *n., f* window 2

ver (yo veo) *v.* to see, to watch 8

verano *n., m* summer 13

verdad *n., f* truth

verde *adj.* green 13

verdura *n., f* vegetable

vergüenza *n., f* shame, embarrassment

verificar *v.* to verify

vestido *n., m* dress 13

vestirse (e→i) *v.* to get dressed

veterinario *n., mf* veterinarian 12

vez *n., m* time

viajar *v.* to travel

viaje *n., m* trip 18

vida *n., f* life

videocasetera *n., f* VCR 2

vidrio *n., m* glass (crystal)

viejo/a *adj.* old 6

viento *n., m* wind; **hace viento** it's windy 13

viernes *n., m* Friday 5

villancicos *n., m* carols 20

vino *n., m* wine 9

violín *n., m* violin

virar *v.* to turn

visitar *v.* to visit 5

vivir *v.* to live 8

volante *n., m* steering wheel

vóleibol *n., m* volleyball 2

volver (o→ue) *v.* to return; to come back 28; **volverse** to become

vuelo *n., m* flight

vuelta *n., f* turn 25

Y

y *conj.* and

ya *adv.* already, still 28

yate *n., m* yacht

yerno *n., m* son-in-law

yo *pron.* I

yogur *n., m* yogurt 9

yuca *n., f* yucca

Z

zanahoria *n., f* carrot 9

zapato *n., m* shoe 13

zoológico *n., m* zoo

English-Spanish

A

able *adj.* capaz; **to be able** poder (o→ue)
aboard *adv.* a bordo
above *adv.* arriba
abroad *adv.* en el extranjero
according (to) *prep.* según
account *n., f* cuenta
accountant *n.* contador(a) 12
across from *prep.* enfrente 26
active *adj.* activo/a 3
actor *n., m* actor
actress *n., f* actriz
advertisment *n., m* anuncio
address *n., f* dirección
adult *n., m* adulto
advantage *n., f* ventaja 11
advice *n., m* consejo 11
advise *v.* aconsejar 27
advisor *n.* consejero/a 2
affectionate *adj.* cariñoso/a 6
after *prep.* después
afternoon *n., f* tarde
again *adv.* otra vez
against *prep.* contra
age *n., f* edad
agent *n., mf* agente 12
agree *v.* aceptar, estar de acuerdo
agreement *n., m* acuerdo
AIDS *n., m* SIDA
air *n., m* aire
airplane *n., m* avión 20
airport *n., m* aeropuerto 8
all *adj.* todo/a
all-boys/girls school *n., f* escuela de niños/as 22
allow *v.* dejar, permitir 11
almost *adv.* casi 8
alone *adj.* solo/a
already *adv.* ya 28
also *adv.* también 18
although *conj.* aunque
always *adv.* siempre 8
a.m. de la mañana
ambitious *adj.* ambicioso/a 3
ambulance *n., f* ambulancia
amusement park *n., m* parque de atracciones 8
analyst *n., mf* analista 12
antiquity *n., f* antigüedad
angel *n., m* ángel
another *n.* otro/a
answer *v.* contestar
anthropology *n., f* antropología 1
antibiotic *n., m* antibiótico 21
anybody *n.* alguien
apartment *n., m* apartamento 18
apologize *v.* disculparse
apple *n., f* manzana 9
application *n., f* solicitud 28
apply for a job *v.* solicitar empleo 28

April *n., m* abril 13
aquatic *adj.* acuático/a
architect *n.* arquitecto/a 13
architecture *n., f* arquitectura
argue *v.* discutir 8
arm *n., m* brazo 21
armchair *n., m* sillón 21
around *prep.* alrededor
arrest *v.* arrestar
arrival *n., f* llegada
arrive *v.* llegar 5
arrogant *adj.* arrogante 3
art exhibition *n., f* exhibición de arte 8
artist *n., mf* artista 12
as soon as *adv.* en cuanto 30
as [adjective] as *adv.* tan [adjective] como 17
as [noun] as *adv.* tanto/a [noun] como 17
ask (questions) *v.* preguntar; **ask (to request)** pedir (e→i) 9
aspirin *n., f* aspirina 21
assemble (a puzzle) *v.* armar (un rompecabezas) 22
astronomy *n., f* astronomía 1
attend *v.* asistir
attractive *adj.* atractivo/a 3
auditorium *n., m* auditorio 2
August *n., m* agosto 13
aunt *n., f* tía 4
avenue *n., f* avenida 26
average *n., m* promedio
avocado *n., m* aguacate

B

baby *n., mf* bebé
baby-sitter *n.* niñero/a 11
bachelor's *n., f* licenciatura
back *n., f* espalda 21
backpack *n., f* mochila 2
backyard *n., m* jardín 18
bacon *n., m* tocino
bad *adj.* malo/a, mal 6
bag *n., f* bolsa
baked *adj.* al horno
balcony *n., m* balcón
ball *n., f* pelota 22
banana *n., m* plátano, *f* banana, *m* guineo 9
bank *n., m* banco
bar *n., m* bar
barbecue *n., m* asador 18
baseball *n., m* béisbol
bathtub *n., f,* bañera, tina 18
bathe *v.* bañarse 14
bathroom *n., m* baño 2
bathroom sink *n., m* lavabo 18
be *v.* estar (yo estoy) 15; **be** ser (irr.) 4; **be able to** poder (o→ue) 20; **be afraid** tener miedo; **be at/in/on** estar en; **be cold (person)** tener frío; **be cold**

(thing) estar frío/a; **be cold (place)** hacer frío 13; **be happy for** alegrarse; **be hot (person)** tener calor; **be hot (thing)** estar caliente; **be hot (place)** hacer calor 13; **be hungry** tener hambre 9; **be in a hurry** tener prisa; **be interested** interesar 19; **be lucky** tener suerte; **be ready** estar listo 15; **be right** tener razón; **be sleepy** tener sueño; **be sure** estar seguro; **be thirsty** tener sed 9
beach *n., f* playa 8
beans *n., m* frijoles 9
beautiful *adj.* bello/a
beauty salon *n., m* salón de belleza
because *conj.* porque
become *v.* ponerse (yo me pongo) 20
bed *n., f* cama 15
bedroom *n., f* cuarto 18
beef *n., f* carne de res 9
beer *n., f* cerveza 9
before *prep.* antes (de) que 30
begin *v.* empezar (e→ie), comenzar (e→ie) 12
beginner *n., mf* principiante
behave *v.* portarse bien 22; **behave oneself** comportarse
behavior *n., m* comportamiento
behind *prep.* atrás 25
believe *v.* creer 17
belt *n., m* cinturón 26
benefits *n., f* prestaciones 11
bet *v.* apostar (o→ue)
better than *adj.* mejor que 17
better (oneself) *v.* mejorar, superarse
beverage *n., f* bebida 8
big *adj.* grande 6
bikini *n., m* bikini 13
bill *n., f* cuenta 9
biology *n., f* biología 1
bird *n., m* pájaro 4
birthday *n., m* cumpleaños; **birthday song** *n. f* mañanitas 20
black *adj.* negro/a 13
blackboard *n., m* pizarrón, *f* pizarra 2
blame *v.* culpar
blond(e) *adj.* rubio/a 6
blouse *n., f* blusa 13
blue *adj.* azul 13
body *n., m* cuerpo 21
book *n., m* libro 2
bookstore *n., f* librería 2
bored *adj.* aburrido/a 15
boring *adj.* aburrido/a 6
borrow things *v.* pedir cosas prestadas 11
boss *n.* jefe/a
bossy *adj.* mandón, mandona
botany *n., f* botánica
bother *v.* molestar 19
bowling *n., m* boliche 8

boy *n., m* niño 4
boyfriend *n., m* novio 4
brake *n., m* freno; *v.* frenar
break *v.* romper; **break (a hand, an arm)** romperse (la mano, el brazo) 21; **break down** descomponerse
breakfast *n., m* desayuno 9
bring *v.* traer (yo traigo) 20
broccoli *n., m* brócoli 9
brother *n., m* hermano 4
brother-in-law *n., m* cuñado 4
brown *adj.* café (color) 13
brunet(te) *adj.* castaño/a
brush (oneself) *v.* cepillarse; **brush one's teeth** lavarse los dientes 14
building *n., m* edificio 2
bus *n., m* autobús 5
business *n., m* negocio, *f* empresa 12
business administrador *n.* administrador(a) de empresas 12
busy *adj.* ocupado/a 15
but *conj.* pero
butter *n., f* mantequilla
buy *v.* comprar 5

C

cafeteria *n., f* cafetería 2
cake *n., m* pastel 9
calculator *n., f* calculadora 2
call *v.* llamar 11
calorie *n., f* caloría
camp *v.* acampar; *n., m* campamento
can *v.* poder (o→ue) 22
candy *n., m* dulce 9
capable *adj.* capaz
car *n., m* coche 5
car accident (crash) *n., m* choque 26
cards *n., f* cartas
care *n., m* cuidado
carols *n., m* villancicos 20
carpet *n., f* alfombra 18
cartoon *n., m* dibujo animado 22
case *n., m* caso
cash register *n., f* caja
casual *adj.* informal 20
cat *n.* gato/a 4
Catholic *adj.* católico/a 22
caution *n., m* cuidado
cave *n., f* cueva
celebrate *v.* celebrar 28
cent *n., m* centavo
cereal *n., m* cereal 9
chair *n., f* silla 18
chance, (by) *n., f* por/de casualidad
change *v.* cambiar 28
character (in book) *n., m* personaje; **character (personality)** *n., m* carácter

charge *v.* cobrar
chat *v.* platicar
cheap *adj.* barato/a
check (personal) *n., m* cheque; **check (bill)** *n., f* cuenta; **check** *v.* revisar
checkers *n., f* damas chinas 22
cheese *n., m* queso 9
chemistry *n., f* química 1
chicken *n., m* pollo 9
child *n.* niño/a 4
childhood *n., f* niñez
chocolate *n., m* chocolate
choir *n., m* coro
chore *n., m* quehacer 18
chose *v.* escoger
Christmas *n., f* Navidad
church *n., f* iglesia 8
citizen *n.* ciudadano/a
citizenship *n., f* ciudadanía
city *n., f* ciudad; **city block** *n., f* cuadra, *f* manzana 26
class clase *n., f* 2
classroom *n., m* salón de clase, *f* sala 2
clean *v.* limpiar; *adj.* limpio/a 5
clear the table *v.* recoger la mesa 18
climb trees *v.* subirse a los árboles 22
close *adj.* cerca
close *v.* cerrar (e→ie)
closet *n., m* clóset 18
clothes *n., f, sing.* ropa 5
cloudy, (it's) *adj.* (está) nublado 13
coat *n., m* abrigo 13
cookie *n., f* galleta 9
coffee *n., m* café 5
cold catarro *n., m*, resfriado 21; **it's cold** *adj.* hace frío 13
color *n., m* color; *v.* colorear 13
comb one's hair *v.* peinarse
come *v.* venir (yo vengo, e→ie) 20; **come back** regresar, volver (o→ue) 28
comfortable *adj.* cómodo/a 20
comic strip *n., f* tira cómica
common *adj.* común
company *n., f* compañía
competent *adj.* competente 3
complain *v.* quejarse
complaint *n., f* queja
complete *adj.* completo/a
compliment *n., m* cumplido
computer *n., f* computadora 5; **computer engineer** *n.* ingeniero/a en computación 12; **computer programmer** *n.* programador(a) 12; **computer technician** *n.* técnico/a en computación 12
concussion *n., f* conmoción
confuse *v.* confundir
consumer *n., m* consumidor
continue *v.* seguir (e→i)
conversation *n., f* conversación
cook *v.* cocinar

cool *adj.* fresco/a 13; **it's cool** hace fresco 13
corner *n., f* esquina 26
cost *v.* costar (o→ue)
cough *n., f* tos 21
cough syrup *n., m* jarabe para la tos 21
count *v.* contar (o→ue)
country *n., m* país
couple *n., f* pareja
court (sports) *n., f* cancha 2
cousin *n.* primo/a 4
cover *v.* cubrir
crash *v.* chocar
crazy *adj.* loco/a
cream *n., f* crema
create *v.* crear
creative *adj.* creativo/a 3
credit card *n., f* tarjeta
cross *v.* cruzar 26
cry *v.* llorar
cry baby *n.* llorón, llorona 22
cure *v.* curar
curios *n., f* curiosidades
custard *n., m* flan
cut *v.* cortar, partir (un pastel) 18; **cut (oneself)** cortarse

D

dad *n., m* papá
daily *adj.* diario/a
dance *v.* bailar 5
dangerous *adj.* peligroso/a
dark-skinned *adj.* moreno/a 6
date *v.* salir (con) (yo salgo); **date (appointment)** *n., f* cita 8; **date (calendar)** *n., f* fecha
daughter-in-law *n., f* nuera
day *n., m* día
December *n., m* diciembre 13
decorate the tree *v.* poner el árbol 20
dedicate *v.* dedicar
defend *v.* defender (e→ie)
defense *n., f* defensa
degree *n., m* título
degree (temperature) *n., m* grado
delighted *adj.* encantado/a 1
demand *v.* exigir (g→j)
demanding *adj.* exigente
demon *n., m* demonio
denim *n., f* mezclilla
dental hygienist *n., mf* higienista 12
depart *v.* salir (yo salgo)
design *v.* diseñar
designer *n.* diseñador(a) 12
desk *n., m* escritorio 2
detail *n., m* detalle
dictionary *n., m* diccionario 2
die *v.* morir (o→ue) 28
diet *n., f* dieta
different *adj.* diferente 6
dine *v.* cenar 9

dining room *n., m* comedor 18
dinner *n., f* cena 9
dirty *adj.* sucio/a 18
disadvantage *n., f* desventaja 11
disappointed *adj.* desilusionado/a 15
disaster *n., m* desastre
disco *n., f* discoteca 8
discover *v.* descubrir
discovery *n., m* descubrimiento
discrete *adj.* discreto/a 3
dish *n., m* plato, platillo 9
dishonest *adj.* deshonesto/a 3
dislike *v.* chocar 19
disobey *v.* desobedecer (yo desobedezco) 22
divorce *v.* divorciarse 28
dizzy *adj.* mareado/a 21
do *v.* hacer (yo hago) 8; **do the dishes** lavar los platos 18
doctor *n.* doctor(a), médico/a 1; **doctor's degree** *n., m* doctorado 28; **doctor's office** *n., m* consultorio
dodge ball *n., m* quemados 22
dog *n.* perro/a 4
doll *n.* muñeco/a 22
dollar *n., m* dólar
donut *n., f* dona 9
door *n., f* puerta 2
dormitory *n., f* residencia estudiantil 2
doubt *v.* dudar
downtown *n., m* centro
drama *n., m* drama 1
draw *v.* dibujar 22
drawing *n., m* dibujo
dream *n., m* sueño
dress *n., m* vestido 13
dresser *n., f* cómoda 18
drink *v.* beber, tomar 8
drive *v.* manejar 26, conducir (yo conduzco)
driver *n.* conductor(a) 26
driver's license *n., f* licencia de manejar 26, *n., m* carnet de conducir
drunk *adj.* borracho/a
dry *adj.* seco/a
dumb *adj.* tonto/a 6
during *adv.* durante
duty *n., f* obligación

E

each *adj.* cada
ear (inner) *n., m* oído 20
early *adv.* temprano 5
earn *v.* ganarse
easy *adj.* fácil 6
eat *v.* comer 8
economics *n., f* economía 1
educator *n.* educador(a) 12
egg *n., m* huevo 9

e-mail *n., m* correo electrónico
embarrassment *n., f* vergüenza
employee *n.* empleado/a 11
end *v.* terminar 28
engagement *n., m* compromiso, noviazgo 27
engineer *n.* ingeniero/a 12
English *n., m* inglés 1; **English** *adj.* inglés, inglesa
enter *v.* entrar 28
enjoy *v.* disfrutar
essential *adj.* esencial
evening *n., f* noche 11
ever *adv.* alguna vez 28
every day *n.* todos los días 5
everything *n.* todo
exam *n., m* examen
excellent *adj.* excelente 3
excess *n., m* exceso
excited *adj.* emocionado/a 15
executive *adj.* ejecutivo/a
exercise *v.* hacer ejercicio 8
exercise *n., m* ejercicio
expect *v.* esperar 27
expensive *adj.* caro/a
expired *adj.* vencido/a
explain *v.* explicar
expressway *n., f* autopista 26
extroverted *adj.* extrovertido/a 3
eye *n., m* ojo 21

F

fascinate *v.* fascinar 19
fall (season) *n., m* otoño 13
fall *v.* caerse; **fall asleep** dormirse (o→ue); **fall in love** enamorarse 28
family *n., f* familia
fan *n.* aficionado/a
far *adv.* lejos
fat *adj.* gordo/a 6
fat (in food) *n., f* grasa
father *n., m* padre 4
father-in-law *n., m* suegro 4
fault *n., f* culpa 25
February *n., m* febrero 13
feed *v.* dar de comer 18
feel *v.* sentir(se) (e→ie) 21; **feel like** tener ganas de
fence *n., f* barda, cerca
fever *n., f* fiebre 21
few *adj.* poco/a
fiber *n., f* fibra
fight *v.* pelear 22
fill *v.* llenar 28
film *n., f* película 8
final *adj.* final
find *v.* encontrar (o→ue) 10
fine *adv.* bien 1
fine (high quality) *adj.* fino/a
finish *v.* terminar 28
fire (from work) *v.* despedir (e→i)
fireplace *n., f* chimenea

firefighter *n., m* bombero 12
first *adj.* primero/a 26
first aid *n., m* primeros auxilios
fish (live) pez *n., m* 4; **fish (food)** pescado 9
fix *v.* arreglar, componer
fixed schedule *n., m* horario fijo 11
flag *n., f* bandera 2
flat *adj.* desinflada/o
flexible *adj.* flexible 3
flexible schedule *n., m* horario flexible 11
flight *n., m* vuelo
floor *n., m* suelo 18
flu *n., f* gripe
follow *v.* seguir (e→i), continuar 26
food *n., f* comida 5
foot *n., m* pie 21
forehead *n., f* frente
foreign *adj.* extranjero/a
foreigner *n.* extranjero/a
forget *v.* olvidar
forgive *v.* perdonar
fork *n., m* tenedor
formal *adj.* formal 20
fracture *n., f* fractura
free *adj.* libre 15; **free (of charge)** gratis
freeway *n., f* autopista 26
freight *n., f* carga
French *n., m* francés; **French** *adj.* francés, francesa
french fries *n., f* papas fritas 9
frequently *adv.* con frecuencia
Friday *n., m* viernes 5
fried *adj.* frito/a
friend *adj.* amigo/a 4
friendship *n., f* amistad
front *prep.* frente a
fruit *n., f* fruta 9
full *adj.* lleno/a
full-time tiempo completo 11
fun *adj.* divertido/a 6
funny *adj.* gracioso/a 6
furnish *v.* amueblar
furniture *n., m* muebles 18

G

gain weight *v.* engordar
gamble *v.* apostar (o→ue)
game *n., m* juego
game (match) *n., m* partido 8
garage *n., m* garaje 18
garden *n., m* jardín 18
garlic *n., m* ajo
gas *n., f* gasolina 26
gas station *n., f* gasolinera
generous *adj.* generoso/a 3
geography *n., f* geografía 1
get (obtain) *v.* recibir 18; **get along** llevarse bien/mal 22; **get divorced** divorciarse 28; **get**

dressed vestirse (e→i); **get good grades** sacar buenas notas 5; **get hurt** lastimarse 21; **get into trouble** hacer travesuras 22; **get involved** meterse; **get married** casarse 27; **get off (at)** salirse (en) 26; **get off (leave) early/late** salir temprano/tarde 11; **get pregnant** quedar embarazada 28; **get sick** enfermarse 21; **get together** juntarse 14; **get up** levantarse 14; **get up early** madrugar; **get upset** enojarse

gift n., m regalo 11
girl n., f niña 4
girlfriend n., f novia 4
give v. dar (yo doy) 11
glass n., m vaso
gloves n., m guantes 13
go v. ir (irr.) 20; **go for a walk** dar un paseo 18; **go on rides** subirse a los juegos 20; **go on the swings** subirse a los columpios 22; **go on vacation** ir de vacaciones 14; **go out** salir (yo salgo) 8; **go to bed** acostarse (o→ue) 14
goal n., f meta
good adj. bueno/a, buen 6; **good afternoon** buenas tardes 1; **good evening (night)** buenas noches 1; **good morning** buenos días 1
good-bye interj. adiós 1
government n., m gobierno 28
grade (temperature) n., m grado
grades n., f calificación, nota
graduate v. recibirse, graduarse 28
graduate school n., m posgrado
graduation n., f graduación 28
grammar school n., f primaria 22
grandfather n., m abuelo 4
granddaughter n., f nieta 4
grandmother n., f abuela 4
grandparents n., m abuelos 4
grandson n., m nieto 4
grape n., f uva 9
graphic designer n. diseñador(a) gráfico/a 12
gray adj. gris 13
green adj. verde 13
green beans n., m ejotes
grind v. moler (o→ue)
grow (up) v. crecer (yo crezco)
guava n., f guayaba
guest adj. invitado/a
guide book n., f guía
guitar n., f guitarra 5
gym n., m gimnasio 2

H

habits n., m hábito
half adj. medio/a
ham n., m jamón 9
hamburger n., f hamburguesa 9

hand n., f mano 14
hand-made crafts n., f artesanía
handsome adj. guapo/a 6
hang v. colgar (o→ue)
happiness n., f felicidad
happy adj. contento/a, feliz 15
hard (difficult) adj. difícil 6
hard-working adj. trabajador(a) 6
hat n., m sombrero 13
hate v. odiar
have v. tener (yo tengo, e→ie) 4; **have a(n) ...ache** tener dolor de... 21; **have a picnic** hacer un picnic 18; **have a flat tire** poncharse una llanta 26, pincharse; **have breakfast** desayunar 9; **have fun** divertirse (e→ie) 14; **have just** acabar de 21; **have lunch** comer 9; almorzar (o→ue) 10; **have to** tener que 20
head n., f cabeza 21
health n., f salud 21
health center n., f enfermería 2
healthy adj. sano/a, saludable
hear v. oír (yo oigo) 17
heat n., m calor 13
heavy adj. pesado/a
heel n., m tacón
hello interj. hola 1
help v. ayudar 11
hi interj. hola 1
hide-and-seek n., f escondidillas, al escondite 22
hiding place n., m escondite
high adj. alto/a 11
high school n., f escuela secundaria, preparatoria 22
highway n., f carretera 26
hike v. ir de excursión 18
history n., f historia 1
hit n., m golpe 25
hit v. pegar 25; **hit (oneself)** pegarse
homemade adj. casero/a
homework n., f tarea
honest adj. honesto/a 3
hope v. desear, esperar 27
hopefully interj. ojalá que... 27
horn n., m claxon
horrible adj. horrible
horse n., m caballo 18
host(ess) n. anfitrión, anfitriona
hot adj. caliente **it's hot** adj. hace calor 13
hour n., f hora
house n., f casa 8
housewife n., f (el) ama de casa 11
how adv. cómo 6
how much (many) adv. cuánto/a(s) 6
hug n., m abrazo
humid adj. húmedo/a
hunger n., m hambre
hurry n., f prisa
hurt v. doler (o→ue)
husband n., m esposo 4

I

idealist n., mf idealista 3
ice n., m hielo
ice cream n., m helado 9
imaginative adj. imaginativo/a
impatient adj. impaciente 3
impolite adj. grosero/a 6
important adj. importante 27
in prep. en, dentro de; **in fact** de hecho; **in front of** enfrente de 26
incredible adj. increíble
indiscreet adj. indiscreto/a
inexpensive adj. barato/a
infection n., f infección 21
information n., f información 5
injection n., f inyección
inside adv. (a)dentro 15
instead of prep. en vez de
instructions n., f direcciones, instrucciones
insurance n., m seguro 26
intelligent adj. inteligente
interesting adj. interesante 3
intersection n., f intersección 26, bocacalle, m cruce
interview n., f entrevista 28
investigador n. investigador(a) 12
invite v. invitar 10
iron v. planchar 18
irresponsible adj. irresponsable 3
irritating adj. antipático/a 6
issue n., m asunto

J

jacket n., m chaqueta, n., m saco 13
jacks (to play) n., f matatena
jam n., f mermelada
January n., m enero 13
jealous adj. celoso/a
jealousy n., m celos
jeans n., m jeans 13, pantalones de mezclilla
jewelry store n., f joyería 27
Jewish adj. judío/a
jigsaw puzzle n., m rompecabezas 22
job n., m trabajo 8
jog v. correr 8
joke n., m chiste
journalist n., mf periodista 12
juice n., m jugo 9
July n., m julio 13
jump v. brincar, saltar 22
June n., m junio 13
just (barely) adv. apenas

K

kind adj. atento/a
kiss v. besar; n., m beso 20
kitchen n., f cocina 18

kitchen sink *n., m* fregadero 18
knife *n., m* cuchillo
know (a person, a place) *v.* conocer 12; **know (about, how)** saber (yo sé) 12
knowledge *n., m* conocimiento

L

lake *n., m* lago
lamp *n., f* lámpara 18
lane *n., m* carril
language *n., m* idioma 12
large *adj.* grande 6
last *adj.* último/a
last (year,…) *adj.* (año,…) pasado/a 15
last name *n., m* apellido
last night *adv.* anoche 15
late *adv.* tarde 5
lately *adv.* últimamente 28
later *adv.* después, luego
law (academic field) *n., m* derecho
law *n., f* ley
lawn *n., m* pasto 18
lawyer *n.* abogado/a 12
lazy *adj.* perezoso/a, flojo/a 6
learn *v.* aprender 19
leave *v.* irse (irr.)14
left *n., f* izquierda 23
leg *n., f* pierna 21
lemonade *n., f* limonada 9
lend *v.* prestar 11
less… than *adv.* menos… que 17
lesson *n., f* lección
letter *n., f* carta
lettuce *n., f* lechuga 9
level *n., m* nivel
library *n., f* biblioteca 2
license *n., f* licencia 26
lie *n., f* mentira 24
life *n., f* vida
lift weights *v.* levantar pesas 18
light *n., f* ligero/a, luz 13
like *v.* gustar 19
likewise *adv.* igualmente 1
limit *n., m* límite
liquids *n., m* líquidos 21
listen *v.* escuchar 5
literature *n., f* literatura 1
little, (a) *adj.* (un) poco 5
live *v.* vivir 8
living room *n., f* sala 18
lobster *n., f* langosta 9
lodging *n., m* alojamiento
long *adj.* largo/a
look *v.* mirar, ver (yo veo)
look for *v.* buscar 5
lose *v.* perder (e➤ie) 17
lot, (a) *adj.* mucho 5
love (a person) *v.* querer 10; **love (something)** *v.* encantar 19
lover *n., mf* amante
luck *n., f* suerte
lunch *n., m* almuerzo 9
luxury *n., m* lujo

M

machine *n., f* máquina
mad *adj.* enojado/a 15
magazine *n., f* revista
Magi *n., m* Reyes Magos
mail box *n., m* buzón
major (field of study) *n., f* carrera
majority *n., f* mayoría
make *v.* hacer (yo hago) 8; **make a decision** tomar una decisión
makeup *n., m* maquillaje
mall *n., m* centro comercial 8
man *n., m* hombre
management *n., f* administración
manager *n., mf* gerente 12
many *adj.* muchos/as
map *n., m* mapa 2
marbles *n., f* canicas
March *n., m* marzo 13
market *n., m* supermercado 8
marketing *n., f* mercadotécnia, *n., m* mercadeo 12
marriage *n., m* matrimonio
married *adj.* casado/a 6
marry *v.* casarse
mass *n., f* misa
Master's degree *n., f* maestría 28
mate *n.* compañero/a 2
materialistic *adj.* materialista 3
maternal *adj.* materno/a
math *n., f* matemáticas 1
mature *adj.* maduro/a 3
May *n., m* mayo 13
maybe *adv.* tal vez
meat *n., f* carne 9
mechanic *adj* mecánico/a
mechanics *n., f* mecánica
memory *n., m* recuerdo
menu *n., m* menú
messy *adj.* desarreglado/a 18
microwave (oven) *n., m* microondas 18
middle school *n., f* secundaria 22
mile *n., f* milla
milk *n., f* leche 9
mini-skirt *n., f* minifalda 13
mirror *n., m* espejo 18
misbehave *v.* portarse mal 22
mischief *n., f* travesura 22
mischievous *adj.* travieso/a 22
miss *n., f* señorita 1
miss (a person) *v.* extrañar; **miss (a flight)** perder (e➤ie); **miss (lacking)** faltar
mister señor 1
misunderstanding *n., m* malentendido
modern *adj.* moderno/a 20
mom *n., f* mamá 4
moment *n., m* momento 28
Monday *n., m* lunes 5
money *n., m* dinero 11
month *n., m* mes 13
mop *v.* trapear

more *adj.* más 17; **more… than** más… que 17
morning *n., f* mañana 11
mother *n., f* madre 4
mother-in-law *n., f* suegra 4
mountain *n., f* montaña
mountain climbing *n., m* alpinismo
mouth *n., f* boca 21
move (change residence) *v.* mudarse 28, cambiarse de casa; **move (objects)** mover (o➤ue)
movies *n., m* cine
mow (the lawn) *v.* cortar (el pasto) 18
museum *n., m* museo 8
music *n., f* música 1
music, (to play loud music) *v.* poner la música muy alta 23
must *v.* deber

N

name *n., m* nombre
narrow *adj.* estrecho/a
near *prep.* cerca (de)
necessary *adj.* necesario/a
neck *n., m* cuello 21
need *v.* necesitar 5
neighbor *n.* vecino/a 23
neighborhood *n., f* colonia, *n., m* barrio
neither *conj.* tampoco 18
nephew *n., m* sobrino 4
nervous *adj.* nervioso/a 3
never *adv.* nunca 8
new *adj.* nuevo/a 6
New Year *n., m* Año Nuevo
news *n., f* noticias
newspaper *n., m* periódico
next (to) *prep.* al lado; **next (close)** *adj.* próximo, cerca de; **next (following)** siguiente
nice *adj.* agradable 6; **nice (friendly)** amable 6; **nice to meet you** mucho gusto 1
niece *n., f* sobrina 4
night table *n., m* mesa de noche 18
not even *adj.* ni siquiera
nobody *n.* nadie 18
noon *n., m* mediodía
north *n., m* norte 26
nose *n., f* nariz 21
not any *adj.* ningún, ninguna 18
notebook *n., m* cuaderno 2
notes *n., m* apuntes
nothing *n.* nada 18
notice *v.* notar
novel *n., f* novela
November *n., m* noviembre 13
now *adv.* ahora 28
nowhere *adv.* a ninguna parte 8
number *n., m* número
nurse *n.* enfermero/a 12

O

obedient *adj.* obediente
obey *v.* obedecer (yo obedezco) **22**
occupation *n., f* ocupación
October *n., m* octubre **13**
of course claro
offer *v.* ofrecer (yo ofrezco) **24**
office *n., f* oficina **2**
office supply store *n., f* papelería
often *adv.* con frecuencia
oil *n., m* aceite
old *adj.* viejo/a **6**
oldest *n.* (el/la) mayor **6**
only *adv.* solamente, sólo
only child *n.* hijo/a único/a **6**
open *v.* abrir **8**
optimistic *adj.* optimista **3**
orange (color) *adj.* anaranjado/a **13**; **orange (fruit)** *n., f* naranja **9**
organize *v.* organizar
origin *n., m* origen
outside *adv.* (a)fuera **15**
oven *n., m* horno **18**
oyster *n., m* ostión

P

pack *v.* hacer las maletas **20**
pain *n., m* dolor
paint *v.* pintar
painter *n.* pintor(a)
painting *n., f* pintura
pajamas *n., mf* pijama **13**
pants *n., m* pantalones **13**
paper *n., m* papel **2**
parakeet *n.* perico/a
parents *n., m* padres **4**
park *v.* estacionar(se) **26**
park ranger *n., mf* guardabosques
parking *n., m* estacionamiento **2**
part *n., f* parte
part-time *adj.* tiempo parcial **11**
party *n., f* fiesta
pass *v.* pasar **26**
paternal *adj.* paterno/a
patience *n., f* paciencia
patient *n., mf* paciente **3**
patio *n., m* patio **18**
pay *v.* pagar **11**; **pay attention** fijarse
peanut *n., m* maní, cacahuate
pear *n., f* pera **9**
pen *n., f* pluma **2**
pencil *n., m* lápiz **2**
people *n., f* gente
perform *v.* desempeñar
perhaps *adv.* tal vez, quizás
person *n., f* persona
personnel *n., m* personal
pessimistic *adj.* pesimista **3**
pet *n., f* mascota
pharmacist *n., mf* farmaceuta
philosophy *n., f* filosofía **1**

physical education *n., f* educación física **1**
pick up *v.* recoger (g→j) **18**
picture *n., f* fotografía
picture (painting) *n., m* cuadro
pill *n., f* pastilla **21**
pillow *n., f* almohada
pity *n., f* pena
place *n., m* lugar **11**
place *v.* poner (yo pongo) **11**
plan *n., m* plan
plan *v.* pensar + [*verb*]
plate *n., m* plato **9**
play (instrument) *v.* tocar **5**; **play (sports, games)** jugar (u→ue) **10**
player *n.* jugador(a)
please por favor
pocket *n., m* bolsillo
poem *n., m* poema
police force *n., f* policía **23**
police (officer) *n., mf* policía **12**
poor *adj.* pobre **6**
pork *n., m* cerdo **9**
position (job) *n., m* puesto **11**
possible *adj.* posible
post office *n., m* correo
potato *n., f* papa **9**
prefer *v.* preferir (e→ie) **10**
pregnancy *n., m* embarazo
present *n., m* regalo **11**
pretty *adj.* bonito/a **6**
price *n., m* precio
principal *n.* director(a)
prison guard *n., mf* oficial de prisión **12**
private *adj.* particular **22**
problem *n., m* problema **11**
profession *n., f* profesión
professor *n.* profesor(a) **1**
program *n., m* programa **28**
promise *v.* prometer **24**
propose (marriage) *v.* pedir la mano
protect *v.* proteger
Protestant *adj.* protestante
proud *adj.* orgulloso/a
psychologist *n.* sicólogo/a **12**
psychology *n., f* sicología **1**
public *adj.* público
public school *n.* escuela pública **22**
pull *v.* jalar, tirar, halar
punish *v.* castigar **22**
punishment *n., m* castigo
purple *adj.* morado/a **13**
purse *n., f* bolsa
pursue a master's degree hacer una maestría **28**
push *v.* empujar **25**
put *v.* poner (yo pongo) **11**; **put on makeup** pintarse **14**; **put on (wear)** ponerse **14**

Q

qualified *adj.* calificado/a
quick *adj.* rápido/a
quiet *adj.* tranquilo/a **3**
quit (a job) *v.* renunciar
quit (a habit, action) *v.* dejar de
quite *adv.* muy, bastante

R

radiator *n., m* radiador
rain *n., f* lluvia
rain *v.* llover (o→ue) **13**
raincoat *n., m* impermeable **13**
raw *adj.* crudo/a
react *v.* reaccionar
read *v.* leer **8**
ready *adj.* (estar) listo/a **15**
real estate *n., m* bienes raíces **12**
realize *v.* darse cuenta **25**
rebellious *adj.* rebelde **22**
receive *v.* recibir **8**
recipe *n., f* receta
recommend *v.* recomendar (e→ie) **27**
recovery *n., f* recuperación
red *adj.* rojo **13**
Red Cross *n., f* Cruz Roja
red-haired *adj.* pelirrojo/a
reef *n., m* arrecife
refrigerator *n., m* refrigerador **18**
refuse *v.* negarse (e→ie)
registration *n., f* inscripción
relatives *n., m* familiares, parientes **4**
remain *v.* quedarse
remedy *n., m* remedio
remember *v.* recordar (o→ue) **10**
rent *v.* alquilar
repair *v.* reparar, arreglar
reprimand *v.* regañar **22**
request *v.* solicitar **28**, pedir
requirement *n., m* requisito
reserved *adj.* reservado/a **3**
residence *n., f* residencia
respectful *adj.* respetuoso/a
responsible *adj.* responsable **3**
rest *v.* descansar; *n., m* descanso **5**
restaurant *n., m* restaurante **8**
résumé *n., m* currículum (vitae) **28**
return *v.* regresar, volver (o→ue) **28**; **return (merchandise)** devolver **27**
rice *n., m* arroz **9**
rich *adj.* rico/a **6**
ride (bikes) *v.* andar en bicicleta **18**
right *n., f* derecha **23**
ring (engagement) *n., m* anillo (de compromiso) **27**
rollerblade *v.* patinar en línea **18**
romantic *adj.* romántico/a **3**
room *n., m* cuarto, *n., f* habitación **5**
rope *n., f* cuerda **22**

routine *n., f* rutina
rude *adj.* grosero/a, maleducado/a 6
run *v.* correr 8; **run a red light** pasarse el alto/el semáforo en rojo 26

S

sad *adj.* triste 15
safety *n., f* seguridad
salad *n., f* ensalada 9
salary *n., m* sueldo 11
salesperson *n.* vendedor(a)
same *adj.* igual 21; mismo/a
sandals *n., f* sandalias 13
Saturday *n., m* sábado 5
save money *v.* ahorrar dinero 28
say good-bye *v.* despedirse (e➔i)
scandalous *adj.* escandaloso/a
scare *n., m* susto
scared *adj.* asustado/a
scarf *n., f* bufanda 13
schedule *n., m* horario 11
scholarship *n., f* beca
school *n., f* escuela 8
scold *v.* regañar 22
scrambled *adj.* revuelto/a
scuba dive *v.* bucear 18
sculptor *n.* escultor(a)
seafood *n., m* mariscos 9
season *n., f* estación 13
seat belt *n., m* cinturón de seguridad 26
second *adj.* segundo/a 26
second *n., m* segundo
see *v.* mirar 5; **see you later** hasta luego 1; **see you tomorrow** hasta mañana 1
self propio
selfish *adj.* egoísta
sell *v.* vender 8
send *v.* mandar, enviar 11
sentimental *adj.* sentimental 3
separate *v.* separarse 28
September *n., m* septiembre 13
serious *adj.* serio/a 3
serve *v.* servir (e➔i) 9
set the table *v.* poner la mesa 18
several *adj.* varios/as
sew *v.* coser
share *v.* compartir 22
shave *v.* afeitarse 23, rasurarse
shift (turn) *n., m* turno 11
shirt *n., f* camisa 13
shoe *n., m* zapato 13
short (length) *adj.* corto/a 13; **short (height)** bajo/a 6
shorts *n., m* pantalones cortos 13
show *v.* mostrar (o➔ue)
shower *v.* bañarse, ducharse 14; **shower** *n., f* ducha 18
shrimp *n., m* camarón 9
shy *adj.* tímido/a 3

sick *adj.* enfermo/a 15
side *n., m* lado 23
sight *n., f* vista
sign *v.* firmar
signature *n., f* firma
silverware *n., m* cubierto
similar *adj.* similar 6
since *conj.* desde
sing *v.* cantar 20
single (unmarried) *adj.* soltero/a 6; **single room** *n., f* habitación sencilla
sister *n., f* hermana 4
sister-in-law *n., f* cuñada 4
sit *v.* sentarse (e➔ie)
size *n., m* tamaño
skate *v.* patinar 18
ski *v.* esquiar 18
skirt *n., f* falda 13
sleep *v.* dormir (o➔ue) 10
small *adj.* pequeño/a 6
smart *adj.* (ser) listo/a 6
snacks *n., f* tapas
snow *v.* nevar (e➔ie) 13
so much tanto
so-so más o menos 1
so that para que 30
soccer *n., m* fútbol 8
sociable *adj.* sociable 3
soda *n., m* refresco 9
sofa *n., m* sofá 18
solve *v.* resolver (o➔ue) 28
some *pron.* algún, alguna 18
somebody *n.* alguien 18
something *n.* algo 18
sometimes *adv.* a veces 8
son *n., m* hijo 4
son-in-law *n., m* yerno
song *n., f* canción
sore *adj.* adolorido/a 21
sorry (to apologize) perdón; **to be sorry** *v.* sentirlo
soup *n., f* sopa 9
south *n., m* sur 26
spaghetti *n., m* espagueti 9
Spanish *n., m* español 1; **Spanish** *adj.* español/a
spare (part) *n., m* repuesto, *n., f* refacción
spare time *n., m* tiempo libre 11
speak *v.* hablar 5
speed *v.* ir a exceso de velocidad 26
speed limit *n., f* velocidad máxima
spend *v.* gastar 19
spider *n., f* araña
spoil *v.* maleducar
spoiled *adj.* consentido/a 22
spoon *n., f* cuchara
sports *n., m* deportes
spring *n., f* primavera 13
stadium *n., m* estadio 2
stage *n., f* etapa
start *v.* empezar (e➔ie) 10
start (a car) *v.* arrancar

stay *v.* quedarse 14
steak *n., m* bistec
stomach *n., m* estómago 21
stop *v.* pararse 26
stop (sign) *n., m* alto 26
store *n., f* tienda 8
story *n., f* historia, *n., m* cuento
stove *n., f* estufa 18
straight *adj.* derecho/a 26
strain *v.* colar (o➔ue)
street *n., f* calle 26
street light *n., m* semáforo 25
strict *adj.* estricto/a
stroll *n., m* paseo
student *n., mf* estudiante 2; **student desk** *n., m* pupitre 2
studies *n., m* estudios
studious *adj.* estudioso/a 3
study *v.* estudiar 5
subject *n., f* materia
subway *n., m* metro
suddenly *adv.* de repente 25
suggest *v.* sugerir (e➔ie)
suit *n., m* traje 13
suitcase *n., f* maleta 13
summer *n., m* verano 13
sun *n., m* sol
sun glasses *n., m* lentes de sol 13
Sunday *n., m* domingo 5
sunny, (it's) hace sol 13
support *v.* apoyar
suppose *v.* suponer (yo supongo)
surf *v.* surfear
surgeon *n.* cirujano/a
sweater *n., m* suéter 13
sweep *v.* barrer 18
sweet *n., f* dulce 9
swim *v.* nadar
swimming pool *n., f* piscina, alberca 2
swimming suit *n., m* traje de baño 13
system *n., m* sistema 12

T

T-shirt *n., f* camiseta 13
table *n., f* mesa 18
take *v.* tomar 5; **take (out)** sacar 18; **take a trip** hacer un viaje 18; **take care of** cuidar 11; **take care of (oneself)** cuidarse 21; **take care of clients** atender a los clientes 11; **take long** tardarse; **take off (clothes)** quitarse 14; **take out (walk) the dog** sacar al perro a pasear 18; **take someone somewhere** llevar 24
talk *v.* hablar 5
tall *adj.* alto/a 11
tank *n., m* tanque
tantrum *n., m* berrinche 22
tape *n., f* cinta
tea *n., m* té 9

teach *v.* enseñar 24
teacher *n.* maestro/a 12
   teaching (profession) *n., m* magisterio
team *n., m* equipo
teaspoon *n., f* cucharita
telephone *n., m* teléfono 5
tell *v.* decir (yo digo), contar 20
tennis (sport) *n., m* tenis 2; **tennis (sneakers)** tenis 13
tent *n., f* tienda de campaña
terrible *adj.* terrible 3
test *n., f* prueba 2
thank you *interj.* gracias 1
that *adj.* ese/a 6
theater *n., m* teatro
theme *n., m* tema
then *adv.* entonces
therapist *n., mf* terapeuta
there *adj.* ahí, allí, allá
there is/are hay
these *adj.* estos/as 6
thin *adj.* delgado/a 6
thing *n., f* cosa 2
think *v.* pensar (e➔ie) 10
third *adj.* tercero/a
thirst *n., f* sed; **to be thirsty** tener sed
this (object) *adj.* este, esta 6
those *adj.* esos/as 6
thousand *n.* mil
throat *n., f* garganta 21
through *prep.* a través
throw *v.* aventar, tirar; **throw a party** hacer una fiesta 18; **throw tantrums** hacer berrinches 22
Thursday *n., m* jueves 5
ticket (plane) *n., m* boleto (de avión); **ticket (fine)** *n., f* multa 26
tidy *adj.* ordenado/a 18
tidy up *v.* arreglar
tie *n., f* corbata 13
tight *adj.* apretado/a
time *n., m* tiempo; *n., f* vez
time, (on) *adv.* a tiempo 5
tip *n., f* propina
tire *n., f* llanta 26, goma, *n., m* neumático
tired *adj.* cansado/a 15
title *n., m* título
toast *n., m* pan tostado 9
today *adv.* hoy
together *adj.* junto/a
tomato *n., m* tomate 18
tomorrow *n., m* mañana 22
tonight *adv.* esta noche
towel *n., f* toalla 18
toy *n., m* juguete 22
track *n., f* pista
traffic *n., m* tráfico
train *v.* entrenar; *n., m* tren
training *n., f* capacitación, *n., m* entrenamiento 28
translator *n.* traductor(a)
trash *n., f* basura 18

trash can *n., m* bote de basura
travel *v.* viajar
tree *n., m* árbol 20
trip *n., m* viaje 18
truck *n., m* camión
true (certain) *adj.* cierto
trust *n., f* confianza
truth *n., f* verdad
Tuesday *n., m* martes 5
tuna *n., m* atún 9
turkey *n., m* pavo 9
turn *v.* dar vuelta, doblar 25, virar
TV *n., f* televisión 2
type *v.* escribir a máquina

U

ugly *adj.* feo/a 6
umbrella *n., m* paraguas 13
unbearable *adj.* insoportable
uncle *n., m* tío 4
understand *v.* entender (e➔ie) 10
understanding *n., f* comprensión
university *n., f* universidad
unless *conj.* a menos que 30
unpleasant *adj.* desagradable
until *conj.* hasta (que) 28
upset *adj.* molesto/a 15, enojado/a
use *v.* usar 5

V

vacation *n., f* vacaciones 11; **on vacation** de vacaciones 13
vacuum *v.* pasar la aspiradora 18
vacuum cleaner *n., f* aspiradora
VCR *n., f* videocasetera 2
vegetable *n., f* verdura 9
very *adv.* muy
very well *adv.* muy bien 1
veterinarian *n.* veterinario/a 12
violin *n., m* violín
visit *v.* visitar 5
volleyball *n., m* vóleibol 2

W

wager *n., f* apuesta
wait *v.* esperar 27
waiter *n., m* mesero, camarero 9
waitress *n., f* mesera, camarera 9
wall *n., f* pared
wallet *n., f* billetera, cartera
want *v.* querer (e➔ie) 27
war *n., f* guerra
wash *v.* lavar 5; **wash (oneself)** lavarse 14; **wash one's hands** lavarse las manos 14
watch *v.* ver (yo veo) 8
watch *n., m* reloj 2
water *n., f* (el) agua 9
water ski *n., m* esquí acuático
watercolor *n., f* acuarela

way *n., m* camino
way *n., f* manera
wear *v.* ponerse (yo me pongo) 14; **wear a costume** disfrazarse 20
weather *n., m* clima; **the weather is nice/bad** hace buen/mal tiempo 13
Wednesday *n., m* miércoles 5
week *n., f* semana 15
weekdays, (on) *adv.* entre semana 5
weekend *n., m* fin de semana 5
weight *n., m* peso
well *adv.* bien 1
west *n., m* oeste 26
what *pron.* qué 6
when *adv.* cuándo 6
when *conj.* cuando 30
where *adv.* dónde 6
which *adv.* cuál 6
while *conj.* mientras
white *adj.* blanco/a 13
who *pron.* quién 6
why *adv.* por qué 6
wife *n., f* esposa 4
win *v.* ganar 12
wind *n., m* viento
windy, (it's) *n.* hace viento 13
window *n., f* ventana 2
windshield *n., m* parabrisas
wine *n., m* vino 9
winter *n., m* invierno 13
wish *v.* desear; *n., m* deseo
witch *n., f* bruja
with *prep.* con; **with me** conmigo; **with you** contigo
without *prep.* sin 26
woman *n., f* mujer
word *n., f* palabra
work *v.* trabajar 5
work (job) *n., m* trabajo 8
worried *adj.* preocupado/a 15
worse than *adj.* peor que 17
wound *n., f* herida
write *v.* escribir 8
writer *n.* escritor(a)

Y

year *n., m* año
yellow *adj.* amarillo 13
yesterday *adv.* ayer 15
yet *adv.* todavía 28
yogurt *n., m* yogur 9
young man/woman *n., mf* joven 6
young person *n.* chico/a 4
younger *adj.* menor 6
youngest *n.* (el/la) menor 6
yucca *n., f* yuca

Z

zero *n., m* cero
zip code *n., m* código postal
zoo *n., m* zoológico

ÍNDICE

Each entry is followed by a citation, **(1)** or **(2)**. All entries followed by a **(1)** are found on the corresponding page in **INVITACIONES: Primera parte**; entries followed by a **(2)** are found on the page noted in **INVITACIONES: Segunda parte**.

Photo Credits: Primera parte

Corbis Images: 2 (tr) © Graham Neden, (bl) © James Marshall, (br) © Darrell Jones. **3** (tl) © Pablo Corral V, (tr) © Francesco Venturi. **15** © Morton Beebe. **48** © Tony Arruza. **66** © Tizziana and Gianni Baldizzone. **119** © Buddy Mays. **142** © Shaul Schwarz. **193** © Nik Wheeler. **216** (l) © Miki Kratsman, (r) © Owen Franken. **239** © Hans Georg Roth. **273** © Wolfgang Kaehler. **320** © Amos Nachoum. **354** © Nik Wheeler. **367** (l) © Michael Freeman. **383** © Doug Wilson. **391** © Rob Lewine. **396** (b) © Reuters NewMedia Inc./Rafael Perez.

CyberSpain: 3 (bl) permission to reproduce J. Carballo.

© Randy Krauss: 3 (br)

Latin Focus: 151 © Jimmy Dorantes. **152** © Jimmy Dorantes.

Courtesy Mabis Robledo: 2 (tl)

Photo Credits: Segunda parte

Art Explosion: 330

Cantomedia: 251 © Frank Cantor 2003.

Rex Cauldwell: 127

Corbis Images: 20 © Jacques Pavlovsky. **49** (l) © Charles & Josette Lenars, (r) © Jeremy Horner. **50** © Barnabas Bosshart. **78** (tl) © Adam Woolfitt, (tr) © Paul Hardy, (b) © Tony Savino. **104** © Tom Bean. **128** © Jeremy Horner. **145** © Bettmann. **154** © Macduff Everton. **173** © Reuters NewMedia Inc./Andrees Latif. **207** © Tom Brakefield. **230** © Joyce Naltchayan. **232** © Charles & Josette Lenars. **278** © Dave G. Houser. **308** © AFP/Daniel Garcia. **329** © Pablo Corral. **359** © Jeremy Horner. **372** (l) © Brooks Kraft, (m) © Bill Gentile, (r) © Reuters NewMedia Inc./Enrique Shore.

© Randy Krauss: 49 (m). **335**

Lucky S. R. L.: 375 Gunter Dittmar.

Courtesy Mabis Robledo: 11

Margorie Stitson: 150

Text and Realia Credits: Primera parte

Pages 6 and 37: *"Catálogo de carreras"* adapted and reprinted with permission from Único – Universidad de la Comunidad, Universidad Autónoma de Guadalajara.
Page 307: "Premio escolar espíritu de superación." Adapted and reprinted with permission from Zubi Advertising.
Page 83: "¡Vivir bien con poca grasa!" ad adapted and reprinted with permission from Rodale Press International.
Page 223: "Estancia Santa Gertrudis." Ad adapted and reprinted with permission from Darío Saráchaga.
Page 316: "The Ultimate Oversees Career," 1997. Translated and adapted with permission from *Hispanic Magazine*.
Page 332: "Instituto Forrester." Ad adapted and reprinted with permission from Instituto Forrester, S.A.

Text and Realia Credits: Segunda parte

Page 495 "Grandes mujeres humildes," 1998. Reprinted with permission from *Revista La Pandilla*.

About the Authors

Deana Alonso-Lyrintzis was born and raised in Mexico City. After graduating from High School and studying for a year at the *Universidad Nacional Autónoma de México* (UNAM) her family moved to the United States. She earned a Bachelor of Arts Degree in Mathematics and a Master's Degree in Spanish from San Diego State University. She also holds a Master's Degree in Teaching English to Speakers of Other Languages from California State University, Los Angeles. She served for four years as consultant and teacher leader at the Los Angeles Area Site of the California Foreign Language Project. In addition, Deana co-authored several texts for McGraw-Hill, Prentice Hall and National Textbook Company. She taught Spanish for five years at Citrus College and she is presently a Professor of Spanish at Southwestern College. She has traveled extensively throughout Europe and Latin America.

Esther Alonso was born and raised in Mexico City. After graduating from High School and studying for two years at the *Universidad Internacional de Turismo,* her family moved to the United States. She earned a Bachelor's Degree in Linguistics and a Master's Degree in Spanish and English Sociolinguistics from San Diego State University. Esther was a consultant and teacher leader for the Los Angeles Area Site of the California Foreign Language Project for a year. She has published her research on language assessment in professional journals. She taught Spanish for five years at California State University, San Marcos where she currently is the Language Proficiency Assessor. She is presently an Associate Professor of Spanish at Southwestern College. She has traveled extensively through Europe and Latin America.

Brandon Zaslow was born and educated in the United States. He holds graduate degrees in Spanish and Education from the University of California, Los Angeles, where he was a University Distinguished Scholar and from California State University, Los Angeles. From 1990 to 1995, he held a teaching position in UCLA's Graduate School of Education where he taught Methods of Foreign Language Instruction and Primary and English Language Development. Since 1995, he serves as Director of the Los Angeles Area Site of the California Foreign Language Project, which is funded by the legislature through the Office of the President of the University of California to improve K–16 foreign, second and heritage language programs. In addition to serving on a team that authored a program for heritage speakers of Spanish, Brandon worked to develop California's Classroom Oral Competency Interview (COCI), Classroom Writing Competency Assessment (CWCA), and Classroom Receptive Competency Matrix (CRCM) and was contributor and consultant to the 2001 Foreign Language Framework for California Public Schools. Recently, Brandon was honored by his colleagues being named California Language Teacher of the Year.